News Writing

News Writing

Fourth Edition

George A. Hough 3rd
The University of Georgia

Houghton Mifflin Company   **Boston**

Dallas   Geneva, Illinois   Princeton, New Jersey   Palo Alto

Printed in the U.S.A.
Library of Congress Catalog Card Number: 87-80261

ISBN: 0-395-35937-6

We would like to thank the following sources for allowing us to use their material in this text:

Facsimile Credits
Page xxiv: Reprinted by permission of The Detroit News, Inc., a Gannett Newspaper, copyright 1986. Page 18: © The Chattanooga Times. Page 38: The Times of Trenton, N.J. Page 56: Reprinted with permission of the Seattle Times. Page 74: © San Francisco Chronicle, 11/20/86. Reprinted by permission. Page 88: Reprinted with permission of The Dallas Morning News. Page 110: Copyright 1986 USA Today. Reprinted with permission. USA Today and its associated graphics are federally registered trademarks of Gannett Co., Inc. Used by permission. All rights reserved. Page 134: Reprinted by permission of The Denver Post. Page 156: The Times (Gainesville, GA). Page 182: The Trentonian, Trenton, N.J. Page 208: Courtesy of St. Petersburg Times. Page 224: Reprinted courtesy of The Boston Globe. Page 242: © 1987 by The New York Times Company. Reprinted by permission. Page 280: Northeast Today — page design by Kimberly Kohlhepp and Jim Gring, Times Publishing Group, Towson, Md. Page 298: Reprinted with permission, The Toronto Star Syndicate. Photographs: Bernard Weil, Toronto Star. Page 318: The Oregonian. Page 338: Reprinted by permission, The Kansas City Star, © 1987, all rights reserved. Page 354: Reprinted from the Milwaukee Journal. Page 368: AARP News Bulletin. Page 402: The Times-Picayune, New Orleans. Page 420: Reprinted by permission from The Christian Science Monitor. © 1986 The Christian Science Publishing Society. All rights reserved. Page 440: © Copyrighted Aug. 15, 1987, Chicago Tribune Company. All rights reserved. Used with permission.

Credit acknowledgments continue on page 507.

CDEFGHIJ-H-9543210-89

Contents

8. Developing the Story 135

9. Some Hard-News Stories 157

Preface

This fourth edition of *News Writing*, like earlier editions, is intended for use in introductory courses in news writing and reporting. It can be used also as a self-teaching text. The book was written for the beginner, but the more advanced student will find that much of the material in early chapters will provide an excellent review of news writing basics and that material in later chapters will prove sufficiently challenging. I have used *News Writing* as a text for courses for beginners, as a review in intermediate courses, and as an introduction to sophisticated writing problems for more experienced students.

This edition of *News Writing* is the product of a lifetime in journalism, a dozen years as a newspaper reporter and editor and nearly 30 as a teacher of journalism. It has been shaped by my own experience in the newsroom and in the classroom both at The University of Georgia and at Michigan State University. Like earlier editions, this fourth edition concentrates on news writing — an important craft that requires the full attention of student and teacher — and leaves detailed coverage of reporting to other texts.

As far as possible, *News Writing* remains a descriptive rather than a prescriptive text. That is, it attempts to describe news writing techniques and practices in use by skilled professionals at well-edited newspapers. Where appropriate, I have tried to show what I consider the best approach to news writing and to suggest, for example, by providing model stories, how I would write it. My biases and prejudices about news writing show through, I am sure, in a number of places.

I have continued the "Suggestions for Further Reading" in the hope that they will be useful to both students and instructors. *News Writing* also includes a glossary of news writing words and terms, a bibliography of useful books and other materials and a style guide.

New to this Edition

News Writing has been extensively revised in this edition:

- A new chapter on ethical and legal matters, Chapter 22, has been added.
- A new chapter on broadcast news, Chapter 14, has been added.
- Examples have been updated, and discussion has been brought into line with current practices in the newspaper world.
- Examples have been selected from a wide range of newspapers as well as from the Associated Press and United Press International in order to make them as representative as possible of contemporary news writing practices.
- Model stories have been added to the discussion of many of the basic writing skills.

The text and my model stories conform to the Basic Guide to News Style in the appendix, and this basic guide is consistent with the *Associated Press Stylebook and Libel Manual*. Many of the examples of news writing practices taken from newspapers, however, do not conform to AP style, since a number of newspapers, for example, *The New York Times* and *The Milwaukee Journal*, follow their own stylebooks — and these frequently differ from AP style.

Practice Exercises in News Writing

News Writing and *Practice Exercises in News Writing*, the workbook of practical exercises that supplements it, have been carefully coordinated chapter by chapter. For example, the subject matter discussed in *News Writing* in Chapter 6, "Writing the Story," is supported by exercises in *Practice Exercises in News Writing*, Section 3, "Writing the Story."

In earlier editions of *News Writing* I acknowledged the guidance and support of people who in a variety of ways have made *News Writing* possible. I continue to be indebted to them all. My friends and colleagues have made helpful suggestions, and I am grateful to the many students whose reactions to the text and to *Practice Exercises* have prompted me to strive for greater clarity and precision.

I especially want to thank Michael E. Abrams, Florida A & M University; R. Thomas Berner, The Pennsylvania State University; Larry Bohlender, Northern Arizona University; Ellie Chapman, University of Missouri, St. Louis; Frank Deaver, University of Alabama; James Fisher, University of Idaho; George L. Garrigues, University of Bridgeport; Robert D. Hilliard, Washington State University; Jeffrey Alan John, Wright State University; Luther Keith, *Detroit News;* Stephen Lacy, Michigan State University; Lamar Matthews, Associated Press; Lois D. Matthews, Western Michigan University; Norman B. Moyes, Boston University; Shirley B. Quate, Indiana University at Indianapolis; Garrett Ray, Colorado State University; John N. Rippey, The Pennsylvania State University; Jon Roosenraad, University of Florida; and Scoobie Ryan, George Mason University.

The various newspapers and the news services from which examples in the text have been taken have been most helpful in their willingness to permit use of copyrighted material, and I am grateful for their contributions.

I am especially appreciative of the help of my wife, Mary Lu Hough, whose skills as an editor have contributed so much to this and earlier editions of *News Writing.* Her advice and critical judgment have been most helpful.

And I am most grateful for the help and patience of my editors at Houghton Mifflin for all their efforts on this and earlier editions of *News Writing.*

George A. Hough 3rd
Athens, Georgia

News Writing

☐ Fighting tampering/**2D** ☐ 'Electronic brokers'/**5D**

The Detroit News
Sunday, August 3, 1986
Business News/222-2738
Home Delivery/222-NEWS
Classified Ads/977-7500

Business

Banking on Martha Seger

Michigan's Fed governor sparks controversy in Washington

By Eric Starkman and Kathleen Kerwin
News Staff Writers

It's been a turbulent ride for Michigan's Martha Seger since joining the Federal Reserve Board 2 years ago

WASHINGTON — Two years after being named to the Federal Reserve Board, Gov. Martha Seger finds herself at a crossroads.

An abrasive woman who stands well over 6 feet tall, the former Michigan bank regulator has earned a reputation as a fractious troublemaker. Ms. Seger's participation in an abortive coup against Chairman Paul Volcker, and her harsh criticisms of Fed staffers, have limited her influence.

Her protests run the gamut from complaints about the way decisions are made to gripes about her office furnishings. Ms. Seger also has rocked the Fed's notions of collegiality and refuses to accept the time-honored tradition that the chairman runs a one-man show. Her record of frequent absences from board meetings draws charges that she is neglecting her duties.

A FEW Fed-watchers have quietly suggested that Ms. Seger should throw in the towel and return to her native Michigan. At the Fed, you play by the rules or you don't play at all.

But events now may be going her way. Economic policy is back on a more even keel and Ms. Seger is gaining ideological allies as new Reagan appointees join the board. She is even getting a new corner office.

For her part, Ms. Seger, 54, is proud of her performance. And she insists that she will serve the 12 years left in her term. The friendlier atmosphere at the Fed these days and the possibility that Volcker will step down next year are added incentives.

Ms. Seger could decide to put past hostilities behind her and forge new alliances to gain a stronger voice in Fed policy. Or she could continue on the path of alienation and be relegated to the role of an ineffectual whiner.

A PICTURE of Ms. Seger's sojourn in Washington emerged in the course of dozens of interviews with present and former Fed staffers and Fed governors, Fed-watching economists, Michigan bankers and sources on Capitol Hill. Current Fed staffers are extremely tight-lipped and many other sources refused to comment on the record for fear of tainting their future dealings with the influential board.

Ms. Seger, who was born in Adrian, Mich., claims her share of accomplishments. She says her lobbying helped lower interest rates and the dollar against other currencies. The weaker dollar makes domestic goods cheaper abroad and foreign imports more expensive here. It has been a boon to the sales of U.S. businesses competing against foreign imports, including the auto industry.

"I haven't done anything bad," Ms. Seger told The News during an interview between connecting flights at Metro Airport, "except my view departed from the majority."

"I haven't done anything bad, except my view departed from the majority."
— MARTHA SEGER

She takes credit "for making people sensitive to the Midwest, smokestack industries and that it is important in this country to maintain a manufacturing base."

MS. SEGER blames her problems on senior Fed staffers who are "dumping trash" on her because "I don't take everything they say as gospel." Among the people who she believes are trying to sabotage her efforts are Steven Roberts, Volcker's right-hand man, Michael Bradfield, the Fed's general counsel, and Joseph Coyne, an assistant to the board. The three men declined to respond to Ms. Seger's allegations.

"There are certain senior staff people there who think they ought to be able to prepare a position" and that governors automatically fall in line, she says. "That's not the way I operate.

"I'm accustomed, (coming from) outside Washington, to dealing with mature adults who can have differences of view and not use those differences as the basis for an attack."

Ms. Seger often has been at loggerheads with Volcker on economic policy and disagrees with him on the Fed's role as regulator of markets. She has lobbied hard for her brand of economics.

SIMPLY PUT, she believes that if more money is pumped into the economy, people will spend more and interest rates will fall, stimulating growth in the economy. Volcker's faction fears that if the money supply grows too fast, it will outpace the production of goods, reigniting inflation.

Ms. Seger's views have won her the praise of some economists. "She was on the side of the angels in arguing for further economic stimulus in 1985," says one economist. He calls her views "intellectually well-founded," adding, "She's very capable at expressing them."

The Federal Reserve's power comes from its ability to steer monetary policy and regulate much of the financial industry. It mans the floodgates that control the money supply — the lifeblood of the economy.

The Fed's actions can raise or lower interest rates, give a sagging economy a shot in the arm or nip a resurging economy in the bud, thus affecting the level of unemployment and inflation. Fed policies also contribute to the strength or weakness of the U.S. dollar, affecting the vitality of domestic industries.

MS. SEGER'S problems are not all of her own making. Her troubles began during the stormy period that followed her nomination to the Fed in June 1984.

The White House and Treasury, on the outs with Volcker, didn't consult him before picking Ms. Seger, the second woman to be named to the Fed board. Her nomination papers were sent to Vice-Chairman Preston Martin, who also occasionally locked horns with Volcker.

Her confirmation hearings were marred by partisan bickering before the presidential elections. She was stung by charges from Democratic senators, including Sen. Donald Riegle of Michigan, that she was unqualified for the Fed job.

Ms. Seger, then a finance professor at Central Michigan University, earned her doctorate at the University of Michigan, where she was a protege of renowned economist Paul McCracken. After a stint as a Fed economist, she worked as a bank economist and as commissioner of the state's Financial Institutions Bureau.

WHEN THE Senate failed to act on the nomination before its summer recess, Reagan appointed Ms. Seger on an interim basis, further antagonizing hostile senators. She was confirmed by the Senate 11 months later.

Ms. Seger, caught in the political cross fire, took a lot of it personally. "She did not have the political experience in living in a tank of piranhas," says Jude Wanniski, an economist at New Jersey-based Polyeconomics and a leading supply-sider who describes himself as a friend of Ms. Seger. "She found herself getting chewed up."

Wanniski noted that Ms. Seger, who has never been married, was forced to go it alone.

When she arrived at the Fed under her interrim appointment, she was treated as only a quasi-official governor, right down to second-hand furniture for her office.

SHE ALSO suffered the usual disdain Fed staffers can show for new governors who haven't yet learned the ropes. The "snooty" staff "probably didn't regard Martha Seger very highly coming in," says Norman Mains, an economist at Drexel Burnham Lambert and a former Fed staffer himself.

"There's a lot of academic snobbery" among the Fed's many Ivy League staffers, who weren't much impressed by a professor from CMU, he says. Ms. Seger's self-description as a "hick from Michigan" and "a garbage collector" of economic theories didn't endear her to staff, either.

She was catapulted into a turbulent period in economic policy that often raised tempers at the Fed to the boiling point. To top it off, she differed sharply on economic policy with the majority of the Fed governors, becoming, at times, the board's lone dissenter.

Ms. Seger is no stranger to controversy. As the feisty commissioner of Michigan's Financial Institutions Bureau, she pleased many big bankers, but aggravated unions, consumer groups and small-town bankers.

ROBERT RASCHE, a Michigan State University economics professor, remembers Ms. Seger as a "somewhat abrasive" administrator who "ran headlong into some legislators," but operated with a large degree of autonomy: "On day-to-day matters, she ran her own show."

In Washington, she chafes at the dominant role of the Fed chairman, whose chief executive role is mandated by law and cemented during 73 years of intermittent financial crises that required a powerful leader. Fed governors who try to buck the chairman's authority usually get left out in the cold. Says MSU's Rasche, "I don't think she's been terribly influential."

The Seger-Volcker feud sometimes flares up in petty ways. She didn't invite Volcker when she was sworn in as a Fed governor. Then staff denied her request for a Fed car, frequently used for chauffering Fed guests, to pick up her mother at the airport before the ceremony.

At a recent appearance in Michigan, Ms. Seger was asked if Volcker always has a cigar in his mouth. She replied tartly, "Yes, he does and they

Please see **Banking/3D**

Hospitals see ads as a cure for clients

But studies challenge campaigns' value

By Carol Cain
News Staff Writer

Patricia McCarthy: "Advertising is ... very much here to stay."
NEWS PHOTO / EDWIN C. LOMBARDO

When the University of Michigan opened a $285-million hospital several months ago, administrators examined the competitive market place and decided that they had better publicize the new facility. The hospital has just launched its first television campaign, highlighting services offered by the institution.

Ford Hospital, one of the more aggressive marketers, is also running a television campaign that features different services it offers patients. One ad discusses its heart-care program, complete with graphic shots of open-heart surgery.

When Sinai Hospital decided on its most recent advertising theme, it opted to focus instead patients' homecomings and stayed away from the usual shots of the hospital.

THE THREE institutions may be approaching the market differently, but at the core of each effort is one thing — winning customers.

In 1983, Medicare stopped paying hospitals based on the institutions' health-care costs. Medicare now pays a flat rate based on patient diagnosis — referred to as Diagnosis Related Groups. Whereas a hospital used to get total reimbursement for whatever they spent to take care of a patient, now they receive a predetermined amount.

The government's decision, coupled with the boom in outpatient services, have resulted in lower hospital occupancy rates. On any given day, approximately a third of all hospital beds in the state and across the country are empty.

Hospitals have been forced to come to grips with the fact they are no longer immune to competition. And the industry is responding by branching out from the operating room into the business world.

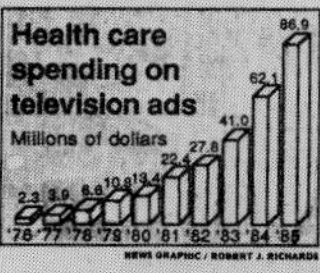

NEWS GRAPHIC / ROBERT J. RICHARDS

MOST BELIEVE that advertising is a necessary survival technique in the fiercely competitive health-care market. Through the use of television, radio and print, hospitals are going after customers in a big way.

Hospital and dental centers across the country spent $86.9 million on television advertising in 1985, up 40 percent from 1984's 62.1 million, according to Television Bureau of Advertising, Inc. from Broadcast Advertisers Reports data.

While all the hospitals interviewed declined to reveal their advertising budgets, industry observers said the larger institutions, such as Ford, Sinai, and Harper Grace, are easily spending more than $1 million each to try and win patients.

But now that those in the medical industry have had a chance to evaluate those marketing efforts, many are beginning to ask whether they're getting their money's worth.

"OUR PATIENT number is increasing," said Sinai's Barbara Lewis. "But is that because of our advertising, or public relations, or having

Please see **Hospitals/4D**

Auto industry gears begin to shift right

Firms brace for cost cutting

By James V. Higgins and Marjorie Sorge
News Staff Writers

Return on equity

Year	Ford	GM	Chrysler
1980	loss	loss	loss
1981	loss	1.9%	loss
1982	loss	5.3	loss
1983	28.4%	18.0	61%
1984	32.6	18.6	72
1985	22.6	13.5	39

The struggle at General Motors Corp. to regain healthy profit levels has brought about a fundamental change in the auto giant's product philosophy, some industry experts are concluding.

After a half-decade of intense innovation, change and investment, GM has gone conservative, they say.

The new emphasis is best reflected in public statements by GM executives hinting that the company will simplify its product lineup in the future, abandoning the traditional goal of meeting every conceivable market need.

OTHERS SEE this new conservatism as an industry-wide trend, prompted by a growing conviction that the industry finally is on the downhill side of the economic cycle and that competition is getting more intense.

There have been these developments in recent days:

■ GM acknowledges that it has trimmed future investment plans, partly because now it is spending more on special sales incentives than it foresaw.

■ GM Chairman Roger B. Smith, in a speech at the Automotive News World Congress, declares that domestic auto companies in the next few years "will be changed in fundamental ways. ... For one thing, it is unlikely that any manufacturer will be all things to all people — in cars or in trucks."

■ Lloyd Reuss, GM executive vice-president in charge of North American Automotive Operations, tells the same gathering that GM has "made a fundamental change" in product planning recently and will concentrate on its core, high-profit car and truck lines, offering fewer body styles in the future.

■ Chrysler Corp. says that its diversification strategy has been placed on temporary hold, and then sells its shareholding in the French auto maker Peugeot to raise cash for future product plans.

■ North American shipments of cars and trucks to dealers declined in the second quarter at GM and Chrysler, and second-quarter profits at those companies were off, respectively, 15.7 percent and 18.1 percent.

All of this, analysts say, is coupled with a growing awareness that the U.S. car market in the future will be more competitive than ever and that survival will require more cost cutting, greater efficiency and better responsiveness to customers than at present.

The second quarter statements drove home the fact that this hasn't

Please see **Autos/3D**

1 News and the News Industry

The basis of our government being the opinion of the people, the very first object should be to keep that right; and were it left to me to decide whether we should have a government without newspapers, or newspapers without a government, I should not hesitate a moment to prefer the latter.

Thomas Jefferson

Before we turn to the main purpose of the text, the business of learning to be a news writer, perhaps we should define a few terms. Just what is news? Where do news writers practice their craft? What kind of work do news writers do?

The Nature of News

News is both a product and a point of view. As a product, news is gathered, processed, packaged and sold by newspapers, news services, news magazines and other periodicals and by radio, television and cable stations and networks. But news is also whatever people think it is. News is what a reporter or an editor or a reader or listener at any particular moment considers interesting or exciting or important. News is something that at a particular moment happens to attract and hold the interest of the reader, viewer or listener.

Definitions of News

A great many people have attempted to define news, not always successfully. One of the great city editors of all time, Stanley Walker of the *New York Herald-Tribune*, didn't think there was a definition of news. News, he said, "is more unpredictable than the winds. Sometimes it is the repetition with new characters of tales as old as the pyramids, and again, it may be almost outside the common experience."

Although Walker's view of the news dates from the 1920s, you will find his observation is still valid. Much news is routine and repetitious, although even then it may be interesting, even exciting to some people. Births, deaths and marriages are common occurrences, but despite this they have news value. Families want to see news of the marriage of children and the birth of grandchildren in their local newspapers both as a matter of record and as news of interest to family members and friends. Deaths — obituaries — have high reader interest.

Some news is so strange that we can hardly accept it. News of medical discoveries, revelations of the secrets of the universe unraveled by theoretical physicists or photographs transmitted over millions of miles from distant planets — these events strain the imagination. Many people were unable to accept the idea that men actually walked on the moon, even though they were able to see the event on their television screens. Some events are truly so far outside human experience that they are hard to comprehend.

Joseph Pulitzer, 19th-century publisher of the *St. Louis Post-Dispatch* and the *New York World,* had his own definition of news. He instructed his editors and reporters to look for stories that were "original, distinctive, romantic, thrilling, unique, curious, quaint, humorous, odd and apt-to-be talked about." Since Pulitzer's newspapers were highly successful — the *World* at one time had a circulation of more than a million — Pulitzer must have had a fairly good insight into the nature of news.

Charles A. Dana, editor of the *New York Sun,* had his eye on his readers when he defined news as "anything that will make people talk." Arthur McEwan, editor of the *San Francisco Examiner* under William Randolph Hearst, is quoted as saying that news is anything that makes a reader say, "Gee, whiz!" And Turner Catledge, a former managing editor of *The New York Times,* called news "anything you can find out today that you didn't know before."

More recently, John Chancellor, senior correspondent for NBC News, suggested that news is a chronicle of conflict and change.

Many editors today are more likely to define news in terms of what their readers want to know — in other words, to give the readers what they ask for, whether it is local news or features or high school football. Some editors define news as information readers ought to have, what they need to know to get along in this complicated and confusing world.

Definitions are not entirely satisfactory, though they touch on some very real qualities of news. News is something that interests people.

Readers and viewers do react to and talk about events and the personalities they consider to be interesting. Readers do turn to the newspaper or to television to learn about events that are out of the ordinary, not routine.

Qualities of News

News is often defined by its qualities, and the qualities often mentioned are *timeliness, proximity, prominence, consequence, rarity* and *human interest*.

News is always a timely matter. The word *journalism* comes from the Latin word meaning *daily*, and journalism has come to mean the current and timely reporting of events. Proximity is always important, since people are more interested in news of local events than in events that happen far away. People are also more interested in major events and prominent people than in trivial occurrences and ordinary people. Consequence is an important element of news. Many events make little impression on our lives. They are isolated occurrences without result. Other events — a presidential election, for example — may have profound consequences. The Vietnam War was a series of events that first disrupted and then drastically changed American society, to say nothing of what it did to Southeast Asia. The rare event is more interesting and exciting than something that happens every day. Human interest is always an important element of news. People are fascinated by other people, and much of the news you read in the newspaper, hear on the radio or see on evening television is built around that interest.

Another kind of quality is described in the terms *immediate reward* and *delayed reward*. Immediate-reward news is news that has an immediate effect on the reader. Examples include the results of a football game in which the reader is much interested, a human interest story that brings a chuckle or the obituary of a friend or acquaintance that generates a pang of regret and loss. Delayed-reward stories are those stories about tax reform, zoning regulations, legal decisions or scientific discoveries that have a long-range rather than immediate impact on readers' lives — important and serious stories, but stories that may lack excitement or emotional impact.

Editors sometimes speak of *hard news* and *soft news*. Hard news is the serious news: fires, accidents, murders, disasters, deaths, the results of elections, the results of battles and the outcome of wars. Soft news is the light stuff: features, human interest stories, news of engagements and weddings, sports, leisure activities and entertainment.

Orientation and Perspective

Another aspect of the news should be mentioned. Much of the news you read in the newspaper and probably most of what you hear on radio or see on television is *event oriented*. Reports of action and conflict — fires, accidents, murders, wars, disasters, political disagreements and so on — tend to fill the pages of newspapers and the minutes devoted to news by radio and television. Much of the news on sports pages and much that is published about entertainment is event oriented, based on events that take place at scheduled times and at scheduled places. A great deal of what we learn about government and politics is event oriented, news of meetings, hearings, trials and sessions of legislative bodies.

Subtle changes in the world around us — *trends* and tendencies — are legitimate and important topics for news stories. Change is difficult to report and write about because changes come slowly and often are not recognized until they are far advanced. One of the major news stories of this century was the cultural change that took place in American society in the 1960s, yet this story was unnoticed and unreported for a long while. News people come to understand trends not by attending events but by developing an understanding of public attitudes and behavior. We identify trends, if we ever do, through public opinion polls, observation over time of voting behavior and examination of statistical data — for example, census data.

Another aspect of news, and an aspect of growing significance, is the personal, especially health and sex. There is increasing coverage in newspapers, magazines and on the air of sex and sexual matters. The social and cultural changes that occurred during the 1960s have enabled newspapers, the most conservative element of the press, to write freely about sex and sexual relations, and the AIDS epidemic has accelerated the shift to frankness and openness. All aspects of health are being given increasing emphasis in the press. Jane Brody of *The New York Times* has earned a national reputation for her reporting on human health. Readers are increasingly concerned about the impact of chemicals in food, the danger in smoking, the effect of cholesterol levels on the heart, the health hazards in polluted air and water.

Special Interests

Most newspapers, daily and weekly, are best described as *general interest* publications. They attempt to satisfy a broad range of readers with varied interests. It is said that there is something for everyone in the newspaper. Another way of looking at it is that everyone reads a different newspaper, that is, people tend to concentrate on what they are interested in or familiar with and ignore other things. Some people read only the sports pages, others entertainment, and others are serious readers who read the front page first, then turn to the editorial page.

The New York Times specializes in broad coverage of world and national affairs and has attracted a million daily readers with this approach. The *Wall Street Journal* concentrates on business and economic news. *USA Today* has found an audience that wants a wide variety of news stories briefly reported. *American Banker* reports only news about banks and of interest to banks. *Women's Wear Daily* reports primarily on news of interest to the apparel industry. *Barron's*, a weekly newspaper, is dedicated to the stock and commodity markets.

What Newspapers Publish

Another way to learn about news is to study newspapers to see what they publish on a daily and weekly basis. The departmentalization of the contents of the newspaper provides important clues to the nature of news. Newspapers reserve the front page for what editors consider the most interesting and significant stories — important local stories and news of state, national and world events. Sections of the newspaper are set aside for sports, business and economic news. Pages and sections are devoted to lifestyle topics — stories centered about the family and the home as well as stories of broader social interest. Some newspapers publish columns, sometimes pages, of news of special interest to children. Many newspapers cater to teen-agers with columns or pages of school news. Most newspapers carry news about food, clothing, fashions, home furnishings and home repairs, gardening, social problems and personal relationships — all of interest to both men and women and to readers of all ages.

Newspapers have developed a number of new approaches to the news to satisfy the specialized interests of their readers. *The New York Times* has developed a series of special sections, including "Sports Monday," "Science," "Home," "Living" and "Weekend." Almost all daily newspapers publish special recreation or entertainment sections reporting on music, film, theater, dining out and other recreational activities. Nearly every daily newspaper publishes a weekly guide to television programming.

Many newspapers have increased the space and attention devoted to business and economic news. *The New York Times* has a separate business section daily, and other newspapers, like the *Chicago Tribune*, the *Detroit News* and the *Atlanta Constitution*, have added business sections or are devoting more space to business news.

A great deal of space is being devoted to sports today, too. Professional sports have multiplied and become a major interest of a large part of the population. The space devoted to sports in the newspaper is a reflection of this preoccupation. Sports pages not only carry news and feature stories about almost every sport or recreational activity imaginable but also carry columns of summaries, statistics, schedules and standings. Fans may watch the game on television, but they turn to the newspaper for background, explanation and the stats.

Newspapers also publish news about books, art, music, architecture, records, stamps, coins, bridge and chess — culture, hobbies and recreational activities. Feature pages or sections tell readers about interesting or unusual people, places and events. And newspapers publish many technical stories about law, business, education, science, religion, medicine and other fields. These topics are also treated in a more popular way for the average reader.

Newspapers may also organize much of their news coverage and the space devoted to news in another way. They look at news as international or world news, national news, regional news and state news and, finally, local news. You will find sections and pages of many newspapers with headings or labels that reflect this compartmentalized view.

The Press Today

Specialization has already been mentioned, and a few specialized newspapers like the *Wall Street Journal* have been identified. But mention of a few specialized newspapers hardly helps us with a description of today's press, a broad, diverse and heterogeneous species, and, except for general circulation newspapers, highly specialized.

And a description of the press won't be easy unless we go beyond thinking of the press as the newspaper and of news as what appears in newspapers.

The press, the mass media of communication, is highly segmented, divided among many different vehicles for the delivery of news and information. There is, first, the division into print and broadcast. Print, of course, includes both newspapers and magazines. Broadcast includes radio, television and cable.

Newspapers

Daily newspapers published in the United States range in size from giants like the *Los Angeles Times*, with a circulation of more than a million, to small city dailies like the *Stillwater* (Minn.) *Gazette*, with a circulation of only 4,989 copies a day.

In 1986 there were 1,767 daily newspapers in the United States and Canada: 1,657 in the United States and 110 in Canada. Of these, 1,187 were evening papers and 500 were morning. Thirty newspapers were classified as all-day newspapers, that is, they published both morning and evening editions. Of the 1,767 dailies, 809 published Sunday issues. Many smaller dailies published four, five or six days a week, but not on Sunday.

The number of daily newspapers has dropped a little over the past decade. There are about 100 fewer dailies today than there were in the mid-1970s. Circulation, however, grew from 60.6 million daily in 1975 to 62.4 million daily in 1986. Sunday circulation of U.S. daily newspapers had grown to 61.5 million in 1986.

Most newspapers are not large. The metropolitan daily — *The New York Times*, the *Washington Post*, the *Chicago Sun-Times* — is not the typical newspaper. Of the more than 1,600 dailies in the United States, about 1,400 have circulation of less than 50,000, as you can see from examining Figure 1.1. Some 650 have circulation of less than 10,000. Average circulation of the nation's 7,600 weekly newspapers is 6,262. Total weekly circulation is 47.6 million.

Few dailies have a really large circulation. In the United States, only 15 dailies have circulation of more than half a million and only five have circulation of more than a million. Newspapers with circulation of more than 50,000 are, in the context of all dailies, large newspapers. The 20 largest newspapers in the United States are listed in Figure 1.2.

The trend over the past 20 years has been the increasing ownership of newspapers by groups. Fewer and fewer newspapers are owned by individuals or operated as individual businesses. Group ownership is becoming the norm. Gannett, the largest group, now owns 92 daily newspapers with a combined daily circulation of more than 5.3 million. Other major newspaper groups include Knight-Ridder with 33 newspapers with a daily circulation of 4.6 million and Newhouse Newspapers with 27 newspapers with a circulation of more than 3.7 million.

Most newspapers are published in one-newspaper communities, and only in the largest cities is there direct, head-to-head competition among the metropolitan dailies. Chicago, Detroit, Boston, Denver and Dallas have competing daily newspapers under separate ownership. In other cities, the metropolitan daily has competition from the suburban dailies and weeklies that ring the central city with aggressive and attractive publications. The *Los Angeles Times*, for example, competes with a dozen other daily newspapers published in Los Angeles and Orange counties.

The United States has three national newspapers. *USA Today*, published by the Gannett Co., appears in nearly identical editions in cities

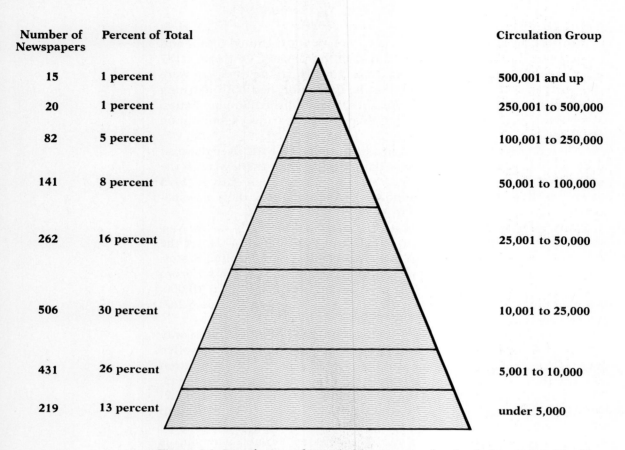

Number of Newspapers	Percent of Total	Circulation Group
15	1 percent	500,001 and up
20	1 percent	250,001 to 500,000
82	5 percent	100,001 to 250,000
141	8 percent	50,001 to 100,000
262	16 percent	25,001 to 50,000
506	30 percent	10,001 to 25,000
431	26 percent	5,001 to 10,000
219	13 percent	under 5,000

Figure 1.1 *Distribution of U.S. daily newspapers by circulation groups. The 35 largest daily newspapers, those with circulation of more than 250,000, represent less than 2 percent of U.S. dailies, but they sell 20 million newspapers a day, nearly a third of the total daily circulation of all general circulation dailies published in this country. (Source:* The Editor & Publisher International Year Book, *1986.)*

from coast to coast five days a week. *The New York Times* publishes a national edition in addition to its New York edition. The *Wall Street Journal* publishes nearly identical editions from satellite printing plants strategically located across the country.

A handful of newspapers stand head and shoulders above the rest in terms of quality rather than size. There is no single standard for judging quality in newspapers, but these newspapers have often been listed as among the nation's best: the *Boston Globe, Chicago Tribune, Los Angeles Times, Louisville Courier-Journal, Miami Herald, Milwaukee*

Newspaper	Circulation
Wall Street Journal m	2,026,276
USA Today m	1,311,792
New York Daily News m	1,278,118
Los Angeles Times m	1,117,952
New York Times m	1,056,924
Washington Post m	796,659
Chicago Tribune m	758,464
New York Post all day	740,123
Detroit News all day	678,399
Detroit Free Press m	639,720
News Day m	624,291
Chicago Sun-Times m	612,600
San Francisco Chronicle m	557,934
Boston Globe all day	500,106
Philadelphia Inquirer m	494,844
Newark Star-Ledger m	461,080
Cleveland Plain Dealer m	454,954
Miami Herald m	437,233
Baltimore Sun combined m and e	410,638
Minneapolis Star & Tribune m	382,832

Figure 1.2 *These are the 20 largest daily newspapers in the United States. Note that most of them are morning newspapers. (Source: Audit Bureau of Circulations, FAS-FAX report for six months ending March 31, 1987.)*

Journal, Newsday, New York Times, Philadelphia Inquirer, Wall Street Journal and *Washington Post.*

Other highly regarded newspapers include the *Christian Science Monitor, St. Louis Post-Dispatch, Minneapolis Tribune, Detroit Free Press, Detroit News, Providence Journal* and *Bulletin, Baltimore Sun, Des Moines Register, St. Petersburg Times* and *Atlanta Constitution.*

Many smaller cities have newspapers of quality and distinction. Among these newspapers are the *Asbury Park* (N.J.) *Press;* the *Berkshire Eagle,* published in Pittsfield, Mass.; the Dubuque, Iowa, *Telegraph-Herald;* the *Jackson* (Mich.) *Citizen Patriot;* the *Jackson Sun,* Jackson, Tenn.; the *Fort Meyers* (Fla.) *News-Press* and the *Eugene* (Ore.) *Register-Guard.* Many other newspapers enjoy excellent regional reputations but are not nationally known. Quality is high, too, in the weekly newspaper field, and weeklies like the *Lapeer County* (Mich.) *Press,* the *Birmingham-Bloomfield* (Mich.) *Eccentric,* the Falmouth, Mass., *Enterprise* and the Edgartown, Mass., *Vineyard Gazette* have long had national reputations. The *Point Reyes Station* (Calif.) *Light,* a weekly with a circulation of less than 3,500, won a Pulitzer Prize in 1979 for a distinguished example of meritorious public service.

Some of the criteria used to evaluate newspapers include quality of news content, the vigor of editorial pages, crusades for better government, community service, size of daily readership, advertising volume and attractiveness and utility of design — makeup and typography.

Special Interest Newspapers

There is a huge specialized press that few of us think about when we think of newspapers. There is a religious press consisting of both newspapers and magazines, a labor press, a collegiate press — your own campus daily or weekly newspaper is a part of it. There is a black press consisting of a great many weekly and several daily newspapers including the *Atlanta Daily World* and the *Chicago Defender*. There is a growing Hispanic press, which includes 51 weekly and daily newspapers. *El Diario–La Prensa*, published daily in New York, has a circulation of 70,000. There is a small American Indian press. There is a Chinese-language press. The Chinese-language *World Journal*, published in New York, has a daily circulation of 70,000.

The Business Page

Another interesting and important area of specialization is the business press, which consists of both newspapers and magazines. The *Wall Street Journal*, usually counted as a general circulation newspaper, is actually the largest and most influential member of the business press. In the past few years this segment of the press has grown and proliferated. Among the better-known business publications are *Fortune*, *Business Week* and *Forbes*, among the magazines, and *American Banker* and the *Journal of Commerce*, both dailies, and *Barron's*, a weekly, among the newspapers.

And there is a growing number of city and regional business publications, for example, *Crain's Chicago Business*, *Atlanta Business Weekly*, published weekly in a tabloid newspaper format, and *Florida Trend*, a high-quality monthly magazine.

The Trade Press

The trade press, largely a magazine and periodical press, specializes in news of narrow segments of the business world. It is a large and growing area of journalism. Among the successful and prestigious trade publications are *Advertising Age*, published for the advertising industry; *Variety*, theater and film; *Editor & Publisher*, newspaper industry; *Broadcasting*, radio, television and cable; and *Billboard*, music. Nearly every industry or segment of the business world has a publication to serve its own special interests.

The Fairchild group of trade publications includes *Women's Wear Daily* and *Metal Market News*, both daily newspapers, and *HFD*, a home furnishings weekly newspaper. *Furniture/Today* is published weekly for the furniture industry. *Computer Reseller News* is published weekly for microcomputer dealers.

Association Publications

Business groups and professional associations also have a vigorous press. For example, there are publications for hardware dealers, automobile dealers and, among many others, truckers, teachers and medical doctors. Every regional and state press association has a publication of some kind. And so do associations of county and city governments, hospitals, dental associations and newspaper publishers.

News Magazines

News not only comes daily from newspaper giants like *The New York Times* and the *Washington Post* but it comes to millions of readers weekly in magazine form. *Time* magazine is the largest of the news magazines, with a circulation of nearly 5 million. *Newsweek* has a circulation of nearly 3 million, and *U.S. News & World Report* has a circulation of about 2 million.

These three publications have developed loyal readerships among those who want the news summarized, organized into topics and freely interpreted.

Magazines

There are very few general interest magazines today, but there is a vigorous specialized magazine press. A visit to the nearest drugstore, supermarket or newsstand will bear this out. There is today a publication for every hobby, every interest, every area of human inquiry or entertainment.

City magazines are a fairly recent entry into the field. Among them are sophisticated, high-quality magazines published in Atlanta, Chicago, Detroit, Boston, Palm Springs, Memphis and Grand Rapids.

News Services

The two major news services, the Associated Press and United Press International, are an important adjunct to the mass communications industry. The Associated Press is a cooperative owned by member newspapers. United Press International is a privately owned news service that sells its services to clients. Together these two news services employ several thousand reporters, writers and editors in this country and around the world and produce and distribute millions of words of news copy every day.

There are, in addition, a number of supplemental news services, including The New York Times News Service; KNT, a joint venture of the Knight-Ridder newspapers, the *Chicago Tribune* and the *New York Daily News;* and the Los Angeles Times/Washington Post News Service. Other supplemental services include the Christian Science Monitor News and Photo Service and the News America Syndicate. These services distribute news and features produced by their newspapers and news bureaus to subscribing newspapers throughout the country. Some newspaper groups — Gannett, Newhouse, Cox, Knight-Ridder, Hearst, Copley and others — have news services that first of all serve newspapers in the group but also distribute news and features to others.

The Audience for News

Truly great newspapers have been in the past and are today edited by able, even brilliant, editors, whose professional expertise has enabled them to produce newspapers that inform and satisfy readers. Today the know-how of even the best editor is supplemented by careful studies of reader interests and reader needs. The form the evening news broadcast takes has been determined by careful study of what attracts and interests viewers. The newer magazines on the newsstands have been created especially to meet the needs and interests of sometimes very small groups of readers who were identified and studied carefully before the publication was launched.

Readership or audience studies vary in approach and complexity, but they all concentrate on one question: What do readers or viewers want to know?

Newspapers seek the answers in several ways. Readers are asked what they read and don't read in the newspaper. They are sometimes asked what they would like to read in an ideal newspaper. Some studies are directed to non-readers and occasional readers in an effort to find out why they don't read the newspaper or why they don't read it regularly.

Readership studies can be simple or complex. The simplest study involves publishing a questionnaire in the newspaper and studying the answers returned by readers. This kind of quick and sloppy study isn't very scientific but can provide understanding of reader interests. One daily newspaper conducted a readership study in this way, and readers returned more than 7,000 questionnaires. *The New York Times'* highly successful "Sports Monday" section was introduced as a direct result of a study of *Times* readers. The Newspaper Readership Project, sponsored by the newspaper industry, questioned a carefully drawn national sample of some 3,000 adults to gather data it later published in a report titled "How the Public Gets Its News."

Gannett, owner of 92 daily newspapers, conducted exhaustive studies of reader interests before launching *USA Today*. A study by Yankelovich, Skelly & White, published under the title "Changing Needs of Changing Readers," has stimulated numerous changes in newspapers.

A provocative study with a slightly different approach was conducted by the American Society of Newspaper Editors as part of its Newspaper Readership Project. The study was directed at newsroom personnel — reporters and editors — in an effort to learn what those who write and edit the newspaper consider to be news and how they approach their work of assigning, reporting, editing and displaying the news. A preliminary report on the study showed a great deal of disagreement among news people about the nature of news and the way it should be handled, another indication that news is very difficult to define.

The Newspaper Advertising Bureau conducts studies of newspaper advertising on a continuing basis, and these studies have revealed a great deal about how newspaper readers go about reading the newspaper.

What Newspaper Readers Read

Readership studies show that everything in the newspaper is read by someone. Few readers, however, read every story. Most read only a part of what is published each day, and the interests of newspaper readers are so diverse that it has been said that every reader reads a different newspaper.

The newspaper industry, citing its exhaustive studies of newspaper readership, contends that nearly everyone reads a newspaper nearly every day. Newspaper readers are, most of them, thorough. Studies have shown that 71 percent of newspaper readers go through the newspaper page by page. Another 27 percent scan the newspaper looking for items of interest. Only 2 percent of newspaper readers are so single-minded that they open the newspaper to read a specific item.

13

The Changing Reader

Attitudes and lifestyles in this country have changed, sometimes dramatically, during the past two decades. There are in this decade both more young people and more older people, and most newspaper readers have new interests and concerns. Newspapers have kept pace by making changes in the way they present the news, in content, page design and organization of newspaper pages and sections.

We find an increasing emphasis in newspapers on news of interest to younger readers — news about film, entertainment, sports and leisure activities. There is more consumer news in newspapers — stories about the best food buys, health and nutrition, medicine, science, personal finance and child care. There has been an increase in the space devoted to soft news — to feature stories and a light, breezy approach to news of the ordinary and routine. Many newspapers are publishing fewer stories in each issue. The emphasis on better organization, the use of larger type and wider columns, the introduction of larger pictures and more graphics and splashy makeup have reduced the space available for reading matter. Newspapers are also using more color these days in direct response to reader interests.

Despite the many changes in newspapers in recent years, the principal business of the newspaper is still news, and news is what readers want in the newspaper. A study by the Newspaper Readership Project found that 59 percent of newspaper readers would rather read a newspaper that is all news than one that offers only brief summaries of the news and emphasizes entertaining features. Newspapers must and do provide readers with information about things they need to know.

Local News

It is often said that all news is local, which really means that there are local and personal implications in nearly all news no matter how remote it might seem at first. We certainly know, for example, that world terrorism eventually has an impact on all of us and that what the oil-producing and oil-exporting countries do about oil production and oil prices affects the price we pay for gasoline at our neighborhood service station.

The great majority of general circulation newspapers — most dailies and practically all weeklies — are local in nature. They serve readers in limited geographical areas and concentrate on local, even neighborhood news. News to the average daily is local, and much of it at first glance is trivial. Yet local news is highly important because it is about people readers know and about events, issues and activities that affect readers and are of immediate interest.

Readers especially want community news: school news, news of service clubs and women's clubs, stories about people, hobbies, store openings and closings, birthdays, school honor rolls, Cub Scout and Brownie activities, anniversaries, newcomers, resignations and retirements, hospital admissions and community programs. One of the best-read stories in many local newspapers is the school lunch menu.

The remarkable growth and financial success of suburban daily and weekly newspapers that give readers news about their community, their neighborhood, even their block, confirm the value placed by readers on local news.

Large city newspapers are so concerned about the competition presented by these successful local daily and weekly newspapers that they have begun to publish special sections and zoned editions devoted to local news. The *Extra* editions, weekly supplements to the *Atlanta Constitution* and *Atlanta Journal,* and the zoned supplements published by the *Chicago Tribune* are examples of this trend.

Localness, even parochialism, of newspapers serves the needs of readers, but it also results in gaps in the coverage of certain kinds of news. Newspaper readers say they are interested in news of national and international affairs, but readership studies show they don't read such news as attentively as they read local news. As a consequence, many newspapers publish very little national and international news.

Good News, Bad News

Newspaper editors are also painfully aware that the reading public professes to prefer good news to bad news. Much of the criticism of newspapers stems from this fact. When the newspaper reports crime, corruption in public office, unemployment figures and increased taxes, readers send letters of complaint to the editor. "Why don't you print some good news?" they ask.

Despite their protests about bad news, however, newspaper readers seem to enjoy it. They relish news of conflict and violence. Stories about violent crimes, murders, battles and wars, conflicts between nations and political parties, staged conflicts in sports arenas and even competition between the sexes attract readers to newspapers and hold their attention.

Striking a Balance

Newspapers try to give their readers a balanced ration of news, and editors make a real effort to report important stories — stories that provide information about an increasingly complex and dangerous world — whether readers like them or not. Newspaper readers also like to be entertained. Crossword puzzles and horoscopes have their following, and there is a hard core of devoted readers for every newspaper comic strip. The phenomenal success of "Peanuts" and "Garfield" attests to both a need for entertainment and a love of children and animals. To a large extent, newspapers are guided by reader interests. Newspapers generally respond to what their readers will pay to read.

News Writing

In this text, news writing means writing about events, activities and people for publication in a newspaper or for distribution by a press association or news service. And this text deals systematically with the problems encountered in writing a variety of news stories found in daily and weekly newspapers.

Excluded from the discussion of news writing are such specialized forms as editorials, columns, reviews and critical articles. However, if you master the techniques discussed in the text, you will find that you will be able to handle other writing problems.

This text is about journalistic writing — effective writing of the type found in the well-written and well-edited daily and weekly newspaper. The intention of the text is to help you master the skills of organization, structure and exposition that will enable you to write about any subject in a variety of ways.

Although they all use basically the same writing skills and techniques, not all news writers write about the same things. Some news writers are generalists and are expected to be able to report and write on a wide range of topics. Others are specialists and write exclusively about subjects like sports, politics, the environment, business or social issues. Some writers have a special touch with feature stories. Some are especially good at explaining complicated matters like school finances or foreign policy. Others are particularly good at writing about people.

Whatever the subject matter, whatever the level — national news, local news, hard news, soft news, features — news writing is a skilled craft and a professional business. This text deals with the realities of news writing. If you master the basic skills in the chapters that follow, you will have a good start on the road to becoming a professional writer.

And while it may seem that the goal is to train you to write for a newspaper, this is not really so. The professional writer will find opportunities to write for a wide variety of publications, to write for broadcasting, to write as a public relations practitioner and for magazines and to write in a wide variety of non-journalistic jobs.

The discussion here of the wide range of newspapers and other publications that offer news and information to the public certainly suggests that anyone interested in a career as a professional journalist — as a reporter, writer or editor — will find a wide range of opportunities. Newspapers provide the greatest number of entry level jobs, but as beginners become experienced professionals, they will find interesting and rewarding jobs on many other publications as well as in other areas of journalism and mass communications.

Suggestions for Further Reading

Here are some sources of additional background on newspaper journalism.

Bagdikian, Ben H. *The Information Machines*. New York: Harper & Row, 1971.
> A survey of the news media against the background of the technological changes taking place in modern society.

Halberstam, David. *The Powers That Be*. New York: Alfred A. Knopf, 1979.
> Inside the *Washington Post, Los Angeles Times, Time* magazine and CBS.

Hulteng, John L. *The News Media: What Makes Them Tick?* Englewood Cliffs, N.J.: Prentice-Hall, 1979.
> A readable and helpful introduction to the nature of the news media and their relation to society.

Hynds, Ernest C. *American Newspapers in the 1980s*. New York: Hastings House, 1982.
> A good introduction to the study of the newspaper industry.

Siebert, Fred S. et al. *Four Theories of the Press*. Urbana, Ill.: University of Illinois Press, 1956.
> Essential introduction to the philosophical basis for the First Amendment and our independent press.

Talese, Gay. *The Kingdom and the Power*. New York: World Publishing Co., 1969.
> This fascinating narrative about *The New York Times* is subtitled "the story about the men who influence the institution that influences the world."

The Chattanooga Times

"To give the news impartially, without fear or favor."   Vol. CXVII No. 289 / Chattanooga, Tuesday, November 25, 1986   ★ Metro Edition ★ / 25 Cents

'1986 Times Printing Co.

Great expectations

Economy puts cloud on horizon of riverport

By Wade Rawlins
The Chattanooga Times

Early in August, about 100 people gathered near the bank of the Tennessee River to attend a groundbreaking. The ground on which they stood — about 385 acres — was planted in corn and soybeans.

The politicians on the white, bunting-draped platform that day predicted the land would be fertile ground for future jobs and millions of dollars of industrial growth.

Stretching along a mile of the river's south bank, the $14 million Centre South Riverport and Industrial Park would provide a port of call for economic prosperity at Chattanooga.

Like many recently built port industrial park complexes, the 385-acre Centre South Riverport was planned on the promise of economic growth from the Tennessee-Tombigbee Waterway and increased trade on the Tennessee River.

But the promises were based on projections. And the projections have changed drastically since the project was first proposed.

Consider these facts:

● The forecast for annual cargo shipments at Centre South have shrunk from 3 million tons projected in a 1976 study to 526,000 tons in 1986 — one-tenth of the initial projections. But the projections still exceed freight movements at Chattanooga's two existing public terminals.

● The Tennessee-Tombigbee Waterway, the $2 billion canal that provides an 885-mile short cut between Chattanooga and the Gulf of Mexico, moved only 7 percent of the 27 million tons of freight forecast for its first year.

● Federal funding for the $14 million Centre South Riverport is behind schedule. Construction on Centre South has begun, although county officials do not have enough money to finish the three-phase project. Hamilton County has received $3.8 million of the $9 million in federal grants promised in 1984 and $750,000 in state grants. It needs at least $4.9 million more.

● County officials and industrial recruiters have not begun to map a strategy to market the riverport.

● Centre South would generate 1,508 to 3,000 jobs, according to former projections. Consultants now say the port will produce about 1,200 jobs. It will produce 848 new jobs within five years, according to the studies.

Revised expectations

County officials such as County Executive Dalton Roberts, engineer Steve Meyer and consultant Ron Coles now concede the costly riverport may operate in the red and may take two decades to break even. But they say the project offers new land for industry and will be an economic tonic for the

See PORT, A7

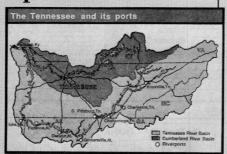

The Tennessee and its ports

● Tennessee River Basin
● Cumberland River Basin
○ Riverports

— John Wood/The Chattanooga Times

Banking on the river

Today *The Times* begins a four-part look at the Centre South Riverport. Planners hope the project will take advantage of a major resource, the Tennessee River, but they're also discovering the project is subject to the ravages of a sagging economy. The story begins on Page A1.

Inside: With the potential for their project to be a huge success, riverport planners like Bob McAuley have plenty of expectations. Still, there are some major concerns about the dark side of the rainbow. The story is on Page A7.

Tomorrow: Two million dollars just won't move as much dirt today as it would in 1982, a fact riverport planners are having to deal with. Wednesday's *Times* takes a look at how an idea blossomed into a $14.5 million project.

Bob McAuley

Public docks: A small share

Annual percentage of commodities moved through Chattanooga's two public-use docks. The overwhelming majority of shipments move through the 19 private docks. The Centre South Riverport would be public.

— John Wood/The Chattanooga Times

White House urged to undo Iran damage

c. New York Times News Service

WASHINGTON — The State Department Monday publicly denounced its isolation from the decision-making process on Iran and called on the White House to "undo the damage quickly."

The State Department's continued dissent from the Iran operation occurred during unusual testimony by John C. Whitehead, the department's second-ranking official, before the House Foreign Affairs Committee.

He said it was time "for the White House to come forward with a positive plan to undo the damage quickly."

"We in the State Department still do not have a detailed record of what happened," he said of the secret Iran dealings. He said Secretary of State George P. Shultz had opposed President Reagan's decision to sell arms, adding that "it is hard to point to major accomplishments" arising from the decision.

The president, speaking with reporters during a picture-taking session, continued to defend his decision to establish contact and provide military arms and spare parts to Iran. He said he had no plans to apologize.

Whitehead's testimony on Capitol Hill was the first public hearing on the Iran situation, and his testimony reflected the continuing divisions within the government on the Iran operation,

See STATE, A2

which was directed by the staff of the National Security Council.

Asked about the use of the National Security Council staff for this purpose, Whitehead said:

"We in the State Department find it difficult to cope with the National Security Council's operational activities."

He said that the department valued the National Security Council staff's advisory role, and its activities in reconciling different viewpoints, but he said that "when they become involved in operational matters, we have concerns, particularly when we don't know about them."

Committee members seemed amused when Whitehead said the State Department was lacking in details on what happened in the secret dealings with Iran.

"I wish I could tell you more of the facts," he said.

He added that it was embarrassing to be in the dark. At one point, he was asked about a statement by Reagan at a news conference on Nov. 13, in which he said that as a result of the secret arms sales to the Iranians, they had moderated their terrorism against Americans.

"I don't like to differ with my president."

See STATE, A2

Stories of backbiting irritating to Reagan

The Associated Press

WASHINGTON — President Reagan made no secret of his unhappiness Monday over news reports about backbiting among his staff, calls for resignations, and suggestions that he admit the Iranian initiative was a mistake.

"I think you'd be happier if I said I'd stop answering questions on that because you wouldn't like my answers," the president told reporters during a picture-taking session in the Oval Office.

Even so, he said, "I'm not firing anybody." Pressed on whether there would be any staff changes, Reagan said, "I'm not commenting either way."

As for whether he would admit it was wrong to approve arms for Iran, the president replied, "I'm not going to lie about that. I didn't make a mistake."

Asked whether he was pleased with his staff, Reagan replied, tight-lipped, "Um-hmm."

One person at least was pleased with the outcome of the arms deal: The sister of hostage Terry Anderson sent an open letter to Reagan expressing "my support and deepest gratitude" for his efforts in behalf of the captives.

In her letter to Reagan, Anderson's

sister, Peggy Say, said, "You placed the lives and freedom of American citizens over all other considerations."

"If your initiative leads to reconciliation with Iran as a prelude to a peace plan in the Middle East, then all of the suffering will have been worthwhile," she said. ". . . A move to bring to an end the suffering of those in the Middle East as well as to stop the victimization of Americans through acts of terrorism should be supported by everyone.

"It is not up to us to determine the method, it is up to us to support the goal," she said.

Anderson, a hostage since March 16, 1985, is chief Middle East correspondent for The Associated Press.

White House spokesman Larry Speakes said the focus of Reagan's meeting with aides and Cabinet officers was "current and future U.S. policy in the light of recent developments."

Secretary of State George Shultz, White House chief of staff Donald Regan and Vice Adm. John Poindexter, Reagan's national security adviser, have been targets of criticism for the Iranian deal, and there have been reports that some or all of them may be

See REAGAN, A2

Don't let TVA's old regime run nuclear program, urges Sasser

By Libby Wann
The Chattanooga Times

Sen. Jim Sasser said here Monday that it would be "criminal" to allow TVA to run its nuclear program with its current managerial line-up.

If former nuclear chief Steven A. White does not return, the agency should begin an immediate search for his successor, Sasser said.

"Why should we turn the nuclear power program back over to the same group who have literally run it into the ground?" Sasser asked during an interview Monday night.

"The people who are now running the nuclear program are many of the same people who have made it a non-producing multi-million sinkhole for the ratepayers," Sasser said.

"If White should for some reason — either failure to clarify his contractual arrangements or re-

solve his ethical problems — leave his post as consultant to the nuclear program, the board needs to look elsewhere for some other expertise to get the program going," the senator said.

White, on a leave of absence pending resolution of concerns raised by the Office of Government Ethics, reportedly will give the TVA board a final answer this week. White must agree to work without direct benefit of advice of experts from Stone and Webster Engineering Co., the company that initially provided his services to TVA.

White must also sever current ties with a group of former Navy admirals and officers who troubleshoot for ailing nuclear utilities. And White must promise that he will receive no future benefits or

See SASSER, A4

Erlanger again halts its burning after visible emissions sighted

By Andy Sher
The Chattanooga Times

Tons of garbage continued to mount at Erlanger Medical Center Monday as the hospital again shut down its waste incinerators after air pollution authorities told officials they still saw violations.

In a letter hand delivered to hospital officials, the Chattanooga-Hamilton County Air Pollution Control Bureau said it is "gathering evidence of apparent continued violations of the Chattanooga Air Pollution Control Ordinance and at least one of the temporary operating permits issued by the Bureau to EMC."

Wayne Cropp, bureau director, said this weekend bureau investigators saw visible emissions from one of the hospital's Basic Model 1250 incinerators. The visible emissions violate city ordinance, including temporary permits issued Friday

Mayor, county executive on Erlanger B1

allowing the public hospital to burn "certain, limited types of infectious hospital waste."

The visible emissions were noticed Saturday and Sunday.

Cropp said he was told the hospital shut down its incinerators Sunday. Efforts to reach Erlanger President Tom Winston were unsuccessful but a hospital source confirmed that the incinerators were idled.

"We did not ask them to shut down the operation," Cropp said. The bureau would not have is-

See ERLANGER, A8

2 Gathering the News

It's not the world that's got so much worse but the news coverage that's got so much better.

G.K. Chesterton

Although this is a book about news writing rather than reporting, it is not easy to separate the gathering of news from the writing of it. News writing depends first on the gathering of information and then on the sorting, analyzing and verifying of the information. It depends on an ability to recognize news and an understanding of news values and reader interests.

The previous chapter dealt with the nature of news, with the values of different kinds of news and with reader interests. It also gave some general background on the newspaper industry and on the broad range of interests served by the mass media. In this chapter, we will look at reporting and the work of reporters in an attempt to put news writing into the proper context.

Reporting and Reporters

Reporting is a journalist's word for research, for the collection of data, for the gathering of facts. This research is topical. It deals with current events and contemporary issues and people. Reporting is the art, the skill, the business of gathering information for immediate use.

The pace at which reporters work and what constitutes immediate use vary a great deal. Reporters who work for the news services — the Associated Press and United Press International — have deadlines almost every minute, since they serve newspapers in several time zones and with varying press times. Broadcast reporters face the deadlines of frequent, sometimes hourly, news broadcasts. Newspapers in large cities may publish several editions a day. Reporters for weekly or semiweekly newspapers work at a different pace. Reporters for magazines may work against a deadline that is from one to several months away. Investigative reporters for newspapers sometimes spend weeks or months on a story. But whatever the pace, reporting deals with the current and the contemporary, and its goal is to deliver news that is fresh and alive and timely.

Where Reporters Work

News is gathered and distributed and finally delivered to the news-hungry public in a variety of ways and by a number of different organizations and agencies.

Newspapers gather news for their own use and deliver it directly to readers.

Wire services, the Associated Press and United Press International, gather news and distribute it to newspapers and other publications. They also distribute news to radio and television stations.

Broadcasting — that is, television and radio networks — gathers news for distribution to network affiliates. Local radio and television stations maintain their own news staffs.

Supplemental news services, like the Los Angeles Times/Washington Post News Service, gather news for the parent organization and for distribution to other newspapers.

News bureaus, like the City News Bureau in Chicago, provide special news-gathering services to client newspapers and others.

Newspapers, news magazines, business publications and many other publications also maintain news bureaus in Washington and other cities to gather news for their own use. Gannett maintains a Washington bureau to serve members of the Gannett group. Gannett also maintains news bureaus in the state capitals of states where it has one or more newspapers.

News magazines maintain extensive networks of news bureaus and correspondents not only in this country but around the world.

The business press, as noted in Chapter 1, is a large and growing segment of the news business. It includes not only newspapers like the *Wall Street Journal* but even more specialized daily newspapers, weekly newspapers like *Barron's,* periodicals like *Business Week* and *Fortune* and regional publications like *Florida Trend.* The business press also includes news services that provide technical and specialized information about stock and commodity markets. The many trade publications might also be included in the business press.

Other periodicals provide work for thousands of reporters and editors. The Magazine Publishers Association estimated that more than 11,000 periodicals were being published in 1987. These publications provide news and information, opinion and entertainment on subjects ranging from agriculture to zoology.

The highly specialized and segmented magazine world relies heavily on the work of free-lance reporters and writers.

Public relations consists of a huge secondary news-gathering and news distribution network. Business, industry, government, social service agencies and educational institutions gather news and write news and feature stories about their own activities for distribution to newspapers, broadcast stations and other primary distributors of news and information. Public relations and public information organizations are an important adjunct to the mass media.

The press and public relations have a symbiotic relationship — they need each other. Public relations people need the press if they are to tell their story. And the press depends on public relations people as news sources.

Despite this close working relationship, the press and public relations are quite different fields of activity. The press has public responsibilities. Its job is to keep the public informed and to serve the public interest. Public relations, on the other hand, serves a narrow, private interest — the interest of a business, government agency or other institution.

The Reporter

Reporters are the foot soldiers of the news world. They are the representatives of newspapers, news magazines, the wire services and radio and television stations and networks. Reporters go out into the world and bring back the news of the day. They are the eyes and ears of the press.

Reporters, like the rest of the human race, come in all shapes and sizes. Probably 40 percent of reporters are women. About 8 percent are members of minority groups. Many are very young, for most entry level jobs in the news business are reporting jobs.

Reporters come to their work from various directions. Many are graduates of schools and departments of journalism. Others were liberal arts majors and arrive in the newsroom with degrees in history or political science or English. You will find a good many reporters — and others in the newsroom — who have changed careers and have moved from teaching, nursing, medicine, the sciences, business or the law into journalistic jobs.

Nearly all news people today have at least a bachelor's degree, and you will find many with master's degrees and some with doctoral degrees.

Reporters and others in the newsroom are a diverse, heterogeneous lot, but they all have one thing in common — a strong belief in the importance of the press and its mission and, for the most part, a sense of satisfaction in their work.

Reporting for Newspapers

The newspaper is a highly organized and specialized news-gathering organization. Figure 2.1 shows how a news staff is organized into desks and departments responsible for various types of news and for special news problems. This sketch presents a representative picture of the division of labor within a newsroom. Newsroom organization varies greatly, and the form it takes depends on the size of the newspaper and the degree of specialization necessary to publish a particular newspaper.

The chief executive officer of a newspaper is the publisher, who is responsible for the overall management of both the news and business sides of the newspaper. The publisher is responsible directly to the owners of the newspaper.

At the top of the hierarchy in the newsroom is an editor, variously titled executive editor or editor. Usually the editor of the editorial page reports directly to this most senior editor. Reporting to the executive editor and responsible for all other newsroom activities is the managing editor. The news editor is generally responsible for selecting stories from the news wires and directs the work of the copy desk, where news stories are edited and headlines written.

Depending on the size of the newspaper, the various editors may have one or more assistant editors working under them, and on larger newspapers like the one shown in Figure 2.1 each editor — sports, features and so on — may also have a separate copy desk. Smaller newspapers usually have a universal copy desk that edits copy for all pages and sections of the newspaper. Some newspapers have additional desks not shown in Figure 2.1 — for example, a national desk to handle national news from news bureaus, correspondents and news services and an international or foreign desk.

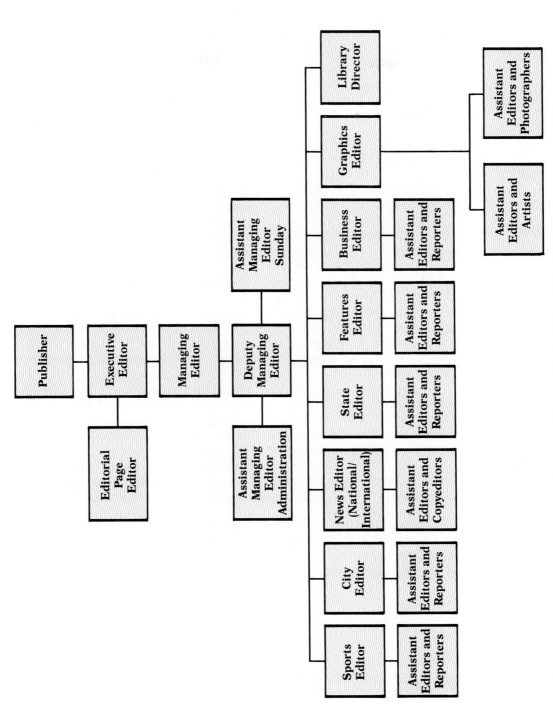

Figure 2.1 *Organizational chart for the newsroom of a 250,000 circulation daily newspaper.*

Some newspapers occasionally set up special desks to handle extraordinary news stories — for example, a special political desk might be organized during a presidential election season.

In addition to the reporters, photographers and artists who work under their respective editors, editors may have their own copy editors. On smaller papers there may be a universal desk that edits copy for all editors.

Newspapers generally use their reporters in two ways. They assign some to specific areas called beats, and they keep others on call as general assignment reporters to work on anything that needs to be done.

Beats were traditionally places. News regularly occurs at city hall, police headquarters, the courthouse, the offices of the board of education and the state capitol, and so reporters were assigned to those places. Newspapers maintained pressrooms, desks and their own telephones for the convenience of reporters assigned to beats in police headquarters, city hall and other places.

The geographical concept of reporting was efficient and provided for thorough coverage of the news as long as news was considered to be what happened in police stations, courtrooms and city halls. In recent years, however, the concept of news has changed and the beat system, based on assigning reporters to places, has been modified and largely replaced by a system that assigns reporters to subject matter or special activities.

Newspapers still cover in a limited way things that happen at police headquarters and in the courtroom, but they are more likely to view police stations and courts as part of the larger problem of law enforcement and criminal justice. The education beat is no longer a matter of covering just the occasional school board meeting but rather of reporting on the whole process of education and on activities throughout the school system. Reporters are assigned now to broad areas like health, environment, consumer issues, lifestyles and the arts, as well as to business, labor and politics.

There is still, of course, some geographical assignment of reporters as a matter of convenience. Newspapers establish suburban news bureaus or state capital bureaus or bureaus in Washington. Reporters still must visit places to cover stories, but the idea of news gathering is to treat news more broadly and to follow it wherever it leads.

Reporting the Expected and the Unexpected

News gathering today is organized to deal with news as it concerns issues, problems and activities, but newspapers, wire services and other news agencies must also be organized on another basis: to cope with both the expected and the unexpected.

A great deal of news is anticipated. It is possible to arrange well in advance to have a reporter available to cover a baseball game, a concert, the monthly meeting of a school board or a primary election or political convention. A considerable amount of news in the daily or weekly newspaper derives from scheduled events in sports, entertainment, government, politics and other areas of human activities.

Newspapers and wire services must also be ready to deal with the unexpected, with spot news. A news staff must be large enough and experienced enough and must be deployed in a way that makes it possible to report on sudden disasters. These tests of news-gathering organizations come in the form of five-alarm fires, train wrecks, plane crashes, hurricanes, tornadoes, blizzards and earthquakes — and more recently in the form of attempted assassinations, hijacking by terrorists and terrorist bombings. Catastrophe never comes at a convenient time. News staffs must and do rise to the occasion.

Made News

There is also a category called made or planned news. Sunday editors plan ahead so as to have feature stories for the front pages of sections in the coming Sunday issue. Editors assign reporters to interview important or interesting people, to write personality sketches or background stories. They arrange for scientific public opinion polls. Biographical sketches needed for eventual use in obituaries are assigned, written and filed away. Major investigative stories are carefully planned and may require months in the reporting, writing and editing before a story is published. None of these fall into the category of either scheduled news or unexpected news. All are created, thought up, by reporters and editors. Some story ideas are suggested by readers or by press releases. All these are planned, developed and written to organize information, to enlighten and inform readers about a variety of things.

The production of the newspaper is a series of carefully planned steps beginning with the reporting and writing of a news story. This production process is shown schematically in Figure 2.2.

What Reporters Do

An editor once defined reporters as people who get what they are sent for.

Some editors define a reporter somewhat more precisely in terms of abilities. Reporters, they suggest, must be able to meet deadlines,

STEPS IN PRODUCTION OF A NEWSPAPER

1. News

. . . is written at the keyboard of a video display terminal. The completed story is transmitted electronically to a computer's memory bank for temporary storage.

2. Editors

. . . and copy editors call up news stories from the computer's memory bank and edit and code the stories for use in the newspaper. Stories then go back to the computer for processing.

3. Composition

. . . begins as high speed computerized photocomposition machines translate electric impulses into images of letters and words. News stories are then printed on strips of photographic paper.

6. Newsprint

. . . in huge rolls is moved from storage to the newspaper presses.

5. Printing Plates

. . . are made photographically from the pasted-up pages as they come from the composing room. These may be offset plates of metal or plastic plates for direct printing.

4. Pasteup

. . . of news stories, headlines, photographs and other copy into full newspaper pages takes place in the composing room.

7. Presses

. . . are equipped with printing plates and newsprint is threaded through the press units in a continuous web. Finished folded newspapers emerge from the press and move on a moving belt to the mailroom.

8. Mailroom

. . . staff counts and wraps finished newspapers and turns bundles over to circulation truck drivers.

9. Delivery

. . . trucks rush newspaper bundles to distributors, newsstands and the carriers who take the newspaper the last few steps to the reader's home.

Figure 2.2 *The flow of news from the reporter's copy to the reader's front door.*

must be able to write, must be able to gather information and to generate ideas. One editor has suggested that reporters are people who know how to dig out information whatever the source and no matter how hidden or obscure.

Another editor, in reminiscing about a friend, a former sports reporter, gives an insight into a skilled and serious reporter's attitudes toward his work.

"Lazy reporters angered John Logue. He watched from the sports department as they sat at their desks, waiting to be sent to cover some press conference. 'That's not newspapering,' he would say. 'Newspapering is war!'"*

How one reporter works and how he views the responsibilities of his job is shown in Figure 2.3.

Reporting Skills

We might also define the reporter in terms of the skills needed to gather information about a wide range of events and human activities. Reporters should be skilled at

- seeing and hearing.
- taking notes.
- finding information.
- asking questions.
- checking and verifying information.
- analyzing and interpreting information.

Editors think themselves especially blessed if their reporters can also write well. Not all reporters do, and not all good writers are good reporters. There are those who can do both well, and these are the stars in an editor's crown. Some reporters don't have to write. They telephone their stories to the rewrite desk, where the story is written by someone else. Some able reporters write only passably well but are excused because of their special talents as reporters. The average reporter, however, would do well to master the skills of both reporting and writing.

A Nose for News

The nose for news is a newsroom metaphor for an understanding of news and news values and the ability to recognize a story when it comes along. The nose for news is not something one is born with. It is acquired, it can be developed and it improves with experience. Experienced reporters often appear to have a good nose for news because they have had long exposure to how editors think and what readers want to read in the newspaper. They also have acquired through experience a knowledge of news sources and, in addition, friends and acquaintances who tip them to news stories. They have learned that much news is

*James G. Minter, "Logue's New Novel Peels the South Like an Apple," *Atlanta Journal and Constitution*, March 1, 1987.

Covering spot news demands quick work and often a lot of luck. But the Shockoe Slip fire offered me something that I seldom get on my job — time.

I live by four rules on this job: Get it right. Get it first. Get it all. And if I can't get it first, then I try to write it better than anyone else.

The fire occurred in the morning. Because of our deadlines, my newspaper would be the last news organization in town to report the event. Before reading the Times-Dispatch the next morning, many people would have seen the fire on television or read about it in the afternoon paper, The News Leader.

We're used to covering news first, but fate wouldn't permit it. If I couldn't do it first, the next best thing was to get it all and do it better.

Before police got to the scene of the fire, I was there. I had seen the smoke blocks away, requested a photographer and rushed to the Slip on the edge of downtown.

What I found there is seldom seen even at the city's largest fires. People rushing from their businesses looked ready to panic. Some were crying. Some were ghostly white.

As I got to the scene I could see and hear explosions. Firemen were calling for help over and over again.

The photographers arrived. My editors were told I'd need some room in the paper for a rather long story. I let them know that Main Street and the Shockoe Slip area were in danger.

This was what I needed to get across to my readers. It was a big fire, but it could have been much worse. I wanted them to feel the tension as firefighters fought the flames, feel the heat as it melted a plastic cover on a fire truck's lights, hear the explosions and see the smoke. I wanted to bring them there. I wanted them to understand why those people rushing from their businesses were upset.

The only way to do this was with details. How many explosions? How many fire trucks? How hot was it? How much water was used? How big an area was evacuated? Because I have covered events like this for two and a half

cyclical or repetitive and are able, because of their experience, to anticipate things that will happen.

A political reporter, for example, may sense because of long experience that a state senator or governor is in political trouble. In a situation like this, an officeholder sometimes decides not to run again rather than risk defeat at the polls. The reporter watches the situation, asks the right question at the right moment and breaks the story that the senator or governor will not be a candidate again.

The reporter in this instance does have a nose for news, but it is less intuition than experience, less instinct than a broad knowledge of the political scene.

Observation: Listening

A great deal of what reporters learn comes from listening to people talk. News is gathered over the telephone, at the scene of an accident, at

years, I have a good understanding of all the emergency workers involved. And because I had extra time, I was able to contact people in the emergency communications room and the water department for that added little bit extra.

Ironically, I used the extra time to gather information and not to write. Once I had my notebook loaded with facts, I sat down and began typing. It was 6 p.m., and I had only an hour and a half to have the story to my editors.

I just went through my notebook. As I found something more important than what I had just typed, I inserted it between paragraphs already written.

I then went through the story smoothing it out so it didn't read like a bunch of paragraphs just stuck together.

I rewrote the first two or three paragraphs about five times. Finally — just moments before deadline — I wrote the final version of the lead, "How ashes rained on Main Street . . ."

A bit dramatic, but the intensity seemed just right. If the readers read the first phrase, they would know they were getting more from us than they had gotten the day before from either the afternoon paper or the broadcast media.

Figure 2.3 *Frank Douglas, a staff writer for the* Richmond (Va.) Times-Dispatch, *not only tells how he reported a major fire but also tells a lot about how a reporter thinks. At the time Douglas wrote his fire story, March 1985, he was 24 years old, a graduate of Ohio University, where he had earned a bachelor of science degree in journalism, and a police-beat reporter with two and a half years' experience. His beat included all the police and fire departments in the Richmond area, the Department of Corrections, the district courts, the U.S. Secret Service, the FBI and other federal police agencies.*

public meetings, lectures and programs. Reporters soon learn to listen with a selective ear and to listen carefully.

Selective listening is important because not everything that is said is important or interesting. Reporters must learn to evaluate as they listen and to take notes only of the useful, interesting and important things that are said. The experienced reporter knows it is not possible to write a story that will include everything said during a long city council meeting. As the meeting proceeds, the reporter's discriminating ear weighs and evaluates, chooses and rejects.

Careful listening is important, too. Good reporters strive to get it right the first time. They zero in on the names, dates, figures, facts and statements that provide the framework for a story. You can't always ask a news source to repeat something, and you don't always get a chance to verify spellings or figures with the source later on.

Listening also requires the reporter to develop an ear not only for what people say but for the way they say it. Direct quotation and dialogue are useful devices for explaining things or making a story more

Reporters listen attentively to the prison warden at a briefing during a riot at the Oklahoma State Penitentiary at McAlester, Okla. (AP/Wide World Photo)

interesting. But you have to hear what people say before you can put a direct quotation or dialogue into your story.

Reporters today frequently use tape recorders to supplement their listening skills, but the tape record is a backup, not a substitute for the human intelligence that goes into reporting. A recording can be extremely useful in verifying a quotation or a figure tossed out during a prolonged city council meeting. Reporters must depend on their own skills first, then take advantage of mechanical help — a tape recorder or an advance text of a speech.

Observation: Seeing

Much reporting is based on asking people what they saw or did and writing a story based on that observation. This is a workable approach and results in acceptable and accurate news stories of a routine nature.

This approach is also acceptable when, because of time, distance or some other barrier, the reporter can't do the observing firsthand.

But reporters are trained observers, and when they are on the scene and can observe things for themselves, a more vivid, more accurate and more interesting story results.

This is partly because experienced reporters know what kinds of things make interesting reading and partly because they know what facts, what details, make a story complete. But a lot of the color and background that make a story come to life is the result of careful observation. The careful and experienced observer sees what people do, notes the weather, the size of the crowd, colors, sounds and background incidents. Out of these bits and pieces the whole picture will emerge, a picture that will enable readers to visualize the scene for themselves.

Finding Things

Reporters, the saying goes, don't have to know everything, they just have to know how to find out. And this is basically true. Through experience reporters learn a great deal about their beats and other subjects they cover regularly. In time they accumulate a lot of knowledge. But no one can know everything, and reporters are no exception. They may not know, but they know how to find out.

Experienced reporters learn as much as possible about their own community. They know something of its history, its geography and its government. They know the names of the principal streets, the names or numbers of the major highways, the airlines and the buses that serve the community. They know the names of public officials and people frequently in the news, and they know how to spell these people's names. They know the titles of public officials, and they know or know where to find their phone numbers.

Against this background of general knowledge about the community, experienced reporters build lines of communication to news sources. They carefully build friendships and develop acquaintances and contacts. They learn who knows what around town and whom to ask when information is needed. An experienced reporter can get on the telephone and pull a story out of the air in a very few minutes.

And experienced reporters know how to use public records and published information available from government and other sources. They know how to use libraries. They know how to locate and read annual reports, budgets, proposals, minutes of meetings, court records and statistical data of all kinds. An experienced reporter knows what kind of information can be found in the city treasurer's office and what is in a court clerk's records. Experienced reporters know that there is a lot of useful information in the records of the registrar of deeds and in the tax collector's office. It may take some digging to get a specific piece of information, but almost always the information is there and can be found by those who know where to look.

Data banks — whole libraries of information available through computer terminals — are a new and increasingly useful source of information. Many newspapers have terminals in their reference libraries, and a reporter can ask for background on the subminimum wage or the status of prisoners on death row and in minutes get a printout of data that might have taken days to dig out of other sources.

On simple things, reporters can find answers quickly because they know whom to ask and where to find the record. Many times the information is not easy to find, and reporters have to use ingenuity and persistence to get what they want. But experienced reporters work on the premise that someone knows, that somewhere there is a book, a record, a report that contains the information needed. They keep asking and digging, and eventually they find what they want.

Verifying Information

Checking, cross-checking and verifying are basic steps in reporting. Reporters often talk of *two-source* or *three-source* stories, meaning that the story was based on information that was verified by two or three knowledgeable and reliable sources.

Careful reporters check everything. They take nothing for granted. They check spellings, dates and figures with news sources. They check facts with other sources and compare their findings with written records. They use city directories and telephone books to ensure the accuracy of names and addresses. Legislative handbooks and state manuals are helpful in checking the names, titles and responsibilities of public officials.

Reporters learn early that it is easy to make mistakes unless information is carefully checked and verified. Editors are impatient with reporters whose copy contains inaccuracies. Complaints from readers, even libel suits, can follow careless reporting.

Accuracy derives not only from careful reporting and painstaking verification but also from the care with which reporters handle the information in their own notes and in their own copy. It is easy to misread your notes and to introduce errors into your copy. It is easy to misread something in an accurate record and to put a wrong name or a wrong figure in your notes. Careful checking at each stage of the reporting process is essential.

Careful reporters verify and cross-check as they go along. And after their copy has been written, they read it carefully, line by line, to be sure it checks against their notes.

The words *all names verified* written across the top of a page of copy are reassuring to an editor. A penciled-in *correct* or *(CQ)* by an unusual spelling or a questionable figure in a story is additional evidence of care and accuracy on the part of the reporter.

Interviewing

Any situation in which a reporter asks someone a question is, in a way, an interview. A dictionary definition describes an interview as a meeting at which a person is asked about his or her views, activities, etc. One of the purest forms of the journalistic interview, of course, is the questioning of knowledgeable and important people about their opinions. Such people are asked what they think because they have special knowledge, expertise or influence. Public officials up to and including presidents are among those most frequently interviewed. Because they are in a position to make things happen, the public is interested in their activities, their views and their plans. The *etc.* in the dictionary definition covers other situations in which reporters question news sources — for example, to gather facts for obituaries, weather stories, announcements of meetings or the standings in a local softball league.

Asking Questions

Interviewing, broadly, involves asking questions that elicit a response. It may be improper for lawyers to ask leading questions of witnesses during a trial, but in reporting, the leading question is everything. The reporter must direct the conversation and ask questions that will get people to supply the information the reporter wants. In every case, however, the question asked by the reporter must be an intelligent question, and the reporter must know something about the subject being discussed.

This is good theory but not always easy in practice. Journalism deals with too broad a range of subject matter for reporters to be knowledgeable about every subject they are likely to discuss with a news source. Reporters in special areas like labor, business or health can in time acquire the knowledge and expertise needed to talk with experts in their own fields. But general assignment reporters get bounced from one subject to another and are all too often at a disadvantage. Few reporters are ready to talk to a film star at one moment and a Chinese industrialist the next and then whip across town to interview an astronomer with a new theory about black holes.

In general, reporters with a good education start out with at least some preparation, and they can often fall back on their education. Exposure during four years of college to the humanities, to literature and the arts, to the sciences and history and economics is bound to provide a basis for talking intelligently with many news sources.

Journalists tend to be self-educated people in the sense that they carry their education beyond the classroom. They read widely and they study the world around them. They read their own newspaper, other newspapers, magazines, books and government reports. They read novels, history, biography and scientific and technical studies. Some study law, others business or economics. Question any journalist closely and you'll find a specialist on some subject.

But education and general knowledge aside, the reporter should be armed with some knowledge about the person to be interviewed and the subject to be discussed. And the reporter should have in mind at least a few specific questions that can be asked as the interview gets under way.

Once the questioning has started, it is essential that the reporter understand what is being said and be able to take careful notes while still keeping one part of the mind free to think of what comes next. The skilled reporter, in a sense, hopscotches along ahead of the person being interviewed and develops new questions based on what has already been said. The skilled reporter is also aware of omissions and asks questions that will fill in the gaps.

Control of an interview is not always easy. Some people gush like fountains once they start talking and can't be stopped easily. Others wander off course and have to be brought back to the subject. And the reporter has to have a sense of when the person being interviewed has been sucked dry and a graceful way of drawing the interview to a close.

Types of Interviews

It has already been suggested that interviews take different forms and have different purposes.

Reporters conduct interviews in order to write personality sketches, light stories explaining what a person is like. Such interviews require a blend of questioning and observation.

Reporters also conduct interviews in order to write detailed and serious biographical sketches, such as the exhaustive biographies that form the basis of *The New York Times'* obituaries.

Still other interviews are conducted so that the reporter can get the views of a knowledgeable person on a subject of current interest.

In some instances, the story comes from the questions asked by the reporter and the answers of the person interviewed. Sometimes an interview is piggybacked on a news event that provides the major part of the story. For example, an enterprising reporter may, after covering a speech, talk to the speaker and ask some additional questions about the speech or even some questions that go beyond the topic of the speech. Good stories can result from this kind of interviewing.

Most interviews are one-on-one situations in which the reporter has the full attention of the person interviewed. There are occasions, however, when interviews are arranged so that several reporters talk with someone at the same time. You don't get exclusive stories this way, but if reporters work together and follow up each other's questions, if they help each other probe and question, a much better story may result. And, of course, all reporters write their own stories so that while the basis for each story will be the same, the way the story is written will in each case be somewhat different.

Press conferences are another thing entirely. Here not just two or three but a dozen reporters, sometimes scores of reporters, attempt to question someone. Here, too, reporters need to work together by following up one another's questions. Otherwise, the questioning may range so far afield and the discussion become so fragmented that nothing useful results.

Interviews ought to be conducted face to face, but that is not always possible. It is possible to interview people over the telephone, and this is often done when time is short or the person to be interviewed is not close by. Interviews have been done in writing, too, by sending written questions to a person who won't meet reporters face to face.

Reporting Techniques

Reporting requires a number of techniques that together make up the news-gathering process. These techniques or methods of reporting are interrelated and complementary. They are not, however, learned or acquired simultaneously but instead are usually learned in stages. Only when reporters are able to work comfortably with all these techniques are they fully competent in their profession.

The first technique is the *stenographic*, which requires only listening and note taking. Every skilled reporter, of course, listens and takes notes, but reporting at this level is often cut-and-dried and uninspired. It is, however, where you start.

The second technique is *interviewing* or *questioning,* which requires not only that reporters listen to what people are saying but also that they ask questions to add to what they have heard. With the ability to ask questions intelligently goes the ability to better select what is important and to weed out what is not important among all the things heard.

Third is *observing.* At this level, reporters add their own powers of observation to the more easily learned techniques of listening and questioning. They learn to see and hear so that they can add what they themselves know to facts gathered in other ways. This is a harder skill to learn, a more advanced technique.

Finally, there is *investigation.* Here the reporter makes use of knowledgeable people and written records as sources. At this point the reporter is not dependent on what people offer in press releases or speeches or what is heard during a city council meeting. Reporters who make use of all these techniques will listen, question, make their own observations and then seek out additional information by knowing who to ask or where to find the written record.

The truly accomplished reporter makes use of all these techniques and operates at all these levels. The ability to ask questions, to observe and to make use of independent sources provides the basis for accurate and meaningful reporting. Presentation of the news of the day in understandable and meaningful form is the purpose of the newspaper. Reporters are the essential element in the process.

Suggestions for Further Reading

These books provide further information about reporters and reporting.

Adler, Ruth, ed. *A Day in the Life of The New York Times.* New York: J.B. Lippincott Company, 1971.
    An hour-by-hour chronicle of newspaper production.

Biagi, Shirley. *News Talk I.* Belmont, Calif.: Wadsworth Publishing Co., 1987.
    Award-winning journalists discuss their work and their professional lives.

Cannon, Lou. *Reporting: An Inside View.* Sacramento: California Journal Press. 1977.
    About newspaper reporters and how they do their work.

Greene, Ward, ed. *Star Reporters.* New York: Random House, 1948.
    A collection of 34 famous news stories.

Liebling, A.J. *The Most of A.J. Liebling.* New York: Simon and Schuster, 1963.

A sampling of the reportage of the gifted writer for *The New Yorker* magazine.

Mollenhoff, Clark R. *Investigative Reporting.* New York: Macmillan, 1981.

A Pulitzer Prize–winning investigative reporter tells how he did it in a text that is partly autobiographical.

JETS BLOW IT
And Washington skins Bears 27-13
Sports/B1

SUNDAY
JANUARY 4, 1987
50 cents

The Times

Serving the New Jersey capital region for more than a century

Partly cloudy
High around 40
Tomorrow sunny, cool
Details/A2

Female trooper critically hurt in turnpike assault

By FRANK McGUIRE
Staff Writer

MOUNT LAUREL — A female state trooper was in critical condition last night with head injuries after she was assaulted by two Virginia men on the New Jersey Turnpike Friday night, state police said.

The assault apparently occurred when the trooper was trying to arrest the men on drug charges, police said.

One of the suspects, Roosevelt Walker, 42, of Petersburg, Va., surrendered to Virginia authorities early yesterday morning and was charged with the aggravated assault of Trooper Susan Marie Smith of the Moorestown station, state police spokesman Lt. Thomas Gallagher said.

Walker also was charged with possession of a controlled dangerous substance, eluding arrest and escape, Gallagher said.

The other suspect, identified as Robert F. Wooden Jr., 48, also of Petersburg, was still at large last night, state police said.

SMITH, 28, of Browns Mills, was in the intensive care unit at Burlington County Memorial Hospital in Mount Holly with a cut to the head and scrapes and bruises to the face, Gallagher said.

Trooper William Sweeney of the Moorestown station discovered Smith about 10 p.m. Friday as she wandered in a daze by her patrol car, which was parked on the shoulder of the New Jersey Turnpike near milepost 37.6 south, just north of the Mount Laurel exit of the turnpike, Gallagher said.

Sweeney spotted Smith's patrol car while he was on routine patrol in the northbound lanes of the turnpike. He radioed her to see if she needed help,

but Smith did not respond, Gallagher said.

Sweeney turned around, rushed to the scene and found the injured trooper.

Sweeney also found a driver's license in the name of Robert F. Wooden Jr., an automobile registration in Walker's name, and marijuana in Smith's pocket, Gallagher said. Smith's handcuffs were also found on the ground nearby, police said.

"WE ARE assuming that she was trying to make an arrest," he said. Smith was semi-conscious and under sedation yesterday and under her authorities what had happened, Gallagher said.

Smith has been a state trooper since June 1985 and was assigned to the Moorestown station in October, Gallagher said.

• see TROOPER, A12

Coastal flooding recedes

Beaches damaged at the Jersey Shore

Associated Press

Most of the flooding caused in New Jersey by the winter's first major storm has receded, but officials still were assessing yesterday what one called "pretty extensive" beach erosion.

Coast Guard officials and Atlantic County marine police said they had no reports of damage to homes or boats in the Atlantic City, though the storm tore loose some planks from the gambling resort's famed Boardwalk.

There was, however, storm-related damage in northern New Jersey to more than 100 homes in the Little Ferry, where the Hackensack River overran its banks Friday, putting about a half mile square under about two feet of water for a time, police said.

The state's emergency management coordinator, state police Capt. Joseph Craparotta, said his office was compiling county damage reports and would not have a statewide dollar estimate until tomorrow.

In Atlantic City, waves created by Friday's fierce coastal storm crashed over the Boardwalk, inundating Ocean Avenue two blocks away with 3 feet of sea water, said Coast Guard Petty Officer Rob Laabs.

ROADS LEADING into Atlantic City were closed for about three hours, but the casinos were not damaged. In all, fewer than a dozen city residents were evacuated.

In Egg Harbor Township, emergency coordinators said at least 55 people were evacuated Friday. Township police said yesterday that there were no

• see FLOODING, A12

▶ New England skiers rejoice over two feet of new snow. A12.

1986 in Mercer County brought trash decision, ethics dispute

By MICHAEL BOOTH
Staff Writer

For Mercer County, 1986 saw the freeholders and the administration end years of political wrangling by deciding on a location for a multi-million dollar trash incinerator.

The year was highlighted by an election campaign fraught with verbal attacks over ethics. The election resulted in one Democrat being ousted and a third Republican freeholder added to the board.

After more than a decade of studies, false starts and arguments over the best location, the freeholders and the administration in October finally compromised on Hamilton's Duck Island for the site of its $200 million incinerator.

Earlier in the year, it had appeared the incinerator would be located at the Trenton freightyards, a site favored by the county's two highest elected officials — Republican county Executive Bill Mathesius and Democratic Free-

holder President Anthony J. "Skip" Cimino. But the Democratic majority on the board rejected the site.

DESPITE THE VERBAL sniping common between political parties, Mathesius and Cimino said last week they believe 1986 was a year in which vital issues were addressed.

"I don't think the political disputes were any greater than in any other

• see MERCER, A12

Budget '88: new binding, old themes

By TOM RAUM
Associated Press

WASHINGTON — President Reagan is ready to submit to Congress the seventh budget of his presidency, but most of the deficit-reduction proposals in the $1.02 trillion document will be variations on themes already rejected by the lawmakers.

The budget, to be formally unveiled at 8 a.m. tomorrow, is expected to look strikingly like the budget Reagan submitted the year before and the year before that.

The color of the cover will be maroon. It was blue last year.

And the contents will be abbreviated — to accomodate the fact that this year the budget is going to Capitol Hill a month early.

LIKE PREVIOUS Reagan budgets, however, it will call for no new taxes but hefty defense increases and wide-ranging cuts in domestic programs — including sharp cutbacks in housing, education, mass transit and student loans.

It will also call for abolition of most of the same 40 programs targeted by last year's budget. Congress ignored that recommendation.

Congressional Democrats, who now control both chambers of Congress, have already served notice that the "dead on arrival" epithet applied to the past two Reagan budgets may be equally applicable this year.

Administration officials don't apologize for the similarity with previous budgets, they boast about it.

"It's the same Ronald Reagan," says Budget Director James C. Miller III. In his weekly radio address, Reagan said yesterday that Congress must avoid "budget-busting legislation" and

MUSKET SALUTE — Commander James Shedlauskas of the Northampton Town Militia barks out the order to fire a rifle salute during a ceremony commemorating the 210th anniversary of the Battle of Princeton yesterday. About 100 people turned out for the event. Story A3.

President Reagan
... urges spending cuts

▶ Reagan shows healthy resiliency. A10.

should any yield to the temptation to raise taxes instead of cutting spending to reduce deficits.

"That budget cuts spending and leaves your family's paycheck alone," Reagan said.

ADMINISTRATION officials say that the budget will propose about $42 billion in cuts and other savings that they claim would result in a federal deficit in fiscal 1988, which begins Oct. 1, of just under the Gramm-Rudman

• see BUDGET, A10

Adults hit the books to earn their diplomas

By PAT PARENTE
Staff Writer

WILLINGBORO — Like the 75-year-old woman who decided she wanted to attend college, most participants in the school district's continuing education program are sorry they dropped out of school.

And, like the 75-year-old woman

who figured it wasn't too late, they turn to the program to finally get their high school diplomas.

According to program director John Celani, about 80 people graduate each year from the township's adult high school program.

"Mostly, they're people who are sorry they dropped out," he said. "Mainly they are adults in their early to mid-20s who dropped out at 16 with a year or a year-and-a-half of schooling to go."

And although the ages and backgrounds vary, the dropouts have one thing in common. Somewhere along the line, Celani said, they realized "they're not going anywhere" in their careers without their high school diplomas.

"SO THEY come back," he said. "Usually it doesn't take more than a year to finish up."

According to Celani, the district will begin second semester night school courses for adult students Feb. 2. Classes meet four nights a week, Monday through Thursday, he said.

In addition, returning students also can begin attending day school at any time of the year for individual study work, Celani said.

"People come in and we evaluate their credits and see what credits are needed to complete a diploma," he

• see EDUCATION, A12

Back to the nest

Many young adults can't afford their dream of independence

By PAT R. GILBERT
Staff Writer

They're like the swallows returning to Capistrano, except they carry college degrees and a few hundred pounds of luggage.

And their visits are not exactly of the short or seasonal variety. They're much more inclined to pull up a comfortable chair and stay a few years.

Known as the "Boomerang Generation," they are young adults who are flocking in increasing numbers back to the nests of their parents.

It's not exactly what they had planned for themselves after graduation.

When Tom Lozowski graduated from Villanova University in 1985, he did not expect to be greeting his parents at breakfast in their Lower Makefield home almost two years later.

"WHEN I graduated, I really didn't think I'd still be here," the 23-year-old Lozowski said. "I didn't have a job at the time, and after traveling in Europe, I was broke."

But Lozowski got a job last January

as a marketing engineer with Public Service Electric & Gas in Princeton.

He still lives in the room where he grew up amid high school letters and some outdated posters on the walls.

"I'm still here, basically, because of the expense," he said. "When I move, I'd like to get a house or a townhouse."

But, for now, he appears happy enough.

"It's all right. There's always a nice dinner, food in the refrigerator, a nice color TV, a washer and dryer, and you don't have to worry about bills too much."

LOZOWSKI'S situation is not unlike those of many young Americans who live with their parents after graduation primarily because they cannot afford to move out on their own.

Some hold out as a way to obtain the style of living in which they have become accustomed. Others return after getting divorced or losing a job.

That's why many of the Baby Boom generation are being likened to boomerangs. Home delay delayed devices which return to their originating points after a hefty throw.

• see BACK HOME, A8

The Martinette family of Pennington is an example of how more young adults live at home with their parents, in this case Charles and Jill in background. Daughters, from front left, are Yvette, Tara, Yvonne and Mary, holding kitten Samantha.

3

News Copy

There is, of course, a certain amount of drudgery in newspaper work, just as there is in teaching classes, tunnelling into a bank or being President of the United States. I suppose that even the most pleasurable of imaginable occupations, that of batting baseballs through the windows of the RCA Building, would pall a little as the days ran on.

James Thurber

There was a time when news writers wrote out their copy in longhand using pen and ink. And for a long period news writers pounded out their copy on a typewriter. Today in newsrooms, news bureaus and wire service bureaus, news writers sit at the keyboard of a video display terminal, a VDT, and write their stories. As they write, their copy appears, line by line, on a screen above the keyboard. No paper. Just keystrokes and little blips of light on the screen.

When the story is complete, the writer touches a control button and the story disappears from the screen and moves instantaneously from the writer's VDT to the memory bank of the newsroom's computer. From this repository, when it is needed, an editor sitting at another VDT will call up the story and edit it in the same way it was written — by means of a keyboard and special controls that enable the editor to change words, delete words or sentences and add words or sentences. The editor can even change the order of sentences or paragraphs at the touch of a couple of control buttons.

The technological revolution that began in the early 1960s continues. New developments in electronic technology regularly bring new generations of computer-driven VDTs and typesetters into the newsroom and the composing room. The next big step, already taken by some newspapers, is *pagination* — the process of composing entire pages by computer.

The electronic revolution has made a great deal of difference to the writer and editor, and not only because of the VDT's advantages over the typewriter as a means of writing and editing news stories. Until the advent of computer-driven typesetters, the mechanical process of setting type and making pages ready for the press controlled and greatly restricted the work of the newsroom. The newsroom was dependent on the typesetting process. Now the newsroom with its VDTs controls the production process. Words, sentences, paragraphs and entire stories written and edited in the newsroom on VDTs are set into type photographically by a computer-driven typesetter controlled from the newsroom. When pagination is also controlled by editors in the newsroom, the entire process, from writing and editing through composition and page makeup, can be accomplished in the newsroom by editorial people.

The fact that newsroom personnel can control not only the editorial process but also the production process right up to the start of the press has enormous implications for newspaper journalists. The additional responsibility implies both challenges and penalties. The newspaper in this electronic age is a better product — more creative, more sophisticated than ever before. Newspaper journalists today and in the future must be more talented, better educated and better prepared in newsroom practices if they are to write and edit and manage not just today's newspaper but the newspaper of the future.

Those who prepare themselves for this new age of electronic journalism will be eagerly sought out by editors. They will be better paid, and they will advance more rapidly to positions of responsibility. And they will have a larger voice in what the newspaper will publish and what it will look like.

VDTs, phototypesetting and pagination are sophisticated electronic systems. They are also expensive systems, and while profitable newspapers can afford such production systems, not all schools of journalism can. More and more departments and schools of journalism have installed VDTs for students to use in learning to write and edit. But for some time to come, many beginning news writers will continue to write news stories on copy paper and use a copy pencil to edit their work.

And there will continue to be a need to know the old paper-and-pencil system of copy preparation. Writing and editing are creative skills that can be accomplished with pen or pencil, on a typewriter or a VDT. The discussion in this chapter of copy preparation and copy editing is intended to introduce you to a basic and necessary journalistic skill. Your instruction will be in terms of paper and copy pencil, but

Reporters and editors at work in the newsroom of the York *(Pa.)* Daily Record. *(© Copyright,* York Daily Record*)*

the skills required for editing in the traditional way will carry over to the VDT when you sit at the electronic keyboard.

Typing Skills

News writers today produce their copy at the keyboard of a VDT. The two-finger artist, the slow typist or the sloppy typist is going to have a hard time of it. It will pay the beginner at the outset to become a better-than-average typist. Speed and accuracy are highly important in the newsroom. Publishers once talked of the cost of producing a galley

41

of type — roughly enough copy to fill one newspaper column — but now they talk about the cost of *keystrokes*. A keystroke is the touch of one finger on a single key of a VDT or typewriter.

Technology is not going to make the reporter and news writer obsolete. But it is going to require that aspiring news writers be able to type quickly and skillfully. They must be able to turn out well-written, clean copy on either a typewriter or a VDT.

Copy Paper

Copy paper is newsprint, the same soft, wood-fiber paper that the newspaper is printed on. It is cheap and it is perishable, but it is ideally suited to newsroom use. Much of it, for reasons of economy, is salvaged from unused paper left on the cores of newsprint rolls taken off the presses.

Copy paper is a standard 8½ by 11 inches. Copy — the story you write on copy paper — is always double- or triple-spaced to make it easier to read and edit. And, of course, copy is always typed on only one side of the sheet.

Margins

Margins on news copy should be generous, at least an inch at left and right. Copy with good wide margins not only looks a lot neater but is easier to read and edit than copy crowded out into the margins.

At the top of the first page of copy it is necessary to leave an extra-deep margin, from 4 to 5 inches, so that your editor has room to write instructions for the copy desk and for the composing room. If a standard sheet of copy paper is folded the short way, no more than two or three lines of copy should show above the fold. On the second and succeeding pages, a margin of 1½ inches or so usually is enough. For utmost clarity, indent generously for each paragraph. Six or eight spaces is about right.

Copy Control

In the days before VDTs came into the newsroom, several hundred to several thousand news stories might be edited and sent to the composing room to be set into type on a given day. Editors had to develop a system for keeping track of all this copy so that each story would be published on the right day, on the right page and in the right edition. A simple system for keeping track of what is now referred to as *hard copy* — news stories on paper — will be discussed here. You will find a similar system in use when you write your copy on a VDT.

Identifying Copy

All copy has to be identified so editors will know who wrote it and what the story is about. The simplest system calls for the news writer's name and an identifying key word on each page of copy. An example is this notation on the first page of copy:

```
sinclair/armed robbery
```

On the second page of the copy, the writer includes a page number:

```
sinclair/armed robbery/page 2
```

These notations tell the editor that the story was written by a news writer named Sinclair and that the story is about an armed robbery. Page numbers serve to keep the copy in proper order, of course. Another example:

```
kennedy center -- with art
sun local -- marcia
```

This tells the editor that the story is about the Kennedy Center and that there are photographs to accompany the story. The second line says that the story is intended for the Sunday paper and for a local news page or section. And the writer is Marcia.

Slug Lines

The identification lines for the story — in the examples just cited, the words *armed robbery* and *kennedy center* — are called *slug lines* or merely *slugs*. They may also be called *guides* or *guidelines*. When an editor tells you to "slug that story *fatal*," he means that you should use the word *fatal* as the identifying slug line.

Slug lines are important because they make it possible to keep track of the story as it moves through production channels from the typewriter or VDT to the printed page.

Slug lines must be concise, no more than four words. One or two words are preferable. The slug line must also be very specific because there may be two stories of a similar nature — two fatal accidents, for example — and editors must be able to tell them apart. It is best to use slug lines like *msu commencement, robber shot* or *dodgeville fatal* that make clear the identity of your story. Your editor wants to know what your story is about. He also wants to know what it is not about. Be as specific as possible. And, of course, slug lines must appear on every page of news copy.

More

When copy runs to more than a single page, every page except the last must be marked with a special symbol to indicate that the copy is not complete. Traditionally, the word *more* serves this purpose.

The word *more* should be centered just below the last line of copy or appear near the end of the last typewritten line — in other words, where it is visible and where editors, copy editors and typesetters will spot it easily.

You can see how this is done by referring to the sample of news copy shown in Figure 3.1.

Thirty

When you get to the end of your news story, you must put an *end mark* so that your editor will know that your story is complete, that there is no more to come. Use of the end mark is shown in Figure 3.2.

The symbol shown in Figure 3.2 is not the only acceptable end mark used by news writers. You may also use the traditional *thirty*, either as an Arabic figure or the word *thirty*, or the word *end*. Some writers use their initials as end marks. Any of these will do. If your editor has a preference in this matter, you'll be told.

When you have finished writing and go back over your copy, circle *more* marks, end marks and slug lines to set them apart and indicate that they are not part of your copy. You'll see this when you study Figures 3.1 and 3.2.

Clean Copy

News writers are expected to turn in copy that is clean and accurate. *Clean copy* means copy that is reasonably free from typing errors, typewritten revisions and penciled changes. Clean copy results not only from practice and experience, but also from following a few basic rules.

Strikeovers

Don't strike over letters. If you make a mistake and you catch it while the page is still in your typewriter, use the capital *X* to obliterate the error. Then type in the word correctly. When you back up and strike over a letter, it is not always possible to tell just what letter you mean. Ambiguity of this kind, especially in names, is dangerous. You can see in Figures 3.1 and 3.2 how words were *X*-d out.

Deletions

Use the capital letter *X* to obliterate and delete. Don't use the virgule, or slant. It doesn't do a good enough job.

When you make an error of one letter in a word or transpose letters, it is frequently best to use the *X* to obliterate the entire word and then type it in correctly rather than to attempt an understandable correction later on in pencil.

Word Division

Never divide a word at the end of a line. It is easier to read whole words than parts of words, and you don't want editors to be guessing at meaning as they read your copy. Compound words that require a hyphen should not be divided at the end of a line.

Spacing

Never single-space copy. Always double-space or triple-space. Don't add extra space between paragraphs, but keep the same spacing throughout your copy.

All Caps

Type all your copy in uppercase and lowercase, capital and small letters. Do not type words in all caps for emphasis or special effects.

Indenting

Indent only for paragraphs. If your editor wants your story or any part of it indented, someone else will mark it, and it will be set in type that way. News writers are not concerned with matters of typography.

frazier
Sunday/B2

The Carolton Board of Realtors has developed a plan to
counter the call for a temporary halt to ~~converting~~ converting
apartments to condominiums.

The board announced ~~XXXXX~~ Monday that it ~~XXXXX~~ will present
its proposal to the City Council this week.

Richard Klein, the realtors' president, said the board
~~XXXXX~~ thinks ~~XXXX~~ its proposal ~~XXXXX~~ is fair to apartment
owners and to tenants.

He was critical of the proposal made in June by the
Carolton Tenants Association that a moratorium be placed ~~XXXXXX~~
on conversions until the vacancy rate in the city reaches
3 percent.

"That would ~~XXXXXX~~ just worsen the housing problem
here," ~~XXXXX~~ Klein said.

The board's proposal would require that:

-- Tenants ~~XXXXXXX~~ of an apartment building to be
converted to a condominium be given 120 days' notice.

Figure 3.1 *A professionally prepared page of news copy. This is clean copy.
Note the clear and unambiguous nature of the editing marks.*

```
frazier -- Sunday/B2 -- realtors -- page 2

     /-- Tenants be given a first right of ~~xxxxxxx~~ refusal
to purchase.
     /-- Housing code violations be removed ~~xxxxxxxxxx~~
before ~~xxxxxx~~ the sale of the first converted unit is
closed.
     /-- Apartment ~~xxxxxx~~ building owners be required to notify
tenants of their intention to convert a building to a condominium.
                              ##
```

Figure 3.2 *The second and other pages of news copy must be identified as clearly as the first page. Every page of copy must carry the writer's name, the slug line for the story and a page number.*

Paragraphing

When you begin to write, you must keep in mind the appearance of the newspaper page on which your story will appear. In the newsroom, paragraphing is not always related to the content of the story. To a great extent, paragraphing is a purely mechanical matter. The length of a paragraph has more to do with the point size of the type and the width of lines than it does with what you are writing about. Editors want the newspaper page to be attractive, inviting and readable. Short paragraphs allow for white space. They look easier to read. Long columns of gray type uninterrupted by white space, subheads or boldface type tend to repel readers.

In news writing, keep your paragraphs short. You may sometimes want to set a single sentence aside in a paragraph. Generally, however, your paragraphs should run to two or three sentences, especially if the sentences are short. Occasionally, you can put four or more sentences into a paragraph.

Be wary of the one-sentence paragraph. Too many one-sentence paragraphs, especially if your sentences are short, will make your copy sound choppy. Variety in sentence length and in the number of sentences in each paragraph will give your writing rhythm.

Newspaper columns are wider today than they were a few years ago now that most newspapers are using a six-column format. Paragraphs can run a little longer where columns are wider. But the basic rule for news writers is — keep your paragraphs short. You will develop a feel for sentence length and paragraph length as you develop your writing skills. In the meantime, study newspaper pages. Get to know the newspaper. It will help you develop a sense of newsroom practices.

Editing News Copy

The last step in writing a news story comes after your story has been completed and the last sheet of copy paper taken out of the typewriter. Experienced news writers at this point take time to read over their copy carefully, word by word and line by line. They look for typing errors, mistakes in spelling and usage and in points of style or writing faults that they can correct themselves before turning their copy over to an editor.

News writers have a responsibility to correct their own copy. They also have a responsibility for accuracy in fact in their news stories. Those who don't take these responsibilities seriously won't last long in newspaper newsrooms.

The usual newsroom practice is to make corrections with a *copy pencil*. This is a rather fat pencil with a broad, soft lead ideal for writing on the soft surface of copy paper. Newspapers supply their staff with copy pencils. Pencils with hard lead are not suitable for use on copy paper. Ballpoint pens are not used in editing copy, for you can't erase or alter inked-in corrections.

Editing Marks

In the newsroom, a set of traditional and standard symbols is used to indicate changes that should be made in copy. These are called *copy-editing marks* and are not always identical to the proofreading marks used to indicate corrections on proofs.

Copy-editing marks are always made within the copy at the place where the error occurs or a change is wanted. They are never made in the margin.

Here's the system.

Paragraph

When you wish to indicate that a paragraph should start where there is no paragraph break in the copy, make a neat right angle like this:

```
       approaching truck. He was issued a ticket for
```

The news writer or the copy desk usually also marks the paragraphs that were indented properly on the typewritten copy, as you can see in Figures 3.1 and 3.2.

Capitalization

When you want to change a lowercase letter to a capital letter, draw either two or three short lines under the letter:

```
       capitalize east in east Lansing
```

Lowercase

When you want a capital letter changed to a lowercase letter, draw a slant line through the letter. The line should slant from right to left, like this:

```
       make this Lowercase
```

Abbreviations

To indicate that a word spelled out in copy should be abbreviated, circle the word:

```
       abbreviate Street as St.
```

To spell out a word abbreviated in copy, circle the word:

```
       spell out St as Street
```

This instruction is usually adequate, but if there is reason to think that the editor or a copy editor might not know the abbreviation or the spelled-out form you want, cross out the word and write it in above the line:

```
                    manufacturing
       spell out mfg. to ensure clarity
```

Numbers

To change Arabic figures to words or vice versa, circle them:

    spell out (9), thus, nine

    make (twelve) an Arabic figure, thus, 12

Transposition

Where words or letters have been typed in the wrong order, indicate the proper order with the transposition symbol:

    change order of words two

    change roder of two letters

When you use the transposition mark to change the order of a couple of letters, as in the example here, the results may not be entirely clear. If not, cross out the word and write it in above the line:

    change ~~roder~~ *order* of two letters

Insertion

To insert a word or a letter within a word, print it neatly above the line and indicate its intended position with a bracket, a couple of slant lines, above the line. Add a small caret below the line to further indicate where the insertion is to be made:

                missing
    insert a word or phrase, thus

                    s
    insert a mising letter, thus

Space

When words or figures are improperly divided by unwanted space, indicate that the space is to be closed up by making short, slightly curved lines above and below the space:

    gave his book to an other person

```
ordered to pay a $10,0 00 fine
```

This mark means to close up and leave no space, so it can be used only to close up space within a word or figure.

When words or figures are improperly run together and there is no space where there should be, separate the words or figures in this way:

```
improperly spaced words are separated thus

or separated in this way

or separated in this way
```

Periods and Commas

A missing period or comma is indicated by an editing mark placed where the period or comma belongs. A period is indicated by a small cross or *x* enclosed in a circle:

```
Always end a sentence with a period
```

A comma is enclosed by a caret:

```
Some commas, you see, come in pairs.
```

Colons and Semicolons

Colons and semicolons, like commas, are enclosed within carets for insertion:

```
War is inevitable if one is attacked all will
fight.

The president responded sharply "That's baloney."
```

Hyphens and Dashes

Hyphens are indicated by double horizontal lines that look like equal signs:

```
Insert a hyphen in H bomb in this way.
```

The dash is indicated by a single, slightly longer line.

```
Insert a dash after the word dash like this.
```

Some copy editors insert a dash in this way:

```
Insert a dash after the word dash like this.
```

Quotation Marks

A missing quotation mark can be inserted at the proper place in the line and enclosed in a small semicircle. Note that the semicircles are different for opening quote marks and closing quote marks.

```
Insert opening quote marks," he suggested.
```

```
"Insert closing quote marks, he suggested.
```

Opening and closing quotation marks may also be inserted in this way:

```
Insert quotation marks in this sentence, he
ordered.
```

Other Punctuation

Question marks, exclamation points and apostrophes are placed above the line. Use slant lines to show where they go, and place a caret below the line to further indicate the point of insertion.

```
"Does a question mark belong here" he asked.
```

```
"Attention" the sergeant shouted.
```

```
Insert an apostrophe in boys.
```

No Paragraph

Where copy has been indented for a paragraph and it is later decided not to start a paragraph at this point, run a guideline connecting the last word of the first paragraph with the first word of the next paragraph. You can see how this is done in Figure 3.3, where a guideline

cooper -- tuesday final -- bridge -- page 2

The old bridge will be torn down ~~XXXXXXXXXX~~ and a new one
built in its place.

While the ~~XXXXXXXXX~~ bridge is closed, traffic ~~XXXXXXXX~~
~~XXXXXXXXX~~ will be diverted onto other routes.

One detour ~~XXXXXXXXXXXX~~ will follow the Lake Lansing
Road, Park Road and ~~XXXXXXXXXXXXXXXXXXXXXXXX~~ Grand Ledge
Road into Oak Ridge and Oak Brook.

The other route will follow ~~XXXXXX~~ Collins ~~XXXXXXXXXXXX~~
~~XXXXXXXXXXXX~~ Road, Jolley Road and Cedar Street into Holt.

~~XXXXXXXXXXXXXXXXXXXXXXXXXXXXXXXXXXXXXXXXXXXXXXXXXXX~~
~~XXXXXXXXXXXXXXXXXXXXXXXXXXXXXXXXXXXXXXXXXXXXXXXXXX~~

The city public works department will erect signs directing
motorists to the ~~XXXXXXXX~~ detour routes.

Some ~~XXXXXXX~~ detour roads -- Collins Road and Lake ~~XXXXXXX~~
~~XXXXXXXXXXXXXXXXXXXXXXXXXXXXXXXXXXXXXXXXXXX~~ Lansing Road,
for example -- are in poor condition because of winter weather.
City ~~XXXXXX~~ officials had hoped to have these roads repaired by
~~XXXXXX~~ now, Coughlin ~~XXXXX~~ said, but wet ~~XXXXXXX~~ weather has
caused a delay in spring road work throughout the county.

Figure 3.3 *This copy has been heavily edited to show how extensive deletions
are handled. Use eye guidelines within the lines. Don't use guidelines at the ends
of lines except as shown here.*

indicates that the second and third paragraphs are to be run in, that is,
run as one paragraph.

Deletions

When you want to delete a single letter, figure or punctuation mark,
the simplest thing to do is to cover it up. Just use your copy pencil.

delete an extra let⌢ter in this way

delete an unnecessary period, or comma, in
this way

delete an unwanted ⁄quote mark in this way

If you want to delete a word, draw a couple of bold horizontal lines
through the word with your copy pencil:

delete an extra w̶o̶r̶d̶ word in this way

    You will note that the deleted matter is also bridged with a
guideline. The guideline says "follow from here to here." You can see
how the bridging line is used in Figures 3.1, 3.2 and 3.3.
    Note, too, that there is a difference between this bridging line,
which means *close up to normal spacing,* and the close-up symbol used
to delete unwanted space within words or figures. The close-up mark
goes both above and below the line. The bridging line goes only over
the line. These marks are not interchangeable.

Extensive Deletions

When a writer makes extensive deletions in typewritten copy, the practice is to use the capital *X* to obliterate the unwanted matter. Later, in
editing copy, it is good practice to draw horizontal lines through the
deleted matter.
    In making deletions in copy that has been removed from the type-
writer, use your copy pencil. Again, draw strong horizontal lines
through unwanted matter.
    If deletions are extensive, guidelines may be necessary to bridge the
gaps. You can see how this is done in Figure 3.3. Note also where bridging is *not* used. You do not need guidelines at the beginning or end of
lines if the eye will naturally move to the next line and the next word.

Stet

If you have, for example, drawn a line through a word to delete it and
then changed your mind, there's an editing mark to undo your change.
You can write in the word *stet* above the unwanted correction. *Stet*
means "let it stand." Circle it, of course, to indicate that it is an instruction, not part of the copy:

Leave this s̶a̶m̶p̶l̶e̶ copy the way it was.

Verification

Names and figures in your copy that might be questioned by the copy desk should be marked to indicate that you have verified them and know them to be correct. Some editors would like you to write "All names verified" at the top of the first page of your copy. Within the copy, a small *OK*, circled, next to the verified word or number will usually do. Some editors prefer that you draw a box around the item. Others use *CQ*, meaning *correct*. You can, of course, type in an *OK* or *CQ* as you write your story. For example:

```
              (OK)
 Dr. Eugene Guthrie, Alfred Newman, John

 P. Parks, Walker Roberts, Mary Ann Small,

 Lyn (CQ) Jennings, Albert Littlefield and

 Russel  Knight.
```

Suggestions for Further Reading

Newspaper journalists should know their roots. These histories of important daily newspapers are worthwhile reading.

Angelo, Frank. *On Guard*. Detroit: Detroit Free Press, 1981.
> A history of the *Detroit Free Press* by a former managing editor. The *Free Press* was the first daily newspaper in Michigan.

Fowler, Gene. *Timber Line*. Garden City, N.Y.: Halcyon House, 1943.
> Colorful narrative about the *Denver Post* and the circus journalism of Bonfils and Tammen.

Johnson, Gerald W. et al. *The Sunpapers of Baltimore*. New York: Knopf, 1937.
> The morning and evening *Sun* have long been important newspapers.

Lyons, Louis M. *Newspaper Story*. Cambridge, Mass.: Harvard University Press, Belknap Press, 1971.
> A history of the *Boston Globe* by the former curator of the Nieman Foundation.

Roberts, Chalmers M. *The Washington Post*. Boston: Houghton Mifflin Company, 1977.
> The first 100 years of one of our most important and influential newspapers.

Wendt, Lloyd. *Chicago Tribune*. Chicago: Rand McNally, 1979.
> The *Tribune* for many years referred to itself as "the world's greatest newspaper."

The Seattle Times Seattle Post-Intelligencer

SUNDAY

SNOW
Temperatures in the 30s. Increasing clouds with snow. Rain later this evening.
DETAILS, E10

$1.00
December 1, 1985
512 pages

WASHINGTON'S LARGEST NEWSPAPER ■ COPYRIGHT 1985, SEATTLE TIMES COMPANY

If you think it's bad now...

Consider the snowstorms of yore

The big snow of 1916 made a cold nightmare of Second Avenue. The view is south near Union Street.

Seattle Times

By Bill Dietrich
Times staff reporter

A w right, you snow wimps.

Yes, last month was the snowiest November on record, with 17.4 inches of the white stuff having fallen at Seattle-Tacoma International Airport.

Yes, it also was one of the coldest Novembers, with temperature records having shattered like puddle ice for eight straight days, Nov. 20-27.

Yes, your car is hibernating on a freeway shoulder, your Christmas shopping timetable is ruined and the 91st schools sent

■ Strong high pressure over western Alaska, the villain behind the record-setting past two weeks, is a hero in summer. **Northwest, D 2.** Storms are hitting much of the U.S. **A 20.**

home your kids. Even the travel brochures for Fargo, N.D., are starting to look good.

But if you think this is bad, consider the storms of yesteryear; back when men were men, women interested such foolishness, the only central heating was one's heart and the potty was a lung, snowbound walk from the back door.

Consider, for example, the winter of 1880 when snowfall

Please see SNOW on A 12

That's sawmill operator John Dunn pushing the Pontiac driven by Mrs. Dunn on a slippery slope on Pine Street near Boren Avenue during snow in January 1950.

Seattle Times

Rain (rain??) is in the forecast

By Greg Heberlein
Times staff reporter

Rain? Can it be possible?

By tonight, or by tomorrow at the latest, rain is expected to fall in the Seattle area, says Larry Kierulff, a National Weather Service forecaster. And it looks as if November's record snows could be only a memory by midweek, when temperatures are expected to be in the 40s.

But today's precipitation is expected to start as snow or sleet, Kierulff cautioned.

"There will be frozen precipitation of some kind," Kierulff said. "It could be snow or sleet."

Kierulff said he was loath to predict accumulations. He said 4 inches are possible, but not necessarily likely in central Puget Sound.

"We're expecting the harsh weather to be away from Seattle," Kierulff said. "It looks like heavy snow and freezing rain in the northern parts of Washington, like Bellingham, and also the southern parts, south of Olympia."

Western Oregon and southwest Washington both reported snow accumulations up to 4 inches yesterday. At midday yesterday, the Weather Service issued a winter storm watch for Whatcom County, on the Canadian border. Severe weather is expected to continue in eastern Washington.

But snow from the coming storm "is expected to moderate quickly enough to escape heavy

Please see WEATHER on A 12

Boeing-Canada deal 'all but wrapped up'

Announcement of de Havilland sale could come tomorrow

by William Gough
Times staff reporter

The Boeing Co. apparently is in the pilot's seat to buy the financially troubled de Havilland Aircraft Co. from the Canadian government, or at least to acquire a share in the firm.

Boeing recently made a bid to buy de Havilland, and a Canadian member of Parliament says he has information that a deal is all but wrapped up.

An announcement is to be made to de Havilland's approximately 3,000 employees at Toronto tomorrow, followed by a news conference in Ottawa. The Toronto Star said Boeing's purchase of the manufacturer of commuter aircraft for about $150 million would be announced.

In Seattle, Boeing spokesman John Wheeler said he could not confirm whether Boeing's bid, of an undisclosed amount, had been accepted by the Canadian government. "The government may have made a decision, but we have not been notified officially of that," he said.

The Progressive Conservative government has been interested in divesting itself of de Havilland for some time. The firm lost $40 million last year on sales of more than $200 million and is expected to lose more than that this year.

Some Canadians are angry that de Havilland, if bought by Boeing,

would be foreign-owned. De Havilland, which manufactures commuter aircraft with short-takeoff-and-landing (STOL) capabilities, represents 23 percent of the Canadian aerospace industry and is an important research and defense arm of Canada.

The member of Parliament, Robert Kaplan, of the opposition Liberal party, is among those who are angry.

"I don't have anything against the Boeing Co., but I am concerned that if (de Havilland) goes back to foreign ownership, the STOL aircraft won't get the kind of priority they have had," Kaplan said in a telephone interview yesterday. De Havilland formerly was owned by a British firm.

Kaplan said he had heard Boeing's bid ranged from $175 million to $525 million, but that the amount of the bid might not be important.

"Whatever Boeing is taking out of one pocket it might get back in another pocket. There are certain understandings, if not outright agreements, that could be involved," he said.

For instance, Kaplan said that in return for concessions granted in the government involving de Havilland, Boeing might stipulate that Air Canada, Canada's national

Please see BOEING on A 9

Tomorrow's Reagan visit is brief but important for GOP

by Jack Broom
Times staff reporter

White House aides are allowing only about two hours to get President Reagan in and out of Seattle tomorrow — but those hours will be precious both to the president and his host, Sen. Slade Gorton.

"It'll raise a bundle of money," said Gorton, who is expecting more than 700 of his supporters to see the president at a $1,000-a-plate luncheon at the Westin Hotel. A visit from a president surging in popularity means cash and attention for the freshman senator up for re-election.

But the visit is by no means unselfish on Reagan's part. Every Senate Republican is important to the president as the GOP next year tries to cling to the slim Senate majority it has held since 1980.

With the House of Representatives in Democratic hands, a Republican senate is seen as vital to enabling Reagan to push his programs during the remainder of his term.

Twenty-two of 53 Senate seats held by Republicans are up for election in 1986, and four GOP veterans already have announced their intentions to retire: Barry Goldwater of Arizona, Charles Mathias of Maryland, Paul Laxalt of Nevada and John East of North

Carolina.

Democrats, on the other hand, have only 12 of their seats up for election. So far only two Democrats, Thomas Eagleton of Missouri and Russell Long of Louisiana, say they are bowing out. Many also expect Colorado's Gary Hart to abandon his Senate post to concentrate a 1988 presidential bid and deal with his $3 million-plus campaign debt from last year.

Reagan's brief Seattle stop comes at the end of a long Thanksgiving weekend the president spent at his ranch near Santa Barbara.

He is scheduled to arrive at Boeing Field from Los Angeles about 11:36 a.m., attend the luncheon an hour later and be back in the sky on his way to Washington, D.C., by 1:30 p.m.

The menu for Gorton's fundraiser features Washington wine, poached salmon, salad, a vegetable, and chocolate mousse cake.

A special, private reception for top campaign officials and Gorton's biggest donors — who've given the legal maximum of $2,000 per person or $4,000 per couple — will be held immediately before the luncheon.

That is the final campaign

Please see REAGAN on A 12

YOU SHOULDN'T MISS . . .

Halley's comet brightening
Astronomers have been watching a dim Halley's comet with telescopes and computers. Now they can see it with binoculars and even the naked eye.
Northwest D 1

Seattle's giant stevedoring firm
Stevedoring Services of America keeps a low profile, but in terms of cargo handled, it is believed to be the nation's second-largest stevedoring firm
Economy H 1

Writing the Lead

If we look intently and listen carefully and read voraciously, in time we begin to discover how a good writer works. We discover the importance of cadence; we learn that a sentence sounds better — to the inner ear — if the accented syllables fall into ordered arrangement.

Harry Hill of *The Milwaukee Journal*

The *lead* is simply the beginning of a news story. Generally, when we use the word *lead*, especially when we are talking about short and uncomplicated stories, we mean the first sentence of the story. And this first sentence, you will see from examples in this chapter and from reading newspapers, is also the first paragraph of a news story.

The lead for a longer, more involved news story, however, often consists of two, three or even four paragraphs. The simplest kind of a lead, although not necessarily the easiest to write, is the summary lead, the most useful and the most used news lead. Learn to write a good summary lead and you will have taken a big step toward becoming a professional news writer. An example of a well-written summary lead is shown in Figure 4.1.

> The Northwest College Board of Trustees Monday approved a master plan for expansion of the campus at a cost of $40 million.

Figure 4.1 *A five-W summary lead.*

The Summary Lead

The summary lead attempts to answer most, if not all, of these questions:

- What happened?
- Who was involved?
- Where did it happen?
- When did it happen?
- Why did it happen?
- How did it happen?

These questions are the five Ws of journalism — actually five Ws and an H — and they provide the news writer with a means of organizing the lead of a story. They also provide a framework or structure for organizing the rest of the story — the body, the development. The five Ws provide a bit more structure if they appear in order of importance. Most news leads emphasize *what happened.* Sometimes when there are people in the story the *who* and *what* are treated simultaneously. *Where* and *when* come next. The *how* and *why* of a story are not always treated in the lead but may be if it can be done concisely. So, now, in order, the five Ws are *what, who, where, when, why* and *how.* Let's see how they work in this news story:

> DELAWARE, Ohio (AP) — A Michigan trucker was killed Wednesday when his tractor-trailer rig blew a tire and flipped over on Interstate 71 in Delaware County.

The lead treats the *what* and *who* questions simultaneously: *what?* a fatality; *who?* a Michigan trucker. The lead also answers the question *how?* when his truck overturned.

The question *when?* is answered by Wednesday, and the question *where?* by identifying the place of the accident: on Interstate 71 in Delaware County.

However, although this lead does answer the questions posed by the five Ws, it is not complete because it does not fully identify the trucker who was killed. Some amplification or some additional details may be needed. So a lead generally needs the support of one or two more paragraphs — sometimes much more — to give the reader the whole story. This lead needs another paragraph to identify the trucker who was killed.

The Highway Patrol identified the dead man as Bruce Hawkins, 33, of Sand Creek, Mich.

This second paragraph adds something else. With the words *the highway patrol identified*, the writer provides *attribution*, that is, tells the reader the source of the story. News stories generally need attribution, but it is often, as it is here, unobtrusive. We'll discuss attribution more fully in Chapter 6.

Now, keeping the five Ws in mind, let's see how the following set of facts can be organized into a summary lead:

Fact 1 — A grant to a local hospital.

Fact 2 — Grant comes from the federal government.

Fact 3 — Grant is for $100,000.

Fact 4 — Purpose: to fund research into early detection of alcoholism among industrial workers.

Fact 5 — The hospital will work with the state Division of Vocational Rehabilitation in the study.

Fact 6 — The grant was announced today by Robert Jackson, director of the hospital's vocational rehabilitation services.

What's this story about? A local hospital — let's call it the Carolton General Hospital — has been awarded a federal grant for research into alcoholism. Let's see if we can put this into a lead:

Carolton General Hospital has been awarded a federal grant for the study of alcoholism.

That's an accurate statement, but a little too general. The hospital is not going to study everything about alcoholism, only one aspect of it. Let's try again:

Carolton General Hospital has been awarded $100,000 in federal funds for research into the early detection of alcoholism among industrial workers.

That's *what* has happened. And this statement also explains *who* was involved: the local hospital and the federal government. The question *why* is also answered: for a specific research project. Is the lead complete? Yes, but there is no attribution, and the reader may well want more details. The body of the story can supply these.

This is a good time to note that summary leads ought to be, as this one is, very specific. No generalities.

Looking at the lead about the truck accident and the one about the federal grant, we can add a little more direction to our definition of the summary lead. Keeping the five Ws in mind, we can now say that a summary lead consists of:

1. A statement of what happened.

2. Identification of people involved.

3. A time element..

4. A place.

5. Something of the circumstances of the event.

That, in order, is the what, who, when, where, and why and how of the story. Leads generally are short on details, but they must provide a good summary of the story.

Attribution is not always necessary in a lead and in fact may clutter the lead unnecessarily. However, when the source of the story is important, attribution becomes an integral part of the lead. For example, when the president speaks, the story is generally of interest because the source is important. So we have leads that begin *President Reagan said today that* . . . But in ordinary circumstances, keep in mind that what happened, who is involved and where and when are more important than the source of the story. '

So we can add a sixth point to our expanded definition of a summary lead:

6. Attribution *in some circumstances.*

Thinking Through the Lead

Good writing is well organized. It has form — for example, the form of the inverted pyramid. And it has structure, the careful arrangement of sentences and paragraphs necessary to explain the story. Before anything is put down on paper, writers think out carefully what they want to say. Experienced news writers may seem to sit at the keyboard and knock out graphic and informative leads without effort, but that is only because the thinking that precedes writing has become instinctive. What you want to do as beginners at the writing trade is develop orderly thought about what to write. If you learn to work systematically at writing, sooner or later much of the system becomes an automatic reaction to the facts available for a news story.

Let's work through a writing problem and establish some guidelines for writing leads. Here's another set of facts, raw material for a summary lead:

Fact 1 — The city of Carolton wants to build a new water treatment plant.

Fact 2 — The new plant would replace the present plant on Territorial Road.

Fact 3 — Cost of the new plant is estimated to be ten million dollars.

Fact 4 — The city has been given $10,000 to start planning the new system.

Fact 5 — The money for planning is being provided by the U.S. Environmental Protection Agency.

Fact 6 — The city was formally notified of the grant today.

Fact 7 — You got the story from Mayor Jane Brown.

Let's assume that you are a careful reporter and that you have the facts right. Now, let's put the story into an orderly sequence: (1) what happened? (2) where? (3) when? (4) who says so? and (5) additional information — how and why?

First, the city has begun planning for a new water treatment plant. Second, some time ago, the city asked for federal funds, a grant, to cover the cost of designing the system. Finally, the city has now been notified that the government will provide the funds asked for.

We can ignore for the moment the fact that the mayor is the source of the story. We know that timeliness is an important news element, so let's put the facts in chronological order. The decision to build a new water treatment plant was made some time ago, and a story about the decision would have been in the newspaper, so the decision is not new or news. Word of the grant came today and clearly has not been in the paper. The award of the grant is a new aspect of the story, and it's the place to start.

The topic, or *subject*, of our story, then, is the grant, so our story should be slugged *grant*. Now, let's match the subject of the story — and the slug — with an appropriate verb. News writing depends on verbs to put pictures in the reader's mind, so we need a verb that will help inform the reader about the story — present a mental image, a quick flash of understanding. What is the appropriate verb? On the one hand, grants are *given* or *awarded*. On the other, they are also *accepted*. Our lead is beginning to take shape:

	(awarded)	
giver	(granted)	*recipient*

The giver is the U.S. Environmental Protection Agency, and the recipient is the city.

The Environmental Protection Agency   awarded/has awarded
(giver)   *(verb)*

the city of Carolton $10,000
(recipient)   *(what)*

to begin planning a new water treatment plant.
(why)

The idea of a grant has led to the pairing of the noun *grant* with an appropriate verb, *awarded*. And the verb requires us to name the giver and the recipient. As we put the lead together in the diagram above, we put the giver, the U.S. Environmental Protection Agency, at the beginning. Whatever goes in this sentence-opening position is, of course, the subject of the sentence we are writing and gets the greatest emphasis. Now, do we want to place greater emphasis on the source of the grant or on the recipient? If we think the recipient, the city, ought to get the emphasis, then we can turn the sentence around:

> The city of Carolton has been awarded a $10,000 grant by the U.S. Environmental Protection Agency to begin planning a new water treatment plant.

Timeliness, we said earlier, is an important news element, and we selected the most recent angle of the story — the award of the grant — as the place to begin. But the verb *has been awarded* is a little vague. It tells us that the city has been given the money, but not when. Let's be more specific:

> The city of Carolton Wednesday was awarded a $10,000 grant by the U.S. Environmental Protection Agency to begin planning a new water treatment plant.

We can, of course, go on from here and tell the rest of the story, add details and include appropriate attribution:

> The new plant will replace the city's present treatment plant on Territorial Road.
> The new plant will cost about $10 million, according to Mayor Jane Brown.

That's the process. The five Ws give you a rough structure for organizing the facts. You know that most of the time, the lead should emphasize what happened. Select the topic or subject that you want to start with. This in turn will lead you to an appropriate verb, as the idea of a grant led directly to the right verbs. Every topic or idea has an appropriate verb paired with it. For example, look at the nouns and verbs listed below:

appropriation	appropriated
injury	injured
fire	burned, damaged, destroyed, killed
burglary	burglarized
robbery	robbed
theft	stole

Develop the knack of selecting the appropriate verb, the verb that best fits with the idea you are trying to explain, the verb that will give your reader the best picture of what happened. Avoid weak and wishy-washy verbs. Don't use innocuous verbs like *occurred* or *took place.* Avoid *received.* For example:

> A fire occurred Monday night at the Acme Laundry on South Sherman Street. It badly damaged the building.

> A smoky fire badly damaged the Acme Laundry building on South Sherman Street Monday night.

Which of these is the stronger and more effective lead? Fires don't *occur* or *take place.* They *burn, damage* or *destroy.* People don't *receive* injuries. They are *injured.* And accidents don't *leave* people injured, they *injure* people.

63

In the interest of better writing, don't use empty verbs like *occur, take place, receive* and *left* in summary leads.

Time Elements

The choice of the *form* of the verb in the leads just developed raises a question about the time element for the lead. If we use the *perfect* form of the verb — usually in the present tense, such as *has awarded* or *has been awarded* — we don't need a time element. The verb allows us to say the event has happened without saying specifically when. If we use the past tense of the verb — *awarded* or *was awarded* — we do need a time element.

> The city of Carolton was awarded a federal grant Thursday to help with preliminary planning for a new water treatment plant.

> The U.S. Environmental Protection Agency awarded the city of Carolton $10,000 Thursday to subsidize preliminary plans for a new water treatment plant.

If we do have a specific day or hour to work into the lead, where does it go? In many leads, the time element fits nicely right after the verb:

> Two 8-year-old boys were kidnapped Saturday from the neighborhood playground where they had been playing.

The time element also may fit comfortably at the end of the sentence after other elements that follow the verb:

> More than 15,000 protesters paraded through downtown streets Saturday.

Newspapers and wire services have a tendency to push the time element as far forward as possible in the first sentence of a news story, often putting it just before the verb, as in this example:

> Members of Local 43 Saturday ratified a new three-year contract with Central States Power Co.

This is generally not the best place to put the time element. Don't place the time element after the subject unless you find that placement elsewhere is confusing. For example:

> The Northwest College Board of Trustees Monday approved a master plan for expansion of the campus at a cost of $40 million.

In this lead, placement of the time element anywhere else would interfere with the sense of the story. It is best in most cases to put the time element *after* the major facts of your lead, thus:

> A special town meeting attracted 50 voters to Town Hall Monday night.

> A trailer was stolen Sunday from the parking lot at the city garage.

Placement of the time element will depend on how the sentence sounds. If you read your lead aloud and the time element sounds out of place — move it. There are several places it can go, as the examples just given show.

Variations of the Summary Lead

The summary lead should be concise, but sometimes there is so much to be said in a summary that the lead becomes long and involved. Two variations on the summary lead, the *blind lead* and the *delayed-identification lead*, offer alternatives that can shorten and tighten up what might otherwise be an awkwardly long or involved beginning.

The Blind Lead

The blind lead permits the writer to hurry into the story without crowding too much into the first paragraph. The purpose of a lead is to both inform and interest the reader. This is a difficult job in an age when readers have so many distractions in their lives and when the newspaper has so much competition for readers' time. Readers spend very little time with newspapers these days and tend to read only stories that look especially interesting. They skim and skip. If a summary lead is packed too full of details, if it looks too formidable, the reader will hurry on to something that looks more appealing.

65

The blind lead, by limiting the information in the first paragraph and picking it up in the second, attempts to give the reader the summary in two stages: a *partial summary* in the first paragraph and details in the second. For example:

> A 4-year-old Carolton boy was injured Saturday when he ran in front of a pickup truck on Main Street.
> William Abbott of 26 W. Main St. is in stable condition at Carolton General Hospital.

Names, long or complicated identifications, specifics like street addresses or large and unwieldy numbers can be omitted in the first paragraph of a summary lead and picked up in the second paragraph. Another example:

> An Iowa planning expert has been hired as Carolton's first full-time community planner.
> James Phelps, who has been assistant planner and project director for the city of Dubuque, Iowa, will begin work here next month.

These examples suggest a good reason for using the blind lead: Although the circumstances of the events reported in these leads are interesting enough to attract a reader's attention, the names may mean very little. By emphasizing the interesting fact or situation and playing down certain details — names and lengthy identifications — the blind lead can hold readers who might not pay attention to an overcrowded lead with the emphasis on an unfamiliar name. A clear and precise description is often more appropriate than name, age, address, title and so on.

The blind lead has the further advantage of brevity. It presents an idea quickly and clearly. But this means that it is effective only if what happened is sufficiently interesting to catch the reader's attention. It is a good lead only when *what happened* is more important or more intriguing than *to whom* it happened. Where the name in the story is an important one or one the reader will recognize immediately, the blind lead is not necessary — indeed, it may be weaker than a lead built around a name. The following, a good example of an effective blind lead, was taken from a sidebar to a story about a plane crash:

> A federal investigator, using white gloves to dig through charred rubble, said yesterday he'll examine every broken piece of the downed plane's wreckage to learn why the accident happened.

Vincent Marcangelli of the National Transportation and Safety Board said it could be nine months before the puzzle is solved.

— *Boston Herald*

The blind lead has a definite order and structure. It places a description at the beginning of the first paragraph and a name at the beginning of the second:

(Description) was injured Saturday when he ran in front of a truck on Main Street.

(Name) (identification) was taken to Carolton General Hospital. He has multiple cuts and bruises and a mild concussion.

This is a form of parallel construction, a structure that makes it easy for the reader to understand the lead and provides an easy way for the news writer to organize the facts of the lead.

The Delayed-Identification Lead

Somewhere between the blind lead and the summary lead lies the delayed-identification lead. Here the name is given in the first paragraph of the lead, but full identification is held back and given in the second paragraph — sometimes later. For example:

Harry Crooks was in critical condition in Carolton General Hospital Monday night. He was struck by a car Saturday.

Crooks, 45, of 311 N. Calhoun St., suffered a broken pelvis, right ankle and collarbone when he was struck while crossing Wisconsin Avenue at Calhoun Street. He was knocked 40 feet from the point of impact.

Delayed-identification leads leave out some information and by so doing make the first paragraph of the lead more concise and more readable. In this example, identification, age and street address of the accident victim are not given until the second paragraph. In delayed-identification leads, as in blind leads, the idea of the story is the important thing. Give the reader the broad outline and fill it in later. Another example:

Andrea Baker will join more than 100 other Michigan and Ohio youths in Guatemala Friday through July 7 for Project Serve, sponsored by Youth for Christ.

Andrea, daughter of Mr. and Mrs. Richard Baker, 1790 E. Midland, a senior at Western High next year, will help rebuild and reconstruct homes, churches and special events buildings.

— Bay City (Mich.) *Times*

Delayed-identification leads are best used when the name has some recognition value of its own. At the time this chapter was written, the names of Larry Bird, the Rev. Jesse Jackson, Dwight Gooden, Oral Roberts and Jim Bakker were being used in leads without identification. Name recognition is topical. A name that was a household word a month ago may have faded from the public consciousness by today. Be cautious in using delayed-identification leads.

Figure 4.2 gives another example of a delayed-identification lead, and Figure 4.3 shows how a summary lead, a blind lead and a delayed-identification lead can be written about the same incident.

John L. Shafter has been awarded a $15,000 National Science Foundation grant for a project to enable high school seniors to conduct research under supervision of scientists.

Shafter, head of the department of physics at Northwest College, will recruit Carolton Central High School seniors for the project.

Figure 4.2 *A delayed-identification lead.*

George Hackett, owner of a Carolton private detective agency, was sentenced to five years in prison Monday after a federal court jury found him guilty of loan sharking.

The owner of a Carolton private detective agency was sentenced to five years in prison Monday.
George Hackett was sentenced by Federal Judge Daniel Curtis after a jury found him guilty of loan sharking.

George Hackett was sentenced to five years in prison Monday after a jury found him guilty of loan sharking.
Hackett, owner of a Carolton private detective agency, was sentenced by Federal Judge Daniel Curtis.

Figure 4.3 *A summary lead, a blind lead and a delayed-identification lead based on the same information.*

Other Aspects of the Lead

Some other aspects of leads should be mentioned here. Datelines, credit lines and bylines are not really part of the lead, but rather precede it. Since they always appear in conjunction with leads on certain types of stories, though, they should be explained before we leave our discussion of leads.

Datelines

The lead on page 58 had what is loosely called a *dateline.* Years ago, datelines included both a place and a date. Today, although it's still called a dateline, the dateline is really a place line. The dateline appears on wire service stories to indicate the place of origin — where an event occurred or sometimes where the story was written. Newspaper practice is to use a dateline when a story originates outside the city in which the newspaper is published or outside the city and its immediate environs. Stories that originate outside the newspaper's own city and suburbs are not local, and a dateline is used to tell the reader where the event took place. In newspaper terminology, such stories are trade area or suburban, state, regional, national or foreign stories.

The dateline precedes the first sentence of a news story. It identifies the story's point of origin and sometimes, but not always, the date the story was written or transmitted. *The New York Times* always includes dates in datelines. Not many other newspapers do.

Datelines appear on all stories originated by the Associated Press and United Press International. Stories originating from other sources — correspondents, supplementary news services, the newspaper's state capital or Washington bureau — are identified by datelines. When staff members are sent on assignment out of town, the stories they bring or send back to the newspaper carry datelines.

Local stories need no dateline. The stories you write for practice in the classroom or as a staff writer for your college newspaper will be local stories and need no datelines.

Credit Lines

The credit line is carried as a separate line that precedes the first paragraph of the lead and gives information not included in the dateline or information that supplements the dateline:

From Our Capitol Bureau

From Our Washington Bureau

Special to the State Journal

From State Journal Wire Services

The last credit line means that stories from both the Associated Press and United Press International were rewritten and combined into a single story.

Wire service stories are identified by the service's initials in the dateline, thus:

NEW ORLEANS (AP) — Fire destroyed a warehouse Monday night . . .

SEATTLE (UPI) — FBI agents said Monday that they had identified . . .

The use of datelines and credit lines varies from paper to paper, and the newspaper's preferences are usually included in a stylebook similar to the Basic Guide to News Style in the back of this book. For the moment, it is enough to remember that local news stories carry no datelines and no credit lines.

Bylines

Bylines on news stories identify the writer. They are not a part of the lead, and they are not casually attached to a news story by the writer. Editors decide who gets a byline and when. You have to earn a byline by doing a good job of reporting and writing.

Creative Leads

All the leads we have discussed so far have been written in normal word order as conventional declarative sentences. Once in a while, however, the nature of the story you are writing demands something different. There are many ways to inject variety in your news writing. Some will be discussed later on. At this point, let's look at one simple way we can make a lead a bit different: variation in grammatical structure.

Questions

News writers sometimes pep up leads by switching from the declarative sentence to the interrogative — by asking a question rather than stating a fact:

> Anyone want a nice cat to give the premises a homey touch?
> > — *Norfolk* (Va.) *Virginian-Pilot*

> Ever wonder how much material goes into one of those new skyscrapers rising above the streets of Center City?
> > — *Philadelphia Inquirer*

The question, of course, is not the entire lead. You must answer the question for the reader or there is no point to the question. For example:

> Guess who wears the pants in the South Carolina House now?
> Everyone.
> > — *Augusta* (Ga.) *Chronicle*

Question leads are appropriate when the question is a topical one, that is, something your readers have been wondering about. They are also appropriate as a device that allows you to provide an answer, for example, in the case of the *Augusta Chronicle* lead above.

Used once in a while, a question lead will provide a bit of variety, but don't try it too often. Master the more usual ways of writing leads first.

The Imperative

Another way to change pace is to shift from the indicative to the imperative and give the reader instructions:

> Don't be in a hurry to retire.
> > — *Asbury Park* (N.J.) *Press*

> Watch out for a swarm of bat-wings and bush-hogs grazing over the shoulders of I-985 this week.
> > — *The Times*, Gainesville, Ga.

Direct Address

Still another variation is direct address, in which the writer talks directly to the reader:

71

> So you're one of more than 16 million Americans expected to quit smoking today in the Great American Smokeout.
> Good for you. But how long will you stay quit?
> — *St. Petersburg* (Fla.) *Times*

These examples are intended only to suggest that there is room for creativity in news writing. Variation in grammatical structure offers one opportunity for creativity. There are others. Later chapters will discuss creativity in leads in more detail. Beginners ought to stick to basics at first — the summary lead — but it is fun, occasionally, to try something different. For example, this lead plays with the difference in meaning between the verb *conduct* and the noun *conduct*.

> SALT LAKE CITY (UPI) — The board of directors of the Utah Symphony says the conductor was fired because of his conducting. The conductor says he was fired because of his conduct — including an admitted affair with a female Mormon missionary.

Originality and creativity are possible even in the most routine news stories. Even leads on obituaries, which generally are pretty staid, can be given a creative touch.

> Bertha Hamlin Boyce died at the Fraser Nursing Home Saturday morning. It was the 56th day of the 102nd year of her life.
> — *The Enterprise*, Falmouth, Mass.

Structure and organization are important. Learn the basics first. Develop the skill of writing a conventional summary lead. What counts in the long run is the skill the news writer brings to the conventional forms of structure and organization.

Suggestions for Further Reading

These books offer thoughtful and provocative discussions of news, news values and the performance of the press.

Epstein, Edward Jay. *Between Fact and Fiction.* New York: Vintage Books, 1975.
Epstein subtitles this study: "The problem of journalism."

Gans, Herbert J. *Deciding What's News*. New York: Pantheon Books, 1979.
A study of news as presented on network television and in the news magazines.

Liebling, A.J. *The Press*. New York: Ballantine Books, 1961.
Liebling's acerbic discussion of the news as presented in daily newspapers. A bit dated, but still valuable criticism.

Mott, Frank Luther. *The News in America*. Cambridge, Mass.: Harvard University Press, 1952.
A distinguished journalism historian analyzes news as history, timely report, sensation, human interest story, interpretation and objective statement.

Roshco, Bernard. *Newsmaking*. Chicago: The University of Chicago Press, 1975.
News as a sociological problem and newsmaking as a social process.

Tuchman, Gaye. *Making News*. New York: The Free Press, 1978.
A sociologist looks at news as a version of reality.

San Francisco Chronicle

The Largest Daily Circulation in Northern California

122nd Year No. 255 ★ ★ ★ ★ MONDAY, NOVEMBER 10, 1986 777-1111 25 CENTS

49ers Win Big

Montana's Back!

Quarterback Joe Montana got a hand from receiver Jerry Rice (right) after the first of their three touchdown passes

BY FREDERIC LARSON, THE CHRONICLE

49ers' Main Man Returns to the Helm

LOWELL COHN

THERE IS something heroic about a man who rises to an occasion. Joe Montana returned to football yesterday in the 49ers' 43-17 win over St. Louis, while the world worried about his back, and we wondered whether he could restore the 49ers to what we've come to expect.

It would have been easy for him to put in a respectable performance — something safe and colorless. Everyone could have said, "Joe looked fine for a guy who was out two months. We can't wait for him to get better."

But Joe wasn't in the least bit respectable. He was glorious.

From the moment he trotted onto the field — elegant, poised — he took possession of the game and put special life into his sagging team. He was the living, breathing definition of the word "superstar," and he reminded us all over again that great quarterbacking involves more than just passing. It is an attitude of attack. With Montana at the controls, a defense had to react to the 49ers' offense for

the first time in two months. With Montana there, the 49ers finally showed a running game. Joe Cribbs gained 105 yards, the first time this season a 49er back had run for more than 100.

Dwight Clark, who was wearing a Joe Montana sweatshirt after the game, said Joe is inspirational in ways he can't even describe. "When Joe ran onto the field for the introduction, it was chillbone," Clark said. "I was ready to play just because he was there. It's terrible to depend on one guy, but this guy's like magic. He is what

Back Page Col. 4

Special Report

Why Far East Is Crucial to State's Future

By John Eckhouse
Chronicle Correspondent

Taipei

California's economy is tilting west. Two-way trade and investment with nations on the Pacific Rim — home of the fastest-growing economies in the world — continue to grow at a torrid pace.

That means events in cities such as Tokyo, Taipei, Seoul and Shanghai now have an effect on California's economy almost as great as policies adopted in Sacramento and Washington.

For example, it took a decision by Japan's Toyota to reopen a General Motors auto plant in Fremont. And Fujitsu's recent offer to buy 80 percent of Fairchild Semiconductor Corp., if it passes government muster, could improve prospects for the troubled Cupertino company.

Most Asian nations are experiencing a dramatic economic recovery and a surge in trade this year. That is good news for California for a number of reasons.

■ Almost one in nine jobs in California — including one in seven manufacturing jobs and perhaps as many as one in four agricultural jobs — relies on foreign trade.

■ California's three largest trading partners are Japan, the Republic of China on Taiwan, and South Korea. Six of the state's top nine trading partners are in the Far East.

■ Last year, 82 percent of California's trade was conducted with Pacific Rim nations. (The figure is somewhat imprecise, because it includes all U.S. imports and exports shipped through California.)

■ The state depends on flows of foreign capital, particularly from Asia, for the creation of thousands of jobs each year. Much of the capital ends up in the pockets of Californians working at local offices and plants of companies like Japan's Sony Corp., South Korea's Hyundai Corp. or Taiwan's Formosa Group.

"One of your own secretaries of state, John Hay, said it best in about 1900," The Mediterranean is the ocean of the past, the Atlantic the ocean of the present and the Pacific the ocean of the future," said Sir Michael Sandberg, chairman of Hongkong and Shanghai Banking Corp.

Looking out from Sandberg's perch high above Hong Kong island toward the second-busiest port in the world, it is clear that Hay's ocean of the future has become the ocean of the present.

California buys consumer goods, electronics, cars and clothing from the Pacific Rim, and the state sends a lot of high-tech production equipment and two-thirds of its $2.8 billion in agricultural exports to the region. Japan, South Korea, Hong Kong, Taiwan and Indonesia purchase hundreds of millions of dollars' worth of California cotton, beef, oranges, raisins, nuts, wheat, grapes and wine.

But beneath all the numbers and reams of trade statistics is the simple fact that California and the United States are not getting their fair share of exports.

Indeed, California has been losing ground in this most important

Page 8 Col. 1

More Asia trade news
SEE BUSINESS, PAGES 28 AND 29

Feinstein's Visit to a Man's World

By Daniel Rosenheim
Economics Editor

Tokyo

As San Francisco Mayor Dianne Feinstein begins her economic mission on the Far East in earnest today, she will encounter a profoundly patriarchal society the likes of which she may never have seen before.

For all its dazzling technological accomplishments, Japan is a nation where attitudes toward women remain rooted in feudalism. Economic success and electronic wizardry have combined to give the nation an almost post-modernist feel, but women remain very much the second sex.

On the sidewalks of this teeming city of nearly 12 million, many women still walk a respectful distance behind their husbands. Outside of academics, it is the rare field where a woman can succeed in obtaining jobs of any professional stature.

Page 9 Col. 1

Record Number Of Doctors Losing Licenses

Washington

The state agencies that discipline physicians revoked a record number of licenses for incompetence or other problems last year, almost 60 percent more than in 1984, a new report shows.

The number of lesser disciplinary actions, such as license suspension or probation, also increased dramatically. The increase appeared to be the largest ever in a single year and larger than the increases for the previous four years combined.

The new statistics came after years of criticism that many state medical boards failed to punish doctors who were drunk, incompetent or impaired.

Officials said the pace of disciplinary actions has increased as local, state and federal agencies have begun to focus more attention on medical incompetence.

The official figures are published by the Federation of State Medical Boards, which represents licensing agencies.

The federation showed that medical boards nationwide revoked

Back Page Col. 4

Shultz Says He Won't Quit Over Arms Deal With Iran

Washington

Secretary of State George Shultz said last night that he will not resign his cabinet post because of the U.S.-Iran arms deal.

Shultz, caught by an NBC News reporter as he left his home, replied "No," when asked if he were going to resign.

Shultz, according to a weekend New York Times report, was on the verge of resigning because the arms transfer violated the public U.S. policy of no negotiations with terrorists and because he had been kept in the dark about the dealing.

The secretary of state made his announcement as controversy continued to swirl around the arms deal that bought freedom for captive Americans, with angry comments from members of Congress and warnings that the deal "guarantees the continued taking of hostages."

U.S. officials, meanwhile, acknowledged yesterday that any American involvement in arms shipments to Iran marked a fundamental policy reversal by the Reagan administration. Officials said Reagan's decision to provide spare parts and arms to Iran came about largely because of his desire to free the hostages.

Officials said the American strategy, approved by Reagan more than 18 months ago and carried out largely by the National Security Council, called for U.S. efforts to improve relations with Iran on several conditions. These conditions are that Iran agree to stop exporting terrorism and revolution in the Persian Gulf, that negotiations lead to an end to the Iran-Iraq war and that Tehran help the United States gain the release of American hostages held by pro-Iranian factions in Lebanon.

Senate Democrats were blunt in challenging the administration tactic, while insisting that they, too, had been kept in the dark. According to news accounts, not only the State Department but also the Pentagon and CIA had been cut out of the deal to avoid leaks and evade requirements for reporting to Congress.

Senator Robert Byrd, D-W.Va., called dealing with terrorists "a serious mistake" and warned that it created a precedent of "arms vs. hostages, arms vs. hostages. And it guarantees the continued taking

Back Page Col. 5

Israel Admits Holding Suspect In Secrets Case

Jerusalem

The Israeli government, reacting to public pressure at home and abroad, confirmed yesterday that it is holding Mordechai Vanunu, a former Israeli nuclear technician accused of selling Israel's atomic secrets to a British newspaper.

It was Israel's first substantive comment on the case since Vanunu was reported missing in London on September 30, just a week before the Sunday Times of London published a report, based on Vanunu's disclosures, that Israel possesses up to 100 atomic warheads.

Unconfirmed reports have said the technician was abducted by agents of Israel's Mossad security service and was brought back forcibly to face treason charges.

Yesterday's surprise announcement, released after the regular weekly meeting of the Israeli cabinet, offered no explanation of how Vanunu returned to Israel but it specifically denied that he was kidnaped on British soil.

The cabinet announcement also made no reference to charges against Vanunu and added that "no

Back Page Col. 1

First Winning Lotto Ticket — $10.7 Million Is Waiting

For the first time since California's Lotto 6-49 began, someone picked all six correct numbers to win a $10.7 million jackpot, a lottery spokesman said yesterday.

All that was known last night is that the winner is from Northern California, according to lottery spokesman Bob Taylor.

Lotto computers keep track of all numbers chosen and record

whether tickets are purchased in the northern or southern part of the state, Taylor said. Winners' names and addresses are not recorded.

"Somewhere out there is a very, very rich person in Northern California," Taylor said.

"This is the fourth week, and lo and behold, we have a jackpot winner, and we're all eager to know

Back Page Col. 1

5 News Story Organization

News is the first rough draft of history.

Benjamin Bradlee

Every writer has to work within the conventions of some literary form, whether it is the novel, essay, biography, play, poem or news story. Whatever information, ideas or emotions the writer wants to communicate, they have to be communicated in that form. News writing is often regarded as highly stylized and conventional. "You have to write everything the same way," the critics charge. Not so. News writing is no more restrictive a form than the short story, the sonnet or the haiku. News writing does make use of a number of conventional organizing devices because experience has shown them to be useful in conveying information to newspaper readers. But once the beginning news writer has mastered these conventions — the inverted-pyramid format, for example — there is ample opportunity to exercise creative urges and imaginative impulses.

News writing demands discipline, but it also demands imagination, perception, humor, sympathy and taste. News writing is more flexible and open to innovation today than it has ever been. Today's news writer relies on the tried and useful news-writing techniques but also uses unconventional and creative ones.

75

Basic Organization

The news story can be organized and told in a variety of ways, but basically news stories consist of a beginning, the *lead*, a middle, the *body*, or *development*, of the story and an end, a *conclusion*. See Figure 5.1.

There are many ways of writing news leads. The basic approach is the summary lead, constructed around the five Ws: who, what, when, where, why and how.

The body, or development, of the story elaborates on the summary provided in the lead. The body of the story may be brief or it may be long. In the one-paragraph news story, the lead and body are one and the same.

News stories may or may not require a conclusion. Some stories tell what they have to tell and then stop. Others have carefully contrived conclusions. Some conclusions carry the point of the story. Others serve to emphasize the significance of the facts presented in the lead and body of the story.

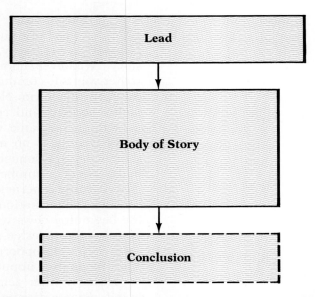

Figure 5.1 *The basic structure of the news story. All news stories have a lead — a starting place — and all have a body, the development of facts introduced or suggested by the lead. Conclusions are not always part of the news story but are common in feature stories.*

Variations in News Story Form

The Inverted Pyramid

Many single-incident stories, that is, uncomplicated stories reporting only one topic or idea, are written in the *inverted-pyramid* format. This consists, as Figure 5.2 shows, of a summary lead and a development that includes details arranged in a descending order of importance or interest. The most important or most interesting facts come right after the lead, the least important or interesting at the end of the story.

The inverted-pyramid story has no conclusion. It just stops. This format has one advantage — the story can be cut from the bottom up, paragraph by paragraph, and the point of the story will not be lost. Put another way, hasty readers will get the gist of the story even if they read only the lead or the lead and the first few words of the development.

Let's look at an example of the inverted-pyramid format:

> General Telephone Co. will invest more than $230,000 to expand and improve service in its Washington County exchange.
>
> The company plans to replace some 70,000 feet of overhead telephone wires with underground cable and install an additional remote switching unit to accommodate growth in the western part of the county.
>
> Work should be completed by the end of the year, the company said.

The first paragraph of this story is a summary lead covering the essential facts of the story. The second paragraph adds specifics, an explanation of exactly what the project will accomplish. The final paragraph adds a useful detail in explaining how long it will take to do the work. If space limitations had demanded that this story be cut, the last paragraph could have been trimmed off and the story would have been intact. If necessary, the second paragraph could have been sacrificed and the story — now consisting of nothing but the original lead — would still stand. The hasty reader, scanning the newspaper and reading only the first paragraph of this story, would at least know what the telephone company was planning. Here is another example:

SACRAMENTO — Most of a 4,200-square-foot warehouse of the River City Van and Storage Co. was destroyed by fire yesterday.

The Sacramento Fire Department said 50 firemen and 15 auxiliaries responded to the three-alarm blaze at 5860 88th St., south of Fruitridge Road.

It took the 12 fire companies about three hours to control the blaze, and firemen stayed on the scene the rest of the day putting out the last embers.

There was no immediate estimate of the damage.

— *Los Angeles Herald-Examiner*

This is a well-organized story. The lead is complete, and the development is carefully arranged in descending order of importance and interest. The lead could stand by itself. The development merely adds details.

Equal-Fact Stories

Many news stories do not lend themselves to the restrictions of the inverted-pyramid form. These are stories whose details are equally important. None can be eliminated to meet the demands of space. Details in the body of the story are not necessarily presented in order of importance, but they always appear in some logical order. (See Figure 5.3.) You can see how this works in the following story:

The Berkshire County Chapter of the American Red Cross will hold three classes in cardiopulmonary resuscitation during December.

Two are at the Chapter House, 63 Wendell Ave. The first, Dec. 8 and 10, will be taught by Sister Jean Bostley, Aline Loud and Senga Trudeau.

The second, Dec. 14 and 16, will be taught by Ed and Sue Lewis. Classes will be from 6 to 10 p.m.

A third class will be taught at St. Mark's Parish Center, Columbus Avenue Extension, Dec. 9 and 16 from 7 to 10 p.m. Instructors will be David Heforth and Garry Rossin.

Registration may be made by telephoning the Chapter House. The Red Cross requests prepayment of the $6 fee because of limited enrollment.

— *The Berkshire Eagle*, Pittsfield, Mass.

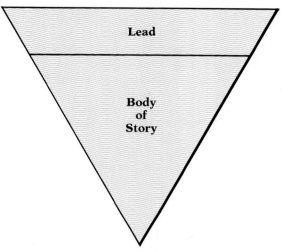

Figure 5.2 *The traditional and useful inverted-pyramid form calls for a summary lead and supporting facts — the body of the story — arranged in a descending order of importance or interest. The facts most easily dispensed with are placed at the peak of the inverted pyramid.*

Since the summary lead mentions three classes, the body of the story must explain three classes. Otherwise readers — who can count, after all — will ask "What about the other class? Where's the rest of the story?"

A number of situations call for the lead-plus-equal-facts format. An accident story may start like this, for example:

> Four Carolton teen-agers were injured Saturday in two separate accidents on Highway 30 west of the city.

This lead must be followed by an explanation of the two accidents and identification of all four who were injured. Similarly, if a lead reports that a speaker made three major points in a speech, the story has to explain all three points. The following lead calls for explanation of five items:

> The City Council will be asked Wednesday to approve spending $165,000 to furnish the new Senior Citizen Center. The five bids Council will consider:

This lead will, of course, list briefly the bids to be considered by the council, and the body of the story will explain each in more detail.

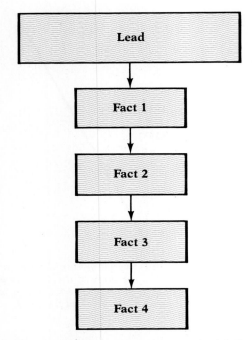

Figure 5.3 *Another news story format, the summary lead followed by facts of relatively equal importance. The last fact is just as important to the story as the first.*

Chronological Accounts

When news stories report action or a series of related events, chronology is the answer to the problem of organization. As Figure 5.4 shows, these stories begin with a lead, then go on to explain the events in chronological order. And the story may be rounded out at the end with material that did not fit in the chronology. Let's look at different approaches to the use of chronology. We'll begin with a hard-news story:

> Boynton Beach police are continuing their search for the lone gunman who held up the Mr. Grocer Store at 3001 N. Seacrest Blvd. Wednesday.
> The robber entered the store around 7:45 p.m., and demanded money from the single employee on duty. He forced the employee to lie on the floor and took an unknown amount of cash from the register, police said.
> Witnesses said the man then ran south on Seacrest.
> — *Miami Herald*

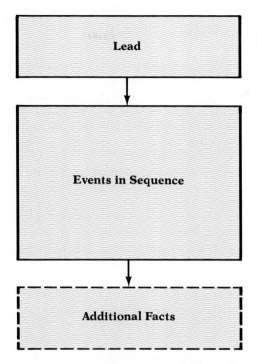

Figure 5.4 *The action story has a summary lead followed by a chronological account of events. It often ends with a concluding segment giving additional information that isn't part of the chronological narrative.*

This story consists of a summary lead that tells concisely what happened. The lead is followed by two paragraphs in which the events of the holdup are told in chronological order, step by step. The story has no conclusion except the last point in the chronological account of the holdup.

Here is another example, this time a somewhat more detailed story. The lead consists of two paragraphs, and the story ends with details that lie outside the chronology.

> A bank robber dropped part of his loot Wednesday morning when a dye capsule exploded, scattering money over the lawn of the Atlantic Bank in Tampa.
>
> But the man picked up some of the money and escaped, police said.

The body of the story is also in chronological order but backtracks to start at the beginning of the robbery:

> The robbery occurred at 8:25 a.m. Wednesday at the Atlantic Bank, 4355 Henderson Blvd. According to a Tampa police spokesman, a man walked up to a teller's counter, pulled a small handgun and demanded money. The man jumped up on the counter and scooped up a handful of money, the spokesman said. No shots were fired and no one was injured.
>
> As the man ran from the bank, a capsule in the bundle of bills exploded. After the man picked up as much money as he could, he ran toward Christ the King School at Henderson Boulevard and Dale Mabry, where police believe he had an automobile waiting.
>
> Police did not have a detailed description of the robber.
>
> — *St. Petersburg* (Fla.) *Times*

The leads of these two stories are quite different. One is a summary lead, the other a chronology. There are other approaches — for example, the *partial summary* lead. The lead of the following story takes this approach. It tells just enough to get the reader interested but not enough to reveal the outcome of the story:

> SUGAR LAND, Texas (UPI) — The burglars were professionals, the sheriff's deputies agreed. They just had a bad day.
>
> The burglars:
>
> Pried open the back door of the Sugar Land State Bank and broke into the cashier's drawers. They were empty.
>
> They used a compressor drill to get into the main vault, but it led only to a storage vault.
>
> Finally, they bored into what they thought was the main vault. Bursting through a wall, the burglars ended up outdoors on U.S. 59.

Stories with a Conclusion

The chronological stories we have just looked at have conclusions of a sort. Now let's look at stories that require a more formal ending, one designed to leave the reader with a specific set of facts or point of view. The *formal conclusion* is more than just a stopping place, a final event in chronology or an additional detail. The function of the formal conclusion is much like that of the summary lead. It is intended to pull the story together in much the same way that the summary lead pulls the story together. The formal conclusion ties together the loose ends of the story. In some instances, as is suggested in Figure 5.5, it points back to the lead by repeating a theme or word from the lead. An example:

> Tuesday night a chair was propped against the rear door of an East Side flat. The 67-year-old woman, sitting inside, had knife scratches on her face.
>
> Earlier in the day, she had been attacked by a knife-wielding man who had slipped into her flat while she worked in her garden. She lost $12 to the assailant, but fought off his attempt to rape her.
>
> "I struggled with all the strength I had," said the woman, who stands 4 feet 11 inches tall and weighs 104 pounds. "I didn't know if I was going to die or not for it, but I struggled."
>
> The woman said the man warned her to be quiet or he would kill her. Despite the threat she screamed whenever she could in the hope that her landlord, who lives downstairs, would hear her. She later learned the landlord had his radio turned on loud and did not hear her screams.
>
> But the assailant apparently was discouraged by the struggle, gave up the assault and instead demanded money. After taking the $12, he fled.
>
> Police were seeking the man Tuesday.
>
> The woman recalled how she had left the rear door leading to her flat unlocked while she worked in the garden.
>
> "I always lock my doors, but I thought, 'Here I am working right by the back door; why should I lock it?'" she said.
>
> As she returned to her flat, she walked to the television and turned it on to watch the news.
>
> "When I turned around, there he was standing right there," she said.
>
> The woman added that from now on doors will always be locked. And, at least for now, the chair will be moved into place for added security.
>
> — *Milwaukee Sentinel*

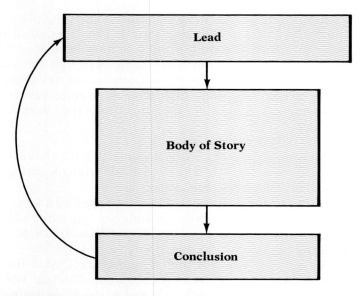

Figure 5.5 *The story with a formal conclusion is constructed like this. The lead gets the reader into the story, and the body of the story reports the facts in some logical order, often a chronology. The formal conclusion often ties back into the lead.*

The lead of this story, with its description of the chair propped against the door for security, sets the stage for the account of the attack on the woman. The story ends with a formal conclusion and repeats the image of the chair against the door. The effect is to swing from the end of the story back to the beginning and to reinforce the feature angle — the vivid picture of the elderly woman besieged in her own home. Lead and conclusion bind the story together and emphasize the feature angle, the human interest element — the vivid picture.

Here is another story with a formal conclusion:

PALO ALTO, Calif. (AP) — All told it was a pretty cool operation.

Jose Garza, 26, told police he was going about his clerking duties in a 7-Eleven store when an armed man walked in and forced him into the beverage cooler so he could rifle the till.

Garza was cooling his heels, and everything else, when the refrigerator door was opened by a customer. The customer was surprised to find the shelf tenanted by other than bottles and things.

"I'm being robbed," Garza gasped. The customer tackled the robber as he was going out the door.

The man was identified as Robert McQueen, 18. Police charged him with robbery.

When Garza defrosted himself, he gave the customer, Spencer Perkins, 22, a six-pack of beer for his help.

The lead on this story characterizes what follows as a *pretty cool operation* but does not offer a summary of what is to come. The story itself is told chronologically and ends with the arrest of the robber. The final paragraph wraps up the story with the reward for the customer who tackled the robber. And the words *defrosted himself* reiterate the *cool operation* theme established in the lead.

Suspended-Interest Stories

Finally, there is a very specialized story form, the *suspended-interest*, or *pyramid*, form. This format is used most frequently to tell short, humorous stories, the kind editors call *page brighteners*. The suspended-interest story is tricky to write because the writer must be careful, as Figure 5.6 suggests, to save the best for last. Just as in telling a joke, if the storyteller gives away too much too soon, the punch line falls flat. Deftly told, a good joke makes the audience laugh at the right moment — after the punch line has been delivered. So it is with the suspended-interest story. Properly crafted, it will make the reader smile, perhaps laugh, at the end.

The following story is deftly told, and the punch line is withheld until the very end:

BALTIMORE (UPI) — Ronald Sapia wishes his dog would bite. Sapia, manager of a local shopping center, was taking his sheepdog for a ride in his automobile when he was approached by a blond youth.

"Does your dog bite?" the youth asked.

"No," Sapia said.

The youth pulled out a revolver, ordered Sapia and the dog out and stole the car.

Beginning news writers are not going to need all these story forms right away. Nor will they be able to write stories like these as deftly as more experienced writers. These stories have been presented here to make the point that news stories are carefully organized structures,

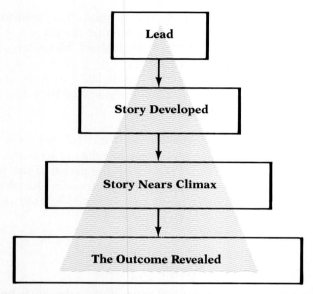

Figure 5.6 *The suspended-interest story is carefully constructed so that the lead does not reveal the outcome. The details are arranged so as to carry the reader on to the final paragraph, where the outcome or punch line is revealed.*

not something thrown together willy-nilly, and to show that there are a number of ways of telling a story.

Most news stories, by their nature, suggest a certain structure — action stories call for chronology, for example. You'll see this as you move through the chapters that follow.

Just keep in mind that there are rules, guidelines for writing news stories. And there are some fairly obvious formats or structures useful in telling certain kinds of stories. But also keep in mind that within the guidelines, within the various structures and formats available to the news writer, there is an amazing amount of room for creativity and imagination.

News writers must develop their own style, their own way of saying things that will put a polish on their stories no matter how ordinary the organization or format.

Suggestions for Further Reading

These anthologies contain some excellent examples of journalistic writing.

Berger, Meyer. *The Eight Million.* New York: Simon and Schuster, 1942.
Stories about people and places in New York by a gifted writer who worked for *The New York Times.*

Clark, Roy Peter, ed. *Best Newspaper Writing for 1979.* St. Petersburg, Fla.: Modern Media Institute, 1979.
Winners of the American Society of Newspaper Editors competition. New collections in this series are published each year.

Gross, Gerald, ed. *The Best of the Post.* New York: Popular Library, 1979.
Ben Bradlee, editor of the *Post,* calls this collection "people, places and surprises" from the *Washington Post.*

Pyle, Ernie. *Home Country.* New York: William Sloane Associates, Inc., 1947.
A collection of columns written before World War II by Ernie Pyle as he traveled around the country for the Scripps-Howard newspapers.

Snyder, Louis L., and Richard B. Morris. *A Treasury of Great Reporting.* New York: Simon and Schuster, 1949.
An anthology of reporting that spans the years from 1587 to 1946. It includes Stanley's account of how he found Dr. Livingstone.

White, William, ed. *By-Line: Ernest Hemingway.* New York: Charles Scribner's Sons, 1967.
A collection of news and feature stories written by Hemingway between 1920 and 1956.

SCIENCE FARE

Seeking the secrets of seismic foresight

Precise earthquake predictions prove elusive for geologists

The Dallas Morning News: Mark Smith

PREDICTING CALIFORNIA QUAKES

In the past 150 years, five "great" earthquakes of magnitude 8.0 or greater on the Richter scale have struck in California. Based on where those and other earthquakes have occurred in the past and how long it has been since one has hit a given area, scientists have estimated the chances for future quakes along various faults in that state. The probabilities were calculated for the 30-year period beginning in 1983. The likely magnitude of the expected quakes are indicated in parentheses.

30-year probability
- more than 60%
- more than 40%
- more than 20%
- more than 10%
- more than 5%
- less than 5%

The Dallas Morning News: Judy Williamson

The ocean's saltiness stems from the early days of the Earth's formation.

SCIENCE Q&A

Q: Why is there salt in the ocean?

A: The most accepted theory is that tremendous rains during the early formation of the Earth washed great amounts of salt and other elements into the oceans, according to Prentice Stout of the Marine Advisory Service at the University of Rhode Island. The concentration of salt in the ocean is now about 35 parts per thousand, Stout said. Almost all elements are represented in the ocean.

Q: Why do women have higher voices (soprano, mezzo, alto) than men (tenor, baritone, bass)?

A: Dr. Peter Albert, chairman of the department of otolaryngology at the University of Toronto, said that the fundamental frequency of the voice is largely determined by the length and bulk of the vocal cords. The shorter, lighter and less muscular the vocal cords, the higher the tone. Men's vocal cords are generally longer, heavier, and contain more muscle than women's, Albert said.

Send your questions to Science Fare, Discoveries, The Dallas Morning News, Communications Center, Dallas 75265.

SCIENCE TALK

KILLER BEES are descendants of honeybees that escaped from a hive in Brazil in 1957. The bees from Brazil had been imported from Africa, so their offspring are often called "Africanized" bees.

Ordinary honeybees common in the United States are descended from a European strain and are sometimes called European bees.

Killer bees are much more aggressive than their European cousins and repeatedly sting upon being disturbed. But they took very much like ordinary bees and are in fact considered members of the same species, *Apis mellifera*. The killers are migrating northward and will eventually

Ordinary honeybees like these aren't easy to tell apart from killer bees.

reach the southern United States.

Identifying killer bees will be important for beekeepers, as an influx of the killer strain will make honey production much less efficient and more expensive. A study reported in a recent issue of *Proceedings of the National Academy of Sciences* offers hope that the two subspecies may be distinguished by a simple DNA test.

Researcher Glenn Hall of the University of California's Lawrence Berkeley Laboratory used gene-splicing techniques on DNA from European bees from California and killer bees from Costa Rica. He found more than a dozen differences in their DNA. With further study, it may be possible to devise an identification test based on those DNA differences.

— Tom Siegfried

TRIVIA PERUSAL

From *Discover* it is possible to go bankrupt in Monopoly after three rolls of the dice, but the odds against it are 21.3 quadrillion to one.

SCIENTIFIC OBSERVATIONS

"Scientists are often regarded as illiterate oafs, unable to write and unwilling to read, captives of their narrow expertise, deserving candidates for humanists' contempt. Yet, most of us are well read and can carry our own with history, literary critics, whomever. Humanists, on the other hand, are often (though not always) extraordinarily mathematically inept, and proudly so. Our conversations must turn on matters of their concern, not our own. We are disadvantaged because we are compelled by their ignorance to match wits on their territory."

— Sheldon Glashow, Harvard physicist, in *The Sciences* (September/October)

By Gayle Golden
Science Writer of The News

GEOLOGY

■ Earthquake preparedness 1A

MENLO PARK, Calif. — One of the finest moments for earthquake prediction came unexpectedly on a chilly February morning in 1975.

After noticing swarms of small tremors and ground deformations around Haicheng, China, scientists warned the city's 190,000 residents to take precautions for an impending earthquake.

As if on cue, five hours later a powerful 7.3 temblor arrived, destroying hundreds of buildings and factories and claiming 1,320 lives. Many more would have died without the warning.

Less than 16 months later, however, that day's promise proved elusive. Without warning, on July 28, 1976, a 7.8 magnitude quake and four powerful aftershocks struck Tangshan, China, virtually destroying that industrial city and killing an estimated 243,000.

Today, scientists say these two events typify the uncertainty of predicting, within hours or even days, precisely when an earthquake will occur, although some are optimistic about doing that someday.

"The lesson from Haicheng is that some earthquakes can be predicted in the short term," said William Ellsworth,

director of seismology at the U.S. Geological Survey in Menlo Park, Calif. "The Tangshan earthquake was, of course, a great tragedy, and it illustrates that earthquake prediction on the short-term has not arrived."

Until a few years ago, scientists searched in vain for a single sign, or geological precursor, that came before all earthquakes. Research has probed tilting, bulges or cracks in the landscape; changes in the magnetic field of rocks; the increased or decreased emission of radioactive gases; the rising or falling of water tables; patterns of smaller earthquakes; or correlations with the moon-induced tides.

Not even the yelping of animals was excluded — for good reason, some say.

One of the earliest earthquake predictions, in fact, was made in 1969 after zookeepers at the People's Park in Tianjin, China, noticed their yaks weren't eating, their turtles were restless and their pandas were screaming. They reported those behaviors to the city's earthquake office. Later that day, a 7.4 earthquake struck east of the city.

In the early 1970s, the U.S. Geological Survey, in connection with Stanford Research Institute of Palo Alto, Calif., cooperated on a study of such pre-earthquake animal behavior. But the program was eventually canceled without any definitive conclusions.

Today, however, the hope for a

Please see QUAKES on Page 7D.

Researchers thinking twice about where lightning strikes

By Walter Sullivan
New York Times News Service

NEW YORK — Using computer-linked networks of observatories and a variety of other devices, scientists are trying to learn what energizes lightning and controls where it hits and how much damage it does.

They hope a better understanding of lightning will enable scientists to forecast where it

METEOROLOGY

will strike with enough accuracy to reroute aircraft and choose the best times for spacecraft launchings, golf tournaments and other events.

Recent observations have cast doubt on some of the most widely accepted theories of lightning formation. While it has long been known that lightning usually occurs when strong negative electric charge accumulates in the lower part of a thunderhead, no theory explaining such accumulation has yet won general acceptance.

According to one group of theories, the electric charge is in some way generated in the heart of the storm by falling raindrops or ice particles. In one version, some of the gravitational energy of precipitation is converted into electrical energy. Other theories emphasize the role of violent updrafts in transporting electric charge.

But Earle R. Williams of the Massachusetts Institute of Technology questions those competing theories. He believes the behavior of ice particles within the storm cloud is critical to lightning formation.

According to the well-established picture of a thunderhead's dynamics, its core of rapidly rising warm air pushes cloud turrets up from its sum-

mit. Moisture in the rising air condenses into ice crystals or rain. The air, cooled as it nears the top, falls back around edges of the cloud, creating the cool blast of air that radiates from the base of the storm.

Williams notes that a number of recent observations suggest that the region of strong negative charge from which lightning originates is normally in a part of the cloud so cold that droplets there must be frozen.

He believes the answer to lightning formation must therefore lie in the special properties of ice particles.

Williams says two basic questions must be resolved: what makes some ice particles in the storm negative and others positive, and what segregates the negative particles at the bottom of the cloud and the positive ones at the top.

In an interview and in *The Journal of Geophysical Research*, Williams cited a growing belief that larger ice particles — hailstones and granular snow pellets — become negatively charged by picking up electrons in collisions with ice crystals riding an updraft. These crystals lose electrons, thus becoming positively charged as they are carried to the top of the cloud. The falling, heavier particles carry their negative charge to the bottom of the cloud.

Updrafts in a thunderhead can reach 100 miles an hour. Acoustic signals and radio emissions in Florida have shown that cloud-to-ground lightning comes almost exclusively from the region of intense updrafts, whereas rain falls primarily from the downdraft region.

Only about 10 percent of lightning strokes, however, are to the ground. The rest are within

Please see SCIENTISTS on Page 7D.

The Dallas Morning News

Lightning bolts, such as these striking Dallas, occur when strong negative electric charge accumulates in the lower part of a cloud.

6 Writing the Story

Journalism is literature in a hurry.

Matthew Arnold

In previous chapters we saw that a news story consists of a lead, the body, or development, and sometimes a formal *conclusion*. In this chapter we will look closely at how the body of the story is developed and how it flows naturally from the lead. As you know by now, although there are some general principles about news writing, there are no absolute rules. Leads can be written in many ways. So can the rest of the news story. What follows here are some workable, easy-to-follow guidelines on writing *single-incident* news stories, which deal with a limited number of facts, in the inverted-pyramid form.

Single-Incident Stories

Single-incident stories are most easily written in the inverted-pyramid format. These stories begin with a summary lead and are developed by adding details in an appropriate order. For example:

A three-alarm fire damaged a vacant furniture warehouse in North Philadelphia Monday.

The blaze in the building at 2306 N. 15th St. — last occupied by Gold's Furniture — was of suspicious origin, according to fire officials.

89

The fire, which was reported at 4:41 a.m., began on the third floor and spread to the top floor of the four-story brick building, according to fire officials. A second alarm was turned in at 4:47 a.m. and the third at 4:59 a.m. The blaze was brought under control at 6:14 a.m.

Two people had to be evacuated from their home at 2302 N. 15th St. because of the flames, fire officials said.

Fifty firefighters and 20 pieces of equipment were called to battle the fire.

— *Philadelphia Inquirer*

This story begins with a concise, one-sentence lead that explains *what happened:* fire damaged a vacant warehouse. The four paragraphs that follow are details — elaboration and explanation. Let's look at the body of the story and see how the writer did it.

The first paragraph of the development, the second paragraph of the story, identifies the warehouse. Note the dual identification: street address and the last occupant of the building. Some readers might be able to identify the building by the street number. Others might recognize it more readily by the name of the business that had occupied it. This paragraph also adds something new: fire officials believe the fire may have been set deliberately.

The next paragraph expands on the description of the fire in the lead: a three-alarm fire. The time of each alarm is given as well as the time at which the fire was brought under control. The specific details, the exact times, contribute to the notion that the fire was a serious one. Another detail is included in this paragraph: where the fire started.

The next paragraph adds information about the danger to people in a nearby building. This is another contribution to the idea of seriousness: human lives were at risk. The final paragraph, too, emphasizes the idea of seriousness, by telling how much equipment and how many firefighters were needed to control the fire.

Appropriate Order

It was pointed out earlier that the facts in the body of a news story must be presented in an appropriate order. From most important to least important is a kind of order, though different writers might disagree about which facts are more important and which less important. Chronology is an appropriate way to order the facts in some stories. Lists of names can be arranged in alphabetical order. Other appropriate arrangements may be suggested by the nature of the story. For example, a news story about the election of club officers follows an order familiar to readers:

> Karen L. Cameron, 36 Sassafras Drive, has been elected president of the Northwest College Newcomer's Club.
> Other officers are Carol S. Reed, vice president; Susan West, recording secretary; Alicia Townsend, treasurer; and Necia Brown, historian.

In this story we have several kinds of organization. First, the overall organization of the story follows the inverted-pyramid format: a one-paragraph summary lead followed by a one-paragraph development. Second, in the body of the story, the names of officers are listed in descending order from president through historian. And, finally, the list of names is arranged so that each officer's name appears first and is followed by the office she will hold.

Here is a slightly different example of the single-incident story:

> Dr. Robert E. Windom, assistant secretary of health for the State Department of Health and Human Services, has been named Distinguished Internist of 1986 by the American Society of Internal Medicine.
> The society, founded in 1956, is a nationwide group with more than 20,000 members concerned with medical care.
> Each year, the group honors a member who has made outstanding contributions to medicine and helped further the goals of the group.
> Windom, formerly of St. Petersburg and son of former city manager Ross Windom, oversees the health and medical research agencies of the National Institutes of Health, the Food and Drug Administration, the Centers for Disease Control, the Alcohol, Drug Abuse and Mental Health Administration, the Health Resources and Services Administration and the office of Surgeon General Dr. C. Everett Koop.
>
> — *St. Petersburg Times*

This story has a summary lead telling what happened and who was involved. The development then answers in turn three questions the reader might ask: First, what organization is making the award?

Second, what does one do to qualify for the award? And, third, who is the recipient?

In these examples of inverted-pyramid, single-incident stories, the lead is a discrete — that is, clearly separate — unit, and the body of the story is also a clearly separate unit. Lead and body belong together, the body logically follows the lead, but there is no overlapping of the two.

Stories with Blind Leads

In stories with blind leads, we find that the separation of lead and body of the story is less clear. The lead, rather than standing apart in a separate paragraph, blends into the body of the story in a bridging paragraph. For example:

> An aerospace engineering professor at Georgia Tech has been named to an advisory panel that will review the Space Shuttle's proposed solid rocket booster system.
>
> Edward W. Price, a nationally recognized specialist in rocket propulsion and propellant combustion, is one of eight experts named by the National Research Council. The Presidential Commission investigating the space shuttle accident recommended that the panel be formed to monitor NASA's efforts to develop an improved booster. NASA, in turn, asked the Research Council to select the panel.
>
> The eight panel members selected so far include authorities in propulsion, materials, structures, reliability . . .

The second paragraph of this story is part of the lead and also part of the body of the story. The description — *an aerospace engineering professor at Georgia Tech* — in the first paragraph is explained or defined by the name in the second paragraph — *Edward W. Price.* And the second paragraph includes other information — that Price is one of eight experts named by the National Research Council — that must be further explained in the next paragraph.

The blind lead also introduces another sort of order to the single-incident story: parallel construction. The first paragraph, the lead, starts with a description. The second paragraph, the bridging paragraph, starts with a name:

A Washington County highway department employee was injured Monday when a scaffold collapsed at a construction site.

Warren E. Foster, 34, was taken to Carolton General Hospital . . .

Attribution

Attribution, the identification of the source of the story or of a fact in the story, is another important element in news stories. We find attribution like the following in general use:

. . . Mayor John Doe said.

. . . according to Judge Jane Doe.

. . . sheriff's officers reported.

. . . police said.

Attribution is important in news stories because a great deal of the time news writers are reporting not what they saw or heard themselves but what others have told them or what they have learned from a written record or other document. It is important that the reader know the source of all the facts, observations and quotations in a news story.

So at least some attribution is required in almost every news story to keep readers informed as to where facts came from or who said what. And every story needs *adequate attribution* — enough to protect the integrity of the story, that is, enough to assure readers the story has a sound basis in fact. A word of warning, however: Too much attribution will clutter up a story, overburden the reader and detract from the effectiveness of the story. Attribution is important to the story, but it is not as important as the who and what of the story. First tell your reader what the story is about, then attribute.

Attribution, then, should be subordinate to the facts of the story. Look back at the story about the warehouse fire and you can see how attribution is used to support the facts but not to overshadow them. And you will note that a lot of information in the story is not attributed. It is not necessary to attribute facts that are easily verified and that no reader is likely to question. Facts like the time at which a fire alarm is sounded or the number of pieces of fire equipment called out can be verified from fire department records. Matters of opinion, judgment or viewpoint, anything that a reader might question, should be attributed.

A sports writer at work in the newsroom of the Arkansas Gazette *in Little Rock. (Bob Roller/Gannett)*

In the warehouse fire story several points were opinion or viewpoint, and these were carefully attributed. The point of origin of the fire and the suggestion that the fire might have been started by someone are matters not of fact but of expert professional opinion. As such they should be attributed.

In the following story, the facts are simple, and one attribution is enough. Once it has been established that the source of the story is the sheriff's office, there is no need for further attribution. The attribution serves two purposes: It identifies the source of all the information in the story as a reliable one, and it gives credibility to the only matter of opinion in the story — the cause of the accident.

> A Carolton man was slightly injured Saturday in a two-car accident on U.S. 210 southwest of the city.
> Ernest Richards, 40, of 127 S. Jackson St., was attempting a left turn off U.S. 210 just as another car was attempting to pass him, sheriff's officers said.

Richards was treated at St. Luke's Hospital for minor cuts. The driver of the other car, John A. Price, 275 W. Ohio Ave., was not injured.

In routine news stories like this accident story, it is not necessary to attribute in the lead. The facts generally can stand on their own. If the reader has questions about the source of information in the lead, words such as *sheriff's officers said* or *police said* will generally make the source clear. Attribution should be brief and it should be unobtrusive. One *police said* in a story is often enough to establish credibility. Sometimes attribution is established by an oblique reference like the following:

Police learned from the driver that he had picked up two passengers . . .

Attribution ordinarily is secondary to the who, what, where and when of the story. Sometimes, however, the source is what makes the story. This is true of stories originating in the White House, where the lead invariably begins:

President Reagan said today that . . .

The source may also be the focal point of local stories. What the mayor or a police chief or the chairman of the county commission says on local issues may be significant because of the source. Comments that might be ignored if they came from others may be controversial and newsworthy when they come from a public official. For example:

Mayor Noel Taylor said City Council is likely to approve a plan for a downtown tax district that would impose a special levy of 10 cents per $100 assessed valuation of property to pay for retention and recruitment of new business downtown.
— *Roanoke* (Va.) *Times & World News*

How Much Is Enough?

Some news stories will need more attribution than others. Where there is conflicting information, it should be attributed so that readers know who is offering each side of the story. In stories where information comes from several sources — even though it may not be questionable or controversial — all sources should be identified.

How much attribution is necessary? Just enough so that the reader is kept informed. In simple stories, one attribution may be enough. In more involved stories, frequent attribution may be necessary to keep the record straight. If you attribute too much, the city editor or the copy desk will delete the excess attribution. If you don't attribute enough, however, your editor may embarrass you by asking: "Who said that?" or "Where did you get this information?"

Too Much Attribution

Too much attribution wastes space and wastes the reader's time. In some cases it may also confuse the reader. An example of this sort of overkill follows:

> A Carolton man was killed Friday in a one-car accident in Bristol County, *police said.*
> *Police said* the accident occurred about 2 a.m. on U.S. 210 just south of River Road and about two miles from Carolton.
> A pickup driven by William Marshall, 35, of 271 W. State Road, went off the road as it approached a curve, then came back on the road, crossed the centerline and struck an embankment, *according to Washington County Deputy Sheriff John Timmons.*
> *Timmons said* the pickup flipped over and Marshall was thrown out. He died at Carolton General Hospital an hour later.
> Police have not determined what caused the pickup to veer off the road, *Timmons said.*

A single attribution would have been enough for this story. Most of the facts are matters of record. The only part of the story that is a matter of opinion or of expert judgment — the explanation of how the pickup left the road — should be attributed. And this one reference to source could have supported all the rest.

Guidelines for Attribution

To summarize the proper use of attribution:

Minimum attribution is required in almost every news story.

Adequate attribution is a necessity in most news stories. Every news story should include enough attribution to assure the reader that the story is accurate and believable.

Attribution should be subordinate to the facts of the story. Attribution that looms larger than the information the story is intended to convey damages the story by confusing the reader as to what is important.

A three- or four-paragraph story with attribution repeated four or five times is a weak story. Excessive attribution wastes precious news space.

Attribution is seldom necessary in the lead of a story. This is particularly true where adequate attribution will follow in the body of the story.

In routine news stories, one attribution may be enough. For example, in a brief story about a traffic accident, *police said* used once will probably be enough to support the story.

The attribution, in instances like this, should come in the second paragraph, certainly no later than the third paragraph. Get the attribution into the story before the reader begins to wonder where the story came from.

Attribution in the lead is necessary where the source of the story is as important or more important than what is being reported. For example, in a story that begins *President Reagan said today*, attribution is a must because the source clearly is determining the importance of what is being reported.

Not all news stories need attribution. Brief stories — for example, the announcement of a scheduled meeting or speech — may be perfectly credible without attribution.

Where facts in a story are obvious or will be accepted by the reader without question — in other words, where the reader will have no reason to doubt the veracity of the newspaper — no attribution is necessary.

Where facts are a matter of public record, generally known to the public or obvious from the context of the story, no attribution is necessary. It would be pointless, for example, in a story about an arraignment to say, "John Jones was arraigned Monday, *court officials said.*"

When a reporter is present at an event and writes from personal knowledge, attribution is unnecessary. For example, a reporter covering a lengthy city council meeting can write from personal knowledge that the meeting lasted three and a half hours. There is no need to seek out the presiding officer and attribute routine information obvious to the reporter, the city council members and anyone else present.

Identification

The people, organizations, buildings, places and events in news stories should be fully identified as early as possible, generally on first reference. The Basic Guide to News Style in this book provides some guidance to identification, use of names and addresses and the proper form of titles. Beyond that there are a number of rules, conventions and practices, all intended to make certain that identification is clear and unambiguous, that readers know for certain who the people in news stories are, where events took place and what the real nature of events and issues is.

People must be identified clearly and accurately. Readers don't want to see their names misspelled or to be given the wrong middle initial, street address, profession or job. So the news writer is faced with a number of problems in accurately identifying the people who appear in news stories.

First of all, you must know who people are. This is a matter of careful reporting. Ask people to spell their names for you. Ask for middle initials. Ask how they usually sign their names. Verify the accuracy of addresses. Verify the correctness of titles. If you intend to use a person's age in a story, be sure you have it right. If your newspaper's style requires the use of courtesy titles, ask women whether to use Miss or Mrs. or Ms. with their names.

If the people you are writing about are not available for this firsthand check, then check against available records: city directories, court records, official printed programs or the telephone book. Who are these people? What are their connections with the story? We need to know not only who people are but who they are not. There are many similarities among names in any community, area or state. We must be concerned about libel, about people's right to privacy, about fairness and about the effect the news story may have on people named in it.

The basic form of identification, of course, is by name. Spell names correctly. Use first name, middle initial and last name unless the person prefers another form — initial, middle name, last name, for example. Use junior, senior, second or third if that is part of the name. If there is no other or better means of further identification, use the person's street address:

John Doe, 30, of 110 Washington St.

Mary Roe of the 100 block on Washington Street

Newspapers and the wire services often use age as a means of identification, especially in stories of injury or death or other circumstances where ages have been officially documented. In most instances, the age doesn't add much to the story, but it may on occasion be interesting or informative to know, for example, that the victim or the criminal was a young person. Or the age may serve to differentiate, to make it clear which of two people with similar names or backgrounds is involved.

Other forms of identification may be more relevant to the story, and it is a good rule to use the identification that has the most relevance, the best tie to the story.

We can identify people by their job, trade or profession:

> Richard Dreyfuss, the actor
>
> Jane Doe, the White House correspondent for CBS

We can identify people by the title of the elective or appointive job they hold:

> Mayor Koch
>
> Justice Sandra Day O'Connor
>
> State Representative Peggy Childs

We can identify people by their accomplishments:

> Henry Aaron, who hit more home runs than any other man in baseball history
>
> Tom Wicker, Pulitzer Prize–winning columnist for *The New York Times*

We can identify people by some local connection:

> Jane Doe, a former resident of Carolton
>
> John Doe, a 1910 graduate of Northwest College
>
> Robert Roe, son of Mr. and Mrs. Richard Roe, 110 E. Main St.

And we can identify people by their involvement in a past news event:

> Lindbergh, the first man to fly the Atlantic alone
>
> John Glenn, the first man in space
>
> Geraldine Ferraro, the Democratic Party nominee for vice president in 1984

In most news stories, it will be necessary to identify a person only once. And that identification should be one that is most relevant to the story. For example:

> The Blue Bird Cafe was held up Monday night by a masked man armed with a shotgun.
> John Doe, the restaurant manager, told police . . .

Here the best identification is, first, the name, second, the job. Doe is in the story because he is manager of the restaurant that was held up. The street address of his residence is irrelevant to the story and should be omitted. Don't pile up identification.

News writers must be careful in identifying women in the news. It would be pointless, pejorative and sexist to identify a woman as someone's wife if the story is about her professional career — a book published, appointment to an important office, promotion to a higher academic rank, an award or a prestigious prize.

And in some stories we must be concerned about invasion of privacy and identification that may place a person at risk. Many newspapers today do not identify victims of crimes by their street address. Criminals have been known to use stories about lucrative burglaries to identify addresses or neighborhoods where they can profitably steal again. Some newspapers routinely use addresses like this:

> John Doe of the 800 block on Main Street

State laws may in some instances prevent the names of young people from being released by police or other authorities. Even when names are available, newspapers often will not identify by name youngsters who are victims of child abuse or sexual molestation. Newspapers in most cases hesitate to use the names of women who have been raped, although exceptions are sometimes made when a woman testifies in open court.

In some stories, the name may not be important, though the circumstances are. The news story in Figure 6.1 is a good example of this. The circumstances, the unusual twist to the story, are interesting. The identity of the woman is not important.

Other Identification

Organizations and businesses, like people, must be identified on first reference if the name might not be readily recognized by the reader. It

SPOKANE, Wash. (UPI) — A woman summoned to police headquarters to help develop a composite drawing of the man who raped her spotted him when she walked into a hallway to get a drink of water.

The suspect, who had been asked by police to file a report on a burglary at his place of employment, was seized immediately.

The 24-year-old victim, working as a clerk at a grocery store when the assault took place Aug. 7, was at police headquarters Tuesday when she saw the young man, pointed at him and, in a shaky voice, told a detective standing nearby: "That's him."

Figure 6.1 *Newspapers often protect the privacy of people in the news by describing the person in general terms rather than by using a name and address. The circumstances are the story here, not the identity of the woman or the man.*

is hardly necessary to explain what the FBI is, or the PTA or the city council. But other organizations, especially less well-known organizations, should be identified by their purpose or nature:

> Ralston Purina Co., the giant pet-food producer
>
> Washington Monthly, a national political magazine
>
> "Up With People," an international cultural and educational program with headquarters in Tucson, Ariz.

Buildings, if they are not well known, should be identified by their location, generally the street address, or their use. The warehouse in the fire story at the beginning of this chapter was, you will recall, identified by its general location, North Philadelphia, by its street address, by its use as a warehouse and by the name of a business that had recently occupied it. No question in this story of what building burned.

Identification and Background

Identification on first reference of people, places, organizations or events should be specific, relevant to the story and limited. You will need to familiarize yourself with the style guide's rules on the use of names and titles. Some short titles, principally the titles of elected public officials and military, police and fire officials, go before the name.

Long titles, job descriptions and other identification go after the name. Once you have identified a person, treat other information as background and use it, if it is relevant, later on in the story. Don't clutter the lead or the early paragraphs of your story with more identification than is necessary.

Punctuation

Identification that follows a name — age, address, job description or other information — is set off by paired commas. For example:

> John Doe, 16, of 125 S. Washington Road, has been elected president of the junior class at Carolton Central High School.

These commas are important, for they set off parenthetical material, facts that can either be included or deleted without altering the grammatical structure of the sentence. The use of paired commas is explained in detail in Chapter 19.

Time and Timeliness

Journalism deals with current events, and newspapers long made a great point of the speed with which they brought news to the reading public. First radio, then television took some of the freshness out of the front page. Newspapers no longer publish extras, and there are fewer late stories marked *flash* or *bulletin* even in metropolitan newspapers, where street sales are still important. Radio and television news programs bring the public the first word of news events. Newspapers recognize this and concentrate on depth and completeness in their coverage of the news. We find that today's newspaper includes more feature writing and more interpretive reporting and that the newspaper places much less emphasis on haste in getting the news into print.

The news writer, however, cannot ignore timeliness in news stories. And events in news stories must be placed in their proper chronological context. First, the story has to be placed somewhere in time, for the reader wants to know when an event took place. Second, the writer must establish a relationship between the time the event took place and the time the story is being read by the newspaper reader.

The Point in Time

With few exceptions, it is necessary to be specific about the time elements in a news story: the date or day, the hour and minute. Depending on the newspaper's style, *today* or the day of the week is made an integral part of the lead:

> The City Council voted $4.5 million for a new disposal plant *Monday* at a meeting that lasted more than four hours.

> Four incumbent council members and one challenger were nominated in a light vote in the city primary *Tuesday.*

> A four-car crash took the lives of four area teenagers *early today.*

> The Senate Finance Committee *Friday* approved a tax bill that would raise the state's income tax and sales tax.

Whether you use *today* or the day of the week is a matter of your newspaper's preference, of its style. Your newspaper will have a rule on this matter. The wire services use the day of the week in most instances.

Note in these examples where the time element is placed. Depending on the sentence, it may come after the subject, immediately after a direct object or after a direct object and other modifying phrases. Placement is up to the writer and depends on the wording of the sentence and its cadence. The time element should fit naturally in the sentence. If you are in doubt, read the sentence aloud. Your ear will tell you if the placement is right. If it is not, move the time element.

Past Tense

News stories about events that have already taken place are written in the past tense and call for active verbs like *elected, injured, proposed, denied* or passive verbs like *was elected, was injured* or *was proposed.*

> Distribution of a half-million pounds of surplus government cheese continued Wednesday as the operation moved into high gear throughout Oregon.
>
> — *The Oregonian*

When you write in the past tense, you must couple the verb with a time element. In the *Oregonian* lead, the verb *continued* is followed by a specific reference to the time: *Wednesday.* Tell the reader when things happened:

> . . . announced *Monday*

> . . . said *Tuesday*

> . . . was killed *early today*

Present Perfect

Some news stories contain no specific reference to the time an event occurred. This is especially true of feature leads or feature stories that put more emphasis on the story and less on timeliness. This is true, too, of stories about past events where the fact that something has happened is important but where the exact time is not known or is relatively unimportant. For example:

> The man who managed Broward County's budget
> for the past two years *has been named* to head Taxwatch,
> a recently formed research group in Palm Beach that
> will scrutinize the county's budget.
> — *The Palm Beach Post*, West Palm Beach, Fla.

The *has been named* is the present perfect form of the verb. The usage is a common one, and verb forms like these are usual in news stories: *has ordered, has told, has announced.* You will also find the present perfect in the passive voice: *has been ordered, has been told, has been arrested.* Note the contrast between use of the present perfect and use of the past tense:

past tense + time element	. . . was killed Monday
	. . . said Tuesday
present perfect	. . . has announced
	. . . has ordered

An example of a news story in which the present perfect is used instead of the usual past tense and specific time element:

> A state appeals court has upheld the additional prison term imposed on a Long Branch man for rioting while serving time in Rahway State Prison.
>
> The Appellate Division of Superior Court yesterday . . .
>
> — *Asbury Park* (N.J.) *Press*

News stories are not always as fresh as we might like, and the writer or editor may want to disguise that fact. The trick is to avoid mentioning the time at all, and the present perfect makes that easy. For example:

> One of Bank of America's top economists has resigned, the latest in a string of departures at the San Francisco bank since its finances worsened this year.
>
> — *San Francisco Chronicle*

The resignation reported here occurred on a Friday. The story was published the following Monday. To avoid use of *Friday* in the lead, the writer turned to the present perfect and thus glossed over the fact that the story was several days old.

Present Tense

Timeliness is sometimes emphasized by use of the present tense. For example:

> Counting on an upswing in the agricultural economy, a Los Angeles developer and a Kansas City businessman plan to open what they term the country's first privately financed agribusiness "shopping center" this fall.
>
> Dick Sneddon and Ralph Wenger are turning . . .
>
> — *United Press International*

The Future

Stories about events that will happen, coming events, require specific time elements, both day and hour, as well as a different form of the verb:

> The Aiken-Barnwell Chapter of the S.C. Genealogi-
> cal Society will meet Sunday at 3 p.m. at the Barnwell
> Museum.
>
> — *Aiken* (S.C.) *Standard*

The future is usually expressed by the use of the auxiliary verb *will:*
will hold, will speak, will arrive.
Sometimes the present tense is used to express futurity.

> The team *leaves* Monday for New Orleans and the
> Sugar Bowl.

> The City Council *meets* Monday to decide on the ap-
> pointment of a city manager.

Day or Date?

The news writer must be sure to make all references to time as clear
and unambiguous as possible. When an event has occurred within a
week in the past or will occur within a week in the future, the day of
the week is specified: Monday, Tuesday and so on. When the event is
more than a week in the past or more than a week in the future, the
date is used. Day and date, according to this rule, are *not* used together.
For example:

> Eligible voters have until Monday to register to vote
> in next month's primary election.

In the following example, both day and date are used because two
performances fall within the week, a third beyond the week:

> More than 40 area children will participate in The
> Augusta Players Children's Wing production of "Not
> Even a Mouse" at 8 p.m. Friday and Saturday and at 3
> p.m. Dec. 7.
>
> — *Augusta* (Ga.) *Chronicle and Herald*

Obituaries often include the day of the week and the month and
year in order to provide an accurate and permanent record. There are

times, too, when both day and date are required to avoid ambiguity. Ordinarily, one or the other will do.

Time and the Reader

One important matter the news writer must keep in mind about time is the reader's point of view. If you write for an afternoon newspaper, a story you write first thing in the morning will be read the same day. If you write for a morning newspaper, what you write on one day will ordinarily not be read until the next day. What will the reader think you mean by *today* or *yesterday* or *tomorrow*? The newspaper helps by establishing a starting place. Every page carries a folio, a line at the top of the page that includes the day and date of publication. If you are reading the Monday paper, you know that Sunday refers to the previous day and that a reference to Tuesday means the next day. There is little ambiguity.

The New York Times also uses dates in datelines, which can be confusing unless you are a regular reader of *The Times*, for *today* in a *Times* news story refers to the dateline, not to the day of publication. To avoid this sort of ambiguity, most newspapers do not include dates in datelines, and most prefer to use the day of the week in news stories rather than *today, yesterday* or *tomorrow*. This is the system suggested in the style guide at the back of this text. Morning newspapers, however, often accept *today* if the reference is to something that will happen later on the day of publication.

In references to months and years, avoid using *next* or *last*. If the reference is to the current calendar year, just use the month: June, November or December. If the reference is not to the current calendar year, use both month and year: June 1989, April 1985, March 1990.

Overemphasis on Timeliness

Many bad leads are written in an obvious attempt to make the story appear fresher than it is. The worst offender is the lead like this one, which has two time elements:

> PRAGUE (UPI) — Western Airline officials said *today* the toll in the crash *yesterday* of the Soviet-built Tupolev 154 tri-engine jet could have gone much higher

if the plane had come down on a highway near the Prague Airport.

Including *today* in the lead is unnecessary. The lead would have been much clearer without it. Use of the present tense would have implied timeliness and resulted in a smoother sentence:

Western Airline officials say that the toll . . .

Don't force *today* on your readers. A good rule of thumb is to avoid including two references to time in the lead. Keep it simple.

The Stylebook

You will find a stylebook — whichever one applies to where you are writing — a great help in solving the problems of identification and time elements. Learn the rules about names, titles and addresses and you will find that identification will to a large extent take care of itself. Learn the rules about time and you will find that many facts in a news story will sort themselves out.

Suggestions for Further Reading

These reminiscences by well-known journalists are both entertaining and instructive.

Carter, Hodding. *First Person Rural.* Garden City, N.Y.: Doubleday, 1963.
> The editor of the *Greenville* (Miss.) *Delta Democrat Times* writes about his newspaper, his town and the South.

Casey, Robert J. *Such Interesting People.* Indianapolis: The Bobbs-Merrill Company, 1943.
> One of the great reporters of all time recalls his early years as a reporter on Chicago newspapers. A classic.

Catledge, Turner. *My Life and The Times.* New York: Harper and Row, 1971.
> Reminiscences of a former managing editor of *The New York Times.*

Hough, Henry Beetle. *Country Editor.* New York: Doubleday, Doran & Company, Inc., 1940.
> A classic account of small-town journalism.

Mencken, H.L. *Newspaper Days*. New York: Knopf, 1941.
    The adventures of young H.L. Mencken on the *Baltimore Morning Herald* from 1899 to 1906.

Murray, Donald. *Writing for Your Readers*. Chester, Conn.: The Globe Pequot Press, 1983.
    Murray, the *Boston Globe*'s first writing coach, has collected a series of essays on news writing by *Globe* staff writers.

Steffens, Lincoln. *The Autobiography of Lincoln Steffens*. New York: Harcourt, Brace and Company, 1931.
    A book that influenced a whole generation of journalists.

DITKA'S TASK

WINNING A REPEAT CHAMPIONSHIP
BEARS' ROUGH ROAD, 3C

HOYT HEADED FOR JAIL 1C
SAN DIEGO PITCHER SENTENCED TO 46 DAYS

Richard Clark
JIM KELLY: Buffalo Bills' frustrated QB, 1C

JIM KELLY'S LONG SEASON 1C

USA TODAY

NO. 1 IN THE USA . . . 4,792,000 READERS EVERY DAY

WEDNESDAY

BEST & WORST AT MOVIES 4D

CAR OF YEAR CONTROVERSY
AUDI 5000 UNDER FIRE, 1B

YEAR'S TOP 10 FRANCHISES; STARTER TIPS 1B

By Lee Anderson
SIGOURNEY WEAVER: 'Aliens' ties for tops, 4D

Voyager exclusive: Lightning big worry

By Mary-Ann Bendel
Special for USA TODAY

MOJAVE, Calif. — Voyager co-pilot Dick Rutan's worst fear: his fuel-laden plane will get hit by lightning, he told USA TODAY Tuesday in an exclusive interview by radio.

"I haven't seen any yet, but there's still a long flight ahead," he said.

Voyager soars over Singapore at 2 p.m. EST today in its record attempt to circle the globe without stopping and without refueling.

The experimental aircraft — completing one-quarter of its journey Tuesday — skirted a Pacific typhoon, riding its tailwinds. Flying at 145 mph, Voyager was about an hour ahead of schedule.

Rutan said crossing the Pacific at night "gave me the first chance to check out Voyager's long-range navigation — it worked fantastic."

He resists comparisons to famed aviator Charles Lindbergh, but said, "There are a lot of similarities and the same kind of problems in our flight."

He peered at the ocean from the cramped cockpit he shares with co-pilot Jeana Yeager: "There's a lot of water out there," he said.

Voyager, which took off Sunday from nearby Edwards Air Force Base, is attempting to make the journey in 10 days.

Two chase planes flying from Singapore and the Philippines are to check the fragile aircraft today.

■ **Voyager path, 3A**
■ **Flight forecast, 12A**

Senator: No immunity 'games'

Homeless have many faces

TODAY: Stories from every state; **THURS.:** These kids have no home

IN HOUSTON: Homeless children found refuge with their parents at the Star of Hope Shelter. These kids were on their way to a Christmas party, decked out in donated clothing.

Photos by Barbara Riks, USA TODAY

■ **Tips on how to help, 2A**
■ **State-by-state report, 6-7A**

Thursday — Suffering grows in study of 26 cities; a visit to Houston shelter

By Johanna Neuman and Juan J. Walte
USA TODAY

WASHINGTON — President Reagan, saying he wants "the full story about Iran (to) come out now," asked Congress Tuesday to give his crew immunity.

The idea, partial protection from prosecution for key witnesses, was quickly rejected by the Intelligence Committee.

"No," said Chairman Sen. David Durenberger, R-Minn. "Playing games . . . isn't going to change anything."

Late Tuesday night, Durenberger conceded the finger firmly at the man the president wanted immunity for: "It's clear . . . that whoever pulled it off did it without proper, appropriate or other authority, and that person is Ollie North."

The White House's Larry Speakes said Reagan "retains the power for executive clemency in any case" but "has no plans at present to do so."

And Nancy Reagan, questioned on a visit to Children's Hospital, said Reagan is "very anxious" for ex-aides John Poindexter and North to talk.

Chief of staff Donald Regan testified Tuesday without immunity or executive privilege. He said R. gan was "shocked" that money from Iran arms deals went to contras.

In other developments:
■ New national security adviser Frank Carlucci continued to clean house. Latest casualty: Howard Teicher, a mastermind of the Iran scheme who also testified.
■ Senate leaders named a new investigating committee, to begin work in January.

More bad news for Reagan: The probe of ex-aide Michael Deaver widened.
■ Committee at a glance, 2A
■ Regan upbeat, 4A

Smoke raises non-smokers' cancer risk

By Steven Findlay
USA TODAY

WASHINGTON — The smoke from other people's cigarettes can cause disease in non-smokers, including children, says the surgeon general's newest report on smoking.

The report, released Tuesday, is the most authoritative yet on the dangers of passive or involuntary smoking.

"It is now clear that disease risk due to inhalation of tobacco smoke . . . can extend to those who inhale tobacco smoke in room air," said Surgeon General C. Everett Koop.

He said he hopes the report spurs efforts to ban smoking in the workplace. Separating smokers and non-smokers reduces, but does not eliminate, the risks, the report says.

Labor leaders opposing the ban respected that environmental smoke "can be relieved to nearly all cases by improved ventilation." The Tobacco Institute called Koop's report political rather than scientific.

The 325-page report says studies show passive smoking increases the risk of lung cancer in adults and respiratory infections in children.

But he said more data is needed to estimate how much disease and illness can be attributed to passive smoking and how much exposure can cause health problems.

COVER STORY

'We bundled up in bed to keep warm'

ST. LOUIS: Evelyn Johnson, Geanovea. 'I've tried everything I know to try.

By Patrick O'Driscoll
USA TODAY

ST. LOUIS — Her wish is simple. All Evelyn Johnson wants is to spend Christmas at home, "with my babies."

Instead, she's taken refuge in a shelter for homeless women and children — a converted old boarding school across the cold Mississippi River in East St. Louis, Ill. She and as many as 3 million others are caught in a nationwide epidemic that blurs the spectrum of age, race and background and stretches from the heartland oilfields outside Houston to the boomtown downtown of Boston.

Advocates for the USA's homeless say it's getting worse. Homelessness wears many faces in many places — a Skid Row alcoholic in a Los Angeles emergency shelter, a

Please see COVER STORY next page ▶

Immigration law slows border flow

By Peg Lofus
USA TODAY

Fears about the USA's new immigration law may be discouraging people from entering the country illegally, U.S. Border Patrol officials say.

The number of illegal immigrant arrests along the border dropped 30 percent last month from November 1985, officials said. That indicates illegal crossings also were down.

"Smugglers are having difficult times getting loads together, and you can't attribute that to anything other than the immigration bill," said Mario Ortiz, spokesman for the Immigration and Naturalization Service's 13-state southern region.

Others say the drop is due to the normal seasonal decline and the Rio Grande running high, making it difficult to cross from Mexico to Texas.

The bill grants amnesty to illegal residents who arrived before 1982 and penalizes employers who hire illegal aliens.

Along the border:
■ Laredo sector saw a 35 percent drop — it's biggest since 1982.
■ Arrests in the El Centro, Calif., sector fell 30 percent.
■ In the San Diego sector — down 2 percent — chief agent Gene Schnblourg said a decline in January, normally a month of big increases, would mean the law is having an effect.

Papers done on computer score higher

Special for USA TODAY

Computerized word processors pay off in higher grades on college papers, a study reported Tuesday.

Of 200 papers by Rider College students:
■ Computer-written papers got an average 3.1 out of 4 — just above a B. None received a failing grade.
■ Typed papers got an average 2.6, or B-minus. A few got Fs.

"Over a college career, a computer could mean the difference between making the dean's list or hovering above academic probation," said Thomas Simonet. His students did the survey.

Women did 76 percent of computer-written papers.
■ Computer buy guide, 4B

Inside USA TODAY
4 SECTIONS

© COPYRIGHT 1986 USA TODAY, a division of Gannett Co., Inc.

USA SNAPSHOTS

A look at statistics that shape the nation

How home ownership varies

Home ownership rates are highest in the Midwest, where home prices are lowest — $61,200 compared with $79,700 nationally. People who own the place they live in, by region:

61.2%   67.2%   66.1%   58.6%
Northeast   Midwest   South   West

*Median price for an existing single family home, '86
Source: Commerce Department, National Association of Realtors

By Heidi E. Caponale, USA TODAY

---

7 Quotation

A good newspaper is a nation talking to itself.

Arthur Miller

The news stories we have discussed so far have dealt primarily with factual material: what happened, who it happened to, where and when it happened. Stories like these are secondhand stories in the sense that they are based on facts told to the reporter but not observed by the reporter. Often they are thirdhand because they were told to the reporter not by participants or witnesses but by others who got the facts from witnesses or participants and passed the information on to the reporter.

This chapter looks at news stories in which people speak for themselves. The use of the exact words spoken by people appearing in news stories is known as *direct quotation*, and the words the speaker used are called *direct quotes* or merely *quotes*. Direct quotation is a useful device, one that breathes life into a story because it enables the participants in an event to speak directly to the newspaper reader rather than indirectly, through an intermediary — the reporter and writer.

When the people in our stories start talking for themselves, new writing and organizing problems arise. Just how do we reproduce in news stories the words people use?

111

Reproduced Speech

When we quote — that is, when we give a written or oral report of what someone says — we are reproducing the words, or an approximation of the words, that the speaker used. We are reproducing speech, not creating it. The speaker's words are the original. What we quote in a news story is a reproduction.

Every direct quotation originates with someone, somewhere, talking. Visualize, if you will, an episode that might have occurred a few minutes ago on a nearby street corner. You were a witness. A traffic policeman is standing on the curb keeping an eye on the traffic and on pedestrians using the crosswalk. A disheveled man comes up to him. His clothes are dirty, his face is cut, his hair is untidy. The police officer turns to him, and you hear the following exchange:

Policeman: What happened?

Man: Officer, a guy just held me up. He took my wallet 'n knocked me down.

Policeman: Ya hurt?

Man: Nope, but I'm plenty mad. Kinda dirty, too.

Policeman: Just a minute. Lemme write this down. What'd this guy look like?

Man: Oh, he was kinda short and heavy.

That's original speech. You hear it yourself. You may watch the speakers as you listen. You know who said what and to whom. Physical movement, relative positions of the speakers, differences in voice and tone identify the speakers and their words. But this exchange reproduced by you later on for a friend needs some explaining. You might say something like this:

Hey, did you hear about the mugging? I was right there when this guy told a cop about it. He said he'd been held up. Said he wasn't hurt. He told the cop he was just mad. Somebody took his wallet and knocked him down.

Later you might see the story in your evening newspaper. This time the man's words are presented in still another form:

A Carolton man was assaulted and robbed Monday near Lexington Road and Jackson Street.

John L. Johnson, 23, of 234 Oak St., told police a short, thickset youth knocked him down and took his wallet. He was not seriously hurt, he told police.

"But I'm plenty mad," he said.

He said he lost about $36.

As you can see, reproduced speech, secondhand speech, simply does not come out quite like the original. An oral report of what was said, like the account you gave your friend, is slightly different from what was said originally: There is a difference in point of view, since you are telling what you heard. There is a difference in tense, since you are speaking about something in the past while the mugging victim and the police officer were often speaking in the present tense. The newspaper version is even more unlike the original exchange, since the location of the mugging and the fact that the man's wallet contained $36 — facts you left out of your report — were added to put the reproduced speech in context.

In the newspaper version, one statement is much like the original and appears as a direct quotation. The rest of the story is *summary* and *paraphrase* in the words of the writer. If we had tape-recorded the original exchange, we could play it back and check the newspaper story against the mugging victim's words.

The newspaper version of the incident quotes the victim as saying:

"But I'm plenty mad."

The original statement was:

"Nope, but I'm plenty mad."

The "nope" doesn't fit very well into the news story as it was developed, so the writer omitted it. The other words — enclosed in quotation marks — are exactly what the speaker said. The rest of the sentence in which the quotation appears is background — a *speech tag* or *attribution* — that identifies the speaker and in this case explains who he was talking to.

The last sentence in the story is *indirect quotation*. Indirect quotation, which is not enclosed in quotation marks, is a slightly edited or altered version of what the speaker said. It has a speech tag, of course, to identify the speaker, just like direct quotation.

If we could turn our tape recorder back on, we would learn that this additional exchange took place:

Policeman: How much d'ya lose?

Man: Oh, about thirty-five, maybe thirty-six bucks.

The newspaper story tightened this up and quoted the speaker indirectly:

He said he lost about $36.

Indirect quotation, then, tells what the speaker said without using his exact words. The speaker's words may be changed very little. The tense, of course, may change from present to past, and the viewpoint changes from first person to second person. Indirect quotations may be *paraphrased*, that is, given in the news writer's words, or *summarized*, that is, reduced to the bare essentials. Although paraphrased or summarized quotes are generally regarded not as quotation but as information, they still must be scrupulously attributed to the speaker.

Direct Quotation

News writers gather information, organize it according to the needs of the moment and set down a story in their own words. They identify the source of the story once or twice, that is, attribute the story to its sources. That's about it. Any of the stories in the earlier chapters of this book can serve as examples of this approach. Most news stories make use of only two basic, useful and important devices of story telling: summary and paraphrase.

Occasionally, however, a news source or someone involved in a news story says something especially interesting or significant or perhaps just says something so well that the news writer finds the speaker's words hard to improve upon. So the writer adds a new element to the story: direct quotes rather than additional summary or paraphrase.

The following, taken from a *Boston Herald* news story about a plane that crashed into a row of houses and started a disastrous fire, shows how the authentic voices of people involved in a news story can add color and drama to a story:

"I kept looking back to make sure the fire wasn't coming towards us. The kids were just looking at it and screaming. I kept saying, 'Get over the fence. Get over the fence.'"

And another direct quotation from the same story:

"When I came back later on, the front of the houses weren't there anymore. They were just ashes."

Direct quotation, the words of spectators and participants, can add a great deal to a news story, which must in large part be secondhand — the writer's version of what he was told by others.

There is one important fact about direct quotation that should be understood from the beginning, however. The fact that someone says it doesn't mean that it is worth quoting. Most of what news writers learn in gathering facts for a story should be presented as summary and paraphrase in the news writer's words. Only when the direct quote is better than anything the news writer could write or comes from a source that is so important to the story that it must be quoted should the news writer use direct quotation.

But as you can see from the direct quotation used in the *Boston Herald* story, direct quotation can add to the impact of a news story. Direct quotation brings the reader into direct contact with the action — directly to the scene of the plane crash, the fire or devastation caused by a tornado. Direct quotation can add authenticity and color to a news story. The direct quotation in the *Herald* story gave the reader something the reporter could not — the emotion of a participant, the terror the mother felt as she tried to get her children away from the fire.

When you hear lively, interesting, colorful and appropriate words from someone, you will want to use these words in direct quotation. Paraphrase the ordinary, the routine, but not the special. A Chicago machine politician some years back exulted at the defeat of a reform ticket and was widely quoted as saying: "Chicago ain't ready for reform." That's real speech. Candidates for office often predict that they will defeat their opponents, and these routine predictions can generally be paraphrased. But when former President Carter told reporters that he expected to defeat Sen. Ted Kennedy and win the Democratic nomination, he said bluntly: "I'll whip his ass." That's real speech, and Carter was widely quoted.

When Winston Churchill died, news stories quoted Harold Macmillan, one of Churchill's successors as prime minister:

> The oldest among us can recall nothing to compare
> with him, and the youngest among us, however long we
> live, will never see the like of him again.

Try paraphrasing that! Keep your ear tuned to the speech of those around you. Listen for the interesting and colorful quote — the quote that adds something to your story. When words have an impact or a ring to them, like Macmillan's tribute to Churchill, quote directly.

Indirect Quotation

Indirect quotation may be very close to the speaker's words, or it may be a very broad paraphrase, the substance of what the speaker said summarized and put into the writer's words. The direct quotations taken from the story about the plane crash could have been handled as indirect quotation, but they would not have been so effective.

Indirect quotation can be a broad paraphrase of what a speaker said. The news story about the mugging used this indirect quotation:

> He told police a short, thickset youth knocked him
> down and took his wallet.

Compare this with the more colloquial and disconnected original statement of the mugger's victim:

> A guy just held me up . . . he took my wallet 'n
> knocked me down . . . I'm plenty mad . . . kinda dirty,
> too . . . he was kinda short and heavy . . .

In the following news story, what is said in the second and fourth paragraphs is indirect quotation. The statements are attributed, but we can safely assume that these paragraphs do not reproduce exactly what the source of the story told the reporter, since the statements are not enclosed in quotation marks:

> The American Association of Blood Banks has
> awarded the West Tennessee Regional Blood Center a
> two-year accreditation.
> Jack Smythe, Blood Center director, explained that
> the accreditation program is voluntary and about 2,000

other centers across the country are also accredited by the association.

The accreditation was awarded after an inspection team from the blood bank organization visited the Jackson facility.

Although the accreditation is not legally necessary, Smythe said, it is a sign of professionalism.

The West Tennessee Regional Blood Center is a non-profit organization that furnishes all the blood to 13 hospitals in West Tennessee and uses only volunteer donors.

— *Jackson* (Tenn.) *Sun*

Indirect quotation adds information, enables the writer to bring the source of information into the story and gives the story authenticity and credibility. To this extent indirect quotation and direct quotation are alike. They differ, however, in that direct quotation is exactly what the speaker said, or as close as it is possible to make it, while the indirect quote is an edited version of the speaker's words, even a summary or a paraphrase.

Attribution

In news stories, almost without exception, it is necessary to identify the source of the story, to tell where we got our information. This is usually done with a brief phrase like *police said*, *she said* or *the mayor admitted*. This is attribution, and we have seen in earlier chapters how attribution is used to pin down the source of a news story. Attribution used with direct or indirect quotation is referred to as a *speech tag*, and it is used to identify the person we are quoting.

The Grammar of Quotations

Don't be thrown by the suggestion that we are going to talk about grammar. All we are going to do is to organize our thinking about the use of direct and indirect quotation and to see how they are handled in news writing. Let's look at the following sentences:

He added: "Can't Mr. Dalton see the need to report honestly and openly what is going on in the city?"

117

"Affluent people are fleeing the city and going to the suburbs," he said.

Bragg said almost everyone who works at Atlantic Sails gets the fever.

"Lyons talks big," Hart said, "but he might make me mad enough to step into the ring with him."

If we analyze these sentences, we will notice several patterns. Some of the sentences are in normal word order with the subject first, the verb second and the direct object — in this case a quotation — third, like this:

Peck said, "This is the regular disciplinary action we've been using."

Bragg said almost everyone who works at Atlantic Sails gets the fever.

One of the sentences has a change in word order with the direct quotation first, the subject second and the verb third and last:

"Affluent people are fleeing the city and going to the suburbs," he said.

Another sentence is turned completely inside out with the subject and verb tucked into the middle of the quotation:

"Lyons talks big," Hart said, "but he might make me mad enough to step into the ring with him."

And finally, we see that sentences including direct quotation and those including indirect quotation may follow the same word order:

Peck said, "This is the regular disciplinary action we've been using."

Bragg said almost everyone who works at Atlantic Sail gets the fever.

There appear to be different ways to structure sentences that include direct and indirect quotation, but there is also some consistency in their use. Let's sort out these consistencies.

Type 1 Quotes

Sentences that follow normal word order we will refer to as *Type 1* quotes. Type 1 quotes follow this order: subject + verb + direct object. In newsroom terminology, we can say that Type 1 quotes put the speech tag first and the quotation second:

> But, he added: "Our city's too big to be a one-man show."

> A Navy spokesman said, "We can confirm that there are no deaths."

These examples of Type 1 quotes are direct quotation. Indirect quotes may also follow Type 1 word order. Some typical examples:

> Hatfield said Los Angeles has stopped growing because of poor planning years ago.

> Reston said he does not believe the United States is on the verge of a new period of isolationism.

The word *that* often appears in Type 1 indirect quotations as a connector between the speech tag and the quotation:

> Hatfield said that Los Angeles has stopped growing because of poor planning years ago.

This connector is optional. It is frequently omitted, as it was in the earlier version of the sentence just given, when in the writer's judgment the sentence will be clear without it. It is generally included when its use will make the sentence easier to understand. Its use depends on the writer's ear for a smooth sentence. Some other examples:

> The president said that in his view the economy of the United States was basically healthy.

> Garcia said that if the auction is successful it will be an annual event.

In both these examples, use of the connector *that* makes the sentences more readable.

Type 2 Quotes

Type 2 quotes are those in which the direct or indirect quotation precedes the speech tag. This is just the opposite of Type 1 word order, but it is a normal usage. In fact, you will find that Type 2 word order is preferable in news writing for direct quotation. Some examples of Type 2 direct quotation:

> "I would hope that legalized gambling doesn't become a reality," Kuhn said.

> "We need a businessman in City Hall," he said.

We find Type 2 word order used frequently in indirect quotations:

> The scarcity of rain in September isn't unusual, Wassall reported.

> A consumer council would be most significant for business in its product complaint services, Hart suggested.

Type 3 Quotes

In Type 3 quotes, the speech tag is placed somewhere within the quotation. This is normal and acceptable grammar and a common arrangement made possible by the fact that the quotation is a complete sentence and can stand by itself. There is nothing complicated about Type 3 quotation. The speech tag is placed at some natural break in the quotation — for example, between the subject and verb:

> "My first love," she said softly, "is the city."

> "The problem before me today," said Judge McGee, from neighboring Amador County, "is whether the editor of the paper who wrote this article is protected under the Constitution."

The speech tag can also be inserted immediately after the verb in either direct or indirect quotation:

> He did not shoot, he said, because he had a can of tear gas in his hand.

"The crux of the matter is," Riley said, "we've changed the concept of the cultural center."

The speech tag can also be inserted between two sentences joined by linking words such as *and, or, for, but* or *so:*

"Well, he told me to go there," she said, "but he wasn't there."

Audiences are used to it now, she said, so we'll have to invent something else to startle them.

Speech tags may also be inserted between the main part of the direct or indirect quotation and a modifying element. For example:

Typically, he said, elderly mental patients sit next to each other without talking or are apathetic, irritable and forgetful.

"If we give them up," he said, "we may be defeated, but we won't be destroyed."

These examples of Type 3 quotation are illustrative but not exhaustive. Anyone who speaks or writes English senses a natural breaking point in a quotation and will put the speech tag in the right place. The real test, of course, is whether the sentence sounds right, whether it is readable. Your ear for the language can tell you that.

Extended Quotation

The examples of direct and indirect quotation we have examined so far have been single sentences. However, in news stories it is often necessary to use several sentences of direct quotation in succession. For example:

"There is mounting distrust, then an outburst, followed by careful rebuilding," she said. "We are at the final stage now."

The first sentence in this example is a Type 2 quotation. The second sentence has no speech tag because the tag at the end of the first sentence identifies the source of both. A single speech tag, then, if it comes no later than the end of the first sentence, will identify the source of quotation in the entire paragraph:

> "One night we made some real good beef stew out of Skippy and baked potatoes and carrots," Arnall said. "For lunch the other day we took cheddar cheese soup and put some Purina in it. Chuckwagon is my favorite dry food."

A Type 3 quotation may also be used to introduce extended quotation:

> "Lyons talks big," Hart said, "but he might make me mad enough to step into the ring with him. All that talk about me eating that crutch is hogwash. He'll need it to walk on when the Mauler gets through with him."

A Type 1 quote may also be used to introduce a paragraph of direct quotation. In such cases, however, the speech tag ends with a colon and the direct quotation is set off in a separate paragraph:

> The governor made the same observation about budget growth:
> "I wonder when the people are going to react adversely. Budgets and taxes can't continue to grow at this rate."

Verbatim texts or long excerpts from texts that run over many paragraphs are generally introduced by a speech tag such as this:

> The text of the president's statement:

The full text or extensive excerpts follow, but without quotation marks. This is a special use of the speech tag, and one that you won't have much occasion to use.

Extended quotation may run over two or three paragraphs but still need only minimum attribution. Note how the single speech tag in the first paragraph below manages to support two full paragraphs of direct quotation:

> "Hunger is much more of a problem with old people than with children," he said. "A hungry child will climb on a cabinet to get some food, but many older people

just don't have the energy to even prepare a meal for themselves.

"Even a borderline competent parent will feed a child as the best way to get him to shut up. Nobody will do that for an elderly person."

Note that there are no quotation marks at the end of the first paragraph. There are opening quotation marks at the beginning of the second paragraph, but the closing quotes come only at the end of the entire quotation. This system of punctuation holds good no matter how many paragraphs of quotation follow.

Fragmentary Quotes

It is best to avoid the use of fragmentary or partial quotes. A fragmentary quote is a word or phrase of direct quotation dropped into a sentence, as in these examples:

The "element" he was referring to consists of young adults who he said "run around with almost no clothes on" and use "terrible language."

Several of the proposals were discussed last year as a "minority party bill of rights" but never voted on.

Breast cancer, it was found, was "highly concentrated" in the New York metropolitan area.

If the speaker's words were clear, concise and informative, you should use the full quotation. If not — paraphrase. Put it in your own words. Do not, as a general rule, use single words or phrases of direct quotation as they were used in these examples. Especially avoid putting quote marks around single words used in their usual and ordinary sense. For example:

Fire officials said they suspect "arson."

There may be occasions when it is necessary to use a fragmentary quote, but don't use fragmentary quotes of one or two or three words used in their normal sense. If you avoid mixing your own words with other people's words, you can avoid impossible sentences like this one:

With inmates waving good-bye and chanting "Give 'em hell, Mitchell," he said he was "looking forward to coming back to Alabama to see all of my friends down here."

Straightforward use of direct and indirect quotation would be better:

The inmates waved good-bye.
"Give 'em hell, Mitchell," they shouted.
Mitchell said he was looking forward to returning to Alabama to see all his friends.

Parenthetical Insertions

Far too often, news writers use incomplete or vague direct quotations and try to patch them up by inserting missing words or phrases in parentheses. For example:

"We intend to enforce them (the mandates) through education," Johnson said.

"It (private donations) is the margin of excellence between a good and a great university," Roberts said.

If direct quotes need to be patched up like this, they aren't worth using. The parentheses are awkward because they are intrusive. They stop readers in their tracks. "How's that again?" It's easy to avoid this situation. Turn the awkward or incomplete quotation into indirect quotation, and work in the missing material or explain the vague references:

The mandates will be enforced through education, Johnson said.

Private donations provide the margin between a good and a great university, Roberts said.

Keep in mind that direct quotation should be used when the speaker says things in more forceful, interesting or unusual form than you might achieve by paraphrase or summary. If the speaker's words are garbled or the syntax awkward — don't attempt direct quotation. Quote indirectly, paraphrase or summarize. Very little is said in such a singular way that it must be quoted directly.

Quotation Marks with Other Punctuation

You will have noticed by this time that the closing quotation marks used in examples always come outside the period or comma at the end of the quotation:

> . . . his friends," he said.

> . . . all the time."

> . . . is that all?" he inquired.

Question marks and exclamation points go inside or outside the quotation marks depending on whether they refer to the quoted matter or the entire sentence.

Quotes Within Quotes

Occasionally you will find quoted matter included in something you want to use as direct quotation. Use single quote marks for the quote within the quote, thus:

> "I don't like to be called a 'nattering nabob' or anything else, for that matter," Smith said.

> "I don't want to be called a 'nattering nabob,'" Smith said.

Speech Tags

Speech tags, or attribution, as you know, are necessary to identify the source of direct and indirect quotations. They are essential, but they should not be obtrusive. They must not be so obvious that they slow readers down or break readers' concentration. Speech tags should be accepted by the reader much as quotation marks are accepted — as quickly understood signals about the nature of the message.

When you use a direct quotation, you place quotation marks at the beginning and end of the quotation. These little punctuation marks are unobtrusive but meaningful. They inform the reader that whatever is included between them is an exact reproduction of what someone said.

The quotation marks are helpful, but they do not intrude. Readers grasp their significance quickly and go on to read for sense and meaning. They are grammatical signals.

The verb *to say* in speech tags — generally in the past tense, as *she said* — is a signal much like the quotation marks. It tells the reader that the name it links to the quotation is the source of the quotation. It is unobtrusive and should be. Its meaning is so limited that it is almost as mechanical a signal as quotation marks.

Most beginning news writers worry about overusing *said*. They sense that it is repetitive and try to avoid using it repeatedly in a news story. They try to find synonyms to substitute for it. There are good reasons, however, for sticking with *said* and avoiding variations. If all the writer wants to do is tag a quote and identify a speaker, it is the best verb to use. It is short and its meaning is not likely to be misunderstood. Its meaning is so limited that the reader catches its signal almost subconsciously and goes on to read the quotation. It doesn't overload the reader with surplus information. Stick to *said*. As a writer, you may be conscious of its repeated use, but your reader won't be.

Meaningful Variations

If, on the other hand, you do want to tell your reader more than just the identity of the speaker, you will have to find a more meaningful verb. For example, in stories about trials, public hearings or other official proceedings, witnesses appear and give testimony under oath. You can, in writing a news story about such proceedings, say that a witness said something, but it would be more accurate to say that the witness *testified*. In this instance, *said* is inadequate because it does not convey the significance of the kind of statement the speaker was making. Here, *testify* is the only verb that will convey that special significance.

Other special situations may call for the use of verbs more colorful and more meaningful than *said*. Accused persons may *admit* or even *confess* their misdeeds. Injured people may *cry out*. Conspirators may *whisper*. You have at your disposal a broad range of useful and descriptive words for special situations. But you must be careful to choose one that conveys the exact meaning you want. And you must be careful not to use verbs that carry too much meaning or a meaning you do not intend. For example, *pointed out* in a speech tag suggests that the speaker is stating a fact. It should not be used if the speaker is merely stating an opinion, for its use might be misleading. Some verbs may put a speaker's delivery in an unflattering light. Verbs like *grumbled*, *insinuated, ranted, stammered* and *whined* suggest that the writer is judging the speaker's words rather than merely reporting them.

Some verbs, like *admitted, confessed* and *conceded* may, in some contexts, imply that the speaker is owning up to a misdeed. Confessions and admissions in many readers' minds are related to wrongdoing. Be careful about using these words.

Some verbs are too formal for casual use. Presidents, governors and other important public officials make statements. To say that the average speaker stated something is usually an exaggeration and always a bit formal. Save *stated* and *announced* for formal and important occasions.

Some verbs may be misleading. *Revealed,* for example, implies that something that has been hidden or kept secret is finally coming to light. *Said* or even *announced* is usually more appropriate. *Added* or *concluded* may be misleading if they give the wrong impression of the order in which a speaker made a statement. News stories generally present the speech in an order somewhat different from the one the speaker used. News writers frequently take something from the end of a speech or interview — the most important part of a speech often comes at the end — and put it at the top of their story. Don't use the words *added* or *concluded* or *went on to say* unless they reflect the order the speaker used.

This is not intended to be an exhaustive discussion of the meanings of the various substitutes for *said.* It is meant only to suggest some of the problems news writers may encounter in using words that go beyond *said.* There are a number of readable and helpful guides to newspaper usage, and news writers, even experienced ones, find them useful.

Nonsense Tags

News writers should avoid nonsensical verbs in speech tags. No one is able to *laugh, cry, chuckle* or *gasp* a coherent statement. For example:

> "I just don't know the answer to that one," he frowned.

It's pretty hard to make a statement like that by wrinkling the forehead. Just stick to *said* or, in this case, perhaps *replied.*

Of course, if the frown is significant, and you want to show that the speaker was having trouble with his statement, you can do this:

Smith paused and frowned.
"I just don't know the answer to that one," he said.

Word Order in Speech Tags

The speech tag is nothing more than the subject and verb of a normal English sentence:

She said that she intends to run for governor next year.

Ordinarily, it is best to stick to the subject-verb word order in speech tags just because it is normal word order:

Smith said

Gov. Harris said

the mayor said

Miss Fonda said

Ordinarily there is little reason to reverse this order. Readers are helped when word order is usual or expected. They have to slow down if they meet the unexpected or unusual. You don't want to confuse your readers, and you don't want to call undue attention to the speech tag. Nothing in the following example calls for shifting the order of words in the speech tag:

"It was what we wanted and what we expected," said the speaker.

Make it simply *the speaker said*. Sometimes, there is a reason for departing from normal word order in a speech tag. In the following example, the name of the speaker and the verb would have been widely separated by a long descriptive phrase if the writer had followed normal word order in the speech tag:

"Frankly, this looks awkward," said Henry Adams, senior vice president of the Southern Ohio Publishing Co., "and I don't like being forced into awkward situations."

Except for this kind of situation, stick to normal word order in speech tags: *he said, she said* or *the mayor said.*

Paragraphing Quotations

It is good practice to keep your own words and the words of the speakers you are quoting carefully separated. You can see how this is done in Figure 7.1. When the writer moved from his own words — paraphrase and summary — to direct quotation, the direct quotation was set off in a separate paragraph:

> She cornered the men in a lot several blocks away and pointed the revolver at the robber who had her necklace.
>
> "He really started begging when he saw my gun," Cross said.

FORT MYERS, Fla. (AP) — A 43-year-old woman who was robbed at gunpoint ran her assailants down, smacked one of them with her own gun and retrieved her stolen necklace before calling police, authorities said.

"Those guys messed with the wrong person," said Martha Kate Cross of LaBelle. "It was a terrible week, and I'd had it."

Cross was on her way to see her 2-year-old grandson in a hospital Sunday when three men approached her in a parking lot, police said. One pulled a revolver and demanded that she drop her purse. She refused.

"It really never occurred to me to give them my purse," Cross told officers later.

One of the men then ripped a heavy gold chain from her neck and the three ran away. Cross jumped in her car and sped after them, reaching for a Smith & Wesson .22-caliber revolver she keeps in the glove compartment.

She cornered the men in a lot several blocks away and pointed the revolver at the robber who had her necklace.

"He really started begging when he saw my gun," Cross said.

The robber threw the necklace at her but she got out of the car and "hit him pretty good" with the gun.

"I was really angry I didn't work him over harder . . . so he would have had to go to the hospital," she said later.

She said she hadn't hit him harder because she had cut her hand earlier and was afraid she might loosen the seven stitches. The robbers ran away and Cross went on to visit her grandson. The men have not been arrested.

Figure 7.1 *This AP story makes effective use of direct quotation to help carry the narrative along.*

When the writer shifted from direct quotation to indirect quotation, again, he started a new paragraph:

> "I was really angry I didn't work him over harder . . . so he would have had to go to the hospital," she said later.
> She said she hadn't hit him harder because she had cut her hand earlier and was afraid she might loosen the seven stitches.

Transitions

Many news stories include only one or two quotes. The quotes are used to add emphasis or to lend support to summary, which may be attributed but not quoted. It is a simple matter to work the quotes into the story if you begin with an indirect Type 1 quote and follow it with the direct quote — either Type 2 or Type 3. The indirect quote is a transitional device that bridges the gap between what went before and the direct quotation. For example:

> Robert G. White, owner of Bob's Pawn Shop, said stolen property is a small part of the pawn business.
> "Out of a thousand loans, we might get one item that's stolen," he said.

Here the first paragraph identifies the speaker and introduces his ideas or viewpoint. The second paragraph then gives the speaker's views specifically and precisely in his own words. Another example:

> Both parents say their son has made remarkable progress since he began attending the special school.
> "He's beginning to read and to write well," his mother said.

You can see in the model story in Figure 7.2 how the use of an indirect quote followed by a direct quote works. The third paragraph of the story tells the reader that the real estate people have figures on housing sales. The indirect quote makes it clear who is going to speak about the figures and gives a couple of specific figures. Then the direct quote tells the reader what the figures mean. There is continuity of thought here, and the direct quote is introduced smoothly into the story.

The reduction in interest rates is already being felt in the housing market in Carolton and Washington County.

After a slow fall and winter, sales are beginning to pick up, according to Henry A. Miller, director of the Carolton Multiple Listing Service.

He cited statistics compiled by the service that reflect daily transactions by 39 real estate firms.

Miller said that in the past two weeks, his office has seen from seven to 13 contracts a day compared with three to five earlier this year.

"Right now the housing market in this area is very good," he said.

Sales are about 20 percent behind last year, according to Miller.

Mortgage rates here peaked at about 10 percent earlier this year. The current rate is 9.5 percent.

Figure 7.2 *This model story shows how quotation can be worked into a brief inverted-pyramid story. The Type 1 indirect quotation in the fourth paragraph serves to identify the speaker and introduce what he is going to say. A Type 2 direct quote follows. The story then returns to other matters in summary form.*

This tactic for easing the speaker and the direct quotation into a story works equally well in longer stories, as you will see when you start writing stories about speeches or interviews, and is very helpful in making it clear who's talking when several speakers are quoted in one story.

When you are writing a story in which several speakers are quoted, always use a transitional paragraph of summary or indirect quotation to introduce a new speaker.

In Figure 7.1 the summary in the news writer's words provides the narrative and prepares the reader for the direct quotations. For example:

> She cornered the men in a lot several blocks away and pointed the revolver at the robber who had her necklace.
>
> "He really started begging when he saw my gun," Cross said.

There is no surprise here. The situation is clear, and the direct quote merely completes the sequence of events.

Don't just toss direct quotation into your story. Set the situation up. Prepare the reader. Let the reader know who's going to talk and give some indication of what the speaker will talk about. Keep the model story in Figure 7.1 in mind when you make direct quotation a part of your news story.

There are no moments when her voice cracks. Only ones when it becomes softer, more pensive. Moments like now.

Lisa Robinson gazes downward.

"God didn't do this to be mean," she says. "He made me this way for a reason."

She refers to her legs. They're withered, still. Her waist sags, ravaged by spina bifida, a spinal defect. She's confined to a wheel chair permanently.

"What possible reason can that be?" she's asked.

"To teach."

"Teach?"

"Yeh, you know, through example. God puts people on earth for a reason. His reason for putting me here was to teach. People see me playing basketball, doing laps around McTyre Park. Doing lots of things."

"They learn from that. Learn you can be — "

"Yes, normal."

"So you don't feel resentment toward God?"

"Why should I?"

"For having the disease."

"Oh, no way. God's done a lot for me. Several times, he's had doctors save my life."

The first occasion was when Lisa, who lives in Hollywood, was an infant. She underwent spinal surgery that could easily have failed. The second time was when she was five and needed an even more delicate operation. Doctors in Nashville gave her only a 50–50 chance of coming through it alive.

She survived, though the braces they'd also applied to her frail legs were of little value. Her bones were simply too brittle to sustain much activity. The bones kept breaking.

"She never had a chance to walk," says her mother, Faye. "The braces helped her stand up. But, really, she couldn't walk."

Figure 7.3 *This excerpt from a feature by Judy Lutz in the Broward County, Fla., Sun-Tattler shows effective use of direct quotation, which appears in this story in the form of dialogue.*

Suggestions for Further Reading

Political reporting is one of the most difficult of journalistic fields. Here are some extraordinary examples of reportorial skill.

Bernstein, Carl, and Bob Woodward. *All the President's Men.* New York: Simon and Schuster, 1974.

> The story of Watergate by the two *Washington Post* reporters who did the most to uncover and report the scandal.

Crouse, Timothy. *The Boys on the Bus.* New York: Random House, 1973.

> Crouse, a reporter for *Rolling Stone*, tells how the national press covers a presidential campaign.

Liebling, A.J. *The Earl of Louisiana.* New York: Simon and Schuster, 1961.
  An informal look at Gov. Earl Long and the politics of Louisiana.

McGinnis, Joe. *The Selling of the President 1968.* New York: Trident Press, 1968.
  An insider describes Richard Nixon's campaign for president in 1968.

Mailer, Norman. *Miami and the Siege of Chicago.* New York: World Publishing Co., 1968.
  A report on the Democratic and Republican presidential nominating conventions of 1968.

Thompson, Hunter S. *Fear and Loathing: On the Campaign Trail '72.* New York: Fawcett Popular Library, 1974.
  One reporter's view of presidential politics during the McGovern and Nixon campaigns of 1972.

AREA STATISTICS

BIRTHS

BOULDER COMMUNITY HOSPITAL

ST. ANTHONY HOSPITALS

LUTHERAN MEDICAL CENTER

PLATTE VALLEY MEDICAL CENTER

SWEDISH MEDICAL CENTER

HUMANA HOSPITAL MOUNTAIN VIEW

PRESBYTERIAN AURORA HOSPITAL

VIEWING THE COMET
Ryan Paterson, 7, views Halley's comet at Gates Planetarium. With him is Midge Kral.

The Denver Post / Susan Biddle

ST. LUKE'S HOSPITAL

HUMANA HOSPITAL, AURORA

SCHOOL LUNCH MENUS

Week of Feb. 17-21
ADAMS COUNTY SCHOOL DISTRICT #12

AURORA

BOULDER VALLEY

BRIGHTON ELEMENTARY

BRIGHTON SECONDARY

CHERRY CREEK

COMMERCE CITY

DENVER

DOUGLAS COUNTY

ENGLEWOOD ELEMENTARY

ENGLEWOOD SECONDARY

JEFFERSON COUNTY

LITTLETON ELEMENTARY

LITTLETON SECONDARY

MAPLETON

SHERIDAN

WESTMINSTER

VOLUNTEERS OF AMERICA

SQUARE DANCING

Today

Thursday

Friday

Saturday

Sunday

Monday

Tuesday

SKIING ON RUBY HILL
Brad Farnan and his dogs Willy and Sadie take advantage of the snow on Ruby Hill.

The Denver Post / Andy Cross

8 Developing the Story

I got something out of working on a newspaper. . . . I used to leave things half written, you know. But things couldn't go in the paper unless they were rounded out.

Robert Frost

The news stories we have discussed so far have been single-incident, inverted-pyramid stories with summary leads. Now we must take a look at some new ways of organizing stories. We are not leaving behind any of the skills or techniques discussed so far. Rather, we are adding a few new concepts and a few new techniques of news writing.

Coming Events

In addition to reporting on events that have happened, newspapers tell about a lot of things that haven't happened yet — coming events, things that *will* take place. These include routine announcements about scheduled events: programs, meetings, parties, weddings, funerals, elections, speeches and lectures, commencement exercises and athletic events. For example:

> State Rep. Martin L. Nesbitt of Asheville will be the speaker at the monthly meeting of the Valley Springs Lions Club at 7 p.m. Monday in the Valley Springs Community Building.
> — *Asheville* (N.C.) *Citizen*

News stories about coming events place greater emphasis on *where* and *when* than do stories about past events. Details that would be unimportant in a story about an event that has already taken place are essential in a story about a coming event. Before an event, it is necessary to tell readers specifically about the day and the hour and precisely where the event will take place. The story must also define the audience. Who will be invited? What will it cost? Where can one get tickets? Explanation of the program, of course, is cast in the future: what *will* happen rather than what has happened. Another example:

> The Heart of the Plains Kennel Club and South Plains Obedience Club will conduct an AKC-sanctioned match today in the Merchants Exhibit Building at the Panhandle–South Plains Fairgrounds.
>
> This is an all-breed show and any purebred dog registered with the American Kennel Club is eligible to enter.
>
> Registration is from 10 a.m. to noon. Judging begins at 12:30 p.m. Entry fees are $3 for the 1st entry and $1 for additional entries for the same dog.
>
> Judges are Jack Krahn of Lubbock and Karen Schultz and Gwen Worley, both of Amarillo. Trophies and ribbons will be awarded.
>
> The public is invited and admission is free.
>
> — *Lubbock* (Texas) *Avalanche-Journal*

These are typical examples of stories about scheduled speeches or programs. In a story about a scheduled speech, the speaker is named and identified, the title of the speech is given or its subject identified, the audience that will be addressed is identified and the place, date and time are given. In stories about programs, like the dog show, the sponsoring organization is named and identified. Another example:

> Union University President Robert Craid will be the commencement speaker for Southwestern Baptist Theological Seminary May 15.
>
> He will address the seminary's largest graduation class of 447 students in the ceremony at Travis Avenue Baptist Church in Fort Worth, Texas.
>
> — *Jackson* (Tenn.) *Sun*

Coming events stories about speeches are quickly and easily organized with the help of a handy formula that says "STOP digging here." This memory jogger tells you to write the story in this order —

speaker, topic, organization to be addressed or sponsor, place, day and hour. For example:

> Charles Mills, district supervisor for Parents Without Partners, will speak on leadership at a general meeting of the local chapter of the organization at the Statler Plaza Hotel Thursday at 7:30 p.m.

The STOP formula practically writes this story. All the writer had to do was put the facts in the right order and add a verb and a few prepositions.

S (speaker)	Charles Mills (and identification)
T (topic)	leadership
O (organization)	local chapter of Parents Without Partners
P (place)	Statler Plaza Hotel
d (day)	Thursday
h (hour)	7:30 p.m.

Use the STOP formula as a guide for organizing coming events stories. The simpler and briefer stories will fall into place without any difficulty. The story above is a good example. In it everything is in the order called for by the STOP formula, and it all fits into one sentence. In writing longer or more involved coming events stories, you may have to vary the formula a bit. Figure 8.1 shows examples of a number of ways the formula can be varied. Where you have too much information for a single sentence, you can save something for another sentence. For example, the name of the sponsor or identification of the audience may be held back and used in a second sentence. The following story follows the STOP formula, but the writer has used a delayed identification lead, and details about the speaker and the conference have been moved down into a second and third paragraph.

> Probate Judge Marilyn Jeffers will give the keynote address at a conference on children at Northwest College Monday at 10 a.m.
>
> Judge Jeffers is the author of "Unwanted Children" and an authority on children and families.
>
> The conference is sponsored by the Carolton Branch of the American Association of University Women.

State Sen. Ralph Faught will speak on "Legislative Response to Tax Reform" at the Downtown Rotary Club at the Chief Pontiac Hotel Monday noon.

Speaker, topic/title of speech, organization/audience, place, day and hour.

State Sen. Ralph Faught will discuss tax reform proposals at a meeting of the Downtown Rotary Club at the Chief Pontiac Hotel Monday noon.

Speaker, topic, organization/audience, place, day and hour.

State Sen. Ralph Faught will speak at a meeting of the Downtown Rotary Club at the Chief Pontiac Hotel Monday noon.

He will discuss the legislature's response to recent proposals for tax reform.

Faught represents the 24th State Senate District, which includes Carolton and Washington County. He is chairman of the senate finance committee.

Speaker, (topic omitted), organization/audience, place, day and hour. The topic is added in a second paragraph. Additional information about the speaker is added in a third paragraph.

The chairman of the state senate finance committee will speak at a meeting of the Downtown Rotary Club at the Chief Pontiac Hotel Monday noon.

State Sen. Ralph Faught will discuss the legislature's response to recent proposals for tax reform.

Faught represents the 24th State Senate District, which includes Carolton and Washington County.

Speaker, (topic omitted), organization/audience, place, day and hour. The lead is a blind lead, and the speaker's name is held back for the second paragraph. The topic is added in the second paragraph. Additional information about the speaker is added in a third paragraph.

Figure 8.1 *These model stories show how the STOP formula can be followed fairly closely yet produce four different versions of the same story.*

The lead here follows the STOP formula: speaker, topic/nature of address, organization/audience, place, day and hour. The second paragraph improves on the identification of the speaker. The third identifies the sponsor.

Not all stories about coming events concentrate on a speaker and the topic of a speech. The Kennel Club story cited earlier did not, but instead it emphasized the nature of the program. A similar example:

Northwest College will offer a workshop on professional burnout — the condition that arises when workers are worn out by the effort they put into their careers.

> Workshop participants will meet at the Center for Continuing Education Saturday from 9 a.m. to 4 p.m.

The order suggested by the STOP formula can be seen here, too: S, the name of the organization sponsoring the workshop, rather than a speaker; T, the nature of the meeting, a workshop, rather than a topic; P, place; d, day; and h, the schedule for the workshop.

After you have written a few coming events stories, you will easily develop workable variations of the STOP formula. Just keep in mind that starting with the name of a speaker or an organization makes it easy to follow with the facts necessary to the story.

Stories with Many Names

Names make news, according to newspaper tradition, and newspapers publish many stories that contain anywhere from two or three names to hundreds of names. These are not difficult to write, once you know how. For example:

> The presidents of the Student Government Associations of four Jackson colleges spoke to members of the Jackson Rotary Club Wednesday.
>
> The association presidents were Karen Trusty, Lambuth College; Ricky Larue, Lane College; Amanda Patton, Union University; and Lareda Dungan, West Tennessee Business College.
>
> — *Jackson* (Tenn.) *Sun*

The trick in handling lists of names is simple parallel construction and the use of commas and semicolons as punctuation:

> name, college; name, college; name, college; name, college; and so on.

Remember that names are people. Name the person, then identify. In the next example, the names are followed by street addresses. Commas separate the names from the addresses. Semicolons separate the sets of names and addresses:

> Members of the board of directors are Robert Anderson, 410 N. Sheridan St.; Glen Barnes, 247 W. Wisconsin Ave.; and Helen Wilkinson, 311 E. Ohio Ave.

139

In some lists there is no particular order to the names, but in others a logical order is suggested by the facts of the story. In a list of newly elected club officers, for example, names are given in an order suggested by the offices.

> New officers are Maria Sanchez, president; Joel King, vice president; Paul Miller, secretary; and Norbert Dubois, treasurer.

The following example shows how more material — here, names, ages and addresses — is handled:

> In satisfactory condition at Carolton General Hospital are:
> Helen Duncan, 65, of 801 N. Lee St.; John Cameron, 25, of 16 S. Jackson St.; Henry O. Grace, 35, of 426 E. Ohio Ave.; Ching Lee, 40, of 245 Virginia Ave.; and Wayne Stoddard, 70, of 840 N. Houston Ave.

This list differs from earlier examples because it is set off in a separate paragraph. This isn't necessary unless the list of names is rather long. Note the use of the colon here in contrast to the earlier examples.

The model story in Figure 8.2 shows the use of commas and semicolons in a list of names.

Localizing

According to the lore of journalism, things that happen nearby are more interesting to newspaper readers than things that happen in the next state, in another country or on the other side of the world. It is important, then, in writing news stories about local people or local events to organize the story in such a way that the *local angle*, the local connection or local nature of the story, is clear to the reader.

Stories that you or others on the newspaper staff report and write are not a problem. They are local by definition. Local names, local addresses, local background are all part of the story, and readers' interests in their neighbors and their own community are easily satisfied. However, many stories with local angles originate in other places. The wire services report them, sometimes very briefly, and that leaves it up to the local newspaper to write the stories, generally in more detail, and to point out the local angle to readers.

A good example of developing the local angle is shown in Figures 8.3 and 8.4. The brief story carried by the wire services (Figure 8.3)

Five Carolton students won letters in spring sports at Northwest College.

They are Eric Rose, varsity basketball; Wayne Bennett, junior varsity golf; Susan Ashburn, women's tennis; Diane Jones, women's track; and Kathryn Mills, women's golf.

Figure 8.2 *This model story shows how commas and semicolons are used to organize a list of names. Note that there is no colon after the introductory phrase* they are *in the second paragraph. Note also that a semicolon follows every group except the last. The* and *in the last group is optional.*

22 identified by Army 39 years after death

WASHINGTON, Jan. 19 (UPI) — The Army said today it had identified the remains of 22 soldiers killed in the World War II crash of a B-24 bomber in the jungles of New Guinea nearly 39 years ago.

The plane and the remains of its crew and passengers were discovered in April on the Pacific island.

The bomber was on a noncombat flight from the capital of Port Moresby to Nadzab when it crashed into dense jungle for "unknown reasons" on March 22, 1944, the Pentagon said.

The remains were identified by the Army's Central Identification Laboratory in Hawaii as being:

Second Lieut. Robert E. Allred of Des Moines; First Sgt. Harold Atkins of Gallatin Gateway, Mont.; Capt. Charles R. Barnard of Wadsworth, Ohio; Sgt. Clint P. Butler of Little Rock, Ark.; Staff Sgt. Thomas J. Carpenter Jr. of Georgiana, Ala.; First Sgt. Weldon W. Frazier of Palestine, Tex.; and Staff Sgt. Frank Ginter of Buffalo, N.Y.

Second Lieut. Stanley G. Gross of Chicago; Second Lieut. Keith T. Holm of Bellevue, Wash.; Technician 4th Grade Joseph E. Kaczorek of Milwaukee; Second Lieut. Harvey E. Landrum of Gladewater, Tex.; Sgt. Stanley C. Lawrence of Eau Claire, Wis.; Pfc. Carlin E. Loop of Salina, Kan.; Cpl. Joseph B. Mettam of Solana Beach, Calif.; and Sgt. Charles Samples Jr. of Smithers, W. Va.

Staff Sgt. William M. Shrake of Mooresville, Ind.; Staff Sgt. John J. Staseowski of Holyoke, Mass.; Second Lieut. Charles R. Steiner of Navarre, Ohio; Staff Sgt. Robert C. Thompson of Anniston, Ala.; Second Lieut. Melvin F. Walker of Racine, Wis.; Second Lieut. Emory C. Young of Good Hope, Ill.; and Second Lieut. Robert J. Geis Jr. of Chicago.

Families of all the soldiers except for Lieutenant Geis have been notified. The Army has asked anyone with information that could help locate Lieutenant Geis's family to notify the Adjutant General's Casualty Office with a collect call to (202) 325–7960.

Figure 8.3 *This brief story written from the national rather than the local point of view contrasts sharply with the local story shown in Figure 8.4.*

listed the names of 22 U.S. servicemen whose bodies had been recovered and identified 39 years after their plane crashed in New Guinea during World War II. Each of these men had a hometown, and in those home-towns, local newspapers reported the story from a local point of view. The *Atlanta Journal and Constitution* story (Figure 8.4) developed the local angle and gave a moving account of the homecoming and burial of a long-missing serviceman.

'Taps' after 39 years

by Mark C. Winne
Staff Writer

ROOPVILLE, Ga. — On the bluff where the weathered tomb-stones of the Roopville cemetery are set, overlooking miles of pasture and pine stretching to Alabama, the only sound was the awning over the casket creaking in the wind.

Then a volley of shots rang out from the black rifles of seven sol-diers standing stiffly in an honor guard. Then another volley, and another.

A bugler standing far off sounded "Taps" as another contin-gent of soldiers with white gloves and white dickeys slipped an Amer-ican flag from a silver casket and slowly folded it into a triangular packet.

A tall U.S. Army sergeant handed it to Mrs. Sue Fransko.

At last, her brother, Sgt. Robert Charles Thompson, was laid to rest.

They buried him Friday, 39 years after his World War II bomber crashed in the dense and steamy jungles of New Guinea.

Only last month did Mrs. Fransko, Thompson's closest living relative, learn that her brother's body had been recovered along with 21 others after New Guineans pointed a search party toward the wreckage of a B-24 in mountainous jungles.

"It's like it has ended," she said after the funeral. "It's a relief."

Gathered in the cemetery, where Thompson's mother's family plot is, were people who had not been brought together for decades.

Off to one side, a trim woman in a blue suit with a fur stole cried. Family members said the former Julia Bishop and the young airman were to be married after the war.

"She's still pretty," said Mrs. Fransko, who last heard from her brother when he sent money in 1944 to buy his sweetheart some flowers.

A dozen members of the Roop-ville High School class of 1938, alerted by class member Travis Lof-tin, were honorary pallbearers at the funeral. About 19 are still living, Loftin said.

Nearly all remembered Thomp-son as very quiet and bright.

"Friendly, help at the drop of the hat," said Ralph Laster of Athens, who himself survived the Bataan Death March early in the war.

Roopville High, long ago aban-doned as a school, was about 200 or 300 yards from the church where the service began, and close to the cemetery.

Martha Barge and Essie Thompson, sisters from Fairburn, last saw Thompson when he was a child of eight, at his grandmother's funeral in the same cemetery plot.

Cousin Eugene Perry, who was a young boy when Thompson went off, echoed Thompson's classmates about his personality.

"I never seen him mad," the Anniston man said, recalling his own experience in the Korean War. "It seems the cream of the crop is always the one that gets killed, looking back. Charles was one of the best men."

Many there had never known the lanky, blond airman.

Over near the Roop family plot, where Civil War Sgt. John K. Roop is buried, stood two dozen Roopville school children.

A car sat up close to the grave-site, so Thompson's two elderly aunts, Mrs. J. G. South and Mrs. Paul Perry, could see.

By them was Lawrence Talton, married to one of Thompson's cousins.

"They say he was killed on his first mission," Talton said. "I was in New Guinea, and I had a lot of those Japs in my sights. So if he didn't get any, I got 'em for 'em."

"This is the first time I've ever conducted a funeral for somebody who died before I was born," said the Rev. Larry Johnson, who was born a few months after the crash.

The small Roopville church, which Thompson himself attended as a teen-ager, was filled. Johnson read from the book of Matthew:

"There is nothing covered that shall not be revealed, and hid that shall not be known."

— *Atlanta Journal and Constitution*

Figure 8.4 *This well-written feature story was a local follow-up to the national news story shown in Figure 8.3.*

The greatest strength of the newspaper lies in the fact that it is local. A newspaper reports on the events of its own community and emphasizes things that are of interest and concern to its readers. Thorough local coverage is appreciated by readers and builds and holds circulation.

Nearly every story has a local angle. When the state board that governs higher education raises tuition for state colleges and universities, the story is carried statewide by the wire services under a state capital dateline. But in the cities with a state college or university, the story is a local story, too. The reporter who covers the education beat hurries to the local college to find out how, specifically, the increase in tuition will affect students at this particular institution.

When the board of regents of the state university system in Georgia announced that tuition would be raised, the *Macon News* localized the story by asking colleges near Macon what effect the higher tuition would have on their institutions. Leads on the stories read:

143

> The coming 15 percent tuition increase at Georgia's 33 public colleges and universities will have little effect on enrollment, officials of two Middle Georgia colleges predicted Wednesday.
>
> Enrollment at Fort Valley State College is expected to rise nearly 15 percent this fall despite a 15 percent statewide tuition increase approved by the Board of Regents Wednesday, school spokesmen say.

When a fire took the lives of 95 guests and employees of a luxury hotel in Puerto Rico, a reporter with the Lawrenceville, Ga., *Gwinnett Daily News* interviewed a local resident who had been a frequent visitor to the hotel. The Lawrenceville resident's observations about safety systems at the hotel added impact to the wire service stories originating in Puerto Rico.

When the state labor department distributes its figures on employment each month, newspapers across the state dig out the figures for their city or county and develop a story that puts the local figures into the larger, statewide picture.

This sort of localizing is a matter of recognizing an undeveloped or unexplored angle. The *Atlanta Journal and Constitution* story in Figure 8.4 is a good example of this. The national story wasn't just rewritten or revised, it was used as a starting point for an entirely new story.

Sometimes, however, *localizing* a story means nothing more than rewriting a wire story or a press release. Wire service copy frequently has to be revised to lift a buried local angle into the lead. This is not because the wire services turn out badly written copy but because they generalize their copy for national, regional or state use in order to serve as many readers as possible with the same story. Few wire service stories out of Washington or a state capital are tailored to individual newspapers. When an editor finds a local angle down in the third or fourth paragraph of a wire story, he turns it over to the rewrite desk for revision. Let's see how this works with this Associated Press story:

> Ann Arbor (AP) — Mary Lou Keppen, 16, of Dearborn, was elected governor of Wolverine Girls State Saturday by 462 teenagers attending the annual girls' exercise in government.
>
> Three other 16-year-old high school students won election to other mythical state government administrative posts. They were Betty Massingill of Livonia,

lieutenant governor; Thea Schwartz of Farmington, secretary of state; and Lynda Martin of Battle Creek, attorney general.

The convention named Kellen Largent, 16, of Lansing, as chief justice of Girls State Supreme Court, and Ruth Travis, 17, of Caro, and Carol Thyer, 17, of Marshall, as justices.

This story, from the state wire, was written from a neutral point of view. The list of elected officers starts with the most important, the governor, and works down. But to a newspaper in Lansing, Battle Creek or Marshall, the story is backwards. Each of those newspapers would want to reach down into the story, pull out the name of the Lansing, Battle Creek or Marshall girl, and put her in the lead. The *Marshall Evening Chronicle* would, no doubt, want the story to start like this:

Carol Thyer, 17, of Marshall, was elected to the Wolverine Girls State Supreme Court in elections held Saturday.

Miss Thyer, the daughter of Mr. and Mrs. . . .

Rewriting wire service copy to emphasize a local angle in a story is common practice. Quite often, localizing requires someone on the rewrite desk to make a couple of phone calls or check clips in the newspaper reference library to provide additional details. In the story about Wolverine Girls State, the local newspaper would want to add the names of the girl's parents and something about her activities at school and in the community.

Hometown news releases are a special kind of press release that floods in to newspaper offices from camps, schools, colleges and the armed forces. These are news stories with a blank space somewhere in the middle or near the end where the name of a local person can be inserted. In this way standardized news stories can be given a local angle with minimum effort on the part of the originating agency. In the newsroom, however, press releases of this type are a nuisance because they can't be edited easily and generally must be completely rewritten. Too, these press releases contain a limited amount of local news — often just one name — buried in a mass of background and detail about a college or an army unit. If such stories are to be used, the local angle must be developed. The kernel of local news must be sifted out, a phone call or two made to the family and the story rewritten.

Localizing is not a different way to write a news story. It is a matter of news judgment — knowing what to put in the lead. Once the local angle is recognized, the story is written like any other story: a summary lead followed by a development that covers the necessary details.

Tying the Story Together

Building on the Lead

Experienced news writers will tell you that quite often the story — that is, the facts of an event or situation — will tell the writer quite plainly how the story must be written. Stories about coming events have their own special emphasis and structure. Brief stories reporting a single event are best written in the inverted-pyramid format. We will see later how action stories require a narrative format and are written in chronological order.

Experienced news writers will also tell you that if you can put a good lead together, the story will write itself. It is not quite that easy, but it is true that many times the lead, once written, provides a sort of rough outline for the story that follows.

A question lead provides a good illustration. If you ask a question at the beginning, the body of the story has to be organized and developed in such a way that the question is answered. For example, this lead from *The Milwaukee Journal:*

What's worse, cigarets or beer?

The story, about proposals for new taxes then under consideration in the U.S. Senate, goes on to say:

The Senate considered that weighty question last week during debate on a bill to raise more than $99 billion in new taxes over the next three years.

Then, at some length, the story presents the two sides of the question as seen by a senator from a state that grows tobacco and by a senator from a state where beer is brewed.

A story from the *Dallas Morning News* about a neighborhood squabble provides a similar example:

The questions were tough Thursday for the Mesquite City Council: Does a goat smell worse than a dog? Is a baa worse than a bark?

The story that follows has to explain what the dispute is about — the background — and the viewpoints of the people who want to keep goats in the back yard and those who object.

A slightly different approach is taken in a lead from the Lawrenceville, Ga., *Gwinnett Daily News*. The writer in this instance presents a problem and a solution.

> The problem: compacting Gwinnett judicial and administrative offices scattered around Lawrenceville into a building they won't soon outgrow.
>
> The solution: for the county commissioners, it was to hire a team of architects, including a judicial/legal specialist, for a space study.

The story follows up this lead by explaining the county's need for office space, the proposed study and the questions the county commissioners hope to have answered. Other leads in a similar vein foreshadow the substance of the story. For example:

> Four persons were treated Saturday at Carolton General Hospital for minor injuries suffered in separate accidents.

The story that follows must identify the four who were injured, explain the nature of their injuries and their condition and tell how the accidents happened. If a lead begins "Eight people were injured" or "Five local residents were appointed" or "Twenty-two colleges and universities will raise tuition," then all eight or five or 22 must be accounted for in the body of the story.

In a blind lead, the descriptive identification must be followed by a name and further identification:

> A Carolton businessman has been elected president of the state Chamber of Commerce.
>
> George Schultz, general manager of the Mid-State Trucking Co., will serve . . .

And the body of the story will include additional details. The lead, as these examples suggest, must be an adequate summary of a news story, and, if it is, it will provide an outline for writing the rest of the story.

147

Linking Lead and Development

The blind lead suggests another unifying device, a link or bridge that ties together the lead and the body of the story. For example:

> A 9-year-old boy was killed Sunday when the bicycle he was riding swerved from behind a parked car into the path of a van.
>
> James Jackson, son of Mr. and Mrs. Wilson Jackson, 217 W. Buena Vista Road, was dead on arrival at Carolton General Hospital.
>
> Police said the boy was riding a bicycle near his home about 11 a.m. when he suddenly swerved into the street. The driver of the van, John Doe, 38, of 278 S. Jackson St., was traveling about 20 miles an hour when the accident occurred.

The story is tied together by the description-name structure that links the first and second paragraphs and by the phrase *9-year-old boy* in the first paragraph, the boy's name in the second paragraph and *the boy* in the third paragraph.

In the following example from the *Augusta* (Ga.) *Sunday Chronicle and Herald,* the lead moves swiftly to a bridging paragraph that connects it to a chronological account of the origin of a lawsuit:

> In the early 1960s, George Anderson and some neighbors agreed to let Thiele Kaolin Co. mine their lands, then sat back and waited for the money to roll in.
>
> And waited . . . and waited . . . and waited.
>
> The waiting ended in 1981 when Anderson and others called their lawyers.
>
> The result is a lawsuit pending before the Georgia Supreme Court . . .

The nature of the landowners' complaint is then explained, an explanation that gives readers the background they need before plunging into the history of the grievance:

> It involves whether or not the kaolin company voided leases with Anderson and six other families by not mining for more than 20 years, even though most of the contracts gave Thiele mining rights for 50 years with an option to renew for another 50.

The history of the contracts and the subsequent lawsuit is then presented in chronological order, beginning with:

At the time the contracts were negotiated . . .

The bridge from lead to development in this example is provided by the paragraph of background and explanation that follows the lead. A few well-chosen words also provide links between the lead and the body of the story. The words *wait* and *waiting* introduce a sense of anticipation, which is satisfied by the opening words of the bridging paragraph: *the result*.

There is also linkage in the words *lawsuit, leases, option* and *contracts*, which tie the bridging paragraph and the first paragraph of the development together.

Repetition

You probably have been cautioned at some time about avoiding unnecessary repetition in your writing. Sometimes, however, repetition may be necessary to make sure your reader can follow the story. Don't be afraid to repeat names or other important words from the lead as you write your story. Some repetition is inevitable and healthy. It keeps the reader on the right track as your story unfolds.

And too strenuous an effort to avoid repetition can lead to trouble, as you will see from the discussion of pointless variation at the end of this chapter.

Attribution

Attribution, if used carefully, can also unify a story. In the story in Figure 8.5, attribution to the sheriff is a unifying thread. There is probably a little more attribution here than the average story needs, but in this case the eyewitness account requires the attribution.

Transitions

Transitions are words, phrases, sentences or paragraphs that lift the reader over gaps in the story. The gap may be the shift from lead to development of the story or it may be a gap where the subject changes, where there is a shift from summary to chronology or where there is a

Woman held after shooting

A 60-year-old Carlton woman is being held in the St. Mary's Hospital psychiatric ward in Duluth following a shooting incident Wednesday, *according to Carlton County Sheriff Terence Twomey.*

He said Marguerite Liimatainen fired three shots from a .38-caliber revolver through the picture window of her home at a caretaker for the nearby Woodland Pines senior citizens' apartments.

Twomey said the caretaker had come to retrieve a broom Liimatainen had taken from the apartment building.

The shooting was reported about 9 a.m. Deputies cordoned off the area and were discussing how to approach the house when Liimatainen emerged and fired a shot at two deputies, *Twomey said.*

The deputies then heard the sound of the gun's hammer striking a spent shell, *the sheriff said.*

"They listened to six clicks and then rushed her," *Twomey said.*

The gun belonged to a Minnesota State Patrol officer who was renting a room in Liimatainen's home but who had left for the holiday, *Twomey said.*

Liimatainen had fired two other shots, *he said* — one into the ceiling of her home and one in the entrance of the apartment building about 3 a.m. Wednesday.

—*Duluth* (Minn.) *News-Tribune*

Figure 8.5 *Attribution can serve not only to identify sources but also to unify the story.*

shift in viewpoint or in time. These gaps have to be bridged or the reader will lose track of what is going on and, having lost the thread of the story, may lose interest and read something else. It is the writer's job to hold the reader's attention, and transitions are one device for doing this. They provide cohesiveness by tying together different elements and parts of the story.

Ordinarily, the shorter the story, the fewer transitions are needed. We have already seen how names, words and phrases can provide a linkage between parts of a story. Linking devices like these are unobtrusive but effective.

A shift in subject, place or time is easily signaled by transitional words like *but, however, nevertheless* and *still*. These words warn the reader to prepare for a shift in subject, viewpoint, direction or point in time.

The following transitional paragraph, taken from a story about a halfway house for ex-convicts, provides a transition between two elements of the story. Up to this point, the story has looked at the halfway house from the point of view of the ex-convicts and their sponsors. The word *meanwhile* introduces a transitional paragraph and tells the reader that the story is going to take a different direction:

> Meanwhile, many residents of Carolton are alarmed at the thought of a halfway house for ex-convicts in their neighborhood.

The reader in this paragraph is being told "now let's see it from the other side." In the following transitional paragraph, the words *at the same time* signal a shift in scene:

> At the same time, outside the high school, students were milling about waiting the start of afternoon classes.

Other transitions that can help the reader over gaps or breaks in a story:

> He also said that . . .
>
> Other suggestions for . . .
>
> In other action, City Council . . .
>
> But others argued that . . .
>
> However, health care officials report that . . .

Rhetorical questions can also serve as effective transitions:

> Have the students been able to keep their mind on their studies?
> Principal Richard Roe says no.
> "All they can think about is Sunday's game," he said.
>
> Will the voters approve the $9.2 million bond issue Tuesday?
> School officials, looking at the growing need for the new high school, hope they will.
> They say . . .

Unnecessary Distractions

We have examined a few useful devices for helping the reader follow the story. Let's look now at a couple of things that distract readers and slow them down — things to avoid.

Parenthetical Insertions

Parentheses are not much used in news writing, because they tend to interrupt the flow of ideas. They are used occasionally to insert explanations in news copy, but the device doesn't work very well. The following is an example of an awkward and unnecessary intrusion in a lengthy and involved sentence:

> The evidence is at the H. George Wilde Sports Center at Bordentown/Lenox School, the home away from home for 200-plus hockey players (and there's a waiting list) and a host of volunteer parent/coaches involved in the Tri-Town Hockey Program.

This is a bad sentence to begin with, but the parenthetical insertion makes it worse. In the following example, the parentheses are both awkward and unnecessary:

> Over 1,600 Carolton families pay more than 35 percent of their income for housing, which Doe said points to the need for decent housing at rents low- and moderate-income families can afford. (Twenty or 25 percent of income going to housing is usually cited as a realistic budget figure.)

The sentence in parentheses contains such routine information that it hardly needs to be set off by parentheses. The writer apparently failed to include this information earlier, so tacked it on as a parenthetical afterthought. The paragraph would have been much better put this way:

> Over 1,600 Carolton families spend more than 35 percent of their income on housing.
>
> Jane Doe, a Carolton financial planner, said that ideally housing costs should represent no more than 20 to 25 percent of income.

And this disparity, she said, shows that Carolton
needs low- and moderate-income housing.

An even more distracting intrusion comes in sentences like this one,
which contains an indirect quotation:

Door said he was comfortable working with the
committee on the issues (athletic reform).

Since the writer put this in the form of an indirect quotation, it
would have been a simple matter to rephrase the sentence and avoid
the distracting parentheses:

Door said he was comfortable working with the
committee on issues connected with athletic reform.

Still more distracting is the parenthetical insertion in a direct
quotation:

"He (Smith) seems to be an excellent candidate,"
Shultz said.

There are two simple remedies here. One is to replace the pronoun,
which the writer apparently thought was not clear, with the name it
referred to. If that sort of editing troubles you, then do the next best
thing. Make the sentence an indirect quote and, again, replace the pronoun with the name. If you have any doubts about making changes in
a direct quotation, ask your editor about it.

Smith seems to be an excellent candidate, Shultz
said.

Unnecessary Variation

Inexperienced writers are often overly conscious of repetition in their
copy, much more so than readers. The reader is learning something
from the story and is interested in what the story says. If the story is
well organized and well written, the reader will not be aware of the
writer's technique — except perhaps to be left with the general impression that the story was informative and interesting. Writers are conscious of technique and until experience teaches otherwise are bothered
by the repetition of words and phrases in their copy. The beginner, for

example, wants to vary the word *said* with *added, explained, concluded, went on to say* and other variations. Actually, *said* is a safe and useful word and so lacking in any special meaning that readers are generally unaware that it is being repeated throughout a news story.

Repetition and redundancy are a necessary part of written and spoken communication. When a writer goes too far out of the way to avoid repetition, the reader gets lost.

A good example of this pointless variation occurred in a news story about the launching of a spacecraft that was to make a voyage to Mars. The writer used 10 different terms to avoid repeating the simple and easily understood word *spacecraft: interplanetary spaceship, Mariner 4, gold and gleaming robot, the 574-pound craft, the streaking craft, the mechanical explorer, the craft, the mechanical marvel* and *the vehicle.* The writer couldn't even refrain from varying the name *Mars* with *the red planet.*

You find this pointless variation in sports stories that identify a player by name in the lead and then avoid the name in later references, referring to the player as, for example, *a 19-year-old sophomore, a potential all-American, the shifty sophomore runner, the team's most valuable player* and other variations.

The writer who can't resist calling Detroit *the motor city* will also refer to oil as *black gold*, to snow as *white stuff*, to legislators as *solons* and to a spade as an *agricultural implement*. Good writers avoid such pointless variation and the ambiguity it causes.

Suggestions for Further Reading

Newspaper readers have an enormous appetite for sports. Sports writing can be very bad, but it is often very good, as the work of writers like Red Smith attests.

Anderson, David, ed. *The Red Smith Reader*. New York: Random House, 1983.
  A collection of columns by one of the great sports writers of all time.

Breslin, Jimmy. *Can't Anybody Here Play This Game?* New York: Viking Press, 1963.
  Jimmy Breslin, the *New York Daily News* columnist, writes about baseball.

Cooke, Bob, ed. *Wake Up the Echoes*. New York: Hanover House, 1956.
  An anthology of sports stories by famous sports writers of the past, including Grantland Rice, Heywood Broun and John Kieran.

Kaegel, Dick, ed. *Best Sports Stories of 1983*. St. Louis: The Sporting News, 1983.

> Sports stories and photographs from newspapers and magazines. Successor to the Marsh and Ehre series.

Kahn, Roger. *The Boys of Summer*. New York: Harper & Row, 1972.

> A book about baseball and growing up by a once-young sports writer. Nostalgia at its best.

Marsh, I.T., and Edward Ehre. *The Best Sports Stories of 1944*. New York: E.P. Dutton, 1944.

> An annual collection of best sports stories. The last in the series was published in 1982.

Smith, Red. *To Absent Friends*. New York: New American Library, 1986.

> An anthology of Smith's columns about people he knew in the sports world.

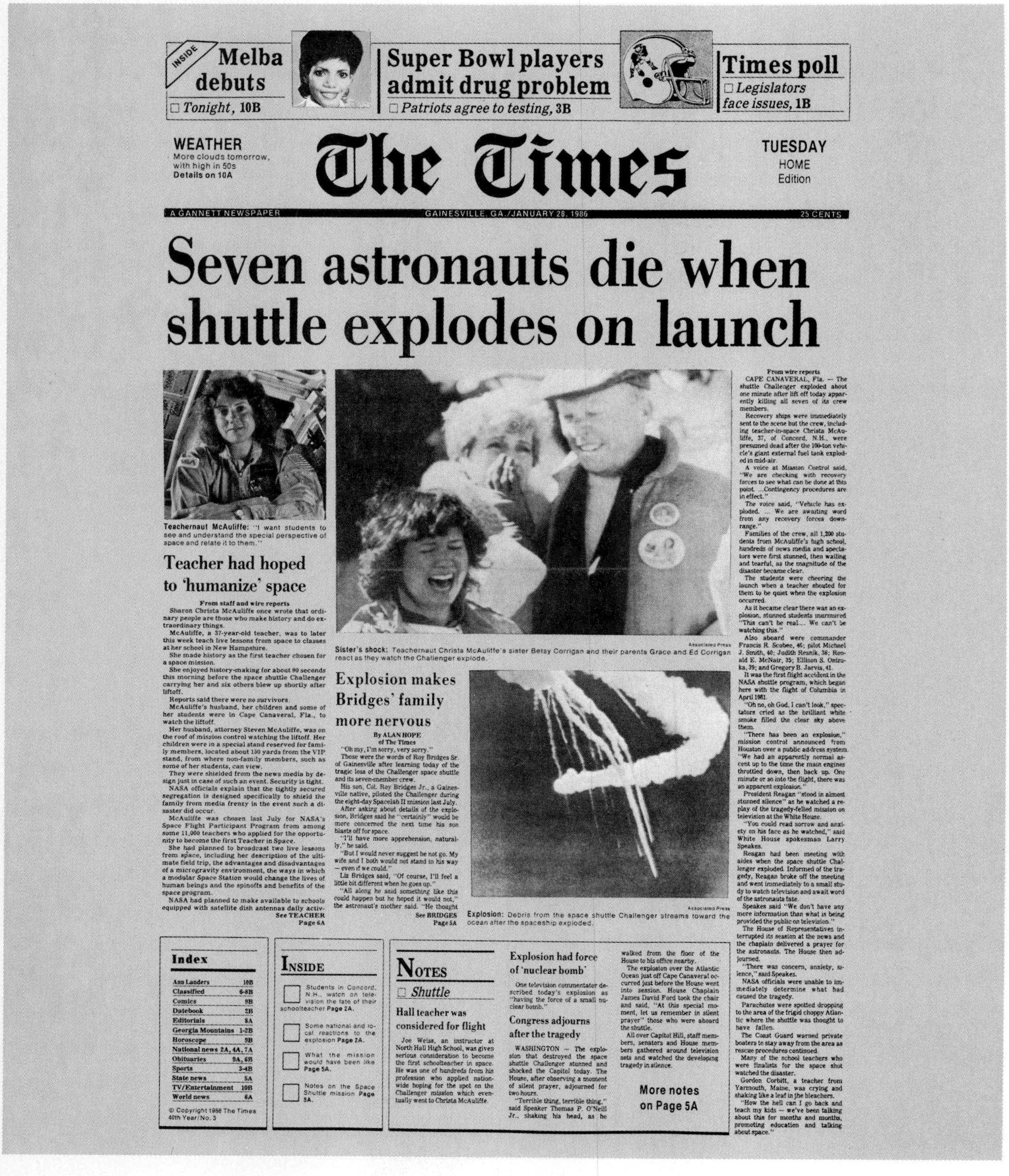

INSIDE **Melba debuts** ☐ *Tonight*, 10B

Super Bowl players admit drug problem ☐ *Patriots agree to testing*, 3B

Times poll ☐ *Legislators face issues*, 1B

WEATHER
More clouds tomorrow, with high in 50s
Details on 10A

The Times

TUESDAY
HOME
Edition

A GANNETT NEWSPAPER GAINESVILLE, GA./JANUARY 28, 1986 25 CENTS

Seven astronauts die when shuttle explodes on launch

Teachernaut McAuliffe: "I want students to see and understand the special perspective of space and relate it to them."

Teacher had hoped to 'humanize' space

From staff and wire reports

Sharon Christa McAuliffe once wrote that ordinary people are those who make history and do extraordinary things.

McAuliffe, a 37-year-old teacher, was to later this week teach live lessons from space to classes at her school in New Hampshire.

She made history as the first teacher chosen for a space mission.

She enjoyed history-making for about 90 seconds this morning before the space shuttle Challenger carrying her and six others blew up shortly after liftoff.

Reports said there were no survivors.

McAuliffe's husband, her children and some of her students were in Cape Canaveral, Fla., to watch the liftoff.

Her husband, attorney Steven McAuliffe, was on the roof of mission control watching the liftoff. Her children were in a special stand reserved for family members, located about 150 yards from the VIP stand, from where non-family members, such as some of her students, can view.

They were shielded from the news media by design just in case of such an event. Security is tight.

NASA officials explain that the tightly secured segregation is designed specifically to shield the family from media frenzy in the event such a disaster did occur.

McAuliffe was chosen last July for NASA's Space Flight Participant Program from among some 11,000 teachers who applied for the opportunity to become the first Teacher in Space.

She had planned to broadcast two live lessons from space, including her description of the ultimate field trip, the advantages and disadvantages of a microgravity environment, the ways in which a modular Space Station would change the lives of human beings and the spinoffs and benefits of the space program.

NASA had planned to make available to schools equipped with satellite dish antennas daily activ-

See TEACHER Page 6A

Associated Press

Sister's shock: Teachernaut Christa McAuliffe's sister Betsy Corrigan and their parents Grace and Ed Corrigan react as they watch the Challenger explode.

Explosion makes Bridges' family more nervous

By ALAN HOPE
of The Times

"Oh my, I'm sorry, very sorry."

Those were the words of Roy Bridges Sr. of Gainesville after learning today of the tragic loss of the Challenger space shuttle and its seven-member crew.

His son, Col. Roy Bridges Jr., a Gainesville native, piloted the Challenger during the eight-day Spacelab II mission last July.

After asking about details of the explosion, Bridges said he "certainly" would be more concerned the next time his son blasts off for space.

"I'll have more apprehension, naturally," he said.

"But I would never suggest he not go. My wife and I both would not stand in his way — even if we could."

Liz Bridges said, "Of course, I'll feel a little bit different when he goes up."

"All along he said something like this could happen but he hoped it would not," the astronaut's mother said. "He thought

See BRIDGES Page 5A

Associated Press

Explosion: Debris from the space shuttle Challenger streams toward the ocean after the spaceship exploded.

From wire reports

CAPE CANAVERAL, Fla. — The shuttle Challenger exploded about one minute after lift off today apparently killing all seven of its crew members.

Recovery ships were immediately sent to the scene but the crew, including teacher-in-space Christa McAuliffe, 37, of Concord, N.H., were presumed dead after the 100-ton vehicle's giant external fuel tank exploded in mid-air.

A voice at Mission Control said, "We are checking with recovery forces to see what can be done at this point. ...Contingency procedures are in effect."

The voice said, "Vehicle has exploded. ... We are awaiting word from any recovery forces downrange."

Families of the crew, all 1,200 students from McAuliffe's high school, hundreds of news media and spectators were first stunned, then wailing and tearful, as the magnitude of the disaster became clear.

The students were cheering the launch when a teacher shouted for them to be quiet when the explosion occurred.

As it became clear there was an explosion, stunned students murmured "This can't be real.... We can't be watching this."

Also aboard were commander Francis R. Scobee, 46; pilot Michael J. Smith, 40; Judith Resnik, 36; Ronald E. McNair, 35; Ellison S. Onizuka, 39; and Gregory B. Jarvis, 41.

It was the first flight accident in the NASA shuttle program, which began here with the flight of Columbia in April 1981.

"Oh no, oh God, I can't look," spectators cried as the brilliant white smoke filled the clear sky above them.

"There has been an explosion," mission control announced from Houston over a public address system. "We had an apparently normal ascent up to the time the main engines throttled down, then back up. One minute or so into the flight, there was an apparent explosion."

President Reagan "stood in almost stunned silence" as he watched a replay of the tragedy-felled mission on television at the White House.

"You could read sorrow and anxiety on his face as he watched," said White House spokesman Larry Speakes.

Reagan had been meeting with aides when the space shuttle Challenger exploded. Informed of the tragedy, Reagan broke off the meeting and went immediately to a small study to watch television and await word of the astronauts fate.

Speakes said "We don't have any more information than what is being provided the public on television."

The House of Representatives interrupted its session at the news and the chaplain delivered a prayer for the astronauts. The House then adjourned.

"There was concern, anxiety, silence," said Speakes.

NASA officials were unable to immediately determine what had caused the tragedy.

Parachutes were spotted dropping to the area of the frigid choppy Atlantic where the shuttle was thought to have fallen.

The Coast Guard warned private boaters to stay away from the area as rescue procedures continued.

Many of the school teachers who were finalists for the space shot watched the disaster.

Gordon Corbitt, a teacher from Yarmouth, Maine, was crying and shaking like a leaf in the bleachers.

"How the hell can I go back and teach my kids — we've been talking about this for months and months, promoting education and talking about space."

Index

40th Year/No. 3

INSIDE

☐ Students in Concord, N.H., watch on television the fate of their schoolteacher **Page 2A.**

☐ Some national and local reactions to the explosion **Page 2A.**

☐ What the mission would have been like **Page 5A.**

☐ Notes on the Space Shuttle mission **Page 5A.**

NOTES

☐ *Shuttle*

Hall teacher was considered for flight

Joe Weiss, an instructor at North Hall High School, was given serious consideration to become the first schoolteacher in space. He was one of hundreds from his profession who applied nationwide hoping for the spot on the Challenger mission which eventually went to Christa McAuliffe.

Explosion had force of 'nuclear bomb'

One television commentator described today's explosion as "having the force of a small nuclear bomb."

Congress adjourns after the tragedy

WASHINGTON — The explosion that destroyed the space shuttle Challenger stunned and shocked the Capitol today. The House, after observing a moment of silent prayer, adjourned for two hours.

"Terrible thing, terrible thing," said Speaker Thomas P. O'Neill Jr., shaking his head, as he walked from the floor of the House to his office nearby.

The explosion over the Atlantic Ocean just off Cape Canaveral occurred just before the House went into session. House Chaplain James David Ford took the chair and said, "At this special moment, let us remember in silent prayer" those who were aboard the shuttle.

All over Capitol Hill, staff members, senators and House members gathered around television sets and watched the developing tragedy in silence.

More notes on Page 5A

9 Some Hard-News Stories

Put it to them briefly so they will read it, clearly so they will appreciate it, picturesquely so they will remember it, and, above all, accurately so they will be guided by its light.

Joseph Pulitzer

Hard news, as Chapter 1 pointed out, is an important category of news, a broad and heterogeneous category. It includes many things of interest and importance: news of politics and government and stories about taxes, science and medicine, the economy and business. Hard news also includes stories about conflict and about death and destruction: house fires and auto accidents; train wrecks and plane wrecks; hurricanes and tornadoes; wars and battles; famine and flood; genocide; assault, murder and rape; robberies and holdups; criminal cases of all kinds; trials, convictions and executions; human tragedies and death.

This chapter will deal with hard news stories in a limited way and do so primarily to re-emphasize the importance of the summary lead, to introduce chronology as a means of telling an action story and to take up an important story form, the obituary.

You must know how to organize and write stories about auto accidents, fires and even robberies and holdups. Newspapers and the wire services often use these hard-news stories as assignments when they give writing tests to applicants for jobs or internships. A summer job on a newspaper or at a radio station may thrust you unexpectedly on the scene of an auto accident or a robbery.

Your college newspaper must report on crime, even occasionally on homicides.

Action Stories

Stories reporting action are often quite involved and require a combination of techniques to keep things straight for the reader. The basic techniques are summary and chronology. The story in Figure 9.1 shows how these techniques are used.

This story has a three-paragraph lead, a chronological account of the police investigation and shooting and a concluding segment that brings the story up to date. The story follows the outline suggested in Chapter 5 and the organization and structure shown in Figure 5.4.

The story in Figure 9.1 shifts smoothly from lead to development — that is, from summary to chronology — with the phrase *Ference gave this account*.

A Bradenton police officer investigating a burglary early Tuesday shot and wounded a man.

The man, identified as Roosevelt Davis, 19, was wounded in the upper right chest. No charges have been filed against Davis.

The shooting happened at the Southern Supply Co., 606 19th Ave. W., about 2:30 a.m. after a burglar alarm went off inside the plumbing supply business. Bradenton police Capt. R.G. Ference said Sgt. Daniel Thorpe and officers Donald Donaghy and Gerry Goglas were sent to investigate.

Ference gave this account:

The officers discovered a broken glass pane in a sliding door on the west side of the business, and saw a man run past the door inside. The officers went inside and called for the man to come out, but got no response.

Goglas, searching the front area of the business, heard a noise and turned to see a man preparing to jump through the broken glass door. Goglas shouted to the man to stop, but the man kept going, and Goglas fired a shot from his service revolver.

With the help of an arriving cruiser, the officers chased the fleeing man and finally stopped him in the 500 block of 17th Ave. W. The man, identified as Davis, said he was shot and the officers called for an ambulance.

Davis, of 1017 Sixth St. E., was in good condition at Manatee Memorial Hospital Tuesday evening.

Davis was not armed when he was arrested. Nothing was missing from the business, although the file cabinets had been rifled and some equipment had been removed.

A police review board will determine whether Goglas was justified in shooting Davis.

— *St. Petersburg Times*

Figure 9.1 *An action story with a summary lead, chronological development and a concluding segment.*

In this story, the fact that the wounded man was hospitalized and in good condition is left to the end of the chronology. In most instances, however, it is good practice to include this information in the summary lead before the chronology begins.

The story in Figure 9.1 is told concisely and specifically. All the names necessary to the story are included. Everyone in the story is carefully identified. Place and time are explicit. The story is carefully attributed to the police captain, but attribution is limited.

The story in Figure 9.2 is another good model of the organization of action stories. It has a complete summary lead and a good transition from the lead to the chronology, and attribution is adequate but limited.

The summary lead has two paragraphs. The first tells about the attempted holdup and the wounding of the liquor-store owner. The second answers the reader's immediate questions: How seriously is he hurt? What happened to him?

The story shifts smoothly from summary to chronology with the opening words of the third paragraph, *police said.* Note how the time is introduced as a starting point:

> Police said Morgan was accosted about 1:15 p.m. by
> a man armed with a pistol.

The concluding segment of the story consists of one paragraph in which a description of the holdup man is given. This information

---

The owner of a West Main Street liquor store was shot Tuesday afternoon during an attempted holdup outside his store.

William Morgan, owner of Morgan's Party Store, 504 W. Main St., was in satisfactory condition at Carolton General Hospital Tuesday night. He was being treated for a superficial bullet wound in the left shoulder.

Police said Morgan was accosted about 1:15 p.m. by a man armed with a pistol. The man demanded a bag containing $2,000 that Morgan had just picked up at the West Main Street branch of the Farmer's and Merchant's Bank.

When Morgan refused, police said, the man shot him and fled.

Morgan ran inside his store and called police. He was taken to the hospital by police ambulance.

Morgan told police his assailant was a white man with reddish blond hair. He was about 5 feet 6 inches tall and about 25 years of age. Morgan said he had a beard and was wearing dirty army khakis and tennis shoes.

Figure 9.2 *This model story consists of a summary lead, a chronological development and a concluding segment. Compare it with the diagram in Figure 5.4.*

follows and is outside the chronology of the attempted holdup, which ends with the wounded man being taken to a hospital by police ambulance.

Descriptions of people being sought by police are not always necessary to a story. Use descriptions when they will be helpful to police or when the public needs to know what the person looks like — for example, in the case of a rapist or mugger who preys on the elderly. When descriptions are so general that they could apply to anyone, omit them.

Attribution is limited to *police said*, which is used twice in the chronological account, and to *Morgan told police*, an oblique reference to the source. Note that there is no attribution in the lead. Facts in the lead came from a reliable source. As the story unfolds, it is clear that what happened is either a matter of record or known to reliable witnesses. The lead does not need any help from words like *according to police*. The body of the story — the chronological account and concluding segment — fully supports the lead.

Here is a similar action story from the Louisville, Ky., *Courier-Journal*. This story also consists of a summary lead, a chronological account and a concluding segment:

> Police arrested two men early yesterday after a clerk was shot in an attempted holdup at Eastwood Market at 16211 Shelbyville Road.
>
> Charlotte Huntington was shot in the left shoulder with a small-caliber pistol, police said. She was admitted to Suburban Hospital where she was in satisfactory condition last night.

The first paragraph of this lead is a concise statement of what happened, where and when. It needs no supporting attribution at this point because the facts reported are all matters of public record. The second paragraph adds necessary details: identification of the clerk and what happened to her, the nature of the wound, where she was hospitalized and her condition. Attribution is included concisely with two words, *police said*, that tell readers where the reporter got the facts. In stories like this one you will find attribution like *witnesses told police* or *police said so-and-so told them*, all clear indications that the facts of the story came from an official and reliable source.

The chronology that follows is concise and neatly begun and ended: the holdup attempt began at 8:45 a.m. and the men were arrested at about 10:30 a.m.

> Ms. Huntington told police that a man came into the store about 8:45 a.m., bought a small amount of

food and left. She said a second man entered a few minutes later and bought a soft drink.

When she opened the cash register, Ms. Huntington said, the man tried to grab money. She said that when she slammed the drawer on his hand, he shot her and fled without taking anything.

The two men were arrested about 10:30 a.m. by Jefferson County and Jefferson town police near Interstate 64 and Hurstbourne Lane, police said.

The attribution in this chronological account not only identifies the wounded clerk as the principal source of this part of the story but also serves to carry the chronological account forward. The facts about the arrest are attributed to police. The story has a concluding segment that identifies the two men arrested and tells what they were charged with:

Mark C. Anthony, 18, of the 800 block of East Muhammad Ali Boulevard, was charged with robbery, assault and wanton endangerment. Frankie Smith, 22, of the 800 block of East Chestnut Street, was charged with robbery, complicity to wanton endangerment and complicity to assault.

The Summary Lead

As it was explained in Chapter 4, the summary lead may be either a naming lead or a blind lead, but it must emphasize *what* happened. Time and place are subordinated to the explanation of what happened. For example:

Fire destroyed a vacant house on West Wisconsin Avenue early Saturday.

Two traffic deaths were reported by the State Highway Patrol Friday, both the result of cars sliding on slushy roads in LaGrange County.

Four people, including a teen-ager shot by police, were arrested early Sunday after they tried to steal an off-duty police officer's car.

A state highway department employee lost control of his pickup truck Wednesday afternoon in an effort to avoid a child on a bicycle and the truck flipped over.

As these leads suggest, many hard-news stories start with a blind lead. What happened is generally more important than who was involved. And it generally is easier to summarize the facts of the story without names and detailed identification. Remember, however, that if a name is well known, one that readers will recognize immediately, it belongs in the lead. The leads discussed so far are simple and straightforward. As you will see in a moment, hard-news leads can be more complicated.

Longer Leads

Leads on hard-news stories often run to two or even three paragraphs. It is not always possible to squeeze all the facts into one paragraph, especially if the story involves several people. For example:

> Martha Green, 41, of 216 W. Arizona Ave., was injured Monday when a pickup truck pulled into the path of her car on West Wisconsin Avenue.
> She was taken to Carolton General Hospital with cuts and bruises and a broken right collarbone. She was released after treatment.
> The driver of the pickup, Harold Lee Hill, 22, of South Airport Road, was not injured. He was charged with driving an uninsured motor vehicle.

When the lead tells of injuries, the reader's first question is "How badly was she hurt? Is she dead?" Answer these questions for the reader before beginning any explanation of how the story developed. Another example:

> A 5-year-old child, playing on Lexington Road, was hit by a car Thursday.
> Terry White, son of Mr. and Mrs. Clarence White, 110 E. Lexington Road, was taken by Mercy Ambulance to St. Luke's Hospital. He has a broken left leg and a concussion. He was in satisfactory condition.

As a rule, in writing the lead on a story involving injuries, give a concise account of what happened in the first paragraph, and in the second identify the injured and explain the nature of their injuries.

Itemizing Leads

When several people are injured or killed, the problem of identifying them and sorting out their part in the story can get involved. The itemizing lead, however, provides an easy way to organize the facts and explain what happened. An example:

> Two Carolton teachers were killed Sunday when their car ran off U.S. 210 east of Carolton and plunged down a 60-foot embankment.
> Killed were:
> Glen Lewis Robinson, 40, of 127 Oak.
> Larry Eaton, 38, of 225 E. Oregon Ave.

As you can see, the itemizing lead is merely an application of the blind lead. Names of the injured or dead are listed in separate paragraphs. This example is comparatively simple, but the itemizing lead can accommodate more complicated events. For example:

> A Carolton woman and her two children were injured Monday when her car went out of control and struck a utility pole.
> Taken to Carolton General Hospital were:
> Roberta H. Fish, 45, of 915 N. Sheridan, fair condition, multiple cuts about the head and a broken left leg.
> Katherine Fish, 15, satisfactory condition, cuts on face and neck.
> Roland Fish, 20, satisfactory condition, cuts and bruises on head, neck and abdomen.
> Another passenger, Rosemarie Cobb, 15, of 907 N. Sheridan, was treated at Carolton General for cuts and bruises and was released.

Note carefully the paragraphing and the punctuation in this lead. Another example of an itemizing lead can be seen in Figure 9.3.

Feature Leads

Taking a somewhat different approach, a story in the Macon, Ga., *Telegraph and News* starts with the first of a series of events rather than with a summary lead.

A spring vacation trip to the Bahamas ended in the deaths of four Wisconsin young people when their light plane crashed while attempting a landing at the Athens (Ga.) airport.

The victims, three of them University of Wisconsin–Milwaukee students, were identified Sunday as:

Roger Papiham, 28, son of Mr. and Mrs. Jerry A. Papiham of 13333 W. Prospect Dr., New Berlin. Papiham was a sophomore at UWM.

Richard W. Pearson, 22, son of Mr. and Mrs. George Pearson of 621 Elm Ave., South Milwaukee. Pearson was a junior.

Michael Scharenbroch, 20, of 3245 N. Oakland Ave. Scharenbroch, the son of Mr. and Mrs. Alphonse J. Scharenbroch of Kiel, was a sophomore at UWM.

Miss Rosemarie Andes, 26, of 1601 N. Farwell Ave. Miss Andes was the daughter of Mrs. Sophie Andes of 4626 W. Concordia Ave.
— *Milwaukee Sentinel*

Figure 9.3 *An itemizing lead on a story about a plane crash.*

> Bank vice president Martin L. Shealy Jr. was writing a letter at his desk Friday morning when he felt a hand on his left arm.
>
> He looked up into the barrel of a .38-caliber revolver held inches from his face.

Further into this chronological account of a bank holdup, the writer turns to summary:

> The Oglethorpe branch of the Bank of Macon County was robbed Friday by two gunmen who minutes earlier had robbed and beaten Police Chief Jessie Jones. One suspect was caught by two Macon County deputies after a gun battle outside this small town's other bank. The second man remained at large Friday night.

This approach is feature treatment rather than hard-news treatment. The writer has chosen to set the stage for the holdup with a description of the bank officer's confrontation with the bank robber rather than to write a five-W lead. You will find a detailed discussion of feature leads in Chapter 16. A feature lead is appropriate on occasion, but the summary lead is usually preferable for hard-news stories. Sometimes, however, there are aspects of a hard-news story that permit feature treatment. The following lead from *The Milwaukee Journal* is an example:

> The woman said she moved her family from the Inner City to a home around 35th and Lloyd Sts. two

years ago because she thought the neighborhood would be safer.

And it was at first, she said.

But now, the 33-year-old mother of four says there is no real escape from crime.

Monday evening, her 9-year-old daughter became the victim of one of the worst kinds of urban nightmares. The child was raped.

Other Hard-News Stories

Not all hard-news stories are action stories. Stories about automobile accidents, for example, are generally handled as inverted-pyramid stories. They require, of course, a summary lead, but the story is summarized rather than being told chronologically. For example:

Two Carolton teen-agers were injured Sunday night when the car in which they were driving went out of control on a curve near Brewster and hit a utility pole.

Ronald E. Howard, 17, the passenger, was in fair condition this morning at Brewster Memorial Hospital.

Zell Don Mitchell, 18, the driver, was treated and released Sunday at West Side Hospital in Brewster.

The accident occurred about 7:30 p.m. Sunday two and a half miles east of Brewster on County Highway D, the Hancock County Sheriff's Department said.

Stories about fires are hard-news stories, but unless the fire is spectacular, fire stories are generally summarized rather than being told in chronological detail. For example:

An early morning fire destroyed a barn on Airport Road Thursday.

Firemen were called about 4:30 a.m. to 849 Airport Road where a 1,700-square-foot barn was burning. The barn, owned by David E. Look, was used for storage.

Harold Jackson, a firefighter from Central Station, was injured when the roof of the barn collapsed at the height of the fire. He was treated for burns and cuts and bruises at Carolton General Hospital and released.

Look said the loss is covered by insurance.

Figures 9.4 and 9.5 provide additional examples of the organization of hard-news stories.

The model story shown in Figure 9.4 presents a problem in conflicting news values. People are more important than property. Death and injury are more important than property loss or damage. In the model story, although no one was killed or injured, the safety of the school children is properly emphasized in the lead. All the children went home and told their families about the fire in dramatic detail. Reader interest in the story will be high.

The model also shows how estimates of damage are attributed to a reliable source and the probable cause of the fire attributed to the proper source — fire officials.

Nearly 1,200 pupils were evacuated from the West Side Elementary School Friday morning when a fire in a first-floor closet damaged classrooms and filled the building with smoke.

Pupils were taken to the school annex until the building was cleared of smoke. Except for those whose classrooms were damaged, they returned to the school later in the day.

Barbara Franco, principal of the school, estimated damage to classrooms at $6,000 and loss of equipment and supplies at $4,000.

The fire began in a walk-in supply closet adjacent to a fourth-grade classroom.

Deputy Fire Chief Clayton Spaulding said the fire apparently started in a fluorescent light fixture.

Figure 9.4 *There are conflicting news values in this model fire story. Which is more important — the $10,000 damage to the building and contents or the danger to the lives of the 1,200 school children?*

An 82-year-old Carolton woman died Wednesday after she was struck by a car while crossing the street.

Yvonne Grace, 811 N. Grant St., died at Carolton General Hospital about an hour after the accident.

Police said Mrs. Grace was struck in the 300 block of West Main Street about 6:15 p.m. while she was crossing the street from south to north. She stepped in front of an eastbound car.

The driver of the car, Patrick Kelley, 31, of 905 Territorial Road, told police he did not see Mrs. Grace until she stepped in front of the car.

Kelley said he was traveling about 30 miles an hour. He tried unsuccessfully to avoid Mrs. Grace, he said. He was not hurt.

Kelley was not ticketed.

Figure 9.5 *This model story has a blind lead — a summary lead — and a development in the inverted-pyramid format.*

There is no need in fire stories to say that fire officials will investigate. They will, of course, as a matter of routine, and the cause of the fire will be officially determined at a later date. Similarly, in accident stories like the ones we have been discussing, there is no need to say anything about investigation. All accidents, like all fires, are investigated thoroughly. But if police do something — arrest the driver or issue a ticket — then say so.

You may recall that in Chapter 4, in the discussion of leads, you were told to avoid using the word *occur* in leads about accidents, that it is always more informative to tell what the accident did — damaged property or killed or injured people. This is good advice, and you can see in the examples of action stories and other hard-news stories in this chapter that the leads employ effective verbs and avoid soft verbs like *occurred*.

Attribution

Notice in the stories we have been discussing that attribution is limited. You might want to compare attribution in these stories with the guidelines for using attribution in Chapter 6. There is usually no need to automatically include attribution in the lead. Some leads not only do not need attribution but are less readable when an awkward *officials said* or *police said* is thrown in. When the lead is a fair, brief and accurate summary of the facts that follow, and when the facts of the story cannot reasonably be questioned, omit attribution.

In the body of the story attribution should be included only where it is necessary. And it is enough to say *police said,* or something equally concise, rather than to use locutions like *according to a police department spokesman.*

"Allegedly"

If an unnecessary *police said* is awkward and intrusive in a hard-news lead, *allegedly* is more so. The word is no defense against libel,* and it tends to weaken the lead. For example:

> A Washington County grand jury indicted a former Carolton Central High School bookkeeper Friday on two charges of theft for allegedly stealing funds from the school.

*See the discussion of libel in Chapter 22.

A conference in the managing editor's office at The Milwaukee Journal.
*(*Milwaukee Journal *photo)*

The use of *allegedly* here is redundant because the indictment is an allegation. Rephrase the lead in this way:

A Washington County grand jury indicted a former Carolton Central High School bookkeeper Friday on two charges of theft.
The indictment accused Sarah Williams, 27, of stealing more than $500 from the school.

Remember, an indictment is an accusation, an *allegation*, so *allegedly* is redundant. Another example:

A Carolton man allegedly supplied the gun that was used to kill his former wife, according to an indictment returned Monday.

This is awkward, and the word *allegedly* merely confuses. Readers might well ask: "Who says so? Did he really?" Omit the word *allegedly* or rephrase the lead:

A Carolton man was indicted Monday on charges
that he supplied the gun used to kill his former wife.

This lead is clear, brief and accurate without the word *allegedly*. It
attributes the facts to the proper source, an indictment, a public record.
The word *indictment* clearly says that the man is accused. There is no
need to equivocate with *allegedly*. State facts concisely. Attribute carefully and to the right sources, public officials and public records, and
there will be no need for *allegedly*.

Obituaries

Obituaries are an everyday fact of life in the newsroom, but they are
more than ordinary news stories. Deaths are reported in newspapers in
several ways. In cases of violent death — in automobile accidents, in
fires, by homicide or in various catastrophes — the death may be reported in a news story. Hard-news stories like these were discussed
earlier in this chapter. In ordinary circumstances, a paid death notice
may be run — advertising ordered and paid for by a funeral home or
the family of the deceased. Paid death notices are usually found in the
back of the newspaper just ahead of classified advertising or, in some
newspapers, on a page with obituaries. All newspapers publish news
stories — *obituaries* — that not only report a death but include biographical background on the deceased, list surviving relatives and give
details about plans for funeral services and burial.

Obituaries are routine in the sense that they are everyday assignments, but they are far from routine in importance. Local newspapers
make certain that all deaths in the newspaper's circulation area are
reported. Larger newspapers may not report all deaths in their circulation areas, but they do report the deaths of the more interesting, the
more important and the better known. Most obituaries are brief, but
the death of a prominent person is treated in more detail.

The detail lies in the biographical background. You can get a hint
of the possibilities of this kind of biography if you read *The New York
Times* regularly. *The Times*, which considers itself a newspaper of record,* includes detailed and extremely well-written biographical
sketches of interesting, prominent and important people in its

---

The New York Times publishes a great deal of information — for example, the text of an
important public document like a president's State of the Union address — for reference
later on, that is, as a historical record. The biographies of prominent people published
as part of an obituary will have historical value and are published as much as a matter
of record as for their immediate news value.

obituaries. This biographical material is gathered in advance of the news of a death by reporters skilled at interviewing and digging out information. The Associated Press prepares biographical sketches of prominent people and has them available to transmit to AP members at a moment's notice. Two collections of *Times* obituaries are listed in the suggestions for further reading at the end of this chapter — examples of good reporting about interesting subjects.

This discussion, however, will deal primarily with the routine obituary, a basic reporting and writing assignment. Let's look at the way the usual obituary is written.

Obituaries are built around four sets of facts:

1. Who died and under what circumstances.

2. A list of surviving relatives.

3. Plans for services and burial.

4. A biographical sketch of the deceased.

The facts in an obituary should be organized into these four categories, but the order in which the categories are presented may vary.

Leads

An obituary may have either a *first-day* or a *second-day* lead. Ordinarily, an obituary is the first story about a death and will have a first-day lead reporting the death. For example:

> Dr. Richard G. Menzel, 52, of Trenton, a veterinarian, died Tuesday in Oakwood Hospital, Dearborn.
> — *The Detroit News*

> David Keiner, 72, of Hamilton Township, died Friday at St. Francis Medical Center.
> — *The Trentonian*, Trenton, N.J.

Occasionally news of a death may be published either when the rest of the information needed for an obituary is not available or when there is no time to get it. For example:

> Reginald VanFleet, 62, of 615 W. Nevada Ave., died Monday at St. Luke's Hospital. Funeral arrangements are being made by Door Bros. Funeral Home.

In situations like this, the obituary published the next day will have a second-day lead:

> Services for Reginald VanFleet, 62, of 615 W. Nevada Ave., will be held Thursday at 3 p.m. at Liberty Baptist Church.
> The Rev. John Duttweiler will officiate, and burial will be in Evergreen Cemetery.
> Mr. VanFleet died Monday in St. Luke's Hospital. He had been ill for several months.

An example of an obituary with a first-day lead can be seen in Figure 9.6, and Figure 9.7 gives an example of an obituary with a second-day lead.

Cause of Death

Newspapers today usually include the cause of death in an obituary. At one time newspaper readers were squeamish about this, but we live now in a more realistic world, and deaths are routinely attributed to cancer, to heart attacks and even to AIDS. For example:

> . . . died Thursday after a stroke

> . . . after a heart attack

> . . . died Sunday of cancer

> . . . died Monday of an AIDS-related illness

Identification

Full and accurate identification is important in obituaries. Include full name, age and other identification in the lead. For example:

> Louis Masso, 77, of 140 Smart St., died Tuesday in Miriam Hospital. He was the husband of Angeline (Imondi) Masso.
> — *The Providence Journal-Bulletin*

> Delores Ann Mask, 44, of Old Peachtree Road, Doraville, died Friday.
> — *The Sunday News*, Lawrenceville, Ga.

171

Margaret Coe, 86, of 205 E. New York Ave., died Thursday at Carolton General Hospital. She had been in ill health for the past year.

Miss Coe was a practicing attorney for many years and was active in local Democratic Party politics.

She was born in Carolton, attended schools here and was a graduate of Northwest College and the Northwest School of Law.

She was admitted to the bar in 1914. She served as city attorney from 1939 until 1951. She retired from active practice in 1968. In 1970 she was elected to the City Council and served until 1976.

She was a member of the Washington County Democratic Women's Organization, the Washington County Bar Association and the Women's City Club. She was a communicant at All Saints Episcopal Church.

She leaves a brother, Henry, Duluth, Minn.; a sister, Mrs. Harriet King, Ottumwa, Iowa; and a nephew, Joseph Coe, Carolton.

Services will be held Saturday at 2 p.m. at All Saints Episcopal Church. The Rev. Edward Evers will officiate. Burial will be in Evergreen Cemetery.

Figure 9.6 *This model obituary is a first-day story with emphasis in the lead on the death.*

Services for Franklin Edison Lee, 73, of 355 S. Scott St., will be Monday at 11 a.m. at the First Baptist Church.

The Rev. Henry Mills will officiate, and burial will be in Mount Olivet Cemetery.

Mr. Lee died at his home Friday after a brief illness.

He was born in Baltimore, Md., and was a graduate of the University of Maryland. He came to Carolton in 1934 to teach mathematics and physical education in the public schools.

He became head football coach at Central High School in 1948. He retired in 1971.

He was a veteran of World War II and an active member of the Veterans of Foreign Wars and the Retired Officers Association.

He is survived by his wife, Eunice; two daughters, Mrs. Walter (Mary) Bryson, St. Louis, Mo., and Mrs. John (Stella) Briggs, Chicago; a son, Frank L., Chicago; and a brother, Robert, Memphis, Tenn.

Figure 9.7 *This model obituary is a second-day story with emphasis in the lead on services.*

Some newspapers prefer to use full names rather than middle initials in obituaries:

> Buford Douglas Smith, 61, of 17 Wallace St., died
> Saturday at a Rome hospital after a long illness.
> — *Rome* (Ga.) *News-Tribune*

Wherever possible, the lead to an obituary should do more than merely identify the person who died by name, age and address. Further identification can be simple: by job, trade or profession, public office held or books written.

Sometimes identification is geographical — that is, the lead identifies the person by pointing out where he lived or his connection with the community. Some people are best identified by some accomplishment or a connection with a past news event. For example:

> Gladys M. Everett, the first woman to serve as a
> municipal court judge in Portland and the first woman
> admitted to practice before the Oregon Supreme Court,
> died Wednesday in a Portland hospital. She was 87.
> — *The Oregonian*

> Frank Cancellare, the photographer who took the
> world-famous picture of Harry Truman holding up a
> newspaper incorrectly declaring Thomas Dewey the
> winner in the 1948 presidential election, died Monday.
> — *United Press International*

Services

Services may be held in a church, at a funeral home or simply at the graveside. In some circumstances only memorial services are held. Sometimes there is more than one service. Some examples:

> Services will be at 2 p.m. today at R.T. Patterson
> Funeral Chapel in Norcross, with the Rev. Frank Led-
> ford officiating. Burial will be in Peachtree Memorial
> Park.
> — *The Sunday News,* Lawrenceville, Ga.

> The funeral will be at 4 p.m. Wednesday at
> Hephzibah Baptist Church, with the Rev. Gerald Miller

and Dr. Mark Wallace officiating. Burial will be in Hephzibah Cemetery.

— *The Augusta* (Ga.) *Chronicle*

A mass will be offered at 9 a.m. Friday in St. Elizabeth's Church, Linden, after a funeral from the Leonard Lee Funeral Home, 301 E. Blancke St., Linden.

— *The Star-Ledger*, Newark, N.J.

A graveside service will be held Saturday at 11 a.m. at the family lot in Prince's Hill Cemetery, Barrington, R.I.

— *The Providence Journal-Bulletin*

A memorial service will be held at 7 p.m. tomorrow at West Acton Baptist Church, 592 Massachusetts Ave.

— *Worcester* (Mass.) *Telegram*

News writers assigned to writing obituaries will find a bewildering amount of technical terminology connected with services. Some examples:

A Mass of Christian Burial will be celebrated Saturday at 9 a.m. in Sacred Heart Church.

Calling hours at the funeral home are 2 to 4 and 7 to 9 p.m. today.

Shivah mourning period will be observed at the family home.

A rosary will be recited Monday at 7:30 p.m. at the O'Rourke Funeral Home.

Survivors

The names of surviving relatives are an important part of the obituary. The list requires care in verifying spelling of names, in getting relationships right and in identifying members of the family clearly. The list is organized according to relationship, beginning with the closest relatives and working outward. For example:

Surviving are his wife, the former Sallie Clancy; one son, William P., Bayonne; one daughter, Alison Marie, Bayonne; two brothers, John, Bayonne, and

Robert, Spring Lake; three sisters, Virginia Dundon, Olga Fedak and Irene La Pilusa, all of Bayonne.
— *Asbury Park* (N.J.) *Press*

Note that in this list of survivors where surnames are the same, they are not repeated. Another example:

Mrs. Morris is survived by a daughter, Mrs. Jean S. Pacifico, two grandchildren and two great-grandchildren.
— *The Star-Ledger*, Newark, N.J.

It is helpful in obituaries to make identification clearer by including a wife's maiden name and the given names of married daughters.

. . . his wife, Margaret (Bradley) Green

. . . a daughter, Mrs. Harold (Emily) Brown

. . . a daughter, Emily (Mrs. Harold Brown)

Note that in lists of survivors, punctuation follows the comma/semicolon arrangement used in other types of lists.

Biography

The biographical part of an obituary may be very brief, or it may be long. The biography of a former president may run to eight columns in *The New York Times*. Many obituaries are only a few paragraphs in length, but even in the obituaries of ordinary people who have led quiet and uneventful lives, there are facts that should be reported: place of birth and family background, education, jobs, membership in clubs or civic organizations, church affiliations and military record. For example:

Mr. Nesnay was a lifelong resident of Bayonne and was captain of the Bayonne Fire Department.

He was the secretary of the Exempt Firemen's Association, Bayonne, a trustee of the Superior Fire Officers Association and a member of the Firemen's Mutual Benefit Association.

Mr. Nesnay was a Navy veteran of World War II.
— *Asbury Park* (N.J.) *Press*

When you are assigned to write an obituary, take special care with the biographical matter. The essentials of age, address, place of birth and date of marriage are easy to get. But probe a little deeper. Ask about education, about hobbies, about jobs, military service, community service and politics. There is something interesting in everyone's life and background. And even one small bit of background will add interest to the obituary.

Anecdotes and Tributes

The biographical part of an obituary can be made warmer and more interesting by the addition of anecdotes, direct quotations and, if appropriate, comments or tributes, as shown in the obituary in Figure 9.8.

A meaningful life in the North End

by Sean Murphy
Special to The Globe

The records at Massachusetts General Hospital show that Jennie Forgione was admitted Thursday afternoon for treatment of heat stroke.

The records show that at the time Mrs. Forgione was admitted the temperature in Boston was 102 degrees and her body temperature was nearly 107 degrees.

The records also show that nearly 100 people were treated in various Boston hospitals for heat exposure or stroke during one of the worst July heat waves in Boston history.

Mrs. Forgione died Saturday, the only known death victim of the historic six-day heat wave.

But the records neglect to show who Jennie Forgione was. That story had to be told yesterday by family members and friends of Mrs. Forgione, who raised eight children and lived for nearly 70 years in Boston's North End.

Jennie Forgione, 85, of 276 Hanover st., was an old-fashioned woman and yesterday afternoon she was waked with much respect.

Not a single wrinkle etched her face; her dignified white hair was neatly combed back and she was clothed in a pretty summer dress. Just above her head were a painting of St. Anthony, her avowed patron saint, a cross and a delicate string of red roses.

A large crowd of well dressed people of all ages, including some 60 relatives, shuffled in and out of the Cincotti Funeral Home on North Cooper street in Boston's North End.

"We are all going to miss Mama," her oldest daughter, Mary Owens, of the North End, said yesterday with traces of tears in her eyes. "I always thought she would always be with us. She was like the Rock of Gibraltar. So solid and reliable. I always thought we'd have her."

Joseph Forgione, one of five sons, and proprietor of Forgione's Meat Market on Salem street, said it would be unfair to say his mother raised eight children.

"You have to consider all the grandchildren loved to go to her house and were particularly fond of my mother plus all the great grandchildren who did and felt the same thing," he said.

Mrs. Forgione owned and operated a typical neighborhood fruit and vegetable stand for more than 30 years on Salem street. She worked for the Rosebud Manufacturing Company until she was 72. She was a devout Catholic and marched in the fiesta parades each year.

"My mother was a beautiful sight marching in those parades. She's be dressed immaculately in white top and slacks with a dark blue sash and hat. And boy! did she smile," Mary Owens said yesterday.

Mrs. Forgione was born in Avellion, Italy, outside Naples, in 1891. She came to the North End as Jennie Giso when she was 17 and finished her high school education. She was soon employed by the Hood Rubber Co. of Watertown and shortly thereafter she married another Italian immigrant, Rocco Forgione.

The couple was happy in Boston's "Little Italy," with Rocco working for the City of Boston Transportation Department and Jennie making a home for their children, cooking and operating a fruit and vegetable stand.

Joe Forgione, her son, is better known in the North End as "Sledgey," because of his football career at St. Mary's High School.

"I'd come home from practice all beat up and hungry and she'd have a table full of roast beef and chicken, stuffed veal, baked potatoes, sausage, cheese, fruit and vegetables. Gee, I'm getting hungry," the broad-shouldered Forgione said.

During those pleasant years, Mrs. Forgione would rise at 4 a.m. and buy produce at the old market near Faneuil Hall. Then she'd set up her stand on Salem street and begin a hard day's work selling fruit and vegetables.

"She was the type to put three pounds in the bag and charge you for two," an old friend said yesterday. "Always pleasant and sincere about getting you the most fresh food."

Before World War II, Mrs. Forgione's husband died and all her sons enlisted in either the Marines, Navy, Army or Air Force. Mary Owens said her mother was often worried, but held it inside herself. "Those were good times."

Mrs. Forgione leaves five sons: Joseph of Marshfield, Anthony, Phillip and Jerry, all of Somerville, and Roland of the North End; three daughters, Mary Owens and Yolanda Forgione, both of the North End, and Mimi Ballite of Medway; 22 grandchildren and 10 great grandchildren.

A funeral Mass will be celebrated for Mrs. Forgione at 10:15 a.m. today in St. Leonard's Church, North End. Burial will be in Holy Cross Cemetery, Malden.
— *Boston Globe*

Figure 9.8 *This obituary includes the routine and necessary facts required of all obituaries, but it does more — it goes on to become a warm and touching story about a rare human being.*

In the obituary of Frank Cancellare, the former White House photographer for United Press International, comments from former colleagues were included. Helen Thomas, UPI's White House reporter, said of Cancellare:

> He was probably the most widely admired news photographer who ever covered the White House.

The obituary of a 100-year-old New York businessman was enlivened by this quotation:

> He said then that his recipe for longevity included an after-work shot of whisky — "No water, no ice. Straight whisky" — and "straight life."
> "No fooling around," he said. "You know what I mean."
>
> — *Associated Press*

Negative Information

Obituaries are news stories and they must report facts, and occasionally there are things in people's backgrounds that they and their families wish were forgotten. Do you include negative facts in an obituary? Yes, if the facts are important to an understanding of who and what the person was. The *Asbury Park* (N.J.) *Press* tells its staff:

> Our longstanding policy is to handle death carefully and with compassion. That doesn't mean previously published negative information need be omitted. However, it does mean negative data shouldn't be emphasized when the subject is better known for other activities or accomplishments.

You may remember that when Woody Hayes, the great Ohio State football coach, died obituaries recalled the 1978 Gator Bowl game during which Hayes, in full view of television cameras, struck a Clemson player who had intercepted an Ohio State pass. The incident, one of a number of examples of Hayes' temper, resulted in his forced retirement. This was one side of Woody Hayes. Obituaries did not play this up or overemphasize it, but Hayes' temper was well known and when he lost it, he did so in very public places. That aspect of Hayes' professional career clearly had to be included in his obituary.

Style

Obituaries don't always follow the rules of style that apply to other stories. For example, *Mr.* is used by some newspapers in obituaries, although it would not be used in other news stories. Women may be given courtesy titles on first reference in an obituary though this would not be proper style in other stories.

> Mr. Allen was well known in veterans' circles.

> . . . and a daughter, Mrs. Emmaline Smith . . .

Some newspapers include a complete date — day, month, year — in obituaries, whereas in other stories only the day would be used:

> Mrs. Spaulding died Monday (Feb. 1, 1988) at her home in Brighton.

Obituaries have a high readership. They are often clipped, pasted in scrapbooks, mailed to friends or relatives living at a distance. They are a matter of family record. The exact date inserted in the obituary makes it a more valuable record.

Feature Leads

Obituaries can be interesting stories in themselves, and as we have seen, they can be made more interesting by the use of anecdotes, direct quotation and comments and tributes. Another device is the feature lead, not common on obituaries but used regularly by the *Detroit Free Press*. An example:

> Mushroom expert Alexander H. Smith shared his expertise with University of Michigan students for 40 years. But he could not share mushrooms with them.
> Despite his discovery and identification of many species of fungi, Mr. Smith was allergic to them.
> Professor Smith, whose "Mushroom Hunter's Field Guide" and related works were used by amateur mushroom hunters and serious mycologists, died Friday in his Ann Arbor home.

The obituary of a World War I veteran published in the *St. Petersburg Times* started this way:

Charles J. Allen was the last man.

His was the final name on a list of 107 World War I veterans, members of Chapter 9 of Disabled American Veterans (DAV), who organized themselves in 1939 into a "Last Man's Club," vowing to meet annually for dinner until only one was left.

Their legacy included a bottle of bourbon, a gift to the club on its charter day from the late James E. "Doc" Webb, founder of Webb's City.

The last man got the bottle.

Mr. Allen, 93, died Saturday (Jan. 24, 1987) at Bay Pines VA Medical Center, where he worked for many years as a painter. He retired in 1953.

Obituaries are important stories. Obituary writers must be careful of details and make a fetish of accuracy. Most obituaries are based on information funeral homes get from the family. It is secondhand information when it is passed along to the news writer. Check facts carefully with the funeral home. You may want to verify some of the information by checking the files in the newspaper's reference library or making phone calls to the family or to friends or associates. Remember, you are writing stories about real people, some of them extremely interesting people, some very important people. A little extra effort, a little feeling for the human side of the story can result in readable and interesting obituaries. Obituaries are not a chore. They are an opportunity.

Suggestions for Further Reading

Experienced journalists look at violence and death.

Gilbert, Ben W., and staff of the *Washington Post*. *Ten Blocks from the White House*. New York: Praeger, 1968.
    Story of the 1968 riots in Washington, D.C., by reporters for the *Post*.

Hersey, John. *The Algiers Motel Incident*. New York: Knopf, 1968.
    A detailed account of one violent episode during the riot in Detroit in the summer of 1967.

Kates, Brian. *The Murder of a Shopping Bag Lady*. New York: Harcourt Brace Jovanovich, 1985.
    Life and death among those who live on the streets.

Morin, Relman. *Assassination: The Death of President John F. Kennedy*. New York: Signet, 1968.
    A retelling of the events of November 1963 by an Associated Press reporter.

Rosenthal, A.M. *Thirty-Eight Witnesses.* New York: McGraw-Hill Book Company, 1964.

> About the murder of Catherine Genovese and the witnesses who did not want to get involved.

Whitman, Alden. *Come to Judgment.* New York: Viking Press, 1980.

> A collection of obituaries from *The New York Times,* including those of such diverse notables as Albert Schweitzer, Norman Thomas and Mary Pickford.

Whitman, Alden. *The Obituary Book.* New York: Stein and Day, 1971.

> An earlier collection of Whitman's skillfully done obituaries from *The New York Times.*

Penn State Beats Miami 14-10 for National Crown
— Back Page

Hotel Blaze Deaths at 95

SAN JUAN, Puerto Rico (AP) — Investigators searching for evidence of arson concentrated yesterday on a blackened corner of the Dupont Plaza Hotel where the ballroom was located. Police said search teams had found 95 bodies.

A few miles away, doctors and forensic experts tried to identified the charred remains of victims, most of whom were so badly burned relatives could not recognize them. Forty-one people remained hospitalized.

Police Superintendent Carlos Lopez Feliciano told

(Related Stories, Photo on Page Six)

reporters outside the darkened hotel last night as searchers quit for the night that 95 bodies had been found. "They consider that 95 is a complete count, but tomorrow they are going to search again just in case. At this moment, 95 is the final total, I hope," he said.

Officials at times have given conflicting casualty estimates. Shortly before Lopez Feliciano spoke, Gov. Rafael Hernandez Colon said 93 had died. Earlier yesterday, officials reported the death toll at 60, then 53, and then 82.

Investigators focused their attention on a ground-
(Continued on Page 35)

Proudly Serving Historic Trenton and the Great Valley of the Delaware

The Trentonian

Trenton's Pulitzer
Prize-Winning Newspaper

Saturday

VOL. 41 NO. 138   TRENTON, N.J., SATURDAY, JANUARY 3, 1987   PHONE 989-7800 25 CENTS

N.J. SURPLUS GROWS $102M

Officials Warn Programs Will Consume Excess

By JUDY ROTHOLZ
State House Reporter

The state government entered this fiscal year with $102 million more in its coffers than originally thought, but administration officials are warning against visions of sugar plums dancing in legislators' heads.

State Treasurer Feather O'Connor yesterday said that tax collections higher than expected and savings in several areas combined in the last fiscal year, which ended June 30, to bring in an additional $102 million. That figure is added to the $233 million surplus the state is expecting from its current budget.

The mandated fiscal report submitted to the Legislature follows a recent meeting between the state's urban mayors, Gov. Thomas Kean and legislative leaders during which the mayors pressed their dire fiscal position and sought the state's help.

The Democratic-controlled Senate recently approved a $68 million program that would use the surplus to help bail out municipalities, but Kean has said there will be no additional aid for municipalities without an additional funding source or the elimination of other programs.

O'Connor yesterday said $24 million of the surplus has already been spent in supplemental programs approved by the Legislature and indicated another $58 million is expected to be spent on other programs,
(Continued on Page 35)

Marcos Loyalist 'Illegal Alien'

By CHUCK DAVIS
Staff Writer

Orlando Dulay, wanted by the Philippine government in connection with six murders and who last summer was found in a Lawrence Township home owned by the Marcos family, has been declared an illegal alien by the U.S. State Department and is facing deportation.

But authorities have lost track of his whereabouts in this country.

Donna Sherman, spokeswoman for the department's Bureau of
(Continued on Page 35)

Snowstorm in the City

Snow makes downtown Trenton a slushy place to be yesterday as it swirls and surrounds bundled-up people at the corner of Hanover and Broad streets. The snow later changed to sleet, icing up roads and sidewalks throughout the area.   *Trentonian Photo By BILL RYAN*

Icy Road Collision; 1 Dead

By PAUL MICKLE
Staff Writer

A Plainsboro woman was killed and three other people were hurt last night when two cars collided on a two-lane bridge into Princeton iced over by an afternoon of snow and sleet, authorities said.

Doris Templin, 35, of the Deer Creek Apartments, was identified as the fatality by Princeton Township police late last night, as the storm that caused the crash blew out to sea and left Mercer-

Bucks-Burlington roadways slick.

Police said Templin was a passenger in a BMW driven by E. Laverne Johnson, 40, of Thoreau Drive, Plainsboro, at 6:28 p.m., when

(See Related Photo on Page Two)

her car spun out on ice and was broadsided by an Audi driven by Thomas E. Nelson, 23, of Darien, Conn.

(Continued on Page 35)

10 Numbers in the News

There are three kinds of lies — lies, damned lies and statistics.

Mark Twain

Newspapers and magazines today are publishing an increasing amount of numerical data. Television and radio, too, are reporting more and more news in statistical terms. Public opinion polls report in terms of percentages what people think about issues, how they intend to vote and what they plan to do in the future — for example, their intention to buy a new car or a major appliance or to take a vacation. Census enumerations report how many people live in Cincinnati and how many U.S. households have bathtubs. The U.S. Bureau of Labor Statistics reports each month on the cost of living and on the number of people at work and out of work. Businesses report on their earnings and profits. Government at all levels announces tax rates and budgets. The economic experts periodically tell us how much inflation has eaten into the value of the dollar.

The press monitors a great many sources of statistical data on a regular basis. You will find stock market reports in almost every daily newspaper. Newspapers report also on commodity markets, on the price of gold, on interest rates paid on money market funds and on the rates being paid on U.S. Treasury notes. Most newspapers will keep you posted on mortgage rates, housing starts, postal receipts and bank clearings.

183

Newspapers, radio and television bombard readers and listeners with statistical data:* inflation rates, tax rates, profits earned by industry, percentages of voters who hold no opinion, won-lost records of professional football teams, allowable levels of pollution, the daily pollen count, salary levels of public employees, foreign exchange rates, unemployment rates, the chance of rain or snow on a given day and the batting averages of major-league players.

Much of the statistical data is published in the form of graphics — charts, diagrams and graphs. *USA Today* fills its pages with colorful graphics. Television presents graphics that move and change as you watch. Numbers are interesting or can be made interesting. They convey information. They have authority. They can also be confusing and misleading.

You have already encountered numbers in the style guide's extensive explanation of the use of numbers in news stories. The basic rule: write out numbers one through nine, and use Arabic figures for 10 and larger numbers. There is a long list of exceptions.

This approach to numbers is mechanical and arbitrary: You *don't* use an Arabic figure when a number is the first word in a sentence. You *do* use an Arabic figure for a percentage.

In this chapter, we will look at the meaningful use of numbers rather than at their mechanical use. Numbers can convey useful and interesting information to readers.

The Routine Use of Numbers

The news writer routinely uses numbers to make news stories specific. News stories give the addresses and often ages of people involved in news events. The scores of athletic contests are reported, as well as the identities of the winners and losers. Weekend accident round-ups tell us how many people were killed or injured on the highways.

News writers avoid words like *tall, fast, near, few* and *many.* They write that John Flanagan threw the hammer 167 feet 4 inches in 1900, that Ferdinand won the Kentucky Derby in 2:02.4, that it is 1,029 miles from Houston to Cincinnati and that paid attendance at last Saturday's football game was 77,402.

The use of numbers enables a news writer to be specific, to give details and convey information in a precise form and to be absolutely

---

Statistics, the dictionary will tell you, means facts or data of a numerical kind, assembled, classified and tabulated so as to present significant information about a subject. The term *statistics,* of course, also refers to the manipulation of data — for example, to test for correlation or significance.

clear in meaning. Words may mean different things to different people, but a number means the same thing to everyone.

Stories Based on Statistics

Statistics compiled by federal, state and local government agencies and by universities, foundations, advertising agencies, trade associations and many others provide an increasing flow of news stories. Some examples:

— The *Atlanta Constitution* used census data to analyze public employment in the metropolitan Atlanta area.

— *Newsday* used public records to compile salaries of school superintendents and other public officials on Long Island and ran a story that revealed among other facts that two Long Island school superintendents were the highest paid in the United States.

— The *Florida Times-Union* used public records to compile a list of salaries paid to public officials in Georgia — including the salaries of faculty at the Medical College of Georgia. The story that resulted was carried in Georgia newspapers and was read with great interest around the state. Taxpayers are much concerned about the way government is spending their money.

— The *Jackson* (Mich.) *Citizen Patriot* compared tax rates in Jackson and neighboring communities and ran a front-page story explaining how the tax burden varied in Jackson County.

— Two *Philadelphia Inquirer* reporters used statistics compiled by Philadelphia courts to identify patterns of police brutality.

— *The New York Times* used preliminary figures from the 1980 census to prepare a series of stories on changes in demographic patterns in the United States.

— The *St. Louis Post-Dispatch* used data provided by the American Statistical Association chapter in St. Louis to put together a story and a chart that analyzed population growth in metropolitan St. Louis.

— The *Detroit News* used data provided on computer tape by the Michigan Department of Corrections to sift

Primary election night in the Associated Press election system headquarters in Chicago. (AP/Wide World Photo)

through the records of nearly 26,000 prisoners to identify 1,830 convicts who were at large after escaping from
state prisons. The analysis, done on a computer, resulted
in a five-part series on Michigan prisons.

The 1980 census has provided data for many interesting and significant stories about the nature of our country and especially about
the changes that have taken place over the past few years. The *Wall
Street Journal*, for instance, put together an interesting story on poverty
levels that reported a shift in poverty from South to North.

Statistics collected by industry provide a basis for many news
stories on business pages. The Associated Press reports regularly on
sales figures for the auto industry. To write her stories, Janet Braun-
stein, an AP auto writer, uses figures from some 30 companies, and she
must make more than 1,400 mathematical calculations to make sense
of the industry's raw figures.

Cost-of-Living Stories

The Bureau of Labor Statistics of the U.S. Department of Labor issues monthly reports on the Consumer Price Index that stimulate newspapers and wire services to produce a variety of news stories on the cost of living.

The Consumer Price Index is a statistical measure of changes, over time, in the price of goods and services that people buy on a regular basis — food, housing, energy, clothing, transportation, health care and recreation. Data compiled each month are compared with the cost of the various items in 1967. The cost of dairy products this month, for example, might be stated as 200, that is, 200 percent. That compares with 100 percent in 1967. In this way, the Consumer Price Index tells us that a quart of milk that cost 30 cents in 1967 now costs 60 cents.

Many newspapers use the monthly Consumer Price Index story as a starting point for their own stories about the cost of living. The *Atlanta Journal* and *Constitution* each month publish a market-basket story reporting on the cost of various food items at Atlanta food stores. The *Florida Times-Union* runs a monthly entertainment-cost index based on data compiled by the economics department of the University of North Florida. In a resort area, the cost of entertainment and recreation is an important economic matter.

Many newspapers conduct similar market-basket and cost-of-living studies. The sudden and spectacular increase in the price of gasoline in early 1979 prompted many newspapers to survey the cost of a gallon of gasoline at service stations in their cities. A survey on gasoline prices conducted by the *Rocky Mountain News* in Denver is shown in Figure 10.1. Newspapers keep track of mortgage rates, housing starts

Gas prices off slightly past 2 weeks

LOS ANGELES (AP) — Retail gasoline prices dipped about a third of a cent over the past two weeks despite rising wholesale costs, according to a survey of 15,000 gas stations nationwide.

The average price for all grades, including taxes, was 84.35 cents a gallon, compared with 84.63 cents a gallon during the previous period.

(Along the Front Range in Col-orado, prices dropped more than 1 cent a gallon. The price of regular, self-service fell 1.2 cents to 73.7 cents a gallon, while the price of unleaded self-service dropped 1.4 cents to 81.8 cents a gallon, according to a survey of 10 stations by the Rocky Mountain News.)

"Retailers had a loss of a penny and a quarter on average as the wholesale increases came through" but did not pass the increases on to consumers, said Trilby Lundberg, publisher of the Lundberg Survey.

At self-service pumps, the average price of regular leaded was 71.43 cents, regular unleaded was 76.27 cents and premium unleaded was 90.88 cents.

At full-service pumps, the average price of regular leaded was $1.016, regular unleaded was $1.073 and premium unleaded was $1.166.

Even if prices rise a penny in December, they will still be far below last year's average price of $1.21 a gallon, Lundberg noted.

Gasoline price survey Service Station	Regular Self-Service per Gallon*	Unleaded Self-Service per Gallon*
1. Downtown Standard 1504 Colorado Blvd. / Denver	69.9¢	79.9¢
2. Fred & Butche's Standard 375 Logan St. / Denver	75.9¢	82.9¢
3. Chatfield Amoco 8321 S. Sangre de Cristo St./Jefferson County	75.9¢	83.9¢
4. Meadowlark Exxon 595 Garrison St. / Lakewood	75.9¢	81.9¢
5. Pester 13694 E. Iliff Ave. / Aurora	71.9¢	81.9¢
6. Road Runner 201 6501 E. Evans Ave. / S.E. Denver	69.9¢	74.9¢
7. Security Conoco 301 Main St. / Colorado Springs	76.9¢	85.9¢
8. 7-Eleven 9201 Federal Blvd. / Westminster	71.9¢	77.9¢
9. Boulevard Amoco 1600 S. Colorado Blvd. / Denver	69.9¢	79.9¢
10. Texaco 5021 S. Jellison Way / Englewood	78.9¢	88.9¢
Average this week	**73.7¢**	**81.8¢**
Average last week	**74.9¢**	**83.2¢**

*Cash price

Figure 10.1 *The* Rocky Mountain News *developed a local angle and a sidebar to bolster this AP story on gasoline prices.*

and applications for unemployment compensation, all indicators of the health of local economies.

Employment Figures

State governments as well as the Bureau of Labor Statistics monitor employment figures. The monthly figures on the number of people employed, out of work and in the labor force make news at all levels. Unemployment figures have both political and economic impact, and federal, state and local figures on how many are at work and how many are without jobs are important stories.

Stories About Taxation

Property taxes represent a major item in the cost of living for anyone who owns a home, and there is increasing irritation and frustration on the part of voters about rising property taxes. In several states, voters have approved a limit on property taxes. Newspapers have made an effort to help readers understand their local taxes by compiling data on tax rates. Individual property owners get tax bills from their local tax collector, but these provide limited information for the taxpayer, since they concern only a single piece of property and the tax rate in a single tax district. Newspapers can collect tax data from larger areas and across a number of tax districts and thus broaden the data base available to individuals.

Such an effort at increasing public understanding of local taxation was undertaken by the *Jackson* (Mich.) *Citizen Patriot* when it compiled a detailed table showing comparative tax rates in Jackson and adjoining counties. A story accompanying the table analyzed and explained how and why tax rates differ even within one county. To make it easy for readers, the study had a base figure: the tax payable on $50,000 worth of real property. Many newspapers print tax lists. These lists include every taxpayer by name and show what his tax bill is. Tax records are public documents, but few property owners take time to visit the courthouse to consult them. The newspaper provides a service for its readers when it makes tax lists available for comparison — and readers will do a lot of comparing between their taxes and those of neighbors and owners of comparable properties.

Graphics — sketches, diagrams, charts or tables — can make stories based on statistics a lot more understandable. A good example of this is the *Chicago Sun-Times* chart shown in Figure 10.2, which showed Cook County, Ill., homeowners how to figure their own property tax

How to figure your property tax bill

Market value is how much the Cook County Assessor says your home is worth. The assessment is updated every four years, with one quadrant of the county updated yearly in rotation.

Assessment level is the fraction of market value that is taxed. Residential property is assessed at 16 percent of market value, commercial property at 40 percent.

Assessed valuation is market value times the assessment-level percentage.

The **multiplier** or equalizer is a number set by the state, designed to make assessments uniform statewide at one-third of market value. This year your assessed valuation will be multiplied by 1.9288.

Equalized assessed valuation is the assessed valuation times the multiplier.

Exemptions, if granted, can lower homeowners' equalized assessed valuation by up to $3,000. Senior citizens may be eligible for another $1,500 exemption. This reduced figure is called the **adjusted equalized valuation.**

The **tax rate** determines the amount of tax you pay for each $100 of adjusted equalized valuation. It is the total billed by the city, county, school board, park district and other taxing authorities. Last year's rate was $9.538 per $100. This year's is $10.053 per $100.

	Examples	Your Figures
Market value	$75,000.00	$ _____
Assessment level	× .16	× _____ .16
Assessed valuation	$12,000.00	$ _____
Multiplier	× 1.9288	× _____ 1.9288
Equalized assessed valuation	$23,145.60	$ _____
Exemption	− $3,000	− $ _____
Adjusted equalized valuation	$20,145.60	$ _____
Divide by 100	$201.46	$ _____
Tax rate (per $100)	× 10.053	× _____ 10.053
Your bill	$2,025.28	$ _____

— *Chicago Sun-Times*

Figure 10.2 *The* Chicago Sun-Times *used a simple chart to show property owners how to estimate their tax bills.*

bills. The chart ran as a sidebar to a story about higher assessments and, inevitably, higher tax bills.

Business News

Newspapers are placing an increasing emphasis on business news. Publishers have taken a cue from the *Wall Street Journal* and now recognize that business news is interesting and important to the average reader as well as to the banker and tycoon. The broad rise of the stock market over the past several years has led thousands to invest in equities — ownership interests in business and industry — through purchase of stocks or investment in mutual funds. Many readers now follow the stock market, avidly read stories on quarterly and annual sales figures of the companies they have invested in and worry about the U.S. trade balance and the success or lack of success of attempts to lure new industries to their communities. The ups and downs of the Dow Jones average, a statistical measure of the direction of the stock market, are reported nightly on both network and local news programs.

The story shown in Figure 10.3, written by a *Seattle Times* business writer, was based on a survey. It is a solid story bound to be of interest to both the business community and the average reader.

Reporters who once needed help to balance their checkbooks have learned how to read financial reports, to understand the gyrations of the stock market, to report knowledgeably about refinancings, leveraged buy-outs and the relationship between the price of bonds and the level of interest rates.

The AP Stylebook now includes a special section on business terminology, a useful guide to the precise use of technical words.

Precision Journalism

Precision journalism is a term coined several years ago by Philip Meyer to describe the process of gathering information through research techniques developed by social scientists. The social scientists, including economists, sociologists and psychologists, have developed quantitative and objective techniques for gathering and analyzing data. They have refined sampling and surveys into an art. Their sampling is done scientifically, and data gathered by survey are analyzed and tested by sophisticated statistical methods. The computer, of course, makes possible the speedy analysis of vast quantities of raw data that would otherwise be nearly impossible to handle.

Social-science research is sometimes referred to as behavioral research because much of it is designed to find out how people behave: what they think, how they vote, their buying habits and preferences and much more.

Much of this research is scholarly in nature and is carried on in colleges and universities and in research centers like the Brookings Institution and the Survey Research Center at the University of Michigan. There is a good deal of commercial research, too, done by firms like Gallup and Harris — best known for their public opinion polls — and

State is split on problems for business

by Svein Gilje
Times business reporter

A lack of qualified workers will hurt the economic development of Eastern Washington in the next 10 years, owners and managers of small businesses east of the Cascades fear.

In Western Washington, however, small business operators said increased competition would be their biggest problem in the years ahead.

"There's an imbalance in the future development of Eastern Washington," said Robert C. Biggs, a partner in Arthur Andersen & Co., which conducted the survey among 2,100 small businesses in the Pacific Northwest. "It was the biggest surprise."

About 14 percent of the businesses in Washington and Alaska responded to the survey, the accounting firm said. Nationally, 50,000 small businesses were surveyed.

Biggs said 37 percent of Eastern Washington executives answering the survey said the lack of qualified employees will be that area's greatest problem in the next decade, while 14 percent in Western Washington felt it was important.

Western Washington business rated the manpower question second most important behind competition.

Small businesses on both sides of the mountains play down the priority rating given by Gov. Booth Gardner to the improvement of education.

The executives said the governor's top priority should be to "stimulate business" and make government more efficient. Tax reform, education and balanced budgets followed in order.

Alaska executives had no worries about finding workers but were concerned about a changing environment, profitability, and increased competition, in that order.

In Washington, 65 percent said they oppose a state personal income tax and elimination of the sales tax. But 48 percent of the executives said they would favor a state income tax on businesses, replacing the existing business and occupation tax.

"Small businesses are most likely to operate at a loss and that's when the B&O tax hits them," said Alan L. Morse of Arthur Andersen.

Local businesses differed little from those nationwide on several questions describing the economy. Locally and nationally, 53 percent said they expected the prime interest rate to be in the 7-to-8.5-percent range next June. This week's rate was 7.5 percent.

In describing the local economy, 44 percent nationally and 46 percent in Washington and Alaska said it was stagnant, while 38 and 33 percent, respectively, said it is expanding.

In Washington and Alaska, 75 percent of the executives said state and local incentives are necessary to attract new business.

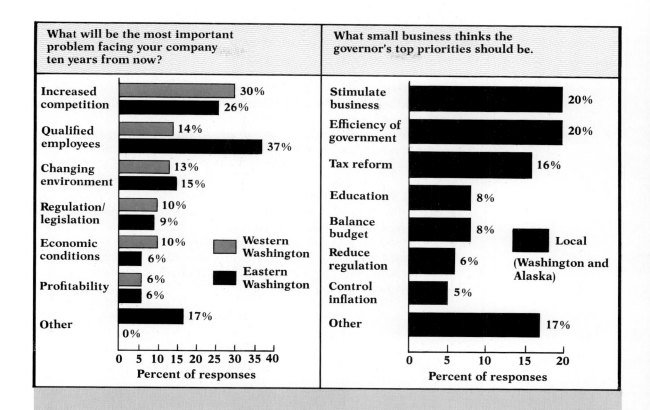

What will be the most important problem facing your company ten years from now?

	Western Washington	Eastern Washington
Increased competition	30%	26%
Qualified employees	14%	37%
Changing environment	13%	15%
Regulation/legislation	10%	9%
Economic conditions	10%	6%
Profitability	6%	6%
Other	17%	0%

Percent of responses

What small business thinks the governor's top priorities should be.

Local (Washington and Alaska)

Stimulate business	20%
Efficiency of government	20%
Tax reform	16%
Education	8%
Balance budget	8%
Reduce regulation	6%
Control inflation	5%
Other	17%

Percent of responses

Other findings:
— Sales and profits will increase moderately with distributors and retailers being the most optimistic.
— Hiring and compensation trends in Washington are nearly identical to overall trends.
— Liability insurance premiums are skyrocketing, often 50 to 200 percent, and small businesses are absorbing the costs and reducing coverage, something which Morse described as "scary."
—Few small businesses deal internationally — 25 percent export and 9 percent import — but there is a growing trend, especially among manufacturers, to sell overseas and expand foreign imports to reduce costs.

Figure 10.3 *The* Seattle Times *reported findings of interest to the Northwest from a national survey of business executives and used charts to highlight some interesting aspects of the survey. (Source: Arthur Andersen 1986 Small Business Survey)*

by less well-known research organizations like Market Opinion Research in Detroit. Advertising agencies also do a lot of consumer-oriented research on behalf of their clients.

The newspaper industry has adapted the research techniques of the social scientists to provide itself with a more careful method of gathering data and a more precise and accurate means of judging what the data may mean.

Among newspapers making use of precision journalism, especially of surveys of reader and public opinion, have been the *Detroit Free Press, Detroit News, Minneapolis Tribune, Newsday, Albany* (N.Y.) *Knickerbocker News, New York Times, Miami Herald, Des Moines Register, Philadelphia Inquirer*, Portland *Oregonian* and *Milwaukee Journal*. In some cases the research has been done by commercial firms under contract to the newspaper, but increasingly newspaper editors and reporters are learning how to do surveys using the newspaper's own staff to gather the data and the newspaper's computer to do the analysis.

Here are some examples of precision journalism carried out successfully by newspapers:

> — *Philadelphia Inquirer:* an analysis of 1,000 criminal cases that enabled the newspaper to demonstrate that the inefficiencies and failures of the prosecutor's office, not the leniency of judges, allowed many persons accused of crime to go free.

> — *Milwaukee Journal:* a public opinion study of the attitudes and concerns of Milwaukee residents about the police department. The results of the study ran as a series.

> — *San Francisco Examiner:* an annual "consumer confidence" poll, which reports the views of residents of San Francisco and surrounding counties on the economy and personal plans to spend and invest.

Many newspapers conduct polls before elections and sample voter opinions on important issues. The *Atlanta Journal and Constitution*, for example, conducted a poll of voter attitudes and opinions in Southeastern states in early 1987, more than a year before the 1988 presidential primary season. The poll surveyed more than 5,000 voters in the 12 Southern states that were to hold primaries or caucuses on Super Tuesday in 1988.

Precision journalism can be expensive. Much depends on the amount of data to be collected and analyzed, and it is more expensive, of course, to hire commercial firms to do the work than for the newspaper to do the research itself. Sometimes several newspapers can pool their efforts in a study, as did four Florida newspapers that worked together to poll voter sentiment shortly before a primary election.

CBS and *The New York Times* together conduct regular polls on a variety of topical issues. For example, one poll sought to find out what political labels like "conservative" and "liberal" mean to people.

Simple surveys can be done quickly and inexpensively, and even smaller newspapers are doing such surveys on a regular basis. Students in many schools and departments of journalism are learning to conduct polls and surveys as part of their public affairs reporting courses.

The methodology for conducting a valid survey is beyond the scope of this text, but there is a reason for introducing the topic here. The press is reporting more and more of the results of social science research of all types and from many sources.

The young journalist today must develop an understanding of numbers and numerical concepts. It is a good idea for journalism students to take courses in statistics and accounting as well as in English grammar and news writing. Editors and journalism faculties have long warned students that they must learn to spell. Now they are asking students to count as well.

When you are reporting on the findings of surveys, you must not only handle the numbers correctly but also establish the accuracy and credibility of the survey. To do this, you must give your readers the answers to a number of questions about the way the survey was done. Figure 10.4 provides a checklist of points that should be explained. Note that the checklist includes a question about the accuracy of the headline that accompanies the story.

The Associated Press's *AP Log* warned AP members recently that every AP poll story must include these facts:

— The identity of the poll's sponsor.

— The dates on which the poll was taken.

— The number of interviews on which the results are based.

— The resulting margin of error in the sample.

— The group interviewed for the poll — just registered voters, for example.

— How the poll was conducted — by telephone, in person or otherwise.

Journalist's Checklist on Polls	Sample Information
1. Who sponsored the survey?	The Canadian Progressive Conservative Party (Federal)
2. Who was interviewed? (What broad group of people is being described?)	Eligible voters living in Manitoba
3. How were the persons selected for interviews? (What was the *sample design*?)	A stratified random sample of households within census enumeration areas
4. How many persons were interviewed?	732 of 800 persons contacted were interviewed
5. What was the response rate?	92 per cent
6. How accurate are the results?	A margin of error of plus or minus 4 per cent can be expected in a sample of this size
7. Who were the interviewers?	Trained personnel of the Western Institute of Public Opinion
8. How were the interviews conducted?	Personal in-home interviews
9. When were the interviews conducted?	Two weeks before the Federal Election and one to three days after Joe Clark's nationally televised address on inflation
10. What were the actual questions asked?	"If a Federal Election were held today, which party's candidate do you think you would favour?"
11. Is the headline or teaser accurate?	"PC's popularity down, poll shows"
12. Is it clear when the results relate only to a part of the full sample?	Only female eligible voters were asked the question on voting intention

Figure 10.4 *"Reporting on Polls: Some Helpful Hints" by Dick MacDonald, manager of editorial services for the Canadian Daily Newspaper Publishers Association. A checklist for news writers for use in writing stories about polls and surveys.*

Misuse of Numbers

Earlier in this chapter it was pointed out that numbers mean the same thing to everyone. This is only partially true. Numbers may mean something, or they may not. It all depends on how they are used. There is some truth in the saying that there are "lies, damned lies and statistics." To mean anything, numbers must be presented in the right form, they must be explained and they must be put into context. That is, they must be placed in an understandable and accurate relationship with other things. Numbers not properly explained or not in proper context not only fail to inform, they mislead.

Exaggeration

News writers are taught early in their careers to be accurate with names, addresses and other everyday facts. Not enough news writers have been cautioned to be careful about the use of numbers. Too frequently news stories make authoritative-sounding statements and cite as evidence numbers carelessly gathered or loosely presented. Too often these statements are misleading or inaccurate.

A common misuse of numbers lies in estimates of crowds. It is interesting, sometimes significant, to know how many people attended a political rally or took part in a protest march. But the crowd figures should be as accurate as possible, or they tend to mislead.

Crowd estimates are not easy to come by when crowds are out in the open. One enterprising reporter after a protest rally in Chicago estimated that the crowd could have been as large as 26,000. This estimate was based on the number of 5-foot squares in the Civic Center Plaza and a generous estimate that 10 people could stand on each square. One Chicago newspaper estimated the crowd at only 8,000. Another newspaper put it at 18,000. A radio station estimated the crowd at 500. Perhaps none of the figures was accurate. A cautious reporter could balance figures from different sources and write that estimates of the size of a crowd ranged from this figure to that.

After an anti-nuclear rally in front of the Capitol in Washington, D.C., newspaper readers were given varying estimates of the size of the crowd. Among the numbers cited were 60,000, 65,000, 70,000 and 100,000. The *Boston Globe* reported the source of various estimates: the organizers of the protest estimated the crowd at 125,000; the police estimated the crowd at 65,000; and reporters found a middle ground, 100,000. Again, perhaps none of these figures was accurate, but *Globe* readers were given some basis for understanding the impact of the rally.

Indoors it is easy to estimate crowds if they are seated. Experienced reporters know the number of seats in an auditorium or a sports arena and can quickly estimate a crowd by how many seats are filled. They make an estimate, but it is based on the fact of the auditorium's or arena's capacity. Or a reporter can count the seats and the number of rows and come up with a fairly accurate estimate of capacity and, again, estimate how many seats are filled. If a 2,500-seat hall is half filled, a fairly accurate estimate of the size of the audience is possible. When the audience pays admission, sponsors usually will provide an accurate head count.

Accuracy in crowd estimates is not easy. But if attendance at a rally, march or program is taken to indicate support or opposition to a politically hot or controversial issue, then some care is needed in presenting the evidence.

Estimates of the street value of drugs seized by police or other law enforcement agencies are, I believe, often exaggerated. When police officials announce after a raid that two pounds or even a few ounces of a particular drug can be translated into millions of dollars in street value, reporters should be cautiously skeptical. A *Chicago Tribune* reporter did a little arithmetic after one drug raid and reduced the police estimates of the dollar value of drugs seized from $10 million to $3 million.

Another figure open to casual and frequent exaggeration is the penalty for crime. News stories reporting the conviction of, for example, a bookkeeper accused of embezzling funds often say that the bookkeeper could be sentenced to 20 years in prison and fined $10,000. The figures given represent the maximum possible penalty. Months later when the bookkeeper is finally sentenced, newspaper readers learn that the penalty was probation and a $1,000 fine. In Atlanta recently, a news story reported that a man convicted in a drug case faced 48 years in prison and a $90,000 fine. A month later the man was sentenced to a year and a day in prison on one charge and to one-year sentences on three other charges, all to be served concurrently. And no fine. It would be more accurate to report not only the maximum penalty possible but also the minimum. It would be even more realistic to report the penalty that is usually imposed for similar offenses in that jurisdiction.

It is not difficult to be accurate in many matters if you think about numbers realistically. When burglars broke into a jewelry wholesaler's vault in Miami a while ago and made off with 875 pounds of gold, wire service stories said the gold was worth, in one story, $9 million, in another story, $11 million. A little arithmetic throws cold water on the figures. There are 16 ounces to a pound, so the 875 pounds of gold weighed 14,000 ounces. The price of gold in various markets that day ranged from $503 an ounce to $506. Using the highest figure, $506, the gold was worth at the most $7,084,000.

Careful reporters and news writers should view numbers with caution. Exaggeration, even if it is unintentional, is not good journalism. Add up columns of figures. Refigure percentages. Verify numbers wherever possible.

Discrepancies

If you are reporting that at a city council meeting the council voted 6 to 1 to approve a motion, you could be in trouble. Your readers know that there are eight members on the council. Six votes for and one against adds up to seven. Where was the eighth member of the council? Absent? Abstaining? You have to account for the eighth member.

In news stories where numbers are supposed to add up, be sure to add them up before you write. If there is a discrepancy, find the error and explain it. In a table, add the columns. Do the numbers add up to the total given? Do the percentages add up? If your lead says that six people were injured in an accident, do you have six names in your story?

The same caution applies to cutlines for news pictures. If there are five people in a picture, be sure there are five names in your cutlines.

Readers can spot discrepancies in numbers and will tell you about them. Reader confidence in the accuracy of your newspaper will be shaken if you make such errors. An example of this kind of discrepancy — numbers that don't add up — is shown in Figure 10.5.

Meaningless Comparisons

In making comparisons based on numbers, you must be sure that your numbers are comparable. For example:

> The Board of Water and Light said the city now pays $37.04 per year for each incandescent street light.
> When the conversion to high-density sodium lights is completed, the city will pay $160,781 for street lighting.

The comparison here between the cost of one street light at present and all street lights at some time in the future is meaningless. What will each light cost after conversion? A figure of $37.04 compared to, say, $40 would be clear. Readers would know that the cost of each street light would increase about $3. It would be informative, too, to compare the total cost of street lighting now and after conversion to the new lights. The comparison of unlike things — of apples and oranges

The average American who lives to the age of 70 consumes in that lifetime the equivalent of 150 cattle, 24,000 chickens, 225 lambs, 26 sheep, 310 hogs, 26 acres of grain, and 50 acres of fruits and vegetables.
— (UPI, Now You Know, Sept. 15, 1978)

"When I first read it, something seemed a bit strange," writes Bob Lentz of Carson City, Nev.

Reader Lentz, after consultation with his local butcher, came up with what he calls "amazing and spectacular" estimates of the dressed weights of the various animals. The cattle would provide 90,000 pounds of meat, the chickens 24,000, the lambs 12,375, the sheep 1,820 pounds and the hogs 46,500.

"Think of it, 222,695 pounds of meat, over 111 tons," Lentz says.

"Now figure how many days there are in 70 years — 365 times 70 equals 25,550 days.

"That figures out to a whopping 8.7 pounds of meat per day!

"Now on top of that we are going to eat 26 acres of grain, and 50 acres of fruits and vegetables.

"No wonder our national debt is so much, and our hospitals are so full of sick people. I want you to know you made my day."

We've retired the reference work from which the item was gleaned for our daily wire opening feature.
— *UPI Reporter*

Figure 10.5 *Someone always notices when your figures don't add up.*

— leaves gaps in information that can confuse readers. If the figures just cited had been arranged in a simple table, the writer would have spotted the gaps in the information presented:

	Present	Future
Cost per light	$37.04	?
Total cost	?	$160,781

Very clearly the writer must go back to the Board of Water and Light and ask a few more questions before the story on lighting costs will have any meaning. Comparisons can make numbers meaningful, but all the figures must be there.

Extrapolations

To extrapolate is to reach a conclusion by speculating or guessing at the consequences of known facts. For example, if your college basketball team has won nine out of its first 10 games, you would be extrapolating if you decided that this record meant that the team would win 18 out of its full 20-game schedule. Not necessarily so. The team might win all its remaining games, half of them or, if a star player were injured, none.

Extrapolating is much like conducting a survey or a poll. It is educated guessing, and if the guessing is a little too free, the results may be highly inaccurate.

For example, a news story in a college newspaper reported what it considered some startling facts about alcoholism on campus. The story quoted an official of a regional council on alcoholism to the effect that 10 percent of the student body had a drinking problem. The official had come to this conclusion on the basis of a study provided by the National Council on Alcoholism that concluded that 10 percent of the adult population of the United States had a drinking problem.

Extrapolation of this kind is dangerous. The project about campus drinking might have been accurate, but in this case it would have meant a campus with some 4,500 problem drinkers of college age. There is room for doubt. Comparison of a heterogeneous adult population with a homogeneous non-adult population could lead to serious error. Be wary of such extrapolation.

Omissions

News stories reporting changes in terms of percentages often fail to relate the percentage to other numbers: percentage of what? There has to be something solid behind the percentage. To say that costs or profits or unemployment have increased 10 percent has a nice ring to it, but it may not be accurate or informative. And it may not be significant. Business leaders have been complaining of late that the press exaggerates the profitability of some industries by reporting profits in terms of percentages. Unless percentages are tied directly to the reality of the sum spread out over the company's shares of stock or to some other concrete figure, they may indeed be misleading. The story in Figure 10.6 handles the concept of profits well. It reports the profits — net earnings — in dollars and cents and as a percentage — up 59 percent. And it pins this down by pointing out that profits for the quarter are $2.74 million and that this figure represents earnings of 90 cents for each share of outstanding stock. Always relate percentages to the numbers they represent. Take this lead from a story in the Portland *Oregonian:*

> Precision Castparts Corp., the Portland-based manufacturer of metal castings, reported a 12 percent decline in sales and a 3 percent drop in profits Friday for the quarter ending Sept. 30.

201

Berkeley's Up-Right boosts its earnings

Up-Right Inc., a Berkeley manufacturer of aluminum scaffolds and platforms, reported net income of $2.74 million (90 cents a share) for 1986, a 59 percent increase from net earnings of $1.73 million (57 cents) in 1985.

Revenue increased by 12 percent to $54.7 million from $49.1 million.

For the fourth quarter, Up-Right announced net income of $165,000 (5 cents), a substantial decline from $728,000 (24 cents) a year earlier.

Revenue decreased 10 percent to $12.7 million from $14.1 million. The company attributed the decline to lower military revenues.
—*San Francisco Chronicle*

Figure 10.6 *This story on a small business's earnings report relates percentages to the numbers they represent.*

Percentages like these, standing alone, are not meaningful. Were the losses in the hundreds, the thousands or the millions of dollars? A story on earnings, the quarterly or annual report story, must relate percentages to actual figures. For example:

	Quarter Ending (Month)	
	This Year	*Last Year*
Revenues	$21,082,000	$23,937,000
Net income	$1,151,000	$1,188,000
Earnings per share	67 cents	69 cents

Now the reader can be sure of the facts. The 12 percent drop in sales is, in dollars and cents, a drop of $2,855,000. The 3 percent drop in net income, as the table shows, amounts to $370,000. And another concrete measure of the change in the company's fortunes is shown in the figure for earnings per share. Each share of stock earned 2 cents less in the quarter just past than in the same three-month period in the previous year. Numbers can be presented in such a way that they are understandable.

Incomplete statistics always lead to confusion. A news story reporting a controversy over inspection of railroad grade crossings included a statement that 26 people had lost their lives in 371 railroad crossing accidents in the first eight months of the year. Without additional data, these figures are meaningless. Do the 26 deaths represent an increase or a decrease over past years? Are highway fatalities from all causes increasing or decreasing? Is highway traffic increasing? Were the crossings where the fatalities occurred guarded or unguarded? Was there more than one fatality at any of the crossings?

In using numbers to make a point, be certain that you are using the right numbers. And don't leave out part of your evidence.

Incomprehensible Numbers

Numbers sometimes mean little or nothing to newspaper readers because they are so large, so unrelated to the experience of the average person. The size of the national debt, the chance that there is life somewhere else in the universe, the distance to the nearest galaxy, large numbers not directly related to everyday experience are unreal.

Numbers can be made clear and meaningful if they are related to things we know. Pollution of air or water and contamination of things we eat are often explained in terms of so many parts of the contaminant per million or billion. What does this mean? Is it something to worry about? Too little to hurt us? Such minute quantities can be explained, for example, like this:

> One part per billion is the amount represented by
> one bad apple in two million barrels of apples.

How much is a trillion? The Associated Press related the sum to five other figures, at least one of which should be familiar to any reader. See Figure 10.7.

How much is a trillion?

— It's a $1 followed by 12 zeros.

— Put another way, it's enough money to give every man, woman and child in the world $250 apiece.

— In miles, it would represent 5,376 round trips to the sun.

— In population, it is 1,000 times the 1 billion inhabitants of China.

— But it would cover less than half of the 2.1 trillion national debt.

— And it's a little less than one-quarter of the nation's current Gross National Product of $4.2 trillion.

— *Associated Press*

Figure 10.7 *This brief story makes numbers easier to understand by relating a hard-to-grasp sum to more familiar concepts.*

203

A news story quoted a builders' association spokesman to the effect that the cost of housing would increase 6 percent by the following spring. Six percent of what? Is that a lot? The figure could easily have been presented in terms understandable to any homeowner or prospective homeowner.

> A 6 percent increase in the cost of a new home would mean that a two-bedroom home that cost $85,000 to build this fall would cost $90,000 by spring.

A United Press International story reporting that the Consumer Price Index had reached 200 explained it this way:

> . . . it means you pay exactly twice as much for life's essentials as you did in 1967.

The story went on to give examples.

An example makes such estimates more understandable. For example, the cost of bread has gone from 40 cents to 80 cents a loaf or a half-gallon of milk has gone from 70 cents to $1.40.

A *New York Times* writer developed an ingenious way to explain international exchange rates. The writer created the *Burger Barometer*, a scale for comparing dollars and foreign currencies based on the cost of a Big Mac, a small order of french fries and a small Coca-Cola. The story is more fun than it is serious journalism, but it does make a point. You can make numbers meaningful if you relate them to things your readers know and understand.

When Skylab, the biggest and heaviest object ever placed in orbit, was about to fall out of the sky, the *Chicago Tribune* carried a news story that, among other things, tried to explain the chance that the falling satellite or a piece of it might hit someone.

> William Pomeroy, news chief of the National Aeronautics and Space Administration in Washington, declared:
>
> "The official NASA position is this: If you had 152 Skylabs all re-entering at the same time, it is calculated that one person — statistically speaking — could expect to be injured."
>
> But, he stressed, this does not mean — as many people have inferred — that there is a "1-in-152 chance" of a chunk of Skylab debris hitting a given individual.

The actual odds of a given individual — you, for example — being struck by a piece of Skylab debris are about "1 chance in 600 billion."

The story further explained that "the chance that you will be struck is almost non-existent."

Metrical Terms

News writers increasingly have to contend with numbers based on two different counting systems: our own inherited system — bushels, acres, fathoms and miles — and the metric system based on precise mathematical relationships. The United States is apparently not going to adopt the entire metric system right away, but we are finding more and more metric measurements in the news. The joint stylebook offers some guidance on metrics, and there are references to the metric system in the Basic Guide to News Style in the back of this text.

For some time to come, newspaper readers will need help in changing over from the familiar concepts of inches, feet, ounces and miles to measurements expressed in metric terms like centimeters and kilometers. Alcoholic beverages were once bottled in pint bottles, quart bottles and bottles holding one-fifth of a gallon. Now they are bottled in liters and milliliters. The weather service has for some time been reporting temperature in degrees Fahrenheit — the old and familiar system — and degrees Celsius — the metric system. Many state highway signs now give speed limits or distances in kilometers as well as in miles. Many of us are driving cars manufactured in other countries whose odometers are calibrated in kilometers rather than miles.

News writers must understand metrics and be able to explain numbers under the metric system. Fortunately, helpful guides are available. The National Bureau of Standards has issued a *Metric Style Guide for the News Media,* and the American Newspaper Publishers Association has distributed a *Metric Editorial Guide.*

Numbers Sense

This discussion has probably raised more questions than it has answered. It is not intended to be, nor could it be, a definitive explanation of all the problems the use of numbers can create for reporters and news writers. I hope to have made one point, however: that numbers can confuse as well as inform.

Starting with that premise, I hope you will see that if journalism is to do what it is supposed to do — inform the public — then the journalist will have to develop numbers sense.

James J. Kilpatrick, a widely published columnist and former newspaper editor, has this to say about journalism and numbers:

> If I were teaching journalism, I would require my students to take one year of statistics for every semester of news writing, and I'd turn out better reporters.

The press has been broadly criticized of late for its inability to explain numerical data: the cost of living, inflation, the profits or losses reported by business and industry, the federal budget, the meaning and validity of polls and surveys.

Serious journalism students ought to take courses in accounting, statistics, public finance and economics. They need a pocket calculator as well as a pocket dictionary. They must be able to write a good lead — and to figure the percentage increase in a company's profits.

Suggestions for Further Reading

Helpful guides to reporting of public affairs, business and economics.

Hage, George S., Everette E. Dennis, Arnold H. Ismach and Stephen Hartgen. *New Strategies for Public Affairs Reporting*. Englewood Cliffs, N.J.: Prentice-Hall, Inc., 1983.
  An introduction to using survey research in public affairs reporting.

Kirsch, Donald. *Financial and Economic Journalism*. New York: New York University Press, 1978.
  The ins and outs of reporting on business and finance.

Kohlmeier, Louis M. Jr., Jon G. Udell and Laird B. Anderson. *Reporting on Business and the Economy*. Englewood Cliffs, N.J.: Prentice-Hall, Inc., 1981.
  A survey of the broad field of business and economic reporting.

McCombs, Maxwell, Donald Shaw and David Grey. *Handbook of Reporting Methods*. Boston: Houghton Mifflin Co., 1976.
  An introduction to social science research methodology and its application to reporting.

Meyer, Philip. *Precision Journalism.* Bloomington: Indiana University Press, 1973.

A successful journalist's explanation of survey research methodology and its application to reporting.

Wilhoit, G. Cleveland, and David H. Weaver. *Newsroom Guide to Polls and Surveys.* Washington, D.C.: American Newspaper Publishers Association, 1980.

A brief guide to the methodology of polling and surveys.

St. Petersburg Times
Florida's Best Newspaper

SUNDAY PARTLY CLOUDY: High, low 80s; low, low 60s; details page 2-A · · St. Petersburg, Florida November 16, 1986 ...... Vol. 103 · No. 115 294 pages **50** cents

Grand Prix

Mike Follmer, driving car No. 16, and Corky Priep in car No. 58 round a curve on the downtown St. Petersburg race course in Saturday's Super Vee qualifying race.

Inside

- Overview of Saturday's St. Petersburg Grand Prix action 1-C
- A look at the Trans-Am feature race for today 16-C
- Saturday's race results 17-C
- Full page of color photos 18-C

St. Petersburg Times — TONY LOPEZ

Hasenfus sentenced to 30 years in jail

■ For the Nicaraguan government, Eugene Hasenfus was a propaganda pawn. 15-A

By STEPHEN KINZER
© New York Times

MANAGUA, Nicaragua — Eugene Hasenfus, the American air cargo specialist whose arms-laden plane was shot down over Nicaragua Oct. 5, was convicted Saturday and sentenced to 30 years in jail by a Nicaraguan tribunal.

Hasenfus had admitted being part of a clandestine operation delivering weapons to anti-government forces in Nicaragua. In the verdict Saturday, the People's Tribunal said such weapons "have been used to kill peasants and other Nicaraguan citizens."

The tribunal ordered the 30-year term after declaring Hasenfus guilty of violating a public security law that bans "actions aimed at subjecting the nation totally or partially to foreign domination, or infringing on its independence or integrity."

The tribunal added a three-year term for illicit association, but limited the sentence to a total of 30 years because that is the maximum allowed under Nicaraguan law. There was no finding on the third charge, terrorism, which carries a maximum sentence of two years.

The State Department said the verdict came "as little surprise."

The verdict took more than an hour to read in Spanish and was then read in English for Hasenfus' benefit.

Hasenfus was asked if he wished to file for an appeal. He was denied a request to consult with his lawyer on this question and then said he would appeal.

"It is very clear that the defendant was fully aware of what he was doing," the three-judge panel said. It found that the rebel groups, especially the Nicaraguan Democratic Force, which Hasenfus was apparently helping, were "supplied, directed and financed by the current government of the United States."

In their decision, the judges said it had been "fully proven" that Hasenfus was associated with the CIA. Hasenfus had appeared to make that admission in an interview with a persistent American television reporter soon after his capture, but at his trial he denied ties to any American agency.

Defense lawyers have said they hope a pardon, commutation or other arrangement might make it possible for Hasenfus to be released soon.

What you can do

Learn the rules, know your rights

■ *Last in a series*
By DIANE MASON and STEPHEN NOHLGREN
St. Petersburg Times Staff Writers

In hospitals and in doctors' offices, the pressure is on. New Medicare rules, which limit hospital reimbursement, have meant fewer admissions, earlier discharges, and a trend toward outpatient treatment, home care and transfers to nursing facilities.

Last week the *St. Petersburg Times* published a series of stories about how people in this community have fared under the new system.

Some do fine.

Others feel helpless. At the mercy of a complicated system, patients and families of patients wonder how they can win back some control over what happens.

If you are a member of your family gets sick, it helps to understand how the system works. The following guide describes your rights and what you can expect from today's Medicare.

Who decides if you get into the hospital?

Your doctor. Hospitals don't admit and discharge patients. Only doctors do that. However, doctors are constrained by new Medicare rules, which specifically spell out standards for admission, treatment and discharge of patients. Hospitals are constrained, too. Medicare can refuse to pay the hospital if the rules are not followed. As a result, there is pressure coming from Medicare that is felt by the hospital and the doctor.

How much will I have to pay for the hospital?

The first time you are admitted in a calendar year, you must make a co-payment of $492. This is rising to $572 on Jan. 1. After the first day, Medicare pays all hospital charges — up to 60 days. Doctor bills for your hospitalization are covered under Part B of your Medicare coverage. They have a different set of rules.

Who enforces Medicare's rules?

Medicare's payments to hospitals are monitored in each state by a Peer Review Organization (PRO). This is a private company under contract with the federal government. The PRO reviews admissions and discharges, and the quality of patient care. The PRO has the power to deny Medicare payment to hospitals if care is inappropriate by Medicare standards. The PRO can also deny payment if a patient's admission is considered unnecessary. The address and telephone number of this area's PRO is:

Professional Foundation for Health Care, Inc.
2907 Bay-to-Bay Boulevard, Suite 100
Tampa, Florida 33629
Telephone: (813) 831-6273

What if you can't get admitted?

In cases of nonemergency or elective surgical procedures, the hospital (with the concurrence of the physician or the PRO) can "deny" your admission.

They would do this by notifying you that Medicare will not pay for your hospitalization. If your doctor says the hospital or the PRO has denied your admission, ask

Please see CONSUMER 10-A

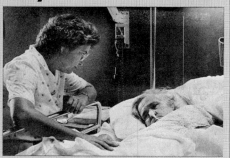

Sarah Griner comforts her mother-in-law, Fannie Griner, in her room at Tarpon Springs General Hospital.

St. Petersburg Times — ROBIN DONINA

When she heard 'Your time's up,' she said 'No'

By DIANE MASON and STEPHEN NOHLGREN
St. Petersburg Times Staff Writers

Sarah Griner hung up the phone, stunned. What the doctor had said didn't add up.

How could he be discharging her mother-in-law, Fannie Griner, from the hospital? The 76-year-old stroke victim, bedridden for over a year, had an open sore — dark red, like a piece of raw beef — that wrapped halfway around her left leg.

Two weeks earlier, when the wound first erupted and formed an infected crater the size of a baseball, Fannie had been taken from a nursing home to Tarpon Springs General Hospital for treatment.

And now, Dr. Javier Bleichner told Sarah on the phone, the wound had been scraped clean, the infection was gone, and Fannie was ready to leave the hospital.

Most disturbing was what Sarah heard next:

Back at the nursing home, Bleichner warned, Fannie would not get the attention she received in the hospital. The wound was more likely to get infected there. And if it did, the left leg might have to be amputated.

"I asked him, wasn't there any way he could keep her there in the hospital?" Sarah says. "He said: No, Medicare will not let us keep her anymore.

They are already pushing me to get her out."

What Sarah Griner heard that morning in September elderly patients and their families have been hearing all over the Bay area since Medicare changed its rules: Your time in the hospital is up. Medicare wants you out.

Bleichner told Sarah that there was nothing more the hospital could do for Fannie.

Sarah thought maybe there was.

The Griners are a tightknit family; they take care of their own. For nearly 30 years, four of Fannie's six children lived in Safety Harbor. Sarah and Fannie's son Charlie lived next door. When

Please see GRINER 11-A

MEDICARE
THE PRICE OF SAVING MONEY

■ People who were more fearful than angry. 10-A
■ Editorial 2-D
■ The painful sweetness of touching lives: Diane Mason's experience reporting on Medicare cases. 1-F

ST. PETERSBURG TIMES
FOREIGN EDITOR

WILBUR G. LANDREY

President's explanation falls short

President Reagan's superb performance on television the other night may have sounded fine to many Americans watching in their living rooms. But it did not convince anyone who takes America's reputation seriously, or the U.S. Congress or the world leaders the President still has to deal with for two more years.

The performance might have sounded even **analysis** better 10 days ago. But it still would have left important questions unanswered about his dealings with Iran. And it only confirmed the amateurism of the men in the White House who, with the President's approval, teamed up with the Israelis in an operation that has gravely damaged American reputation and credibility.

The question is not, as the President tried to make it, whether to try to patch up relations with Iran. Some day we'll have to, just as some day, an American government will have to deal again with Syria.

The question is whether the

Please see LANDREY 2-A

Islamic Jihad says demands must be met

Compiled from Times wires

AMMAN, Jordan — The Islamic Jihad group said Saturday that it will not release its remaining American hostages in Lebanon until its demands are met, apparently dashing hopes for a quick release of the captives.

■ Reagan, Thatcher talk arms. 12-A
■ Joint Chiefs said in dark on arms deal. 12-A
■ Iran deal stirs Arab rage. 29-A
■ Pointcexter in eye of storm. 30-A

In a statement released in Beirut, the terrorist group also decried the "propaganda furor" raised in the West following the recent release of David P. Jacobsen, a hostage held in Lebanon for 17 months.

After Jacobsen's release, it was disclosed that U.S. officials had engaged in secret contacts with Iranian officials for the purposes of improving relations and possibly gaining release of the Lebanon hostages.

The reports culminated Thursday in President Reagan's admission in a speech that the United States had sent a "small amount" of defensive arms and spare parts

Please see HOSTAGES 12-A

Guru triggers moves to Northwest

By ROBERT LINDSEY
© New York Times

YELM, Wash. — George Hain, a millionaire businessman from Cheyenne, Wyo., attended a seminar in Colorado last year and listened to a slender blond woman, J. Z. Knight, tell how a 35,000-year-old-man uses her body to speak words of wisdom.

The next day Hain returned to Cheyenne, sold his five Burger King restaurants and moved to a rural area in Northern California. He now is building a house that is shaped like a pyramid, he says, to "manifest the energy" of the universe.

"I'm happy beyond my wildest dreams," Hain said of his decision to abandon his old life because of the teachings of the 35,000-year-old man called Ramtha.

Hain is part of a curious migration to the northwestern corner of the nation. Over the past two years hundreds of Americans have moved to rural areas in Washington, Oregon, Idaho, Montana and Northern California. In some cases, the decision to move has divided families and led to divorces.

The migrants say they were motivated by

Please see GURU 7-A

11
Second-Day Stories and Other Organizing Devices

The only thing that stops me is when I get a sentence that strikes me as real good. That makes me feel so fine that I get up and walk around and can't do any more writing for an hour.

T.S. Stribling

U p to this point, we have talked about news stories of several types, but always as if the story were the only one of its kind, as if it were an isolated example and had little if any relationship with other news stories or the other news of the day.

New stories are not isolated events. Each is part of the whole panorama of the day's news. A number of stories each day will be, in a sense, chapters of stories, perhaps the fourth or fifth chapter in a series. Others will be one part of a mosaic of similar stories that together make up a larger picture of some part of the day's news.

Stories that continue the telling of events that started the day before are *second-day* stories. Stories that began with events several days or even weeks ago are *follow-up* stories or *folos*. Second-day and follow-up stories not only require new leads, but they also require a *tie-back* — that is, background information to remind the reader of what went on before.

Several stories on similar topics — for example, auto accidents or the weather — can be pulled together into a larger story called a *round-up*. *Sidebars* are another way of pulling together different parts of a larger story. *Shirttailing* is a device for uniting smaller parts of a story with larger parts.

Second-Day Stories

We have already encountered the concept of the second-day story in our discussion of obituaries. You will recall that an obituary has a second-day lead if news of the death has already been published.

Many stories are written every day about new developments in stories that occurred the previous day. Sometimes news stories continue over several days. A trial may last for several days, even weeks, and a new story is written every day to keep readers informed of progress in the courtroom. Coverage of an election campaign is a continuing story that goes on for months. Let's look at how the *San Francisco Chronicle* handled a kidnapping. The first-day story:

> A wealthy Novato woman was kidnapped at gunpoint from her home at an exclusive tennis club yesterday by two masked intruders who forced her into the trunk of her new Mercedes and sped away.
>
> Novato police said the kidnappers, dressed in black and armed with a shotgun and a knife, escaped with an undisclosed amount of cash, furs and jewelry after first tying up the woman's husband and a caretaker.
>
> The kidnapped woman is Edith A. Quartaroli, 62, who, with her husband, Attilio, owns and manages the Olive Ridge Tennis Club at 301 Olive Avenue.

The rest of the story follows, another 18 paragraphs of details and explanation. This story ran on a Tuesday. The next day, Wednesday, there were new developments. The lead, with the tie-back in italics:

> A kidnapped Novato woman was found bound and gagged yesterday in a locked storage compartment in Gilroy after being threatened with death by the men *who forced her from her home at gunpoint.*
>
> Novato detectives said Edith Quartaroli, 62, "was shaken but does not appear to have been physically harmed" during the ordeal *that began at her home Monday morning.*

This, of course, is a second-day lead. It begins with new information about the kidnapping but includes a tie-back, just enough about the beginning of the story to tell a reader who had not read the earlier story how the story began. Three days later, on Saturday, the *Chronicle* reported new developments.

> An 18-year-old Milpitas youth was arrested yesterday in the kidnapping of a wealthy Novato woman after police found what they said was the getaway car in his garage.

This third-day lead was followed by four paragraphs about the investigation of the kidnapping and the arrest. Then the story turned back to what had gone before — to the tie-back or background.

> The arrest came four days after *Edith Quartaroli, 62, was kidnapped by two masked intruders who broke into the Olive Ridge Tennis Club, which she owns with her husband, Attilio. She was found Tuesday bound and gagged — but unharmed — in a Gilroy storage locker.*

The story then returns to the new developments and reports in detail on the arrest of the 18-year-old. The structure of this story is shown in Figure 11.1.

Let's look now at three stories from the *Atlanta Constitution*. The stories report the last days of a murder trial and, like the stories in the *Chronicle*, blend new and old material. A number of stories about the trial preceded this lead on the story of the final day of the trial.

> Conflicting stories about who pulled the trigger in the fatal shooting of a College Park high school student concluded the evidence Wednesday in the trial of two teenagers accused of murder and armed robbery.
>
> Fulton County Superior Court Judge Luther Alverson said the jury would begin its deliberations Thursday after closing arguments by attorneys.
>
> Anthony Robinson, 16, one of the two remaining defendants and the last witness in the trial, testified Wednesday afternoon that 14-year-old Travis Slayton, *who apparently committed suicide by hanging himself last month in a jail cell, fired the bullet that killed 15-year-old Andrew Reid Martin on the night of Dec. 3.*

211

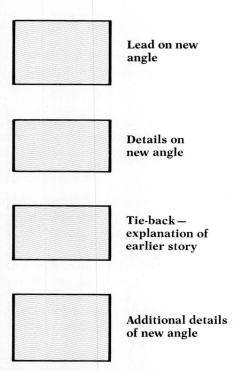

Lead on new angle

Details on new angle

Tie-back — explanation of earlier story

Additional details of new angle

Figure 11.1 *Overall organization of a second-day story — for example, a story on the second or third day of a long trial or a story on developments in a murder case. The* San Francisco Chronicle *second- and third-day stories on the kidnapping follow this scheme.*

The third paragraph of this lead ties the trial to the background, the shooting that began the series of events. The next day the lead read:

> A Fulton Superior Court jury was unable to reach a verdict Thursday after more than three hours of deliberation in the murder case against two teenagers accused of *the Dec. 3 slaying and armed robbery of a 15-year-old College Park high school student.*
>
> The jury of nine women and three men was sent home for the night by Judge Luther Alverson. Deliberations resume at 8:30 a.m. Friday.
>
> In his closing argument to the jurors . . .

The first two paragraphs of the lead report developments since the previous day's story was written and give a little background on

A compositor pastes up the front page of the Lewiston (Pa.) Sentinel. *The finished page will go to the camera room where an offset plate will be made. (*The Sentinel, Lewiston, PA, 17044)

the trial. The third paragraph begins an account of the final hours of the trial before the jury was charged and began its deliberations. The next day's lead:

> A mother and other family members wept uncontrollably Friday when her teenage son was found guilty of the murder and armed robbery of a College

Park student, but the crowded courtroom exploded in shouts and applause when a second young defendant was acquitted.

The next two paragraphs continue the account of the verdict and its aftermath. Then the writer once again writes a tie-back and explains the background of the case:

> *The two youths had been indicted with two other teen-agers in the fatal shooting Dec. 3 of 15-year-old Andrew Reid Martin, a high school student who was on his way home at the time from his job at a church.*

After this bit of background, the story continues with additional details about the end of the trial — including comments from attorneys and others.

The Tie-back

Background is very important when events are reported over a period of days or weeks. You can't assume that newspaper readers have read anything about the beginning of the story. And you can't assume that even if they have, they will remember much about it. When you write a developing story on the second or third or a later day, always bring your readers up to date. Tell them briefly how the story started, what happened before the events you are writing about in today's story. As you can see in the preceding examples, the writer has included some details of earlier events in the lead. Then, before going into the details of new events, the writer has taken time, written a paragraph or two, to refresh readers' memories on what went before. Background does not go at the end of the story. It should be fitted in early in the story.

Other Second-Day Leads

Sometimes second-day leads take a different approach. In this second-day lead on a jailbreak, the writer is not presenting new developments. The first-day story was largely devoted to what happened. The second-day lead explains how it happened before going on to report on developments in the search for the missing prisoners:

> It took 15 minutes over the weekend for three prisoners to chip through a cell wall at the new Clayton County

Detention Center, and once outside they were cloaked in darkness to complete their escape because no lights had been erected outside the $9.5 million jail.

Five paragraphs giving additional details of the escape follow, and then the story turns to new material, thus:

Still at large from the Saturday escape were . . .

Follow-ups

Follow-up stories are much like second-day stories, but they may appear not the next day but days, weeks or even months later. They are like second-day stories because they, too, report new developments in an earlier story. But they can differ from the type of second-day stories we have just looked at when the news story does more than update the earlier story. The *Milwaukee Journal* follow-up in Figure 11.2 reports on the reaction of a small town in the wake of a brutal attack on an elderly couple. The story includes the necessary tie-back or background on the attack, but the follow-up was created by the writer, who did more than just ask police "what's new?" The lead:

Caledonia — An uneasy mood has gripped this semi-rural town in the wake of the savage beatings that claimed the life of a 68-year-old man and left his wife severely injured.

The tie-back is included in these paragraphs:

Jacob Vogel died Tuesday night at St. Mary's Medical Center in Racine. His wife, Edith, 65, remained in serious condition at St. Mary's Wednesday.
The couple was beaten Monday night after they discovered burglars at their home and chased the burglars' car. Police issued a bulletin naming a 27-year-old man as a suspect.

The rest of the story, which is not included in Figure 11.2, includes more about the attack on the elderly couple, tells about two similar attacks in the same community and gives some background on the community and its limited police force. Hardly as cut-and-dried as the second- and third-day stories on the kidnapping: woman kidnapped, woman found and kidnap suspect arrested.

215

Caledonia residents uneasy after attack

Caledonia — An uneasy mood has gripped this semi-rural town in the wake of the savage beatings that claimed the life of a 68-year-old man and left his wife severely injured.

Jacob Vogel died Tuesday night at St. Mary's Medical Center in Racine. His wife, Edith, 65, remained in serious condition at St. Mary's Wednesday.

The couple were beaten Monday night after they discovered burglars at their home and chased the burglars' car. Police issued a bulletin naming a 27-year-old man as a suspect.

One of the Vogels' neighbors, who asked not to be identified, was keeping a shotgun and shells in the kitchen.

"There are no street lights here," the neighbor said. "When there isn't a full moon, it's black at night."

Bill Beresford, another neighbor, said residents in the area had always watched out for each other's property. But they are more alert now than ever, he said.

"What are you going to do?" Beresford asked. "You can't have a cop in front of everybody's house."

Another Caledonia resident, Herb Kauth, who was doing repairs Wednesday on the home of one of the Vogels' neighbors, said he was shaken up by the incident.

"Having some stranger pull off the freeway and pick a house at random, it gives you an eerie feeling," he said.

In the nearby hamlet of Franksville, several residents at Bob Tyler's barber shop said the Vogels were widely known in the community through church and other social activities.

"It shocked the whole community," Tyler said. "It's like one big family out here."

The man named as a suspect came to the attention of police when officers questioned the owner of the car used by the burglars, a 1977 Buick Electra. They said the owner told them the suspect and a companion had asked to borrow the car Monday night while they were in a bar in the 3400 block of W. Lisbon Ave. in Milwaukee.

Police said he told the two men he did not want them to use his car. But while he was in the men's room, someone stole his car keys, which had been left on the bar, police said.

Police said when the man looked outside, his car was also missing. Milwaukee police recovered the vehicle in the 1800 block of N. 24th St. Evidence taken from the car linked it to the Caledonia incident.

Police speculated that the fleeing burglars saw the Vogels following them and returned to the home to beat them because they feared the couple might be able to identify them.

"I suppose we can logically come to that conclusion," said Caledonia Police Chief Phil Stanton.

But Stanton said that "at this point in the investigation, that motive is purely speculation."

Jacob Vogel was beaten with a hedge trimmer and was found lying face down in the garage. Edith Vogel was beaten on the face and head with a wine bottle and was found in the kitchen of the home. The home had been ransacked, Stanton said. . . .

Figure 11.2 *A follow-up story from* The Milwaukee Journal.

A Carolton woman who was struck by a car on Main Street and dragged nearly two blocks was still in critical condition Thursday at St. Luke's Hospital.

Donna James, 62, has a broken pelvis and broken ribs, police said.

She was struck by a vehicle driven by Carl Robertson, 217 N. Grant St., about 2 a.m. Sunday.

Robertson was heading west in the 200 block of Main Street when he struck Mrs. James, who was crossing the street, police said.

Police said Mrs. James was dragged to the 500 block.

Robertson, who left the scene of the accident, surrendered at police headquarters Sunday afternoon.

He has been charged with leaving the scene of an accident and operating a motor vehicle after his license had been revoked.

Figure 11.3 *A follow-up on an accident story published earlier in the week.*

Another follow-up is shown in Figure 11.3, a story published on Friday to bring readers up to date on an accident that occurred the previous Sunday.

Follow-ups frequently use the original story only as a news peg. For example, a story reporting a zoning variance might trigger a long follow-up, perhaps even several follow-ups, on the background and present status of zoning bylaws in the community. A story about an auto accident at a railroad grade crossing might be followed by a story looking at accidents at other grade crossings in the vicinity. Follow-ups can do more than add details to an earlier story. They can and often do add depth and perspective far beyond the original story.

Round-ups

A round-up story is one that pulls together under one lead several stories of a similar nature — for example, the round-up on weekend auto accidents that generally runs in your newspaper on Monday. The lead may report, for example, that four people were killed in accidents on county or area highways over the weekend. The story that follows will explain each of the several accidents that caused the deaths. A diagram showing how a round-up story is organized is shown in Figure 11.4. A round-up story of this kind is shown in Figure 11.5.

An accident round-up story in the *Augusta* (Ga.) *Herald* started like this:

> Ten people died in weekend accidents on Georgia and South Carolina roads, including an Augusta teenager who was killed in a head-on collision in Richmond County.

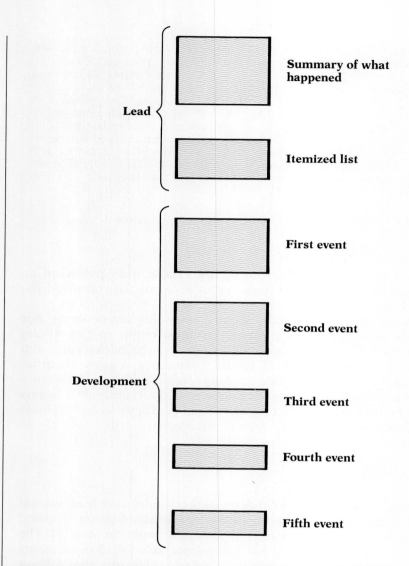

Figure 11.4 *Overall organization of the round-up story — for example, a round-up of weekend traffic accidents. Compare this sketch with the story shown in Figure 11.5.*

Four state residents, including a Dairyland father and one of his 13 children, drowned during the weekend in Wisconsin waters.

The victims:

Eugene W. Sikorski, 53, Dairyland.

Miss Rose Sikorski, 19, his daughter.

Florian L. Schellinger, 40, West Bend.

Earl Koehnke, 38, Menasha.

Washburn County Sheriff Arnold Drost said Sikorski had taken several of his 13 children to Bear Track Lake near Minong Friday to swim.

When his daughter Rose disappeared while swimming, Sikorski tried to rescue her.

One of the other children ran to a nearby public beach and summoned help when he failed to reappear. Six youths recovered the bodies and attempted to revive them.

The young men told authorities that both victims seemed to respond for a brief period. The father, however, was dead at the scene when the ambulance arrived. His daughter died in an ambulance en route to a Spooner hospital.

Schellinger drowned Saturday when he fell off the rear of a boat about 100 feet from shore on the Iron River.

Bayfield County authorities said several persons were standing on the shore of the river when Schellinger fell into the water.

His body was recovered within a few minutes by a bystander.

The body of Earl Koehnke, who drowned Friday off the north shore of Lake Winnebago, was recovered Saturday.

The Menasha Police Department said Koehnke was in a boat with four other persons when he stood up near the rear of the craft and tumbled into the lake.

Efforts by his companions to rescue him failed.

— *Milwaukee Sentinel*

Figure 11.5 *A round-up of weekend fatalities from a Monday morning issue of the* Milwaukee Sentinel. *Note that an itemized list of victims is part of the summary lead.*

The lead was followed by an account of the accident in which the teen-ager was killed. Then the other accidents were grouped, first two other accidents in Georgia, then four accidents in South Carolina.

Round-ups are most frequently used to pull together accident and crime stories, but there is no reason why several stories of any nature can't be pulled together under a round-up lead.

Other Organizing Devices

Second-day stories, follow-ups and round-ups are devices for pulling stories together, for making connections, for helping readers see the news in broader perspective.

Two other useful organizing devices are sidebars and shirttailing.

219

Sidebars

Sometimes because a story is lengthy or involved not everything that needs to be reported will fit conveniently under one lead. In other instances two aspects of the story may not fit well under one lead — for example, a hard-news story that also has a feature angle. In cases like these, the writer may produce two stories, a main story and a second story, a sidebar, perhaps with a feature lead on the sidebar. The story in Figure 11.6 is a sidebar that ran in *The Milwaukee Journal* with the follow-up shown in Figure 11.2. It is another aspect of the main story, written as a result of the attack on the elderly couple but treating another matter. It deals not with the attack or its aftermath or the mood of residents in Caledonia but with something of direct and immediate concern to other newspaper readers — what should you and I do in case we find burglars in our home or apartment?

When a man hijacked and threatened to blow up a commuter plane in Oregon, the Portland *Oregonian* carried a story on the hijack attempt across the top of page one. The story jumped to an inside page, where *The Oregonian* placed three sidebars alongside the continuation of the hijack story. They were:

— A column-long transcript of FBI and police conversations with the hijacker on the commuter plane.

— A list of seven other recent hijackings in the Northwest.

— A chronological account of the hijacking pieced together from the accounts of passengers on the plane.

The sidebar device is simple. If a story is too long or too complicated or has too many angles — break it up. Write a main story and give the reader an overview. Then write separate accounts of other aspects of the story.

Shirttailing

Shirttailing is another simple device for organizing a lot of miscellaneous material. The story in Figure 11.7 is a good example, despite its brevity. The story first reports on the principal matters to be discussed at a board of education meeting, then says that the board will also discuss other matters and lists them. The device is frequently used in stories about city council or board of education meetings. After the story has taken up the more important events of the meeting, other

Best weapon is phone, police say

After fatal assaults on three Wisconsin senior citizens who had confronted burglars, police on Wednesday urged homeowners to use their most effective weapon: the telephone.

In the most recent case, Jacob and Edith Vogel returned to their Caledonia home Monday night and found a strange car in their driveway and burglars in their home. The Vogels parked in a neighbor's driveway and followed the burglars when they left in the car. The Vogels apparently were trying to get a license plate number, police said.

When the Vogels returned home, the burglars also had returned. The couple were beaten with a hedge trimmer and a broken bottle, police said. Jacob Vogel, 68, died Tuesday night. His wife, 65, was in serious condition Wednesday at a hospital in Racine.

In Milwaukee, Police Inspector Kenneth Hagopian said:

"You don't know what you're confronting. Sometimes you have a real tense situation. What if you pull a gun on the burglar and he has one too?

"Or the person may be a juvenile, a 13-year-old kid. Are you going to kill him? How can you justify it?"

Hagopian said it was his experience that a burglar generally would try to escape when confronted.

"That happens often when older people confront a burglar," he said. "But we're not encouraging them to do it."

Instead, use the phone to alert police, Hagopian said.

"You may be attacked or beaten severely if you confront him," Hagopian said.

Phil Stanton, Caledonia police chief, said that in the past eight months there had been three incidents in the town in which residents returned home to confront burglars.

"To me, the bottom line is my life is worth more than my property," said Stanton, who also suggests that people who find intruders in their homes call police.

"From what I've observed," Stanton said, "if a person can just be as observant as possible, get all the information in a subtle way, and get the police, that's the best."

He said he wasn't sure older people would be safer with a gun in the house.

"That's a personal question," he said. "I personally have guns at home. But I do not promote confrontation with people like burglars."

The two other victims of fatal attacks this year were Edward Langbecker, 74, and his 66-year-old wife, Ruth, who were beaten and stabbed to death in Wausau Feb. 28. A 22-year-old Merrill man is charged with two counts of first-degree murder in the slayings.

Figure 11.6 *A sidebar to* The Milwaukee Journal *follow-up shown in Figure 11.2.*

School board meets Tuesday

BEAUFORT — Topics on the Beaufort County Board of Education's agenda for its 6 p.m. meeting Tuesday include the district facilities improvements plan and a financial update.

The meeting is scheduled for the school administration office on King Street in Beaufort.

According to the agenda, the board also expects to:

— Approve a contract with the Beaufort-Jasper County Water Authority for sewage treatment at Bluffton schools.

— Give third-reading approval to the school district's student-promotion policy.

— Approve a Beaufort County Recreation Commission project for a softball field at Michael C. Riley Elementary School in Bluffton.

Figure 11.7 *Additional information about a school board meeting is shirttailed to a story from the Hilton Head, S.C.,* Island Packet.

matters are shirttailed — that is, added on at the end of the story. The shirttailed matter is introduced by a transition like these:

> The Council also voted to:

> In other decisions Tuesday, the court:

> Others who pleaded guilty and were sentenced Thursday included:

> Others named in the suit were:

The items that follow generally are single sentences or short paragraphs, much like those you can see in Figure 11.7.

Suggestions for Further Reading

Investigative reporting goes back to Lincoln Steffens and the muckrakers of the 1890s. Here are some recent and instructive books on the subject.

Anderson, David, and Peter Benjaminson. *Investigative Reporting.* Bloomington: Indiana University Press, 1976.

A textbook on reporting methods by two successful investigative reporters.

Behrens, John C. *The Typewriter Guerrillas.* Chicago: Nelson-Hall, 1977.

Sketches of the top 20 investigative reporters, including Carl Bernstein, Seymour Hersh and Clark Mollenhoff.

Downie, Leonard, Jr. *The New Muckrakers*. Washington: The New Republic, 1976.

A study of some successful investigative reporters and their work.

Mitford, Jessica. *Poison Penmanship*. New York: Vintage Books, 1980.

Selected examples of investigative reporting and an interesting discussion of method in the introduction.

Smith, Zay N., and Pamela Zekman. *The Mirage*. New York: Random House, 1979.

How the *Chicago Sun-Times* bought a tavern and used it in an investigation of official corruption.

Wendland, Michael F. *The Arizona Project*. Kansas City: Sheed, Andrews and McMeel, 1977.

Story of the probe of organized crime in Arizona conducted by members of Investigative Reporters and Editors.

News and feature guide on Page 2
Telephone 929-2000
Classified 929-1500
Circulation 929-2222

© 1987 Globe Newspaper Co.

The Boston Globe

Chilly con blarney
Tuesday – Cloudy, windy, 35
Wednesday – Mostly sunny, 45
High tide – 12:05 a.m., 12:37 p.m.
Full report – Page 40

Vol. 231: No. 76   TUESDAY, MARCH 17, 1987   84 Pages • 25 cents

Dukakis launches presidential bid

Gov. Dukakis announces that he will seek the presidency.
Globe staff photo/Bill Greene

Governor to set up campaign committee

By Joan Vennochi
Globe Staff

Gov. Michael S. Dukakis yesterday ended nearly four months of speculation about his political future with a dramatic announcement that he will seek the presidency of the United States – an effort he likened to a marathon that he said he is ready and eager to run.

After a series of morning meetings with senior staff members and legislative leaders and a dozen or more courtesy calls to politicians across the country, Dukakis announced he will set up a committee to begin his fledgling campaign for the presidency.

"I have the energy to run this marathon, the strength to run this country, the experience to manage our government and the values to lead our people. With your help and your prayers, a son of Greek immigrants named Mike Dukakis can become the next president of the United States," he said at a packed State House news conference.

The governor said he plans to formally announce his "run for the White House" May 4. He acknowledged it will be a long shot, but said he would not be running unless he believed he has a chance of winning. He also defended his decision to run while a sitting governor, saying he dislikes the idea that "public servants are somehow disqualified from seeking the presidency."

Stressing his personal qualities along with his political achievements, Dukakis said he invites Americans to test his "character and competence." He said he wants to be weighed not only on his positions on issues but by the integrity and judgment he said he would bring to the presidency.

Immediately after the news conference, Dukakis moved to the House chamber, where he was greeted by a sustained ovation from legislators of both branches. Democrats and Republicans alike stood to cheer the 53-year-old governor, who began his career in state politics as a representative from Brookline 24 years ago but who at times has had rocky rela-

tions with legislative leaders. House Speaker George Keverian (D-Everett) welcomed Dukakis as a "family member."

"It is fitting that we hear him here . . . where he fought so many battles," said Keverian, who introduced Dukakis as "the next president of the United States."

In his address to the joint session, Dukakis reached back

DUKAKIS, Page 14

Another long shot enters ring

By Thomas Oliphant
Globe Staff

It's plausible, but in the words of the candidate himself, "a very, very long shot."

Michael Dukakis shares with the other likely aspirants for the Democratic presidential nomination next year the fact that his papers as a national figure and plausible president are in good order.

Where he is weak, what makes him a long shot, are two factors – one he cannot directly control, the other he can.

Regardless of the stirrings of candidacy on Beacon Hill yesterday, Gary Hart remains the increasingly imposing obstacle over which every other candidate must hurdle. Dukakis cannot directly influence Hart's fortunes. Hart may soar to the nomination next year, or he may crash, but the 1988 story begins with him, and if he's good when it all gets serious, it may not matter what anyone else does.

As of this morning, Dukakis is one member of a group of candidates who occupy what has become known as the "second tier."

ANALYSIS, Page 14

NEWS ANALYSIS

Michael Dukakis: his own politician

An irregular but essentially pragmatic politician, Michael S. Dukakis, 53, is 5 feet, 8 inches tall and weighs about 160 pounds. He has never smoked, and drinks only an occasional glass of wine. He is serious, analytic, intensely disciplined, naturally aloof – definitely not one of the boys. A devoted family man and a devotee of the work ethic, he is also a hands-on manager who immerses himself in policy details of government. One thing that gives political observers pause is the question of his ability to step back and speak thematically of his vision for the future. A profile by Ben Bradlee Jr. begins on Page 12.

★ THE DUKAKIS RUN

Gov. Dukakis and his wife, Kitty, at the State House yesterday.
Globe staff photo/Bill Greene

Enthusiasm and caution

Gov. Dukakis' decision to run for president drew an enthusiastic response from his family and from Democratic political colleagues in Boston, New York and Washington yesterday. A Massachusetts Republican leader introduced a note of caution, saying "there is no clear answer on how the state will operate while the governor is running for president, which is essentially a full-time job." Page 14.

Voters interviewed in downtown Boston yesterday said Dukakis earned his run for the presidency by performing well as governor. Page 15.

AIDS risk seen for 12,000

By Richard A. Knox
Globe Staff

About 12,000 unsuspecting Americans may harbor the AIDS virus as the result of blood transfusions they received between 1978 and 1985, according to a draft of a document scheduled for publication on Thursday by the federal government.

In Massachusetts and Maine,

the two states served by the Boston-based American Red Cross Blood Services regional system, 166 transfusion recipients may unknowingly be infected by the virus and are capable of infecting sexual partners, Dr. Peter Page of the Red Cross estimated yesterday.

This hidden reservoir of AIDS virus infection is the target of an

expected federal recommendation that many Americans who received blood transfusions in the 7½ years before May 1985 seek testing to determine if they were exposed to the AIDS virus.

In May 1985, US blood banks began screening donated blood for AIDS virus antibodies (an indirect

AIDS, Page 42

SURVIVOR'S CHRISTENING

Beryl Zutic holds her 10-week-old granddaughter Carly Zutic, the youngest survivor of the Zeebrugge, Belgium, ferry disaster, after her christening Sunday. Carly, her mother and father all survived the sinking of the ferry Herald of Free Enterprise on March 6.
UPI/Reuters photo

Inside
Today: Business Extra

Opportunities for state GOP

The future of the Massachusetts Republican Party is cloudy, but chances for growth are beginning to shine through. Last of series, Page 19.

Boston's seaport renaissance

The Massachusetts Port Authority has spent $12.5 million to update Boston's seaport facilities. Labor cutbacks have been negotiated, cargo-handling costs have been cut, an atmosphere of cooperation has taken hold. The result: Boston has logged a third straight year of handling record tonnage. A look at the seaport renaissance, Business Extra, Page 8.

Rep. Biaggi of New York indicted

US Rep. Mario Biaggi (D-N.Y.) and former Brooklyn Democratic Party leader Meade Esposito were accused yesterday in a federal indictment of peddling influence on behalf of a ship repair firm. Page 8.

Baldness drug gets initial OK

By Larry Tye
Globe Staff

Federal officials yesterday gave preliminary approval to the most effective drug yet tested to treat male baldness, and the drug could be approved for commercial use within months.

"It's exciting to have a drug that works after so many years of all the phony stuff around," said Dr. Howard P. Baden, a dermatologist at Massachusetts General Hospital. "There's no question this drug has an effect that's measurable."

Baden and others say the drug could stimulate hair growth in a third of the 30 million to 50 million American men suffering so-called

MINOXIDIL, Page 4D

Study says acid rain toll may grow

EPA: Lakes severely damaged could double to 600 if pollution persists

By Jerry Ackerman
Globe Staff

A federal acid-rain study said yesterday that the number of United States lakes severely damaged by acid rain will double to more than 600 in the next 25 to 50 years unless the air pollution that causes this damage is reduced.

The study by the US Environmental Protection Agency, although not final, said the lakes in danger include a cluster in southeast Massachusetts, Rhode Island and eastern Connecticut, which

are sensitive to acid rain but so far have escaped the severe acidification seen in lakes in the Adirondack Mountains.

An EPA spokesman in Washington said that although the findings have been presented to the agency's administrator, Lee Thomas, they won't become official until after a review meeting this week in Oregon.

"Any interpretation that would suggest significant shifts in the administration's policy on acid rain would be premature,"

the spokesman, Christian Rice, said in a telephone interview.

Nevertheless, the report's completion three weeks before a meeting between President Ronald Reagan and Canada's prime minister, Brian Mulroney, is considered politically timely.

The two days of talks scheduled between Reagan and Mulroney in Ottawa include discussions of what the United States is doing to reduce air pollution that flows north and is blamed by

ACID RAIN, Page 42

12 The Speech Story: Leads

Democracy depends on information circulating freely in society.

Katharine Graham

Speech stories are basic to news writing. They require so many of the techniques and skills of news writing that they provide excellent training for beginners. Schools of journalism have traditionally started off young news writers with assignments to cover sermons, speeches and meetings.

In this chapter we will discuss a variety of news stories, all grouped under the general heading of speech stories because they all depend on what people have *said* rather than on what they have done. Speech stories in this sense, then, include stories about speeches, lectures and panel discussions but also stories based on press conferences, trials, public hearings and interviews. News stories based on city council meetings, school board meetings or sessions of the state legislature are also speech stories because so much of what is reported about them is what was said rather than what was done. Many speech stories report only what one speaker said, but others must incorporate what two, three or even half a dozen speakers said.

News writers must have considerable reportorial skill to get this material together — handouts of the text of a speech are not always provided, and city council meetings are often long and involved — but they have to have a lot of writing tricks up their sleeves as well.

Turning the spoken word into the written word and using direct and indirect quotation were discussed in Chapter 7. In this chapter and the next we will analyze news stories that are made up almost entirely of direct and indirect quotation and summary based on what a speaker or speakers said.

This chapter will deal primarily with stories about speeches and explain in some detail the writing of leads. The chapter that follows will discuss the writing of a variety of stories based on speech — public meetings, trials, hearings, panel discussions, interviews and, of course, speeches.

The Speech Story Lead

The lead of a story reporting a speech is the first unit or section of the story. It may consist of a single paragraph in a very brief story, or it may be as long as three or four paragraphs. For example:

> The U.S. Supreme Court does not have the last word on the constitutional questions it decides, Justice Sandra Day O'Connor told a University of Wyoming audience yesterday.
>
> Citizens — through lawsuits, elected officials and public opinion — have the final say on how the Constitution is interpreted, she said.
>
> "Much as it might seem otherwise, the Constitution was not written as a full employment plan for the judiciary," O'Connor told a packed auditorium audience.
>
> "On the contrary, the Constitution is interpreted first and last by people other than judges."
> — Denver *Rocky Mountain News*

The first paragraph of this lead is a summary statement that presents in a few words the major point that the speaker made. The second paragraph clarifies or makes the point just presented a bit more specific. The third and fourth paragraphs, direct quotation from the speaker, add emphasis to the points made in the first two paragraphs.

The four-paragraph structure of this lead moves from the general to the very specific. It gives the reader a little more information at each step. As a whole it tells the reader clearly what the speech was all about: major emphasis, identity of the speaker and where and when the speech was made. The writer can now go on and give readers a fuller explanation of the speaker's views in the body of the story.

The Summary Lead

The starting point of a speech story, as this lead shows, is a one-paragraph summary. It consists of a *statement* of what the speaker said and *attribution*. In this example, the attribution comes first, the statement follows:

> Civil rights activist James Meredith said here Sunday that subtle racism in the North is much more difficult to overcome than the overt racism of the South.

The first part of this summary is attribution:

> Civil rights activist James Meredith said here Sunday that . . .

The statement of what the speaker said is linked to the attribution by the word *that*. The attribution is brief, limited to the speaker's name, a three-word identification of the speaker and a time element.

The statement is the meat of the lead:

> . . . subtle racism in the North is much more difficult to overcome than the overt racism of the South.

This is the news writer's version of what the speaker told his audience. It is brief, but it gives essential information about the subject of the speech, the speaker's point of view and the general tone of his remarks. It is a good starting place.

The statement in this first paragraph is a summary. It can be derived from the speech in one of several ways. It may be a concise statement of the general thrust of the speaker's remarks. It may be a summary of the major point that the speaker made. Or it may be a summary of one of the major points in the speech. The statement, too, is in the news writer's words, not the speaker's — it is a paraphrase, not a direct quotation. Some further examples of summary statements follow, with the statements italicized for emphasis:

> *Secondary school teachers must give their students more individual attention*, the state superintendent of public instruction told the faculty of the College of Education here Monday.

> *Pollution must be controlled if the Great Lakes are to survive*, John Coleman, director of the Department of Natural Resources, said here Monday.

227

> *Farmers are facing the worst economic crisis since the Depression,* the dean of the College of Agriculture said here Friday.

The attribution, as you can see from these examples, is concise. It should identify the speaker either by name or by a descriptive statement and tell where and when the speech was given. Although the word *here* is redundant in stories with datelines, in local stories words or phrases like *here* or *on campus* can be used in the lead to point out briefly that the story is a local story. If further explanation is necessary, it can be inserted in the body of the story. Sometimes the nature of the audience should be indicated, at least in a general way.

Variation in the Lead

This first paragraph of a speech story lead consisting of a summary statement and attribution can be arranged in a number of ways. The arrangement the writer chooses will depend on which of the various elements the writer wants to emphasize. The writer may want to give the speaker more emphasis. Or the thrust of the speech may seem to require the greater emphasis. Sometimes it makes the story more meaningful to emphasize the audience.

The beginning news writer will soon see that there are a number of fairly standard approaches to the writing of speech leads. Certain recognizable and re-usable patterns provide a framework and guide for the beginner learning to write about what people say.

Attribution plus Statement

One of the most common patterns — and probably the easiest to use — is the attribution-plus-statement structure, which puts the speaker's name first. This arrangement obviously emphasizes the identity of the speaker. It recognizes the fact that the importance of the speaker frequently accounts for the importance of what was said, that the source of the story has a great deal to do with its importance and credibility. A diagram of an attribution-plus-statement lead looks like this:

_____ said _____ _____
speaker's name   *where*   *when*

(that) _____
                        statement of what was said

The opening paragraph of speech leads that take this approach looks like this:

> Gov.-elect Roy Romer yesterday said he'll pull talent from private industry into government service and restructure the state hierarchy to spur economic development in Colorado.
> — Denver *Rocky Mountain News*

> Cook County Board President George W. Dunne Thursday said the campaign in which he is involved with board member Bernard Carey is the dirtiest in his political career.
> — *Chicago Sun-Times*

Note that in these leads the attribution not only names the speaker but further identifies him by giving the title of the office he holds.

Statement plus Attribution

A shift in emphasis is accomplished when the statement is placed first and the attribution after it. Now the emphasis is on what was said rather than on who said it. We can diagram this statement-plus-attribution lead like this:

statement of what was said		
_____ said	_____	_____
speaker's name	*where*	*when*

Leads of this type are generally used when the subject matter of the speech, what was said, is interesting or significant and when the speaker's name might not be immediately recognizable by newspaper readers. This is the news first–source second approach we have followed in other types of news stories. For example:

> Tennessee's rural communities have been shaded from the Sunbelt growth around them in the state's urban areas, Tennessee's senior U.S. senator said Tuesday.
> — *Chattanooga Times*

> Black Americans are paid less than whites for their work, are more often unemployed, and more of their families are below poverty level, a University of Michigan professor said Sunday.
> — *United Press International*

Audience plus Statement

In some stories about speeches, it is important to emphasize another element: the nature of the audience the speaker addressed. This is often interesting, sometimes highly significant, and when it is, we emphasize who was being addressed rather than who was doing the addressing or what the speaker said. We can diagram this lead like this:

_____ was told _____ _____
audience *where* *when*

(that) _____
statement of what was said

This type of lead puts the emphasis on the audience by putting it first. The speaker's name is not even included in the first paragraph, so this lead is in a sense a blind lead. An example:

> More than 1,750 South Carolina Baptists were urged Tuesday to lobby Gov.-elect Carroll Campbell and the state Legislature to stop sex education in public schools and to oppose abortion on demand.
> — *Greenville* (S.C.) *News*

Audience and Speaker

It is possible to include both an identification of the audience and the name of the speaker in the speech lead, thus:

_____ told _____ _____ _____
speaker *audience* *where* *when*

(that) _____
statement of what was said

> The chairman of the House Banking Committee told members of the nation's savings and loan industry on

Monday that they must clean up the problems in their
industry or Congress will do it for them.
— *Associated Press*

This lead could also be turned around to put greater emphasis on
the audience:

Members of the nation's savings and loan industry
were told Monday by the chairman of the House Banking Committee that they must clean up their act . . .

The lead could also be handled this way:

Members of the nation's savings and loan industry
heard the chairman of the House Banking Committee
Monday say that they must clean up their act . . .

To review briefly, the first sentence — the first paragraph of the
speech story lead — consists of two elements: a statement of what the
speaker said and an attribution. The statement represents the contents
of the speech. The attribution identifies the speaker and also identifies
at least in a general way the time and place of the speech. The attribution may sometimes include the audience.
Further, remember that the statement is a summary. It gives in the
writer's words the gist of what the speaker was telling the audience.

Brevity in the Lead

One of the essentials of a good lead is conciseness. This is not always
easy to achieve, of course. For example, while it may be possible to
present a brief and succinct statement of what the speaker said in the
first paragraph, it may not always be possible to be concise in the
attribution. Including the name of the speaker, some further identification and the where and when may make that first sentence too long and
complicated for easy reading. To keep the first sentence short, concise
and readable, the writer can fall back on two useful devices: the *blind
lead* and the *delayed-identification lead*. We have seen how these devices
work in other types of leads.

Blind Leads

Like other blind leads, the blind lead on the speech story fully identifies the speaker in the second paragraph:

A nationally known nutrition expert said here Monday that malnutrition threatens the unborn of American middle class women as well as those of poor women.

Dr. Myron Winick, director of the Institute of Human Nutrition at Columbia University College of Physicians and Surgeons, said that . . .

A blind lead makes it possible to avoid starting off with an unfamiliar name, a name either not known to readers or not easily recalled by readers. Another example:

A Toronto psychiatrist said here yesterday that girls are three times as likely to attempt suicide as boys, but boys are four times as likely to succeed.

Dr. Barry D. Garfinkel, of Toronto's Hincks Treatment Centre, told the Ontario Psychiatric Association that of 505 teenagers and children he studied, 381 girls and 124 boys had tried to kill themselves.

— *Toronto Star*

Holding Back Attribution

In all the leads we have examined so far attribution has been closely linked to the statement of what was said. Sometimes, it is possible to separate statement and attribution and present the statement unsupported. The attribution can be brought into the lead in a second or even a third paragraph. The link between statement and source is not as strong in this type of lead, but the reader can reasonably be expected to make the connection, as the examples that follow will show. This is not a common approach, but when the news writer has trouble writing a concise statement of what the speaker said, it may be the best way to keep the first paragraph of the lead short and snappy. For example:

There's more than a glimmer of hope that by the turn of the century, Michigan's population count will have stopped climbing.

That was the good news brought to members of Lansing's Zero Population Growth group Sunday night by Dr. Kurt Gorwitz, chief of the center for health statistics of the Michigan Department of Public Health.

— *Lansing State Journal*, Lansing, Mich.

In this example, the writer has presented a concise statement of what the speaker told his audience, but the attribution was unwieldy.

By separating statement and attribution, the writer managed to keep both paragraphs short and readable. Holding back attribution this way is acceptable on occasion and should present no problems for the reader. Of course, the writer could have written a different type of lead — a blind lead or a delayed-identification lead — but this approach worked. Another example:

> Blacks must be invited to live, work, shop and play in Forsyth County.
> That's the message Roger Crow gave to some 350 business leaders Friday night as he took office as president of the Cumming-Forsyth County Chamber of Commerce.
> — *The Times*, Gainesville, Ga.

Other Considerations

The speech lead that places the statement first emphasizes what was said. It is a *what* lead. The lead that puts the name first, either the attribution-plus-statement lead or the delayed-identification lead, is a *who* lead. There are some dangers in overdoing the use of the *who* lead.

Names in the Lead

Names are supposedly the stuff of which news is made, and the *who* lead pays honor to this journalistic cliché. But the news writer must remember that the name must mean something to the reader. It must be more than a space filler. It must be a genuine attention getter. If the name of the speaker or news source is important, if it is well known, the reader will recognize it and it won't need a lot of explanation. In this case the *who* lead makes a perfectly good beginning for a speech story. If the name won't command the reader's attention and by itself lend some significance to the story, then the lead ought to be written in another way. To exaggerate a little, unless you are reporting a speech by the president, or, perhaps, the governor or a big-city mayor, don't use the *who* lead. Take another approach.

Direct-Quote Leads

Some years ago it was fashionable to use direct quotes in the lead of speech stories. Today it is not. Generally, the summary lead with its concise statement of what was said will tell more and tell it better than

233

a direct quote. The summary gives a broader view of the speech. The direct quote can usually cover only one point the speaker made. However, direct-quote leads can be used occasionally and when they are properly used can be highly effective. The following direct-quote lead sums up the speaker's thoughts quite as well as a summary statement could have:

> "Successful people don't quit," Marilyn Van Derbur, a former Miss America, told a group of high school journalists attending the Northwest Regional Media Conference in Sun Valley.
>
> — *Boise Idaho Statesman*

Direct-quote leads are not always practical. Usually, in fact, almost any other kind of lead would be better in summing up the point of a speech and directing reader attention to the body of the story that follows. The example given here suggests an appropriate use of the direct-quote lead. Where the writer has a colorful or emotional statement to use, the direct-quote lead can be very effective. Don't use this approach too often, however.

Characterizing Leads

Every lead we have discussed so far has included both a statement of what was said and an attribution. The characterizing lead is different. It describes or characterizes the speaker's message instead of presenting a summary of what the speaker said. It comments, interprets, analyzes the effect or potential effect of the speaker's message or tells how the audience was affected. The following leads show how this is done. They explain the import or impact of the speech rather than quoting from it. They avoid the statement-plus-attribution structure and find other verbs to take the place of *to say*. For example:

> North Carolina Gov. James E. Holshouser Jr. used his inaugural address Friday for another strong denunciation of the North Carolina Highway Department and for a reiteration of his campaign promises.
>
> — *Charlotte* (N.C.) *Observer*

This lead describes or characterizes the content of the gubernatorial address but does not quote from it. There is no summary of what was said, just a descriptive note. Another example:

A group of criminal justice officials Friday heard a college professor tell them what they were doing wrong.

But they didn't buy it.

Gesturing with a cigar to punctuate his points, Dr. Eugene Czajkoski told more than 100 persons attending a state criminal justice conference that "the criminal justice system is working against itself."

— *St. Petersburg Times*

The first two paragraphs of this lead explain what the speaker was doing and what effect his efforts had on his audience. The third paragraph, after a bit of description, picks up the attribution-plus-statement format and begins to deal with the content of the speech.

The characterizing lead is a perfectly good way to get into your story when the effect or import of the speech is as interesting — or more so — than the speech itself. If what the speaker said needs some clarification, the characterizing lead may be a good way to start your story.

Creative Variations

News writing, at least when it deals with routine stories, is pretty much a matter of averages. There are routine ways of doing things, workable and useful ways of saying things, basic ways of organizing various kinds of news stories that will work most of the time. But as long as news writers are human beings and not computers, the ingenious or creative news writer will find new ways of putting words together and of organizing stories. You have seen in this chapter some of the standard approaches to writing leads on speech stories and have been introduced to a couple of occasionally used variations. Here are a few more creative leads — non-standard approaches:

If you had hopes that the nation's weather might get back to something approaching normal one of these days, Dr. Iben Browning, a controversial climatologist from Albuquerque, N.M., says not to bother.

It has already happened. The erratic rainfall (or lack of it) in the West and the subfrigid weather last winter in much of the East are what he considers normal.

Bankers who heard Browning speak Friday in Lincoln found this was one of his sunnier observations.

The others ranged from bad to ominous.

— *Lincoln* (Neb.) *Journal*

235

Another approach, the question lead, is not often used but occasionally provides a good beginning for a story:

> Do Americans mean to include everyone in the American Dream?
> If so, when and how?
> That was the central question tossed in the laps of affirmative-action professionals Thursday night by still-strident Julian Bond, the Georgia legislator.
> Bond said the task before these professionals — to secure equal job and promotional opportunities for blacks and women — is made harder by enemies such as personal selfishness, the American corporate structure and "collaborators" like the NAACP.
> — *St. Petersburg Times*

There are infinite possibilities in news writing and, while the tried and trusted may generally be best, there are times when a story cries out for different treatment. You should not be afraid to experiment. It may not work, but if it does — and your editor and the copy desk like your approach — then you can take pardonable pride in your creativity and imagination.

The Lead as a Unit

For much of this chapter, we have been talking about the first paragraph of a speech lead — the statement and attribution — as if that paragraph were the entire lead. If you look back at the first example of a speech lead, you will see that it had a four-paragraph structure. The first paragraph consisted of a statement and attribution, the second of a more detailed statement of the speaker's views, the third and fourth of a direct quote building on the first two paragraphs and making the speaker's views explicit.

Let's look at another example of speech lead, in a three-paragraph structure:

> The president of the National Bureau of Economic Research said here Monday that the American economy is not in a recession, and there is no clear evidence of a recession in sight.

Dr. Martin Feldstein said economists have been talking about being in a recession for the past year, but the evidence is still fuzzy.

"So much of business still looks strong," he said.

The first paragraph is in the attribution-plus-statement format. The second paragraph names the speaker and adds to the speaker's views about the possibility of a recession. The third paragraph gives, in the speaker's own words, the clincher — his reasons for believing that there will be no recession. There is a natural flow of the speaker's views from a general statement through added detail to a specific conclusion. Another example:

Democratic gubernatorial candidate Allen E. Ertel said here Monday that his first priority as governor will be to declare war on criminals who prey on the elderly.

The elderly live in fear, he said at a news conference during which he released a position paper on the elderly.

"The elderly fear crime," he said, "because they are especially vulnerable."

Here again is a careful one, two, three buildup of the speaker's views. This three-paragraph structure is a useful one. It is shown in Figure 12.1 as a blank form into which the writer can plug the main points of a speech. The model speech leads in Figures 12.2 and 12.3 follow this format.

The speech lead, as we can now see, does a number of things all at once:

— It gives the reader a brief idea of what the speaker said. In the statement-plus-attribution format, the first paragraph gives a tight summary of what the speaker said. The second and third paragraphs enlarge on the first-paragraph summary but like the first paragraph are concise and brief.

— It identifies the speaker. The first paragraph may include a complete identification or, as in the blind lead, a partial one that is completed in the second paragraph.

— It explains the circumstances of the speech. Often it is enough in the lead to say *said here*.

_____

_____

_____, Leo Bogart said on campus Friday.

Bogart, executive vice president of the Bureau of Advertising, said

(that) _____

_____

_____.

" _____

_____

_____," he said.

Figure 12.1 *The three-paragraph structure of a speech lead. The attribution provides a framework. The writer's job is to fill in the blanks with the appropriate material from the speech.*

Gov.-elect Lewis Dexter said here Monday night that he will work with high technology industries to improve the state's faltering economy.

Dexter said that any attempts to improve the economic climate of the state must take into account the central role of the high technology industries.

"They alone," he said, "have prevented the full impact of the national recession from being felt here."

(more)

Gov.-elect Lewis Dexter said here Monday night that he will work with the state's high technology industries to improve the state's faltering economy.

Dexter, speaking at the annual meeting of the Carolton Chamber of Commerce, said that any effort to improve the economic climate of the state must take into account the central role of the high technology industries.

"They alone," he said, "have prevented the full impact of the national recession from being felt here."

(more)

Figure 12.2 *Two versions of the same lead. The second adds details about the nature of the speech in the second paragraph. Both are attribution-plus-statement leads.*

238

> The governor-elect said here Monday night that he will work with the state's high technology industries to improve the state's faltering economy.
>
> Lewis Dexter, speaking at the annual meeting of the Carolton Chamber of Commerce, said that any effort to improve the economic climate of the state must take into account the central role of the high technology industries.
>
> "They alone," he said, "have prevented the full impact of the national recession from being felt here."
>
> (more)

Figure 12.3 *A blind lead. The speaker is identified but not named in the first paragraph.*

The lead is a unit, complete in itself. It is a prelude to the body of the story. In Chapter 13, you will see how the lead is tied into the rest of the story and how the rest of the story is developed.

No-News Leads

Every lead discussed in this chapter has been a device for telling the reader something, for providing information about a speech, a press conference, an interview, a meeting. The leads have been factual and newsy. They have had content. Except for characterizing leads, the leads have all told what the speaker said. They have all used the verb *said* or an equivalent verb.

Beware of the lead that doesn't say anything — the *no-news lead*. For example:

> Flying saucers and other unidentified flying objects were the topic Sunday night at Trinity Church parish house.

> A widely known Protestant clergyman discussed the errors of the younger generation Sunday in his sermon at St. Stephen's Church.

> The state Republican chairman discussed his party's program for improving the nation's moral and economic climate in a speech on campus Monday.

To leads like these, apocryphal but entirely possible, the average reader is sure to say: "Yup, but what did he say?" These leads don't tell what was said. They hint. They go around the content, not into it. Writers who can't find anything more for their lead than the topic or title of a speech or can say only that the audience was delighted to hear the speaker's views aren't saying much.

Before a speech is given, as you will recall from the discussion of coming events stories, you tell your readers what the speaker will talk about, the topic or the title of the speech. After the speech has been delivered, you tell your readers what the speaker said.

What did these no-news leads have in common? Each of them had a weak and wishy-washy verb. You will remember the discussion in the chapter on news leads about pairing the subject of a story with an appropriate verb. The appropriate verb for a speech story is the verb *said* or appropriate alternates like *told* or *heard*. As you saw in the diagrams of speech leads earlier in this chapter, the right verb leads inevitably to a statement of what the speaker said:

> The dean of the school of journalism *said* here Monday that . . .

> Journalism students *were told* Monday that . . .

If you follow the statement-plus-attribution format suggested in this discussion and if you use the right verb — *said* or an appropriate substitute — it will be impossible not to write an informative lead. Avoid weak and non-productive verbs like *discussed*. Stick to *said*.

Remember: a no-news lead contains little more information than an advance story written days before the speech. If you don't give readers something more than they could have learned in a story published before the speech was given, then you haven't given them enough news.

Suggestions for Further Reading

Women have long had a place in — and an impact on — journalism.

Geyer, Georgie Anne. *Buying the Night Flight*. New York: Delacorte Press, 1983.
>Autobiography of a distinguished foreign correspondent who began her newspaper career on the *Chicago Daily News*.

Marzolf, Marion. *Up From the Footnote*. New York: Hastings House, 1977.
>A history of women in journalism.

Rittenhouse, Mignon. *The Amazing Nellie Bly*. New York: E.P. Dutton and Company, Inc., 1956.
>Biography of a flamboyant woman journalist of the last century.

Ross, Lillian. *Reporting.* New York: Dodd, Mead, 1982.
Seven classic pieces, including her famous "Portrait of Hemingway."

Sanders, Marion K. *Dorothy Thompson: A Legend in Her Time.* Boston: Houghton Mifflin Company, 1973.
Biography of a distinguished woman journalist whose reporting and commentary on foreign affairs was highly influential in the pre–World War II years.

Thomas, Helen. *Dateline: White House.* New York: Macmillan, 1975.
Miss Thomas reports on her years as White House correspondent for United Press International.

Transcript of President's Message to Nation on State of Union

Following is a transcript of President Reagan's State of the Union Message, delivered to Congress last night in Washington, as recorded by The New York Times:

May I congratulate all of you who are members of this historic 100th Congress of the United States of America. In this 200th anniversary year of our Constitution, you and I stand on the shoulders of giants, men whose words and deeds put wind in the sails of freedom.

However, we must always remember that our Constitution is to be celebrated not for being old, but for being young, young with the same energy, spirit and promise that filled each eventful day in Philadelphia's State House. We will be guided tonight by their acts and we will be guided forever by their words.

Now, forgive me, but I can't resist sharing a story from those historic days. Philadelphia was bursting with civic pride in the spring of 1787, and its newspapers began embellishing the arrival of the Convention delegates with elaborate social classifications.

Governors of States were called "Excellency." Justices and Chancellors had reserved for them "Honorable" with a capital "H." For Congressmen, it was "honorable" with a small "h." And all others were referred to as "the following respectable characters."

Well, for this 100th Congress, I invoke special executive powers to declare that each of you must never be titled less than Honorable with a capital "H."

Incidentally, I'm delighted you are celebrating the 100th birthday of the Congress. It's always a pleasure to congratulate someone with more birthdays than I've had.

Now, there's a new face at this place of honor tonight, and please join me in warm congratulations to the Speaker of the House, Jim Wright. Mr. Speaker, you might recall a similar situation in your very first session of Congress 32 years ago. Then, as now, the Speakership had changed hands, and another great son of Texas, Sam Rayburn — "Mr. Sam" — sat in your chair. I cannot find better words than those used by President Eisenhower that evening: "We shall have much to do together; I am sure that we will get it done, and that we shall do it in harmony and good-will."

Tonight, I renew that pledge. To you, Mr. Speaker, and to Senate majority leader Robert Byrd who brings 34 years of distinguished service to the Congress, may I say: Though there are changes in the Congress, America's interests remain the same. And I am confident that, along with Republican leaders Bob Michel and Bob Dole, this Congress can make history.

Six years ago, I was here to ask the Congress to join me in America's new beginning.

Well, the results are something of which we can all be proud. Our inflation rate is now the lowest in a quarter of a century. The prime interest rate has fallen from the 21½ percent the month before we took office to 7½ percent today and those rates have triggered the most housing starts in eight years.

The unemployment rate, still too high, is the lowest in nearly seven years and our people have created nearly 13 million new jobs. Over 61 percent of everyone over the age of 16, male and female, is employed, the highest percentage on record.

'Roll Up Our Sleeves And Go to Work'

Let's roll up our sleeves and go to work and put America's economic engine at full throttle.

We can also be heartened by our progress across the world. Most important, America is at peace tonight and freedom is on the march. And we've done much these past years to restore our defenses, our alliances and our leadership in the world. Our sons and daughters in the services once again wear their uniforms with pride.

But though we've made much progress, I have one major regret. I took a risk with regard to our action in Iran. It did not work, and for that I assume full responsibility.

The goals were worthy. I do not believe it was wrong to try to establish contacts with a country of strategic importance or to try to save lives. And certainly it was not wrong to try to secure freedom for our citizens held in barbaric captivity. But — but we did not achieve what we wished and serious mistakes were trying — made in trying to do so. We will get to the bottom of this and I will take whatever action is called for.

But in debating the past in debating the past, we must deny — not deny ourselves the successes of the future. Let it never be said of this generation of Americans that we became so obsessed with failure that we refused to take risks that could further the cause of peace and freedom in the world.

Much is at stake here and the nation and the world are watching, to see if we go forward together in the national interest, or if we let partisanship weaken us.

And let there be no mistake about American policy: We will not sit idly by if our interests or our friends in the Middle East are threatened nor will we yield to terrorist blackmail.

And now, ladies and gentlemen of the Congress, why don't we get to work?

I am pleased to report that, because of our efforts to rebuild the strength of America, the world is a safer place. Earlier this month, I submitted a budget to defend America and maintain our momentum to make up for neglect in the last decade. I ask you to vote out a defense and foreign affairs budget that says "yes" to protecting our country.

While the world is safer, it is not safe.

Since 1970, the Soviets have invested $500 billion more on their military forces than we have. Even today, though nearly 1 in 3 Soviet families is without running hot water, and the average family spends two hours a day shopping for the basic necessities of life, their Government still found the resources to transfer $75 billion in weapons to client states in the past five years, clients like Syria, Vietnam, Cuba, Libya, Angola, Ethiopia, Afghanistan and Nicaragua.

With 120,000 Soviet combat and military personnel and 15,000 military advisers in Asia, Africa and Latin America, can anyone still doubt their single-minded determination to expand their power? Despite this, the Congress cut my request for critical U.S. security assistance to free nations by 21 percent this year, and cut defense requests by $85 billion in the last three years.

'There Is No Surer Way To Lose Freedom'

These assistance programs serve our national interests as well as mutual interests, and when the programs are devastated, American interests are harmed. My friends, it's my duty as President to say to you again tonight that there is no surer way to lose freedom than to lose our resolve.

Today, the brave people of Afghanistan are showing that resolve. The Soviet Union says it wants a peaceful settlement in Afghanistan, yet it continues a brutal war and props up a regime whose days are clearly numbered. We are ready to support a political solution that guarantees the rapid withdrawal of all Soviet troops and genuine self-determination for the Afghan people.

In Central America, too, the cause of freedom is being tested. And our resolve is being tested there as well. Here, especially, the world is watching to see how this nation responds.

Today, over 90 percent of the people of Latin America live in democracy. Democracy is on the march in Central and South America. Communist Nicaragua is the odd man out, suppressing the church, the press and democratic dissent and promoting subversion in the region. We support diplomatic efforts, but these efforts can never succeed if the Sandinistas win their war against the Nicaraguan people.

Our commitment to a Western Hemisphere safe from aggression did not occur by spontaneous generation on the day that we took office. It began with the Monroe Doctrine in 1823 and continues our historic bipartisan American policy. Franklin Roosevelt — Franklin Roosevelt said we " . . . are determined to do everything possible to maintain peace on this hemisphere." President Truman was very blunt: "International Communism . . . seeks to crush and undermine and . . . destroy the independence of the Americans. . . . we can't let that happen here."

And John F. Kennedy made clear that " . . . Communist domination in this hemisphere can never be negotiated."

Some in this Congress may choose to depart from this historic commitment, but I will not.

This year— this year — this year we celebrate the second century of our Constitution. The Sandinistas just signed theirs two weeks ago, and then suspended it. We won't know how my words tonight will be reported there, for one simple reason: there is no free press in Nicaragua.

Nicaraguan freedom fighters have never asked us to wage their battle, but I will fight any effort to shut off their lifeblood and consign them to death, defeat or a life without freedom. There must be no Soviet beachhead in Central America.

We Americans have always preferred dialogue to conflict and so we always remain open to more constructive relations with the Soviet Union. But more responsible Soviet conduct around the world is a key element of the U.S.-Soviet agenda. Progress is also required on the other items of our agenda as well, real respect for human rights and more open contacts between our societies, and, of course, arms reduction.

In Iceland last October, we had one moment of opportunity that the Soviets dashed because they sought to cripple our Strategic Defense Initiative, S.D.I. I wouldn't let them do it then. I won't let them do it now or in the future. This is the most positive and promising defense program we have undertaken. It's the path, for both sides, to a safer future; a system that defends human life instead of threatening it. S.D.I. will go forward.

The United States has made serious, fair and far-reaching proposals to the Soviet Union and this is a moment of rare opportunity for arms reduction. But I will need, and American negotiators in Geneva will need, Congress's support. Enacting the Soviet negotiating position into American law would not be the way to win a good agreement. So I must tell you in this Congress I will veto any effort that undercuts our national security and our negotiating leverage.

Today, we also find ourselves engaged in expanding peaceful commerce across the world. We will work to expand our opportunities in international markets through the Uruguay round of trade negotiations and to complete an historic free trade arrangement between the world's two largest trading partners, Canada and the United States.

Our basic trade policy remains the same: we remain opposed as ever to protectionism because America's growth and future depend on trade. But we will insist on trade that is fair and free. We are always willing to be trade partners but never trade patsies.

Now from foreign borders, let us return to our own because America in the world is only as strong as America at home.

This 100th Congress has high responsibilities. I begin with a gentle reminder that many of these are simply the incomplete obligations of the past. The American people deserve to be impatient because we do not yet have the public house in order.

We've had great success in restoring our economic integrity, and we've rescued our nation from the worst economic mess since the Depression.

But there's more to do. For starters, the Federal deficit is outrageous.

For years I've asked that we stop pushing onto our children the excesses of our Government. What the Congress finally needs to do is pass a constitutional amendment that mandates a balanced budget and forces Government to live within its means. States, cities and the families of America balance their budgets. Why can't we?

Next, the budget process is a sorry spectacle. The missing of deadlines and the nightmare of monstrous continuing resolutions packing hundreds of billions of dollars of spending into one bill must be stopped.

We ask the Congress, once again: Give us the same tool that 43 Governors have, a line-item veto so we can carve out the boondoggles and pork — those items that would never survive on their own. I will send the Congress broad recommendations on the budget, but first I'd like to see yours. Let's go to work and get this done together.

Keeping 'Commitment' To Balance the Budget'

But now, let's talk about this year's budget. Even though I have submitted it within the Gramm-Rudman-Hollings deficit reduction target, I've seen suggestions that we might postpone that timetable. Well, I think the American people are tired of hearing the same old excuses. Together, we made a commitment to balance the budget, now, let's keep it.

As for those suggestions that the answer is higher taxes, the American people have repeatedly rejected that shopworn advice. They know that we don't have deficits because people are taxed too little; we have deficits because big government spends too much.

Now next month, I will place two additional reforms before the Congress.

We've created a welfare monster that is a shocking indictment of our sense of priorities. Our national welfare system consists of some 59 major programs and over 6,000 pages of Federal laws and regulations on which more than $132 billion was spent in 1985.

I will propose a new national welfare strategy, a program of welfare reform through state-sponsored, community-based demonstration projects. This is the time to reform this outmoded social dinosaur and finally break the poverty trap. Now e will never abandon those who, through no fault of their own, must have our help. But let us work to see how many can be freed from the dependency of welfare and made self-supporting, which the great majority of welfare recipients want more than anything else.

Next, let us remove a financial specter facing our older Americans, the fear of an illness so expensive that it can result in having to make an intolerable choice between bankruptcy and death. I will submit legislation shortly to help free the elderly from the fear of catastrophic illness.

Now, let's turn to the future.

It is widely said that America is losing her competitive edge. Well, that won't happen if we act now. How well prepared are we to enter the 21st century? In my lifetime, America set the standard for the world. It is now time to determine that we should enter the next century having achieved a level of excellence unsurpassed in history.

We will achieve this: first, by guaranteeing that Government does everything possible to promote America's ability to compete. Second, we must act as individuals in a quest for excellence that will not be measured by new proposals or billions in new funding. Rather, it involves an expenditure of American spirit and just plain American grit.

The Congress will soon receive my comprehensive proposals to enhance our competitiveness, including new science and technology centers and strong new funding for basic research.

The bill will include legal and regulatory reforms and weapons to fight unfair trade practices. Competitiveness also means giving our farmers a shot at participating fairly and fully in a changing world market.

Preparing for the future must begin, as always, with our children.

We need to set for them new and more rigorous goals. We must demand more of ourselves and our children by raising literacy levels dramatically by the year 2000. Our children should master the basic concepts of math and science and let's insist that students not leave high school until they have studied and understood the basic documents of our national heritage.

There's one more thing we can't let up on. Let's redouble our personal efforts to provide for every child a safe and drug-free learning environment. If our crusade against drugs succeeds with our children, we will defeat that scourge all over our country.

Finally, let's stop suppressing the spiritual core of our national being. Our nation could not have been conceived without divine help. Why is it that we can build a nation with our prayers but we can't use a schoolroom for voluntary prayer? The 100th Congress of the United States should be remembered as the one that ended the expulsion of God from America's classrooms.

The quest for excellence into the 21st century begins in the schoolroom but must go next to the workplace. More than 20 million new jobs will be created before the new century unfolds, and, by then, our economy should be able to provide a job for everyone who wants to work.

We must also enable our workers to adapt to the rapidly changing nature of the workplace and I will propose substantial new Federal commitments keyed to retraining and job mobility.

Over the next few weeks, I'll be sending the Congress a complete series of these special messages, on budget reform, welfare reform, competitiveness, including education, trade, worker training and assistance, agriculture and other subjects.

The Congress can give us these tools, but to make these tools work, it really comes down to just being our best. And that's the core of American greatness.

The responsibility of freedom presses us toward higher knowledge and, I believe, moral and spiritual greatness. Through lower taxes and smaller government, government has its ways of freeing people's spirits. But only we, each of us, can let the spirit soar against our own individual standards.

Excellence is what makes freedom ring. And isn't that what we do best?

We're entering our third century now, but it's wrong to judge our nation by its years. The calendar can't measure America because we were meant to be an endless experiment in freedom, with no limit to our reaches, no boundaries to what we can do, no end point to our hopes.

The United States Constitution is the impassioned and inspired vehicle by which we travel through history. It grew out of the most fundamental inspiration of our existence: that we are here to serve Him by living free, that living free releases in us the noblest of impulses and the best of our abilities. That we would use these gifts for good and generous purposes and would secure them not just for ourselves, and for our children, but for all mankind.

Over the years — over the years, and I won't count if you don't — nothing has been so heartwarming to me as speaking to America's young. And the little ones especially, so fresh-faced and so eager to know. Well, from time to time, I've been with them, they will ask about our Constitution. And I hope you members of Congress will not deem this a breach of protocol if you'll permit me to share these thoughts again with the young people who might be listening or watching this evening.

I have read the constitutions of a number of countries, including the Soviet Union's. Now some people are surprised to hear that they have a constitution, and it even supposedly grants a number of freedoms to its people. Many countries have written into their constitution provisions for freedom of speech and freedom of assembly. But if this is true, why is the Constitution of the United States so exceptional?

Well, the difference is so small that it almost escapes you, but it's so great it tells you the whole story in just three words: We the People.

In those other constitutions, the Government tells the people of those countries what they are allowed to do. In our Constitution, we the people tell the Government what it can do and it can do onlb those things listed in that document and no others.

Virtually every other revolution in history has just exchanged one set of rulers for another set of rulers. Our revolution is the first to say the people are the masters and government is their servant.

And you young people out there, don't ever forget that. Someday, you could be in this room, but wherever you are, America is depending on you to reach your highest and be your best, because here in America, we the people are in charge.

Just three words, some words.

'This Unique Breed We Call Americans'

We the people. Those are the kids on Christmas Day looking out from a frozen sentry post on the 38th Parallel in Korea or aboard an aircraft carrier in the Mediterranean. A million miles from home. But doing their duty.

We the people. Those are the warm-hearted whose numbers we can't begin to count who'll begin the day with a little prayer for the hostages they will never know and M.I.A. families they will never meet. Why? Because that's the way we are, this unique breed we call Americans.

We the people. They're farmers on tough times, but who never stop feeding a hungry world. They're the volunteers at the hospital choking back their tears for the hundredth time caring for a baby struggling for life because of a mother who used drugs. And you'll forgive me a special memory, it's a million mothers like Nellie Reagan who never knew a stranger or turned a hungry person away from her kitchen door.

We the people. They refute last week's television commentary downgrading our optimism and our idealism. They are the entrepreneurs, the builders, the pioneers, and a lot of regular folks, the true heroes of our land who make up the most uncommon nation of doers in history. You know they're Americans because their spirit is as big as the universe, and their hearts are bigger than their spirits.

We the people. Starting the third century of a dream and standing up to some cynic who's trying to tell us we're not going to get any better.

Are we at the end? Well, I can't tell it any better than the real thing, a story recorded by James Madison from the final moments of the Constitutional Convention, Sept. 17, 1787. As the last few members signed the document, Benjamin Franklin — the oldest delegate at 81 years, and in frail health — looked over toward the chair where George Washington daily presided. At the back of that chair was painted the picture of a sun on the horizon. And turning to those sitting next to him, Franklin observed that artists found it difficult in their painting to distinguish between a rising and a setting sun.

Well, I know if we were there, we could see those delegates sitting around Franklin, leaning in to listen more closely to him. And then Dr. Franklin began to share his deepest hopes and fears about the outcome of their efforts, and this is what he said:

"I have often . . . looked at that picture behind the President without being able to tell whether it was a rising or setting sun: But now at length I have the happiness to know that it is a rising and not a setting sun."

Well, you can bet it's rising, because, my fellow citizens, America isn't finished, her best days have just begun.

Thank you. God bless you and God bless America.

The Reagan Years: How He Viewed the State of the Union

1982

President Reagan, buoyed by his early success in winning a 25 percent cut in income taxes over three years, announced a sweeping plan to give states and localities control over Federal programs costing $47 billion a year by 1984. He spoke of what he called the "truly ominous" situation when he took office a year before. "Americans' faith in their governmental process was steadily declinining," he said, a result of "decades of tax and tax spend and spend." But he insisted that "an era of American renewal" had begun.

1983

With the economy having just pulled out of a recession that lasted most of Mr. Reagan's first two years, the President's message dealt heavily with economic problems, and he urged Congress to support a broad freeze in non-military domestic spending. He called for a "standby" tax increase of up to $50 billion a year for the fiscal years 1986-88. But polls showed that many Americans did not support some of the President's policies, particularly the military buildup and the soaring budget deficits, and that they believed he had not done enough to reduce unemployment.

1984

In a speech that would set the tone for the Presidential campaign, Mr. Reagan said the nation had gained renewed hope since he took office, and he again focused on reducing Federal spending. Declaring that the United States was "safer, stronger and more secure" than before, he said his Administration was ready to negotiate in earnest with the Russians on all issues.

He endorsed the idea of large increases in military and economic aid to Central America and defended the American presence in Lebanon.

1985

Mr. Reagan urged the nation to forge "a second American revolution of hope and opportunity," with an agenda of economic growth and elimination of the threat of nuclear war. He also proposed a sweeping overhaul of the nation's tax code.

In a year in which Americans increasingly blamed foreign trade for the loss of jobs and supported restrictions on imports, Mr. Reagan said the Administration would study potential changes in trade policy and urged a new round of trade negotiations next year.

1986

The President's message was delayed for a week by the explosion of the space shuttle Challenger. Mr. Reagan singled out the American family as a major theme of the remainder of his term. He proposed a study on the nation's welfare system and what he termed the "web of dependency" among recipients.

The speech, shorter and with fewer specific domestic proposals than usual, came shortly after passage of the budget-balancing law and reflected uncertainty as to its impact on spending.

The New York Times

The President on Iran

Nov. 24 "I am not going to lie about that. I did not make a mistake."

Nov. 25 "I believe our foreign policy goals toward Iran were well founded. However, the information brought to my attention yesterday convinced me that in one aspect, implementation of that policy was seriously flawed."

Nov. 29 "So, while we've been occupied with the Iranian issue over the past two weeks, let's not forget that there are many other issues that concern us."

Dec. 1 "If actions in implementing my policy were taken without my authorization, knowledge or concurrence, this will be exposed and appropriate corrective steps will be taken."

Dec. 6 "While we are still seeking all the facts, it's obvious that the execution of these policies was flawed and mistakes were made."

Dec. 16 "There is urgent need for full disclosure of all facts surrounding the Iranian controversy. I want to get this information out. We must get on with the business at hand and put this issue behind us. It is my desire to have the full story about Iran come out now — the alleged transfer of funds, the Swiss bank accounts, who was involved — everything."

Jan. 27 "But though we have made much progress, I have one major regret. I took a risk with regard to our action in Iran. It did not work, and for that I assume full responsibility. . . . We did not achieve what we wished, and serious mistakes were made in trying to do so. We will get to the bottom of this, and I will take whatever action is called for."

13 Writing the Speech Story

Good reporting, what the reporter observes, experiences, reacts to, provides the reader with the rich details, the examples, the adroit similes — drawn from the action not the old cliché basket — that put him at the scene of the story, make him a part of it or at least a front row spectator.

Hugh Mulligan
of the Associated Press

One way to let newspaper readers know what was said at a speech, meeting, public hearing or trial is to print a verbatim text. Then readers, if they have the time and patience, can pick out the points that interest them and make their own decisions as to what in the text was significant.

This is not done very often in the newspaper world. In the first place, most newspapers do not have the space to print long transcripts. In the second place, it is the newspaper's job to evaluate and select what is interesting and significant in the day's news and to present it to readers in a concise and readable form. The success of *Time* magazine and *USA Today* ought to convince any skeptic that the reading public appreciates news that is selected, edited and presented in a readable and even entertaining fashion.

So reporters who cover speeches, meetings, trials or public hearings must take notes, tape the speech or verify a prepared text and then prepare a short, edited version for their readers. Some newspapers will, as a matter of record, publish the text of a significant speech — and occasionally verbatim testimony from a trial or public hearing — but they also invariably print a story that digests the text. Some readers will read both text and news story. Most readers will prefer the news story.

The New York Times, which considers itself a newspaper of record, publishes many verbatim texts. For example, the *Times* always publishes the text of the president's annual State of the Union address to Congress. But, at the same time, the *Times* also publishes a detailed news story about the president's address, reporting what he said, what the various points meant, the reaction of members of Congress and the impact of the speech on the public and various political constituencies.

In this chapter, we will look first at stories reporting speeches, then at other stories based entirely or in large part on the spoken word. Many speech stories — that is, stories based on the spoken word — are routine once you get the hang of writing a good lead, of summarizing and paraphrasing. Other speech stories — for example, city council meetings, public hearings or trials — will require careful reporting not only of what was said but also of what was done — votes on issues before the council, decisions by planning boards or hearing examiners, a judge's decision or other matters that may affect the outcome of a trial. This chapter deals only with the reporting and writing of what was said, with the problems of dealing with quotation, with paraphrase and summary.

The Single-Speaker Story

If you are assigned to report a lengthy and perhaps technical speech, your job will be to select, to summarize and to interpret the speech for your readers. You will have to edit the speech, select the interesting and important parts and structure your story so that it is clear and coherent. Above all, you will have to reduce the great many words in the speech to the few words you will be allowed for your story. You will have to select what ought to be included and eliminate what ought not to be included. To do this well, you must, first of all, understand what was said. You must summarize lengthy passages and paraphrase much of the speaker's message. And you must include, when appropriate, some of the speaker's words in accurate direct and indirect quotation.

The job of boiling down a long speech, of condensing a whole day's testimony at a trial or summarizing the often confusing give and take of a city council meeting is not an easy one.

Roger Tatarian, former vice president and editor of United Press International, had this to say about reporting in general and the speech story in particular:

> Far more is involved than getting the exact number of dead or quoting the man's exact words. It also involves tone, emphasis, nuance, juxtaposition and similar

difficult-to-define factors that very distinctly affect the credibility of the press. If a journalist is not sensitive to these he can produce a story that may be technically correct in specific detail, but a bad story nevertheless.

The longer the speech and the more controversial the subject, the greater the dangers inherent in trying to condense to a few paragraphs or even a few hundred words.

Structure

Figure 13.1 is an example of the end product of such a process of selecting, eliminating, summarizing and paraphrasing. The speaker's text may have been 10 or 12 typewritten pages long, but the published story runs to just over 400 words, including three paragraphs of biographical background at the end.

The story consists of a three-paragraph lead, a bridge, the development and a concluding section of background information. The diagram in Figure 13.2 makes this structure clear. In this story, since most of the background is not directly related to what the speaker said, it is held back until the end. In other stories, it may be appropriate to include background material earlier and to tie it to the subject matter of the speech.

In the Clark speech, for example, some of the background could easily have been added to the lead to make clearer to readers who the speaker was. Compare the following paragraphs to the second paragraph of the speech as it appears in Figure 13.1:

> The Hon. Tom C. Clark, who served on the U.S. Supreme Court from 1949 to 1967, spoke at the Rio Rico Inn.
> He told his audience that one of the main problems besetting the justice system is that the public does not take an interest.

In the speech story in Figure 13.3, background or explanation is brought into the story immediately after the three-paragraph lead and serves as a bridge or springboard for moving the reader into the body of the story.

Development

In the story about the Clark speech, the development is a series of blocks or units, each dealing with a separate topic. The story covers five topics in all, including the first, which is covered in the lead.

Improved justice in Arizona called responsibility of public

NOGALES — An improved quality of justice in Arizona is the responsibility of the people of Arizona, a retired associate justice of the U.S. Supreme Court told Town Hall participants here yesterday.

Speaking at the Rio Rico Inn, the Hon. Tom C. Clark said one of the main problems besetting the justice system is that the public does not take an interest.

"They do not want to get involved," he said. "They want to stay away from the courthouse."

Clark complimented the sponsor of Town Hall — The Arizona Academy — for selecting "The Adequacy of Arizona's Court System" as the discussion topic, but asked why it waited until the 22nd semi-annual meeting to wrestle with the subject.

Clark attacked the traditional election of judges. He called for the establishment of an "Arizona plan, a merit plan" for the selection of judges.

"It costs money for a judge to run for election," he said. "It cost one judge I know $500,000 for a campaign.

"Where does he get the money? From lawyer friends mostly. I tell you it's dangerous to have the subconscious knocking in the back of a judge's head when one of his financial supporters is trying a case before him.

"We must abolish this system of electing judges."

Clark asked the delegates to consider structural changes in the court system that would include bringing justice of the peace courts and municipal courts under the control and supervision of state rules of order and procedure.

"The structure of Arizona's courts is good," he said, "except for this base, this foundation."

He also suggested that Arizona Town Hall panelists look into the possibility of establishing conciliation courts to handle the large number of domestic relations cases clogging Superior Court calendars.

Another area needing examination, he said, is to consider the omnibus hearing prior to criminal trials. In this hearing, attorneys will make all the pretrial motions.

"I guarantee that by use of this type of hearing you'll get from 90 to 95 percent guilty pleas without having to plea bargain," he said.

Clark, 74, was born in Dallas, Tex., and received his law degree from the University of Texas in 1921. In 1922, he was admitted to the Texas Bar Association and the Texas Supreme Court.

He served as civil district attorney for Dallas County from 1922 to 1927. He was appointed assistant attorney general in charge of the anti-trust division of the Department of Justice in 1943 and held that post until he became U.S. Attorney General in 1945.

He served as Associate Justice of the U.S. Supreme Court from 1949 to 1967.

— *The Arizona Republic,*
Phoenix

Figure 13.1 *This well-organized speech story follows a topical outline. The fourth paragraph provides a bridge from the lead to the body of the story.*

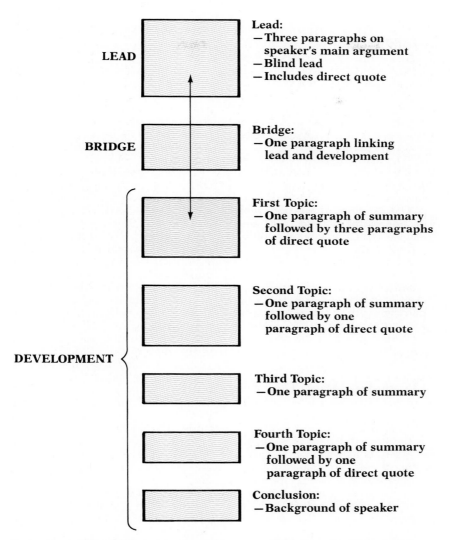

LEAD

Lead:
—Three paragraphs on
 speaker's main argument
—Blind lead
—Includes direct quote

BRIDGE

Bridge:
—One paragraph linking
 lead and development

DEVELOPMENT

First Topic:
—One paragraph of summary
 followed by three paragraphs
 of direct quote

Second Topic:
—One paragraph of summary
 followed by one
 paragraph of direct quote

Third Topic:
—One paragraph of summary

Fourth Topic:
—One paragraph of summary
 followed by one
 paragraph of direct quote

Conclusion:
—Background of speaker

Figure 13.2 *A diagrammatic outline of the Tom Clark speech in Figure 13.1, showing the organization and structure of the story and calling attention to the use of summary statements and direct quotation.*

1. The need for an improved quality of justice in the state.
2. The need for a better system for selecting judges.
3. The need for structural changes in the court system of the state.

Lead

Civil rights activist James H. Meredith said here Sunday that subtle racism in the North is much more difficult to overcome than the overt racism of the South.

Meredith, speaking at a memorial mass for Dr. Martin Luther King Jr., urged blacks to remember Dr. King by continuing his struggle for equal rights.

Bridge

"Dr. King's dream is not a reality," Meredith told a crowd of about 200 at St. Martin Church, 5842 S. Princeton. "We are not free."

The Roman Catholic ceremony was one of many held in Chicago to honor Dr. King, who would have been 49 Sunday.

Meredith, the first black to attend the University of Mississippi, argued that blacks are provided a lower quality of education in Northern public school systems such as Chicago's.

Body of the story

"You can be enslaved by not being given the proper opportunity to get an education. . . . That is a freedom denied just as much as when (former Mississippi Gov.) Ross Barnett didn't want me to go to the University of Mississippi," Meredith added.

Because the type of racism in the North is less visible, he said, it probably will last longer.

"If I wanted to discriminate, I would do it the way they do it in Chicago," Meredith later told reporters. "It is much more smooth and likely to succeed."

Meredith, who now lives in Jackson, Miss., called Mississippi "the most integrated state" in the country.

"But while Dr. King's work changed the South," Meredith said, "I don't think he made any dent in Chicago."

He praised Dr. King, whom he first met in 1960, as a "man of action."

Meredith said he met Dr. King again in Jackson in 1961 after black college students were arrested for using the city's public library. Dr. King had been invited to back the students.

"The people had invited him to come, but everyone in Mississippi was afraid to pick him up at the airport," Meredith recalled. "They were afraid that the police might do something, afraid that the Klan might do something." Meredith said he drove out to meet Dr. King and found him alone at the airport.

Meredith said the young people in the audience might find this story hard to believe, but fear "still pervaded and controlled" blacks in the Deep South throughout much of the 1960s.

He also recalled that after he was shot by a sniper in Mississippi in 1966 while on a march from Memphis to Jackson, Dr. King visited him in the hospital and continued the march.

"He came because he also wanted to alleviate this fear. . . . He pledged to continue, and he did," Meredith said. "I only went 23 miles. He went 200."

Meredith said part of Dr. King's power was his ability to relate to everyone, no matter how poor or uneducated. "He was indeed a simple man and he dealt with people on a simple basis."

— *Chicago Sun-Times*

Figure 13.3 *This speech story has a block of transitional paragraphs that form a bridge tying together the lead and the body of the story.*

4. A suggestion for a new kind of court, a conciliation court.

5. A suggestion for a new kind of pretrial hearing, an omnibus hearing.

Each block begins with a summary statement, and all but one of the summaries are followed by a direct quotation that enlarges upon and supports the summary, as you can see by studying Figure 13.1.

Think back for a moment to the three-paragraph structure of the speech story lead. It started with a concise summary followed by two paragraphs of supporting information in the form of direct and indirect quotation. The development of the speech story can be handled in much the same way. Each point the speaker made is introduced by a concise summary statement. This is followed by one, two, three or more paragraphs of supporting matter. Each point or topic and its supporting paragraphs form a block or unit. The length of each unit will depend, of course, on how much time the speaker devoted to it and on how important the writer considers that particular point.

Now let's look again at the story about the Clark speech. The speaker's main point, that the state needs an improved system of justice, is covered in the three-paragraph lead.

The fourth paragraph is a bridging paragraph that takes the story on from the lead with its introduction of the main thrust of the speaker's message to other points the speaker made. The other topics are clearly introduced.

1. Clark attacked . . .

2. Clark asked . . .

3. He also suggested . . .

4. Another area needing examination, he said . . .

The block in the Clark story beginning *Clark attacked*, for example, consists of a paragraph of summary that includes a partial quote and three paragraphs of direct quotation. The next block, beginning *Clark asked*, consists of a single paragraph of summary followed by a single paragraph of direct quotation. The block beginning *He also suggested* consists of a single paragraph of summary.

Another example of a topic block appeared in an Associated Press story about an interview with *Washington Post* editor Ben Bradlee:

> The most noticeable change in Washington in 20 years has been an increase in deception by government, Bradlee said.
>
> "Under the veil of national security the government tries to slip past the people an awful lot that has nothing to do with national security," he said.

These examples suggest a simple approach to organizing the development of a speech story. Break the speech down into a number of topics or points to be covered. Treat each of these as a block or unit. Introduce each block with a summary statement explaining the point the speaker is making. Follow that with one or more paragraphs of direct quotation, indirect quotation or additional summary. Make an effort to use direct quotation in each block.

The lead of the Clark speech fairly summarized the speaker's main point, that he wanted to see improvements in the state's courts. Each point made in the body of the story represented an example of the changes or improvements the speaker sought. Every topic related clearly to the summary statement in the first paragraph of the lead. Quite often, however, a speaker will make several interesting or important points, and the writer will have to pick one of these for the lead and treat the others in the body of the story.

It is important, too, to remember that a three-paragraph lead may not cover all that should be said about the topic you selected for the lead. If there is more to be said, go on, write a few more paragraphs before moving to other matters.

It is most important, finally, to understand the structure and organization of the speech you are reporting. Speakers start out slowly. They present less important ideas first and build up to their main point at the end of the speech. A news story does just the opposite. News stories put the best stuff in the lead, the less interesting or important toward the end. In writing about a speech, keep in mind that you can't go through the speech as it was presented and write it in that order. You are more likely to find your lead in the last few minutes of a speech than in the speaker's slow introduction to the topic. Your story must be organized logically, not chronologically.

Selecting and Eliminating

As important as knowing how to write a speech story is knowing what to write about. In other words, out of the mass of material at hand, the news writer has to decide which ideas to include in a story and which to eliminate. There is always much more material available than can be included in a story. The text of a 30-minute speech is a formidable document. The text of a presidential press conference could fill two newspaper pages.

It is essential that the writer understand the speech, know what the speaker was saying. If the writer has a firm grasp of the speaker's message, he can select the main points the speaker is making, summarize, select appropriate direct quotes and indirect quotes and discard the details.

Something is certainly lost in this process: some of the speaker's ideas, many details, various nuances and shades of meaning and the color and vigor of the speaker's words in their original sequence and in their oral presentation. However, something is gained: a concise news story covering all the speaker's main points in a form that may be read quickly and easily by hundreds, thousands or millions of people who were outside the range of the speaker's voice when the speech was delivered.

Paraphrasing and Summarizing

Once the news writer has decided what parts of a speech to use, the next job is to write as concise a story as possible. Concise does not necessarily mean brief. It does, however, mean direct and precise. The news writer must make use of summary and paraphrase to a large extent and, to a much lesser extent, of direct and indirect quotation.

Direct and Indirect Quotation

Direct and indirect quotation play an important part in any speech story. Direct quotation of the participants in a news event puts them into the story and enables them to speak directly to the newspaper reader. This point and some of the mechanics of handling direct and indirect quotation were discussed in an earlier chapter. Now we want to look at some other aspects of the use of quotation.

You will find as you write stories about speeches, public meetings, trials and hearings that a news story is not the same thing as a transcript. A transcript is an exact report of what was said — in other words, a verbatim report.

A news story about a speech, a trial or a public hearing will include some of the speaker's exact words — that is, direct quotation. It will also include indirect quotation, paraphrase of what a speaker said and summary that condenses lengthy passages of direct quotation. The news story may also add explanatory matter and will, of course, include attribution.

Liman: You testified that one reason that Mr. Casey was excited about the plan for use of the residuals was that he wanted to have a funded organization that he could pull off the shelf to do other operations. Is that what in essence his view was?

North: Director Casey had in mind, as I understood it, an overseas entity that was capable of conducting operations or activities of assistance to the U.S. foreign policy goals that was a "stand alone," it was . . . self-financing, independent of appropriated monies and capable of conducting activities similar to the ones that we had conducted here. There were other countries that were suggested that might be the beneficiaries of that kind of support — other activities to include counterterrorism.

Liman: Now, Director Casey was in charge of the CIA and had at his disposal an operations directorate, correct?

North: Certainly.

Liman: And, as I understand your testimony, Director Casey was proposing to you that a CIA outside the CIA be created, fair?

North: No.

Liman: Well, wasn't this an organization that would be able to do covert policy to advance U.S. foreign policy interests?

North: Well, not necessarily covert. The director was interested in the ability to have an existing — as he put it — off-the-shelf, self-sustaining, stand-alone entity that could perform certain activities on behalf of the United States.

Liman: You understood that the CIA is funded by the United States government, correct?

North: That is correct.

Liman: You understood that the United States government put certain limitations on what the CIA could do, correct?

North: That is correct.

Liman: And I ask you today, after all you've gone through, are you not shocked that the director of central intelligence is proposing to you the creation of an organization to do these things outside of his own organization?

North: Counsel, I can tell you that I am not shocked. I don't see that it was necessarily inconsistent with the laws, regulations, statutes and all that obtain.

WASHINGTON — Lt. Col. Oliver North yesterday rejected suggestions that he had helped run "a secret government within our government," but acknowledged that the late CIA Director, William J. Casey, had wanted the Iran-contra initiative to spawn a permanent apparatus that could run a wide range of secret operations.

North said Casey, who died in May, "was interested in the ability to have an off-the-shelf, self-sustaining entity to do certain activities on behalf of the United States."

Arthur L. Liman, the Senate counsel who did most of yesterday's questioning, asked North whether he was "shocked" that Casey had wanted to create "a CIA outside the CIA."

North said he was not.

Figure 13.4 *At left, from United Press International, excerpts from testimony by Lt. Col. Oliver L. North during the Iran-contra hearings conducted by a joint Senate and House committee of the Congress. At right, excerpts from a* Boston Globe *story reporting this part of North's testimony.*

You can see an example of this in Figure 13.4, which shows a portion of testimony given during a Congressional hearing and excerpts from a news story in the *Boston Globe* based on the testimony. In this instance, the *Globe* published the verbatim testimony in addition to its news story — a sort of sidebar — because of the considerable reader interest in the witness.

Problems with Quotation

Reporters covering speeches occasionally have an advance text to follow as the speech is given. But reporters covering public meetings, trials or hearings must depend on their own ability to hear and understand what is said, to take notes that summarize and paraphrase but also to get some passages of direct quotation.

When you do have a prepared text in front of you, you may find some difficulty in making use of the speaker's words. Speeches are made for oral delivery and include many rhetorical devices that help speakers in their delivery and enable them to relate more closely to their audiences. Such devices usually have to be edited out or revised in writing a news story about the speech. Here, for example, is a verbatim passage from a speech:

> All these rights come from the people, and in their Bill of Rights combined with the Fourteenth Amendment, they say they want both — a free press and a fair trial — and it is up to the responsible people in law and in journalism to see that the people have both.
>
> And if we don't see to it — you in your profession and I in mine — then we are both false to our responsibility, and democracy is in trouble.

Now, look at the news writer's version of this passage:

> Kavanaugh, addressing the kick-off luncheon of the 98th annual Michigan Press Assn. meeting at Kellogg Center, said the American people by virtue of the Bill of Rights want both a free press and a fair trial.
>
> "It is up to the responsible people in law and in journalism to see that the people have both," he said.
>
> "And if we don't see to it, then we both are false to our responsibility and democracy is in trouble."
>
> — *The State News*, East Lansing, Mich.

253

The first paragraph of the text becomes two paragraphs in the news story. The first paragraph of the news story paraphrases the text. The second picks up a direct quotation. The writer has taken advantage of the break in the speaker's long sentence provided by the insertion "a free press and a fair trial" and has broken off the last part of the sentence and quoted it directly. The second direct quotation is altered a bit, too. But there has been no alteration in the meaning of the speaker's words. All the writer did was eliminate the parenthetical phrase "you in your profession and I in mine," which may have been an effective device in the oral presentation of the speech but is not effective or even necessary in conveying the speaker's ideas to the newspaper's readers.

It is not only permissible but often necessary to do this kind of smoothing out when you use direct quotation in a news story. Unless you overdo it and alter the meaning of the speaker's words, no one will question your revisions. You will find that you have to do much more smoothing out when you work from your own notes or from a transcript of a spontaneous or unrehearsed speech than when you have a prepared text to work from. The average person does not speak in complete sentences nor in direct and concise language.

Indirect quotation, of course, does not purport to be a speaker's exact words and so can be edited or revised somewhat more than direct quotation. The following sentence, for example, comes from the prepared text quoted earlier:

> That citizen wants his press to be free and he wants his trials to be fair, and I don't think he has much patience with the idea of either one infringing on the other one.

The news writer paraphrased it in this way:

> The citizen wants his press to be free and his trials to be fair, and he has little patience with the idea of either one infringing on the other, the editors were told.
> — *The State News*, East Lansing, Mich.

The changes are minor. The news writer changed the original from "I don't think he has much patience" to "he has little patience." Here is another sentence from the text:

> If an attorney makes statements that convict a defendant before he is tried, the fault lies with the sense of responsibility of that attorney, and not with the newspaper which prints the remark.

The news writer revised this sentence a little more heavily than the last one.

> He said that if an attorney makes a prejudicial state-
> ment that convicts a defendant before he is tried, the
> fault lies with the attorney's lack of responsibility and
> not with the newspaper which prints the remark.
> — *The State News*, East Lansing, Mich.

One of the revisions that usually has to be made in lifting direct or indirect quotes out of context and putting them into a news story is a substitution of nouns for pronouns of reference. In a speech, everything is in context. When the speaker says *you*, everyone present understands that the reference is to the audience. In a long discussion of freedom of the press, the speaker may say *they* in referring to the press — newspapers, magazines and broadcast news. The audience can follow the reference without difficulty. But a news story based on only a portion of the speech will be hard to follow if the writer picks up every *we, they, you, us* and *it* the speaker used. The writer must replace the pronouns with the nouns they stood for.

The following excerpt from the text of a speech provides a good example:

> Their freedom to rage at us with accusations of cen-
> sorship, repression and McCarthyism is adequate proof
> that the alleged "chilling effect" or threat to their free-
> dom is fictional.

The pronoun *their* in the text was clear to the audience, which knew that the speaker was talking about the press because of what had been said before. The newspaper reader might not know this, however, and so the writer carefully substituted *the media* for the pronoun *their:*

> The vice president said the media's freedom "to rage
> at us with accusations of censorship, repression and
> McCarthyism is adequate proof that the alleged 'chilling
> effect' or threat to their freedom is fictional."

Transitions

Transitions are words, phrases or sentences, sometimes paragraphs, that link separate parts of a story — for example, the topic blocks in a speech story. Earlier in this chapter, in Figure 13.3, we looked at the bridge paragraphs that provided a transition from the lead to the development of a speech story. The bridge paragraphs were a device to help the reader move from the lead to the new material presented in the body of the story. In the same way, in the development, when the subject changes or when one speaker stops talking and another begins, the reader needs help in moving from one topic to another or from one speaker to another. The Clark speech in Figure 13.1 used transitional phrases to introduce two topics on which the speaker commented. They were:

He also suggested that . . .

Another area needing examination, he said, is . . .

When you find a word like *also* or *another* in something you are reading, it is immediately clear that something new or different is about to be brought to your attention. Transitions are simply signals to the reader that some shift is coming. Get ready, they say, we are about to change the subject. Transitions may be single words like *also, but, however* or *nevertheless*, or they may be phrases or complete sentences.

The following paragraphs show how a transition can be used to shift from one speaker to another in a story in which several people are quoted:

Williams said that only then could he draft the provision to legalize the present system of classifying real estate in the county.

Another speaker, Mrs. John B. Mullen, a legislative representative of the League of Women Voters, called the amendment's language confusing.

"The amendment would do nothing for the public," she said.

The transition is effected with the words *another speaker*, followed by the second speaker's name. This paragraph is, of course, an indirect quote or possibly a paraphrase of the new speaker's words. It serves to introduce and identify the new speaker and to begin a presentation of her views. This arrangement of a paragraph of indirect quote or paraphrase followed by a direct quote was the arrangement suggested in the chapter on quotation for introducing a direct quote into a news story.

Transitions are necessary when you shift from one speaker to another, as in the example just given. They are also necessary when you are dealing with only one speaker, in order to shift smoothly from one topic or idea to the next. You must give some signal that a shift in ideas is coming and tell the reader what the next topic will be. For example, in the following sentence, the phrase *the governor also called* clearly tells the reader, here comes another topic:

> The governor also called on the public universities and community colleges to better coordinate their programs and to eliminate inefficiencies as student enrollments decline.

Questions are often used as transitional devices, but they must be handled carefully or they will get in the reader's way. The *when asked if* approach is to be avoided. It puts the reporter in the story, and reporters are supposed to be observers, not participants. Furthermore, the reader is more interested in the answer than in the question, so keep the question short. If you use a question as a transitional device, make it a rhetorical question. Here, for example, is a rather clumsy and obtrusive *when asked if* construction:

> When asked how many votes he anticipated, he said "1509," the number needed for nomination.

Here is the same passage, revised so that the speaker's answer is introduced by a rhetorical question:

> How many votes did the candidate expect?
> "Fifteen-oh-nine," he said.
> A candidate needs 1,509 votes to be nominated.

The question here is short and provides a smooth transition to what's really important — the candidate's answer. Another example of obtrusive questioning and a revision:

> Asked if she thought her pilot training could lead her to the astronaut corps, Lt. Neufer replied: "I haven't given it any thought — I have to take one step at a time."

> Lt. Neufer was asked if her pilot training might lead to the astronaut corps.
> "I haven't given it any thought," she said. "I have to take one step at a time."

That's not bad, but here again, a rhetorical question would be preferable:

Will pilot training lead to the astronaut corps? Lt. Neufer says she hasn't given it any thought.

"I have to take one step at a time," she says.

Another approach is possible, one that makes it clear that the speaker's statement was actually a response to a question:

Young was asked if he had been hurt by criticism of his remarks.

"It hurts," he said, "only because I am anxious over the possibility of having hurt my country or President Carter."

Redundancy

In presenting summary followed by direct quotation, avoid unnecessary repetition or awkward redundancies. It wastes space to tell readers the same thing in only slightly different forms in two successive paragraphs. Note the redundancy in the following paragraphs:

If the firm were to be found guilty at the trial, the door would be open to bring criminal action against the top executives.

"If the corporation is found guilty, the next logical step may be to prosecute on individual responsibility," the prosecutor said.

That could have been handled without unnecessary repetition.

If the firm were to be found guilty at the trial, the door would be open to bring criminal action against the top executives.

"That would be the next logical step," the prosecutor said.

Partial or Fragmentary Quotes

Let's turn now to a couple of mechanical problems in the use of quoted material. First, the problem of quoting single words or isolated phrases, a practice sometimes called "using orphan quotes." For example, note the unnecessary and pointless use of quote marks in these paragraphs:

He said Raoul, an unfound and never fully identified "accomplice," never touched the rifle.

Despite these potential "land mines," he said, schools must develop ways to measure student competencies.

He noted that overly protective chest devices could make a player into a "weapon."

In none of these examples are the quote marks needed. The quoted words are being used in their usual sense, and their meaning is clear. The only justifiable use of quote marks around single words or short phrases is to call attention to something unusual about their use. When this is not the case, avoid the use of orphan quotes. A couple of additional examples of bad usage:

He blamed a "permissive society" fed by banks offering "easy money."

Dr. Langmuir said the hospital is "the weak link in the chain" of smallpox prevention.

Many editors also consider it a bad habit to mix direct and indirect quotation in the same sentence. For example:

One aspect of the fiscal goal, he said, is to increase the school's income by 5 percent "to provide needed and realistic increases for faculty and staff."

It is better to keep direct and indirect quotation apart. When you use direct quotation, use it in complete sentences. When you are through with direct quotation and shift to paraphrase — your own words — or to indirect quotation, start a new paragraph. The example just given could quite easily have been handled in this way:

He said one aspect of the fiscal goal is to increase the school's income by 5 percent.
"We must provide needed and realistic increases for faculty and staff," he said.

You can get trapped in a syntactic quagmire by mixing direct and indirect quotation. One of the stickiest is the mixed quotation that also mixes pronouns:

He added that he didn't know what the political consequences might be since "I know what I did was right."

This awkward sentence shifts not only from indirect to direct quotation but from third person to first person. It could have been better handled in this way:

He said he didn't know what the political consequences might be.
"I know what I did was right," he said.

Another example of awkward syntax:

He said he was moving on "because I don't get the satisfaction I want from television."

This could have been rewritten to say:

He said he is looking for something else to do.
"I don't get the satisfaction I want from television,"
he said.

Editing the Speaker

The idea behind direct quotation is that it represents the exact words of the speaker, not the words of the news writer. This means, very clearly, that you report what the speaker said exactly the way the speaker said it.

But what if the speaker uses loose or awkward syntax, makes a mistake in grammar or gets so wrapped up in pronoun references that the referents get lost? What do you do, in short, if the speaker's words need editing?

The first approach is simple. Don't quote directly. Paraphrase what the speaker said. Put it in your own words so you can straighten out or simplify the message. Just because someone said it doesn't mean you have to use direct quotes.

A second approach, and a common one, is to edit the speaker's words carefully and judiciously. Unless you intend to show that the speaker is an ignoramus, correct his grammar. We all speak colloquially, and the spoken language is not as precise and formal as the written language. So fix up colloquialisms that might be acceptable in speaking but less acceptable in writing. If your speaker slips, patch up the syntax or correct the error in usage. And though policy varies, you generally will be expected to delete profanity or vulgar words. It may sometimes be a good idea to do a little editing to make meaning clear.

Speakers talking directly to an audience — even an audience of one, in the case of an interview — tend to use personal pronouns that may be clear references at the moment but that become less clear when the speech or interview is reported in a news story. An example:

> "Down here in a big town, they (surgeons) have to make a real effort to do their job right and build rapport," he said.

In the context of the interview, the speaker's reference was probably clear. The conversation was about surgeons, and both the speaker and the reporter understood who *they* referred to. In a news story, a shortened and largely paraphrased version of the interview, the reference *they* was not as clear, and the writer attempted to repair the ambiguity by including after the pronoun the word *surgeons* in parentheses. This is an awkward and halfway measure. In situations like this, you can edit the speaker's words without altering the meaning. Merely remove the unclear pronoun and replace it with the word the speaker was referring to:

> "Down here in a big town surgeons have to make a real effort to do their job right and to build rapport," he said.

The result of this minor editing is a neater, cleaner and clearer sentence. And because there is no alteration in the speaker's meaning, there is no misquotation. Parenthetical insertions like *surgeons* in this example are unwelcome intrusions. They interrupt and slow the reader down. A little careful editing will clarify things and make such insertions unnecessary.

If this sort of editing bothers you, and it does bother some editors, then paraphrase or summarize. But don't pepper your story with parentheses.

Editing Prepared Texts

Speeches are prepared to be heard, not to be read. The text of a carefully prepared speech often has long sentences tied together with a variety of punctuation — colons, semicolons and dashes. For example:

261

> A newspaper has responsibilities to three masters: its owners and stockholders; the public; and a standard of journalism which is in some respects the most demanding taskmaster of them all.

This is a long sentence, but it is easy to translate into more informal language.

> A newspaper has responsibilities to three masters, Mrs. Graham said.
> These are its owners and stockholders, the public and a standard of journalism which, she said, is in some respects the most demanding of all.

Avoiding Ellipses

Avoid if at all possible — and it usually is — the use of the ellipsis in direct quotation. First, if the direct quotation is too long or too awkward, it should be handled as indirect quotation or paraphrased to avoid the dot-dot-dot remedy. In this example, the writer left something out and indicated the omission with ellipses:

> "There are a few I haven't purposely sought out, though . . . and I'm going to be careful not to run into certain people at the next meeting," he said.

There is no gap in the speaker's thought in this passage, and the ellipsis apparently represents something that the writer considered irrelevant to the point the speaker was making. Or perhaps the speaker mentioned a few names, and the writer thought the point was made well enough without resorting to personalities.

The awkward gap in the quotation can easily be fixed by replacement of the ellipsis with a speech tag.

> "There are a few I haven't purposely sought out," he said, "and I am going to be careful not to run into certain people at the next meeting."

Here's a passage from a speech from which a few words can be deleted:

> Of course, we never do a perfect job — and even if we did one day, we'd have to start over again the next

morning. But I think it's in the nature of the news business to be continually unfinished.

The words "but I think" aren't adding much. Let's remove them.

> Newspapers never do a perfect job, Mrs. Graham said, and even if they did, they would have to start all over again the next day.
> "It's in the nature of the news business to be continually unfinished," she said.

Judicious editing and the use of speech tags at the appropriate places can often tighten up a quotation — and clean it up — without being obtrusive.

In the following example, the ellipsis is unnecessary, and the writer should have found a way to get rid of it.

> The confusion of youth is only a mirror of the hypocrisies of the older generation and its studied refusal to acknowledge that a problem . . . exists," he said.

> "The confusion of youth is only a mirror of the hypocrisies of the older generation," he said.
> It also reflects refusal by older people to acknowledge the existence of the problem, he said.

Smooth out syntax. Tighten up sentences where they need it. Leave out unnecessary words or phrases if it will make the sentence more understandable. But avoid ellipses.

Other Stories

Not all speech stories — that is, stories that deal primarily with what was *said* rather than with what *happened* — are simply a shorter version of a speech. The news writer will have to write stories about panel discussions, where several speakers must be quoted. A regular assignment, for example, is the city council meeting, where half a dozen people may say something that should be reported. During public hearings or trials, a number of people may speak, and the proceedings may last not half an hour but all day.

When you have more than one speaker you have a stage management problem. Instead of one actor, you have several — a whole cast

263

of characters. How to get them on and off stage without confusion and without losing track of who they are and what they say?

Panel Discussions

Let's look at stories about panel discussions, one of the simpler kinds of stories in which more than one speaker must be quoted. Various strategies can be used to handle this kind of story, but the most practical pulls the whole story together in the lead and then deals with each speaker separately. Here is the lead from a speech story organized in this way:

> Congress must enact a law that will restore the absolute protection of newspapermen guaranteed by the First Amendment to the Constitution, speakers agreed today at the closing session of the annual convention of the American Newspaper Publishers Association.
>
> This view was expressed by Clayton Kirkpatrick, editor of the Chicago Tribune; Earl Caldwell, a reporter for the New York Times; and Len H. Small, publisher of the Kankakee (Ill.) Journal.
>
> — *Chicago Tribune*

The first paragraph of this lead summarizes the views of three speakers, noting that they agree, and explains where and on what occasion the panel discussion took place. Change the word *agreed* to *said* and substitute a name for the word *speakers* and this lead would be just like the leads written for single-speaker stories. So far, you can see, it's an easy jump from one-speaker stories to stories reporting the words of several speakers.

The second paragraph, of course, identifies the several speakers. After this, the writer can add to what was reported in the lead or go on to report what the individual speakers had to say. This story is shown in Figure 13.5 and diagrammed in Figure 13.6.

If you will look at this story, you will see that the writer was very careful about transitions and made it clear who was speaking at every point in the story. The views of each speaker were attributed: *Small said, Kirkpatrick said, Caldwell said.*

Another approach to the panel discussion is to focus on one speaker in the lead and the first part of the story, then pick up the other speakers. Stories organized in this way are written as if they were single-speaker stories up to the point where the other speakers are brought in.

In this case, a transitional paragraph is necessary to help the reader from the first part of the story to the second. For example:

Other speakers were . . .

The writer can then deal with these speakers individually or can summarize their views, much as the views of the panel were summarized in the lead on the story in Figure 13.5.

U.S. news shield law is vital, publishers assert

by Vincent Butler
Chicago Tribune Press Service

NEW YORK, April 26 — Congress must enact a law that will restore the absolute protection of newspapermen guaranteed by the First Amendment to the Constitution, speakers agreed today at the closing session of the annual convention of the American Newspaper Publishers Association.

This view was expressed by Clayton Kirkpatrick, editor of the Chicago Tribune; Earl Caldwell, a reporter for the New York Times; and Len H. Small, publisher of the Kankakee (Ill.) Journal.

Caldwell was the reporter whose citation for contempt for refusing to appear before a grand jury in California led to the United States Supreme Court decision that said the First Amendment does not specifically protect newsmen from disclosing confidential sources of information.

Since that time a number of newsmen have gone to jail rather than reveal their sources. Fears have been expressed that unless new legislation is passed to nullify the court's decision, freedom of the press and the public's right to know would be imperilled.

A number of states have passed laws to protect newsmen, but they are not considered adequate. Congress also is considering a number of bills.

Small, who moderated today's discussion, said the A.N.P.A. has not changed its position on what kind of law Congress should pass. He said it was one that would grant "Absolute privilege" as proposed in a bill sponsored by Senators Alan Cranston (D., Cal.) and Edward Kennedy (D., Mass.), which A.N.P.A. helped prepare.

"We feel that any legislation to protect the free flow of information ought to be as broad as possible and simple enough for anyone to understand," Small said. "Otherwise it will likely turn off rather than encourage news sources.

"Publishers today are greatly concerned over this issue. They are deeply committed to the struggle which they recognize as one which

265

may change the course of American journalism and ultimately affect our form of government."

Kirkpatrick said, "What we want is a charter that gives us the opportunity to fulfill our duty." He called for a bill containing "simple, direct language to prohibit any action by a government that interferes with a newsman in the performance of his duties."

He said that since 1968 the Tribune has been forced to answer 107 subpoenas. And while officials in Illinois, ranging from a former governor to aldermen, were being sent to prison for "moral turpitude," reporters were being threatened with jail for serving a "principle."

Caldwell said that there must be "some kind of relief from the government now." He said that unless there is "we're going to be reduced to dealing with handouts from the government."

He recounted how he had been harassed by government investigators and asked to produce his records and tapes concerning the Black Panther movement in 1968 and 1969, though he insisted that everything he knew he had told in his stories.

He was convicted of contempt for refusing to appear before a California grand jury, but his conviction was overturned by the court of appeals. Two years later his case was ruled on by the Supreme Court.

Caldwell said that his tapes, notes and files, which he said had great "historical value" and could have had great news value in the future, now have been destroyed.

— *Chicago Tribune*

Figure 13.5 *A news story based on a panel discussion in which three speakers give their views of First Amendment concerns.*

Stories reporting panel discussions are commonly written like the story in Figure 13.5. They are organized around the speakers — first speaker, second speaker, third speaker — rather than topically.

It is also possible to organize a story in which a number of people speak around topics — for example, pro and con. A good example of this is a story about a panel discussion in which speakers took opposite views. You might write a summary lead and then organize the story so as to first present the views of the several speakers on one side of the issue and then take up the speakers who argued the opposite view.

The story on a panel discussion in Figure 13.7 emphasizes the agreement of the panelists in the lead but places greatest emphasis on the views of the panelist the writer considered more newsworthy than the others. The other speakers are brought into the story gradually, first one other speaker, then the list of all the panelists. The views of two of the panelists were taken up only in the second half of the story. Here the news value of what was said changed the structure from that seen in Figure 13.5, where all speakers were given more or less equal treatment.

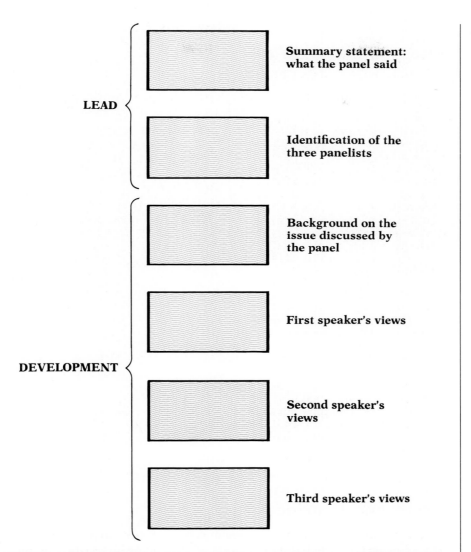

Figure 13.6 *This diagram shows how the First Amendment story in Figure 13.5 was organized. This is a highly functional structure, easy for the writer to write and for the reader to follow.*

Reagan had right to sell arms, ex–cabinet officers say

Four former secretaries of state meeting in Atlanta agreed Friday that the Reagan administration's secret arms sales to Iran have left U.S. foreign policy in turmoil, but they defended the president's right to take such initiatives.

The lead pulls together the views of the four speakers on the panel.

Alexander Haig, who resigned from the Reagan Cabinet in 1982, said corrective measures in the wake of the Iranian affair "should not cripple the presidency."

Views of one of the panelists.

Haig said the duty of Cabinet members is to "support the president, and if they can't — like one secretary of state I know — to leave."

Haig would not elaborate on whether he was referring to himself or to Secretary of State George Shultz, who opposed the arms deals.

Former Secretary of State Henry Kissinger said Reagan's stated aim of reaching out to moderates in Iran was a laudable idea that "got off the track" when missiles became involved.

Views of a second panelist.

Trials and Hearings

Stories about trials and public hearings present several problems. First, the news writer is faced with a mass of material representing as much as eight or 10 hours of statements, questions, answers and other verbal exchanges. Second, several — sometimes many — speakers are involved, and the problems of identification, background and transition become more difficult. Third, the subject matter often tends to be complicated. There may be conflicting views, long chronological accounts, sometimes even lengthy exchanges of questions and answers before a significant point is made. Finally, the story may be obscured by so many wearisome details and such roundabout presentation that it takes great skill on the part of the writer to summarize it all.

"The sale of arms to a radical revolutionary government is not the best way to show good faith," Kissinger said. "Nor was the obligation to show good faith primarily on the United States."

Kissinger and Haig were joined by Edmund Muskie and Dean Rusk at the fourth annual "Conference with the Secretaries of State" sponsored by the Atlanta-based Southern Center for International Studies.

Bridging paragraphs give background on the conference before story moves to details.

The conference, filmed before an audience of more than 1,000 at the Atlanta Civic Center, will be aired Dec. 23 at 10 p.m. on public broadcasting stations.

In a three-hour discussion sprinkled with both profundities and one-liners, the Reagan administration received both harsh criticism and sympathy for its recent foreign policy moves.

Figure 13.7 *This excerpt from a story on a panel discussion has an organization different from that of the story in Figure 13.5. The body of the story (not included here) follows the bridging paragraphs and takes up the views of all four panelists in more detail.*

Q. and A.

Stories about trials frequently require the reporting of long exchanges between witnesses and the attorneys examining or cross-examining them. This kind of exchange can be handled in the form of a series of questions and answers referred to as Q. and A. This form of direct quotation doesn't need speech tags, since the identity of the two persons involved is established before the Q. and A. begins. For example:

Q. And that's where you made the first phone call?
A. Yes.
Q. OK. Now, you also testified that you wanted to go home by a route of I-285, is that correct?
A. Yeah, I said that.
Q. All right. Now, my question is, if you wanted to take the I-285–I-20 route home, why not after using the telephone at the Racetrac right at 285, why not get

269

on 285 there rather than coming south toward the bridge?

A. Man, look, what in the world has that got to do with killing somebody?

— Atlanta Constitution

This is an excerpt from a long passage of verbatim testimony from a murder trial. The identity of the questioner and the person being questioned was made clear earlier in the transcript. In this kind of exchange, the quoted statements are not enclosed in quotation marks. In the following example, the questions and answers are attributed and placed within quotation marks:

"Are you positive?" Assistant District Attorney Tasca Babcock asked the girl.

"I'm positive," she replied.

"There's no mistake?"

"I'm not mistaken," she said.

— Columbus (Ga.) *Enquirer*

Sometimes Q. and A. is handled another way:

Singer: "Have you lost your faith?"

Lockhart: "No, sir."

In news stories of trials in which the proceedings last a considerable period of time — hours each day — you will find a great deal of summary. This is necessary to keep the story under control and to provide transitions linking the bits of verbatim testimony. An example of a trial story is shown in Figure 13.8.

Occasionally when a trial or public hearing is of special interest, a newspaper will publish full or partial transcripts of testimony. These may take up as much as two or three full newspaper pages. Transcripts do not, however, take the place of a news story that summarizes and explains the proceedings. Transcripts, even full ones, are only adjuncts to a well-organized news story. They are not substitutes for the work of the news writer, who must summarize, synthesize, condense and explain. The news story will make extensive use of summary but will include direct quotation of interesting or important points in the trial and may include extensive passages of Q. and A. The well-balanced news story of a trial or a lengthy public hearing will be brief and interpretive. It should in a sense predigest the lengthy proceedings for the reader who doesn't have time or patience to wade through columns of verbatim testimony.

Closing arguments in Chagra murder trial set today

By Lilla Ross
Times-Union Staff Writer

Testimony in the murder conspiracy trial of Jamiel "Jimmy" Chagra ended yesterday after the defense took only 10 minutes to present its case in the 13-day-old trial.

Chagra is charged with arranging the 1979 murder of U.S. District Judge John H. Wood Jr. in San Antonio, Texas.

Chagra's attorney called only two witnesses before resting his case. The 39-year-old defendant did not testify.

Habitual criminal Jerry Ray James, the government's star witness, was recalled by defense attorney Oscar Goodman, who questioned him about his earlier testimony that Chagra had told him he had killed a man in an Austin, Texas, bar.

"The conversation arose out of Jimmy being mad at a Jack Stricklin," James testified. "He said, 'Jack knows what I'll do to him because he was there when I killed Mark Finney.' I think he said he shot him."

Goodman then called Martin E. Finney of Austin to testify. The difference in first names was never resolved in testimony.

Finney testified that he first met Chagra at the funeral of his older brother, Lee Chagra, who was murdered in December 1978 in his El Paso, Texas, law office.

Finney said he saw Chagra two other times, the last time in Austin with Stricklin.

"I assume that you are alive and well?" Goodman asked Finney.

"I feel pretty good," Finney said.

"Did Jimmy Chagra ever point a gun at you or shoot you?" Goodman asked.

"No, sir," Finney replied.

"Your honor, ladies and gentlemen of the jury, the defense rests," Goodman said.

U.S. District Judge William Sessions recessed court until 9:30 a.m. today, when the two sides will present closing arguments. Sessions told the jurors to come prepared to be sequestered during their deliberations.

The government closed its case yesterday against Chagra, a Las Vegas gambler, after calling 87 witnesses, presenting more than 100 pieces of evidence and playing more than six hours of tape-recorded conversations between Chagra and his wife, his brother and James.

James testified for a full day about his relationship with Chagra at the federal prison in Leavenworth, Kan., where Chagra was serving 30 years on a narcotics conviction.

James testified last week that Chagra told him, "Jerry, you know I'm the one who had Judge Wood killed."

The 43-year-old James was serving a life sentence at Leavenworth when he became a government informant in return for parole and $250,000 in reward money.

Before the government rested its case, several witnesses were

271

called to review the evidence regarding the movements of Charles V. Harrelson, who was convicted of being a hit man, around May 29, 1979, the day Wood was killed by a single gunshot outside his San Antonio apartment.

The government played a tape yesterday of a telephone conversation between Chagra's brother, Joe, and Harrelson in which Harrelson said Chagra had nothing to do with the judge's murder.

"I just wanted them [authorities] to know that neither you nor Jimmy or Virginia or any of your family was in any way culpable," Harrelson said in the conversation that Joe Chagra, an El Paso lawyer, taped at Harrelson's request.

"I wanted them to take note that Jimmy didn't have a damn thing to do with it," Harrelson said.

An FBI agent testified that the tape of the Aug. 30, 1980, conversation was taken from Joe Chagra in February 1981. Joe Chagra later pleaded guilty in the Wood case and was sentenced to 10 years.

After the prosecution rested its case, Goodman filed motions for acquittal and dismissal of murder and conspiracy charges against Chagra. He also asked Sessions to recuse himself because the judge presided at the trial of Harrelson, Harrelson's wife, Jo Ann, and Chagra's wife, Elizabeth, last December. The three were convicted and will be sentenced March 8.

Sessions denied all the motions.

The judge moved the trial to Jacksonville because of massive pre-trial publicity in Texas. Jacksonville was chosen for its size and court accommodations.

— *Florida Times-Union,* Jacksonville

Figure 13.8 *This story about a trial makes effective use of direct and indirect quotation, of Q. and A. and of summary.*

Public Hearings

Public hearings are covered in detail in newspapers more frequently than are trials. Hearings may be quite informal, merely involving the presentation of views by interested citizens, or they may be extremely formal and involve sworn testimony and cross-examination of witnesses. The Congressional hearings into the sale of arms to Iran is a good example of this kind of hearing. Stories dealing with this kind of hearing have to be organized topically — that is, around some point in contention. The story, in other words, is organized logically rather than following the testimony as it unfolded chronologically.

Other Meetings

Meetings of county boards, city councils and school boards are also stories based in large part on the spoken word, but they generally require more summary than stories of speeches or panel discussions. And they usually also include background information and facts about actions taken by the council or board. A further complication is the fact that any number of people — members of the board or council, public officials, sometimes members of the public — may speak during the meeting. Meeting stories require care in organization, skill at summary and knowledge of the subject matter. Examples of such stories are shown in Figures 13.9 and 13.10.

Committee members ready to do some traveling now

The school committee has selected three finalists for Falmouth school superintendent and created a five-member subcommittee to travel to the finalists' communities for additional interviews.

The board's top three choices are Dr. Ralph H. Lataille, deputy commissioner of education in New Jersey; Dr. John J. O'Neill, superintendent of schools in Sudbury; and Dr. Seldon V. Whitaker Jr., superintendent of schools in Concord.

The board selected them Tuesday night after three nights of interviews with the six semifinalists.

The vote to narrow the candidates from six to three called for board members to name their three favorite candidates in no particular order.

Four committee members agreed on all three finalists and a fifth member, who listed only two top choices, included Dr. Whitaker and Dr. Lataille.

Every board member named Dr. Whitaker; eight named Dr. Lataille, and six named Dr. O'Neill. The student representative to the board, Douglas Jones, also named Dr. Whitaker, but his vote was to play no official role in the proceedings.

Dr. Charles F. Ritch Jr., the board consultant in the search and selection process, named Dr. Robert J. Lane, superintendent of schools in Haverhill, Dr. Whitaker and Dr. O'Neill, in that order, as his top three choices.

The procedure now calls for the subcommittee to visit each candidate in his home community to interview teachers, administrators, school board members, students and parents.

Those interviews are expected to take place on Feb. 8, 9 and 12, and are being arranged by Dr. Ritch.

The board agreed to name its top choice at a scheduled budget hearing on Feb. 12 at Falmouth high school following the interviews.

At one point during the evening, several members of the board appeared ready to visit Dr. Whitaker first and offer him the job if the interviews in Concord satisfied the subcommittee.

Caroline E. Blake objected.

"That's exactly how we hired someone else," she said, apparently referring to Dr. Richard L. Sheely, superintendent of Falmouth schools from 1971 to 1973.

Both Mrs. Blake and Anthony R. Spagone continually pressed the notion that the committee has so far based its decision only on data and references supplied by the candidates.

"I can't believe anyone can be perfect," Mr. Spagone said. "There must be something wrong with them."

Dorothy Hahn asked: "What disparaging information are we trying to find?" She said it was "incredible" to cast the on-site interviews on such a negative base.

Robert L. Rabesa took issue with Mrs. Blake's and Mr. Spagone's concern for finding something — anything — negative about the candidates.

"If you look far enough, I'm certain you'll find they received a 'C' in a course at some time," he said.

Mrs. Blake countered: "Had it been investigated thoroughly, we wouldn't have had one candidate come and go so quickly."

"Preliminary interviews — which were preliminary — is what we're going to decide on," she added.

"Absolutely," replied Chairman Edwin L. Medeiros, nodding his head in agreement.

Finally, Mrs. Hahn moved that the traveling subcommittee visit Dr. Whitaker and offer him the position if they agreed he was the best man for the job.

"What kind of a motion is that?" asked Edward F. Westgate.

A critical factor

John M. Connolly took a few minutes to explain that time is a critical factor. He said the top candidates may take another offer if the selection procedure takes too long.

"We're dancing on ball bearings," he said. "How long is it going to take us to get on firm ground?"

Mrs. Hahn's motion, which was seconded by Dr. Frank Egloff, "just

to see what happens," passed on a six-to-three vote.

Mr. Connolly, Mr. Rabesa, Mr. Medeiros and Mrs. Norton joined Mrs. Hahn and Dr. Egloff in support of the motion.

Moments later, the committee nullified Mrs. Hahn's motion because they agreed that the vote was too close and might have the effect of unfairly eliminating two candidates.

Dr. Ritch also advised the committee to move fast.

"After they've been here and seen how you folks operate, they may have other ideas," he said.

He said Wednesday that he knows that several of the candidates are being seriously considered in other communities.

"Each has other irons in the fire," he said.

"If we're going to capture them before the other iron strikes, we're going to have to act soon."

The subcommittee that will travel to Sudbury, Concord and Trenton, N.J., is composed of Mr. Medeiros, Mrs. Blake, Mr. Spagone, Mrs. Norton and Mr. Connolly. Their expenses will be borne by the school department.

Mr. Spagone was most emphatic about visiting representative groups in the finalists' communities. When it appeared that his work schedule might preclude his traveling with the subcommittee, he said he would visit the communities on his own.

"I want to talk to people on the street and get some input," he said. "I would be abdicating my responsibility if I didn't."

Mrs. Norton objected.

"Talking with people on the street is a dangerous precedent, Tony," she said. "You have no idea where they're coming from."

She added that independent

visits by members of the committee would place too much pressure on the candidates, who would have to arrange too many interviews.

Mr. Connolly agreed.

"It's bogus," he said, referring to individual visits. "I think we ought to show a little class."

In the end the subcommittee arranged its travel dates so that Mr. Spagone will be able to travel with the group.

Establishing that schedule resulted in still another clash.

Mrs. Blake accused Mr. Medeiros of arranging the travel dates to fit Mr. Connolly's schedule.

"What makes him so special?" she asked.

That offended Mr. Connolly. "Let's show a little civility," he said.

The three candidates who did not appear on the list of finalists are Richard G. Gallivan, superintendent of schools in North Kingstown, R.I., Mr. Lane of Haverhill and Vincent B. McGee, superintendent of schools in Chelsea.

The committee instructed Dr. Ritch to inform these three candidates that they will be reconsidered if the committee's list fails to yield a superintendent.

— *The Enterprise*, Falmouth, Mass.

Figure 13.9 *A tightly organized and readable news story about a public meeting. Note the extensive use of direct quotation. What other organizing devices can you identify?*

Aurora tower OK'd despite objections

Aurora — A handful of residents implored the city council last night not to build a 110-foot radio tower virtually in their backyards, but the council unanimously approved the tower, saying it is critical to the safety of the rest of the city's 240,000 residents.

The vote overturned the planning commission's denial of the tower, which is to be built in a stretch of open land next to the city's fire station at 17200 E. Mexico Ave.

The commission, like area homeowners, was concerned that the tower is not compatible with the surrounding residential neighborhood.

"I don't want to have to look at it every day," said resident Linda Blankenship. "That may be a dumb reason, but I just don't want to look at it."

Residents also said the tower would lower their property values and be a danger to the youngsters who use the greenbelt as a park.

But city officials told the council the tower is imperative if Aurora is going to provide adequate emergency assistance to current and future residents.

"We rely on emergency communications systems to work every time we need it," said police Chief Jerry Williams. "I don't think it's an overstatement to say that people's lives depend on that."

Williams said the tower will eliminate some of the "dead spots" in the city's communications network where radio signals do not reach.

The tower will allow Aurora to use 20 new high-frequency channels approved by the Federal Communications Commission. But if the city doesn't begin using at least five of those channels by February, the FCC could take them away, warned deputy city manager Jim Mullen.

Mullen said the proposed site is the best place for the tower because it is one of the highest points in the city. It is also accessible, can be easily maintained, and is in clear sight of firefighters in the station so is unlikely to be vandalized, he said.

The tower itself will be moved from the fire station near Peoria Street and Mississippi Avenue and the city will construct a $65,000 to $75,000 communications building enclosed by an 8-foot wall next to

it. The cost of the electronic equipment for the tower will be about $1 million.

In other action, the council unanimously elected councilwoman Peggy Kerns as mayor pro tem for the upcoming year. She replaces Frank Weddig, who has served since last November.

The council also approved, by a vote of 7 to 2, a change in the city's telephone tax that will mean an extra $3 a year for the average phone user. The change is expected to generate an additional $300,000.

During its study session last night, the council also gave tentative approval to a new ward boundary map, which expands the number of wards from nine to 11. The two new city council seats are necessary to keep up with the city's rapid growth.

—*Rocky Mountain News*, Denver

Figure 13.10 *This story about a public meeting relies heavily on summary and uses only a few quotes. Note that the story not only reports on what was said at the meeting but also reports decisions made by the council.*

Interviews

You will find that interviews present more complex reporting problems than other kinds of speech stories. When you interview someone, you initiate the discussion, guide the speaker along the lines you want followed and generally take charge. You have to ask intelligent questions and prod and pull until you get the material you are after. This is a different situation from the lecture or panel discussion, where the reporter merely takes notes on what is said. However, once you have your notes, you will find that stories about interviews require much the same techniques as those about speeches.

It is usually a good idea to write explicitly that your story is based on an interview — a conversation between a reporter, sometimes several reporters, and an interview subject. For example:

> In an interview before stepping down from the job
> he has held since 1968 to become president of the Corpo-
> ration for Public Broadcasting, Fleming said . . .

This is, as you can see, just a matter of clear attribution, of telling the reader not only who spoke but what the circumstances were. Since interviews frequently have a tone different from that of other speech stories, the reader ought to be prepared.

Published Sources

Quite often news stories are based on published reports, an article in a scholarly journal or a popular magazine or a copyrighted story that appeared in another newspaper. These are speech stories, but they are based on a published record rather than on an oral source. Stories based on published sources are handled exactly like other speech stories, except that it is essential to tell the reader the source. This is a matter of clear attribution. For example:

> In a letter released Monday, Cranston said . . .
> — *United Press International*

Identifying the Platform

Speech stories, as must be apparent now, are stories based on what people say under many different circumstances. They include not only stories about speeches and panel discussions but also stories reporting on conventions, public hearings, various public meetings, trials, inquests, press conferences, interviews and formal and informal announcements and statements. They also include stories about television and radio programs and a variety of published sources and texts including press releases, official reports, scholarly studies, copyrighted stories in newspapers, magazine stories and books.

Whatever the source of the material, it should be identified clearly and early in the story. In a story based on a speech, the writer tells in the lead who spoke, where and when. Generally, too, early in the story the nature of the audience and the circumstances of the speech are made clear. In stories drawn from other sources, it is important that these also be identified. The circumstances under which a statement is made may have a lot to do with the significance of the statement. There may be quite a difference, for example, in what a politician says in answer to a reporter's hurried question in an airport waiting room and what the same politician might say under oath at a public hearing.

277

The following paragraph illustrates this. The story differs from routine stories about speeches only in the circumstances under which the statements were made. The speaker was holding a press conference so as to get public attention for his views. There was an obvious bias in what he had to say, and readers had to be warned about it:

> Fogel, in a press conference called to explain his reasons for resigning to become corrections director in Illinois, said either man is qualified to continue the programs set in motion since his appointment in March 1971.
>
> — *Minneapolis Tribune*

The following excerpt makes it clear that the speaker's remarks were made under carefully controlled circumstances:

> Anderson made his remarks during a meeting with reporters at his Overlea home, where he is recuperating from a recent illness that hospitalized him for five days.
> Under the ground rules, questions were to be limited because of the county executive's health.
>
> — *Baltimore Sun*

Sometimes reporters add to a story, or get an entirely different story, by interviewing a public official or prominent person who has just delivered a prepared speech. The fact that the resulting story did not come from the scheduled address should be made clear.

> Mrs. Cynthia Wedel of Washington, D.C., gave her views in an interview after she had spoken to the 27th annual Laymen's Conference here.
>
> — *Milwaukee Sentinel*

Reporting

The discussions in the chapters on quotation, speech story leads and developing the speech story are about writing, not about reporting. Not much has been said, either, about news values, although some inferences might be drawn from the news stories used as examples.

Do not be misled, however, into thinking that mechanics and organizational skills are all you need to know about handling the speech story, that a tape recorder or a prepared text will give you the story and all you have to do is write it. Far from it.

Covering a speech, a political debate, a heated discussion at a city council meeting, a public hearing on a controversial zoning issue, a late-night legislative session, the national convention of the American Medical Association or a speech by a Nobel physicist — or interviewing Ralph Nader — can be hard work. Knowledgeable reporting requires education, experience and an awareness of current affairs. It requires a sense of what makes news and what readers want to know or need to know.

A good reporter has to be a good listener as well as a skilled asker of questions. A good reporter must be able to think quickly and must have good judgment.

This discussion of writing about what people say is important, but it will be useful to you only if you first learn how to report.

Suggestions for Further Reading

Interviewing — asking the right questions — is one of the highest of journalistic skills.

Brady, John. *The Craft of Interviewing.* Cincinnati: Writer's Digest, 1976.
A useful discussion of interviewing by an experienced editor and writer.

Fallaci, Oriana. *The Egotists.* Chicago: Henry Regnery Company, 1968.
Sixteen interviews conducted by a reporter who is said to be able to make the most reticent talk and the most verbose tell the truth.

Metzler, Ken. *Creative Interviewing.* Englewood Cliffs, N.J.: Prentice-Hall, Inc., 1977.
A valuable how-to-do-it book by an able journalism teacher. Includes a comprehensive bibliography.

Reed, Rex. *Do You Sleep in the Nude?* New York: New American Library, 1968.
A collection of Reed's interviews with entertainment-world personalities. Good examples of expert reporting.

Terkel, Studs. *Working.* New York: Pantheon Books, 1974.
An expert interviewer talks to people about their jobs and the effect of work on their lives.

Walters, Barbara. *How to Talk With Practically Anybody About Practically Anything.* Garden City, N.Y.: Doubleday, 1970.
A skilled interviewer gives some useful tips on how to ask questions.

NORTHEAST TODAY

Volume 1, Number 19
Thursday, June 11, 1987

CUB HILL   ROSEDALE   PARKVILLE   CARNEY   OVERLEA   FULLERTON   PERRY HALL   WHITE MARSH

Still Waters...4

Graduation Day...18

Shining Stars...32

Staff Photo by Richard Tomlinson

The Fighting Fourth
of World War II

See story, Page 14

14 Broadcast News

A language less rugged than the English would have been destroyed long ago.

Bert Leston Taylor

The news you hear on radio or watch on television is the same news that you read in the newspaper — reports of events and incidents, stories about people and places and accounts of tragedies and successes, stories about people and stories about government.

Despite this fact, news written for radio broadcast or integrated with pictures for television is not the same thing as news written for publication in a newspaper.

The broadcast reporter and the newspaper reporter will cover the same stories — fires, accidents, city council meetings or political rallies — but the broadcast version of the story is not going to be the same as the newspaper version. The broadcast journalist writes news copy to be read aloud and to be *heard* by a listener or viewer. The print journalist writes to be *read*, for the reader who absorbs the news visually.

One writes for the ear, the other for the eye. The difference is substantial.

The news story that appears on the printed page is read by readers at their convenience. If readers don't have time to read a story, they can put the paper aside and return to it later. If readers lose track of details in the lead or the early part of a story as they read the last few paragraphs, they can turn back to the beginning of the story and re-read it. The facts that the newspaper can be read when readers want to read, that stories on the front page can be read in any order, that the reader can re-read a lead or an entire news story — or choose not to read a story — are unique to the printed page.

Broadcast News

Broadcast news when it is delivered to the listener and viewer must be accepted in the order in which it is presented. Once the sound of the broadcaster's voice or the picture on the screen has faded away, it is gone for good. It can't be called back. Nor can reception of broadcast news be slowed down. The pace of delivery is the same for the listener of quick comprehension and the listener who doesn't quite catch what is said.

So those who write news for broadcast have to write in such a way that the ear can catch and the mind absorb the facts of the story the first time. No going back. No second chance to check a name or a figure.

News With and Without Pictures

There are, of course, two kinds of broadcast news. Radio news is for the ear alone. Television news is for both the ear and the eye.

News for television places heavy reliance on camera work and visual images. News for radio is more closely related to news written for newspapers. Indeed, a great deal of the news broadcast by radio is written by news writers who also write for newspaper publication. At Associated Press and United Press International bureaus, news writers are trained to write news two ways — first for the newspaper, where it will be read, second for radio, where it will be heard.

Writing News for Radio

Let's look first at news written for radio. Stories written for radio, first of all, must be brief and they must be concise. Most radio news broadcasts last no longer than five minutes. An experienced broadcaster can read about 18 lines of copy in a minute. A five-line story will take 15 to 20 seconds of air time. Six or seven five-line stories will fill a two-minute newscast. Longer stories, those of 10 to 15 lines, will fill a five-minute newscast much more quickly.

News for radio must be concise in order to get the essential facts of a story into five or six lines of copy. News for radio must be written simply and informally, in easily understood words and terms.

Journalism student in broadcast studio at the University of West Florida. (© 1986 University of West Florida/Tom Carter)

And news for radio must be written so that it can be read aloud. Reading copy aloud is a good test of copy written for newspapers as well as for broadcast. But it is essential to writing for broadcast. Broadcast news must be written so that it is free of awkward phrasing, unnecessary clauses and long sentences that might cause a newscaster to stumble in reading the copy on the air.

These are generalities, broad statements about the way broadcast news writers approach their writing. Keep them in mind as you learn to write for broadcast. Now, let's look at some specific points on which broadcast writing differs from newspaper writing.

283

Broadcast Leads

When we speak of the lead of a broadcast news story, we really are talking about the first few words of the story rather than a first paragraph. If you were to compare a broadcast news story with a story written for newspaper publication, you would find that the lead of the newspaper story and the five- or six-line broadcast story are comparable. The newspaper lead is a concise introduction to a news story and merely precedes a more detailed account. The five- or six-line broadcast story is all there is. Here is an example of a broadcast news lead, the first words of this Associated Press radio story:

> The news on inflation hasn't been this good in 25 years.

The entire story, five lines in all:

> The news on inflation hasn't been this good in 25 years. The Labor Department says consumer prices rose just one-point-one percent last year — the best showing since 1961. The tiny rise in the cost of living is due mainly to the sharp drop in crude oil prices that followed last winter's collapse of the "OPEC" cartel's production quotas.

The newspaper writer might call this approach a feature lead or even suggest that the writer is backing into the story, but in writing for radio, it is essential to lay out as quickly as possible the nature of the story, then present the facts more precisely. For example, another AP radio wire story:

> Still no word from Anglican Church envoy Terry Waite — well over a day after he left his Beirut hotel for face-to-face talks with kidnappers holding two American hostages. But one of his bodyguards reported Waite held marathon negotiations in secret with the kidnappers who hold two American hostages.

Compare the radio news lead below with the newspaper story in Figure 14.5:

> A news conference in Harrisburg, Pennsylvania, turned into a horror show today.

Broadcast leads must in the first few words give the listener a point or two — a couple of mental images to hold onto while the story is read. In this lead the key words are *news conference* and *horror show*. What happened? Something horrible. Where? At a news conference in Harrisburg, Pennsylvania. In the same way, the news story on Terry Waite tosses a quick insight at the listener — *still no word* about Terry Waite — before giving the details.

Attribution

Attribution, the source of the story, very often comes at the beginning of a broadcast news story and consequently gets a good deal of emphasis. Putting attribution first may also tell the listener where the story came from, establish credibility for the story and to some extent tell the listener what the story is about. Broadcast stories often start like this:

> Michigan transportation officials say . . .
>
> Experts in family violence say . . .
>
> The national weather service says . . .
>
> The chairman of the special senate panel set up to investigate the White House arms scandal says . . .

Starting with attribution alerts the listener to what's coming. By the time the five Ws are reached, the listener is in a position to hear and understand the story.

Quotation

Direct quotation, so useful in stories written for newspapers, is difficult to handle in copy written for broadcast. Quotation marks, the use of speech tags and paragraphing make it clear to newspaper readers what is direct quotation and what is not. It isn't that easy in writing for broadcast to make it clear where a direct quote begins and where it ends. Broadcast news writers prefer to paraphrase rather than quote directly. When it is necessary to use direct quotation, the broadcast writer must use words rather than quotation marks to make clear to listeners whose words — those of the person in the story or those of the newscaster — are being heard. Here is one example of direct quotation from an AP radio news story:

As one official looking into the collision of two military reconnaissance jets yesterday put it: "someone zigged when they should have zagged." Officials say the planes were taking part in a practice dogfight near Lake Brownwood, Texas, when they crashed. Two crewmen died — while two others parachuted to safety.

The writer indicated the beginning of the direct quote by the words *put it* and indicated that the quotation was complete by the words *officials say,* which made it clear that what followed came from another source. Other examples:

Hooks said the N-A-A-C-P will resort to the courts because civil rights marches alone won't be enough, as he put it, to "eliminate the white racist attitude in that county." Hooks made his comments in Columbia, South Carolina, on his way to make a scheduled speech in Myrtle Beach.

Williams says the demonstration will take place, in his words, "whether it's cold as ice or hot as it is in hell."

Often it is clearer to paraphrase rather than quote directly, and it is a good idea to limit direct quotes to a single sentence so that the reader doesn't lose track of who is speaking.

Punctuation

Punctuation is used in broadcast news copy in pretty much the same way it is used in newspaper copy. Examples of punctuation shown in Chapter 19 and in the Basic Guide to News Style will serve with some exceptions for broadcast as well as newspaper use. There are some important differences, however.

Broadcast writers avoid the use of paired commas to set off ages.

Newspaper usage: Jane Doe, 48, was . . .

Broadcast usage: Jane Doe, who is 48, was . . .

Punctuation is a device for the eye. In words we hear, as when we listen to a radio news broadcast, punctuation comes in the form of a pause, of a raising or lowering of the voice. Any punctuation used in writing broadcast news copy must aid the person who will read the copy in reading smoothly, with clarity and with proper emphasis.

Hyphens, as you may already have noticed, are used to set off abbreviations that are to be pronounced letter by letter — for example, N-B-C or D-D-T.

And a.m. and p.m., in newspaper usage lowercase and with periods, are hyphenated in broadcast copy: 9 p-m and 10 a-m.

Acronyms like NATO or DEW line are enclosed in quotation marks: "NATO" and "DEW" line.

Miscellaneous Differences

You should have noticed in these examples from radio news stories that broadcast writing differs from newspaper writing in a number of other ways. State names are spelled out after city names to make it easier for the newscaster to read the copy. And as much as possible broadcast news stories are cast in the present tense rather than the past. *Say* or *says*, for example, are preferred to *said*.

Numbers are handled differently. In writing for a newspaper, you would write *2.5 percent*, but in writing for broadcast, you would make it *two and a half percent*. And *72.5* would be written as *72-point-five*. Large numbers are written as, for example, *872-thousand-600* and *nine-thousand*. Newspaper style requires you to write *$25*, but broadcast style makes it *25 dollars* to make it easier to read. And when large numbers are used, the writer helps the newscaster keep numbers straight by marking millions with an *M* and billions with a *B* in this way: *The 20 (B) billion dollar measure* or the *10 (M) million dollar loss*.

Identification

In the newspaper, only a few titles, generally the short titles of elected public officials, military titles and courtesy titles, come before a name. Long titles, job descriptions, ages and other identification are placed after a name. In writing for broadcast, even long identification is generally placed ahead of the name. For example:

"NASA" Administrator James Fletcher

Former Tennessee Senator Howard Baker

House Minority Leader Johnny Isakson

However, long titles and job descriptions go after the name just as they do in the newspaper.

> Brenda Hucks, executive director of South Carolina Citizens for Life
>
> Jim Ledbetter, Georgia Human Resources director

In broadcast writing, identification is sometimes held back. For example:

> Terry Waite has broken two days of silence to report he's o-k and that he's continuing his talks with Moslem terrorists in Lebanon.
> The British churchman and hostage negotiator is trying . . .

Ages generally precede rather than follow a name:

> 42-year-old Fred Gary
>
> 17-year-old Tony Reed

Abbreviations are avoided in broadcast copy except for abbreviations or acronyms that are familiar to listeners. Several acceptable abbreviations and acronyms were used in stories just cited. But many titles that would be abbreviated in the newspaper would be written out in broadcast copy. For example:

> the reverend Hosea Williams
>
> major general John Jones
>
> police lieutenant James Oaks

Names

To help the newscaster who must read unfamiliar names on the air, broadcast news writers insert keys to pronunciation of unfamiliar names in their copy. For example:

> Ali Hamadi (Hah'-muh-dee)
>
> Shiite (shee'-eyet)
>
> Corazon Aquino (kor-ah-zohn' ah-kee'-noh)

Negatives

Contractions are commonly used in both newspaper writing and writing for broadcast, but broadcast writing avoids contracting the word *not*, for the *n't* in *isn't* or *aren't* may be missed by an inattentive listener. An example of careful attention to the negative:

> Carolton Detective Lieutenant Thomas O. Maher says he has decided — not — to take the job of police chief in Henderson, North Carolina.

Datelines

As you may notice, some of the radio wire stories shown below have datelines and some do not. Where the datelines are carried, they are in parentheses.

Datelines are not read, and the place where an event occurred is woven into the story. If you look at Figure 14.4, you can see how this is done. In the story broadcast at 11:42 a.m., the reference is a little vague — the word *Pennsylvania* alone. In the 12:33 story, the reference is specific — Harrisburg, Pennsylvania.

The dateline on the longer story transmitted at 12:48 carries a dateline in parentheses for information only. Again, the reference to place is a little vague but probably specific enough to satisfy the listener.

This discussion of the differences between writing for newspapers and writing for radio is highly selective. The *AP Broadcast News Handbook* is as detailed as the *AP Stylebook*. For answers to style problems, the best counsel is to have the *Broadcast News Handbook* at hand and to look things up.

Writing to Space

As noted earlier, broadcast news copy must be brief and it must be concise. The *Newswatch* copy shown in Figure 14.1 ranges from a four-line story to a seven-line story. No wasted words in this copy. The *Newsminute* stories shown in Figure 14.2 are similarly brief and concise.

The AP radio wire is a 24-hour service, and quite often stories that are treated fully early in the day are cut back as they are repeated for later broadcasts until, sometimes, at the end of the day only a couple of lines remain. Almost any news story can be trimmed by the skilled broadcast news writer. A good example of this can be seen in Figure 14.3. An early version of this story was 21 lines long. Later versions were trimmed until at the end of the day the story had been reduced to six lines.

EARLY ESTIMATES INDICATE THE ECONOMY GREW LAST YEAR AT THE SLOWEST
PACE SINCE THE LAST RECESSION. THE COMMERCE DEPARTMENT ESTIMATES THAT
THE GROSS NATIONAL PRODUCT GREW AT AN ANNUAL RATE OF ONE-POINT-SEVEN
PERCENT DURING THE FOURTH QUARTER OF THE YEAR. IF THAT FIGURE HOLDS
UP, IT WOULD MEAN THE ECONOMY GREW JUST TWO AND A-HALF PERCENT LAST
YEAR -- THE WORST SINCE 1982, WHEN THE G-N-P SHRANK TWO-AND-A-HALF
PERCENT.

THE ONLY HINT OF WHAT ANGLICAN CHURCH ENVOY TERRY WAITE IS UP TO
IN LEBANON IS COMING FROM THOSE WHO ARE PROTECTING HIM. AN OFFICIAL
OF THE DRUSE (DROOZ) MILITIA THAT'S PROVIDING SECURITY FOR THE
MISSION SAYS WAITE WAS LAST SEEN TUESDAY WHEN HE LEFT FOR AN APPARENT
MEETING WITH THE KIDNAPPERS HOLDING TWO AMERICANS HOSTAGE. THE
SECURITY OFFICIAL SAYS WAITE HASN'T CALLED FOR AN ESCORT BACK TO HIS
HOTEL -- SO HE ASSUMES THE MEETING IS CONTINUING.

BONN OFFICIALS SAY THEY STILL CAN'T CONFIRM THAT A SECOND WEST
GERMAN MAN HAS BEEN KIDNAPPED IN BEIRUT. BUT LEBANESE POLICE SAY
THEY'RE CLASSIFYING HIS DISAPPEARANCE AS AN ABDUCTION. AND THE GERMAN
GOVERNMENT IS URGING ITS CITIZENS TO LEAVE LEBANON FOR THEIR OWN GOOD.

ATTORNEY GENERAL ED MEESE IS SAID TO BE IN AGREEMENT WITH A
RECOMMENDATION BY A JUSTICE DEPARTMENT REPORT ON THE 1966 SUPREME
COURT MIRANDA RULING. THE REPORT SUGGESTS THE RULING, WHICH REQUIRES
POLICE TO ADVISE SUSPECTS OF THEIR RIGHTS, BE DONE AWAY WITH. IN THE
PAST, MEESE HAS SAID THE MIRANDA RULING ''ONLY HELPS GUILTY
DEFENDANTS.''

EDUCATION SECRETARY WILLIAM BENNETT IS CALLING ON SCHOOL BOARD
LEADERS TO INSIST THAT SEX EDUCATION COURSES ALSO TEACH KIDS THAT
HAVING SEX BEFORE MARRIAGE IS WRONG. HE SAYS SEX EDUCATION COURSES
THAT DON'T TEACH SUCH MORAL VALUES ARE WORTHLESS. IN REMARKS PREPARED
FOR DELIVERY THIS MORNING IN WASHINGTON, BENNETT SAYS HE DOUBTS MUCH
OF THE SEX EDUCATION IN THIS COUNTRY IS DOING ANY GOOD BECAUSE MORE
THAN HALF OF TEENS LOSE THEIR VIRGINITY BY AGE 17.

A SENATE PANEL IS EXPECTED TO HAVE SOME TOUGH QUESTIONS FOR TOP
OFFICIALS OF THE SPACE PROGRAM TODAY. THE OFFICIALS OF ''NASA'' AND
MORTON THIOKOL (THY'-OH-KOL) ARE TO EXPLAIN HOW THEY'RE REDESIGNING
THE SPACE SHUTTLE BOOSTER ROCKET SYSTEM. THE PANEL INVESTIGATING THE
''CHALLENGER'' DISASTER ORDERED THE REDESIGN AFTER DETERMINING THAT
THE ACCIDENT WAS CAUSED BY A FAULTY BOOSTER.

A REAL-LIFE MEDICAL DRAMA IS BEING PLAYED OUT IN PHILADELPHIA.
DOCTORS AT CHILDREN'S HOSPITAL ARE PREPARING TO SEPARATE TWINS JOINED
AT THE HEART, LIVER AND INTESTINES -- KNOWING THE OPERATION WILL KILL
ONE OF THE INFANTS. THE DOCTORS SAY BOTH OF THE
THREE-AND-A-HALF-WEEK-OLD BOYS WOULD DIE WITHOUT THE OPERATION.

SHE HAD LONG BEEN RENOWNED AS THE ''QUEEN OF SOUL.'' AND LAST
NIGHT, ARETHA FRANKLIN WAS INSTALLED AS ONE OF THE QUEENS OF ROCK 'N'
ROLL. SHE WAS AMONG 15 FOUNDING MEMBERS OF THE ROCK 'N' ROLL HALL OF
FAME HONORED DURING CEREMONIES IN NEW YORK CITY. AMONG OTHERS
INDUCTED WERE RICKY NELSON, BILL HALEY, SMOKEY ROBINSON AND MARVIN
GAYE.

NEWSWATCH BY OSCAR WELLS GABRIEL III

Figure 14.1 *Associated Press* Newswatch *copy.*

```
     (ATLANTA) - EARL SHINHOSTER, SOUTHEAST REGIONAL DIRECTOR OF THE
NATIONAL ASSOCIATION FOR THE ADVANCEMENT OF COLORED PEOPLE, SAID
YESTERDAY HE IS NOT SATISFIED THAT STATE AND LOCAL AGENCIES ARE DOING
ENOUGH TO PROTECT THOSE IN THIS SATURDAY'S CIVIL RIGHTS MARCH IN
FORSYTH COUNTY; MEANWHILE SENATOR SAM NUNN SAID HE'LL BE IN CUMMING TO
WELCOME THE MARCHERS, ALTHOUGH HE WILL NOT PARTICIPATE IN THE MARCH
ITSELF.

     (ATLANTA) -- A PROSECUTOR TOLD THE GEORGIA SUPREME COURT YESTERDAY
THAT DEATH ROW INMATE CARLTON GARY WAS CONVICTED IN THREE OF THE
''COLUMBUS STOCKING STRANGLINGS'' BECAUSE OF CONVINCING EVIDENCE
AGAINST HIM; BUT A DEFENSE LAWYER ARGUED THAT GARY WAS THE VICTIM OF A
ONE-SIDED TRIAL.

     (BETHESDA, MARYLAND) -- GEORGIANS AGAINST NUCLEAR ENERGY (OR GANE)
TOOK ONE MORE SHOT YESTERDAY AT THE VOGTLE NUCLEAR POWER PLANT; THE
GROUP ASKED A FEDERAL APPEALS BOARD IN BETHESDA, MARYLAND, TO OVERTURN
A DECISION BY THE ATOMIC SAFETY AND LICENSING BOARD; THAT BOARD
REJECTED A SERIES OF SAFETY ALLEGATIONS THE GROUP HAS RAISED AGAINST
VOGTLE.

     (ATLANTA) -- TWO KEY MEMBERS OF A STATE HOUSE COMMITTEE SAY A HUGE
LOBBYING CAMPAIGN BY THE STATE'S CHURCHES PROBABLY HAS DOOMED ANY
CHANCE GEORGIANS MIGHT HAVE HAD TO VOTE FOR THEMSELVES ON WHETHER THEY
WANT PARI-MUTUEL WAGERING; HOUSE INDUSTRY COMMITTEE CHAIRMAN SONNY
WATSON OF WARNER ROBINS AND BARBARA COUCH OF ATLANTA, CHAIRMAN OF A
SUBCOMMITTEE THAT WILL CONSIDER THE BILL TODAY, NOW SAY THEY DOUBT THE
BILL HAS ENOUGH SUPPORT TO BE PASSED BY THE COMMITTEE.
```

Figure 14.2 *Associated Press* Newsminute *copy.*

An AP radio wire story on the controversial W-4 tax withholding form provides a good example of concise writing. The story in one version was as follows:

> (Washington) — Treasury Secretary James Baker is asking the Internal Revenue Service to revise the new W-4 tax withholding form.
>
> Because of the new tax law, workers are required to file a new W-4 so the right amount will be withheld from their paychecks, but taxpayers and lawmakers who've seen the new form say it's too complicated. The instructions for the new W-4 form are twice as long as for the old one.
>
> Baker told the house budget committee he was on vacation when the form came through for approval.

291

```
   (MANILA, PHILIPPINES) -- MARINES OPENED FIRE TODAY WHEN THOUSANDS
OF MILITANT FARMERS TRIED TO BREAK THROUGH A SECURITY CORDON THROWN
UP TO PREVENT THEM FROM MARCHING TO PRESIDENT CORAZON AQUINO'S OFFICE.
   THERE WAS NO OFFICIAL WORD ON CASUALTIES BUT REPORTERS COULD SEE
THREE PEOPLE LYING ABOUT 300 YARDS FROM THE PRESIDENTIAL PALACE.
   THE MARCHERS, WHOM POLICE SAID NUMBERED ABOUT TEN-THOUSAND,
SCATTERED IN TERROR WHEN THE MARINES BEGAN FIRING IN THE AIR.
SECURITY FORCES TRIED TEAR GAS, AND TWO JEEPLOADS OF TROOPS CHASED
AFTER THE FLEEING DEMONSTRATORS.
   THE PROTESTERS, ORGANIZED BY THE MILITANT MOVEMENT OF PHILIPPINE
FARMERS, HAD VOWED TO MARCH ON MALACANANG PALACE TO PRESS THE
GOVERNMENT FOR LAND REFORM. THE CHAIRMAN OF THE FARMERS' GROUP SAID
AQUINO SHOULD REDISTRIBUTE LAND FROM HER FAMILY'S 14-THOUSAND-800
ACRE ESTATE IN CENTRAL LUZON AS A MODEL FOR LAND REFORM.
   ABOUT 500 RIOT POLICE AND ELITE MARINES WERE DEPLOYED TO BLOCK THE
FARMERS FROM REACHING THE PALACE. WHEN THE MARCHERS REACHED THE
BARRICADES, THEY LINKED ARMS AND BEGAN PRESSING AGAINST THE POLICE
AND MARINES, WHO SHOVED BACK AT THEM WITH THEIR SHIELDS. ROCKS WERE
THROWN -- AND SUDDENLY THE MARINES OPENED UP WITH A VOLLEY. MOST OF
THE TROOPS APPEARED TO HAVE FIRED INTO THE AIR. A POLICEMAN, WHO
REFUSED TO GIVE HIS NAME, SAID THE MARINES ''FIRED TOO SOON.''
   PHILIPPINE ARMED FORCES OFFICIALS ARE BLAMING A LACK OF DIALOGUE
BETWEEN DEMONSTRATORS AND TROOPS FOR A BLOODY STREET CLASH. A
STATEMENT RELEASED IN MANILA CONCEDES. HOWEVER, THAT MARINES
OVERREACTED WHEN THEY FIRED ON A CROWD OF LEFTISTS WHO TRIED BREAK
THROUGH POLICE BARRICADES. AT LEAST 12 DIED AND 94 WERE WOUNDED IN
THE BLOODIEST CONFRONTATION SINCE CORAZON AQUINO CAME TO POWER.
```

Figure 14.3 *The 21-line story written for broadcast early in the day had been trimmed to six lines by the end of the day.*

Now he's asking the I-R-S to take another look at the form and try to come up with a better one.

A considerably shorter version got to the point of the story — the need for a simpler form — more quickly.

Treasury Secretary James Baker is telling the I-R-S to come up with a simpler W-4 tax withholding form. Baker says the new form is too complicated. In the meantime, Baker says taxpayers should keep muddling through the current form. Everyone who works for an employer has to fill out a new W-4 form because of the tax reform law.

An even more concise version followed later in the day.

Treasury Secretary James Baker has told the Internal Revenue Service to revise the new W-4 tax withholding form. The form has been criticized as too long and complex.

Another example: An AP radio wire story about the sale of stock in the Turner Broadcasting System was 25 lines long when it was written for broadcast at 8 p.m. It was reduced to 15 lines an hour later and to seven lines an hour after that. When it was transmitted for the final time, just before midnight, the story had been cut to four lines:

(Atlanta) — To keep an influx of cash, Turner Broadcasting System said today it will sell 550 (M) million dollars worth of stock to financier Kirk Kerkorian and 14 major cable-tv systems. T-B-S said Ted Turner still will own more than half the company.

Figure 14.4 follows a breaking news story, the suicide in front of reporters and television cameras of R. Budd Dwyer, state treasurer of Pennsylvania. You may recall seeing news photos of Dwyer moments before he shot himself. Because his act was so sudden, reporters and photographers were caught by surprise. But photographers react instinctively in moments of crisis, and a series of still photos captured the shooting from the moment Dwyer pulled the pistol out of an envelope to the moment only seconds later when his body lay crumpled on the floor. At least one radio mike was open, and AP later in the day offered an *actuality*, a recording for broadcast. However, the following advisory was sent out ahead of the actuality:

Producers, news and program directors note:
As part of the hourly 2:00 pes newscast, AP Network News will air an actuality of the seconds during which a Pennsylvania state official took his life at a news conference.
This piece of sound is extremely graphic.
You may want to preview the tape, which will air first on the 1:32 pes closed circuit update as cut 182.

Restraint and good taste are problems for broadcast journalists as well as for journalists who write for newspapers. There was considerable controversy over use of the photos of Dwyer's suicide. Some newspapers used them, some did not. A photo of Dwyer with the pistol muzzle in his mouth was widely used. Photos taken in the next few seconds were not. Would you have aired the actuality?

Pennsylvania State Treasurer Budd Dwyer was expected to announce his resignation at a news conference in Harrisburg this morning. But at the end of a long, rambling statement proclaiming his innocence in a bribery case, he pulled out a gun and shot himself. (11:42 a.m.)

Reporters who showed up at a news conference in Harrisburg, Pennsylvania, thought they'd be covering the state treasurer's resignation announcement. Instead, they watched in horror as he shot himself to death. Budd Dwyer was to be sentenced tomorrow for a bribery conviction. (12:33 p.m.)

(Harrisburg, Pennsylvania) — As cameras and tape recorders rolled, Pennsylvania state treasurer R. Budd Dwyer shot himself to death this morning. It happened during a news conference where he was expected to announce his resignation because of a bribery conviction.

At the end of a long, rambling statement in which he proclaimed his innocence, Dwyer pulled a revolver from a manila envelope he was holding, put the gun in his mouth and pulled the trigger.

When he pulled the gun, reporters yelled for him to stop, but Dwyer warned everyone, "Stay away, this thing will hurt someone."

Dwyer and former state Republican chairman Robert Asher were convicted of conspiring to accept bribes in awarding a no-bid computer contract. He was scheduled to be sentenced tomorrow in federal court. The state attorney general had determined that Dwyer would lose his job as state treasurer as soon as he was sentenced. He faced up to 55 years in prison. (12:48 p.m.)

With reporters looking on in horror, Pennsylvania's state treasurer R. Budd Dwyer shot himself to death at a news conference in Harrisburg. He'd been expected to announce his resignation because of a bribery conviction. Instead reporters say he launched into a long, rambling statement of innocence and then pulled a gun out of an envelope, put the barrel in his mouth and pulled the trigger. (1:45 p.m.)

A news conference in Harrisburg, Pennsylvania, turned into a bloody horror show today. State treasurer R. Budd Dwyer, who was expected to announce his resignation, shot himself in front of a crowd of reporters and died a short time later. Dwyer and a former state Republican chairman were convicted last month in a bribery case. In a rambling statement before he shot himself, Dwyer said he was being punished for a crime he did not commit. (3:30 p.m.)

While shocked reporters looked on — Pennsylvania's state treasurer shot and killed himself during a news conference today. R. Budd Dwyer, who was facing jail for defrauding the state, declared his innocence before pulling the trigger. (5:47 p.m.)

Pennsylvania's treasurer was facing jail for defrauding the state. Budd Dwyer called a news conference today, and most people assumed he would announce his resignation. Instead, he shot himself to death as horrified reporters, photographers and government aides looked on. (9:11 p.m.)

Figure 14.4 *An example of a breaking news story carried through the day on the AP radio news wire.*

HARRISBURG, Pa. — Pennsylvania's treasurer, facing jail for defrauding the state, proclaimed his innocence at a news conference yesterday but said "It's too late for me," then pulled a pistol from a manila envelope, put it in his mouth and killed himself.

R. Budd Dwyer died instantly after he fired a single shot from a .357 Magnum pistol in front of two dozen horrified reporters, photographers and aides, said Dauphin County Coroner William Bush.

"No, No! Budd, don't do this!" people gathered in Dwyer's office in the state Finance Building screamed just before he pulled the trigger.

Dwyer's son, Rob, 21, said his father had given the family no indication of what he intended to do.

"We're pretty broken up," he said. He said he heard the news with his mother, Joanne, 47, and his sister, Dyan, 18.

A jury in December convicted Dwyer of awarding a $4.6 million contract to a firm called Computer Technology Associates in return for a promised $300,000 payoff. No money ever changed hands.

He faced up to 55 years in prison on five counts of mail fraud, four counts of interstate transportation in aid of racketeering, one count of perjury and one count of conspiracy to commit bribery.

Figure 14.5 *The Associated Press story on the state treasurer's suicide as it was written for newspapers and published in the* Asbury Park *(N.J.)* Press.

Television: Words and Pictures

Television news is a more complicated business than radio news because of the need to weave words and pictures together. A number of examples of copy prepared for radio are included in this chapter. An example of copy prepared for a television news broadcast is shown in Figure 14.6. The copy shown was prepared by James Polk, an NBC investigative reporter with the NBC bureau in Washington, at the end of the trial of John Gotti in Federal Court in New York. Polk was given two minutes and 15 seconds for his story. He actually used two minutes and 14 seconds.

The numbered copy at left indicates the film to be shown as Polk tells the story of the verdict in the Gotti trial. Pictures — the visuals — included bits of video tape used as evidence during the trial and copied earlier by NBC News for just this occasion; tape made by NBC News during the trial and earlier; sketches made by an NBC News artist on the last day of the trial; and videotape made after the verdict and transmitted to NBC studios from a sound truck just before air time. The words "He's a hoodlum's hoodlum" and the other copy typed in capital letters indicate where other voices, recorded earlier, interrupt the narration of the reporter. Reporters' stories like this one are not broadcast live but are edited onto tape before they are broadcast. Polk's Gotti

FRI 3/13   POLK

POLK -- GOTTI

1. Surveillance tape B & W

   N. Y. Police Dept.
   April 1979

Investigators spent years watching John

Gotti's rise to power in the Mafia, using

hidden cameras, and tape recordings as

mobsters talked about him with respect:

HE'S A HOODLUM'S HOODLUM.

2. sketches at trial/wide shot

   Sketches by:
   IDA LIBBY DENGROVE

The jury deliberated seven days.

Gotti wore black on this Friday the 13th.

The verdict:

3. sketch/ Gotti & jury

innocent of the racketeering charges,

and murder conspiracy.

innocent of loansharking

broad

4. sketch/ Gotti smiling

Gotti broke into a smile.

5. sketch/ wide/ hugging

Other Mafia defendants hugged their lawyer:

6. sketch/ clapping

They applauded as the jury

left the courtroom,

7. sketch/ embrace

then walked up, one by one, to embrace

Gotti.

8. film tape yellow ribbons
   at home

Gotti left the courthouse by a back door.

His home was decorated with yellow ribbons

for his return.

9. Eugene Gotti & lawyer

His brother, Eugene Gotti, was also acquitted.

His lawyer:

SOT: WE'RE FEELING GOOD. WE FEEL LIKE THE
            JURY GAVE A CORRECT VERDICT AND A
            JUST VERDICT.

10. John Gotti's lawyer

John Gotti's lawyer said the jury

rejected the parade of criminals called to

testify against him:

SOT: BRUCE CUTLER
        Defense Attorney

...PAID WITNESSES, WITNESSES WHO HAVE LIED
IN THE PAST, WITNESSES WHO HAVE GOTTEN NEW
IDENTITIES, WITNESSES WHO HAVE SOLD DRUGS,
WITNESSES WHO HAVE KILLED PEOPLE.

Figure 14.6 *A page from a television reporter's copy.*

story was finished just two minutes before it was broadcast on the evening news. This margin, Polk says, is not unusual.

Learning to Write for Broadcast

Beginners who want a career in broadcast journalism are often restive when they are required to take courses in news writing and reporting where the principal emphasis is on writing and reporting for the newspaper.

News writing for the newspaper, however, is a basic skill, and the beginner who masters it can move to another field and learn to write equally well for broadcast. This text is about writing for newspapers, but there is very little in it that won't be helpful to the beginner who wants to go on to radio or television reporting and writing.

Broadcast journalism has its roots in newspaper journalism, and the stars of radio news from the early 1920s until very recently were first newspaper journalists, then broadcast journalists. And the radio journalists who got their first training on newspapers later pioneered television journalism.

Basic training in newspaper writing will provide a solid base for writing in other fields — including broadcasting.

Suggestions for Further Reading

Biagi, Shirley. *News Talk II*. Belmont, Calif.: Wadsworth, 1987.
State-of-the-art conversations with 12 broadcast journalists.

Chancellor, John, and Walter R. Mears. *The News Business*. New York: Harper & Row, 1983.
Good advice about many aspects of the news business by two experienced reporters.

Cohler, David Keith. *Broadcast Journalism*. Englewood Cliffs, N.J.: Prentice-Hall, 1985.
An introduction to writing news for radio and television.

Friendly, Fred W. *Due to Circumstances Beyond Our Control*. New York: Vintage Books, 1968.
An insider discusses the conflicts within the world of broadcast journalism.

Kendrick, Alexander. *Prime Time*. New York: Avon Books, 1969.
A biography of Edward R. Murrow, one of the giants of broadcast journalism.

Shorr, Daniel. *Clearing the Air*. Boston: Houghton Mifflin Co., 1977.
A personal account by a controversial broadcast journalist.

LONDON'S
ALISTAIR BLAIR

■■■■■■■

Above, Alistair Blair's cocktail outfit in crepe de chine with contrasting lining showing at hem and matching, lined two-tone stole. Right, Blair's double-faced wool coat with kimono collar over tartan jacket and slim skirt.

LONDON — Britain's Alistair Blair has learned from the masters. And it shows.

In a season when virtually every international ready-to-wear designer is creating clothes with a finely detailed custom-made look, Blair is one of the few who can claim couture credentials.

Blair's training is impeccable. He studied the rigors of couture's made-to-measure mystique with the great designers of Paris, starting with a six-year initiation with Christian Dior's Marc Bohan, followed by a succession of much-coveted design posts from Givenchy to Chloe and three years as assistant to designer Karl Lagerfeld.

Blair, one of the designers who dresses Sarah Ferguson, Duchess of York, and who has a shop of his own in the offing, is exceptional in Britain for a look that is Parisian in its femme-fatale chic.

His first showing in London a year ago caused a minor sensation — substantial orders were placed by all the top North American shops, including Toronto's Simpsons and Chez Catherine.

"I started off in couture," said the 30-year-old Blair in an interview following the showing of his collection this week at the London fall/winter designer collections. "I hope that I have learned and understand the quality of that, and what you can do with good fabric. I would like to think that what I've just done is as near to couture as ready-to-wear can get."

When Lagerfeld left Chloe to establish his own house, Blair was posted in New York with Karl Lagerfeld Sportswear, but America's Polyester City wasn't to his taste.

Back in Britain — Blair hails from Helensburgh, Scotland — he was approached by Danish fashion financier Peter Bertelsen, owner of Aguecheek.

Bertelsen offered to back Blair's British design debut, and swept his latest investment up and away from a Chelsea basement and into a grand. See BLAIR/page B5

BY NANCY HASTINGS
PHOTOGRAPHY BY BERNARD WEIL

sensational!

Scottish-born designer Alistair Blair with model wearing his full-skirted, double-breasted coat in rich red cashmere. Blair aims for couture cut and quality in his ready-to-wear designs.

15 Features

It is hard news that catches readers. Features hold them.

Lord Northcliffe
British newspaper proprietor

News stories can be written so as to emphasize one of the conventional news elements: what, who, why or even how. You can localize a story to emphasize a tie to your own community in order to satisfy reader interest in local news. And you can play up the most timely, the most recent aspects of a story so as to satisfy the reader's demand for up-to-the-minute news.

In the same way, you can emphasize the unconventional: the unusual, the odd, the humorous, the pathetic or sometimes even the commonplace. Stories of this type can be called human interest stories because they deal with matters that are of basic interest and concern to people. If the stories are light and humorous, they may be called *page brighteners*. Such stories are also called *features*.

Feature is a term with a number of meanings.* In this chapter, we are using the term to describe human interest stories, stories that are neither important nor significant but that appeal to readers because of some special quality, a *feature angle*, that will amuse them, entertain them or touch their emotions.

---

*The various meanings and uses of the word *feature* are explained in the glossary.

The great appeal of the feature story, whether it is funny or sad, is that it involves the reader. Features deal with qualities of human nature that we all understand. And they deal with the kind of things that happen, or could happen, to anyone. The feature exploits our interest in other people and reminds us that we all share common experience.

Feature Angles

Feature stories may be long or short, may be organized in a variety of ways and may have many different kinds of leads, but they are all alike in their emphasis on a feature angle. Here are some typical feature angles that were developed into entertaining human interest stories:

— Police raid a cockfight in a rural area.

— A city council proposes to outlaw tattooing.

— A youngster makes nitroglycerin with his chemistry set and causes an explosion.

— A surprised driver finds a boa constrictor in her car.

— A local resident calls police to get help in finding the owner of a large sum of money found in the street.

— A political message turns up in a batch of fortune cookies.

— University students stage a "study-in" to protest limited library hours.

— A thief is caught fishing money out of a bank's night depository using a line equipped with fish hooks.

— Movers make a mistake and move the wrong building.

— A demolition crew makes a mistake and tears down the wrong building.

— A large number of small boys and girls turn up to buy bicycles at a police auction.

— A young couple marries under unusual circumstances — up in a balloon.

— A mistake is made in a newspaper ad and customers rush to a local store for a "bargain."

The list is endless. Don't forget the lost child; the puppy that needs a home; the family reunited after many years; the child orphaned by an automobile accident or plane crash; the ring found after all those years; the two-headed calf; the chicken with four legs; the quintuplets born to a local couple; the surprised parents who expected one child and got twins or triplets; the cat in a tree; the man, woman or child who fights back against some real or fancied wrong perpetrated by a bank, the Internal Revenue Service or the telephone company; the fraternity that does good deeds instead of hazing its pledges; the divorced couple that remarries; the naive elderly person bilked in a confidence game; the repentant criminal . . .

All kinds of things happen to people, and human events run in cycles. The same things happen, generation after generation, year after year, but since people are always interested in what happens to other people, these things make news, or more properly, they make features. It doesn't matter that the events and situations we are talking about are not really important, except perhaps to the people involved, for they are interesting. They are something to laugh about, to sigh or cry over, and newspapers publish and will continue to publish such stories and readers will continue to read and enjoy them.

The Feature Touch

The following story shows how a routine event can be developed into an entertaining feature:

> BENTON HARBOR (UPI) — Two Benton Harbor men have decided that a professional towing service has its advantages.
>
> Robert Ross, 27, had trouble with his car, which stalled.
>
> Sampson Sally, 22, started towing Ross' car Sunday night. Sally's car, a convertible, ran out of gas. There were no gas stations nearby.
>
> The two men took a felt hat and drained gasoline from the Ross car for the Sally car. They had no flashlight and Ross struck a match to guide the operation.
>
> Sally's convertible was destroyed by flames.

How dull this story would have been if the news writer had not taken advantage of the reader and held back the outcome. The story would have lost its entertainment value — its feature qualities — if it had started out:

> A convertible belonging to Sampson Sally, 22, of
> Benton Harbor was destroyed in a fire last night.

A story written in this way is not a feature. It belongs in the police briefs if it gets in the paper at all. The misfortune of the two Benton Harbor men is not unique. Things like this have happened before and will happen again. The situation is a frequent subject of humor. But properly told, it has an impact on the reader, and it is this impact that the feature writer is after.

Recognizing Feature Angles

The first problem you face in dealing with features is learning to recognize the situations, the little twists in events, that represent feature angles. You have to develop a nose for feature angles just as you have to develop a nose for other kinds of news, and this chapter will provide you with some guidelines as you develop your skills as a reporter and news writer. Then, of course, you will have to develop a knack for writing the feature in such a way that it has maximum impact on the reader. Feature stories require a special touch. Some news writers have a natural ability for recognizing feature angles and writing bright and lively features. Others must learn the technique.

The treatment of features in this chapter is brief but suggestive and should be enough to help you on your way toward developing your own instincts about features. *Featurizing* is a concept, just as *localizing* is a concept. If you can learn to recognize a feature angle, then you can learn to write the feature story.

Writing Features

Feature stories may be written in a number of ways, but one of the simplest is to write a brief summary lead and then tell the story chronologically.

In the following feature, the summary lead tells us all that we need to know about the story. The chronological development provides the details, and the conclusion is simply the final step of the chronology.

> A 24-year-old Pontiac man told police he was bilked
> of $65 yesterday after another man approached him at a
> downtown bank and asked for "help" in making a deposit.

Elden O. Lloyde Jr., who gave his address as 16 S. Perty, said he was making a deposit at the Community National Bank, 30 N. Saginaw, when a man sought his assistance.

Lloyde said the man then walked outside the bank, showed "a large sum of money," and offered Lloyde $50 to help him deposit the money in the bank if Lloyde would put up $65 "security."

The man then wrapped Lloyde's money and the $50 into a blue handkerchief and left, according to the victim.

Lloyde said he opened the handkerchief only to find some folded newspaper sheets.

— *The Oakland Press*, Pontiac, Mich.

This feature story's effect depends first of all on the feature angle. The story itself is interesting, and all the writer has to do is tell it simply. The straightforward summary lead followed by a concise chronology is a reliable format. It is almost a matter of just letting the story write itself. Adding unnecessary details or forced cleverness or explaining things readers can grasp for themselves can easily ruin a good feature. Keep it bare, keep it brief.

The feature that follows is handled in much the same way. The summary lead consists of two brief paragraphs that make simple statements about the events in the story. But the summary lead does not spoil the story by telling too much — just enough to stimulate the reader's curiosity. "That's odd," the reader thinks. "Now how did it happen? It never happened to me." Here's the story:

MEMPHIS, Tenn. (UPI) — C.B. Roach has discovered what that funny noise was in his car.

It was a turtle, and it had been living behind a panel for four months.

"I thought I was going nuts," Roach said. "I'd be driving along and hear this scratching, then kerplunk. I looked a hundred times and couldn't find anything."

Finally, Roach decided he'd had enough. He took the car to a mechanic and told him "I don't care what you do. Take the car apart. Just find the noise."

The mechanic found the turtle behind an upholstery panel.

Roach was so happy to solve the mystery that he fed the turtle, then gave him to the zoo.

The final episode in the turtle story, the conclusion, is an important element in many feature stories. It wraps up the story and answers the reader's obvious questions. In this case, if we hadn't been told, we would certainly have asked: "What did he do with the turtle?"

Keep It Simple

Keeping a story simple may mean, in some instances, dispensing with the lead. The feature about George Jefferson and the big shootout, Figure 15.1, is an interesting example of this technique. This story has no summary lead and consists only of a chronological account. The story starts at a convenient point in the chronology and goes on from there. The first paragraph does identify the principal actor in the story and tell what he was doing, but it contains no other lead elements. And the start of the story is certainly not a summary, for there isn't the slightest hint as to how the story came out. This story is a little longer than the two previous examples and is told to a large extent in the first person, in the words of the central figure in the story. Only here and there does the writer insert a few words to keep the story moving along properly. As the story reaches its end, we see that it is going to come out all right, but the writer adds a concluding statement, still in the words of the man involved in the story.

6 policemen arrive, big shootout fizzles

By Richard S. Vonier
Of The Journal Staff

George Jefferson parked his car at N. 18th st. and W. Wisconsin av. Tuesday and walked off carrying a toy pistol for his 7 year old son in nearby Milwaukee Children's Hospital.

"First, I put it in my pocket," he explained, "but then I went to light my cigar. When I slipped my hand in the pocket for my lighter, there was the gun sticking out. So I pulled it out and folded it in the newspaper I was carrying."

In the hospital lobby, Jefferson met his wife, Ruby, who was waiting for their son, Lawrence. The son was having X-rays taken.

"I sat down in a chair, you know, and laid the newspaper on a table," Jefferson continued. "Then, when I started to read the newspaper, I gave the gun to my wife, and said, 'Here, put this in your purse.'

"I forgot to bring him the gun Monday, and me being so forgetful, I figured I'd better give it to my wife so she'd remember."

While they were waiting, the

Jeffersons decided to get coffee in the cafeteria. Jefferson made a stop in the men's room.

"There was a big cop standing there with his hand on his gun when I came out," he reported. "He was looking at me awful hard. Then he went in the rest room.

"Then we went into the coffee shop and he came in there and looked at me again. Then he went out again, but came back with another uniformed policeman and a detective.

"The detective showed me his badge, and wanted to know if I was George Jefferson. He said to come along with them.

"He said, 'You'd better get your cap,' so I guess that meant I was on my way.

"When we got outside the coffee shop, my wife wanted to know what this was all about. The detective said they had a call that I put a gun in my wife's purse.

"Suddenly, it all began to unfold."

(Actually, Jefferson learned later, there had been two reports. The first one said a man carrying a gun in a newspaper walked into the hospital. A caller had noted Jefferson's license number, and that's how the police — six responded — knew his name.)

"I took it out of the purse by the barrel — very carefully," Jefferson said. "They was looking pretty serious, and I wasn't going to take no chances that they'd think I was going to come out shooting.

"The detective kinda looked at the gun. Then he looked at the officers. Then he said, 'Well!'

"It was one of those plastic jobs. A six shooter, you know, with a big hammer on it. I guess it looked like an old .45.

"One of the officers asked a doctor if he had a bag. He said, 'Let's keep it in the bag until you get it up to the room, so someone else doesn't make a mistake.'"

Jefferson, 50, of 57334 N. 75th st., an overhead crane operator at the Harnischfeger Corp., said he had to leave for work so he couldn't stay to see his son.

"I also had to go get me something for my nerves," he added.

Figure 15.1 *An artfully told story from* The Milwaukee Journal. *Much of the effect of this story comes from the use of the principal actor's own words.*

Involve the Reader

The conclusion of the story about George Jefferson is a direct bid for reader reaction. "Boy, so would I," says the reader. "So would I." Again, note the simplicity of the story: a straightforward account in the first person with only a few additions by the writer. The first-person account involves the reader. We just listen as George Jefferson tells what happened to him. And the conclusion is a final, subtle touch. It pulls us right into the story. The reader can only let out a sigh of relief and say: "If it happened to me, I'd feel the same way."

Hold Something Back

A useful kind of summary lead for a feature is not the complete summary that we would write on a hard-news story. Instead it is a *partial summary* that tells just enough of the story to stimulate the reader's curiosity without completely satisfying it. The partial summary lead sets the stage and hints at the nature of the story but holds back enough of the details to force the reader to read on. The following feature has a summary lead that reveals the outcome of the story but tells it in such a way that we have to read on to satisfy our curiosity about how and why:

> CINCINNATI (UPI) — Jerry Held, 27, of suburban Delhi Hills rang up $90 worth of apologies in police court Saturday.
>
> Held was arrested Friday night as he walked across a downtown street against a red light and yelled at a passing police cruiser.
>
> Patrolman Charles Greenert said Held continued to argue loudly when he stopped. He charged Held with disorderly conduct.
>
> In police court Saturday Held told Judge Robert V. Wood he had apologized to Greenert Friday night.
>
> "That cuts the fine from $100 to $50," said Wood.
>
> "I also apologized again this morning," Held said.
>
> "That cuts it to $25," Judge Wood said. "Now if you will apologize to me that will cut it to $10."
>
> Held apologized to Judge Wood and paid a fine of $10 and costs.

Another way to write a feature story is to write a partial summary lead and then develop the story in the suspended-interest format with the punch line carefully withheld until the very end. The story about Robert Ross and Sampson Sally was written in this way. Not every story lends itself to this treatment, but when the situation is right, the suspended-interest story can be very effective.

Another good example of the suspended-interest format can be seen in this feature:

> GRANT (UPI) — Jimmy Morrison, a local restaurant operator, made sure he was well prepared before setting off on a three-day deer hunting trip to Michigan's northland.
>
> He made a thorough check of his maps, made sure his camping equipment was in good shape and packed

plenty of ammunition and warm clothing before driving 75 miles to the hunting grounds north of Baldwin.

Morrison returned to Grant Wednesday empty-handed.

He had left his rifle at home.

The story is simply told in chronological order. The punch line is held back until the final sentence. And the writer has added to the impact by deliberately misleading the reader with the words *well prepared* in the first paragraph.

One more example. This feature is also a suspended-interest story, although it doesn't have a punch line. We are led into the story with what appears to be an informative summary lead. The second paragraph reveals the point of the story to be one we hadn't expected at all. The lead misled us.

SAN FRANCISCO (AP) — More than 100 physicians whose specialty is the study of why and how folks get fat dined Wednesday night at the Mark Hopkins Hotel. They had:

Beef stroganoff, shrimp newburg, cold cuts, cheese, chicken salad, green salad, potato salad, bread, butter and pastries.

Playing with Words

In the feature stories examined so far, the emphasis has been on simplicity. The leads have been brief and revealed just enough to draw the reader into the story. In each case, once the lead was written, the story practically told itself, usually in simple chronological order. There was no need for trick writing. Indeed, overwriting or trick writing would have spoiled those stories, for the feature angle was inherent in the event or situation itself. The main problem for the writer was to do as little as possible and to let the story tell itself.

There are times, however, when some aspect of the story, some little twist, allows the writer to add a creative touch. This added touch may be necessary to attract the reader or it may just be a bonus. A good example of this is the following lead on a story about high meat prices and a housewives' boycott:

LIVERMORE, Calif. (AP) — The meat boycott is a lot of tripe, and housewives deserve the higher prices they are getting, says Margie Thompson, who has been in the butchering business for 30 years.

Here the writer is playing with words to add interest to the story. It's a useful device to pep up a routine story as well as to add luster to stories that are inherently interesting. The feature that follows is a perfectly good story in itself, but the writer has taken pains to add a little something in the lead:

> BALTIMORE, Md. (AP) — Only by sticking to his guns, standing his ground and keeping a stiff upper lip did George Gorney emerge victorious in his battle with the U.S. Internal Revenue Service.
>
> It started in September, when Gorney watched a friend at a boatyard fill out a form for a rebate of the excise taxes he paid on gasoline for a powerboat.
>
> Gorney, 38, a salesman, claimed a similar rebate for gas used in operating his mechanized lawn mower.
>
> Back came a letter from IRS, rejecting the claim.
>
> "I called the fellow who signed the letter," he said.
>
> "Then I got disconnected or something. I thought he got mad or something so I hung up."
>
> Then came another letter, saying his claim had been reconsidered.
>
> And last Thursday, Gorney received a check covering the rebate, which — figured on the basis of the three gallons of gas he used in the mower — totaled six cents.

A familiar saying, proverb or aphorism or a line from a popular song or poem often can provide a bond of immediate understanding between writer and reader. The tax story lead used several clichés: *to stick to one's guns, to stand one's ground, to keep a stiff upper lip.* It's generally best to avoid clichés, but in this case, the effect was to make the point about Gorney's determination. There is a fine line between catching a reader's attention with a familiar phrase or metaphor and turning off the reader with a cliché — words so overused that they no longer have impact. Make use of the familiar, but don't overdo it. Develop a light touch. The following feature lead depends on a pun, the contrast between the colloquial meaning of the word *dough* and the conventional meaning. The writer is playing a verbal game with the reader:

SHERWOOD, Ore. (AP) — A woman opened a box of cake mix Saturday and found a lot of dough — nearly $4,000 in U.S. Savings bonds.

The writer of a story about a man who dreamed he was Superman and stepped out of a second-story window was playing with words in this description of what happened:

Slower than a speeding bullet, he thudded to earth 15 feet below.

Another example of the right word in the right place, in a story from the *Atlanta Constitution* about a man who was seen jogging in the nude:

The naked jogger was described as a very cold white male, about 5 feet 11 inches tall and about 180 pounds.

In the feature story in Figure 15.2, the writer plays with words. The word play here could have been overdone, but the writer stops just short of the danger point. It is a competently done feature with a nice beginning and an effective conclusion.

Allusions

Sometimes a literary, historical or topical allusion serves as a good starting place. For example:

IOWA CITY — Well, folks, there may be trouble in River City . . . lots and lots of trouble . . . but it was nothing compared to the trouble in Iowa City.
You spell it with a "T" and rhyme it with "P" and "P" stands for pass . . . and that's how Iowa beat Michigan Saturday.

— *Detroit Free Press*

Allusions are useful if the reference is immediately recognized by the reader. They are a kind of shortcut to understanding between writer and reader. The allusion in the *Free Press* lead to a song from "The Music Man" works only if readers know the song. Allusions and references must either be very current or topical, or they must refer to something that is part of our common language or culture — for example, a verse or a name from the Bible.

Purr-fect stranger; why the whole chorus thought it was Morris

By Alexander Friedrich

What has 99 lives and measures 44 feet?

Eleven cool cats, of course.

Which is just exactly how many finicky felines were entered yesterday during a Morris the Cat Look-Alike Contest in Gainesville.

Before continuing our tail, let's paws for this message: The contest was sponsored by the Hall County Humane Society.

The 11 kitties — Peaches, Stripy, Benson, Fozzie and the rest — all attempted to impress judges Shuri Slater of the Humane Society and B.J. Williams of radio station Y-106 FM.

One of the entrants insisted he was Morris. And he was — that's the name of the office cat at the Animal Medical Center.

"He's the one who sits and glares at you when you come in the office," explained Angela Brisendine of the not-so-famous Morris.

The competition included its share of catty puns, but once it had moved a fur piece it became clear only one of the 11 was as debonair as TV star Morris.

That was Stripy, owned by 4-year-old Bethany Martin, daughter of Nick and Mae Martin. Once the kitty had been fed, it was Stripy who held the purrfect hand and was proclaimed "Cat Most Like Morris." He also received his own supply of cat toys.

That seemed OK by Blackie, the office cat at Gainesville Scrap Iron and Metal. Blackie was named "Cat Most Unlike Morris."

"I entered Blackie because Blackie's a cat, and they can't discriminate," said Sanford Loef. "It's just like the Miss America Pageant."

Well, sort of.

— *The Times*, Gainesville, Ga.

Figure 15.2 *The writer played with words to brighten this feature.*

More will be said about this widely used literary device in a later chapter.

Creative Leads

Some features depend not so much on playing with words — verbal trickery — as on using language that is imaginative and creative. Here are some leads that have that creative touch:

One of the last of the great nonspenders, Alfred J. Tennyson of Pawtucket, is about to retire after nearly 20 stingy years in the state budget office.
— *Providence* (R.I.) *Journal-Bulletin*

"Ruly teenagers entering the building . . . 9,280."
"Unruly teenagers entering building . . . 17."
— *The New York Times*

A seven-foot water snake went out for a writhe yesterday, it being that kind of a day.
— *Associated Press*

Richard Hays was in jail, while his twin brother, Kenneth, was out. But for a while, Kenneth was in and Richard was out when Richard was supposed to be in and Kenneth was supposed to be out.
— *Associated Press*

Anyone can forget where he parked his car for a day. Or maybe even for a week. But for one year, six months and 22 days?
— *Reuters*

If there's anything that makes a bear mad, it's to be standing in a road in the middle of nowhere minding its own business and be hit with a motorcycle.
— *Charleston* (W. Va.) *Gazette*

Justice is supposed to be swift, but a Gaston County Superior Court jury was so swift it delivered a not guilty verdict before hearing testimony from the defense.
— *Charlotte* (N.C.) *Observer*

The well-done feature is a work of art whose success depends as much on the telling as on the facts. The facts are usually simple, as in the feature in Figure 15.3, which tells how a college student insured his guppy and, when it died, talked the insurance company into paying a death benefit.

The writer who wove the facts into this entertaining story, who embroidered and gave life to the bare facts, first of all recognized the feature possibility in the story. Then came the selection of details, the attention to organization, the choice of words and phrases — in short, the application of writing talent and skills.

There is usually a special tone to a feature story, and the story about Fred Finn has that special quality — in this case, a tongue-in-cheek sense of humor. There is little news in the Fred Finn story, but it has strong entertainment value.

Guppy dies; insurers are hooked for $650

OKLAHOMA CITY (AP) — After Fred Finn Mazanek gulped his last, Globe Life & Accident Insurance Co. paid off — but not before trying to wriggle off the hook.

After all, Fred was just a guppy.

The whole thing started last year when Globe offered Stan Mazanek, then a senior at the University of Arizona, a special, once only, student-discount life insurance policy.

For just $1, the company offered, the insured could purchase a $5,000 policy good for six months.

Mazanek, 24, figured to be around longer than six months, so he decided to sign up his guppy, Fred Finn Mazanek.

Before sending in the application, Mazanek made sure to answer all the questions accurately:

Age of insured: "6 months."
Weight: "30 centigrams."
Height: "3 centimeters."
Good health: "Yes."
In the military service? "No."
Relationship of beneficiary to insured: "Owner."

Mazanek figured Globe Life would return his check, but instead it issued policy No. 3261057. So when Fred died, Mazanek notified Globe.

That's when Globe took a closer look at the application. A special representative was sent to Tucson, Ariz., to see whether Mazanek was the kind of man who would take advantage of a "clerical error."

Yes, said Mazanek.

No jury would award $5,000 for the death of a guppy, the Globe man argued.

Mazanek offered to settle for $1,000.

Not a penny more than $650, the Globe man replied.

Mazanek said no, but then reconsidered and accepted. He said he used part of the settlement to buy two more guppies and a fish dinner for his family.

Globe Life president John N. Singletary was reached Friday at a fishing lodge where he and other company executives were meeting.

"It's sort of funny, you'll have to admit," Singletary said.

"You know, we mass-produce these policies and we have about 340,000 of them in effect. He put a strange name on there for a fish, and our computer just isn't trained to catch fish, I guess you could say."

Figure 15.3 *The writer of this entertaining feature used a play on words in the lead, but the rest of the story is a straightforward account in chronological order. There is extensive quotation and a slight touch of exaggeration. The point of view of the insurance company provides an appropriate conclusion.*

More Than One Way

As you can see from the examples in this chapter, there are a number of ways of writing human interest stories. Given the same facts, different writers, or the same writer, can find different ways of writing the story.

The *Detroit Free Press* story in Figure 15.4 makes use of a simple literary device, putting the reader into the story. Just imagine, the writer coaxes the reader, that this was your idea. Then he continues to talk out loud to the reader as the story is developed.

The writer has, as you can see, involved the reader. "Imagine this, get that, do this," the writer urges. "Wouldn't it be a good idea? Why not?" And the writer makes good use of conversation. He talks out loud to himself as he tells the story so that the reader may follow his thoughts:

> Voila!
> Cognac. Tomato juice. A drink. Call it a "Bloody Napoleon."

And he talks directly to the reader:

> Quick, Henri, more Cognac. Forget the bloody tomato juice. I'll drink it straight.

Fragments of high school French help jazz up the story: a *voila* here, a *zut alors* there.

The feature in Figure 15.5 employs a great deal of direct quotation and colloquial language. The writer clearly is reconstructing dialogue and embellishing the story with the punning references to raspberries and peanuts. The creative use of imagination to tell a story, the reconstruction of dialogue, the re-creation of scenes the writer most certainly did not witness are perfectly legitimate in their place. Daniel DeFoe did it in "A Journal of the Plague Year." Tom Wolfe, Gail Sheehy, Hunter S. Thompson and other new journalists have done it more recently. The banana feature was obviously written from a basis of fact. The dialogue surely has been re-created by the writer. There is a touch of exaggeration, another useful literary device. But the story is true and the feature touches — the creative or fictional touches — have made the story more readable and more entertaining. Just as important, the feature touches have not changed the facts or the meaning of the story.

The professional news writer does not make up stories — doesn't fake. But the skilled writer can heighten the effectiveness of a story by

313

NAPOLEON, Ohio — Imagine for a moment that it is your job to promote the sale and consumption of a good French brandy, a Cognac called Courvoisier and known as the "brandy of Napoleon."

Wouldn't it be a good gimmick to somehow tie that brandy into a solid little northwestern Ohio community bearing the French emperor's name?

Voila!

Napoleon, Ohio, population 7,300, is about to celebrate the 150th anniversary — more or less — of its founding by French-Canadian fur trappers and also to mark the opening of the annual Tomato Festival and the Henry County Fair.

Why not somehow combine all these ingredients? Yes, but how?

Voila!

Cognac. Tomato juice. A drink. Call it a "Bloody Napoleon."

Get all the 7,300 residents — or at least all those old enough to drink — and have them toast the festival and fair with "Bloody Napoleons."

Zut alors!

Contact the Chamber of Commerce. Call the French consul. Bring in some prominent people from Toledo, 40 miles to the northeast. Contact the newspapers.

Change the name of Main Street to Rue de Courvoisier.

All set. Raise the glasses. Clink. Clunk.

Only 17 people turned out for the toast.

At the crowded fairgrounds where most of Napoleon's 7,300 residents — at least those old enough to walk — are milling around looking at the prize tomatoes, a woman says:

"Napoleon Bonaparte? Oh, yes. I remember the name from school. He was some Frenchman, wasn't he?"

Quick, Henri, more Cognac. Forget the bloody tomato juice. I'll drink it straight.

— *Detroit Free Press*

Figure 15.4 *An amusing feature story about a promotion that failed.*

the use of creative techniques commonly used by the novelist or short story writer and also commonly used by the news writer. Creativity is an important ingredient of all good writing, and you will find further discussions of its use in Chapters 16 and 17.

The feature in Figure 15.6 is simple and conventional. It has a partial summary lead, three paragraphs explaining how the speeding problem was solved and an anecdotal concluding paragraph. Very straightforward. No tricks. No gimmicks.

The feature in Figure 15.7 has only one feature touch. This story is written in the familiar inverted-pyramid format with a summary lead. Again, no tricks, no gimmicks.

Many news stories lend themselves to the feature touches we have discussed in this chapter. Sometimes a news writer, faced with writing a story that has obvious feature possibilities, just doesn't feel clever — can't turn on the creative mood. As you can see from the features shown

BRISTOL, Conn. (UPI) — The housewife and the car dealer have come to terms on the late model sedan and all agree the deal was just the bananas. She gets the car. He gets the 1,395 bananas.

Dealer Joe Degone said he's also been getting a few raspberries for being outmaneuvered so handily by Mrs. Bernice Wyszynski.

And, he said, he still means bucks when he advertises cars "for only 1,395 bananas," even though he will take the fruit for the car this time.

Mrs. Wyszynski snapped up Joe's offer and plopped down a 25-banana down payment on his desk. She told the salesman she wanted the car. They started eating the down payment.

"Your bananas are very delicious, lady, but you got to be putting us on," she said the salesman told her.

Mrs. Wyszynski said she wasn't.

She complained to state Consumer Protection Commissioner Attilio J. Frassinelli.

Degone then called Mrs. Wyszynski and said she could come down and get the car, but "bring the bananas."

"Don't worry," the housewife said. "I called the fruit man and he said he could get them for me on a moment's notice."

"I figure that at 18 cents a pound and three to a pound, those bananas cost me $75 to $100."

Degone said he will give the bananas to the Newington Home for Crippled Children and that, after a long talk with Mrs. Wyszynski, "we're the best of friends."

He said he did not think anyone put her up to the deal.

"She just saw a way to get a car and took it. It was a sharp deal on her part."

Degone said business has picked up and that now everybody calls his agency about a car and wants to buy it for peanuts.

Figure 15.5 *This feature makes effective use of dialogue and colloquial speech.*

in Figures 15.6 and 15.7, it isn't always necessary to be bright, witty or funny. If the story is good, it can be told simply, with routine structure and organization. A good summary lead, a chronological development or even the ordinary inverted-pyramid format may do very well. If the feature twist is there, the reader will see it and respond to it whether the writer dolls it up or presents it without any frills.

In Summary

This chapter has introduced a new element — the imaginative, creative use of language — to the discussion of news writing. There will be more to say on this subject in Chapters 16 and 17.

Another new element — human interest — has also been added to our list of news values. News writing deals with real events and with

Police work: the world's slowest cruiser

Gary Gleason, a sign builder, was upset because people coming through the central Kansas town of Hedville rarely slowed to the 30 m.p.h. speed limit.

Hedville doesn't have a police department. So with the consent of the Kansas Highway Patrol and the county sheriff, Gleason built a full-sized plastic squad car. It's got the standard black and white paint job, a red light on top, and even a profile of a man's head in the side window.

About a week ago, he placed his creation, which has a "Hedville Police" sign on its door, near the railroad tracks at the edge of town.

"When they see it, they slow down," he said. "When they get to the tracks, they're usually doing 5 m.p.h. It seems to be working real well."

Gleason has watched several evenings as motorists cruise down a hill from an intersection with Interstate 70 about a mile away.

"At night, you can't tell the difference between the fake police car and a real one," he said.

It fools non-speeders, too. One man stopped at the phony car to ask directions.

— *Philadelphia Inquirer*

Figure 15.6 *A humorous story told simply and without any special feature touches except the anecdotal conclusion.*

The stuffed dog case

Miami night watchman T.J. Stephenson is holding Dade County officials responsible for separating him for three days from his stuffed German shepherd, Whisker.

Stephenson, whose pet has been immortalized by a taxidermist in a sleeping position, has sued the county for $5,001, claiming that on Feb. 9, while he was in a bar having a drink, police improperly towed away his car with Whisker stretched out on the back seat.

He is seeking compensation for loss of his auto, towing bills and anxiety over Whisker.

A passer-by, thinking Whisker had suffocated in the locked car, called the police. The car was towed away and Whisker was taken to the Humane Society, where he remained three days before being returned to Stephenson.

— *Atlanta Journal and Constitution*

Figure 15.7 *This light feature is written in the inverted-pyramid format with a straightforward summary lead. There is only one feature touch — the description of the dog as immortalized by a taxidermist.*

real people, but as this chapter suggests, there is no reason that news writing cannot be interesting and entertaining as well as factual and informative.

News writing does have some restrictions and some limitations. These have been apparent in earlier chapters. Now you are being invited to shake off some of the usual restrictions and to enjoy the real freedom to be found in professional writing by developing your own writing style, a style that includes not only accuracy and precision but also creativity and imagination.

Suggestions for Further Reading

These collections include some classic examples of reportage by major journalistic writers.

Breslin, Jimmy. *The World According to Breslin*. New York: McGraw-Hill Book Company, 1984.

> An anthology of Breslin's columns from the *New York Daily News*.

Capote, Truman. *The Dogs Bark*. New York: New American Library, 1973.

> Capote is both a novelist and a journalist.

Mills, Nicolaus. *The New Journalism*. New York: McGraw-Hill Book Company, 1974.

> An anthology of new journalists, including Jimmy Breslin, Pete Hamill and Norman Mailer.

Sheehan, Susan. *A Missing Plane*. New York: G.P. Putnam's Sons, 1986.

> A brilliant piece of reporting. An account of what happened after the wreck of a World War II plane was found in the jungles of New Guinea nearly 40 years after it had crashed. (See Chapter 8, Figures 8.3 and 8.4.)

Thompson, Hunter S. *The Great Shark Hunt*. New York: Rolling Stone Press, 1979.

> Includes some fine examples of Thompson's reportorial skills.

Wilkinson, Alec. *Moonshine*. New York: Knopf, 1986.

> The story of Garland Bunting, a federal revenue service agent who hunts moonshiners in and around a small town in North Carolina.

Wolfe, Tom. *The New Journalism*. New York: Harper & Row, Publishers, 1973.

> Wolfe's critical analysis of new journalism and an anthology of some representative reportage.

The Oregonian/NANCY PULLMIER

YOUNG VOICES
A YOUTH FORUM

Suicide, alcohol, pregnancy, drugs and fatal accidents loom over today's pressured teens

STRESS

By JUDY McDERMOTT
of The Oregonian staff

Child psychologist David Elkind calls them "hurried children" — miniature adults garbed in sophisticated designer-label costumes, exposed to gratuitous sex and violence, expected to cope with an increasingly bewildering social environment.

Today's teen-ager, says the Tufts University professor, has become the unwilling, unintended victim of overwhelming stress — the stress born of rapid, bewildering social change and constantly rising expectations.

Staggering numbers of teen-agers, says Elkind, lack the adult guidance, direction and support they need to make a healthy transition to adulthood. They are, in effect, "unplaced," denied the special recognition and protection that society previously accorded their age group.

Harsh words. But judging by comments from The Oregonian's Youth Forum, sadly true.

The 13 high school juniors and seniors, who gather monthly to discuss a subject of concern to today's teen-agers, point in several directions as they attempt to trace the origins of that stress.

Blame it on parental expectations, they say. Blame it on inner drive. Blame it on today's hyper-competitive society.

Blame it on the rat box.

"It's the little things," says Jon Cawthorne, a senior at Jefferson High School whose responsibilities include cleaning the kitty litter. "It's amazing what an issue the cat box can become," confirms Krista Lamvik, a junior at Portland Christian High School.

"Parents, if they can't find something big, will find something little," agrees Arah Erickson, a senior at Catlin Gabel School.

The comments produce laughter all around, but the forum (whose discussion continues in the accompanying story) is deadly serious. "I do not know anyone who is not under stress," Lamvik says.

Sobering statistics

No one disputes the fact that the teen-age years, full of confusion, stress and insecurity, can be turbulent. Figures from

With additional reporting by Knight-Ridder News Service

the National Center for Health Statistics paint a grim picture of the growing risk of adolescence.

● Every 78 seconds, an adolescent in this country attempts suicide. Every 90 minutes, one succeeds. That adds up to nearly 5,000 teen-age suicides a year, triple the number in 1960.

● Every 20 minutes, an adolescent is killed in an accident.

● Every 31 seconds, an adolescent becomes pregnant.

● Nearly half of all high school seniors have used an illegal drug at least once, and almost 90 percent have used alcohol. An estimated 1.5 million teen-agers are problem drinkers.

Dr. Daniel Offer, chief of psychiatry at Michael Reese Hospital and Medical Center in Chicago, estimates that 20 percent of young people suffer from serious mental disorders. Among "normal" adolescents, he says, 20 percent tend to feel emotionally empty and view life as an endless series of problems without solutions; another 20 percent confess to being confused most of the time.

For the young person in today's fast-paced world, the stresses take many forms: family problems and pressures, the loss of a loved one, despair at the threatened loss of an important relationship, financial pressures, the identity problems that come with the transition from adolescence to the adult world, the increased availability of drugs and alcohol, and high academic competition.

"The whole spectrum of what is normal

for adolescents is moving in a direction that is socially pathological," says Mihaly Csikszentmihalyi, head of behavioral sciences at the University of Chicago.

"Our society has come to the point where it feels that using marijuana and alcohol are pretty normal, that sexual intercourse at a younger age is pretty normal and that teen-age pregnancy is becoming almost normal."

Expectations and reality

At Providence Medical Center, William Thorne, coordinator of employee assistance services, says single-parent households with insufficient income to meet family needs are a major source of stress for teen-agers.

In such a household, the working parent is never as "available" as the child would like, Thorne says. "Kids tell me, 'Gosh, when my mom is home, she's so tired.' And kids in that situation hesitate to burden a parent with their problems."

While Thorne describes himself as "essentially an optimist," he thinks that "too many kids end up feeling very pessimistic about whether there will be a position for them in society." Add to that the existential worry — "Is there going to be a world to inherit?" — and Thorne says it's not difficult to understand the sense of powerlessness.

Fifty years ago, young people's choices were made for them — occupation, education, recreation, maybe even life partner, notes Geordie Knapp, an adolescent and family therapist at Lutheran Family Service.

"Drugs were no problem at all, there might be an occasional beer sneaked out of the refrigerator, smoking was looked down on, sexual preference was a hidden issue.

"Your life was pretty much laid out." Not so anymore. Now, the number of choices has mushroomed, and the young person often has no help in making them. "I've worked with 24- and 25-year-olds who are still struggling with adolescence," Knapp said.

Stress, '80s style

Tuft's Elkind has identified four stressful situations he considers unique to adolescents of the late 20th century:

● **Responsibility overload.** Instead of "chores," the teen-ager in today's increasingly common single-parent household often has adult responsibilities, for young-

See **STRESS,** Page B6.

Q: Why do young people feel so stressed out?

"It's impossible to do everything, and friends want you to do things you don't want to do."

—Dottie LaBenske
Roosevelt High School

"My parents say, 'Do what you want.' They know (if I fail) I'll be disappointed with my own performance."

—John Ohnstad
Lakeridge High School

Test your stress

This a simple test to help teen-agers determine if they are under too much stress and should seek help before tragedy strikes.

Circle the numbers of all the events that have happened to you in the past year. Do not attempt to evaluate how stressful you think each event was.

The test key and an explanation of what your score means are on Page 6 of Living.

1. Rape
2. Suicide of parent
3. Death of parent
4. Divorce of parents
5. Sexual abuse (past or present)
6. Physical abuse (past or present)
7. Parents separating
8. Death of family member
9. Abortion
10. Serious illness in family
11. Dependency on drugs/alcohol
12. Death or suicide of friend
13. Remarriage of parent
14. Dependency by parent on drugs/alcohol
15. Emotional illness in family
16. Emotional abuse (past or present)
17. Illness or injury to self
18. Pregnancy
19. Formation of stepfamily
20. Sexual relationship of a single parent
21. Difficulty in child-parent relationship
22. Breakup with serious boy/girl-friend
23. Parental expectations for academic or sports achievement
24. Death of pet
25. Running away
26. Formation of stepfamily
27. Fear of nuclear war
28. Being placed in special education
29. Move to a new home
30. Moving out of home
31. Witnessing a violent event
32. Failing/repeating grade
33. First sexual encounter
34. Inability to refuse sexual advances
35. Mother returning to work
36. First date
37. Court involvement
38. Addition to family (stepsiblings/parent)
39. Applying to college
40. College rejections
41. College acceptances
42. Looking for a job (summer job included)
43. Fear of AIDS or VD
44. Athletically unsuccessful
45. Vacation
46. Christmas season

Tips ease pressure

For teen-agers, there is no such thing as a stress-free existence. The pressures come from every direction: peers, parents, conflicting feelings, waiting for independence, having to make important life decisions.

In "The Teen-Age Survival Guide (Simon & Schuster)" Kathy McCoy offers 10 constructive ways of dealing with the inevitable stresses of life.

● **Know your stress limit.** Recognize what the stresses are in your life and how much you can take before you start feeling exhausted, trapped and overwhelmed. Take your life stresses in moderate doses (particularly by keeping reasonable limits on part-time work and extracurricular activities) and you'll reduce anxiety and banish that helpless, out-of-control feeling.

● **Start small.** Don't try to change your life or lifestyle all at once. Take on one problem or challenge at a time. Solve the problem, meet the challenge and move on to the next.

● **Get a fresh perspective.** If you're a stress-prone person, you feel everything intensely and see every pressure as a life-and-death matter. Learn to ask yourself: "Is this really worth all the anxiety? What is my nervousness accomplishing?" And recognize that life does go on. It isn't the end of the world.

● **Try to separate who you are from what you do.** Realize your own diversity — your traits, strengths, weaknesses, feelings and ideas — and the innate value of who you are. Avoid hinging your self-image totally on what you do and achieve. You would still be you without any honors and prizes.

● **Make time to have fun.** Fun is a vital part of your emotional health and must be a part of your daily routine. Pursue a hobby, read for pleasure, go for a long walk, listen to music, talk to a friend, meditate, write a long letter to a pen pal — whatever is fun for you.

● **Work out a simple, basic daily routine.** With so many variables in your life right now, a little sameness and stability in your daily routine — things you don't have to decide constantly or things you can look

forward to — can be soothing. Establish a regular bedtime, get-up time and study time and eat well-balanced meals on a regular schedule.

● **Exercise.** All forms of vigorous exercise (sports, running, walking, dancing) are excellent tension reducers.

● **Realize that you're in control.** You can choose to be nervous or you can choose to alleviate some of your stress. Taking responsibility for your anxiety in the first step toward changing the situation.

● **Use your imagination to relax.** Peaceful fantasies can be wonderful stress-reducers. One suggested relaxation exercise: Close your eyes. Imagine that you're floating, nestled in a fluffy white cloud. You're safe, happy and content. Stay there for a few minutes. Breathe deeply and open your eyes slowly.

● **Let others help you.** Don't suffer silently, talk about your stress and anxiety with someone you trust. You will feel less alone, your feelings will be out in the open and your confidante may be able to help you explore ways to lessen stress or cope with it more effectively.

16 Creative Writing: Feature Leads

A writer's problem does not change. . . . It is always how to write truly and, having found what is true, to project it in such a way that it becomes a part of the experience of the person who reads it.

Ernest Hemingway

News writing is often criticized for its lack of creativity. News writing, critics say, is stiff and formal. It relies on formulas. There is even a word to describe news writing as seen in these terms: *journalese.*

By this time, I hope you know better. Of course, there are routine story forms — for example, the inverted pyramid. And news style is an arbitrary collection of rules.

But though there are constraints on news writing, the constraints are intended to encourage writers to organize their thinking and their writing so as to tell a story clearly and concisely. News writing is disciplined writing, but, as you found in Chapter 15, there is ample opportunity in journalistic writing for creativity.

If you read enough newspapers, you will find some bad writing. But you will find far more bright, creative and exciting writing in today's newspapers. Editors today are more concerned than ever about the quality of writing. Good writing is demanded of news writers, and good writers are much in demand.

This chapter is intended to remind you that creativity and imagination are important in news writing and to suggest a few ways to put a little magic into news leads.

Summary leads and speech story leads, as you know, are straightforward and uncomplicated. They summarize and present facts quickly and clearly. They are generally devoid of emotion or human interest.

Many other stories, however — straight news stories and features — offer ample opportunity for creativity. Leads can be written imaginatively. A good feature lead will attract readers and draw them into the story. Seasoned news writers try to make their stories not only informative and understandable but interesting. Feature touches should not only attract readers and hold their interest but should touch readers in some way — emotionally, intellectually or both.

Writers and editors work under difficult conditions these days. Newspaper readers spend less time with their newspapers than they did a few years ago, and newspapers are using more sprightly page makeup and design and catchier headlines to attract reader attention. To hold that attention, they are demanding better and brighter writing from their writers.

Better writing is in demand for another reason — today's newspaper must report a broad range of complex and technical subjects. Inflation, pollution, energy, the problems of education, national security, transportation, corruption in government, the economy, astronomy, space exploration, science — these can be pretty heavy stuff. The news writer's best efforts are required to make serious and technical subjects clear and interesting so that readers will not only read but understand and react.

The discussion in this chapter and the next is about writing readable and interesting stories for newspapers. It could as well be about writing for magazines. And the point I hope to make is that almost any story can be improved by brighter writing.

Feature Leads

A good lead is half the battle. If readers can be drawn into a story and led into its substance through well-written opening sentences and paragraphs, they will probably read the entire story.

There is no easy-to-follow formula for putting creativity to work and writing attractive and interesting leads. News writers are storytellers and creative writers. They develop leads out of an understanding of what the story is all about and out of a feeling for their subject. And every story is different.

There are no formulas, but if you read newspapers regularly and study the way feature stories are written, you will find that there are ways to describe some of the approaches writers take with their leads. Some of these approaches are categorized informally here for purposes of discussion. But despite the labels, the categories are not clearly defined and in some cases clearly overlap. And as you study more newspaper features, you will find feature leads that don't fit any of the categories in this chapter.

Writing is an art and a craft. Any attempt to explain how a writer writes must not be taken as a blueprint for building identical productions. Writers are not workers on an assembly line. The categories of leads and the examples presented here are merely suggestive of the wide range of creativity and the variety of techniques available to skilled writers. There are, you will see, a number of ways to go beyond the five Ws to make the news more interesting and more meaningful.

Simplicity

Longer stories don't necessarily need longer leads. Nor do more complicated stories necessarily need more involved leads. Frequently the best approach is a short, simple statement of fact presented abruptly and concisely. Such a statement provides the writer with a place to start and establishes a common ground with the reader. Look at this lead, for example:

> Augusta places well in a race nobody wants to win.
> — *Augusta* (Ga.) *Chronicle and Herald*

That is a provocative statement, but tantalizing. One has to read on.

> People living in the coastal plains of Georgia and the two Carolinas have the dubious distinction of having one of the highest death rates in the country, especially when it comes to cardiovascular disease.

The following lead introduced the reader to an interesting story about a summer jobs program for low-income youths.

> Confidence and a fighting chance.
> This, say Harry Porter and Raymond Peralt, is what a summer youth-employment program has given them.
> — *The Arizona Republic*, Phoenix

Another lead of the same general type:

An editor at Gannett's Westchester Rockland Newspapers works at the keyboard of a pagination terminal to make up the entire newspaper page. The image composed on the screen will become a full-page negative and then an offset plate ready for the press. (Gannett Westchester Newspapers)

Doug Russell gets so mad when he sees "ugly American" misused in a publication that he fires off a letter.

Again, this kind of abrupt beginning needs following up. The writer goes on:

That he almost universally is ignored does not deter Russell, who remains firmly in control of "The Ugly American Defense League" as its founder, chief executive officer and recording secretary.

Russell contends — and rightly so — that too many people use "ugly American" to describe those Americans who go abroad and give us all a bad name by behaving with arrogance and insensitivity.

If you aren't sure if you've been using the words correctly, listen to Russell:

— *Seattle Times*

The body of the story begins here, an explanation of Russell's interest in the correct interpretation of the title of William Lederer's novel *The Ugly American.*

A short and simple beginning works, but as you can see, you can't drop the idea after a few words. You can provoke the reader's curiosity with an opening statement, but you must provide additional details to feed that curiosity before you move on to the body of the story.

Stage Directions

Playwrights, at the beginning of a play, provide stage directions. They explain what the stage setting looks like, who the characters are and what the audience should expect of them. Stage directions can be adopted as a convenient way to organize a feature lead. For example:

It's 8 p.m. on a cool, clear Tuesday.

School Supt. Richard N. Percy pulls into Winchell School's parking lot, grabs his brief case and darts into the auditorium.

At the same time, Board of Education President Donald C. Smith greets a Hillside Junior High PTA audience.

Carl Czuchna, administrative assistant to the superintendent, who gulped down a quick dinner, arrives at Edison just as parents assemble for a monthly PTA meeting.

School Board member Robert Cooper has ducked out of the postmaster's office a little early to get home, eat and meet Czuchna at Edison.

— *Kalamazoo* (Mich.) *Gazette*

This lead set the stage for a story telling how school board members spent their evenings explaining a complicated tax question to voters in the few days remaining before a school election. The following lead is similar:

323

It was Sunday morning on Anderson Avenue and the Mt. Hermon Primitive Baptist Church was jammed. People were standing in the aisles and crowding outdoors, a little restless, but still hanging on the words of the Rev. Preston Daymon.

His resonant voice, which had been marching through a Biblical story, paused for a moment and softened.

"We have some church business to take care of," he said, producing an envelope of money.

— *Fort Meyers* (Fla.) *News-Press*

The stage is now set, and the story moves into the first episode of a lengthy feature about the support their church has given to the people of a black community.

Narrative

Narrative is an effective and useful device for telling a story. You have seen how it is used in hard-news stories to explain action. Now let's see how narrative can be used to introduce a story. For example:

Rienzi B. Lemus, an 87-year-old bachelor who is frugal, but not always, walked into Children's Hospital the other day and asked if he was in the right place to give away money.

Joyce Buck, assistant to Alfred Lawson, the hospital's director of development, allowed as how Children's was a good place for that.

Lemus held out a check. "How much do you think it's for?" he asked.

"Twenty dollars?" guessed Mrs. Buck.

— *Washington Post*

Could you stop at this point? Probably not, for the writer has introduced elements of the suspended-interest story into a narrative lead. Something has been held back. The narrative is made more real by dialogue and by use of the colloquial expression *allowed as how*. The story itself more than holds up a strong lead, as you can see in Figure 16.1.

A similar narrative lead introduces another kind of feature story.

Roughly once a week, 15 men carrying long billy clubs meet secretly in the small chapel located in a corner of the top floor of the Wayne County Jail.

$5,000 visitor at children's 'getting old' at 87; he gives half his savings to hospital

by Phil Casey
Washington Post Staff Writer

Rienzi B. Lemus, an 87-year-old bachelor who is frugal, but not always, walked into Children's Hospital the other day and asked if he was in the right place to give away money.

Joyce Buck, assistant to Alfred Lawson, the hospital's director of development, allowed as how Children's was a good place for that.

Lemus held out a check.

"How much do you think it's for?" he asked.

"Twenty dollars?" guessed Mrs. Buck.

She was wrong by $4,980.

Lemus, who doesn't look 87 any more than he looks rich, said it was nothing, really. He still has $5,000 left.

"I always wanted to send them a little change," he said yesterday. "It was getting time to straighten things out. I'm getting old and I figured I'd better do it now."

There was something else, he said. He wanted to be remembered a little before things got posthumous. He'd heard how grateful Children's Hospital is to people who leave money in their wills, and he decided not to wait. It was a good idea. The hospital is going to give him a plaque.

The $5,000 was just about half his savings, he said, but he has a small federal pension and he figures he'll get by.

Lemus served in the Army in the Philippines just after the Spanish-American War and worked as a railroad dining car waiter most of his life. He went to work as a clerk in the Interstate Commerce Commission when he was 62 and retired 10 years ago.

"I never had sense enough to get married," he said. "I have no dependents and I've seen a lot of suffering children and helpless parents. Something happened a long time ago, I forget what, that made me want to send the hospital a little change."

Lemus, a slender, surprisingly agile man who looks and acts much younger than he is, reads a great deal and is interested in everything. He is a prolific writer of letters to editors and figures he must have written more than 200 of them to Arthur Krock, the former New York Times Washington bureau chief and columnist. He got answers to them, too.

Figure 16.1 *A narrative lead draws the reader into this warm human interest story.*

The men sit restlessly on the wooden pews as a supervisor gives instructions from a small podium usually reserved for the dissemination of the gospel.

Then, followed by a man carrying a small videotape camera and a power pack, they sneak down the stairs and gather quietly in a small hall near one of the entrances, taking great care to stay out of sight of the inmates.

A ward deputy opens the iron door in an ostensibly routine action. He gives a silent signal and in a flurry of brown uniforms, long nightsticks, voices giving quick, curt instructions, and clanging bars, a shakedown squad of the Wayne County Jail makes its move.

— *Detroit Free Press*

The narrative continues, but the lead that has built up suspense — what *is* going on here? — ends with the words *shakedown squad* and the entry of the squad into the cell block. You will find a similar approach, a narrative lead, on the feature story in Figure 16.2.

Randy Thomas wants to play basketball; death is averted in the afternoon

By Rick Hammerstrom
News Staff Writer

It was about 4 Sunday afternoon when Riley Williams and his wife wheeled their car into Dale's Union 76 Station on Lawyer's Rd.

Leslie Dieth, a part-time employee at the station, was off that day, but thought it would be a good time to wash his car.

It was a picturesque Indian summer afternoon, with unseasonably high temperature and a pleasant, soft breeze.

The serenity, however, was broken several seconds later as a car slid into the station, its brakes locked, its tires screaming.

Inside the car were three teenagers, including Randall Wayne Thomas, a 14-year-old junior high student whose very life was slowly ebbing away.

Williams looked over at the two youths helping Thomas toward the station.

"That's when I saw the blood," Williams said. "It was all over him."

Thomas' throat had been slashed by flying glass when a friend had attempted to throw a soda bottle out the car window.

The bottle had struck a post in the car and shattered, sending a piece of jagged glass into Thomas' throat. It cut through his jugular vein.

Dieth, a 20-year-old Central

Piedmont Community College student, immediately dashed for a phone and called police and an ambulance.

Williams, 45, ran to the youth, who was slowly slumping to the pavement in front of the station.

"I usually get a little nervous about blood," Williams said. "But some things you just have to do."

Williams, a former FBI agent, bent over the youth and began searching for ways to stop the bleeding.

"The blood was just spurting out from a gash about the size of a pencil," Williams said. "I guess I could have put my fist into it."

He finally pinched the right place and the bleeding subsided.

While this was going on, Thomas remained calm, Williams said.

"One time he looked up at me and told me he would have to be at basketball tryouts tomorrow," Williams said.

"He told me not to worry — that he wasn't going to give up. He never asked me how bad it was or told me it hurt."

When the ambulance arrived and took Thomas to Memorial Hospital, the battle to save his life was just beginning.

Waiting at the hospital was a team of six doctors with countless pints of blood.

Thomas immediately went into surgery. Pint after pint of blood was pumped into his body to replace the 50 per cent loss he had suffered.

There were tense moments — and he stopped breathing. The amount of blood transfused ran into quarts, but today it appears that Randy Thomas will live.

He's still listed in serious condition in the intensive care unit and his parents, Mr. and Mrs. Edsel Thomas, are continuing a 24-hour vigil at the hospital, but they are breathing easier.

"I don't know how to thank all the people who have helped Randy," Thomas said.

"It's hard to explain it . . . everyone has been so great . . . the people at the hospital, the police, the doctors . . . everyone."

Most of all, Thomas said, he has God to thank.

"I know a lot of prayers were said," he said. "We said a lot and I know a lot of Randy's friends were praying."

Due to the breathing apparatus applied to him, Randy still cannot talk to his parents.

But through sign language and notes, they are able to communicate.

"The first question he asked once he could write notes was if he could play basketball again," Thomas said.

"He just loves basketball. His coach came to visit him here — of course he couldn't have visitors — but it made him feel great.

"They are announcing his condition all the time at Albemarle Rd. Junior High. All the kids are interested in him."

Thomas hasn't been back at his job as a district supervisor for Sealtest since the accident and neither has his wife gone back to work at the cafeteria of Albemarle Rd. Junior High.

"We plan to stay by his side as long as he's in trouble," Thomas said. "I've only been home one time — that was to take a shower."

Figure 16.2 *A low-key narrative lead introduces a story filled with tension and drama.*

Anecdote

An anecdote is a little story, an episode rather than a full-length narrative. The anecdote generally used in a feature lead should be interesting, entertaining and illustrative. It should suggest to the reader something of the nature of the larger story to follow. An example:

> "Run, run," two little boys shouted to a Marquette University coed.
>
> But the warning was too late. A gang of about 10 girls jumped the coed as she was turning to see what the shouting was about.
>
> One girl grabbed her by the hair while the others began hitting her in the face. The beating was continued as she was forced to her knees.
>
> "I kept waiting for them to break my contact lenses in my eyes and blind me," the coed said later. "I tried to fight back, but I couldn't . . ."
>
> When she began screaming for help, her attackers halted to laugh at her.
>
> The coed broke away and ran the few remaining feet to the door of her apartment house.
>
> Later at the hospital she was treated for a broken nose and two black eyes.
>
> — *Milwaukee Sentinel*

This is an anecdote, an episode in a feature story about youth gangs. It is narrative in form, but it provides an illustration of the kind of things that happen in the streets of a large city. Another example:

> Sandy Babb was making her rounds in a chicken house picking eggs one day last summer, when her left hand got caught in an automatic feeder. Before she could do anything about it, the gears were ripping at her fingers and the back of her hand. By the time one of her children heard her cries, and got someone to turn off the motor, she was in so much pain she thought they might have to cut her hand off.
>
> — *Atlanta Constitution*

This anecdote introduced a story about families who work on poultry farms in northeast Georgia, one in a series of stories on the working poor. The anecdote relates an ugly incident, but it is an anecdote that is bound to get the reader's attention. Here is another example:

Tri-Met bus driver Larry Morgan was trying to explain to the blind man how to get to Gladstone High School after he let him off. But it was obvious to Morgan that the man was confused and would have trouble getting to the school.

"I finally just stopped the bus a moment and asked the others aboard if any of them was in a big, fat hurry," Morgan recalled. "They weren't, so I drove the bus three or four blocks off its route and took the man to the high school."

— Sunday Portland *Oregonian*

Flashback

The flashback is a familiar device to moviegoers, and it is a useful device in writing. In the lead, a flashback provides a contrast between a previous situation and a present situation. It can also provide a starting point for an account of a situation that has changed or developed over a period of time: *then* and *now* or *from then* to *now*. For example:

Later, some of the 30 or so employees at the Sophisticated Data Research company picnic would remember several men watching from a distance as the co-workers fished, ate and played volleyball along the shore of Lake Lanier.

One of the strangers circled the park in a pick-up truck, a scowl on his face. Miguel Marcelli assumed the man looked that way all the time, and paid no more attention.

It was July 27, 1980, a sunny Saturday in Forsyth County, Georgia.

— *Creative Loafing,* Atlanta

In this lead, the writer goes back in time to tell how several years before a black Atlanta man had been shot and wounded after a company picnic. The story then goes on to discuss at length present-day racial conflicts in Forsyth County.

Contrast

The flashback lead, as you can see, provides a kind of contrast, the past as opposed to the present, although sometimes the contrast is more implied than stated. In the following lead, the contrast is explicit.

329

From his tenement window in Long Branch, Dennis Moore, a black resident of public housing, watches the drug pushers and the street thugs who rule his neighborhood. He lives in fear that the ghetto will erupt in violence.

Vilma Morton, 82, a white resident of public housing, looks out her front window onto a quiet street with tidy houses and well-manicured lawns.

The dividing line between these two lives is racial segregation. Outlawed more than 20 years ago, it is still a way of life for residents of the city's public housing projects.

— *Asbury Park* (N.J.) *Press*

The following lead, from a story written in 1971, offers a contrast between then and now in the life of a young Milwaukee black:

Richard Green might have laughed four years ago if you had told him that he would be working for the Association of Commerce.

He might even have punched you in the mouth.

Four years ago, Green, then 23, was a member of the Commandos, the muscle of the NAACP Youth Council. In that tumultuous summer of 1967, Commando became synonymous with militancy.

During that summer, the Commandos and Father James E. Groppi took to the streets in a series of marches to force open housing on the so-called establishment.

Today 15 of those black men who marched across the 6th St. Viaduct into a barrage of rocks and bottles sit behind desks in a storefront office at 2134 N. 3rd St.

— *Milwaukee Sentinel*

In addition to the *then* and *now* contrast, the *Sentinel* lead offers contrast between the former militancy of the young blacks and their later approach to civil rights and open housing from behind a desk in cooperation with the Association of Commerce.

Description

Describing the scene where your story or some significant incident in the story takes place or the appearance of a leading character in the story can be an effective way of interesting the reader. Action stories and human interest stories provide excellent opportunities for description. A good example is this lead from a story about the closing of a Waukesha, Wis., manufacturing plant.

> With paper shopping bags stuffed full of old, sooty foundry clothes in each hand, Robert Delgado, 53, walked out of the General Casting Corp. gates here Friday, probably for the last time.
> Delgado is among the 128 steelworkers at the plant at 706 E. Main St., which is headed toward a shutdown next week.
> — *Milwaukee Journal*

Another example, this one from a feature story about a 79-year-old expert on gospel music:

> A gas heater burns in the pastor's small office at the rear of East Trigg Baptist Church. It is warm.
> After a few minutes talking to the man who has led this church for nearly half a century, it becomes apparent the real warmth in the room comes not from the heater, but from Dr. W. Herbert Brewster.
> Dr. Brewster, now in his 80th year, sits with accustomed dignity in a black easy chair. He is slim and immaculately dressed in a black vested suit and sparkling white shirt.
> When he speaks the room is filled with melodious bass. He has a preacher's instinct for emphasis.
> — *Commercial Appeal*, Memphis, Tenn.

This lead is more complicated than it seems, for it presents description not only of tangible things — the room, the easy chair, clothing — but of intangibles — atmosphere and character.

Chronology

You have seen chronology used before in short features and in hard-news stories. It is an effective storytelling device and is useful in feature leads. The following lead, although it makes obvious use of chronology, is also descriptive and anecdotal:

> 6:56 a.m. Thursday. It is still dark and cold outside Shy and Red's Bar in Hamtramck. The few people on

Dequindre seem hunched low to the ground as they hurry off to early-morning jobs along well-memorized routes.

6:59 a.m. Shy Piasecki kicks the door of the bar ajar and admits Frank and Arlo, two Fleetwood Cadillac workers who have been waiting outside. He sets up the usual: A shot of vodka for Frank and blackberry brandy for Arlo. He draws each a beer.

7:08 a.m. A lanky man called Bill walks in wearing a UAW "Square Deal" jacket. He is trailed by two other workers who are giving him a good-natured hard time. They all order a shot and a beer and Bill heads for the telephone to make a customary morning call to his wife.

"Are y'up Nancy?" shouts bartender Piasecki, anticipating Bill's standard telephone question as if he's heard it a hundred times before.

"Y'up Nancy?" Bill says into the phone and all the others laugh. It's all part of a simple, jovial early morning routine.

— *Detroit Free Press*

Reference and Allusion

Sometimes a familiar saying, a line of poetry or a familiar quotation provides a starting place for the feature writer. You have seen how this device is used on short features. It is also used as an attention-getter or illustrative device in writing the longer news story or feature. For example:

"Money won is twice as sweet as money earned."
— Paul Newman in *The Color of Money*

"My kid once watched me make six grand in a night. That's bad, because I don't want him to think it's easy money. I want him to grow up different."
— Ray Silby, former pool hustler

Thwack! Ray Silby breaks so hard the cue ball pops up in the air and flies off the table, cracking loudly onto the floor. Everybody gathers around. Two of the best bar players in Denver are about to shoot a little nine-ball at $200 a rack.

> Sixteen games, two Coke-and-limes and seven
> Marlboros later, Silby collects $400 cash from his old
> friend, Roger Kimmel, and finally allows himself a beer.
> Kimmel has a Jim Beam and Coke.
> Both men once made a living hustling pool . . .
>
> — *Rocky Mountain News,* Denver

Another example, this time from a feature written in the aftermath of a multiple shooting on the University of Texas campus:

> It was a very hot noon;
> That fatal noon.
>
> — Thornton Wilder
> *The Bridge of San Luis Rey*

> At high noon a man's shadow in early August on the
> University of Texas campus stands out only a foot and
> a half to the northwest, a little rounded thing that would
> shade a passing grasshopper but little else.
> The sun comes down just about straight. The wea-
> ther bureau figures it's at least 110 degrees out in the
> sun on a day like last Monday, when the temperature
> stood at 98 degrees in the shade.
>
> — H.D. Quigg
> *United Press International*

Direct Quotation and Dialogue

The use of direct quotation in a lead usually results in a lead that is weaker in impact than a lead based on a summary. This is a rule of thumb, no more. And in the case of feature leads, it is a rule to be broken occasionally. You can use direct quotation and even dialogue in a feature lead, and you will find that it makes an effective and interesting beginning. Feature leads are more leisurely than the leads on hard-news stories. They don't have to summarize the stories they introduce. Try a direct quotation or a dialogue lead and see if it works. For example, this lead from a story about a victim of Alzheimer's disease:

> Lawrence Day grabbed the telephone.
> "Who are you calling?" asked Hazel Day.
> "My wife," he said.
> "But I'm your wife, honey."
> "Oh . . ."

> Hazel Day thinks her husband remembered last year who she was. Maybe it was the year before. It doesn't matter anymore.
>
> For the last six years . . .
>
>   — McClatchy News Service

Dialogue is highly effective in this feature lead on a light story about a band rehearsal:

> "Drums, get me more fill," said music director Ed Logeski to the CP Telethon Orchestra's drummer at practice at the Civic Center.
>
> "You mean boom-boom?" asked the drummer.
>
> "No, more like whack-whacka-whacka-whack. OK? One, two, three . . ."
>
>   — *Jackson* (Tenn.) *Sun*

Another example of quotation in a lead, although this lead might be termed both anecdote and narrative:

> "Bye!" the man with the shepherd's crook shouts across the huge field.
>
> The dog obediently turns left. The three sheep head in the same direction.
>
> "Away!" the master shouts. The dog turns right, herding the disgruntled sheep across the field toward an empty pen.
>
>   — *Macon* (Ga.) *Telegraph & News*

When you can capture the voices of people talking, naturally and in their own voices, your readers will listen.

Questions

The question lead has been discussed in previous chapters. It has its place in the news writer's bag of tricks, but it shouldn't be overused. Like the direct quotation lead, however, it can be tried once in a while. Sometimes it is the only way to get into a story worth telling:

> How can the poor share in America's wealth?
>
> By organizing, say welfare rights spokesmen. Give the poor a voice in programs that affect them, they plead.

> Align with sympathetic groups and press for change,
> say lawmakers and community workers.
> Reorder national priorities; spend less for space and
> more for people, says a concerned taxpayer.
> Give us more money, say the poor.
> — *Milwaukee Sentinel*

The writer of this feature, one of a six-part series on the poor in Milwaukee, used a question as a device to present four possible answers to the problem of providing the poor with a greater share of the nation's wealth. In fact, each installment in the six-part series started with a question and several answers. Repetitious? Perhaps, but the parallel construction of leads in the series served also to tie the leads together. Another example:

> Why would 154 people live in Riddleville, Ga.?
> — *Macon* (Ga.) *Telegraph & News*

This question enabled the writer to tell an entertaining story about a small town where "there is no industry, little commerce and seemingly nothing to do."

Other Methods

The labels and the categories in this chapter help define and explain the idea of the feature lead but certainly don't say everything about creativity and imagination. The categories are artificial. Some leads could just as well go in one category as another. Some categories overlap others. And some leads won't fit neatly into any of the categories. Here are several excellent feature leads that belong in a final category we might call *and there are other ways of writing a feature lead*.

> All his life, he has shaken off the punches. All his life
> he has kept bouncing back.
> Born poor. Shook it off.
> Lost his mother while he was still a baby. Shook
> that off, too.
> Blind from birth. That just meant he got used to not
> seeing early.
> He was barely school age when his aunt and uncle
> packed him off to boarding school in St. Augustine.
> "It was the only school for the blind they knew
> about," he says.
> — *St. Petersburg* (Fla.) *Times*

> Louis Kahn owns and operates a worldwide computer network, a computer mail-order catalog, a service company for real estate brokers, a fledgling book publishing company and an in-house ad agency. And in two years he'll be old enough to buy a drink and celebrate his success.
>
> — *Atlanta Constitution*

Creative Writing

The point behind this discussion should be clear. There is room for imagination and creativity in news writing. The leads presented in this chapter came from a wide variety of feature stories and from a number of quite different newspapers. In each case the writer was attempting to attract readers and capture their interest through the use of an imaginative beginning that made a statement about the story to follow.

A word of warning, however: You can't use leads like these on every story. There are stories, many of them each day, that require a straightforward, five-W summary lead. It is extremely frustrating to readers who come to a story for information to be put off by a feature lead. Good examples of overuse of feature leads can be found in the sports pages of many newspapers. If the point of a story, for example, is to tell readers how many passengers were killed in a train wreck, don't write a lead based on an episode in the early life of the engineer. There's a time and a place for every approach to organizing and writing a story.

Creativity is needed every day in the newsroom. Newspapers are reporting a greater variety and range of news stories than ever before. Readers are hungry for information about a great many things that affect their lives and their lifestyles. News writers coming into the business today will find they need a great deal of imagination to keep up with the needs and interests of their readers — and a great deal of creativity if they are to make their copy interesting as well as informative.

Suggestions for Further Reading

There is an immense journalistic literature of war. These are representative and readable.

Emerson, Gloria. *Winners and Losers*. New York: Random House, 1976.
> Vietnam recalled by a *New York Times* reporter, who calls the book "battles, retreats, gains, losses and ruins from a long war."

Herr, Michael. *Dispatches.* New York; Knopf, 1977.

  Distinguished reportage on the Vietnam War.

Hersey, John. *Hiroshima.* New York: Knopf, 1946.

  A moving account of the day the first atomic bomb was dropped and its tragic aftermath. A major piece of journalism.

Liebling, A.J. *Liebling Abroad.* New York: PEI Books, 1981.

  Includes Liebling's war reportage: *The Road Back to Paris* and *Mollie & Other War Pieces.*

Pyle, Ernie. *Brave Men.* Henry Holt and Company, 1944.

  Pyle's reporting from Sicily, Italy and France in 1943 and 1944. Pyle is still regarded as a reporter and writer to emulate.

Sack, John. *M.* New York: New American Library, 1967.

  Sack lived with and followed an infantry company from training at Fort Dix., N.J., into combat in Vietnam.

STAR HOME

Housing news
Mortgage rates
Decor
Classified sales and rentals

Sunday, March 22, 1987   Page 1F

Theda and Roger Wilson's house was assembled from pre-numbered, Southern pine logs shipped from a Missouri factory.

Novel game boards on the wall and an antique secretary, at top, add a country look to the dining area. The wife designed the folk-art towel rack and wallpapered the bathroom, above.   (photos by Marianne Maurin/special to The Star)

Reflecting the rustic spirit

Friends and family raise log house from a kit

By Marjean Busby
STAFF WRITER

Roger Wilson thinks his friends and neighbors in rural Miami County, Kan., can never be thanked enough. Through a rainy fall and Thanksgiving ice storm, they helped his family build a log home from a kit. But the job wasn't finished until the group of 20 had labored for 18 months.

At home this week

"This was basically all done on weekends," the electrician said. "I'd just do what I could do by myself in the evening. The logs took six weeks to put up, and we had the house pretty well closed in by November 1985."

At a 10-month milestone, he and folk artist Theda Wilson moved into the home with their college-age children, Royce and Janette.

Their daughter acted as hod carrier for the bricklayer who did the fireplace furnace for pay but volunteered his muscle for other work.

The Wilsons hired out several jobs, including the excavation, concrete foundation work, plumbing, heating system and custom cabinets.

"We brought the house up from the foundation to the peak, including the roofing, and we did all the interior work clear to the finish," Roger said. "We had the cabinets built to our design, but we did the finish and installation on those to save some money.

"Probably the hardest part for me was doing the electrical work. Because I hadn't wired a house since 1961, I had to think. I was used to doing big buildings. I got a lot of teasing about it."

Wilson has worked through Local 124 of the International Brotherhood of Electrical Workers for contractors on large commercial and industrial buildings in the Kansas City area since 1959.

After the subfloor was laid, a company based in New England sent three 60-foot flatbed tractor-trailers from its factory in Houston, Mo. The 180,000-pound load included hand-peeled South-

The quaint kitchen stove is electric.

ern pine logs, as well as windows, doors, trusses, roofing and other materials.

The logs had a tongue-and-groove configuration so they would fit together easily and tightly. To make the house more energy-efficient, the men stapled foam sealant strips between the logs.

"We unloaded the trailers with the help of a friend who brought a boom truck," Roger Wilson recalled. "We had to sort the logs, which were coded and numbered for their exact location. To me, it was kind of like putting a puzzle together."

Many logs were 12 feet long.

weighing up to 300 pounds. "If a certain number was called out, you knew the log was going to be long and heavy," he said. "The dealer spent the first day here to help us get started, and we had a construction manual and comprehensive instructions.

"We had no trouble in figuring it out because most of us had construction experience. Those who didn't have it did the grunt work."

No more than eight persons worked at the site at the same time, he said.

"A number of the men were fellow electricians I had worked with for years on commercial and industrial buildings. Others were close friends and neighbors. We also had college girls on weekends. Theda's lady friends and neighbors also helped. Even our insurance guy and his wife came out once with another couple. They brought food so we had a barbecue."

Theda's role was "to worry a lot," mainly about someone getting hurt, and to cook. She also handled the cleanup.

"Janette, her roommate and I took a wire brush and a scraper to get the residue off the interior walls," Theda said. "Then we applied a Danish oil finish. I also stained the woodwork and cabinets, painted the conventional interior walls and put up the wallpaper.

"My other job was to run around finding bargains, such as the marble counter tops for three bathrooms. I got the carpeting at wholesale through a friend and bought the lights at a sale. Fortunately, we were able to buy all of our construction materials at contractors prices."

The Wilsons had ordered a larger house than the basic plan, and the higher-than-usual ceiling required special trusses. The main section is 30 by 48 feet. A 24- by 36-foot extension holds the mud room, third bedroom and garage.

The house is rustic outside and inside, complemented by small-scale country wallpapers in dark rose and blue. The varying diameters of the logs, from 7 to 12 inches, keep them from looking like "uniform telephone poles," Theda said.

Even before entering, visitors are captivated by the home-on-the-range

See Wilson, pg. 16F, col. 3

Dangers of indoor pollution often are overlooked

Knight-Ridder Newspapers

Wayne and Karen Schultz had a mission when they set out to build their dream house in rural Connecticut.

They knew that many modern American homes are filled with potentially harmful chemicals that seep from building and household products. So they teamed up with architect Paul Bierman-Lytle to build a pollution-free home.

The Schultzes used pine for their subfloor and oak for their kitchen cabinets instead of particleboard and plywood containing formaldehyde, a toxic and potentially cancer-causing chemical. Knowing that oil-based paints, varnishes and polyurethane floor finishes often contain toxic chemicals, they used latex paint and natural stains and covered their oak floors with beeswax.

When the Schultzes and their 6-year-old son moved into their home in September 1985, they were greeted by the smell of sawdust and pine, not the odor of a chemical factory.

"Substances like formaldehyde really concern me," said Wayne Schultz, a 36-year-old electronics technician with Sikorsky Aircraft. "They don't really know the long-term effects of small doses. And I didn't want to find out for my family, not if I could eliminate it. Why take the risk?"

The Schultzes are not part of a mass movement sweeping the country. But they do represent a growing number of people who realize that many Americans face a bigger threat from inside pollution than outside pollution.

"For a long time the whole pollution-control effort was focused outward," said Joseph O. Minott, executive director of the Philadelphia Clean Air Council. "I think it's easier for people to look at a smokestack and say to a company: 'Don't pollute. You're killing me.' When you start telling people to look at pollution in their homes, there is more resistance. But it's a national health problem we have to come to grips with. It may well be the up-and-coming environmental issue."

No one knows the full extent of the health effects of indoor pollution, which can range from eye irritation and headaches to the possibility of increased risk of cancer.

But indoor pollution dangers have come into sharper focus recently with the discovery that harmful levels of radon—a gas produced by the breakdown of uranium in the soil and rock—might be leaking into as many as 8 million American homes. The U.S. Environmental Protection Agency has estimated that radon is causing 5,000 to 20,000 new cancer cases a year in the United States.

While the risks from radon have been publicized, many environmentalists and government officials point to growing evidence that homeowners also may face a threat from hundreds of commonly used products and building materials. The Environmental Protection Agency recently completed a study in which it monitored the presence of dangerous chemicals in the homes and on the breath of 650 persons across the country.

Among the surprising findings:

● Using air fresheners, toilet-bowl cleaners and moth crystals can fill homes with high levels of paradichlorobenzene, a toxic chemical that causes cancer in animals.

● Taking a hot shower can fill a home with levels of chloroform that are four times greater than outdoors. Chloroform, a byproduct of the chlorination of water, is suspected of causing cancer in humans.

● Bringing clothes home from the dry cleaner can fill a home with high levels of tetrachloroethylene, a toxic chemical used to dry-clean clothes. The levels of tetrachloroethylene, a known animal carcinogen and suspected human carcinogen, often remain high for days and can be detected in substantial amounts on the breath of a person who makes a two-minute stop at the cleaner.

Another EPA study of nine randomly chosen homes in Jacksonville, Fla., showed that the air in three of the homes had measurable levels of more than a dozen pesticides and that the other

homes each had measurable levels of one or two pesticides. Many pesticides contain chemicals that are suspected of causing cancer, neurological damage or genetic defects in humans.

No one is urging Americans to flee their homes and patch tents. But the findings should alert Americans to a potential problem that has long been ignored, experts say. Many scientists think more money should be spent to research indoor air pollution and to develop less-toxic building materials and improved ventilation systems.

"We're spending $200 million a year trying to reduce outdoor air pollution and $2 million a year on indoor air pollution," said Lance A. Wallace, an EPA scientist who has headed research into indoor air pollution. "Frankly, I think it should be reversed. Air pollution is generally much higher indoors."

Industry officials said, however, that the threat of indoor air pollution from building products such as formaldehyde

See Pollution, pg. 2F, col. 1

17

Creative Writing: Pictures from Words

Organization, precision, clarity — these are the three virtues of readable prose. To these one might add a sense of cadence, a sense of imagery, a feeling for simile and metaphor.

James J. Kilpatrick

Organizing a story is one thing. Making it interesting is quite another. Some stories are so interesting in themselves that the facts are enough. Others may be important to the reader, but the facts by themselves are unappealing unless the writer makes some special effort to make them interesting and meaningful. Any story can be improved by the creative use of language.

Illustration

News writers as well as novelists can add creative touches to their stories. They can use the right words in the right way and paint pictures for their readers. Sometimes this is referred to as adding color to the story. Sometimes it is called adding human interest. A good term might be *illustration* — using the written word in such a way that readers can see people, places and events in the mind's eye. A creative writer can *show* readers the story, not just tell them what it is about.

339

Let's look now at some of the ways news writers can use words to paint pictures for their readers — show their readers the story. All these devices are readily available to any writer who will look for them. All are commonly used by short story writers, novelists, dramatists and poets. They are commonly referred to as literary devices, but they are not the exclusive property of the writers of fiction. Many skilled news writers routinely make use of literary devices to add color and interest to their stories. Their use and the use of other illustrative devices can make the difference between a dull and routine news story and one that is read with appreciation by newspaper readers. Figure 17.1 lists some illustrative devices.

Details

An important illustrative device, and one almost too obvious to mention, is the specific detail. News stories are built out of details, from the initial who, what, where and when to the last name and date, but news writers are so used to working with details that they sometimes forget that details do more than ground a story in fact.

News stories should avoid generalities and build on specifics. And they should include the small, additional details that paint pictures for the reader. The late Richard Bissell in one of his novels about life on the upper Mississippi quoted a river boat captain on his preference for newspaper stories over broadcast accounts of events. The secret is in the details, the captain said. If a man murdered his wife with a shovel, the newspaper would even tell you the brand name of the shovel. A picturesque exaggeration, perhaps, but a point that should be taken seriously. Specific details make the story.

Do you remember what Frank Douglas said about covering the Shockoe Slip fire? (See Chapter 2, Figure 2.3.)

> The only way to do this was with details. How many explosions? How many fire trucks? How hot was it? How much water was used? How big an area was evacuated?

Douglas' story in the *Richmond Times-Dispatch* was filled with specific details. For example:

> Fourth and fifth alarms were sounded at 11:29 and 11:32. The sixth and seventh were sounded at 11:38 and 11:51. And the eighth was sounded four minutes later.

Alliteration	Repetition of sounds at the beginning of words.
Allusion	A reference to a real or fictional character, situation, event, proverb or topical saying.
Analogy	A comparison of similarities — for example, an explanation of an unfamiliar event or situation in terms of something familiar.
Anecdote	A little story used as an example or to illustrate a point.
Description	Words used to provide a mental image.
Detail	A small point or particular of the whole.
Dialogue	Conversation between two or more people.
Example	A case or situation that can serve as a model for a larger group of similar cases or situations.
Hyperbole	Exaggeration, overstatement.
Meiosis	Understatement, the opposite of hyperbole.
Metaphor	An implied comparison — for example, calling someone *a lion* because he is courageous.
Quotation	The use of someone else's words.
Simile	A clearly stated comparison using *like, as* or *as if.*

Figure 17.1 *A few illustrative devices. Some of these are, of course, routine journalistic devices — for example, the use of quotation. Others are literary, or rhetorical, devices.*

And he gave other specific details: explosions caused by 30 cases of lubricants; between 300 and 400 gallons of cutting oil spewed out black smoke; firemen were using 13,000 gallons of water a minute, 700,000 gallons an hour; the fire was declared under control at 12:54 p.m. Read that list again. Douglas not only told his readers how many gallons of oil spewed out black smoke, but he told them what kind of oil it was. Details add to the impact of a story. Look for them. Use them.

Nearly every example used in this chapter, although most are only brief excerpts from news stories, demonstrates the use of the specific rather than the general.

Description

Description, the use of a word picture of a situation or an event, is a basic device for illustrating a news story. This doesn't mean the wholesale use of adjectives but rather the exact use of appropriate words, a piling up of details, the use of specific words, especially nouns and verbs, and the use of familiar words and terms. This calls for good reporting, of course, because good description requires careful observation. For example, look at this excerpt from a story about Southerners who had emigrated to Chicago:

> Small children, ill-clothed and unescorted, raced along the sidewalks and ducked in and out of doors. A young couple, hand-in-hand and unmistakably American Indian, windowshopped their way around the same block at least four times in an hour and a half without seeming to notice the wind or snow flurries.
>
> A former citizen of Tennessee, out of work temporarily, he said, cadged a cup of coffee on the strength of his great knowledge of the area and then got distracted. He had eased onto a counter stool just behind a departing customer and just ahead of the counter-cleanup man.
>
> His mind was on the paper tray half full of french fried potatoes left by the previous customer. Casually, expertly, he slipped his hand around the paper tray to claim possession without ever touching it. The counterman cleaned around the tray and moved on.
>
> — *Charlotte* (N.C.) *Observer*

The writer is a good observer and is able to describe what he sees with clarity. In a lighter vein but equally descriptive is this excerpt from a story in *The New York Times*.

> It was, to put it mildly, bedlam, and according to one guest who was delicately removing an oily lettuce leaf that had been jostled into her somewhat remarkable cleavage, the scene at the club made "sardines look like pikers."
>
> But amidst the young girls in strategically cut dresses who spent part of the evening trying to meet Mr. Hartford, the young men in velvet and ruffles who spent part of the evening trying to meet each other, and the older couples who spent most of the evening wondering why they were there at all, there were a few genuine celebrities past and present.

Examples

Another useful illustrative device is the example. The writer makes a statement but, instead of expecting readers to accept it at face value, says, in effect: "See, like this." Examples are graphic verification of the writer's statements. In a story about the end of rail service from the Union Depot in Milwaukee, the writer doesn't just say that the loss of rail service affected people but cites examples to make the point clear.

> When the 7:40 a.m. North Western Road streamliner clacks out of Milwaukee's Union Depot for the last time Friday, the lives of many persons will be upset.
>
> A 65-year-old Racine man may be forced to give up an office job in Chicago and, at his age, he fears the prospects are poor for finding another one.
>
> The operator of a women's apparel shop in Lake Forest, Ill., will have to move out of her fashionable apartment on Milwaukee's East Side and move into another in Chicago.
>
> An advertising man living in Racine will have to start rising an hour earlier each morning in order to report on time to his job at the Carson-Pirie-Scott Co. department store in Chicago's Loop.
>
> The three commuters . . .
>
> — *Milwaukee Sentinel*

Another *Sentinel* story makes effective use of a hypothetical inner-city family to explain how a federal program worked:

> To help put the plan in perspective, here is an example of how the massive program might affect a hypothetical family.
>
> A 40-year-old maintenance worker — let's call him John Jones — lives in Milwaukee's Model Cities neighborhood. He is married and has six children.
>
> The family needs are many — and largely unfulfilled.
>
> Jones lives in a shabby three-bedroom flat, for which he pays a hefty portion of his meager income.
>
> His health and that of his family is poor.
>
> His kids go to inner city schools where tempers are short and the educational gap between those in the outer city and suburbs is great.

Jones never got beyond the 8th grade himself, and, because of this, is locked into a dead-end job, pushing a broom.

His wife, Marie, would like to work, but is tied to her household by youngsters.

Jones' world is pretty much Milwaukee's core area. He has no car, and little reason to take a bus elsewhere.

The cataloging of the problems of this hypothetical family goes further, but this excerpt gives you an idea of how it was done. After describing the family, the writer turns to an explanation of how Model Cities programs will help the family and its various members and in what ways. This device — a hypothetical, or made-up, example — can be used effectively when it is important to relate abstractions to real situations. The background of the hypothetical family in this story was apparently drawn from census data and perhaps also from the files of public agencies working with inner-city people.

Another approach is the composite — another kind of made-up example. A composite family might, for example, represent some of the characteristics of three or four real families. The result of assembling these characteristics into a composite is much the same as the hypothetical family, even though the hypothetical family's characteristics are drawn from statistical data and the composite family's characteristics are drawn from life. Hypothetical people or situations and composites are useful devices, but the writer must make it very clear to readers that the figures are not real, that although based on fact, they are hypothetical or composite. Many newspapers will not permit the use of a hypothetical or composite figure, but properly used this is a legitimate storytelling device.

Here is another instance of the effective use of examples, this time in a news feature from the *Miami Herald* that tells how jewel thieves work in the resort area in and around Miami:

There are other ways for thieves to select their victims:

Befriend the wealthy who wear jewels in bars of class hotels, follow them home, then pass along the vital information for a share of the take.

Get names from newspaper society pages which report when the social set will be away from home attending balls and other events.

Obtain information from children in the family, between 15 and 21 years old, who set up their own homes for robbery in order to finance drug habits.

Enlist the help of people in a position of trust — such as employees at country clubs and hotels or security guards for exclusive residential sections.

Anecdotes

The anecdote — a little story, an episode — adds color and human interest to a news story. Anecdotes are, of course, especially effective in stories about people: interviews, personality sketches, biographical sketches and obituaries. This anecdote from Stanley Woodward's obituary in *The New York Times* provides insight into character.

> A Herald-Tribune legend about Mr. Woodward has him recoiling in horror when the managing editor suggested that an exclusive sports story was worth page 1 play.
>
> "Why bury a good story like that?" retorted Mr. Woodward in his querulous, high-pitched voice. He considered sports pages to be the heart of the paper.

An obituary in the Falmouth, Mass., *Enterprise* included the following anecdote:

> In the last summer of his second term in the House, Mr. Albro gave up a trip to Florida with the Shrine band to be in his seat while the representatives considered impeachment proceedings against Attorney General Reading. Near the end, the Republicans caucused. The leaders announced they expected a unanimous vote to ask the Senate to try Reading.
>
> Mr. Albro spoke up and said he did not think the case for impeachment had been proved. "I'm a Republican and I won't vote to impeach a Republican attorney general on this evidence. I'll go on the floor and fight against it."
>
> "We won't recognize you," said the leaders.
>
> "I've got a big voice and you will," said Mr. Albro.
>
> He opposed the impeachment on the floor and got 17 votes for Reading.

A story in *The New York Times* about civil defense programs in New York City included this anecdote:

> Mr. Cooney's headquarters staff has an average age of 65, he said, and is made up primarily of retired Army officers who call each other "general" or "colonel" or the like. One man who had not been in military service was given a captain's commission in the auxiliary police so that the others would have something to call him.

In a light story about the wiles people use in trying to avoid traffic tickets, the writer included this anecdote:

> Officer John Rosemeyer told of a pretty school teacher he ticketed one day for speeding down Portland Ave.
> "You're mean," the woman said to Rosemeyer.
> "If your students act up you punish them, don't you?" replied Rosemeyer.
> "Yes," said the teacher.
> "Well, you're acting up," said Rosemeyer.
> — *Minneapolis Tribune*

Quotation and Dialogue

When we quote people directly, we bring them into the story and let them speak for themselves. The way people talk, what they say for themselves or to each other, can reflect character and personality. Their words can illustrate a point in a story or shed light on an obscure or complicated matter. Writers who let the people in their stories speak for themselves add color, human interest and detail to their copy.

You will find effective use of dialogue as a storytelling device in the *Chicago Sun-Times* feature in Figure 17.2.

Another example, this one from a reporter's reminiscences about a former Chicago alderman:

> One day Paddy got in to see Kennelly (some called him St. Martin) and said, "Mr. Mayor, the little businessmen in my ward are screaming. You got to lay off 'em. You got to quit harassing 'em. I helped get you elected — you got to do it."
> "We're not bothering anyone," said Kennelly, not knowing what on earth Paddy was talking about.

"The hell you're not," Paddy yelled back.

"Who are these little businessmen?" asked the mystified Kennelly.

"The bookmakers, the bookmakers!" Paddy screamed.

Helping Mickey Rooney over bumps (and grinds)

by Paul Galloway

The young woman, who looked as tall as the Statue of Liberty, stood there with her long blond hair falling over her shoulders and her tan jersey clinging for dear life.

Mickey Rooney gazed up at her, much as Norm Van Lier would gaze up at Kareem Abdul-Jabbar, only with more warmth.

"Beautiful, just beautiful," he said. He kissed her hand. "Thank you, darling. You were great. Excellent."

She turned and walked up the red-carpeted runway.

"Next!" Rooney shouted. "Whoever's coming out of the chute. And remember, just have fun. We're here to have fun."

The music flowed out of the loudspeaker again, the bump-and-grind brass and cymbals of "The Stripper."

Show biz. It's no fun, not a lot of it.

This was Friday afternoon at the Drury Lane East Theater in McCormick Place, auditions for a stripper in a comedy chestnut called "Goodnight Ladies."

"You have to have a lot of guts to come out and do this," Rooney said into the darkness at the edge of the stage, where reporters sat. "This is not easy."

Vernon Schwartz, who will direct this play in which Rooney will star and draw the customers, jotted notes with a felt-tip pen on a notebook after the names of each "auditionee," as the voice on the loudspeaker referred to the young women who vamped down the long ramp to dance in front of Rooney and Schwartz.

Schwartz had written "Moves fair, reads well" by one name, and "All-round plus" by another.

The music blared. The next young woman danced. Rooney sat on a sofa on the set, silent and watching. This is noteworthy. Niagara Falls and the conversational style of Rooney have something in common. Both are endless torrents. Rooney earlier had held court with a temporary audience, touching upon the nonsolidarity of actors, his belief that only two female actresses are allowed to do musicals, the story line of a Disney film in which he will appear, an enactment of a TV commercial he has filmed, and his disaffection with Metro-Goldwyn-Mayer, golf, Chicago weather and the machinations of putting a movie together these days.

He is quite a talker. But he is also kind. With each of the 15 young

347

women who danced and read lines for the part, he was patient, funny, complimentary and reassuring.

"Wonderful, my dear. You're great. Great."

"Lovely. You're very good."

Fifteen young women tried out. One was a professional stripper, the rest aspiring actresses. Rooney was gracious to all.

In the top row, director Schwartz explained how the choice would be made.

"Mickey and I'll get together. We'll have our minds made up and we'll give the winner a call."

Those who don't get the part won't hear anything. "That's right," Schwartz said. "It's still, 'Don't call us, we'll call you.'"

— *Chicago Sun-Times*

Figure 17.2 *This feature from the* Chicago Sun-Times *uses a number of illustrative devices, including description, direct quotation and figurative language. What other creative touches can you identify?*

Lengthy quotation is not always necessary. Sometimes just a few words will serve to illustrate some point. For example:

He spoke of the accuracy of the stenographic record of town meetings.

"Believe me, they take down every burp."

— *The Enterprise*, Falmouth, Mass.

This vignette from a *Washington Post* story by Mary McGrory added color to a story about former House Speaker Tip O'Neill on election night.

He gestures toward the food.

"Beef stew," he says and turns to his 33-year-old son, Christopher. "I've been eating beef stew on election night since before you were born, Kip."

The young waiter at the table looks slightly pained.

"It's beef burgundy," he murmurs.

Literary Devices

Illustrative devices include figures of speech, like metaphor and simile, references and allusions and images. These enliven our speech and writing and provide colorful and understandable illustration. Take this description, for example:

Mrs. Cloyd Heck Marvin rattles off discursively in all directions like the chatty clubwomen in a Helen

Hokinson New Yorker cartoon. In manner she rather resembles Agatha Christie's bumbling detective, Miss Marple.

A small hat perches perilously on the back of her still brownish hair. Her clothes flutter about her small plump figure with timeless skittishness. Words flutter from her in a rush of rosy tea-party platitudes.

— Atlanta Journal and Constitution

The writer says her subject is "like the chatty clubwomen in a Helen Hokinson New Yorker cartoon" and "resembles Agatha Christie's bumbling detective." If we know the characters to whom the writer refers, the relationship, the similarity, is quickly established. The allusion to a tea party, too, is intended to suggest a familiar or understandable image. Many younger readers, however, may not know what a Helen Hokinson clubwoman is like. Some may not have read Agatha Christie's Miss Marple stories. A reference or an allusion that is not immediately understandable is of no value. If literary devices are to be useful, they must be short cuts to understanding that quickly establish a bond between writer and reader.

Frederick Allen, writing in the *Atlanta Constitution*, made effective use of simile in a column on television evangelists:

It is no wonder viewers stop dead in their tracks. The Bakkers are like a roadside car wreck, a bug in a jar, someone having an epileptic fit: It is impossible not to look, and in the case of most of us who belong to the cult, to wonder how in the world Jim and Tammy Bakker get away with their act.

Analogies of all kinds are useful — for example, this lead on a story by Robert Boyd, Knight-Ridder Washington bureau chief, about charges and countercharges in Washington:

The squid, it is said, emits a cloud of black ink when it is attacked and then it vanishes in the murk.

The White House, under attack, sometimes imitates the squid.

— Detroit Free Press

Measuring a cat in terms of cats enlivens this Associated Press feature story:

> The Valley Empire Cat Fanciers, Inc., has a championship cat show coming up in Fresno next month, and the whole thing is a problem to Pierre.
>
> Pierre is a house cat roughly three cats long and two cats wide. He's 40 inches from nose to tail tip and weighs 32 pounds. The problem is how to get all this into one ordinary cat cage.

Playing with words is another useful device — for example, this lead from the *Atlanta Journal and Constitution:*

> One thing about feeding alligators, says Steve Ruckel, is that they tend to hang around for the next meal. And that can be a problem, largely because alligators make no distinction between hand and handout.

And this lead, on a story in *The Milwaukee Journal* about a man who not only walks on hot coals but teaches others how to do it, uses alliteration.

> Anthony Robbins, the pied piper of pyromania, was in Milwaukee Friday night, and about 260 people took off their shoes and followed him barefoot across a 12-foot bed of red-hot, 1,200 degree coals.

Nan Robertson has a good eye for detail and for colorful language. Writing in *The New York Times*, she provides a vivid description of a White House reception:

> The first shock wave of flowered hats hit the White House at 12:45 p.m. today, only 21 hours after the last Daughter of the American Revolution had departed the premises.
>
> Mrs. Richard M. Nixon was entertaining the ladies again — 4,702 of them, all Republican — in the biggest party held there since Andrew Jackson's riotous inaugural brawl in 1820. They were girdle to girdle in the East Room and all over the state floor.

In a story in the *Times* about a Democratic campaign blitz through Southern states, Miss Robertson wrote:

> The den mother, the conductor and orchestrator of the tour was Elizabeth Carpenter, Mrs. Lyndon B.

Johnson's press secretary. She proclaimed at each stop that she was a "footwashing, psalm singing, total immersion Democrat" . . .

There are other illustrative devices, most of them commonly used in both the journalistic and literary worlds. Exaggeration was discussed in Chapter 15. It is a useful device in writing and was used effectively in several of the light features shown in Chapter 15. Understatement, the opposite of exaggeration, can be useful. Sometimes it is better to understate rather than overstate. The point was made in Chapter 15, for instance, that some stories are so good that all the writer has to do is report the facts in simple terms — let the story tell itself — without embellishment.*

Maps and Diagrams

News writers mostly work on their own. They use words to convey an understanding of the simple and the complex, to describe people, emotions and attitudes. By skillful use of dialogue, example, anecdote, description and literary devices, the writer helps readers see things they have never seen and know people they have never met. To be sure, a headline, a photograph, sometimes a sketch accompanies the story, but the story is the thing.

Sometimes, however, the writer needs a sketch, a diagram or a map — graphics — to provide the kind of illustration that is beyond the power of words to convey. The use of a diagram or a sketch with a story in no way implies that the writer did not submit a clear and understandable story. But a diagram frequently makes a complex event more understandable. A sketch is a useful illustrative device and is as acceptable as description, dialogue or a figure of speech.

Elaborate sketches and diagrams must be prepared by a staff artist, of course, but news writers can do a certain amount of illustrative work with the aid of the typewriter or terminal. It is easy enough to put figures into two columns and type in a heading, for example. Simple tables are sometimes extremely helpful in making complicated stories easier to understand.

News writers are routinely responsible for a lot of charts and tables. Box scores and other sports summaries are good examples. So are tables of election returns. Like the other illustrative devices discussed in this

*For an easily understood discussion of literary, or rhetorical, devices, see Theodore Bernstein, *The Careful Writer* (New York: Atheneum, 1977).

chapter, they are merely added touches to the story — additional illustrative details.

Newspapers are making much more use of graphics today and with changes in the production process, charts and graphs — even elaborate charts and graphs reproduced in several colors — are becoming routine. News writers provide the data for the chart or graph, and a staff artist does the rest. The routine availability of computers to digest and analyze data makes it possible to reproduce fairly complex charts, graphs and tables, too. Another indication that news writers must be number conscious as well as word conscious.

Reporting and Writing

These last chapters have tried to show the possibilities for creativity and imagination in news writing. Nothing has been said, however, about the reporting that has to be done before creative writing is possible. Good reporters who are also good writers must be able to find information. They must also be perceptive — able to see and to hear and to understand what goes on around them. Good dialogue appears in a news story only after careful and discriminating listening. Good description is possible only if the writer is also a careful observer. Figurative language is possible only if the writer has the education, the experience and the perceptivity necessary to understand relationships and to make comparisons. Interesting and compelling stories about people are possible only if the writer likes and has empathy for other people.

I cannot promise that the mere reading of examples of good writing will make you a good writer. But if you read widely, keep an eye out for the well-written news and feature story, read and absorb and think about good writing — you can learn.

You must first, however, learn to be a reporter — a trained observer of events and a people watcher. And you must be concerned and interested in the people and activities around you — a participant not only in journalism but in human affairs.

Suggestions for Further Reading

A sampling of journalistic treatment of people, places and events. The five Ws brought to life by some very creative writers.

Davis, Richard S. *The Best of Davis*. Milwaukee: Milwaukee Journal, 1961.
Selections from the reportage of a gifted storyteller and an able writer.

Didion, Joan. *Slouching Towards Bethlehem.* New York: Dell Publishing Co., 1968.

> Scenes from the '60s as seen by a writer with a keen interest in human behavior.

Jacoby, Susan. *The Possible She.* New York: Farrar, Straus & Giroux, 1979.

> Insightful writing about the changing status of women. Includes "The Flatbush Feminists" from *The New York Times Magazine.*

Lukas, J. Anthony. *The Barnyard Epithet and Other Obscenities.* New York: Harper & Row, 1970.

> Lukas, a Pulitzer Prize–winning reporter, calls this essay on human behavior "notes on the Chicago conspiracy trial."

Talese, Gay. *A Serendipiter's Journey.* New York: Harper & Row, 1961.

> Stories about people and places in New York City written when Talese was a reporter for *The New York Times.*

Wolfe, Tom. *Radical Chic and Mau-Mauing the Flak Catchers.* New York: Farrar, Straus & Giroux, 1970.

> Tom Wolfe, the original "new journalist," at his very best with stories about high and low society.

THE MILWAUKEE JOURNAL **Sports/Business** Friday, March 20, 1987 — Section C

49ers seek Lofton

Special to The Journal

Kaanapali, Hawaii — San Francisco 49ers Owner Edward DeBartolo Jr. said Thursday that his team was interested in trading for troubled but talented wide receiver James Lofton of the Green Bay Packers.

"If there is going to be a deal, it's going to be wrapped up in the next two weeks," DeBartolo said at the National Football League meetings here.

Lofton's professional football future, however, is clouded by a second-degree sexual assault charge he faces in Green Bay. His trial is scheduled for May 18. If convicted, Lofton could face a penalty of 10 years in prison and a $10,000 fine.

DeBartolo would not say what the 49ers were willing to trade for Lofton but it most likely would involve 1987 college draft picks. The Packers have the fourth pick in the first round of the draft, and the 49ers have two first-round picks, their own (22nd) and Washington's (25th), and

James Lofton

two-second round picks, their own and Philadelphia's (ninth). Speculation is that the 49ers might try to package some of their draft picks for Lofton and the Packers' fourth selection in the draft.

Of Lofton's problems, DeBartolo said, "If we make a deal I don't think people will be concerned about that. We'd be bringing Lofton to San Francisco as a football player."

Friars go downtown for upset

By DON BURKE
of The Journal staff

Louisville, Ky. — From the NCAA's Southeast Regional, the region that features the well-known "Reggie and the Miracles," comes the lesser known but continually surprising "Billy and the Beaters," aka Billy Donovan and the Providence Friars.

The Friars, a long shot when this 64-team tournament began a week ago, used just that — *long shots* — to beat Alabama, 103-82, Thursday night at Freedom Hall, drowning the Crimson Tide in a sea of three-point baskets.

The Friars shot an amazing 69% for the game and an even more amazing 64% on three-pointers, making 14 of 22.

Providence, not exactly the least but certainly not the beast of the Big East, where they finished with an 11-5 record this season, will meet conference foe Georgetown for the fourth time this season in Saturday afternoon's regional final here.

Georgetown, thanks to Reggie Williams' 34 points and a defense that never rests, advanced by beating Kansas, 70-57, in Thursday's second game.

"Reggie and the Miracles," the Big East tournament champs, beat the Friars two of three times this season, including a second-round victory that eliminated Providence from the conference tourney two weeks ago.

NCAA SOUTHEAST

"Coach gives us the freedom offensively to take any open shots we have."

— **Billy Donovan**

The Friars-Hoyas matchup assured the Big East of having at least one team in the Final Four. And — are you comprehending this Big Ten fans? — Syracuse, another Big East team, is still alive in the East Regional.

The 6-foot Donovan, a Scott Skiles clone without the police record, scored 26 points, making five of six 3-pointers. His 10 assists moved him past Ernie DiGregorio, making him Providence's all-time assist leader.

Donovan's backcourt mate, Delray Brooks, added 23 points. The transfer from Indiana made five of eight shots from three-point range, several from so far away the very thought would make Michael Jordan blush.

Brooks did most of his damage when Donovan, who fouled out with 1 minute 43 seconds left, was on the bench with foul trouble.

"Billy did a great job of penetrating, and I was open and the shots just fell," said Brooks. "Billy is a great floor leader. When he is not out on the floor somebody else has to try and take over from a leadership standpoint, and I decided to do the job."

Donovan has been the Friars' main offensive weapon all season long. He scored 35 and 25 points, respectively, in Providence's earlier National Collegiate Athletic Association tournament victories over Alabama — Birmingham and Austin Peay.

"Coach gives us the freedom offensively to take any open shots we have," said Donovan.

Smart man that coach. Rick Pitino, in only his second season at Providence, has taken the Friars to within a game of their first Final Four appearance since DiGregorio starred for Providence in 1973.

While enamored with the long-range artillery unloaded by Donovan and Brooks, Pitino said the key to the game was the defensive job done on Alabama center Derrick McKey. McKey, the center who helped the Tide roll to the Southeastern Conference title, took only six shots Thursday and finished with 11 points.

Please see **Friars**, Page 5C

MICHAEL BAUMAN
SPORTS COLUMNIST

Selig wisely finds allies

MILWAUKEE BREWERS PRESIDENT Bud Selig is convinced that his franchise needs a new or renovated stadium to make a go of it in Milwaukee into the 21st century.

Selig's feelings on this issue run every bit as deeply as they did when he opposed a state prison in his franchise's neighborhood and when he opposed the building of the Bradley Center on the County Stadium parking lots. He was, you will recall, two-for-two on those controversies. So, as ambitious as the notion of a new stadium might be, he might well be on something of an operational roll.

The problem for Selig, particularly in the Bradley Center brouhaha, was that, while he believed he had to go to the wall for the well-being of baseball in Milwaukee, the perception in some quarters was that he was merely whining, complaining and being petulant. There were plenty of people around town in positions of considerable influence who also saw problems with the Stadium site, but Selig became the point man for this particular operation and suffered the attendant abuse.

This time around, again with his perception that nothing less than the future of the franchise is at stake — Selig's thoughts and emotions regarding his ballclub do not come to us in muted tones — he will not be going it alone. Selig has enlisted the support of the captains of industry, the economic leaders of the community, the big guys. They appear to be only too happy to help.

THE GREATER MILWAUKEE COMMITTEE, a group of corporate, professional and educational leaders, announced earlier this week that it had formed a task force to aid Selig in this undertaking, an undertaking that is, at once, immense and delicate. Apart from the specific form this assistance could take, this arrangement means that Selig would not be doing a solo act on the stage of another complex issue. Behind him, around him, will be this accumulated expertise and influence. Selig is hardly without expertise and influence, but in an operation of this magnitude, you cannot compile too much clout.

"In a way, the experience Bud went through with the Bradley Center is the kind of thing we'd like to avoid," said Robert Milbourne, executive director of the Greater Milwaukee Committee. "We'd like to build support for this project and we want to communicate with the community in a way that doesn't make it appear as though Bud is begging for help."

Consultants working for the Brewers are studying the feasibility of several options, among them a new stadium and a complete renovation of County Stadium. If we are to speak of a new stadium, then we must also speak of magnificent sums of money. Pick a figure — $80 million, $100 million, $125 million, it's far too early to say, but it won't be pocket change. Even a Stadium renovation, such as the one at New York's Shea, a decade younger than County Stadium, is reportedly a $40 million job. Selig stressed that begging won't be on his agenda, even at these prices.

"There is no question in my mind, in all of this, that the economic linchpin has to be the Milwaukee Brewers," he said.

Said Milbourne: "Nobody is suggesting that we are going to go to the government for a huge subsidy. That is not the objective here."

BUT IF THE GMC will not be begging — these people are not experienced in that area, anyway — the organization will be brainstorming, suggesting, lobbying. The various levels of government will eventually be involved, whether in specific areas such as access roads and parking, or the larger, considerably more intricate questions of "creative financing," in which government ideally assists with the financing without sticking the taxpayers for the whole bill.

Getting the simultaneous cooperation of city, county and state government is a much trickier undertaking than getting the business community together for lunch. The path to a new stadium will not be a smooth multilane freeway, but much more of a two-lane county trunk road, complete with curves, bumps and potholes.

But Bud Selig could be doing nothing less than betting the franchise on this project. All the more reason why he needs as much influence behind him as possible. It is not unknown for the various elements of this community to pitch in on a sports project. The very return of major-league baseball to Milwaukee was a combined effort of the public sector, the private sector and the baseball interests.

In the end, the various studies on the stadium options could show that a new stadium is beyond the realm of possibility, that even a renovated Stadium is a stretch. But for the moment, the involvement of the Greater Milwaukee Committee in the stadium situation means that this is bigger than a Bud Selig project, bigger than a Milwaukee Brewers project. Given what baseball means to this entire community, this is as it should be.

Journal photos by Benny Sieu

Antigo's Todd Frisch (left) tried to steal the ball from Washington's Brian Garner at the WIAA tourney

Quickly, Purgolders advance

WIAA BOYS

THURSDAY'S RESULTS
Class A Quarterfinals
Fond du Lac 41, Racine Case 32.
Sussex Hamilton 53, Eau Claire North 49.
Madison East 51, Beloit Memorial 50.
Milwaukee Washington 67, Antigo 55.

FRIDAY'S SCHEDULE
Class C Semifinals
Elk Mound 68, Florence 59.
Fennimore (23-3) vs. Oostburg (24-1), 11:20 a.m.

Class B Semifinals
Clintonville (17-7) vs. Phillips (23-2), 2 p.m.
Elkhorn (18-7) vs. Wisconsin Dells (23-1), 7 p.m.

Class A Semifinals
Fond du Lac (19-6) vs. Sussex Hamilton (18-8), 3:45 p.m.
Madison East (14-11) vs. Milwaukee Washington (23-2), 8:50 p.m.

By BOB BERGHAUS
of The Journal staff

Madison, Wis. — The last quarterfinal game of the Wisconsin Interscholastic Athletic Association Class A tournament here Thursday night was a classic mismatch: the gutsy, but slow Antigo Red Robins against the lightning-quick, high-jumping Milwaukee Washington Purgolders.

Quickness won this battle hands down as Washington raced to a 67-55 victory.

"We figured they'd be quick; that was no surprise to us," said Antigo Coach Robert Anderson, whose team finished with a 16-9 record. "I think what happened was their quickness intimidated us. They had fast breaks and some dunks, but that quickness had my kids worried more than anything else."

It was that quickness that Washington used to make three steals and force five turnovers on its way to a 21-8 lead in the first quarter,

WIAA BOYS/A

taking away any thoughts Antigo had of playing a control game.

It was that quickness Washington used to end any momentum the Robins tried generating after scoring a couple of baskets for a brief run.

It was quickness and overall talent the Purgolders used to improve their record to 23-2 and gain a berth in the semifinals Friday night opposite Madison East.

"I thought our defense was an important factor in the game," said Washington Coach Clyde Rusk, who was wearing a fish tie for the fifth game in a row. "I was pleased with it as far as coaching goes. We came out in a tough man-for-man defense and took them out of their ball game."

Washington's offense wasn't that bad, either. The Purgolders made 17 of 26 shots in the first half in racing to a 37-21 lead. They finished the game making 29 of 50 for 58%.

Please see **Quick**, Page 3C

Reserve sparks Sussex's victory

Staff correspondence

Madison, Wis. — Todd Becker, Sussex Hamilton's version of John Havlicek, played his sixth-man role to perfection here Thursday afternoon.

Becker, a senior guard who started most of last season and the first four games this season, proved his value off the bench in leading the Chargers to a 53-49 victory over

WIAA BOYS/A

Eau Claire North in a quarterfinal game of the Wisconsin Interscholastic Athletic Association Class A basketball tournament.

Becker scored a season-high 17 points, including six in the final 1 minute 38 seconds, to finish off North, which had chopped a 10-point deficit to two.

Becker, who had been averaging about six points, sank five of seven field-goal attempts and seven of nine free throws. He also made his presence felt on defense, forcing a couple of turnovers and getting his hand in on just about every loose ball possible.

"Todd's like an assistant coach on the bench," said Hamilton Coach Jim Lawinger. "He says we should be doing one thing and goes into the ball game and does something different. He says, 'Boy, we should be passing the ball around more,' then he gets in and shoots it."

Please see **Sussex**, Page 3C

Hamilton's Kevin Loken (right) awaited D.J. Pophal

Who shot J.R.? Not the Irish

East Rutherford, N.J. —AP— The initials J.R. have come to mean bad dude, and many a Notre Dame player would say the North Carolina version may be the worst of all.

"J.R. showed he was a man tonight," North Carolina Coach Dean Smith said after J.R. Reid, the Tar Heels' sensational freshman, scored 31 points to lead North Carolina to a 74-68 victory over Notre Dame in the NCAA tournament East Regional semifinals. "He certainly scored a lot of tough points. J.R. had played very well of late and considering the importance of the game, this may have been his best performance."

The victory avenged a regular-season loss to the Fighting Irish and

NCAA EAST

put the second-ranked Tar Heels in Saturday's East Regional final against Syracuse.

The Orangemen, ranked No. 10 nationally and second in the region behind the Tar Heels, held off upstart Florida, 87-81, in the opening game at the Brendan Byrne Arena behind a career-high 33-point performance by center Rony Seikaly.

The final matchup on Saturday pits the regular-season champion of the Atlantic Coast Conference against one of the three champions of the Big East. Syracuse shared that title with Georgetown and Pitt.

In North Carolina's victory, the toughest stretch came in the final eight minutes, when Reid took over and became the Tar Heels' offense. The 6-foot 9-inch center, who has the moves of a guard, scored 16 of the Tar Heels' final 17 points with a variety of turnaround jump shots, power moves on the baseline, follows off rebounds and rim-shaking dunks.

"All good players want the ball down the stretch," said Reid, who has given new meaning to the initials "J.R." popularized by television's bad guy, J.R. Ewing of "Dallas."

"I was just getting the ball in great scoring position from my teammates. This team has a lot of great players. I think any one of them could have done it."

The performance left Notre Dame Coach Digger Phelps impressed.

"J.R. put on a great show, especially in the second half," Phelps said. "He has a lot of confidence for a freshman. You could see this summer he was going to be a dominant college player."

Twice in the final four minutes, Notre Dame pulled within three points of North Carolina, the first at 65-62 with 3 minutes 45 seconds left on a jump shot by Mark Stevenson. However, Reid slammed home a dunk with 3:26 left.

Gary Voce hit a layup with 2:20 to play to make it 67-64, but Reid came back 20 seconds later with a 10-foot jump shot and the Fighting Irish, 24-8, never got closer than four points the rest of the way. Their 11-game winning streak and season came to an end.

The victory was the 32nd in 35 games for North Carolina, and it more than made up for a 60-58 loss to Notre Dame on Feb. 1. In that game, the Tar Heels played without guard Kenny Smith, who was injured, and blew a lead in the late stages.

"As a team, we were determined not to let the same thing happen to us that happened at South Bend," said Reid, who hit 15 of 18 shots and matched his career high, set earlier this year against North Carolina State.

North Carolina took control in the first half with a 16-4 run that gave it a 28-19 edge. Reid had seven points in that run and North Carolina never trailed again.

Joe Wolf scored 13 points and Dave Popson added 11 for North

Please see **East**, Page 5C

18

Style and the Stylebook

I learned on the Journal *the value of high standards on apparently small matters. Details taken together become large matters, so that high standards on details almost dictate high standards on larger matters.*

Tom Wicker

Beginners in the newsroom are confronted almost immediately with the need to spell, punctuate, capitalize and abbreviate — among other things — in a certain way. If they ask why, as they ought to, they will be told, "That's our *style.*"

Style is the way things are done around the newsroom. Style is the way you are supposed to do things. And style, you will quickly find out, is often arbitrary, unreasonable and confusing. But it is important, and the first thing beginners should do is get a copy of the stylebook that governs writing practices and usage in the newsroom where they work and learn its rules.

All newspapers follow a stylebook of one kind or another. Many use the stylebook prepared jointly by the Associated Press and United Press International. Larger newspapers often have their own stylebook, agreeing in most cases with the press associations' joint stylebook but often differing in one way or another. Book publishers, public relations agencies, magazines, radio and television newsrooms, the Government Printing Office and the armed forces also have stylebooks. Most books on news writing, including this one, include a basic style guide for beginners.

355

The Joint Stylebook

One of the major influences on news style today is the joint stylebook published by the Associated Press and United Press International. The first joint stylebook was published in 1960, revised in 1968 and completely rewritten and enlarged in 1977. A new and updated edition was published in 1987. Most newspapers follow its lead, either using it as their own stylebook and making locally written copy conform or basing their own stylebook at least in part on preferences set forth in the joint stylebook.*

The rapidly changing technology of newspaper production has favored the general use of the joint stylebook. Today news copy is transmitted by the wire services from computer to computer. That is, a news story is transmitted from the wire service computer via satellite to the newspaper computer. The story can then be sent directly to a computer-driven phototypesetter. News copy is edited less and less, and newspapers have found it faster and less expensive to follow the style of the joint stylebook than to edit wire service copy to follow a different stylebook.

For the beginner, there is some advantage in the dominance of the joint stylebook. Once you learn style, you will find you can follow it most of the time in most of the places where you will work.

Why Have a Stylebook?

The development of printing in the late fifteenth century brought a great tide of intellectual activity first to Europe, then to England and finally to the American continent. With printing and scholarship came an interest in language, which led to grammar books, dictionaries, spellers and stylebooks. All are similar in that they are attempts to describe the written language and to devise rules for its use.

A Need for Consistency

Stylebooks are devices for enforcing consistency in writing throughout the newspaper. This does not mean that the newspaper wants every one of its reporters, writers and editors to write exactly the same way. Far from it. No newspaper wants its pages to sound like the homogenized

---

*Although the Associated Press Stylebook differs from the United Press International version in typography, occasionally in wording and occasionally by citing different examples, the two stylebooks are essentially the same. Examples in this chapter are quoted from *The Associated Press Stylebook and Libel Manual.*

columns in *Time* magazine or *Reader's Digest*. But it does want consistency in punctuation, capitalization, abbreviation, spelling, the use of numbers and related matters. The press associations' joint stylebook, for example, says:

> Use the abbreviations *Ave.*, *Blvd.* and *St.* only with a numbered address: *1600 Pennsylvania Ave.* Spell them out when part of a formal street name without a number: *Pennsylvania Avenue.*

This rule is intended to ensure that every news story originating with either press association, or published in the newspapers that have adopted the joint stylebook, will abbreviate or spell out these words in exactly the same way every time. In this and other matters of style, consistency is considered both a virtue and a necessity. Editors want capitalization, punctuation, abbreviations and numbers to appear in the same form on every page of the newspaper all the way from the front page to the market news on the inside of the back page. They want business writers and police reporters and columnists to follow the same rules in the use of titles and nicknames. They want locally written stories to follow the same spelling rules that the press associations follow.

Preference and Tradition

Style is basically a preference for one way of doing things over another way when there are two or more acceptable ways of doing it. You could, for example, capitalize the word *Street* in addresses, or you might not. You could abbreviate it or spell it out. In any case, the word would be understandable to your readers. The choice you make is a matter of preference, not a matter of one way being right and another wrong.

Style, in the sense of providing rules for spelling, punctuation, capitalization, abbreviation and the use of numbers, is a product of the printing press. It is a visual matter. In the case of punctuation, periods and commas and question marks provide visual clues to meaning that we hear and interpret when we listen to someone talk. In the case of spelling, the various rules of English spelling reflect what was originally an attempt to indicate how words sounded.

Style is to a large extent traditional. It grew up with the development of printing and with the growth of the printing and publishing industries. The earliest printers and editors sought consistency as they created a new written form of the English language. There is a long tradition that language ought to be consistent, that there must be true and correct forms and that the correct way to use the language should

357

be preserved and the rules enforced. This view does not take into account the reality of change. All language changes over time. Sounds change, meaning changes and usage changes. But attempts at establishing the "correct" forms have persisted. Style falls within this tradition as it attempts to establish certain forms and usage.

Style is *prescriptive* — that is, it tells you how you ought to use the language if you are to conform to what have come to be regarded as standard practices among well-educated writers and editors.

Mechanical Rules

The most mechanical and least interesting aspects of news style have to do with punctuation, capitalization, abbreviations and the use of numbers. In all these matters, the written language allows for considerable variation, and stylebooks attempt to provide consistency. Stylebooks needn't bother to remind news writers that the first word of a sentence is capitalized, nor that a sentence ends with a period. But the joint stylebook does provide helpful guides to consistency in less certain areas. For example:

> Periods always go inside quotation marks.

Capitalization is an area in which there are few well-understood rules and a lot of leeway for personal choice. For example, we all agree that the initial letters of personal names should be capitalized: John, William, Henry. But the joint stylebook instructs us in some other matters not so generally agreed upon:

> Capitalize formal titles when they are used immediately before one or more names: *Pope Paul, President Washington, Vice Presidents John Jones and William Smith.*

> Capitalize common nouns such as *party, river, street* and *west* when they are an integral part of the full name for a person, place or thing: *Democratic Party, Mississippi River, Fleet Street, West Virginia.*

Abbreviations are anybody's game, and stylebooks have much to say about them. For example, the joint stylebook allows the abbreviation *U.S.* as an adjective but not as a noun. *U.N.* for United Nations is treated the same way. Stylebooks set rules for abbreviation of state names, legislative titles, military titles and religious titles.

Numbers are a problem, but the stylebook has one generally accepted rule: Write out numbers one through nine and use Arabic figures for 10 and larger numbers. That sounds easy, but when you start using numbers in news copy, you will find that there are a good many exceptions. For example:

> Use figures for amounts under 10 in dimensions, formulas and speeds: *The farm measures 5 miles by 4 miles. The car slowed to 7 mph. The new model gets 4 miles more per gallon.*

> Spell out casual expressions: *A thousand times no! Thanks a million. He walked a quarter of a mile.*

These examples turn the basic, one-through-nine rule upside down. Yet you will find that the rules for the use of numbers are fairly simple and, because we use so many numbers in news stories, not too difficult to master. And, when in doubt, refer to the stylebook.

Many rules found in stylebooks are there to make news stories easier to read and understand. Once learned, the more frequently used style rules make it easier to write, too, for they provide formulas for handling routine information. Knowing style rules for using names, titles, ages and addresses, for example, makes it easier to organize facts in an understandable way. Consistency in these matters helps the reader, too. Figure 18.1 shows just how many style rules are involved in even a brief news story.

News style is gradually eliminating unnecessary punctuation as a means of keeping sentences uncluttered and flowing smoothly. The joint stylebook asks you to eliminate the comma before *and* and *or* in a series:

> He saluted the red, white and blue.

> She asked for apples, pears or oranges.

The joint stylebook also does away with the apostrophe in plurals of numbers and letters:

> The airline had no 727s in the 1950s.

> The children knew their ABCs.

News style calls for the use of *a.m.* or *p.m.* with all references to clock time. Readers should not be confused about when things happened or will happen.

```
01        A Carolton police officer was shot Sunday by a man he
02   had surprised siphoning gasoline from a school bus parked
03   on West Main Street.
04        Patrolman Edward Look, 30, a four-year veteran of the
05   Carolton Police Department, said he saw Robert Anchor, 30, of
06   91 N. Meade St., taking gas about 8 a.m. from a car parked at
07   a service station at 511 W. Main St.
08        Anchor fired one shot at Look from a .32-caliber pistol,
09   before Look subdued him.
10        Anchor is wanted by the FBI for questioning about a bank
11   robbery in New Iberia, La., and a bar holdup in Houston,
12   Texas.
```

Figure 18.1 *This story suggests the importance of knowing style when you write even the simplest news story. Look up the rules followed in this story in the Basic Guide to News Style at the end of this text.*

Line 1	*day of week, 6.5*
Line 3	*addresses, 1.5*
Line 4	*ages, 3.5; hyphens, 4.4*
Line 5	*capitalization, 2.1; ages, 3.5*
Line 6	*addresses, 1.5 and 1.7; time, 6.1*
Line 7	*addresses, 1.5 and 1.7*
Line 8	*weapons, 3.6 and 4.4*
Line 10	*abbreviations, 1.1*
Line 11	*state names, 1.9 and 1.10*
Line 12	*state names, 1.9, 1.10 and 1.11*

News style is also particular about the use of names, and although there are some exceptions, the basic rule is to identify people by their first name, middle initial and last name:

John C. Smith and Mary L. Hamilton

News style tells us that ages are always written in Arabic figures and that numbers in street addresses are always in Arabic figures:

John C. Smith, 37, of 8 W. Circle Drive

Where street addresses follow a person's age, as in this example, news style requires the insertion of the word *of* between the age and the address. The word *of* is a safety precaution against getting the numbers in the age and the address mixed up. It might be awkward placing Smith at 378 W. Circle Drive.

The joint stylebook is explicit about the use of courtesy titles:

> In general, do not use the courtesy titles *Miss, Mr., Mrs.* or *Ms.* on first references. Instead, use the first and last names of the person: *Betty Ford, Jimmy Carter.*

> On news wires, use courtesy titles for women on second reference, following the woman's preference.

As you become familiar with the contents of the stylebook, you will find many rules and suggestions that will make it easier for you to write your story and will also make your story easier to read and understand. Rules about style help structure and organize news writing. Although style takes away some freedom of choice, it does speed up production. You don't have to stop whenever a decision is called for. The decision has already been made for you. Once you have learned the rules, style becomes second nature and the copy rolls out much faster.

Style and Usage

In addition to the more mechanical matters like punctuation, stylebooks tend to get into meanings and uses of words and phrases. There are some good reasons for this, although reason and logic do not account for all the rules of usage enforced by stylebooks. In the first place, the newspaper is concerned with the clear, accurate and truthful presentation of information, so that precise meanings of words are important. Do you mean *imply* or *infer*? Are you sure it is *convince*, or should it be *persuade*? Second, the newspaper is seeking to present the news in readable, informal and understandable prose. Through the stylebook and its strictures on usage, newspapers attempt to strike a balance between informal, slangy, irreverent popular speech and the stiff, formal language of scholarship or technical writing. You will notice, however, that journalism has a conservative streak, and stylebooks to some extent represent resistance to change in language.

Precision in the use of words is important if our readers are to understand what we write. News writing must be so accurate that readers get the same meaning out of a story that we put into it. Hence, suggestions such as the following from the joint stylebook:

> **couple of** The *of* is necessary. Never use *a couple tomatoes* or a similar phrase.

The *Washington Post Deskbook on Style* cautions:

> *Verbal* means related to words, either written or spoken, rather than to action. It is often erroneously used to contrast with *written;* the correct expression of contrast is *oral* versus *written.*

Popular speech, of course, is the real source of the written language, and journalism has always drawn on the everyday language of the street, the police station, the theater, sports, politics — and everywhere else — to enrich its language.

Some words may be banned by stylebooks because they are too slangy or too undignified, but there has been a general easing up on slang and popular speech in the past few years. Stylebooks are becoming more tolerant, but the joint stylebook cautions that *cop,* for example, should be used only in quoted matter. And while *OK* is OK, *okay* is not.

Many of the prohibitions in stylebooks are, unfortunately, due to tradition and conservatism, even prejudice, and some are due to a refusal to accept the fact that English is an ever-changing language. Many stylebooks object to the coining of new verbs from existing nouns: for example, *shotgunned* and *hosted.* Other proscribed usages include *-ize* words like *finalize* or *utilize.* Such prohibitions are grammatical nonsense, since speakers of English have been creating useful new verbs from nouns and making verbs out of adjectives by adding *-ize* for many generations. It is true that some newly coined words are awkward, some grate on the ear and some are not as familiar as older words or phrases. Many coinages won't last. However, others will survive because they meet the needs of our times. Newspapers are full of such words. Nevertheless, stylebooks continue to ban some from newspaper columns, and we have to follow the stylebook.

Many stylebooks ban the use of *contact* as a verb and other coinages like *guested, premiered, debuted* and *readied.* Other prohibitions are traditional but difficult to explain logically:

> The use of *feel* for *believe; following* as a preposition in the sense of *after; sustained* in the phrase *she sustained injuries; lady* for *woman; over* for *more than; Xmas* as an abbreviation for *Christmas.*

Spelling is a problem for the stylebook since there are sometimes two acceptable and commonly used spellings for a word — *employe* and *employee,* for example — and consistency within a publication demands that one spelling be selected as the preferred usage. Most stylebooks include a list of preferred spellings, and news writers must follow the stylebook. Many stylebooks include lists of frequently misspelled words and words similar in form or meaning that are commonly confused. The joint stylebook has many such entries, and the Basic Guide to News Style in this book includes a section on spelling and usage.

Style and Policy

Stylebooks usually include some rules or guidelines to the newspaper's policy on such matters as courtesy titles, racial descriptions, sexual stereotyping, the use of epithets, vulgarities, profanity and obscenity and the use of legal, technical and scientific terminology.

The joint stylebook goes into considerable detail on courtesy titles. In the past few years, there have been changes in community attitudes toward the use of courtesy titles — Mr., Miss, Mrs. and Ms. — and the stylebook reflects this to some extent. However, the joint stylebook continues to require the use of courtesy titles for women on second reference, although many newspapers no longer require them.

Most stylebooks ban racial descriptions unless they are clearly relevant to a news story.

Sexual stereotyping is a matter requiring the attention of all writers and editors, so stylebooks are explicit on the subject. For example, the joint stylebook says:

> Women should receive the same treatment as men in all areas of coverage. Physical descriptions, sexist references, demeaning stereotypes and condescending phrases should not be used.

The *Washington Post Deskbook* has an excellent chapter titled "Taste and Sensibilities," which deals with sexual stereotyping, courtesy titles and other matters.

The use of words or phrases that may be offensive to some readers is a problem. Very few words or phrases are banned outright today, although many readers are still a bit squeamish. *Rape*, for example, long felt to be too strong a word to appear in a family newspaper, is now preferred to such circumlocutions as *statutory offense* and *sexual assault*. The cultural revolution of the 1960s and the more recent spread of AIDS have brought frank discussion and reporting to the columns of the newspaper. There is very little that may not be reported these days, and very few words that can't be used in the proper context.

Vulgarity, profanity and obscenity continue to be a problem for the newspaper. Stylebooks are explicit about the use of vulgarities, profanity and obscenity, for newspapers generally are locally oriented and sensitive to community standards and attitudes. Words that many

363

people use and most know are simply not used in print. The joint stylebook warns about vulgarities, profanity and obscenities:

> Do not use them in news stories unless they are part of direct quotations and there is a compelling reason for them.

The *Los Angeles Times Stylebook* also takes a conservative stand on questionable language. In its discussion of vulgarity, profanity and obscenity, it says:

> None of the terms in these categories should go into the paper without the knowledge of either the managing editor, the associate editor of the editorial page or one of the assistant managing editors.

The *Washington Post Deskbook* also urges caution and says:

> The test should be "why use it?" rather than "why not use it?"

The position of *The New York Times* is clear and unequivocal:*

> The Times does not violate standards of taste unless the quoted material makes an overwhelmingly important point that cannot be made as clearly and forcefully through paraphrase.

The Authority Behind Style

Although stylebooks tend to be arbitrary and conservative about language, there is both authority and scholarship behind their rules. Stylebooks follow well-established standards. The joint stylebook bases its rules on spelling and usage on *Webster's New World Dictionary of the American Language*, a well-edited and up-to-date dictionary. Second or backup reference is *Webster's Third New International Dictionary of the English Language*, which despite carping by some editors about its permissiveness is *the* standard dictionary of American English.

Military titles and designations are based on the official usage of the armed forces, and rules on religion are based on the *Handbook of Denominations in the United States*. The use of place names in the United States is based on the *U.S. Postal Service Directory of Post Offices*.

---

*Winners and Sinners, No. 441, June 25, 1987.

On grammar and usage, the joint stylebook relies on a number of authoritative sources, including Theodore M. Bernstein's *The Careful Writer* and *The Chicago Manual of Style.*

Other Stylebooks

A number of larger newspapers have developed and follow their own style. Among them are the *Boston Globe, Indianapolis News, Kansas City Star, Los Angeles Times, Miami Herald, Milwaukee Journal, Milwaukee Sentinel, Newsday, New York Times* and *Wilmington* (Del.) *News-Journal.*

Many of the examples of news stories in this text are from newspapers whose style differs in some way from wire service style.

"A Basic Guide to News Style"

This text includes what might be called a basic stylebook. It includes many statements on style and newsroom practice that are too basic and well understood to be included in the joint stylebook or in many newspaper stylebooks. It also includes some guidance on matters that are important on smaller, local newspapers but that don't affect the wire services. It omits a great deal that you will find in the joint stylebook or in the stylebooks of other newspapers, especially typographical matters that are not of immediate interest to the beginning news writer. Because most beginning news writers are writing in college classrooms, the Basic Guide covers a number of matters that are of greater interest on college campuses than elsewhere — for example, treatment of academic titles, degrees and rank and identification of students.

As far as possible, this guide to style agrees with the rules and preferences of the press associations' joint stylebook, either specifically or by analogy.

Personal Style

News style as we have just described it deals with mechanical matters and with consistency. It smacks of history and tradition. It presents some guidelines for clear and accurate writing and it establishes some matters of newsroom policy. News style offers some useful and workable guidelines for organizing and writing news stories, but it should not inhibit you from developing your own style of writing. You can obey the newsroom stylebook and still develop your own style, your own way of saying things. Personal style is not the same thing as style

rules you find in the newsroom stylebook. Personal style is choice —
your choice of words, of idioms, of sentence structure and grammatical
alternatives.

The writer's choice of words, the writer's own writing style, resulted
in this lead from the *Detroit Free Press:*

> A 23-year-old man, clad only in raindrops, tried to
> climb the Scott Fountain on Belle Isle Sunday.

Nude or *naked* might have been obvious words to describe the Detroit man. Some writers might have said *unclothed*. But the writer of
this news lead out of his own sense of appropriate language found a
different way of saying something quite ordinary.

Your personal style will develop over time, and it will probably not
start to grow until you have mastered the arbitrary and structured
aspects of news style and the basic news story structures. Once you feel
comfortable with the basic matters of news writing, you will begin to
reach out, to be more creative, to develop a style and approach to writing that is uniquely your own.

This personal style will not be a matter of punctuation, capitalization or abbreviation. It will be a matter of your choice of words, the
range of your vocabulary, your ability to coin figures of speech, your
ear for speech and for dialect, colorful words and apt expressions. It
will be a matter of sentence length and the rhythm of your prose, of the
clarity of your thinking and the logical presentation of your ideas. This
style will not come out of a newsroom stylebook — it will come out of
you. It will not be a matter of rules, it will be a matter of feeling. Accept
the newsroom stylebook for what it is, a help and a guide, and go on to
learn to write in your own style.

Suggestions for Further Reading

Stylebooks are not easy reading, but they are exceedingly useful as
reference books. These are some of the standard and authoritative references used by professional journalists in their daily work.

French, Christopher, ed. *The Associated Press Stylebook and Libel Manual.*
New York: Associated Press, 1986.
    The Associated Press version of the wire services' joint stylebook.

Holley, Frederick S., ed. *Los Angeles Times Stylebook.* New York: New American Library, 1981.
    A useful reference, especially on usage. Authoritative.

Jordan, Lewis, ed. *The New York Times Style Book.* New York: McGraw-Hill Book Company, 1962.

> *The New York Times* has its own rules on style.

Miller, Bobby Ray, ed. *The UPI Stylebook.* New York: United Press International, 1981.

> The UPI version of the wire services' joint stylebook.

Strunk, William, Jr., and E.B. White. *The Elements of Style.* New York: The Macmillan Company, 1959.

> An idiosyncratic discussion of style. This is not a complete guide to style like others listed here, but it is useful, and professional writers use it and recommend it.

Webb, Robert A., ed. *The Washington Post Deskbook on Style.* New York: McGraw-Hill Book Company, 1978.

> An extremely readable and useful book on style, usage and newspaper practices.

AARP NEWS BULLETIN

Vol. 28, No. 1   Washington, D.C.   January 1987

Volunteer matchmaker

AARP Talent Bank helps volunteers find jobs they love

Dorothea Brayer knows how to get things done.

"I like working with people and I like to see them succeed . . . I've spent most of my life helping people through difficult situations," says the AARP member who is among the retirees who have found volunteer jobs to match their special skills through the AARP Volunteer Talent Bank (VTB).

At 74, Brayer says she is eager to tackle new assignments though the VTB. "We all need to sharpen our skills and I'm in the process of helping other volunteers become better in their jobs." She offers management and administrative advice in workshops for AARP Tax-Aide volunteers.

"Each assignment is a real challenge and I really enjoy helping people get organized and get into something worthwhile . . . I hate to see people struggle," she explained.

Brayer brings a range of skills and experience to her assignments. A former teacher, she also served as an administrator in the Rochester, N.Y., area schools, established and directed a halfway house for young people who were called "underachievers," and counseled alcoholics and mentally retarded persons.

Patty Jane Stockman of Marina Del Rey, Calif., is another AARP member who has found her niche through the VTB. A former human resources specialist with a large aerospace corporation, she is serving as community liaison volunteer and works with

Talent Bank volunteer Alma Humphrey works with AARP's Legal Counsel for the Elderly in Washington, D.C.

employers in the Association's Worker Equity Department's Business Partnership program.

Stockman is another example of how
continued on page 10

AARP offers to help 'improve' new catastrophic health plan

Calling a catastrophic care proposal by Health and Human Services Secretary Otis R. Bowen a "step in the right direction," the Association pledged to work with the administration and Congress to improve key provisions of the plan.

AARP cautioned, however, that the plan does not go far enough to help people who currently cannot pay for nursing home care or lengthy illnesses. For example, last year older Americans paid over $7 billion out-of-pocket for medicines.

Bowen proposed an expansion of Medicare and some tax breaks that would increase protection for all persons with catastrophic medical expenses.

The Bowen plan focuses on three main areas of catastrophic illness:

1) acute care costs for people over 65; 2) long-term care costs for people over 65; and 3) acute care costs for people under 65.

Expanded Medicare coverage for acute care would be financed through a $4.92 monthly increase in the Medicare Part B premium. Medicare beneficiaries would pay no more than $2,000 each year out-of-pocket for co-insurance and deductibles.

However, AARP pointed out that costly services and products, such as physical examinations and outpatient prescription drugs, would not count toward this $2,000 limit.

"Gaps in Medicare coverage of acute illnesses leave older people vulnerable to huge medical costs," said AARP Executive Director Cyril F. Brickfield. "Medicare must be strengthened if beneficiaries are to be protected from potentially catastrophic costs not currently covered."

The second part of the Bowen plan would combine a private savings approach with a private long-term care insurance feature. For instance, individuals placing $1,000 into an individual medical account (IMA), similar to
continued on page 10

IN THIS ISSUE

Workers get support for burden of love

A woman in her mid-50s with teenage children and a full-time job, Annette has managed the stress of caring for frail relatives in her home without asking for special consideration from her employer.

But thanks to a new AARP pro-

AARP is developing a variety of programs to assist caregivers. See Executive Director's Report, page 8.

---

gram, those in similar situations may find support in the business world for their concerns.

Annette's mother, crippled with

rheumatoid arthritis, lived with her daughter's family for five years before she died. Within a year, Annette's father became ill and lived with the family for three years before his death. Two years ago, when her mother-in-law became too frail to live alone, Annette knew her family and job would suffer once again as she tried to balance household duties, a full-time job and the care of relatives. "There's a limit, even for a strong person," she says.

The Association's new "Caregivers in the Workplace" program will help employers understand the needs of employees like Annette whose responsibilities for elderly family and friends
continued on page 8

A publication of the American Association of Retired Persons

19 Newspaper Grammar and Punctuation

Punctuation marks are a part of the vocabulary of civilization; a misunderstanding can be created or erased by them.

Karen Elizabeth Gordon
The Well-Tempered Sentence

The English language takes many forms. It is a spoken language and it is, as well, a written language — each form with its own conventions and rules. The language used in the newspaper is a special form of English in the sense that it has some conventions and rules that differ somewhat from the way things are done in other varieties or dialects of the language.

In this chapter, we will take a look at some of the special problems of newspaper language. These include matters of syntax and usage that are peculiar to news writing as well as some grammatical problems that tend to cause difficulties for many news writers. The discussion will include punctuation problems common in news writing.

Word Order

The words in English sentences are arranged in a consistent manner. In the most common sentence structure, we find nouns first, verbs second and another noun after

369

the verb: the familiar arrangement of subject + verb + direct object, like this:

Subject	Verb	Direct Object
The boy	hit	the ball.
The ball	struck	the fence.
The president	addressed	the Congress.

Normal Word Order

This word order has distinct advantages in communicating, because it is normal, usual and familiar. Listeners or readers encountering a noun/ subject are able, because they recognize familiar word order, to know what is coming. They expect a sentence to get somewhere — to provide information. After the subject they expect a verb, and then they expect to get information explaining the subject and the verb. Ordinary journalistic usage calls for writing in normal word order — subject first, then verb, then a completion of the thought. In addition to the *subject + verb + direct object* sentence, there are other common sentence types, in which something other than a direct object follows the verb:

The accomplice ran away.

The witness was unresponsive.

The thief was arrested by the detective.

Because sentences put together in this way are straightforward, simple and understandable, they are commonly used in news writing. If you study the front page of almost any newspaper, you will find that probably four out of five news stories begin with sentences that consist of a subject + verb + direct object. Beginning news writers should follow this pattern. Master the simple sentence. Strive for clarity and conciseness.

Remember the discussion of news leads. We emphasize what happened — start with the subject — then select the appropriate verb and finally complete the thought with a direct object or other appropriate grammatical structure. Details — where and when — come, as you know, most generally somewhere after the subject and verb:

Burglars broke open a safe in the Administration Building Monday night.

An armed man held up the Old Madrid Restaurant Monday.

> Mayor John Lane was re-elected Monday by an over-
> whelming majority.

Special Effects

Occasionally, for effect, we change things around and arrange words in a way that is a little out of the ordinary. We change emphasis and with it some elements of meaning. For example, take this sentence from a story in *The New York Times:*

> Rare is the Vietnamese in Saigon who buys Tin
> Song, the small pro-government afternoon newspaper.

Putting the adjective at the beginning instead of at the end of the sentence has the effect of emphasizing the key word, *rare*. Note the difference when the sentence is restructured and its elements put in normal word order:

> The Vietnamese in Saigon who buys Tin Song, the
> small pro-government newspaper, is rare.

We use normal word order most of the time because it is predictable. We change word order when we want some special effect — for example, to call special attention to some word or phrase in a sentence. Non-normal word order also has the effect of waking up readers and making them pay closer attention to what we are writing. Here's another example, a lead from a United Press International story:

> Backward ran machines in this northern port city
> when an engineer a wrong switch pulled.
> On movie screens, actors in reverse maneuvered;
> from oil tanks in the harbor flowed oil back into tankers.

Obviously the opportunity to use this kind of sentence, and make sense, doesn't come along every day. But there are occasions when a shift in normal word order can be a useful trick.

Lists of Names

Newspapers frequently have to publish lists of names in news stories: names of dead and injured in accidents, names of people elected to office, names of people competing in various events, names of people charged with crimes. A useful journalistic device is a reversal of normal word order. You start the sentence with the verb. For example:

> Charged with murder and armed robbery were Michael Clark, 21, of 7624 S. Normal Ave.; Nathaniel Burse, 23, of 50 W. 71st St.; Reuben Taylor, 22, of 9719 S. Prairie Ave.; and his brother Donald Taylor, 21, of 7000 S. Parnell Ave.

Few readers would wade through that list of names if it preceded the verb — as it should in normal word order. And until they get to the verb, readers aren't going to know what is going on. Here is the same paragraph rewritten in normal order with the subject — the list of names — first:

> Michael Clark, 21, of 7624 S. Normal Ave.; Nathaniel Burse, 23, of 50 W. 71st St.; Reuben Taylor, 22, of 9719 S. Prairie Ave.; and his brother Donald Taylor, 21, of 7000 S. Parnell Ave. were charged with murder and armed robbery.

Normal word order is not always satisfactory. In presenting lists of names, a non-normal order works best. Here are some other examples of verb-first sentences with the names omitted:

> Treated at Carolton General Hospital were . . .
>
> Dead are . . .
>
> Found innocent of the same charges were . . .

Many newspapers, including some of the most carefully edited ones, accept these inverted constructions. Other newspapers prefer normal word order and introduce lists of names like this:

> Those charged with murder today were . . .
>
> The dead are . . .
>
> Four men were found not guilty of the same charges Monday. They were . . .

Sequence of Tenses

Ordinarily the principal verb in a sentence determines the tense of the verbs that follow it. For example:

He *tried* to do a good job whenever he *was asked.*

He *does* whatever he *likes.*

This is normal and expected usage. When the first verb in the sentence is in the past tense, the second verb is usually in the past tense, too. When the first is in the present tense, the second is, too.

But sometimes strict adherence to normal usage can cause confusion in meaning. Look at this sentence:

> The governor said that his state was rapidly becoming an urban state.

Because the verb *to say* was used here in the past tense, *said,* the writer followed normal usage and made the verb *to be* past tense, *was.* But since the governor was not talking about history but about the present and the immediate future, his views would be more properly presented in this form:

> The governor said that his state is rapidly becoming an urban state.

Another example in which the present tense may be more accurate:

> The police chief *said* he *had* information that the suspects would be arrested in a matter of hours.

Here the writer should have made it *has* instead of *had:* The chief had information, and, unless he has mislaid it, he still has it.

> The police chief said he has information that the suspects will be arrested in a matter of hours.

The Passive Voice

Every construction, usage or tense has its uses. And so with voice. The active voice has its place. And when you need it, the passive voice is also highly useful. In the example that follows, the first sentence is in the passive voice, the second in the active voice. Which, in this instance, is the more usual?

> Smith was struck by a pitched ball.

> A pitched ball struck Smith.

Clearly, for the subject matter, the first sentence is the more usual. It is in the passive voice, a construction that gives the injured player the emphasis. Note the emphasis in the following sentences:

The president was told Monday that Congress will almost certainly over-ride his veto.

Congress will almost certainly over-ride his veto, the president was told Monday.

Because the elements closest to the front of the sentence get the most attention, the writer has to decide which element to emphasize and then select the grammatical construction that will do the trick. The passive voice provides an option. For example, the following sentence is in the active voice, and the emphasis is on the university board of regents. The coach's name is subordinated.

The Northwest College Board of Regents Wednesday approved the appointment of Jack Gaines, former Carolton High School coach and Ohio State University freshman defensive coordinator, as assistant football coach.

If the writer had wished to give more prominence to the new assistant coach, he would have used the passive voice:

Jack Gaines, a former Ohio State University freshman defensive coordinator, was appointed assistant football coach by the Northwest College Board of Regents Wednesday.

The passive voice is a useful variation. It can and should be used to put emphasis where it belongs. Learn to use it where it can help you tell your story more effectively.

Note the contrast in the following leads:

The small fire that damaged the Quick Coin Laundry, 204 E. Main St., early Monday injured a woman employee.

An employee of the Quick Coin Laundry, 204 E. Main St., was slightly injured in a fire that caused minor damage to the building early Monday.

In the first lead, written in the active voice, the fire is the subject of the sentence and gets the main emphasis. In the second, written in the passive voice, the employee is the subject and gets the greatest emphasis. Minor damage has little news value. Death or injury to human beings does. News values, the emphasis you want to put on events, will indicate the need for either the active or passive voice.

Empty Subjects

When *there is, there are* or *there were* is used as a sentence opener, the result is often awkward. This is not always the case, since we can find a good many excellent sentences that begin in this way. For example:

> There were giants in the earth in those days . . . mighty men which were of old, men of renown.

> There are more things in heaven and earth, Horatio, Than are dreamt of in your philosophy.

> There were in the same country shepherds abiding in the field, keeping watch over their flocks by night.

It would be difficult to improve upon these well-known passages from the King James Bible and from *Hamlet*. But the following awkwardly constructed sentences are not in the same class:

> There is a good portion of advertising that is done in color.

> There are more than 20 federal agencies that have data about individuals in the United States.

> There were only a handful of people living in the endangered area, he said.

> There are 3,150 new students expected on campus next year.

These sentences can be quickly and easily revised by getting rid of the *there are* or *there were* openers:

> A lot of advertising is done in color.

> More than 20 federal agencies have data about individuals.

> Only a handful of people are living in the endangered area, he said.
>
> About 3,000 new students are expected on campus next year.

Avoid the *there is, there are* or *there were* opening. Identify the real subject of your sentence and begin with it.

Placement of Modifiers

In normal usage, writers have a stylistic choice: They may place modifiers before or after the words they modify. Look, for example, at these two sentences — both grammatical and acceptable to native speakers of our language:

> He demanded a jury trial.
>
> He demanded a trial by jury.

In the first sentence the modifier *jury* is placed in front of the word it modifies, *trial*. In the second sentence, the modifier is a prepositional phrase, *by jury*, placed after the word it modifies. Both of these arrangements are acceptable and, in this instance, clear. Sometimes, however, modifiers placed in front of the words they modify are not clear. For example:

> wood substitute
>
> Chinese teacher

Are we speaking of a substitute for wood or of something made of wood that is intended as a substitute for some other material? Do we mean a teacher of the Chinese language or a teacher who is a native of China? In these examples, it might be better to use a prepositional phrase and place it after the word to be explained:

> a substitute for wood
>
> a teacher of Chinese

If the one-word modifier and the prepositional phrase are interchangeable — that is, convey the same meaning quickly and easily — use either one. You might prefer to use the single word, however, in the interest of saving space: income tax rather than tax on income, for instance. If there is the slightest possibility that a reader might hesitate over your meaning, use the longer prepositional phrase — usually the more precise form: *vote by secret ballot* rather than *secret ballot vote*. And where placing modifiers in front of a noun results in the accumulation of more words than a reader can easily assimilate, then place the modifiers after the noun. Compare these sentences:

> a two-car rural intersection accident
>
> an accident between two cars at a rural intersection

Don't let too many modifiers pile up in front of the noun. Strike a balance between those that more properly belong in front of the noun and those that can be placed after the noun:

> a 15-cents-an-hour wage increase
> a wage increase of 15 cents an hour
>
> an attempted July 16 gas station robbery
> an attempted robbery of a gas station on July 16

Misplaced Modifiers

Although modifiers can be placed either before or after the words they modify, their placement is guided by meaning, not whim. A modifier in the right place means one thing. In another it may mean something entirely different. Take the following example:

> . . . reported that someone stole a $15,000 diamond ring and five $100 bills from his motel room, which he had left in a dresser drawer.

It is doubtful that this unfortunate person left his motel room in a dresser drawer. The sentence should be revised to read:

> . . . reported that someone stole a $15,000 diamond ring and five $100 bills from a dresser drawer in his motel room.

Another example of a misplaced modifying phrase:

> Ten years ago, a coin worth $4 would sell today for as high as $500.

This should be revised to read:

A coin worth $4 some 10 years ago would sell for as much as $500 today.

In the following example the writer has inserted a long modifying sequence in the middle of a sentence when it should more properly have come at the end:

Elaborate security arrangements, to protect Pope Paul VI from the moment he leaves the Vatican for India until his return, were set in motion Saturday.

This sentence makes more sense written in this way:

Elaborate security arrangements were set in motion Saturday to protect Pope Paul VI from the moment he leaves the Vatican for India until his return.

If we assume that the following sentence is grammatically correct, we might wonder about the county nurse:

After a discussion of making diapers for the county nurse, the meeting was adjourned.

The writer probably intended to say:

The meeting was adjourned after a discussion of making diapers to be distributed by the county nurse.

Split Infinitives

The split infinitive is not a very important problem, but since so many beginning writers seem to worry about it, it will be treated here briefly. An infinitive is, of course, any combination of the word *to* and a verb: *to go, to run, to speak, to say* and so on. Splitting the infinitive means placing an adverb between the word *to* and the verb, a practice that is not ordinarily an indictable crime:

to immediately run

to quickly go

to subsequently hide

to eventually leave

to immediately return

It is not wrong, ungrammatical or immoral to split an infinitive. Put the adverb where it sounds best. Meaning or the rhythm and flow of your sentence may suggest that you split the infinitive. Go ahead. If it sounds right and your sentence seems clear, good. If the construction seems awkward or unclear, recast it. You must develop your own ear for what is clear and readable.

Right and Wrong Words

We have discussed a number of problems involved in getting words in the right order in a sentence. Now let's look at some of the problems of selecting the right word. Mark Twain has been quoted as saying that the difference between the right word and the wrong one is the difference between lightning and the lightning bug. The right word communicates — the wrong word fails to communicate. It may also mark the writer as careless or illiterate or both.

The Wrong Suffix

We ought to be able to assume that beginning news writers — and certainly seasoned news writers — know the difference between a noun and an adjective. Experience, however, shows that this is not so.

Confusion arises partly because both nouns and adjectives are regularly used in a modifying position before a noun:

> We had a *nice* time. (adjective)
> We had a *fun* time. (noun)

Both of these sentences are acceptable in today's spoken idiom. However, where there are two related forms that differ only in the suffix, it is best to use the form with the adjective suffix in what is more properly an adjective position in front of a noun:

> He expected to get the *Democrat* vote. (noun)
> He expected to get the *Democratic* vote. (adjective)

Democrat, the noun, and *Democratic*, the adjective, are not interchangeable. For example:

> He voted for the *Democrat* candidate. (noun)
> He voted for the *Democratic* candidate. (adjective)

379

The adjective *Democratic* with its characteristic *-ic* suffix sounds better than the noun in this sentence because it is filling a position where native speakers of English expect to find an adjective. In an adjective position, use an adjective when you have a choice:

He plans to vote for the _____ candidate.

Democratic (adjective)

Democrat (noun)

Another example where, again, the adjective sounds better than the noun when the word is used as a modifier:

She was studying *journ-alism* ethics. (noun)

She was studying *journ-alis-tic* ethics. (adjective)

In each of the pairs of sentences below, the second sentence would be accepted as more usual, more grammatical, by careful writers. These examples have all been gleaned from newspapers. The mistakes in these sentences are common ones, generally the result of pure ignorance of meaning or usage:

an *old-fashion* picnic	(unacceptable)
an *old-fashion-ed* picnic	(acceptable)
an *alum-ni* of the state college	(unacceptable)
an *alum-nus* of the state college	(acceptable)
a *doctor-ate* degree	(unacceptable)
a *doctor-al* degree	(acceptable)
the county *prosecut-ions* office	(unacceptable)
the county *prosecut-or's* office	(acceptable)
an indigent *defend-er* who . . .	(unacceptable)
an indigent *defend-ant* who . . .	(acceptable)

Precision is lost, if not some degree of meaning, when writers carelessly or from ignorance use the wrong suffix. There's a world of difference between a *defender* and a *defendant*, between a *mortgagor* and a *mortgagee*.

Confusion of Forms

Strangely enough, some of the commonest words in the language are often used incorrectly in writing, though not in speech. The words that cause trouble for many writers are those that sound alike but have different written forms. These words are called *homophones* — that is, words that have the same sound. Be on guard in using these:

He went to the classroom.	*to*, preposition
John went, too.	*too*, adverb
Two boys went.	*two*, number
It's a nice day.	*it's*, contraction (it is)
I like its looks.	*its*, pronoun
It's been a nice day.	*it's*, contraction (it has)
The meeting was held there.	*there*, adverb
They held their meeting.	*their*, pronoun
They're all here for the meeting.	*they're*, contraction (they are)
Your book is here.	*your*, pronoun
You're the new reporter.	*you're*, contraction (you are)
Whose book is that?	*whose*, pronoun
Who's going with me?	*who's*, contraction (who is)

A good many other homophones are problems for writers. Can you distinguish between *sight, site* and *cite*? Writers must learn to use words correctly in both the spoken and the written language.

Empty Words

Some words in the language have a functional rather than a semantic utility. Suppose, for example, we say to someone:

My teacher told me to go home quote unquote.

This is one way of telling someone who is listening to you that the teacher said what in writing we would put this way:

My teacher told me to "go home."

"Go home," my teacher told me.

The word *said* is used in much the same way in news writing. It is a word that carries very little semantic meaning. Its main use is to link a statement with an identification of the speaker:

The mayor said that taxes are much too high.

The words *quote/unquote* and *said* as they were used in these examples have very little meaning but serve a useful function. Other empty words may be less useful — for example, the words *et cetera*, usually written *etc.*, which mean *and so on and so forth*. Writers often use *etc.* when they don't know what to say next or how to cut off a sentence. For example:

> The mayor said that taxes are too high, expenditures are excessive, the budget is unbalanced, etc.

The *etc.* in this statement means nothing. If the mayor cited other examples of the city's fiscal problems, the writer should have included them. If no further examples were cited, the writer should not have implied that they were with *etc.* Avoid such empty words. If there is something to say, say it. If there is nothing more to add, end the sentence.

Empty Verbs

Empty verbs are a continuing problem. There are fads in language as in other cultural matters, and one of the current fads among news writers is the verb *to receive*. This is a word of limited meaning, which produces awkward, wordy sentences and blurred meanings. For example:

> The store did not receive an inspection by the state.

What the writer means is that the store was not *inspected* by the state. *Receive* here is a weak and unsatisfactory substitute for the verb *inspected*. The writer is leaning on the noun *inspection* instead of putting the accurate verb *inspected* to work. Here are some other examples of awkward sentences built around *receive*. In each case the sentence would be stronger, the meaning more precise and accurate if the right verb were put to work.

> He was the second man *to receive* a sentence of capital punishment.
> He was the second man *to be sentenced* to death.

> He pleaded guilty and *received* a $100 fine.
> He pleaded guilty and *was fined* $100.

> He *received* the doctor of philosophy degree.
> He *was awarded* the doctor of philosophy degree.

Avoid *receive*. It generally precludes the use of a stronger, more meaningful verb. Here are some other examples of empty verbs that could be replaced with stronger, more accurate verbs:

> The boys got ready *to take* a swim.
> The boys got ready *to swim*.

> There *was* a heavy snow Sunday night.
> It *snowed* heavily Sunday night.

> The Smiths *were* in attendance at the wedding.
> The Smiths *attended* the wedding.

> The board *reached* a decision on the matter.
> The board *decided* the matter.

False Possessives

Another writing fad and a bad habit among writers is the overuse of the *-'s* that ordinarily indicates possession. We find usages such as these:

> Detroit's chief executive
>
> Florida's governor
>
> the board's vote
>
> the university's fencing team
>
> the association's membership

The use of these so-called false possessives is widespread and growing. It is probably too late to restrict this usage, in which possession is credited to inanimate things. We cannot argue with idiomatic usage like *the nation's capital, at day's end* or *states' rights*. But where there is a more direct and more precise way of saying something, the possessive *-'s* should not be used. Two examples of the unnecessary and awkward use of the *-'s:*

> More than half of those at the meeting left after the board's vote.
> More than half of those at the meeting left after the board voted.

> He cited the reasons for the planning commission's denial of the special use permit.
>
> He cited the reasons the planning commission gave for denying the special use permit.

In many instances the -'s is substituting for a more usual and more readable construction using the preposition *of*. For example:

> *the mayor of Houston*, not *Houston's mayor*
>
> *the governor of Florida*, not *Florida's governor*
>
> *the president of Harvard*, not *Harvard's president*

In other instances, the -'s is superfluous and can be deleted without any change in sentence structure:

> the University of Oregon's School of Journalism
>
> the University of Oregon School of Journalism

Resist the temptation to use the -'s where you are not indicating genuine possession. *Mother's Day* is fine — the day belongs to mothers. But make it *the vote by the board*, not *the board's vote*. The board didn't possess the vote. It used its authority or responsibility to vote.

Agreement

In standard English, verbs and subjects are supposed to agree — that is, we use singular verbs with singular subjects and plural verbs with plural subjects. Most people don't have much trouble with this, though a few oddities like collective nouns do cause occasional confusion. And in standard English, pronouns are supposed to agree with their antecedents — that is, with the nouns they refer to. Pronoun agreement does cause problems.

Subject and Verb Agreement

A collective noun must be followed by a singular verb when the noun refers to a group or unit:

> The *team* leaves tomorrow. (The team/it)
>
> The *audience* was enthusiastic. (The audience/it)

Some words, like *economics, news, scissors* and *athletics*, are plural in form but singular in meaning. They are followed by singular verbs.

Agreement of Nouns and Pronouns

The grammatical rule is that singular pronouns must refer to singular nouns and that plural pronouns must refer to plural nouns. For example:

> The *girl* is lost. *She* can't find *her* way.

Here the singular pronouns *she* and *her* refer to and agree with the singular noun *girl*. For some reason, nouns like *board, committee, council* and *team*, among others, cause difficulties. All are singular nouns, and all must be followed by singular verbs:

> The board is meeting only once a month this summer.
>
> The committee is in session right now.
>
> The city council is writing a new budget.
>
> The team is leaving for Auburn tomorrow.

These nouns must also be followed by singular pronouns. For example:

> The board is meeting only once a month this summer. *It* will resume weekly meetings in September.
>
> The committee is in session right now. *It* will meet for another hour.
>
> The city council is writing a new budget. *It* expects to have the budget ready tomorrow.
>
> The team is leaving for Auburn tomorrow. *It* plays Auburn on Saturday.

Because the spoken language is casual about this, we hear the pronoun *they* used a great deal to refer to singular nouns. Perhaps someday the written language will conform to everyday speech in this regard, but right now it does not. Be extremely careful about this. When the noun is singular, the pronoun that refers to it must be, too.

Other Syntactical Problems

It is easy to get tangled up in one's own prose — and not always easy to untangle one's self. Sometimes the tangled syntax can be cured by breaking up long sentences into shorter sentences. At other times tangled prose can be untangled by a change in the form of the verb. Parallel construction is another device for tidying up syntax.

Parallel Construction

Parallel construction is used a great deal in news writing and is neither mysterious nor difficult to execute. Examples of parallel construction include itemized leads listing dead and injured in accident round-ups, lists of names and itemizations of one kind or another in the body of a news story. For example:

> Promotions effective with the beginning of the fall semester:
> James R. Smith, instructor, to assistant professor.
> Robert L. Jones, assistant professor, to associate professor.
> Elizabeth R. Deeds, assistant professor, to associate professor.
> Mary E. Laird, associate professor, to professor.

The list might go on, but you can see the way it is done. Each item in the list — in the series — is in exactly the same order and form: name, present rank, new rank.

Here is another example of parallel construction, this time a series of phrases starting with a figure:

> Other major projects in the budget include:
> $5.1 million for a new bridge over the Indian River at Battle Road.
> $4 million for widening Airport Road from River Road north to Perimeter Road.
> $2 million for work on crossing where Airport Road, Western Avenue and Battle Road cross Territory and Western Railroad tracks.

There could be more items in the list, but this is enough to show the parallelism. The blind lead offers another example of parallel construction:

The owner of a Carolton private detective agency was sentenced to five years in prison Monday.

George Hackett was sentenced by Federal Judge Daniel Curtis after a jury found him guilty of loan sharking.

The parallelism lies in the beginning of the two sentences. In the first sentence the subject is a description, in the second it is a name.

Participial Constructions

Many, probably most, sentences that use subordinate elements introduced by a present participle — a verb ending in *-ing* — can be improved by rewriting. For example:

The State Department refused to send speakers, contending the conference was set up to be one-sided.

The clause introduced by the present participle *contending* seems like an afterthought. The simple past tense is most used in news writing and would work better here. Two possible solutions:

The State Department decided the conference was one-sided and refused to send speakers.

The State Department refused to send speakers because it viewed the conference as one-sided.

If you have used a verb in the past tense in the first part of your sentence, use the past tense in the part of the sentence that follows. This is a form of parallel construction, of course, and makes for smoother sentences. Another example:

The fire broke out in the basement, filling the structure with smoke.

The fire broke out in the basement and filled the building with smoke.

Periphrasis

Periphrasis merely means putting things in a roundabout way — using more words than necessary. For example, the following sentence:

The team will be playing Wake Forest next Saturday.

Will be playing — three words, 15 keystrokes. Let's tighten it up:

The team will play Wake Forest next Saturday.

Avoid the *will be -ing* construction. Drop the *be* and the *-ing*. For example:

They will be going soon.	(padded)
They will go soon.	(concise)
They will be competing for the title.	(padded)
They will compete for the title.	(concise)
The students will be expecting a test.	(padded)
The students will expect a test.	(concise)

In the same way, *are expecting* can be written more concisely as *expect* and constructions like *are feeling uneasy* can be more concisely put as *feel uneasy.*

The Writer and Grammar

This chapter has treated only a very few common problems, grammatical matters that frequently cause difficulties for untrained writers. Along the way to becoming a professional writer, you will have to learn a great deal more about the language and ways to use it effectively. Dictionaries and stylebooks can be helpful. So can handbooks of grammatical usage. A few that have proved their value are listed at the end of this chapter. But you can't always depend on others to tell you what is right or wrong with your writing, what is euphonious or discordant. To write well requires an ear for language. You must learn to listen — with your ears when you are around other people and with your mind when you read. Hark to the well-turned phrase, the apt use of the appropriate word. Develop your own sense of what is well said and what is not.

Good writing is an art. The good writer is a creative artist who knows the language and how to manipulate it for the desired effect.

Punctuation

Punctuation is not a serious problem for most beginning news writers. There are, however, a few specialized uses of punctuation in news writing, and these will be reviewed here.* For the most part, common sense and the rules one already knows provide adequate guidance. When in doubt, consult the stylebook.

Linking Punctuation

The colon, the dash, the hyphen and the semicolon are used to link things.

The Colon

The colon is widely used in news writing and causes little difficulty. The most frequent use is in clock time, where it links the hour and the minute:

> 1:12 a.m.   4:15 p.m.   12:01 a.m.

The colon is also used to link an introductory statement and a list that follows in a separate paragraph or paragraphs:

> The class winners were:
>
> Those elected to the board were:
>
> Those killed in the crash were:
>
> Police identified the arrested men as:

The colon also links an introductory statement and a list or itemization of points, which may be numbered or marked by dashes, bullets or some other typographical device. Examples of this punctuation were given earlier in this chapter in the discussion of lists.

The colon is also used to link an attribution or speech tag to quoted material:

> A spokesman said:
> "The main objection is that no one knows the freshman candidates."

The quoted material may be a single sentence, several sentences or the complete text of a speech, but the device is the same. In this

---

*I am indebted to the *Associated Press Stylebook* and to various newspaper stylebooks for suggesting some of the punctuation problems discussed in this chapter. The organization of punctuation into linking, separating and enclosing marks follows Harold Whitehall's *Structural Essentials of English.*

example, as in earlier examples of itemized lists, the writer began a new paragraph after the colon. In the following examples, the speech tag and the quotation were run together in the same paragraph. This is acceptable form and saves space:

> He had this to say of his opponents: "The only thing I have against the Democrats is that there are too many of them."

> Rep. Walter Fuller, D-Mass.: "This appears to be just another extension of the federal power over interstate commerce."

The Dash

A single dash is used to connect the main part of a sentence with a subordinate part. For example:

> He will quit Common Council next month to become a higher-paid Council employee — city deputy auditor general.

> Jack Church is a successful student — he has a 3.5 grade point average, is president of his class and tutors other students in math in his spare time.

> Worse than that — the firm's out of business.

The Hyphen

The hyphen is used to link two or more words together, to link numbers and words, to link letters and words and to link prefixes to words.

Hyphens are used in word combinations like the following, when they are used as modifiers:

right-to-work laws	a do-it-yourself kit
a well-to-do neighborhood	a come-as-you-are party

But note the contrast with this usage:

> He has a right to work.

> I think you can do it yourself.

A pressman adjusts the flow of ink in the press room of The Milwaukee Journal. *(*Milwaukee Journal *photo)*

Hyphens are used in combinations like these with numbers and a noun:

6-inch pipeline	10-pound hammer
2-ton load	one-year contract
half-mile back	three-quarters completed
12-6 score	20-20 vision

And with these longer combinations:

2-year-old boy	6-inch-wide crevice
6-foot-6-inch athlete	

Note the contrast between these:

The boy is 2 years old.

He is a 2-year-old boy.

Hyphens are used in double names where both elements are of equal importance:

German-American	Landrum-Griffin Act
City-County Building	city-county reporter
East-West Center	north-south axis

Hyphens are also used in noun + noun combinations that describe dual jobs or dual qualities:

actor-manager	writer-director
soldier-statesman	secretary-manager

Hyphens are used in some political titles and designations:

ambassador-at-large	ambassador-designate
secretary-general	

Hyphens are used in compound units of measurement:

foot-pound	light-year
kilowatt-hour	

Hyphens are used in compound words where the two parts of the compound represent separate ideas or concepts:

serio-comic	socio-economic

Hyphens are used in compounds of family relationship:

great-grandfather	mother-in-law
great-great-grandfather	father-in-law
son-in-law	

Hyphens are commonly used in word combinations that include a present or past participle:

labor-saving plan   half-baked idea

hard-working team   twice-told tale

man-eating tiger   new-driven snow

Hyphens link combinations of letters and words or numbers:

H-bomb   X-ray

A-bomb   A-1

Most words with prefixes are set solid — that is, without a space and without a hyphen, as in *unrecorded, supermarket, transoceanic.* In newspaper usage, however, the following require the hyphen:

all-   all-university, all-America, all-star

ex-   ex-champion, ex-president

self-   self-defense, self-government

non-   non-stop, non-aligned, non-degree

anti-   anti-labor, anti-aircraft, anti-war

When in doubt about the use of the hyphen, go to a dictionary. The AP/UPI standard reference is *Webster's New World Dictionary.*

Hyphens are used in words with prefixes or suffixes to avoid doubling vowels or tripling consonants:

pre-empt   shell-like

re-elect

It is *co-op,* but there is no hyphen in *cooperation* or in *cooperative.*

Hyphens are used to distinguish a word with a prefix from a homonym:

re-cover, as opposed to recover

re-sent, as opposed to resent

re-view, as opposed to review

Hyphens are used where a prefix precedes a noun that begins with a capital letter:

un-American	Pan-American
trans-Atlantic	pre-Columbian

Hyphens are used in compounds consisting of a verb and a preposition or adverb:

sit-in	hoped-for
once-over	put-on
head-on	put-down
lean-to	

Combinations with -*like* are hyphenated if the usage is colloquial or if there is a need for clarity:

crazy-like	flu-like

Hyphens are not used with adverbs formed with the suffix -*ly:*

fully informed	recently named
newly elected	wildly excited

Hyphens are used in suspensive hyphenation:

a three- to five-year term in prison

a one- to two-mile distance

Suspensive hyphenation is awkward and can be avoided by recasting the sentence:

He was sentenced to three to five years in prison.

The distance was one to two miles.

The Semicolon

The semicolon is used to link closely related ideas into a single sentence. For example:

The maximum sentence for perjury is seven years; the sentence for subverting justice is left to the judge.

Because this use of semicolons leads to long sentences, news writers seldom use the semicolon in this way. If you are tempted to — don't. Use a period and start a new sentence.

In news writing, the semicolon in most often used in lists to separate items. This usage will be treated later.

Separating Punctuation

The use of the period and question mark are so common and so widely understood that it is pointless to recapitulate here. Some journalistic uses of the period — for example, its use in initials like U.N. — are adequately explained in the Basic Guide to News Style at the back of this book.

The use of the exclamation point is also simple and well understood. However, it is rarely found in news writing.

The comma and the semicolon, however, are extensively used in news writing. Some of the journalistic conventions for their use follow.

The Comma

As a separating punctuation mark, the comma can be disposed of quickly. It is used to separate figures:

Aug. 1, 1984   10,000

$1,150

The comma is also used to separate words in a series, but in news writing the final comma before *and* and *or* is omitted.

The student was tall, handsome, intelligent and neatly dressed.

She could choose red, white or blue.

A comma is always used in direct quotations like the following to separate the quotation from the speech tag or attribution:

> All qualified persons should register to vote, the city clerk said.

> "All qualified persons ought to register," City Clerk Mabel Smith said Monday.

The Semicolon

The semicolon is used in lists to separate items grouped together — for example, in lists that include names, ages, addresses, titles or other descriptive items. For example:

> Those arrested were James Nixon, 510 N. Scott St.; Kelly Mills, 608 E. Ohio Ave.; Aaron O. Lund, 48 S. Meade Ave.; Elwayn Fereira, 708 E. Main St.; and Theodore Davis, 850 N. Stuart Ave.

A similar list shows again how the semicolon separates groups of related items and makes for clarity:

> Others on the television panel included Kenneth A. Gibson, Newark, N.J.; Neil Goldschmidt, Portland, Ore.; Ben Boo, Duluth, Minn.; and Pete Wilson, San Diego, Calif.
>
> — *United Press International*

Lists of names, ages and addresses also require the semicolon for clarity:

> John Smith, 17, of 103 E. Grand River; Myron Brown, 44, of 234 MAC Ave.; Harris O'Connor, 26, of 723 Michigan Ave.; and Max Cohen, 22, of 442 Western Ave.

Enclosing Punctuation

Enclosing punctuation includes paired commas, paired dashes and parentheses. Paired commas are used extensively in news writing, paired dashes occasionally. Parentheses are generally avoided in news writing since they tend to interrupt the flow of thought, although they do have a couple of specialized uses.

Paired Commas

Commas come in pairs when they enclose and set off what are properly parenthetical insertions. For example, a grammatical and complete sentence:

John Smith was arrested Monday.

Additional information can be inserted parenthetically after the name:

John Smith (a railroad employee) was arrested Monday.

Since parentheses tend to slow down the reader — interrupt the flow of the sentence — newspapers prefer to use a pair of commas to set off the parenthetical information:

John Smith, a railroad employee, was arrested Monday.

The nature of Smith's job is optional information. That is, it can be included, as in this example, or it can be omitted without changing the grammatical structure or meaning of the original sentence. This is a common construction. Newspapers use a lot of parenthetical information in identifying people in news stories.

Addresses or hometowns are commonly used as identification and when they follow a name are set off by paired commas:

John Smith, 1227 High St., was arrested Monday.

John Smith, Carolton, was arrested Monday.

This is the preferred way to do it, but paired commas may also be used to set off identification in this way:

John Smith, of Carolton, died Monday.

Newspapers for the most part, however, drop the paired commas when the word *of* is used:

John Smith of Carolton died Monday.

John Smith of 1227 High St. was arrested Monday.

Whenever a person's age is used as part of an identification and the age is followed by a street address, the Arabic figures must be separated by the word *of*, so that *John Smith, 1227 High St., was arrested Monday* becomes:

> John Smith, 37, of 1227 High St., was arrested Monday.

The addition of the word *of* in a series like this one — age, address — is a safety precaution. It insures against running the figures together and producing an erroneous address. But the addition of the word *of* does not change the nature of the added material — the age and address. They are still optional information, parenthetical insertions, and must be set off by paired commas.

One of the commonest errors in news writing is the omission of the comma after the parenthetical construction. However, if you keep in mind that the commas enclose a parenthetical insertion, it is easier to remember the second comma. Parentheses come in pairs, so the commas must come in pairs. Parenthetical insertions that may be omitted without changing the grammatical structure of the sentence must be set off by a pair of commas.

Paired commas are also used to set off the name of a city after a street address:

> John Smith, 37, of 1227 High St., Carolton, died early Monday.

Paired commas are also used to set off the name of a state that follows a city or other political division:

> The student lived in Madison, Wis., before coming to the university here.

> Washington, D.C., is a beautiful city.

Paired commas, of course, are used to set off other parenthetical matter used as identification:

> Ann Garells, NBC News correspondent in Washington, joined in the discussion.

> John Smith, a railroad employee, was seriously injured.

Paired commas are also used to set off other kinds of parenthetical information:

> The students, despite the fact they felt unprepared, did well on the examination.

Paired commas are used to set off appositives like the following:

> Her son by a previous marriage, Eldon McKee, is the manager of the boat line.

> His opponent, Sen. Shattuck, would not debate.

Paired commas are also used to set off a year inserted after a month and date:

> The eclipse occurred on June 30, 1973, over a wide area of the African continent.

Paired commas are also used to set off attribution in direct and indirect quotations like the following:

> "My first love," she said softly, "is the city."

> He did not shoot, he said, because he had a can of tear gas in his hand.

Paired Dashes

Paired dashes can be used instead of paired commas or parentheses to set off matter inserted in a sentence. They represent a somewhat more emphatic break and are generally used to set off material that is explanatory or interpolative:

> Four nations — the United States, Russia, Great Britain and China — are the powers to be watched.

> The president — it was generally conceded — owed the Congress an explanation.

> Smith — at bat for the first time this season — faced the pitcher warily.

Paired dashes are a nice compromise between commas, which are all right for routine use, and parentheses, which are usually too abrupt an interruption in a smoothly flowing sentence. Paired dashes are informal, easy for the reader to accommodate and well suited to the general tone of news writing.

Parentheses

Parentheses are not much used in news writing because they interrupt the reader in the midst of a sentence. Paired commas or paired dashes are better for setting off parenthetical matter. Parentheses are most used for enclosing and setting off single words, initials or brief interpolations:

> The program began shortly after noon (EST) on the Capitol steps.

> Smith was a reporter for the Marion (Ind.) Tribune.

> The bill was sponsored by State Sen. Frank Perkins (R-8th) and Rep. James Meek (R-31st).

> The land-use bill (House Bill 1122) was approved by the committee Monday.

Not all of these examples of parentheses follow the Basic Guide to News Style in this book, nor do they all conform to the joint stylebook. They are all, however, structurally correct and suggest the kinds of use to which parentheses can be put. It is best when in doubt about the use of parentheses to consult the stylebook.

Suggestions for Further Reading

Some useful discussion of writing, editing and the effective use of language.

Bernstein, Theodore M. *The Careful Writer*. New York: Atheneum, 1965.
   An indispensable handbook on good usage by a former managing editor of *The New York Times*.

Born, Roscoe C. *The Suspended Sentence*. New York: Charles Scribner's Sons, 1986.
   A few of the notes on language written by Born during his stint as a writing coach at the *Detroit News*.

Capon, Rene J. *The Word.* New York: Associated Press, 1983.
A guide to good writing and a few words about bad writing by an Associated Press editor.

Copperud, Roy H. *American Usage: The Consensus.* New York: Van Nostrand Reinhold Company, 1970.
A useful guide to usage by a respected critic of journalistic writing.

Garst, Robert E., and Theodore M. Bernstein. *Headlines and Deadlines.* 4th ed. New York: Columbia University Press, 1982.
A manual for copy editors, but helpful to the news writer, too.

Kilpatrick, James J. *The Writer's Art.* Kansas City: Andrews, McMeel & Parker, 1984.
An entertaining and useful discussion of good grammar and good writing by a writer who knows his grammar.

Newman, Edwin. *Strictly Speaking.* Indianapolis: The Bobbs-Merrill Company, 1974.
An entertaining commentary on various abuses of the English language. Fun to read.

OUR TOWN

Business employees inspire children

By VALERIE FACIANE
Staff writer

Stay in school — that was the message from a group of Freeport-McMoRan Inc. employees to youngsters in the city's summer day camps.

The 115 employees recently visited 20 of the 39 day camps around the city to encourage youngsters, who are primarily economically disadvantaged, to get a good education.

The meetings were rewarding, not only for the youngsters but also for the employees — many of whom never before had given inspirational talks.

Curtis Robinson, an administrative aide at the company, remembers the first question asked of him when he visited the George Washington School day camp at 3819 St. Claude Ave.

"Are you a millionaire?" he recalled one youngster asking.

"I looked at him and I said, 'no,'" Robinson said with a chuckle.

The meeting had such an impression on Robinson that he hopes he will again be asked to speak to young people. And other employees, such as Cathy Hock, an executive secretary for the president of Freeport Sulphur, who participated in the program at Robert E. Lee School, feels the same.

"It made you feel like if you reached just one of the 30 or 40 children you talked to then you had done something," said Hock.

The Freeport-McMoRan employees' visits were part of the "Summer Youth Opportunity Program." The program, which involves recreation and a jobs program, was financed through the efforts of Freeport-McMoRan Chairman and Chief Executive Officer James R. Moffett, who volunteered to raise $1 million for the city's summer youth program.

Of the $1 million, $300,000 went to the Rescue 1 project of the Urban League of Greater New Orleans and the city. This program has provided 500 13- and 14-year-old black youths with summer jobs and seeks to give them inspirational counseling.

The remaining $700,000 was used to add 1,000 summer jobs to the 2,500 summer jobs that the city could finance; and to keep the city's summer recreational program alive.

In addition to asking area businesses to donate to help the summer youth program, Moffett called on these businesses to provide a group of their employees to go to the youngsters and talk about what it means to get an education. His company kicked off the talks.

He wanted role models — people the youngsters could look up to who could persuade them to stay on the right track.

"He wanted it to be not only financial but philosophical," said Nancy Link, public affairs coordinator for Freeport-McMoRan who spearheaded the program.

"We need to spend time and energy with these kids, not just the money to have their programs," she said.

Last week Coca-Cola employees went to 13 day camps, Link said.

In all, 10 groups will participate, she said.

"When you go in and the little kids

ask you questions you really have to be on the ball with them," Robinson said. "It really made me feel very good to go out and talk with them. They were so beautiful sitting there, and they were really listening."

Robinson recalled the questions: How much do you make? How did you start with the company? Where were you born? Why did you leave New York?

"I explained that I started on the ground level and worked my way up," said Robinson, who has been with the company for 21 years.

"One of them wanted to know how did I get to work in the morning," Hock said. She said another wanted to know where she learned to type.

Hock recalled that one 13-year-old girl, impressed after meeting a Freeport-McMoRan engineer, said: "I want to be either a beautician or an engineer."

Monica Boll of Freeport McMoRan talks to students about future opportunity.
STAFF PHOTOS BY BRYAN S. BERTEAUX

'It made you feel like if you reached just one of the 30 or 40 children you talked to then you had done something.'
Cathy Hock

Freeport McMoRan administrative aide Curtis Robinson speaks to children at the Washington School camp.

Centenarians are reunited for birthday

By LYNNE JENSEN
Staff writer

The two old men held hands like children, having learned much about life these past 100 years.

Joseph Schroeder's 100th birthday brought his 100-year-old friend William Childress to his side at the Lutheran Home of New Orleans last week. The men had not met since retiring from South Central Bell in 1952, after working together for about 50 years.

It was more a reunion of spirit than body. Schroeder is blind and seemed unable to comprehend that Childress sat beside him.

"It's Bill Childress," he said sweetly, over and over into Schroeder's good ear.

"Bill Childress?" Schroeder answered.

"Yes, I know Bill Childress."

Childress remained vigilant, seldom turning his face from his friend of more than 80 years.

For several hours, friends and members of the Schroeder family streamed by, echoing happy birthday wishes.

"You've got lots of friends here," Gloria Schroeder said to her father-in-law.

"Everybody comes to see you when you're going to die," Schroeder said. "Can I lie down now?"

The small room where the party was held was packed with people and gifts of baby powder, Old Spice cologne and blue pajamas.

As the room temperature rose, guests began spilling into the hallway for fresh air.

"We used to fight plenty, him and I," Clarence Johnson said, recalling days

spent living next to Schroeder on Franklin Avenue in Gentilly. "We had an old wooden fence between us," he said. "I wanted to tear it down. He didn't."

"He taught me the dial system at the phone company," Wilbur Sumners said about his former boss. "Before New Orleans went dial you had to go through the operator."

Schroeder, a native of New Orleans, began working for the telephone company at 15, driving a mule-drawn wagon. He retired 50 years later as a plant manager.

"One of the things I have to admire about my father is that he had a second-

grade education and when he left the phone company he had 500 people under him," Wesley Schroeder said.

The party continued with cameras capturing kisses and handshakes.

"All the ladies are kissing you," Helen Cortese, Schroeder's sitter said. "You're full of lipstick today. Do you like that?"

"No," Schroeder said.

The party ended, Schroeder was asked to say something about the event.

"When you're 40, you want to die," he said. "When you're 60, Oh, my God. And 100, that's a long time to live.

"Goodbye, Mr. Childress," Schroeder said with outstretched arms. "Where are you? I'm glad you came."

Williams Childress, 100, left, talks to his friend, Joseph Schroeder, at Schroeder's 100th birthday party.
STAFF PHOTO BY KATHY ANDERSON

Schools

20 Be Clear, Complete and Accurate

The hardest job of reporting is listening. But it is the must. By listening a reporter can pluck a story. Listening destroys preconceived ideas of a story.

Richard H. Growald
of United Press International

The purpose of the newspaper is to inform the reading public — to present news of events, trends and ideas in such a way that readers know more when they put their paper down than they did when they picked it up. To inform, the news must be written clearly, understandably and accurately. It must be organized so its meaning is readily apparent.

Clarity is not easily attained, but it is an ideal for which news writers should strive. Facts, even when verifiable, can often be interpreted in different ways. News writers can write only from the vantage point of their own knowledge and experience. Some bias is inevitable. So with this built-in limitation on our writing, it is essential that we write as clearly and as accurately as we can.

How Much Do Readers Know?

In addition to the writer's human limitations and the varying interpretations that can be drawn from any set of facts, the newspaper and the news writer must consider the limitations of the readers, the people we are trying to inform, educate, entertain or persuade.

Newspaper readers are, by and large, intelligent and knowledgeable. The average American has more education today than ever before. In many communities — college and university towns, for example — the average reader is very well educated. The readers of specialized newspapers like the *Wall Street Journal* are not only well educated, but they have a special understanding about the very technical world of business and economics. *The New York Times* boasts of the high educational level and sophistication of its readers.

But whatever their audience, news writers must consider two factors. First, newspaper readers are intelligent. Second, they are probably not as well informed on any given subject as we might expect. There's a well-known rule of thumb in newsrooms: "Never underestimate your readers' intelligence, but don't overestimate their information."

Older readers have forgotten things that happened in their youth, and younger readers have never heard of some things that older readers take for granted. Newcomers to a community won't know the names of pioneer settlers or be able to identify the local hero for whom the high school was named. College freshmen will be ignorant of important events that took place on campus just the year before. News writers must remember that some readers know a great deal about whatever it is they are writing about — and some do not. We must write for our entire readership — informed and uninformed.

People in the business world often complain that newspapers oversimplify stories about business and economics. To them, many business stories are simple, perhaps even superficial. But to readers who are not specialists, the same business story may be instructive — even illuminating. Newspapers have to write for all types of readers.

Newspapers seek to appeal to the largest possible audience. News stories must be written so clearly, facts explained so precisely, terms defined so carefully, that no reader, no matter how uninformed on the subject, will wrinkle his brow and mutter, "How's that again?"

This is an age of specialization and of highly complex technology. News writers are called upon to write about many highly technical subjects, and they write for the most part for readers who are generalists, not specialists. If newspapers are to hold these readers, news stories must be clear, complete and accurate.

Define and Explain

It is not enough to arrange facts in a news story in a logical order — as an inverted pyramid, in chronological order or as a feature story with a well-developed conclusion — for the facts alone may not be understandable to all readers. Sometimes a story will need additional facts — background — to remind readers of things that they may have forgotten. Obscure names, references or dates may need to be explained. New words or technical terms may need to be defined for readers encountering them for the first time. Readers are helped to better understanding by care in these matters.

Context and Background

A basic tenet of clear, understandable writing is that the background or context of the story should be made clear to readers. Second-day and follow-up stories include a brief re-cap or résumé of earlier events so that readers can place the new developments in their proper context. As an aid to better understanding of the news, *The New York Times* regularly publishes biographical sketches of people connected with major news stories. Knowing more about the people who make the news or are involved in the news, the *Times* believes, makes the news itself more understandable.

Another example: When Charles H. Kuhl died in Mishawaka, Ind., several years ago, the Associated Press identified him as the soldier who had been slapped by Gen. George S. Patton Jr. The slapping incident was a sensation in 1943, but readers who followed the story at the time might easily have forgotten the details after three decades. The AP story gave the background so that the most uninformed readers would understand the story.

Another example: When an engineering firm billed the town of Falmouth, Mass., some $2,000 more than the amount it had originally estimated for doing a study for the town, *The Enterprise* published a lengthy story about the situation. The story explained how engineers, supposedly accurate people, could make such an error. The newspaper was not satisfied merely to report that the cost would be higher than anticipated. Editors knew readers would ask why. *The Enterprise* felt an explanation was in order and published the story.

A *New York Times* story about three railroad officers who were jailed and fined for taking kickbacks explained in detail just how the scheme worked. And an Associated Press story about the excavation of the ancient Italian city of Sybaris included a detailed explanation of the importance of Sybaris in ancient times and an account of its destruction. Not all newspaper readers know ancient history, but if such a story is given enough background, many will read it with interest.

The experienced news writer is careful to provide the background of a story, to place people and events in context, to explain how things came about, how things work. The experienced news writer does not ask readers to remember, to guess or to look it up in the almanac or encyclopedia.

Technical Words and Terms

New words and terms, technical terms, unfamiliar words and references ought to be explained in news stories. Don't let your readers stumble over an unfamiliar word or term. They may get discouraged and stop reading. Do you know what *Antabuse* is? What does *nunc pro tunc* mean? What exactly is *salmonella*? How loud is a *four-decibel sound*? What are *pork barrel funds*? What is a *yarmulke*? What are *antibodies*? You cannot expect your readers to know everything, and when new words or technical terms crop up in news stories, they must be explained. Sometimes it is possible to substitute a more understandable or commonly used word for the unfamiliar one. Short, everyday words are often better than longer, more learned words. But you can't always write in words of one syllable — nor should you.

The newspaper is a great educational force because it makes new facts, new ideas, new words familiar and understandable. Thirty years ago, *astronaut, orbit, perigee, apogee* and many similar technical words were not part of the vocabulary of the average newspaper reader. Since 1957, when the first manmade satellite was lofted into the sky above the earth, newspapers have reported on space and space programs, and reported them in the kind of detail that has made these and other terms a part of everyone's vocabulary.

The excerpts in Figure 20.1 contain technical terms that were important to a story and had to be used. But each story included a brief and clear explanation of what the term meant. And, you will notice, no matter how technical the term, the explanation is in familiar, everyday language.

Obscure Details

Harold Ross, the founder and long-time editor of *The New Yorker* magazine, was a stickler for clarity in articles that appeared in the magazine. James Thurber, in his biography of Ross, recalled that whenever Ross did not recognize a name, he would pencil in the margin "Who he?" Don't give your readers the opportunity to ask, "Who he?" Tell them. The following excerpt shows how a United Press International story handled a reference to a name that might be unfamiliar to some:

To clear up the confusion, Miss Hash has proposed to Superior Court Judge Laurens Henderson that he file all 200 decrees nunc pro tunc — in other words, doing now what should have been done in the first place.
— *Associated Press*

A candy company official said Wednesday a day's production of two of its products was being withdrawn from the market because some of it was contaminated with salmonella.
Salmonella is a micro-organism that can cause violent stomach upsets.
— *United Press International*

In the suit, the plaintiffs alleged that the brokerage concerns violated federal and state securities laws by conspiring to sell Unioil's stock "short," causing the stock's value to plummet. Short selling occurs when investors borrow stock, then sell it into the market, hoping to profit by repaying the borrowed shares with stock bought later at a lower price.
— *Wall Street Journal*

The appoggiatura is a pesky little feature of musical execution that's easier to demonstrate than to describe. Here's an example that may help: Try singing the song "Wouldn't It Be Loverly" from "My Fair Lady." The note on "lov-" is a step above "-erly" each time. That's an appoggiatura.
— *The New York Times*

Figure 20.1 *Technical words or terms can be made clear for readers.*

He told a Senate subcommittee investigating snooping and wiretapping activities:
"I can sit here and point to George Wilson and I can say that he was the Dr. Strangelove of the Boston office."
Mr. Wilson is a group supervisor of intelligence in the Boston revenue office.
Dr. Strangelove was a fictional evil nuclear mastermind in a motion picture.

Several years ago James J. Kilpatrick, then editor of the *Richmond* (Va.) *News Leader*, created the Beadle Bumble Fund, a modest trust to give a helping hand to the victims of official stupidities. A story about the fund explained the odd title of Kilpatrick's fund. Most newspaper readers today are not familiar with minor characters in Charles Dickens' works, and the stories about the fund had to identify Mr. Bumble. He was, it was explained, the parish officer in "Oliver Twist" who called the law "a ass . . . a idiot" for supposing that a wife acted under the direction of her husband.

Jargon and Gobbledygook

Jargon and gobbledygook are much the same thing — nonsensical, incoherent and meaningless language. *Jargon* is an old word, *gobbledygook* a more recent one. Both apply to a very real problem for the news writer. If we are to communicate with our readers, we must write clearly, precisely and intelligibly. Jargon and gobbledygook are roadblocks.

Obscure language — jargon and gobbledygook — originates with people in specialized trades, professions, groups or classes: with doctors, lawyers, teachers, public officials and politicians, the military and scientists. It originates in sports, politics, the sciences, government bureaucracy, in police stations and on military bases. It is "in" language, understandable to members of the profession, trade or group but generally unintelligible to the rest of us.

Since newspapers are written for the rest of us, the news writer must learn to avoid jargon, to use words and terms that the average reader can understand. But in many cases, the reporters and news writers get their stories from people who use jargon, so they must learn to translate. The news story in Figure 20.2 will give you an idea of the problem.

Examples of jargon are easy to come by. The Bureau of Public Roads referred to an "impact attenuation device" that turned out to be oil drums placed around obstructions to warn motorists away or soften the bump if they did run into the obstruction. When questioned, a brigadier

Reading a report about a family on relief, County Judge Christ T. Seraphim was stopped Wednesday by this sentence:

"In the area of functional failure, our prognosis is 'modification.' This modification we expect to take place at a very slow rate."

"Explain this gobbledygook to me," Judge Seraphim demanded of the report's author, George Gochinas, a welfare department case worker.

Somewhat flustered, the case worker began: "There should be some kind of modification here. . . ."

"Don't use that word 'modification.' Nobody here knows what it means," said the judge.

What the report was trying to say, Gochinas explained, was that the parents lacked education and the welfare department was trying to help them improve.

The case involved a 30-year-old mother charged with the neglect of her 14 children. Judge Seraphim adjourned the case until the father could be found.

— *The Milwaukee Journal*

Figure 20.2 *It takes a little effort, but gobbledygook can be translated into plain language.*

general explained that when a program is "definitized" the army means that it makes a "definite list of equipment. . . . So many this, that, the other thing, and it becomes definite." In this case, the explanation is as much jargon as the original.

Checking into a neighborhood school district's application for federal funds, a newspaper questioned an item about "self-contained learning packages." A self-contained learning package, it was explained, is a book. Another newspaper, reporting on affairs in Washington, found that in government circles, reading a government notice to reporters is referred to as a "verbal posting." And a press briefing is known as a "verbal information opportunity."

A famous example of bureaucratic gobbledygook came to light at one of President Roosevelt's press conferences during World War II. The president read a blackout order which he said had been prepared by the director of civilian defense:*

> Such preparations shall be made as will completely obscure all federal and nonfederal buildings occupied by the federal government during an air raid for any period of time from visibility by reason of internal or external illumination. Such obscuration may be obtained either by blackout construction or by terminating the illumination. This will of course require that in building areas in which production must continue during a blackout, construction must be provided that internal illumination may continue. Other areas, whether occupied or not by personnel, may be obscured by terminating the illumination.

Roosevelt directed that the order be rewritten as follows:

> Tell them that in buildings that will have to keep their work going, put something across the windows. In buildings that can afford it, so that work can be stopped for a while, turn out the lights.

President Johnson, too, had difficulties with bureaucratic jargon. Bill Moyers, at one time Johnson's press secretary, recalled this incident:

> Another time he ripped into a group of Government lawyers who had drafted an Appalachian assistance bill.

*Quoted from Roy H. Copperud, "Editorial Workshop," *Editor & Publisher*, Nov. 28, 1959.

"Who the hell can read this gobbledygook?" he thundered. "But that's a technical document, Sir," one of the men replied. The President gave him a long merciless stare, then with his own black felt pen he rewrote the establishing clause. "There!" he said, holding the document out before him with a flourish. "Now they'll know down in Morgantown what we're talking about."*

Presidents Roosevelt and Johnson were articulate speakers who used plain language to get their ideas across to the American public. Like them, experienced news writers avoid jargon and are expert at translating obscure language into easily understood words. Editors and copyreaders are generally quick to catch offending language and return it to the writer for translation. But jargon does occasionally slip through.

A newspaper recently referred to a grade school child who "underachieved in school and socialized poorly." Apparently the child wasn't learning anything and couldn't get along with the other kids. Another newspaper said that in Pennsylvania a presidential candidate was "stepping into as many media markets as he could." Presumably, the candidate was visiting cities where there were newspapers and broadcasting stations and skipping the little places where there wouldn't be any reporters to cover his appearance.

Be wary of words, phrases, sentences and paragraphs that you don't understand. If you don't understand them, neither will your readers. Ask the source to translate. If you understand the idea yourself, you can find plain language, simple terms, in which to explain it to your readers. This doesn't always make the experts happy, however, for they like jargon. A reporter for a Michigan newspaper told me of this encounter with an expert:

At a press conference I attended some time back, an expert on water pollution scolded the press for saying that Lake Erie was dying and that it was dying because it was dirty.

"It's not dying," he said. "It is slowly deteriorating in terms of natural plant and animal growth because of an increase in the amounts of effluent poured into it."

"That's what we've been saying in the papers," one reporter replied. "It's dying because of all the crap that's being tossed into it."

*From Bill Moyers, "Across the Pedernales," *The New York Times*, Jan. 26, 1973.

Translation is not hard once you get the hang of it. To *finalize* is to finish, to *annualize* is to put something on a yearly basis, *civilianization* means that jobs once done by members of the armed forces will now be done by civilians and *dichotomy* just means that there are two sides to a question.

Accuracy Always

"Accuracy always" has long been the slogan of the journalist. The careful professional checks and cross-checks the facts. In the newsroom, copy goes through the hands of several editors and copyreaders, all of whom read with a critical eye, searching for missing details, factual errors, misspelled words and awkward or ambiguous phrasing.

Verifying Facts

Considering the staggering number of facts and bits of information that even one issue of a newspaper contains, it is surprising that more errors do not creep into the pages of the newspaper. The computer that sets copy into type and lays out pages may juggle lines, split words at awkward places and mistake *sight* for *site*, but it doesn't make mistakes in fact. Any errors that escape the watchful eye of editors and copyreaders are the result of human error — carelessness, inattention, failure to verify — and sometimes ignorance.

The first line of defense against errors, of course, is the reporter who first gathers the facts. Careful reporters check facts with sources. You can usually count on your sources to know how to spell their names, to know how old they are and to remember their street address or a wife's or husband's first name. Other information, even that obtained from reliable and trustworthy sources, should be double-checked with other sources. If you are working on the rewrite desk and take a story over the phone from a reporter, you must check the facts carefully with the reporter. Be sure you both have the same set of facts and that you both understand them. Then recheck names, addresses, highway numbers, references to localities and similar facts with a city directory, almanac, map or gazetteer.

Experienced editors always warn beginners in the newsroom: "Never take anything for granted." That means check and check again. Check spellings of names. Check addresses. Check the location of streets. Check titles of public officials. Check dates. Check figures in the city or county budget. Check the accuracy of direct quotes. Verify the wording of a state law. Add up the column of figures. Refigure the percentages. Be ready to stand behind all the facts of the story when you turn it over to your editor. Don't depend on other people — editors, copyreaders or proofreaders — to do your work for you. Verification and accuracy are the primary responsibility of the reporter and news writer.

Where and how do you verify facts? Some you can check quite easily by asking the source for verification. Other facts can be readily verified in published sources. Your newspaper library will have some of these, and others will be right there in the newsroom. You should have in your own desk such obvious sources of information as a city street map and a state highway map. Your newspaper library may also have a detailed county map, and many newsrooms have large-scale local maps on their walls. You should also have ready access to a telephone book, a city directory and, if one is available, a directory of local public officials.

Your newspaper library should have a copy of the most recent state government manual. There is in many states also a state government telephone directory. For verifying information about the federal government, there are the *U.S. Government Organization Manual* and the *Congressional Directory*. Statistical data taken from the census can be found in the *Statistical Abstract of the United States*. Much useful data is also found in the *Historical Abstract of the United States*. Much useful demographic data is broken down in the *County and City Data Book*, published by the Census Bureau. In most states, a state statistical abstract is also available.

Your newspaper library should also have a large atlas with enough detailed maps to enable you to check geographical facts. Atlases usually include a gazetteer, a list of place names by state and country, and many other useful data. *The World Almanac* is authoritative and useful. Another important source is your newspaper itself. Many major newspapers are indexed, chief among them *The New York Times*. If your newspaper library does not have *The New York Times Index*, a large public library or university library near you will. The index won't tell you much more than the date a story was published, but once you know the date, you can go to a microfilm file and read the original story.

A word of warning, though, about verifying facts from newspaper files. Errors do get published — and are sometimes repeated by reporters who rely on clippings or newspaper files alone. Treat all sources with skepticism. Do your own verifying.

Computerized data banks have become an important resource, and many newspaper libraries have terminals and access to data banks. Libraries, of course, are tying into data banks, and you can search through a vast amount of material in a surprisingly short time once you learn how to ask the data bank for information.

Verifying Quotations, Allusions and References

In addition to checking and verifying facts learned from news sources, news writers frequently must verify the accuracy of quotations from literature, the names of literary figures, the meaning of words or phrases or the titles of plays or songs. You cannot depend on memory or on the helpfulness of the person at the next desk. What you or your colleague are surest of may be quite inaccurate. For example, even the best-known quotations tend to be slightly twisted in popular use. "Gilding the lily" is a common expression used to describe something done to excess. It is not an accurate quotation. Shakespeare's words were "to gild refined gold, to paint the lily." If you are going to be accurate, you will have to look things up. Newspaper reference libraries have most of the basic tools needed for verifying information, and beyond that there is the reference desk at the public or university library.

If you need to check the spelling of a word or are seeking a more precise definition, you go to the dictionary. The joint stylebook specifies as its first reference the second edition of *Webster's New World Dictionary of the American Language*, a desk or abridged dictionary. The joint stylebook's choice of a second reference is the standard and unabridged *Webster's Third New International Dictionary of the English Language*. Another useful dictionary is the *American Heritage Dictionary of the English Language*, not as large as Webster's Third but published more recently. An unequaled reference on American English is H.L. Mencken's *The American Language*, a useful source of information about words, either in the original study with its two supplements or in the one-volume revised and abridged edition.

There are also useful dictionaries of slang and specialized dictionaries of acronyms, space terminology, military words and terms, foreign words and phrases, scientific terms, political words and even words used by journalists and printers. If a word is in use anywhere, it is likely to be defined for you in some dictionary.

The standard reference for verifying the accuracy of quotations is Bartlett's *Familiar Quotations*.

If you want to check the spelling of a name from literature — that is, the name of a fictional character or the title of a work of fiction — you take a different tack. If you are verifying a reference to a literary classic — the King James Bible, for example — you may find what you need in a *concordance*. A concordance is an index of all the principal words in a work with a reference to their location. A concordance is a useful tool if you want to check on the chapter and verse of a biblical quotation or name or the act and scene of a reference to Shakespeare. There are also dictionaries of fictional characters, which may be useful if there is no concordance for the work or author you are checking. Another useful reference work is the *New Century Handbook of English Literature*, which contains some 14,000 articles on British authors, literary works, fictional characters and common literary allusions.

If you are checking on a real person of more than local importance or interest, you start with *Who's Who in America*. There is also a *Who Was Who in America*, useful if the person is no longer living. Another source is *The New York Times Obituaries Index*, and there are more specialized sources like the *Directory of American Scholars*.

Other helpful references include for speeches, *The New York Times* or *Vital Speeches of the Day*; for presidential press conferences, *The New York Times*; for book reviews, *Book Review Digest* and *The New York Times*; for sports, the *Baseball Encyclopedia* and similar volumes; for legal terms, *Black's Law Dictionary*.

You can verify many facts yourself, quickly and easily, once you get the hang of it. However, you will occasionally be stumped. You can be almost certain that what you need to know is recorded somewhere. Go to a professional librarian in your newspaper library, public library or university or state library. You may not even have to go in person. Often a phone call will do. Librarians are remarkably adept at finding information. There is nearly always a handy source, and the librarian knows the source and how to use it.

Unanswered Questions

Reporters, writers and editors do their best to see that the stories you read in the newspaper are not only clear and accurate but also complete. Most of the time they succeed. But all too frequently there are gaps in the story, missing facts, unanswered questions that leave the reader wondering. If the story raises questions that it fails to answer, the story has a hole in it. It is important to plug the holes in your story before your readers write or telephone your editor for more information.

A story widely published in the Southeast, for example, reported that heavy rains were washing quantities of fire ants into streams and ponds and that fish were eating the ants and dying. The story warned readers not to eat the fish that had eaten fire ants. Although the story ran to some 500 words, it never explained what substance in the fire ant made it lethal to fish and dangerous to people. The story had a hole in it.

Stories with Holes

Some other examples of stories with holes in them:

> — A story about tax loopholes that identified in the headline and in the story a dodge called "the Mexican vegetable rollover." Nowhere in the story was the reader told how this tax dodge worked or how taxpayers benefited from it.

> — A story about a new strain of rice developed in Japan. According to the story, a single grain of the seed can produce 57,000 grains of rice. The story did not explain how this botanical marvel works.

> — A story about a labor contract calling for wage increases of 15 cents an hour for the first year and 10 cents an hour annually for four more years. The story did not, however, say what kind of wage the employees had been earning, how much the increase would mean in weekly or monthly terms or what the wage increase would cost the employer. Figures in isolation have little meaning.

Readers are unnecessarily puzzled when explanations are omitted from news stories. A news story reported that customs officials had seized 10 rare birds smuggled into the United States and were, following federal law, about to quarantine the birds for 120 days. Cost of the quarantine, the story said, would be $120,000. Let's see — that's $1,000 a day. Ten birds. Wow! It's going to cost Uncle Sam $100 a day to keep a Tahiti blue lory in quarantine. Sounds expensive. Either the figures in the story are wrong or the reader should be told why the cost of quarantining a bird is so high.

"Allegedly" and "Reportedly"

When news writers lack a specific fact or detail needed to make a story complete and clear, they ought to go get the missing information. They shouldn't pretend. That is, they shouldn't evade responsibility for holes in their stories. If the missing information is unavailable at press time — or unobtainable — the news story should say so. The writer shouldn't fuzz the issue.

Too many news writers producing copy for daily newspapers and wire services do fuzz the issue — inexcusably, in my opinion — with words like *reportedly*, *alleged* and, especially, *allegedly*. The first, *reportedly*, clearly says that the reporter isn't sure of the facts. That's sloppy

415

reporting and bad journalism. The following lead is a good example of evasive reporting and writing:

> A light plane reportedly low on gasoline made a forced landing Monday night two miles south of Metropolitan Airport — 25 feet above ground and in a tree.

Someone was guessing about the plane's gasoline supply or failed to pin down a news source or, perhaps, was just writing in a hurry. It would be much better to ascertain the facts or find a source for the guess — or opinion — that the plane was low on fuel:

> Three occupants of a light plane were unhurt Monday night when the plane made a forced landing in a tree two miles south of Metropolitan Airport.
> Fire Chief Tom King said he was told by the pilot of the plane that he was low on gas.

The writer, of course, had to give some explanation for the forced landing, but things that "reportedly" happen aren't very convincing explanations. A few questions asked of the right people generally will provide a factual answer or an educated guess that can be attributed to a credible source.

News writers also write around things with *allegedly*, under the impression, perhaps, that it will protect them against libel suits. It won't. All *allegedly* does is fuzz up a story and twist syntax. For example, this lead:

> A West Side man who allegedly injured a city police officer was indicted Thursday by a Circuit Court grand jury for second-degree assault.

Allegedly is used here to avoid putting the newspaper in the position of stating categorically that the West Side man is guilty when he is only being charged with the offense. Its use is awkward and unnecessary. The indictment — an accusation — is a fact, verifiable at the courthouse, and the lead should have been written this way:

> A West Side man accused of injuring a city police officer was indicted by a Circuit Court grand jury Thursday on charges of second-degree assault.

In the following example, *allege* is properly used in the sense *to assert without proof:*

Also indicted was Lawrence Lowell, 18, of West Bend, also accused of assault. The indictment *alleges* that Lowell . . .

The absurdity of the use of *allegedly* is clearly shown in the following excerpt:

Metro police are winding up an investigation of why an off-duty homicide detective allegedly fired his handgun in a South Side neighborhood during the weekend.

The detective, Jay Savage, admitted he fired several rounds from his revolver, the police report shows.

If the detective admitted the facts, and if a police report exists as evidence that he did admit the facts, then it is silly to insert *allegedly* in the lead. Verifiable facts merely have to be attributed, in this case to the police report.

Another example of unnecessary wavering:

A local man who has periodically harassed a 17-year-old girl is under arrest after allegedly holding the girl, her mother and three sisters hostage.

If you read only this far in the story, you might be excused for thinking that there is a reasonable doubt about the man's actions. But read on:

Police and a neighborhood priest spent 14 hours trying to persuade the man to give himself up, and were able to talk him into releasing four of the hostages, one by one. But the arrest came early Wednesday when he dozed off and police stormed the house.

Allegedly? This lead should be rewritten to state the facts clearly and attribute to reliable sources:

Police stormed a South Side home early Wednesday and arrested a man who had held five occupants of the home hostage for more than 14 hours.

John Doe, 25, of 136 Baker St., is being held at city jail for investigation of kidnapping.

Police said that Doe . . .

Remember what was said in Chapter 6 about attribution. The whole neighborhood knew about the hostage taking and the siege of the South Side home. The arrest is a matter of public record. Details can be attributed to police officials who were present and in command of the police who besieged the home and finally arrested John Doe. Other participants, like the neighborhood priest, can provide details that can be attributed to them.

The best advice for news writers is: Don't use *allege, alleged* or *allegedly* at all. Establish the facts, attribute to reliable sources — participants, witnesses, public officials and public records. And if you do, sometime, feel compelled to use *allege*, then understand what it means and how it can be correctly used. The following examples show legitimate use:

> The indictment *alleges* that . . .
>
> The complaint *alleged* that . . .
>
> Smith *alleged* in his statement that . . .

The joint stylebook cautions about the use of *alleged* and *allegedly* but does permit their use in some circumstances. It would be best to avoid using these words. If you know the facts and attribute carefully, they won't be necessary.

And avoid all such uses as *alleged* burglar, *alleged* killer, the accused *allegedly* robbed a supermarket, the two are *allegedly* linked to organized crime. Find out who says so, then attribute.

Confessing Error

There was a time when newspapers only reluctantly acknowledged their mistakes, for journalists generally don't want readers to doubt their reliability.

However, over the past decade increasing criticism of the press, libel suits and suits over invasion of privacy have led newspapers especially to be more accommodating, to more readily concede that they make mistakes and to do their best to straighten out errors in reporting.

Some newspapers have ombudsmen to whom readers can take complaints about errors. Others simply make corrections a matter of routine, even to the point of having a daily paragraph or two in a regular corrections column. The daily confession of error on the part of newspapers may, perhaps, lead readers to consider newspapers just a bit careless about facts but probably also gives readers a sense that the

Correction

A story in Friday morning editions of the *Star-Telegram* incorrectly identified the location of a fire that destroyed a home at 929 Gettysburg late Thursday afternoon. According to fire officials, the blaze occurred in Bedford, not Benbrook as was reported in the paper.
— *Fort Worth Star-Telegram*

Figure 20.3 *Correction notices are now routine in most newspapers. When errors occur, it is important to set the record straight.*

newspaper is less remote, less impersonal, more responsive to its public than critics have charged.

You will find corrections in almost any newspaper. A typical correction is shown in Figure 20.3.

Suggestions for Further Reading

Some interesting examples of good reporting and creative journalism.

Agee, James. *Let Us Now Praise Famous Men*. Boston: Houghton Mifflin Co., 1960.
> Classic reportage by a novelist-journalist. The lives of tenant farmers in Alabama in the 1930s.

Babb, Laura Longley, ed. *Writing in Style*. Boston: Houghton Mifflin Co., 1975.
> A collection of features from the *Style* section of the *Washington Post*. Readable and instructive.

Conway, Mimi. *Rise Gonna Rise*. Garden City, N.Y.: Anchor Press/Doubleday, 1979.
> An able investigative reporter's portrait of Southern textile workers.

McPhee, John. *The John McPhee Reader*. New York: Farrar, Straus, Giroux, 1976.
> McPhee has established himself as a superlative writer of non-fiction. Much of his work was first published in *The New Yorker*.

Roueche, Berton. *The Medical Detectives*. New York: Washington Square Books, 1980.
> A medical journalist reports on bizarre, puzzling and startling medical cases.

THE CHRISTIAN SCIENCE MONITOR

COPYRIGHT © 1986 THE CHRISTIAN SCIENCE PUBLISHING SOCIETY
All rights reserved   VOL. 79, NO. 8   AN INTERNATIONAL DAILY NEWSPAPER   FRIDAY, DECEMBER 5, 1986   A TWO-SECTION PAPER   50¢ (60¢ Canadian)

Youth: front line against Pretoria

As they struggle against white rule, young blacks bid childhood goodbye

By Ned Temko
Staff writer of The Christian Science Monitor

Johannesburg

For thousands of young South African blacks, there is no childhood anymore.

There is "the struggle" – against white political domination. There are the makeshift barricades, or stones, or even gasoline bombs. And for an estimated 1,300 to 1,800 youngsters, there is arrest without charge, or trial, or appeal – and prison walls.

In black "townships," children, some not yet teen-agers, have moved to the forefront of opposition to the South African government. And children, it seems, are emerging as

a prime target in the authorities' state-of-emergency offensive against unrest.

Initially overshadowed by the general debate over the state of emergency, the issue of jailed minors is becoming the central concern of antiapartheid, human rights, and political-opposition organizations. A "Free the Children" campaign has been launched. Public meetings – a rarity these days, since many such gatherings violate emergency restrictions – have been held to press the issue.

The government has declined publicly to comment on specific cases of jailed youths

Please see S. AFRICA back page

Black protest wears a youthful face

R. NORMAN MATHENY - STAFF/Soweto township

Iran probe shines into dark corners

Was US intelligence lax – or worse?

By Gary Thatcher
Staff writer of The Christian Science Monitor

Washington

Four words have started a furor in the United States intelligence community: "a number of intercepts."

They suggest that US eavesdroppers learned about the Iran arms scandal long before it became public. That raises some tough questions for US intelligence agencies. What did they know? When did they know it? And what did they do about it?

Those who have held senior US intelligence posts say the phrase – uttered by Attorney General Edwin Meese – refers to

intercepted communications signals concerning arms sales to Iran. Mr. Meese said they led to the disclosure that proceeds from the sales had been diverted to Nicaragua's contra rebels.

(Iran-contra update, Page 2.)

The existence of such "intercepts" places US intelligence agencies on the horns of the same dilemma that's bedeviling senior officials of the Reagan White House: If they didn't know about US arms shipments to Iran and the diversion of profits to Nicaraguan rebels, why didn't they? And if they did, what did they do with the information?

Please see PROBE back page

Swiss banks: private or secret?

By Ellen Wallace
Special to The Christian Science Monitor

Geneva

It seems that whenever an international scandal involves hidden financial treasures, otherwise-quiet little Switzerland finds itself in the news – to its chagrin.

Fugitive Marc Rich, deposed dictators "Baby Doc" Duvalier and Ferdinand Marcos, inside trader Dennis Levine, and now arms dealers in the United States-Iran imbroglio: All have in recent months found their Swiss bank accounts the source of much international speculation. And the Swiss, to their dismay, find themselves once again trying to explain and defend their banking laws.

Please see BANKS back page

Last article
in a three-part series

The impact of technology

New technology has made it easier to tap information on our personal lives. Laws are being passed to protect people from such high-tech intrusions. But some warn that technology is changing too fast for safeguards to keep pace.

By Curtis J. Sitomer
Staff writer of
The Christian Science Monitor

Washington

BIG Brother's data-based wings have been singed – but not clipped.

The Electronic Communications Privacy Act, signed recently by President Reagan, places for the first time strict limits on government and other intrusions of individual privacy by technological means.

Among other things, this law makes it illegal to eavesdrop on electronic mail, com-

puter-to-computer data transmissions, private video conferences, and cellular car phones.

But strong advocates of privacy, such as the American Civil Liberties Union (ACLU), still see technology outpacing regulation in many areas – leaving individual citizens vul-

nerable to possible limits on their personal freedoms.

These rights groups continually lobby for new laws and rules. But restrictions on computer matching – sharing computer files containing personal data, such as credit or health information – are still minimal, if they exist at all.

Further, an increasing number of questions relating to privacy invasions are being raised about use of computers to monitor the efficiency and productivity of workers.

PRIVACY
AND
PERSONAL
FREEDOMS

Story continues
on Page 24

These grads come with warranties

By Scott Armstrong
Staff writer of The Christian Science Monitor

Los Angeles

Americans, who like guarantees on everything from hot tubs to Hondas, are now getting them on an unusual new commodity: the high school graduate.

A handful of public schools across the country are beginning to send students out into the world with the equivalent of a product warranty.

They are telling businesses: If a student proves deficient in reading, writing, or performance of other basic tasks at a high school level – send him or her back. We will retrain the individual – at our expense.

"It is simply a constructive effort on the part of schools to assure the public that their graduates are well prepared," says Scott Thomson, executive director of the National Association of Secondary

Please see GRADS page 43

BOOKS
Critics' choices
for Christmas
gifts

B1

TELEVISION
Two mystery
tales vie for
viewers

33

21 Editing, Revising and Rewriting

In my own somewhat narrow experience, the value of writing seems to be in inverse proportion to the ease of writing. Whatever flows freely and bubblingly turns out to be sorry stuff a week later.

H.L. Mencken

Copy flows to the editor's desk from a number of directions. Some of it comes in publishable form. Some of it needs a touch here and there. Some of it needs extensive revision. To cope with this never-ending task of editing, revising and rewriting copy, the newspaper has developed a staff of specialists.

Editors responsible for pages and departments — city editors, metro editors, news editors, state editors, lifestyle editors, business editors, sports editors, among others — all have assistant editors, a rewrite desk and copy editors.

Editors make decisions about how copy is to be handled and do some editing themselves, although an editor with a staff to supervise rarely has time to do more than make minor changes in copy and perhaps rewrite an occasional lead. Assistant editors do some of this minor editing, too, and may also rewrite and revise copy. The copy desk and copy editors work mostly with copy after it has been written, revised and rewritten.

Larger newspapers have a rewrite desk that works under the direction of the city editor. On smaller newspapers the work of a rewrite desk may be shared by editors, copy editors and reporters. A rewrite desk is staffed by highly skilled writers who rewrite — revise and reshape — news copy.

But anyone assigned to rewrite must also be a reporter. The rewrite desk is often asked to follow up stories, to develop new leads on running stories or to develop sidebars to go with stories already in hand. The principal tool of the rewrite desk is the telephone, for rewrite must sandwich reporting in between other work. The rewrite desk also writes stories telephoned in by reporters working outside the newspaper office. Many reporters get credit for skillful writing when it is the rewriteman, working from notes phoned in by a reporter, who has given the story its bright lead or clearly developed chronology. Reporters often get the bylines where the rewrite desk does the work.

Need for Revision

Much of the time and effort spent on editing, revising and improving news copy would not be necessary if the news writer had done a better job in the first place. News writers should be aware of the standards for publishable copy in their newsrooms and should do their best to deliver well-written copy to their editors.

All copy submitted to an editor is subject to change and to some revision. No one writes a perfect story, and editors have a knack for spotting weaknesses and knowing ways to improve raw copy.

Several categories of copy account for most of the work of revision that falls on editors and the rewrite desk:

— Stories published in earlier editions that need improving or updating.

— Stories originating with the wire services, supplementary news services and the newspaper's own bureaus, regional correspondents and stringers.

— Stories originating with public relations or public information people who work for businesses, industries, state and local government, the federal government, universities, the armed forces and service agencies like the Red Cross or the Community Chest.

Common Weaknesses in News Copy

No two news stories are alike, and it is impossible to draw up a hard and fast list of writing problems that weaken news copy. But there are some common weaknesses:

— *Badly written copy.* Much news copy submitted by news writers is so badly written that it must be revised or rewritten to tighten it up, improve the lead, eliminate clutter and make the story clear and readable.

— *Wordy copy.* Some copy is too long because it is padded with unnecessary details, uninteresting quotation and superfluous words.

— *Wrong leads.* Many news stories have the wrong lead. Sometimes the writer uses the wrong angle, and the story has to be turned around to bring a more interesting or more important fact into the lead. Wire service copy and press releases are often rewritten to bring local angles into the lead.

— *Unprofessional copy.* Much news copy, especially that written by stringers, club publicity chairmen and other outsiders, must be revised to conform to news style, to eliminate padding and details that are too commercial and to improve organization and structure.

— *Out-of-date copy.* News copy is often rewritten to update it. A continuing story, a trial, criminal investigation or major disaster may require a new lead for every edition of the newspaper over several days. Yesterday's stories are frequently revised and updated to bring new information to readers.

— *Missing facts.* News stories often have to be revised to fill gaps in information. People in the story may be inadequately identified, technical terms may not be fully explained, background that would make the story more understandable may be omitted.

Many of these weaknesses could be avoided if news writers took the time to read their own copy more carefully, to correct small errors in usage and style, to take out unnecessary words and details, to simplify involved sentences, to eliminate clutter in leads and to clarify and simplify their language. If news writers did these things, fewer stories would be returned to their VDT screen with instructions to "fix this up."

Forms of Revision

Revision may involve editing, rewriting or updating. All of these processes may involve the editor, the rewrite desk, the copy desk and the writer who first wrote the story.

Three newsmen work on a news story at a computer. (Photo by Joe Abell. Courtesy of the San Angelo Standard-Times.*)*

— *Editing.* Editing involves minor changes and minor revision: a word changed here and there, a sentence shortened, a long word replaced with a simpler one. All this can be done with a copy pencil or a few keystrokes on the typewriter or the VDT. Editing should improve the story, but it does so without making major changes. This kind of editing ought to be done by news writers before they turn their copy over to an editor, but unfortunately the burden for this type of cleaning up falls on editors and copy editors.

— *Rewriting.* Rewriting involves major surgery to the entire story or some part of it. Sometimes, in the case of a breaking story, it may mean rewriting the entire story from one edition of the paper to the next.

— *Updating.* Updating is minor surgery and may mean changes to a story still in the editor's hands, revision of a story already set in type or updating of a story that appeared in an earlier edition. Updating may mean merely writing a *new lead* to incorporate newly reported facts. It may mean writing an *insert* to add something to a story or to replace sentences or paragraphs that are outdated or erroneous. Or it may mean tacking an *add* to the story, new copy that will go at the end of the story.

Improving Copy

Experienced news writers never turn in their copy without editing it carefully, revising it where necessary and even rewriting it. They go over their copy carefully, checking for typing errors, reviewing words and sentences, verifying names, dates and details from their notes. Only when they are satisfied that they have done the best possible job do they turn their story over to an editor.

When there is no time for this careful second look, however, news writers may turn in their copy with little or no review. When time is short, editors may also hustle copy to the copy desk without giving it much attention. There is a term for this — *railroading* — and news writers and editors know they are flirting with danger when they don't have time to carefully edit, revise and improve copy. Copy is railroaded only under extreme deadline pressure. It's not a good way to produce a well-written and accurate newspaper.

News writers who edit their own copy carefully and editors and copy editors who review it after them can eliminate redundancies, substitute specific words for vague ones, find short words to replace long ones, substitute single words for whole phrases, straighten awkward sentences, clear up ambiguities and explain jargon and gobbledygook.

Common Mistakes

Stylebooks, grammar handbooks and textbooks on news writing all include lists of common mistakes in grammar and usage. Several years ago the Associated Press Managing Editors drew up a list of some 50 common errors in language. Every editor has a few of these in his head and searches them out in news copy. Some typical errors in usage:

— *Congressman* when the writer means *state legislator*.

— *Ceremony* when the writer means *fanfare*.

— *Excessive* when the writer means *extensive*.

— *Conclave* when the writer means *conference*.

— *Profane* when the writer means *vulgar*.

— *Irregardless* when the writer means *regardless*.

Careful editing should catch misspellings that arise through haste, carelessness, poor typing or ignorance:

— *Knit-picking* for *nit-picking*.

— *Site* for *cite*.

— *Alright* for *all right*.

— *Hearty* for *hardy*.

— *Pension* for *penchant*.

Careful editing should eliminate redundancies:

— *Is currently* for *is*.

— *Consensus of opinion* for *consensus*.

— *Past history* for *history*.

— *Future plans* for *plans*.

— *Might possibly* for *might*.

Careful editing should replace vague or neutral words with precise words. Fad words often contribute to vagueness or inaccuracy in news stories. One of today's fad words is *received,* which leads to such bland sentences as these:

He pleaded guilty and *received* a $10 fine.

He pleaded guilty and *received* a sentence of 10 years.

In both instances a more precise word, a more accurate word, exists.

He pleaded guilty and *was fined* $10.

He pleaded guilty and *was sentenced* to 10 years.

Situation is another fad word, especially among the sports announcers on television who are fond of saying "We seem to be in a first-down situation" instead of simply saying "It's first down." Television weathermen are fond of the word *activity*. They almost invariably say "There's going to be some thundershower activity" when it would be more direct to say "There may be thundershowers later today."

If there is a roundabout way of saying things, too many speakers and writers will find it. This roundabout approach, or *circumlocution*, can be fixed easily by the alert editor:

— *For the purpose of* means *for*.

— *In most cases* means *usually*.

— *A sufficient number* means *enough*.

— *Despite the fact* means *although*.

Ambiguity can be cleared up by careful editing, usually by a change in word order or the elimination of a word or two. Ambiguities — words or phrases that are not clear, that could be read more than one way — are often hard to detect in one's own writing. A writer may know what his sentence means and may not realize that someone else could misinterpret it. For example, think of two ways to read this sentence: "A Viet Cong prisoner was listed as killed by the Pentagon." The writer who said that a woman had been injured "in a rear-end collision" may have meant a collision between two automobiles, but the reader could wonder. A wire service story about a hurricane reported that "more than half a million people fled from North Carolina to Maine." A reader might wonder where Maine would put all those people. And the writer who spoke of "smoking students" when he meant students who smoke paints a picture of a truly unusual sight.

Careful editing can save space by substituting short words for long ones:

— *Meet* is better than *encounter*.

— *Buy* is better than *purchase*.

— *Job* is better than *employment*.

— *Begin* is better than *commence*.

— *Person* is better than *individual*.

Careful editing can also eliminate jargon, gobbledygook or the use of technical or specialized language. News writers who use sports terminology in stories about politics or religion are likely to confuse their readers. The writer who said that a candidate "racked up two-thirds of the Republican total" was using jargon. Why "racked up"? It would be clearer to say that the candidate got two-thirds of the Republican vote. And this:

> McCarthy's delegates were leading as well as some
> running under Johnson's colors.

We can assume the writer meant that delegates pledged to McCarthy and Johnson were leading in early returns. Jockeys wear the colors of the owners whose horses they ride. Delegates to political conventions may be pledged to a particular candidate, but it is doubtful if they are wearing anyone's colors, unless it might be a brightly colored scarf or necktie. Attempts to be clever often fall flat. Familiar language, familiar metaphors are best. Sports terminology doesn't belong in political copy, and academic jargon does not belong in stories on the economy. Why talk of a "downward revision of prices" when you can say simply that "prices will go down"? Military jargon should be explained. Who outside the army would know what a *riff* is?

> In the second riff since large numbers of U.S. troops
> began coming home from Vietnam . . . each riffed officer
> will get 10 days notification before his release.

Police jargon crops up all too often in news stories. Police reports refer to *suspects, citizens, the scene, white males* and *victims.* News writers who pick up jargon may write nonsense like this:

> The suspect shot the bank guard and ran out the
> door.

Hardly. The bank guard was shot not by a suspect but by a bank robber. Later on when someone who fits the description of the bank robber is arrested, he may be referred to as a suspect, but the person who entered the bank, stole the money and shot a bank guard is a bank robber — in person — and not a suspect. And the newspaper that published this lead confused quite a few readers, for nowhere in the story were *fi fas* explained:

> The Jacksonville firm that bought up some fi fas in
> Washington County a few weeks ago hasn't been back in re-
> cent weeks, Tax Commissioner John Duke said this week.

You may have heard it said that this or that writer has a tin ear. This colloquialism means that the writer has a poor ear for language, that he doesn't hear the rhythms of speech, fails to understand nuances of meaning and mistakes one word for another. There are, unfortunately, a good many tin ears in newsrooms, and some odd things get into print.

The writer with a tin ear will write *pornographic* when the right word is *photographic*. Such a slip did get into print, much to the embarrassment of a college professor who was to lecture on "Photographic Possibilities with a Christmas Theme." Or the writer might use *flaunt* when the correct word is *flout* or confuse *nauseous* and *nauseated*.

The news writer who said that "trespassers will get their comeuppins" had a tin ear. The word is *comeuppance*. It is colloquial, but it is in the dictionary.

The wire service staffer who wrote this and the editors who allowed it to get into print had tin ears:

> The Senator did not charge the calls to his home phone, he said, because he lives with his parents, and his mother would have "knipschen" if calls to Scotland appeared on her bill.

The word isn't *knipschen*, although the writer may have considered it local dialect like, perhaps, *gemutlichkeit*. The word is *conniption*, a fairly common colloquialism. *Conniption* is in the dictionary, and it means a fit of anger or other violent emotion, perhaps a tantrum.

A reporter with a tin ear wrote that mice and shrimp were being placed in effluent as a test for the toxicity or lack of it of the effluent. If, after four days, at least half of the creatures survive, the effluent is considered harmless. Actually, the test was being conducted with *mysid shrimp*.

A tin ear is probably incurable, but beginning news writers can avoid developing one if they will read widely, listen carefully and develop the ability to distinguish between similar words. When you hear something that doesn't sound familiar or has an odd ring to it — ask questions. Remember the mice and shrimp!

This discussion is meant to be suggestive, not exhaustive. I have introduced it here only to make the point that writers should learn to monitor their own news copy and to check style, language, spelling and facts before submitting a story to an editor. News writers are part of the editing process. Editors and copy editors are there to back up news writers, as one line of defense against errors, not to write the story. Post-mortems on bad copy are embarrassing. News writers don't want to see their stories posted on the newsroom bulletin board with funny remarks attached.

Badly Written Copy

A good rule of thumb in news writing is to keep things together — that is, present the facts in an orderly way, keeping related matters together. One shouldn't hop, skip and jump around. It confuses readers when irrelevant details are dropped haphazardly in places where they don't belong.

Avoid scattering background through your copy. For example:

> An ardent golfer and fisherman, Smith was born in California and moved to New York in his teens.

There is no connection between Smith's love for golf and fishing and his birthplace. If there were a connection, the writer certainly hasn't made it clear. The writer here is mixing entirely different subjects: Smith's hobbies and interests and an explanation of where he was born and lived. The story in which this sentence appeared should have been revised to put Smith's hobbies in one place and biographical data in another. Another example:

> Dr. George Nichopolus, long-time physician to the swivel-hipped, throaty baritone who was known as the King of Rock 'n Roll, said an autopsy revealed a constriction in one of the main arteries to the heart which restricted blood flow and brought on a heart attack.

The background matter — the description of Elvis Presley as a swivel-hipped, throaty baritone who was known as the King of Rock 'n Roll — should not have been dropped into this paragraph. It has no connection with the subject of the autopsy report. The sentence might have been rewritten in this way:

> Dr. George Nichopolus, Presley's physician, said an autopsy revealed a constriction . . .

Other examples of hop-skip-and-jump writing like this make it clear that unrelated information interrupts the flow of the story, and if it does not confuse readers, it certainly doesn't help them:

> The tall, broad-shouldered John Doe, who now lives in Mason City, is the first of the three men to be tried.

If he is convicted on either count, Doe, who still hopes to play professional football, could spend the rest of his life in prison.

Don't take the scatter-shot approach to writing. Arrange things in logical order. Identify people as they are introduced into your story. Keep like things together. Don't interrupt your story with details that are clearly irrelevant to that part of the story.*

The Newsroom as Classroom

Newspapers and wire services clearly expect reporters they hire, even the beginners, to be educated and trained and to have some experience — work on a college daily or experience gained on an internship. But, still, newspapers do a lot of on-the-job training.

Good editors are generally also good teachers and work with their staffs to improve the quality of the newspaper. A great many newspapers today have writing coaches to help writers improve their work. Some writing coaches are part-timers, others full-time staff members. Newspapers send reporters and editors to workshops and seminars on writing and editing.

Some newspapers publish regular newsletters for the newsroom staff that comment on both good and bad writing. *The New York Times* issues its *Winners and Sinners* on an occasional basis. Editors at the *Asbury Park* (N.J.) *Press* publish a monthly report called *Second Takes*, which compliments good writing and points out errors and misjudgments on the part of the staff. Paula LaRocque, assistant managing editor and writing coach at the *Dallas Morning News*, produces a detailed monthly critique called *F.Y.I.* for the *News* staff.

Revising the Lead

Badly written leads can be found in almost any newspaper. Most of them could be improved by a little careful editing. For example:

Mapleton's Village Managers' Association (VMA) chose a 45-year-old insurance salesman and a native of Mapleton Monday as its candidate for Mapleton village president in the April 3 election.

*I am indebted in part in this discussion to "Prose and Cons," a discussion of writing problems by Rene J. Capon, general news editor of AP Newsfeatures, taken from the *AP Log*.

> The powerful group, whose selections normally win easily, chose Walter P. Mulligan, 15 Droste Circle, to head the board.

This lead tries to give too much information and is repetitive. It could be easily rewritten to read:

> A 45-year-old insurance salesman has been selected by the Mapleton Village Managers' Association as its candidate for village president in the April 3 election. Walter P. Mulligan, 15 Droste Circle, will . . .

Not all leads are as cluttered as this one, but writers frequently try to do too much in a lead, often making two points instead of one or including qualified statements or unnecessary details. For example:

> An agreement for broadly expanded cable television in East Wilmington, with all its potential for public service and entertainment, is set for approval at Tuesday's City Council meeting.

This lead would be much more to the point if the aside about the potential of cable television had been saved for use somewhere else in the story. The lead could be written to read:

> City Council is expected to approve a broadly expanded cable television service at its meeting Tuesday night.

Another lead that needs trimming:

> Four foreign correspondents criticized the American press Wednesday for what they see as its failure to come to grips with important issues in America and a failure to use one of its best weapons, writing, effectively.

This lead presents two points made by the correspondents. It should have stopped after the word *issues*. The second point distracts and lessens the impact of the first point. The lead would have been more effective if it had been rewritten to read:

> Four foreign correspondents criticized the American press Wednesday for what they considered its failure to come to grips with important issues.

Another weakness in many leads is the use of attribution where none is necessary. For example:

> Fire seriously damaged a two-story brick building used by the Washington County Highway Department to house road machinery, fire officials said Monday.

Attribution is unnecessary in this lead. The fire is a matter of public knowledge and record. That the building was used as a highway department garage would be known to many people and a fact that others would not readily question. Delete the attribution and save it for later in the story where some matter of opinion, perhaps the amount of damage, must be attributed.

Leads like these are weak because they are poorly organized, are cluttered with unnecessary details or try to say too many things at once. Earlier chapters in *News Writing* have shown how leads ought to be written: concisely, to the point, built around accurate, compelling verbs and making just one point. The examples just cited are a warning. Revise, improve, rewrite before you turn in your story, not after the editor returns it and asks you to.

Updating a Story

News stories often must be revised to add information that was not available at the time the earlier story was written. Usually this means revising a story that appeared in the previous day's paper. Or it may mean a revision of a story that appeared in an earlier edition. On morning-evening combinations, stories that appeared in the morning paper may need to be updated and freshened for the afternoon paper. The wire services update stories on an hourly basis to keep up with the deadlines of newspapers and broadcasters across the country.

Large metropolitan newspapers still publish four or five editions each day and commonly update stories from edition to edition. If a serious plane crash or train wreck occurs just before press time for an early edition, the newspaper will update the story in every edition the rest of the day. When a serious storm — a blizzard or hurricane — strikes, newspapers may revise and update the storm story from edition to edition for several days. On election night, the wire services will update stories hourly as votes are counted and returns come in.

Let's follow the updating process through three versions of a news story written in the course of a morning before the first edition of a newspaper goes to press. The first story is written by someone on the

433

rewrite desk from notes called in by a police reporter making an early visit to his beat:

> A two-car collision at Lexington Road and South Grant Street tied up traffic for half an hour Tuesday morning.
> A car driven by J.R. Gordon, 413 N. Grant, collided with a car driven by Marvin G. West, 20, of Brewster.
> Police said neither driver was injured and neither was ticketed.

A little later in the morning the story changes: one of the drivers is hospitalized. The first story is given a new lead and additional details are added to the story:

> The driver of a car involved in a minor accident Tuesday morning was hospitalized after he collapsed in his office on the Northwest College campus.
> John R. Gordon, a professor of mathematics, was taken to Carolton General Hospital about 9 a.m. from his office in the Physics-Math Building.
> The hospital said that Gordon may have suffered a concussion.
> Police said Gordon's car went out of control and struck a utility pole after it collided with a car driven by Marvin G. West, 20, of Brewster.
> Gordon was driving south on South Grant, and West was headed west on Lexington Road. The vehicles collided at the intersection.

A couple of hours later and shortly before the deadline for the first edition, the story changes again:

> A Northwest College faculty member died at Carolton General Hospital Tuesday morning a few hours after he collapsed in his office on campus.
> John R. Gordon, 45, was taken to the hospital about 9 a.m. He died an hour later.
> Gordon had been involved in an accident shortly before 8 a.m. as he was driving to the campus from his home at 413 N. Grant St.
> Campus police said Gordon's car collided with a car driven by Marvin G. West, 20, of Brewster at the intersection of South Grant and Lexington Road.

Gordon may have been injured when his car went
out of control and struck a utility pole, police said.

Police said neither driver appeared to be hurt. No
tickets were issued at the time of the accident.

In this hypothetical example, the updating required an entirely new
story at every stage. In some instances, a story can be updated with a
new lead, which is substituted for the earlier lead. The rest of the story
is left intact. Sometimes the new information affects only a later part
of the story. In such cases a couple of paragraphs of the earlier story
might be deleted and an insert written to replace them.

In the third version of our accident story, further updating might
have changed the last paragraph. This paragraph might have been deleted and these paragraphs added to the story:

add fatal

John C. Chin, the police officer who was at the scene
of the accident, said neither driver appeared to be injured and both refused medical assistance.

Chin said Gordon had failed to yield to oncoming
traffic on Lexington Road. West will not be ticketed.

Revising Handouts

Handout is a catchall term for news stories originating from public
relations or public information sources. Handout is a descriptive term,
not a pejorative one, and reflects the fact that press releases are literally
handed out to the press. Handouts or press releases can be a valuable
source of news, but they must be screened carefully to determine what,
if any, news value each has. Many handouts are too self-seeking, too
trivial or too specialized for newspaper use. Others are newsy and can
be published with a little editing.

Some handouts contain the germ of an idea or an element of news
that can be converted into a readable news story with a certain amount
of revision. Sometimes a new lead will do the trick, but sometimes a
complete rewrite is necessary. Some handouts are much too long or
too detailed but are organized well enough that they can be easily
edited to conform to newspaper standards. Others require considerable revision. The press release in Figure 21.1 is illustrative. It was
distributed by a state highway department a few days after a truck
hauling toxic chemicals overturned on an interstate highway during
the morning rush hour and tied up traffic for the better part of the day.

**News from the
Georgia Department of Transportation**

For Immediate Release

State Transportation Commissioner Tom Moreland has expressed concern and chagrin that the thousands of motorists who suffered loss of time, and in many cases money, due to the truck accident and chemical spill in the I-75/I-285 Interchange during rush-hour Tuesday morning have no recourse through which to gain compensation. Under existing regulations the shipper, Ashland Chemical Company, must pay for clean-up and disposal of the toxic substance. The Georgia Department of Transportation (DOT) can recover their cost for traffic control and other assistance during the incident, also.

Commissioner Moreland said, "It seems grossly unfair that those who suffered inconvenience, were late for work or lost business through no fault of their own must bear those losses themselves."

Prior to the next Session of the Georgia General Assembly, the DOT intends to recommend to the appropriate legislative committees that additional legislation concerning the transportation of hazardous materials in and through the state be considered. The DOT will recommend that public hearings be held to identify the problems that arise in the transport of these materials, and to help formulate the solutions to these problems. The Tuesday chemical spill emphasizes that the solutions must address more than clean-up and disposal of the substance. They must also address the inconvenience, cost and danger to the traveling public and those who live and work in adjacent areas. The carrier should be held liable for these aspects of such incidents in the opinion of the Georgia DOT and Commissioner Moreland. The public hearings should help in the determination of the extent of that liability, and the mechanisms of collection.

Public Information Office
(404) 656-5269

Figure 21.1 *A typical press release from a state government agency's public information office. Handouts like this one, though they may have news value, generally must be reworked by the rewrite desk. Handouts often contain errors in style, spelling or grammar.*

The important part of the handout is buried in the fourth paragraph. The lead of a news story developed from this handout might read:

> State Department of Transportation Commissioner Tom Moreland said Thursday that truckers should be held financially responsible for accidents that tie up traffic on major highways.
>
> "It seems grossly unfair," Moreland said, "that those who suffered inconvenience, were late for work or lost business through no fault of their own must bear those losses themselves."
>
> Under existing regulations, shippers must pay for clean-up and disposal of toxic substances, for traffic control and for assistance provided by the DOT.
>
> Moreland thinks they should do more.
>
> "They must also address the inconvenience, cost and danger to the traveling public and those who live and work in adjacent areas," he said.

The revision of this press release should also refresh readers' memories about the accident and report that the DOT will ask for new legislation.

The DOT press release suggests the nature of the problems press releases present. This one clearly had news value. Many do. But press releases often fail to get the most important part of the story in the lead. They are written from the point of view of the issuing agency, and the agency's idea of news often differs from the newspaper editor's view of the news. Many press releases, like the DOT press release, tend to start with attribution, identification of the source of the press release, before getting to the point of the story. The rewrite desk routinely has to dig the news out of the wordy and roundabout approach of the press release and restructure the story.

Buried Angles

The rewrite desk is frequently called on to revise stories in which the news that ought to be in the first paragraph is buried somewhere down in the middle of the story. This often happens with press releases, as we have just seen. It also happens with wire service stories and with stories originating with correspondents. Even experienced writers make mistakes in judgment and bury something good far down in a story. When this happens, the editor turns to the rewrite desk with instructions to "rewrite and put *this* in the lead."

An example of a buried angle is shown in Figure 21.2. The original version of the story about a school board meeting in a nearby community is at the top. In the revised version, routine business of the meeting was deleted and a school's loss of accreditation, a significant development, became the story.

A lot of copy needs revision. For example, a story that starts out with a lengthy feature lead may need to be rewritten to bring the outcome

PORT WASHINGTON — All officers of the Port Washington school board were re-elected Monday night at the board's reorganizational meeting.

Robert Hall will continue as board president; Mrs. Earl Thomas as secretary; and James Bookbinder as treasurer.

The board was told by school officials that plans for the district's new elementary school are progressing. The voters approved plans for the $1.9 million school in July.

The First National Bank of Eastville was retained as financial consultant and preliminary plans have been drawn by Wolfe, Reed and Cook, who have been retained as architects.

Superintendent Walker Roberts said topographical surveys are being completed and ground will be broken in October.

The board discussed a letter received from the Midwest Schools Association which said that the Port Washington High School had been dropped from the association's list of accredited schools as of July 1. The decision was based on an evaluation of the high school made last spring and cited several violations of the association's accrediting standards.

The association particularly objected to split shifts which have been necessary for the past three years because of increased enrollments.

PORT WASHINGTON — Port Washington High School is no longer accredited by the Midwest Schools Association, the school board was told Monday.

Superintendent Walker Roberts told the board the high school lost its accreditation July 1.

The Midwest Schools Association evaluated the high school last spring, Roberts said, and the high school was cited for several violations of the association's accreditation standards.

The association especially objected to the split shifts which have been in effect for the past three years. The split shifts have been forced on the high school because of increased enrollments.

The school board will ask the association to restore accreditation on the grounds that the district's building program will make the split shifts unnecessary.

Figure 21.2 *An error in judgment is rectified by the rewrite desk after it was decided that the loss of accreditation was more newsworthy than the routine re-election of school board members.*

of the story up to the top in a concise summary lead. No newspaper reader should have to wade through four or five paragraphs of background or color before being told who won a football game and what the score was.

Localizing

The importance of local news and the need for stressing local angles in stories were discussed in Chapter 8. The examples given in Chapter 8 showed how newspapers can follow up national stories by developing local angles. Wire service copy frequently has to be revised to lift buried angles into the lead — another job for the rewrite desk. An example of revision necessary to localize a wire story was discussed in Chapter 8.

Suggestions for Further Reading

Reporters and editors discuss their daily routine — and some unusual events.

Adler, Ruth, ed. *The Working Press*. New York: G.P. Putnam's Sons, 1966.
New York Times reporters and correspondents write about their work. Includes Tom Wicker's account of the day President Kennedy was assassinated.

Babb, Laura Longley, ed. *Of the Press, by the Press, for the Press (and Others, Too)*. Washington, D.C.: The Washington Post Co., 1974.
A critical study of the inside workings of the news business as told in news stories, editorials, columns and internal staff memos.

Brown, David, and W. Richard Bruner, eds. *How I Got the Story*. New York: Dutton, 1967.
Members of the Overseas Press Club tell how they covered memorable news stories.

MacDougall, Curtis D. *Reporters Report Reporters*. Ames, Iowa: Iowa State University Press, 1968.
A collection of first-person accounts of the daily work of newspaper reporters.

Providence Journal. *How I Wrote the Story*. Providence, R.I.: Providence Journal Co., 1983.
News stories by Journal reporters and their explanation of how they wrote the story. A book by writers for writers.

Thiem, George. *The Hodge Scandal*. New York: St. Martin's Press, 1963.
A detailed account of an investigation into political corruption in Illinois state government. The author won the Pulitzer Prize for his work on this story.

Sports

Tribune photo by Bob Fila

Cubs turn back Mets
Scott Sanderson (above) picks up the win and Keith Moreland, Andre Dawson and Jerry Mumphrey homer in the Cubs 6-1 victory over New York. Sec. 2, pg. 1.

Blue Jays trip White Sox
The White Sox stop George Bell's 17-game hitting streak but fall to the Blue Jays 3-2 in Toronto. Sec. 2, pg. 1.

$11 million for Bosworth
Former Oklahoma linebacker Brian Bosworth signs a 10-year guaranteed contract with Seattle for $11 million, a record for an NFL rookie and a defensive player. Sec. 2, pg. 1.

Bosworth

Cubans in Pan Am scuffle
Members of the Cuban boxing delegation go into the stands to fight spectators after a Cuban flag is burned. Sec. 2, pg. 1.

Inside

100 S. African strikers hurt
Authorities wound more than 100 striking black miners in the worst violence so far in the nationwide walkout. Page 3.

New trial for ex-judge
The mail-fraud and racketeering convictions of former Cook County Judge James Oakey and three lawyers are overturned on appeal and new trials are ordered. Page 7.

Oakey

Secrecy sails with tankers
The departure details of a reflagged tanker convoy that will be ready to leave Kuwait Saturday is under wraps. Page 3.

DeLorean debts settled
Creditors of John DeLorean's defunct car company will split $9.35 million under an agreement approved by a judge. Page 3.

Business

'People mover' moves
The city ends talks with the Pentagon over an O'Hare land swap and changes the "people mover" route. Sec. 2, pg. 7.

Economic news mixed
The U.S. trade deficit widens, but a modest wholesale price rise suggests inflation is still in check. Sec. 2, pg. 7.

C&NW eyes restructuring
The holding company of the Chicago & North Western discusses the firm's possible sale or restructuring. Sec. 2, pg. 7.

WEATHER
CHICAGO AND VICINITY: Saturday: Partly cloudy, humid, thundershowers likely; highs 85 to 91 degrees. Saturday night: Partly cloudy; lows 70 to 78. Sunday: Partly sunny; highs 90 to 96. More on pg. 20.

Vehicles are stranded Friday on the Kennedy Expressway at Addison Street while a southbound CTA train on the O'Hare line stays put on tracks leading to deep water.

Tribune photo by Anne Cusack

City awash in record rain

At O'Hare, it's fly, walk or forget it

By Joel Kaplan and John Camper

A flash flood Friday turned O'Hare International Airport into a strange sort of island, accessible only by foot and by air.

Thousands of passengers landed there between 9 a.m. and 6 p.m., only to discover there was no way out. The lone access road, I-190, was six feet deep in water beneath the Mannheim Road overpass, blocking cabs, cars and buses.

The Chicago Transit Authority's O'Hare rapid-transit line, the one form of transportation that usually makes it to the airport when others fail, also was under water at Mannheim, as well as at Addison Street. The CTA ran shuttle buses between the Jefferson Park and Belmont Avenue stops. The line fully reopened shortly after 6 p.m., and cars and buses began to trickle into O'Hare a short time later.

"I don't think the airport has ever been more isolated in its history," said Rev. John Jamnicky, O'Hare's chaplain. "And my Boss is the one most responsible."

It was easier to get to O'Hare from Los Angeles than from downtown Chicago. The trip from the West Coast took only about 4 hours; the trip from downtown Chicago took 9 hours, 15 minutes for a Westin Hotel bus.

"All the hell I wanted to do was get back to Alabama," moaned Sam Hardin, of Montgomery, a passenger on the bus.

Hundreds of others drove their cars or rode CTA buses and trains as far as River Road, then grabbed their luggage and slogged three miles on foot along

Continued on page 6

Record rainfall hits Chicago area, smashing 24-hour record. Old record falls in just 12 hours.

At least 300 cars stranded on Kennedy Expressway. Parts of Eden, Eisenhower, Tri-State impassable.

Sanitary District opens locks at Wilmette and Chicago River, dumping record volume of water and sewage into Lake Michigan.

Guard units requested by Addison, Elmhurst, Bensenville.

Roadways to O'Hare closed; passengers stranded. 8½ miles of CTA rapid transit shut.

Gov. Thompson declares Cook and Du Page Counties state disaster areas and calls out National Guard troops.

Chicago Tribune Graphic

A new day of infamy enters Chicago legend

By Robert Davis

An all-time record 9.35 inches of rain deluged the Chicago area late Thursday and most of Friday, causing millions of dollars in damage and millions of miles of frayed nerves in a chaotic day that extended the morning rush hour into the early evening for thousands.

And the National Weather Service said there could be more of the same early Saturday in a weather report it issued shortly before it closed down after its electrical power was knocked out by flooding in its offices near O'Hare International Airport.

The rains came at about 9 p.m. Thursday and, in a freakish pattern, continued at a pace of nearly an inch an hour until mid-Friday morning when the storm turned to drizzle. The official 24-hour record rain accumulation had been 6.24 inches accumulated on July 12-13, 1957. But that record had become ancient history in just

Full coverage
- Flooding makes sure no one goes anywhere fast. Page 5.
- Storms create a nightmare that lasted all day. Page 5.
- Flood doesn't faze Western Open officials. In Sports.

slightly over 12 hours in Chicago Friday, when, at 10 a.m., a total of 8.58 inches already had fallen. By 4 p.m. Friday, the record had climbed to 9.35 inches.

The storm's effects were as staggering as its statistics.

According to National Weather Service conversion formulas, if the rain had been snow, Chicago and its northern suburbs would have been buried under about 93 inches, about as much as during the entire infamous winter of 1979, when it took several weeks to accumulate that amount.

Gov. James Thompson, in response to calls from suburban

Continued on page 6

Workers from the Happy Foods store in Skokie ferry improvised sandbags across Oakton Street to put in front of the store.

Tribune photo by Frank Hanes

Special envoy Habib resigns unexpectedly

By Nathaniel Sheppard Jr. and George de Lama
Chicago Tribune

President Reagan's special envoy to Central America, Philip Habib, resigned abruptly on Friday in the midst of negotiations between the U.S. and Central American leaders on a peace plan for the region.

There was wide speculation that Habib was irked at having had no major role in drawing up the peace proposal advanced jointly last week by congressional leaders and the Reagan administration. Nor did he have a chance to press his ideas at a subsequent meeting of five Central American presidents in Guatemala City, from which another peace proposal emerged.

Salvadoran rebels agree to cease-fire talks. Page 2.

Habib has been an advocate of direct negotiations between the U.S. and Nicaragua.

Habib's resignation came without warning, a week after Secretary of State George Shultz said the special envoy stood ready to go to Central America to assist in the peace negotiations.

The veteran diplomatic troubleshooter packed his belongings and left his office with no public comment, in keeping with his usual stoic silence outside the negotiating room.

"Ambassador Habib has decided that this is the appropriate moment for him to return to

private life," State Department spokesman Charles Redman said in Washington. "The progress that has been made on the path to peace in Central America is a tribute to his efforts in 1986 and 1987."

Another diplomatic source

Continued on page 2

Philip Habib

Reagan close call seen as inevitable; pilot jailed

By Glen Elsasser and George de Lama
Chicago Tribune

White House officials said Friday that there was no sure way to prevent a recurrence of the midair close encounter between President Reagan's helicopter and a small plane near his California ranch Thursday.

"It's open airspace, you can't build a fence," White House spokesman Marlin Fitzwater told reporters at a Santa Barbara, Calif., briefing.

Meanwhile, the pilot of the plane, identified as Army Pvt. Ralph William Myers, 32, was jailed Friday on charges of being absent without official leave from an Army base in Ft. Lewis, Wash. In addition, his pilot's li-

cense was revoked Friday by the Federal Aviation Administration.

Fitzwater rejected suggestions that intruding airplanes approaching Reagan's ranch would be shot down. "There isn't a war going on. Do you believe we should shoot down civilian planes?" he said.

Under repeated questioning, Fitzwater said there was no foolproof way of protecting the airspace around the Reagans' mountaintop ranch about 30 miles west of Santa Barbara, short of erecting "a 6,000-foot wire fence."

When asked what would prevent a terrorist from flying a kamikaze mission against the presidential hideaway, Fitzwater said: "Nothing. You can't close

Continued on page 2

22 Legal and Ethical Considerations

Always do right. This will gratify some people, and astonish the rest.

Mark Twain

The First Amendment to the Constitution of the United States is the foundation on which modern journalism is built. It is for journalists a sacred artifact. It supplies an answer when the performance of the press is questioned, when readers or public officials ask: Why did you print that? Why do you behave the way you do? Why do you want to know? It supplies a philosophy and a historical justification for what in many ways is only sophisticated and highly technical business.

The First Amendment says:

> Congress shall make no law respecting an establishment of religion, or prohibiting the free exercise thereof; or abridging the freedom of speech, or of the press; or the right of the people peaceably to assemble, and to petition the Government for a redress of grievances.

The First Amendment, as you can see, provides for considerably more freedoms than just freedom of the press. And it should be understood that the freedom of the press guaranteed under the First Amendment is not a right granted only to *The New York Times* or to other newspaper publishers but to the people, to you and me as citizens.

Despite its very specific guarantee against restraints on the press, the First Amendment has never guaranteed absolute freedom for the press. Since the early days of the republic, the right to publish and disseminate news and opinion has been hedged with legal restraints, some to protect the government in the conduct of the people's business, some to protect other freedoms of the people themselves.

The legal restraints imposed on the press and the privileges won by the press under the law are of two kinds. First, some restrictions are imposed on reporting — that is, on gathering news — and on publishing. Second, certain laws and decisions by the courts make the press responsible for what it publishes, but only after the fact of publication.

Behind all this is the protective bulwark of the First Amendment, which has historically protected the press from restrictions on its activities by government.

The Watchdog

The press has a very important role in a democratic society. In some respects, as the press carries out its responsibility of informing the public and providing a forum for discussion of public affairs, it becomes one of the checks and balances of our democratic system and, hence, is very much like a fourth branch of government. On the other hand, the press acts a great deal of the time as an opponent or adversary of government.

The role of the press, as the press sees it and in the view of others, is to inform the people. The press has assumed the responsibility of reporting on public affairs and providing a forum for the discussion of public affairs. Without knowledge of public affairs — of the management of our government, of economic matters, of cultural and social phenomena — people would find it difficult not only to vote intelligently but to manage their own lives. We as individuals cannot do what the press does for us — that is, bring the news of the world to our doorsteps so that we can understand what is happening around us.

The role of the press as an adversary or watchdog, as a lookout keeping an eye on the world and reporting back to readers and listeners, is not an easy one. The public, the readers of newspapers and magazines and the viewers and listeners of television and radio, is often critical of the way the press does its job. Many people think the press is too pushy, that it prints too much bad news, that it is too critical of government and public officials. Many others, to the contrary, consider that the press is too much a part of the establishment.

From the early days of the printing press in Western Europe, the publication of news about government and public affairs and the forum for discussion of ideas provided by the printing press — now simply *the press* — has caused grave concern to governments.

Governments from the first tried to regulate the press, to limit its access to information, to censor it, to ban publications and to punish editors for publishing news the government preferred to keep from the public.

Out of this background, of course, came the First Amendment, which in the United States established the freedom of speech and of the press. And out of this background, too, has come the adversarial relationship of press and government.

The press has come to regard itself as a watchdog and its principal task to be keeping an eye on the performance of government. And government at all levels has, though limited by the First Amendment, tried through the years to limit and circumscribe the activities of the watchdog press.

Out of the tug-of-war between these two adversaries, press and government, have come a variety of rules, laws and court decisions giving first one side, then the other, a momentary advantage.

Access to the News

In order to publish and disseminate news, the press believes, it should have freedom to go where things are happening, to travel freely at home and abroad, to have access to places, to be able to see public records, to sit in court and on the sidelines at city council meetings, school board meetings and the meetings of legislative committees.

In insisting on access to places and records, the press generally asserts that it seeks access as representative of the public, that it is an agent of the public, that the public has a right to know and that the press is the single agency in society that has the resources and ability to see that the public does know.

And though in some ways the press has established some special privileges for itself, in general the press has been found by the courts to have no more special privileges than the average citizen — you or I. But it does have at least as much right to go places and to see records as anyone else.

Access to Places

If the press is to report the news, reporters must have access to the places where news occurs. Access to public places — the streets, sidewalks, public parks and public buildings — is not a problem. Where the public goes, the press can go.

There are times, however, when access to public places is limited. Firefighters and police set up barriers at the scenes of major fires or accidents and the public is kept behind the barriers. Reporters cross fire lines and police barriers only when the authorities are willing for them to do so. Police have, on occasion, arrested reporters and confiscated the film of press photographers attempting to report on an accident, a fire or an arrest. Courts generally have upheld the rights of the press in these cases and prohibited authorities from interfering with reporters or photographers working in public places.

Access to private property is another matter. The press has no more right to trespass on private property than has any citizen. Problems of trespass have arisen when reporters have tried to report on demonstrations at nuclear plants — private property — or on plane crashes on military bases or sometimes to cover stories on the grounds of shopping malls — private property, though with a distinctly public flavor.

Open Meetings

All states, the District of Columbia and the federal government have open meeting laws that require that nearly all meetings of public bodies be open to the public. Statutes require not only that the press and the public be admitted to meetings but that there be adequate public notice that meetings are to be held.

There are exceptions to the open meeting laws, however. Public bodies may close meetings and go into executive session to discuss sensitive matters — generally personnel matters but sometimes financial matters like plans for purchasing property. The justification for closing some meetings to public scrutiny is that publicity might embarrass individuals or infringe on their right to privacy or that premature publicity might increase the cost of buying a piece of property.

Public officials have not welcomed open meeting laws and frequently try to circumvent them. The press has a right to protest, and usually does, when meetings are closed. And public officials have been reprimanded by the courts, fined and in at least one instance sent to jail for violating an open meeting law.

Open Records

Every state, the District of Columbia and the federal government have laws defining public records and establishing the right of press and public to have access to them. These laws vary from state to state, and there are numerous exceptions in the definition of public record.

Among matters excepted by states are sensitive personnel records, medical records, trade secrets, student files, records of welfare recipients, adoption records and academic and scientific research.

However, the best open record laws are based on the idea that everything is public unless it is specifically excepted, and reporters should assume records are open and act accordingly.

Freedom of Information

When reporters are barred from seeing what they consider to be public records, they do have recourse. If the records sought are records of the executive branch or of regulatory agencies of the federal government, the reporter can use the federal Freedom of Information Act, which was enacted in 1966 to provide public and press with a legal basis for obtaining access to public records when public officials attempt to withhold them. Too many public officials have a habit of stalling and may use devious excuses to avoid releasing records. Records can be obtained — and are, regularly — by the press under the Freedom of Information Act.

State open record acts can be used to gain access to state records. Where state officials balk, newspapers have gone into court and secured the records they sought.

Access to Courts

The courts and the press have been at odds for a number of years over several issues of access. The major controversy has been the so-called *free press–fair trial* issue, which has pitted the First Amendment with its free press guarantee against the Sixth Amendment, which guarantees a fair trial. To a large extent the controversy centers on a tendency on the part of judges to protect the right of a defendant to a fair trial by closing or attempting to close pretrial proceedings and trials.

The right of the press and public to attend criminal trials has been clearly established by a number of recent court cases. And the U.S. Supreme Court has ruled that pretrial proceedings, jury selection and criminal trials are public. There is a presumption that civil proceedings are also public, but the Supreme Court has not ruled on this.

Courtrooms may be closed to press and public under some circumstances, but there must be a compelling need for such closing. The press vigorously protests the closing of any proceeding in court because it believes the public has a right to know what goes on in courtrooms as well as in other areas of government. Attorneys for newspapers and press associations stand ready to go into court and argue against closure.

Cameras in the Court

For many years cameras were barred from courtrooms, much to the irritation of newspaper photographers and later of television camera crews. In 1981, however, the Supreme Court held that states may adopt their own rules on allowing cameras and tape recorders into courtrooms. Forty-three states have established their own rules, but these vary considerably from state to state. Still cameras are more likely to be admitted to courtrooms, but recently television cameras have been permitted into some courtrooms. The federal courts do not allow cameras and tape recorders in the courtroom.

Gag Orders

Occasionally a court has ordered attorneys and others involved in civil or criminal cases not to discuss a case. And sometimes these orders have been extended to the press, and judges have ordered newspapers not to publish anything about a case.

The Supreme Court has held that orders prohibiting publication of information about court proceedings are unconstitutional under most circumstances, yet from time to time a judge will issue such an order.

These so-called gag orders are a nuisance, and in most cases newspapers appeal the order to a higher court and are able to get the ban on publishing lifted. However, in the meantime, the newspaper has to assume that the order is a valid order and must obey it. Even when gag orders are eventually lifted, days or weeks may have passed with the newspaper effectively barred from reporting on an ongoing case.

Responsibility for Things Published

As you can see, though there are some limitations on access, the press pretty generally is able to report on public affairs and on the activities of public bodies, including courts. But once the newspaper has published a news story, it is faced with another legal problem: It must take responsibility for what it has published. If a news story libels someone or invades someone's privacy, that person may sue the newspaper. The First Amendment protects the press against prior restraint, but libel laws and court decisions on the right to privacy place serious constraints on the press after publication.

Libel

Libel is a tort, a wrongful act against a person — or sometimes a business firm or corporation. Libel is today generally a civil matter, not a criminal offense. That is, you can be sued for damages by someone who claims to be libeled, but you are unlikely to be arrested for it.

The offense consists, in simplest terms, of defaming someone — that is, injuring the person's reputation by making a false statement that holds that person up to hatred, ridicule or contempt. Damage to a reputation can be a serious matter. It can mean the loss of a job or failure to get a job or to be promoted. It can cause financial loss to the owner of a business or a professional man or woman. It can result in the loss of friends.

Despite uneasiness in the newsroom, newspapers are not often sued for libel, and a great many of the libel suits that are filed against newspapers are either dropped or settled out of court for modest sums. Occasionally there are serious suits, and sometimes substantial damages are levied against a newspaper, a magazine or a broadcaster.

The worst part of libel laws is the fact that they can be expensive for a newspaper — even if the plaintiff, the person who claims to be libeled, either drops the suit or loses in court. Newspapers and broadcast stations today spend a great deal of money trying to avoid libel suits and trying to abort threatened suits before they reach court.

Newspapers and broadcast stations have attorneys on retainer and sometimes on the newspaper staff who consult on a daily basis with editors before stories are ever published. This is expensive and runs up the cost of gathering the news. If libel cases get into court, the cost can be staggering. CBS and *Time* magazine spent millions defending themselves in the Westmoreland and Sharon cases.*

---

*CBS was sued by Gen. William Westmoreland over allegations in a CBS documentary that Westmoreland had knowingly reported erroneous figures on enemy strength during the Vietnam War. Westmoreland dropped the suit just before the end of a lengthy trial. Westmoreland claimed that evidence introduced during the trial vindicated him. CBS, of course, insisted that in dropping the suit, Westmoreland admitted that he had not been libeled. *Time* was sued by Ariel Sharon over a story charging that Sharon as defense minister of Israel encouraged Lebanese retaliation against occupants of a Palestinian refugee camp. The verdict in the case was ambiguous enough to allow both *Time* and Sharon to claim vindication.

There are a number of simple, before-publication protections against libel suits — safeguards readily available to all news writers and applicable in any newsroom. The best of these are accuracy and fairness in reporting and writing — that is, accuracy in reporting facts and a concern for the feelings of both public and private people.

Accuracy will go a long way in guarding against libel. Scrupulous accuracy in reporting about people and events is, of course, good, honest journalism. It is also, usually, safe journalism. Libel suits can result when addresses are garbled, when names are misspelled or incompletely given, when a name appears in a wrong context or when meaning is confused. Be accurate in identification. Be accurate in quoting and careful in attribution.

Fairness is also important if the news writer would avoid libel suits. If newspapers, news writers and editors treat figures in news stories fairly, they will seldom get into trouble. People may not like the story, but they will seldom claim libel unless they believe they are not being treated fairly, that they are being hurt intentionally, that a false statement has been published purposely and with malice.

Not to be forgotten, either, is the fact that truth is an almost absolute defense against libel. A recent Supreme Court decision has helped the defendants in libel cases by reaffirming that private individuals must prove that what was published was false. Public figures have been held to this standard since the *Times* vs. Sullivan decision in 1964.*

The most obvious libels are those statements that are defamatory on their face — for example, saying falsely that someone is a criminal, that he has a loathsome disease or that a particular bank is financially unsound.

Defenses Against Libel Actions

There are a number of valid defenses against libel suits. Truth has already been cited as a defense. Other defenses:

Statute of Limitations

In most states libel actions must be started promptly, and suits are barred after two or three years. In some states suits can be filed as long

---

*In this case, the Supreme Court ruled that public officials cannot recover damages for reports on their official duties unless they can prove actual malice — that is, that at the time of publication, those responsible knew the report was false and published it with reckless disregard of whether it was true or false. In 1967, the court extended this ruling to public figures as well as public officials.

as five years after publication. The plaintiff who waits too long may not have a case.

Privilege

Anyone, public official or member of the public, who speaks in a legislative forum, in a meeting of the Congress, a state legislature, a county board, a city council or a school board or in court enjoys immunity for whatever he says even though the statements might be held libelous if they were made somewhere else. This immunity is absolute. The speaker cannot be sued no matter how outrageous his remarks.

The press enjoys a qualified or conditional privilege in reporting what happens or what is said in legislative forums and at official governmental meetings. Reports, however, must be accurate and complete or a fair summary to enjoy this qualified privilege.

Stories about public meetings, trials, court decisions, verdicts of juries, court opinions, judicial orders and grand jury indictments are protected by qualified privilege even if they include false or defamatory statements.

Fair Comment

This conditional privilege allows news writers to say things on matters of public interest that might otherwise be libelous. The most usual area for fair comment or criticism is in reporting on public performances by professional actors or musicians. Fair comment also applies to reviews of books, plays and recitals and other musical events. It applies to comments a sports writer might make about the quality of coaching or the performance of a football team. Food critics are protected in their reporting on restaurant meals. Consumer reporters are protected when they discuss the virtue or lack of virtue of goods available in the marketplace.

Mitigation

If someone claims to have been libeled, the newspaper can choose to stick by the story, go into court and vigorously defend itself. Or, if it seems likely that a libelous statement has indeed been published, the newspaper can try to mitigate — that is, to lessen — the offense.

The first step is to publish a retraction, to take back the statement. About half the states have retraction laws of some kind. In some states people who claim to have been libeled must give the newspaper an opportunity to retract the statement.

Retractions frequently satisfy the offended person. In some cases retractions will reduce or cancel damages obtained in a libel suit.

To return for a moment to fairness, newspapers have found that many times potentially serious complaints of libel can be headed off by a little sympathy and a genuine apology. Most people just want a fair shake. A few sympathetic words from whoever answers the telephone may be all that is needed.

Most newspapers, as you know, publish a lot of corrections. They have found that it is not enough to be as accurate as possible but that it is also necessary to be viewed by readers as accurate. Most newspapers will quickly correct any error called to their attention by readers, and most of the errors are harmless ones in the sense that they are not libelous.

Privacy

Privacy, a relatively new concept, is becoming as serious a threat to the press as libel, perhaps more so. Only in the past several years has it become a hazard for the press, and nearly every state now recognizes some right to privacy. In most states statutes try to balance the right of the press to report matters of public interest and the right of individuals to be let alone.

Privacy is a personal right. It belongs to individuals, not to businesses or corporations, and it is not a right easily claimed by public figures or public officials.

When private citizens, people who are not public figures, become involved in newsworthy situations, they lose some of their claim to the right to privacy. However, if the newspaper intrudes on someone's privacy, publishes what should be private information about a person or puts a private person in a false light, the newspaper may be liable for damages.

It is important to be accurate in reporting, to be fair and to be certain that what is being reported is actually newsworthy when private individuals are involved in the news.

Understanding the Law

This has been a brief, even superficial, review of some of the legal problems of the press. No one should begin reporting or writing for newspapers, even student publications on a college campus, without some grounding in press law. The very least the beginner should do is enroll in a course in press law. Beyond that it would be wise to keep up with court decisions that may change the rules as they now stand.

Many state press associations have published small handbooks on state laws. Some have pocket-size cards summarizing state press laws. The Reporters Committee for Freedom of the Press has published a handbook on First Amendment law and a guidebook to using the federal Freedom of Information Act.

Several studies of press law are listed at the end of this chapter.

Journalistic Ethics

Ethics, your dictionary will tell you, has to do with the rules and standards of behavior governing the conduct of members of a profession. Ethics has to do, too, with morality — understood and accepted choices between right and wrong in personal and professional behavior.

Journalism today is a responsible and an ethical calling, but this was not always so, and it is still subject to ethical lapses of one sort or another. Journalism shares its ethical sensitivities with society as a whole and with other groups — for example, the medical and legal professions and the ministry. All areas of journalism have developed and subscribe to codes of ethics or statements of ethical standards and behavior. The various professional organizations in the newspaper industry have such codes — for example, the codes of the Associated Press Managing Editors and The Society of Professional Journalists, Sigma Delta Chi and the statement of principles of the American Society of Newspaper Editors. There are codes of ethics, too, for advertising, public relations and broadcasting.

These codes or statements of principles are much the same in purpose: to establish acceptable professional behavior, to encourage honesty and fairness and, in some instances, to police an organization's membership and punish those who do not live up to the standards of the group.

Newspapers were not always paragons of either responsible conduct or honesty. Newspapers aggressively took sides in politics, fabricated news stories, lied about their circulation, used news columns to manipulate public opinion or to punish their enemies. Newspaper reporters accepted bribes to get stories in the paper and sometimes to keep stories out of the paper. These things were not universally done, but they did happen, as a study of newspaper history will show.

In the 1920s, however, things began to change. The growth of the newspaper industry and a need to be more broadly read and accepted in the community led publishers, editors and rank-and-file journalists to begin formulating standards of ethical behavior.

The American Society of Newspaper Editors adopted a code of ethics in 1923. Widespread interest in establishing formal codes of ethics did not develop overnight, however. SPJ,SDX adopted its first code of ethics in 1926. Other groups followed over the years. APME adopted its code of ethics only in 1975.

The ASNE Canons of Journalism

The code adopted by ASNE in 1923, usually referred to as "The Canons of Journalism," was brief and simple. It called for responsibility on the part of publishers and newspaper staffs; it emphasized the freedom of newspapers to report and discuss public affairs; it called for an independent, non-partisan press; it described truth and accuracy as a cornerstone of journalistic behavior; it urged that news and opinion be kept strictly separate in the newspaper; and it urged fairness and decency in dealing with news sources and the public.

Newspaper codes of ethics and professional standards, including the revision of the ASNE code in 1975, pretty much follow this outline.

Responsibility

Newspaper journalists generally agree that the newspaper, despite the fact that it is a business like any other business, is vested with a special kind of responsibility to the general welfare. "The purpose of distributing news and enlightened opinion," the SPJ,SDX code says, "is to serve the general welfare." The APME code puts it slightly differently: "The public's right to know about matters of importance is paramount."

The ASNE's 1975 code, called a statement of principles, says:

> The American press was made free not just to inform or just to serve as a forum for debate but also to bring an independent scrutiny to bear on the forces of power in the society, including the conduct of official power at all levels of government.

These and other statements about the responsibility of the press recognize that the press serves an essential function in our society by informing and educating the public. In doing this, today's journalists believe, the press must be scrupulously honest and scrupulously fair.

Freedom of the Press

Freedom of speech and of the press is established under the First Amendment. And it is to the First Amendment that journalists turn in defining their role in society. The freedom of the press established in the First Amendment refers to the right of anyone to write, publish and disseminate information and opinions. Somehow this sense has been obscured to the point where many believe that this right belongs mainly to newspapers. Newspapers have attempted to counter this viewpoint — and to justify the obvious fact that newspapers have accumulated considerable wealth because of their First Amendment protection — by talking about the *public's right to know.*

The newspaper industry is, admittedly, a prosperous and extremely profitable industry, and it is given special privileges under the First Amendment. But, the industry points out, the First Amendment ensures not just the newspaper's livelihood but also the public's right to news and information.

Actually, freedom of the press and the public's right to know are two sides of the same coin. The public's right and need to know about public affairs and the conduct of government is essential in a democratic society. And the freedom of newspapers to gather and publish news and opinion is necessary to that public need.

Journalists feel strongly about their rights under the First Amendment, but they feel that way because they believe journalism serves an important public purpose.

Truth and Accuracy

Journalists have a determined approach to accuracy in reporting on the affairs of the world and a passion for truth. And codes of ethics reflect this. The APME code says: "The newspaper should guard against inaccuracies, carelessness, bias or distortion through either emphasis or omission."

The ASNE principles say that every effort should be made to be certain that reporting is accurate and free of bias and that all sides of issues are presented fairly. The SPJ,SDX code calls truth "our ultimate goal."

The various codes spell out in detail how accuracy and truth can be maintained. The essential point is that journalists believe in truth and accuracy and do their best to be both accurate and truthful. And those who don't live up to this professional and ethical standard are eased out of newspaper journalism — sometimes publicly and sometimes painfully.

News and Opinion

One of the tenets of journalism, spelled out in different language in the various codes of ethics, is that news and opinion should not be mixed. Opinion, newspapers believe, belongs on the editorial page, on op ed pages and in signed columns. That is, opinions and viewpoints, personal on the part of individual journalists or those representing the view of the newspaper itself, must be clearly recognizable to the reader. The reader, newspapers believe, should have confidence that what appears in news columns is as accurate as possible, as unbiased as possible and fair to all sides.

Fair Play

Another aspect of fairness dealt with in journalistic codes of ethics is fairness to people in the news. An essential part of this is understanding that many people who get involved in the news are private individuals not always comfortable being in the spotlight and often upset and unhappy to be the focus of attention by the press. Sensitivity in dealing with people is important. And journalists must recognize the right to privacy. Privacy is a legal matter, as we have seen, but it is also an ethical concern. Journalists must do their work in such a way that people — the public, newspaper readers, individuals who become part of a news story — are treated fairly, decently and with compassion. Fairness is a balancing act. The press must be fair to people in the news, but it must also be fair to the reading public by seeing that the public is adequately informed about situations, events, issues and people.

Conflict of Interest

Conflict of interest, either the interest of the individual journalist or of the newspaper, has become a central issue in discussions of journalistic ethics and the formulation of codes of journalistic behavior.

As we have seen, newspaper journalism assumes a mantle of social responsibility. It presumes to serve the public welfare in the process of gathering, writing, editing and disseminating news and opinion. Newspaper journalism, therefore, must be disinterested. Journalists must stand apart as observers. They must not be involved in the news. They must not be on one side or the other.

Codes of ethics spell out in detail the kinds of activities that may cause conflicts of interest for newspapers and newspaper staff. Some codes developed by newspapers are very specific in these matters.

Gifts and freebies are generally prohibited by codes of ethics. Newspapers and newspaper people should not accept things of value from sources outside journalism. These include gifts from news sources or others, free or reduced-rate travel for reporters and writers, free meals or entertainment or lodging.

Years ago it was acceptable practice for major league baseball teams to foot the bill for sports writers to go to Florida in late winter to report on preseason practice. Theater critics were given tickets for the opening nights of plays they were to cover. Free movie tickets and free circus tickets were regarded as newsroom perquisites. No more. Newspapers by and large ban gifts and subsidies. They pay their way.

Outside employment that causes a conflict of interest is generally banned. Too-active participation in community affairs, especially in politics, is considered a no-no by many newspapers. Business reporters are specifically forbidden to invest in companies they may cover during the course of their work.

Newspapers, too, try to avoid institutional involvement. The Gannett newspapers, for example, are heavy supporters of community activities and community social services and charitable organizations. But financial support in Gannett cities comes not from the newspaper but from the Gannett Foundation, which has no direct local ties.

Matters of Taste

Newspapers are painfully aware that they are guests each day in readers' homes. Readers are especially sensitive to matters of good manners and taste in the columns of their newspapers. The newspaper enters the home on a regular schedule and is available to and read by the whole family. Probably for this reason, readers can object to words, to news stories, to pictures in the newspaper when they aren't bothered by the same material in a book or a magazine or on television.

Expletives, vulgarities, profanity and obscenities can, when they appear in the newspaper, rile the newspaper reader. Never mind that the child may hear or use the word on the playground, that the parent may use the word at work, that it may be in this week's *Time* magazine or on tonight's NBC News. Readers don't like those words in their newspapers.

Newspaper readers are especially sensitive to what they regard as invasion of privacy or callous treatment of people in trouble, of the ill, the bereaved or those shocked by natural catastrophes. They are especially upset by news photos. Photos of people injured in auto accidents, of parents crouched over the body of a child, of violence and situations clearly embarrassing to those pictured have in recent years caused vehement reader reaction.

News writers have been fired for including a vulgar word in a news story. Editors have been fired by newspaper owners for permitting a four-letter word to get into print. Newspapers have been sued over news pictures that the subject regarded as an invasion of privacy.

Newspaper journalists are engaged in a vigorous and continuing debate about the use of vulgar, obscene or profane language in the newspaper. They continue to argue over the use of pictures of violence or pictures that show people in moments of extreme emotion. There is a fine line between the word or the picture the reading public should see and the word or picture that needn't be published. There is a right of the public to know, but there is also a necessity for the newspaper to show restraint.

You will find a statement on the use of vulgarity, obscenity and profanity in the Basic Guide to News Style, at the back of this text. It is worth thinking about.

Good taste is good manners. Newspapers as institutions and journalists who work for newspapers must understand the viewpoint of readers, must recognize differences in perception and attitudes.

Suggestions for Further Reading

The press today is facing new challenges to its ability to report and publish the news.

Denniston, Lyle. *The Reporter and the Law*. New York: Hastings House, 1980.
    Techniques for covering the courts. Includes a discussion of libel, privacy, contempt, prior restraint and postpublication penalties.

Fink, Conrad. *Media Ethics: In the Newsroom and Beyond*. New York: McGraw-Hill, 1987.
    A discussion of the ethical problems facing reporters, editors and publishers.

Gore, Joel M. *The Rights of Reporters*. New York: Avon Books, 1974.
    A handbook for reporters, prepared by the American Civil Liberties Union.

Hulteng, John L. *Playing It Straight*. Chester, Conn.: Globe Pequot Press, 1981.
    A practical discussion of the ethical principles of the American Society of Newspaper Editors.

McCulloch, Frank. *Drawing the Line.* Washington, D.C.: ASNE Foundation, 1984.

    Newspaper editors tell how they solved their toughest ethical problems.

Middleton, Kent, and William Chamberlain. *Law of Public Communication.* White Plains, N.Y.: Longman, 1987.

    A broad discussion of legal problems affecting the press, advertising and public relations.

Pember, Don R. *Mass Media Law.* Dubuque, Iowa: Wm. C. Brown Company, 1977.

    A readable and instructive textbook on legal problems.

Sanford, Bruce W. *Synopsis of the Law of Libel and the Right of Privacy,* rev. ed. New York: World Almanac Publications, 1981.

    A handbook written for the Scripps-Howard companies by the legal counsel for the Society of Professional Journalists, Sigma Delta Chi.

Swain, Bruce M. *Reporters' Ethics.* Ames: The Iowa State University Press, 1978.

    A study of ethical problems reporters face in covering the day's news.

A Basic Guide
to News Style

These basic rules and guidelines conform to practices of the Associated Press and United Press International as set forth in the most recent revisions of the joint stylebook. They reflect as much as possible the current practices in the newspaper world.

Abbreviations

1.1   Spell out, do not abbreviate, the names of organizations, firms, agencies, universities and colleges, groups, clubs and governmental bodies the first time the names are used.

There are a few common exceptions like IQ, FBI, NBC and PTA where an abbreviation is acceptable.

Note that these and most other abbreviations take no periods. Learn the commonly used exceptions. See 4.6.

1.2   The names of organizations, firms, agencies, universities and colleges, groups, clubs and governmental bodies may be abbreviated in second and subsequent references if the abbreviation is standard and will be easily understood by readers. For example, first reference might be:

> Civil Aeronautics Board
> National Organization for Women

Second and later references would be:

> CAB
> NOW

Note that these are standard, well-known abbreviations or acronyms.

1.3   Do *not* use an abbreviation or acronym in parentheses after a full name. If the abbreviation or acronym would not be clear without this arrangement, do *not* use it. Do *not* reduce names to unfamiliar initials or acronyms to save a few words. Do *not* create initials or acronyms.

Right: The Humane Society of the United States has accredited the new animal shelter.

Wrong: The Humane Society of the United States (HSUS) has accredited the new animal shelter.

1.4   A short form of a name should be used in second and subsequent references rather than an unfamiliar abbreviation or acronym. For example, first reference might be:

European Economic Community
University of Notre Dame
International Court of Justice

Second and subsequent references would be:

the Common Market
Notre Dame
the world court (lowercase)

1.5   In street addresses, abbreviate these:

street	St.
avenue	Ave.
boulevard	Blvd.

However, in general references where a street number is not used, spell out and capitalize *street*, *avenue* and *boulevard*. See also 1.6 and 2.1.

on West Grand Boulevard
at the Grand River Avenue crossing
but at Massachusetts and Pennsylvania avenues

1.6   Do *not* abbreviate these:

alley	drive	plaza
road	terrace	place
circle	lane	

1.7   Abbreviate points of the compass in street addresses:

> 1813 S. 59th St.
> 600 Oakland Road N.E.

However, in general references where no street number is used, spell out the compass point:

> on South 59th Street
> in the 400 block on West Main Street

See also 1.5 and 2.1.

1.8   Do *not* abbreviate points of the compass used to indicate direction:

> Snow fell south of the city.
> He lived north of the railroad tracks.

See also 2.3.

1.9   Names of states are abbreviated when, but only when, they are used with a city name or with a political party affiliation:

> He lived in Memphis, Tenn., for many years.
> All were present except John Smith, D-Ga.
> She lived in Illinois for a year, then moved to Iowa.

1.10   Use these abbreviations for the names of states:

Ala.	Ill.	Miss.	N.C.	Vt.
Ariz.	Ind.	Mo.	N.D.	Va.
Ark.	Kan.	Mont.	Okla.	Wash.
Calif.	Ky.	Neb.	Ore.	W.Va.
Colo.	La.	Nev.	Pa.	Wis.
Conn.	Md.	N.H.	R.I.	Wyo.
Del.	Mass.	N.J.	S.C.	
Fla.	Mich.	N.M.	S.D.	
Ga.	Minn.	N.Y.	Tenn.	

1.11   Do *not* abbreviate the names of the states of Alaska, Hawaii, Idaho, Iowa, Maine, Ohio, Texas and Utah.

Do *not* use the abbreviations recommended by the U.S. Postal Service for use with zip codes.

He lives in St. Paul, Minn. *Not* St. Paul, MN.

1.12   Do *not* abbreviate the months of March, April, May, June and July. Other months are abbreviated only when they are used with a date:

> Oct. 21, 1984   *but*   in October 1984
> Sept. 25   *but*   fine September weather

1.13   Names of countries are usually not abbreviated, although there are some exceptions. United States is abbreviated when it modifies a noun:

> Mrs. White visited the United States last year.
> She served on the U.S. Court of Appeals.

1.14   Do *not* abbreviate days of the week, given names, points of the compass in city names, parts of city names or city names:

> Monday or Tuesday, *never* Mon. or Tues.
> William or Charles, *never* Wm. or Chas.
> East St. Louis, *never* E. St. Louis
> Los Angeles or Grand Rapids, *never* L.A. or Gd. Rapids

Do *not* abbreviate these: *associate, association, assistant, attorney* or *attorney general, assemblyman, assemblywoman, department, professor.* Do not use *Xmas* for *Christmas*. Do *not* abbreviate the courtesy title *father*, as in *Father Smith*.

1.15   Names of earned or honorary academic degrees are spelled out and in lowercase:

> He earned a bachelor of arts degree.
> She earned a master of arts degree in journalism.
> He earned a doctor of philosophy degree at Johns
>   Hopkins.

It is acceptable to use *bachelor's degree* or *master's degree* or merely *bachelor's* or *master's* or *doctorate*.

In a list or in tabular matter, degrees may be abbreviated and in uppercase:

> . . . John Jones, Ph.D.; Marilyn Thompson, Ph.D.; Jane
> Smith, Ed.D.; Donald Wright, Ph.D.; Richard Roe, J.D.

1.16 Abbreviate and capitalize *Mr.* and *Mrs.* before names:

> Mr. and Mrs. Henry Clay Smith
> Mrs. Walker

1.17 Titles of certain elected or appointed officials are abbreviated:

> Gov. Joe Frank Harris
> Sen. Sam Nunn
> Lt. Gov. Martha Griffiths
> State Rep. Peggy Childs

Others are always spelled out, among them, *judge, mayor, treasurer, city clerk, registrar of deeds.*

1.18 Abbreviate military titles and titles of police and fire officials before names:

> Sgt. Harry Hood
> retired Army Gen. Louis Look
> fire Capt. John Williams
> detective Lt. George Foreman
> Navy Capt. Ann Jewett

President is never abbreviated.

> President Ronald Reagan
> President Reagan
> former President Jimmy Carter

1.19 Spell out *fort* in names of cities or military establishments. Spell out *mount* in all uses:

> Mount Pleasant, Mich.
> Mount St. Helens
> Fort Atkinson, Wis.
> Fort Benning, Ga.

1.20 Do *not* abbreviate *World War I* or *World War II.* Note that the numbers are Roman numerals, not Arabic figures.

Capitalization

2.1 As a general rule, capitalize both distinguishing and non-distinguishing words in the names of places and things:

> Renaissance Center
> Missouri River
> Cedar Shoals High School
> Golden Gate Bridge
> Hilton Hotel
> Democratic Party

2.2 Capitalize names of holidays, historic events, church feast days, special events and so on, but not seasons:

> Mother's Day   fall weather
> Labor Day   autumn days
> Orientation Week   winter storm
> Honors Day   spring flowers
> Veterans Day   summer showers

These do *not* take quotation marks. See 4.7.

2.3 Do *not* capitalize points of the compass in usages like these:

> an east wind
> a southerly breeze
> a northern exposure

But *do* capitalize points of the compass in names of recognized geographic areas:

> the Middle West   the South
> the Eastern Shore   the West Coast
> the Southeast   Western Ocean

See also 1.7 and 1.8.

2.4 Capitalize trademarks, brand names and service marks, that is, names in which a manufacturer, distributor, inventor or originator has a property right:

> *Coke* and *Coca Cola* are registered trademarks.
> *Astroturf* is a registered trademark.

Scotch tape is a trademark.
Xerox is a registered trademark.

Generic equivalents should be used in preference to trademarks unless the protected name is essential to the story.

soft drink	cellophane tape
artificial turf	photocopy

2.5   Capitalize the names of nationalities, peoples, races and tribes:

Canadian	Arab
Caucasian	Negro
Asian	Asiatic
Hispanic	Standing Rock Sioux
Oriental	Yoruba

Do *not* capitalize descriptive words like *black* or *white*.

2.6   Capitalize the titles of books, plays, poems, songs, lectures or speeches, hymns, movies, television programs, holidays and special days and historic events:

"NBC Nightly News"	(television program)
"The Age of Uncertainty"	(book title)
"Hiawatha"	(poem)
"The Fantasticks"	(play)
"America the Beautiful"	(song)

Note that these are also enclosed in quotation marks. See 4.7. Names of holidays, special days and special events are capitalized, but not enclosed in quotation marks:

Mother's Day	(special observance)
Labor Day	(national holiday)
Boston Marathon	(special event)
Newspaper Week	(special event)

2.7   Names of newspapers, magazines, sacred books and reference works are capitalized but not enclosed in quotation marks:

the Bible	Webster's Dictionary
The New York Times	Ms. magazine
USA Today	Atlanta Journal
World Almanac	Who's Who in America

Note that the word *the* is capitalized in the names of newspapers when the newspaper prefers that usage: *The New York Times*, but *the Times* on second reference. The word *magazine* is capitalized only when it is part of the name of the publication: *Green's Magazine*, but *Time magazine*. See also 4.7.

2.8   Do *not* capitalize occupational descriptions before names:

> columnist Art Buchwald
> author Martha Grimes
> feminist Patricia Carbine
> visiting editor Harold Hughes

It is better, generally, to use descriptive matter *after* a name, thus:

> . . . including James Baldwin, the author, who . . .
> . . . and Mary Brock, an active candidate, who . . .

Do capitalize official titles before a name:

> Sen. Sam Nunn
> Justice Sandra Day O'Connor
> Sen. Nancy Landon Kassebaum

See also 1.16 and 5.12.

2.9   Capitalize the names of universities and colleges and independent schools, institutes and programs within a university:

> Howard University   Kalamazoo College
> School of Journalism   College of Education
> Survey Research Center

But do *not* capitalize the names of academic and administrative units within a college or university except where a word should ordinarily be capitalized:

> department of Romance languages
> department of history

2.10   Do *not* capitalize general references to subject matter, areas of interest or political philosophies:

466

air navigation	computer science
democratic system	communist system
socialism	radical right
political science	

2.11   Names of campus and other public buildings are capitalized:

Old College Hall	Journalism Building
the Pentagon	Atlanta Market Center
Memorial Hall	Widener Library
Alumni Chapel	Senate Office Building
the Capitol	

2.12   Capitalize the full names of all courts:

the U.S. Supreme Court
federal District Court
County Court

Numbers

3.1   As a general rule, spell out both cardinal and ordinal numbers from one through nine. Use Arabic figures for numbers 10 and larger. For example:

one woman	10 women
nine years	11 years
first day	10th day

Other rules in this section are exceptions to this basic rule.

3.2   Use commas in numbers with four or more digits except in years and street addresses:

1,500	23,750
1985	1703 S. Washington Road
$1,500	

3.3   Exact numbers of more than a million are expressed in Arabic figures:

The population of New York City is 7,867,760.

However, the words *million* and *billion* may be used with round numbers:

> 5 million miles or more
> at least 10 billion years

And numbers over a million are rounded off and expressed thus:

> 2.75 million rather than 2,750,000
> $3.2 million rather than $3,221,000

3.4 Arabic figures are used in street addresses:

> 129 S. Stratford Drive
> 1600 Pennsylvania Ave.
> 6 W. Circle Drive

3.5 Arabic figures are used in ages:

> Neil Greene, 7, who . . .
> Smith, 60, was . . .
> a 4-year-old boy

3.6 Arabic figures are used to express caliber, dates, dimensions, heights, highway numbers, latitude and longitude, percentages, scales, scores of sports events, speeds, temperature and time:

caliber	.32-caliber pistol
dates	Jan. 4, 1989
dimensions	5 feet by 9 feet
	11 feet by 23 inches
height	7-foot-4-inch basketball center
	5 feet tall
highways	Interstate 95
latitude	45 degrees north
longitude	80 degrees west
percentages	1 percent
scales	4.1 on the Richter scale
scores	Army 6, Navy 7
speed	5 miles an hour
temperature	93 degrees
	temperature in the 30s
time	8 a.m., 9:15 p.m.

Zero is spelled out except in scores:

The temperature fell to zero at 5 a.m.
Michigan State defeated Michigan, 7-0.

For uses not listed here or cited elsewhere in this section, consult the *Associated Press Stylebook and Libel Manual.*

3.7 Arabic figures are used to express sums of money:

5 cents	$250,000
$1	$100

Sums of money over a million may be rounded off and expressed thus:

$2.5 million	$1.7 billion

Do *not* round off or express in words sums of money under a million:

$22,000	$115,000

3.8 Fractions are written out except when they form part of a modifying unit:

three-quarters of a mile
half an acre
a 3/4-inch pipe
a 1/2-ton shipment

3.9 In a series, follow the basic style rule for numbers:

10 dogs, six cats and 14 hamsters
two books, three magazines, nine newspapers and 11
 radio stations

3.10 When a number is used at the beginning of a sentence, spell it out. Do *not* use an Arabic figure to start a sentence:

Seventy-six trombones led the big parade.
Ten thousand jammed the stadium.

If it is awkward to spell out a number at the beginning of a sentence, rephrase the sentence:

The parade was led by 76 trombones.

469

Sometimes you can round off a number and use a word like *nearly,* *almost* or *more than* to start the sentence:

> More than 10,000 spectators jammed the stadium.

But it is acceptable to start a sentence with a year in Arabic figures:

> 1980 was an election year.

3.11   Casual numbers, obviously inexact, are spelled out:

> A thousand times no!
> I've said it a hundred times.

3.12   In news writing, do *not* use signs or symbols for these: cents, degrees, inches, feet, number, percent and so on. Always spell out. The only exception is the dollar sign:

> 5 feet 2 inches   12.6 percent
> 32 degrees   12 cents
> $50 $100,000

3.13   Dates are written in Arabic figures:

> July 4, 1776   Feb. 12
> Nov. 11, 1918   Feb. 22
> Oct. 12, 1492   Nov. 1

Note that dates are written as cardinal numbers.

3.14   Plural numbers are written as Arabic figures followed by a lower-case *s*. Do *not* use an apostrophe:

> the 1890s
> temperatures in the 90s

But use the apostrophe to indicate any omission, thus:

> during the '70s

3.15   References to decades that have acquired popular names are spelled out:

the Gay Nineties
the Depression-ridden Thirties

3.16   Centuries follow the general rule for numbers given in 3.1 and are expressed in ordinal numbers:

ninth century
20th century

Note that the word *century* is *not* capitalized.

3.17   Metric terms are spelled out but not capitalized:

100-meter yachts	10 kilometers
3 metric tons	5 kilos

However, *Celsius* is capitalized:

9 degrees Celsius

Metric terms in photography and ordnance are abbreviated:

35mm camera
8mm film
105mm cannon

Note that these abbreviations do not require a period and that there is no space between the number and the metric term.

Punctuation

4.1   The apostrophe is used to indicate omissions in contractions and certain other forms:

it's	it is
can't	cannot
the '60s	the 1960s

4.2   Use the apostrophe to form the plural of single letters:

Mind your p's and q's.
The A's won the second game.

Omit the apostrophe in forming the plural of Arabic figures:

> three 7s
> the 1920s
> temperatures in the 60s

4.3   The colon is used in clock time:

> 8:15 a.m.
> 10:20 p.m.

4.4   The use of the hyphen is complicated. When in doubt, it is best to refer to the dictionary. Here are some basic rules, however.

The hyphen is used in compound words like these:

> an off-the-cuff opinion
> a new right-to-work rule
> a not-so-easy task
> a two-man submarine
> a well-known actor

A hyphen is necessary in compounds consisting of a number plus a unit of measurement. For example:

> a 7-year-old boy   a 4-yard gain
> a 2-foot-thick wall   a 20-mile hike
> a 25-mile-an-hour speed   a 2-foot drop
> a 6-foot-2-inch athlete   a .32-caliber pistol

A hyphen is also necessary in compounds consisting of a number plus other nouns. For example:

> a two-base hit   six-man football
> a four-lane highway   six-day wonder

The hyphen is *not* used in phrases like the following where the adverb ends in *-ly* because the reader can expect the phrase to modify the word that follows:

> a gravely ill patient
> a relatively easy solution

The hyphen is necessary for clarity when compound words like these are used as modifiers:

> well-known   well-educated
> little-known   soft-spoken

Note the contrast in these sentences:

> Mary Jones is well educated.
> Mary Jones is a well-educated woman.

Where prefixes are usually not hyphenated, *do* hyphenate if they precede a word that is normally capitalized:

> unbecoming   un-American
> unknown   un-British
> unlovable   pre-Raphaelite

A hyphen is always used with the prefix *ex-*, as in:

> ex-president   ex-chairman

A hyphen is used to separate vowels in words with prefixes like:

> pre-empt
> re-elect
> co-op

A hyphen is used when numbers ending in *-y* are spelled out:

> seventy-six
> twenty-four

A hyphen is used, with some exceptions, in words beginning with *anti-* and *non-:*

> anti-intellectual
> non-stop

4.5   The comma is omitted before *Jr., Sr.* and Roman numerals in names:

Adlai Stevenson II
Franklin D. Roosevelt Jr.
H.D. Metcalf Sr.

4.6 Periods are used in certain abbreviations, among them:

U.S.   the U.S. marshal
U.N.   a U.N. delegate

After points of the compass in street addresses:

16 E. Wabash Ave.
600 Connecticut Ave. N.E.

Periods are used in certain lowercase abbreviations: a.m., p.m., c.o.d.
    Periods are used in abbreviations of academic degrees: Ph.D., D.D., M.D., M.A., B.A., Ed.D., D.V.M., D.D.S.
    In many other instances, abbreviations in the form of initials do *not* take periods:

Military abbreviations: ROTC, RAF, MiG 70, USS
    Texas
Organizations, businesses and universities: AFL-CIO,
    OAS, GOP, NBC, ACLU, AT&T, AP, UPI, UGA, BU
Certain lowercase abbreviations: 35mm, 20 mpg, 50ips
Time zones: EDT, CST
Acronyms: NOW, CARE, NASA, UNESCO, CORE, radar
Initials standing for a person's name: JFK for John F.
    Kennedy, LBJ for Lyndon B. Johnson, ET for the
    Extraterrestrial

4.7 Quotation marks are used to enclose direct quotations and the titles of books, plays, poems, songs, lectures, speeches, television and radio productions, editorials and similar titles:

"I'm in trouble," he said.
"What," he asked, "is the meaning of this?"
"What's the Matter with Kansas?" (editorial)
"The Today Show" (television program)
"What Now, My Love" (song)
"Timberline" (book title)

Note that in direct quotation, periods and commas are always arbitrarily placed *inside* the closing quotation marks. Other punctuation marks are placed before or after as logic demands.

Names of newspapers and magazines are *not* enclosed in quotation marks:

> Kansas City Star Time magazine
> Boston Globe Computer World

Names of holidays and special observances are *not* enclosed in quotation marks:

> Mother's Day Veterans Day
> Orientation Week Commencement

See also 2.2.

Names of sacred books and reference works are *not* enclosed in quotation marks. For example, the Bible, the Talmud, the Koran, Webster's New World Dictionary, The World Almanac, Editor & Publisher International Year Book and Encyclopaedia Britannica. See also 2.7.

4.8 Avoid the use of quotation marks with slang expressions or single words where meaning is clear without them:

> He called the youth a "hippie." (Wrong)
> He called the youth a hippie. (Right)
> He said the word was "slang." (Wrong)
> He said the word was slang. (Right)

4.9 Use parentheses to set off names of states when they are used to complete identification of newspapers:

> the Boston (Mass.) Globe
> the Augusta (Ga.) Chronicle

4.10 In a series, omit the final comma before *and* or *or:*

> red, white and blue
> the numbers six, seven, eight and nine
> bell, book or candle

4.11   Nicknames are enclosed in quotation marks:

> Ruggiero "Richie the Boot" Boiardo
> W.C. "Pug" Pearson
> The other players called him "Slim."

Where a nickname has become better known than the person's given name, omit the quotation marks:

> He remembers Babe Ruth's 300th home run.
> Democrats honor Old Hickory at Jefferson-Jackson
> dinners.

4.12   Do *not* underline in news copy. Use quotation marks to set off titles. See 4.7.

Names and Titles

5.1   Identify people in news stories by their first name, middle initial and last name:

> Gerald M. O'Neil
> James A. Bailey
> Christy C. Bulkeley

However, when people prefer and follow some other usage, follow their preference:

> Richard Cooper   James MacGregor Burns
> T. John Lesinski   Pat Schroeder
> P.D. James   C.D.B. Bryan

5.2   Use full identification in first reference and follow the usage described in 5.1.

In second and later references to men, use last name only:

> Richard Cooper (first reference)
> Cooper (second reference)

In second and later references to women, use courtesy titles. Follow the guidelines provided in 5.3.

5.3   Courtesy titles are used by the wire services and by newspapers that have adopted the joint stylebook to make identification certain and to make all references to people named clear to the reader. Some newspapers no longer use them, but courtesy titles have been retained by the joint stylebook, apparently because a majority of newspapers consider them useful. In wire service style courtesy titles are not used on first reference:

>   Jane Smith   John Smith

The preferred form on first reference to a married woman is to identify her by her own first name and her husband's last name.

Courtesy titles, *Miss, Mrs.* or *Ms.,* are used on second and subsequent reference to women.

If a woman prefers *Ms.,* do not include her marital status in your story unless it is relevant.

It is acceptable to use *Miss* on second reference where a woman's marital status is not known or is not relevant to the news story, for example, in stories about the accomplishments of professional or business women:

>   Diana Ross, the singer, was . . . (first reference)
>   Miss Ross was . . . (second reference)

Mr. is not used in news copy unless it is used with *Mrs.,* as *Mr. and Mrs. John Doe* or *Mr. and Mrs. Doe.*

Although the joint stylebook does not say so, *Mr. and Mrs.* is in general use in newspapers, especially in establishing relationships, for example:

>   . . . son of Mr. and Mrs. Richard Roe . . .
>   Mr. and Mrs. Henry Doe have announced the
>   engagement of their daughter Margaret to . . .
>   visiting their parents, Mr. and Mrs. Robert Walker, . . .

Newspapers generally refer to married couples as *Mr. and Mrs. So-and-so* when the fact of the relationship is relevant to the news story. At the same time, you will find news stories in which husband and wife are referred to by their own names, for example:

>   . . . son of Mary and Roger Brown
>   . . . her parents, Jane and Robert Roe

Courtesy titles may be used in obituaries where they would not be in other copy.

Courtesy titles are generally not used in sports copy.

For usage not covered in this section, see *The Associated Press Stylebook and Libel Manual.*

5.4 In news stories involving both men and women, if titles are used for men on second reference, use them for women on second reference as appropriate. Do not, for example, on second reference, refer to a male faculty member as *professor* and to a woman faculty member as *Miss* or *Mrs.* if she, too, has faculty rank and is entitled to the title *professor.*

5.5 College and university students can be identified by class and hometown:

> John P. Wintergreen, Little Rock, Ark., senior, was . . .
> Mary Williams, Pittsfield, Mass., senior, said . . .
> Abdul Jamal, Lansing, Mich., senior, was . . .

On some campuses, students are identified by class and major:

> Janice Keith, journalism junior, was . . .
> Eli Whitney, graduate student in history, was . . .

5.6 Identify faculty by rank and department, thus:

> Nancy Perkins, professor of psychology, said . . .
> John Bulfinch, instructor in economics, was . . .
> Elton Henry, food science technician, said . . .
> Russel B. Nye, professor of English, was . . .

Note that it is professor *of* but instructor and graduate assistant *in.*

Omit the title *Dr.* for faculty holding the degree of doctor of philosophy when they are identified by academic rank and department.

5.7 Use *Dr.* with the names of doctors of medicine, doctors of osteopathic medicine, doctors of veterinary medicine or doctors of dentistry or divinity.

> Dr. Ellsworth West, dean of the college of human
>   medicine, said Monday that . . . (first reference)

Omit *Dr.* on second reference:

> West said that . . .

5.8 In referring to Protestant or Catholic clergy, first reference is *the Rev.* followed by full name:

> the Rev. John C. Smith (Episcopal, Baptist and others)
> the Rev. Patrick McGuire (Catholic)

On second and later references, omit *the Rev.:*

> the Rev. John A. Knox (first reference)
> Knox said that . . . (second reference)

Use *Rabbi* before a name on first reference. On second reference use only the last name:

> *Rabbi James Wise* (first reference)
> *Wise* (second reference)

Follow the usage cited here. Do not refer to clergymen as *Rev.* Smith or *Rev.* Jones. Where the adjective *reverend* is used it should be abbreviated and preceded by the word *the*.

Do not in referring to Catholic clergy use *father* except in direct quotation. There is no abbreviation for *father*.

For second reference to women clergy, follow 5.3.

5.9 It is customary to identify members of state legislatures and members of the U.S. Senate and House of Representatives by giving some idea where they are from: state, hometown or legislative district. In many news stories it is useful to identify them by their political party as well.

Here are some general guidelines on legislative titles and identification.

For members of the legislature in your own state, use a hometown identification, for example, *Rep. John Doe, Midland.*

If party identification is relevant to the story, use *Rep. John Doe, Midland Republican.*

Members of the U.S. House of Representatives from your own state may be identified in the same way, for example, *Rep. Donald J. Pease, Oberlin,* or *Rep. Donald J. Pease, Oberlin Democrat.*

U.S. senators are seldom identified by hometown, probably because they have a statewide constituency. Just write *Sen. Wyche Fowler, Sen. Robert Dole* or *Sen. Barbara Mikulski.*

Do not use *congressman* or *congresswoman* as a title except in direct quotation, although it is permissible and customary to speak of congressmen in general references to members of the U.S. House of Representatives.

Do *not* confuse the Congress of the United States with state legislatures. There is only one Congress, and it sits in Washington, D.C. Members of state legislatures are state senators, representatives or legislators, but *never* congressmen.

5.10 Party affiliation is not always necessary in identifying members of state legislatures or the Congress. When it is relevant to a news story, you may use these forms:

> Democratic Sen. Daniel K. Inouye, Hawaii, said . . .
> Sen. Daniel K. Inouye, D-Hawaii, said . . .
> Inouye, a Democrat, said . . . (second reference)
> Inouye said . . . (or this on second reference)

5.11 In a list of names and titles, place the name first and the title second:

> Harry C. West, president; John Elmer, vice president;
> Walter Meyers, secretary-treasurer

5.12 Short official titles of elected public officials, members of the armed forces, police officers and firefighters are placed before the names:

> City Clerk Donna Williams
> fire Capt. James Donahue
> Circuit Judge Olga Bennett
> Gov. Michael S. Dukakis
> Gen. Paul X. Kelley

These titles as well as others already cited are omitted on second and subsequent reference.

5.13 Do not pile up long, unwieldy titles before names. Short titles precede names, as *Mayor Andrew Young,* but long titles follow names and are lowercase:

> Dr. W.T. Door, Washtenaw County coroner, said . . .
> Beverly Sills, general director of the New York City
> Opera, said . . .

5.14 Occupational descriptions before names are not capitalized:

> actor Marlon Brando
> columnist Mary McGrory

Occupational descriptions or job descriptions, especially lengthy ones, should be placed after names and set off by commas:

> John Doe, assistant corporation counsel, said that . . .
> Flora Lewis, the syndicated columnist, was invited . . .

Time

6.1 Time in newspaper usage is always *a.m.* or *p.m.*

> 8 a.m.   8:15 a.m.
> 9 p.m.   9:20 p.m.

Note that it is 8 a.m. and not 8:00 a.m. Keep it short and simple. Note that *a.m.* and *p.m.* are lowercase and take periods.

6.2 Midnight and noon are neither *a.m.* nor *p.m.* Write:

> noon
> midnight

The Arabic figure 12 is omitted: The ship sailed at *noon*.

6.3 Use the day of the week rather than *last night, yesterday* or *tomorrow. Today* and *tonight* are acceptable where their meaning is clear, and they are commonly used in morning newspapers.

6.4 Using *tonight* with *p.m.* or *this morning* with *a.m.* is redundant. Don't do it.

6.5 In reference to events within seven days of the date of publication — before or after — use the day of the week only.

481

In reference to events more than one week ahead or previous to the date of publication, use the date only and omit the day of the week.

Use either day or date, according to this rule, not both, although there may be occasions when both day and date will be necessary to the story.

6.6   In dates, do not use a hyphen to indicate *to* or *through*.

They will meet June 11 to June 15.
They will meet June 11 through 18.

Note that *to* and *through* mean different things. The hyphen could be ambiguous.

6.7   Dates are written as cardinal numbers:

Nov. 15   Oct. 20   July 9

6.8   When month, date and year are used together, set off the year with commas:

He was born on Feb. 14, 1838, in a log cabin.

Spelling

7.1   Words ending in *-ent* or *-ant* and in *-ence* or *-ance* cause spelling difficulties because of the unstressed vowel in the suffix:

acquiescent	acquiescence
competent	competence
consistent	consistence
different	difference
exorbitant	exorbitance
	grievance
independent	independence
insistent	insistence
precedent	precedence
relevant	relevance
resistant	resistance

7.2   Words ending in *-ible* and *-able* that frequently cause difficulty:

accessible   accessibility
admissible   admissibility
compatible   compatibility
discernible
indispensable
inseparable
resistible   irresistible

7.3 These words are often troublesome because of doubled consonants:

accommodate   inflammation
affidavit   innuendo
bailiff   miscellaneous
ballistic   occurred, occurring, occurrence
bookkeeper   parallel
colossal   questionnaire
dissertation   sheriff
drunkenness   surveillance
embarrass   tariff
harass   uncontrollable

7.4 Words ending in *-er* or *-or* that are often misspelled:

adviser*   debtor
conquer   impostor
coroner   observer
councilor   sponsor
counselor

7.5 Words of Greek or Latin origin that frequently appear in news stories:

deity   hygiene
diphtheria   nonagenarian
fluoridation   rhetoric
hemorrhage   subpoena*

7.6 There is a rule in English spelling that says: Keep the silent *e* before a suffix beginning with a consonant and drop it before a suffix beginning with a vowel. These words are exceptions:

---

*Words marked thus are preferred spellings, that is, there are two acceptable spellings, but this one is preferred by the stylebook.

changeable   mileage
judgment   wisdom
knowledgeable

7.7 These words cause trouble when -*ing* is added:

die   dying
dye   dyeing
eye   eyeing*
tie   tying

7.8 These words have doubled consonants because of their prefixes:

innocuous   misspelled
irreligious   offense

7.9 When it is used as one element in a compound word, *full* is spelled with a double *l*. When it is used as a prefix or suffix, spell it with one *l*.

fulfill   armful   masterful
fulsome   awful   playful
                       skillful

7.10 Words with *ie* or *ei* may cause difficulties despite the spelling rule that says *i* before *e* except after *c* or in words like *neighbor* and *weigh:*

ei after *c*	deceive	
	perceive	
	receive, receipt	
ei	foreign	sleigh
	leisure	sleight
	neighbor	weight
	seize	weird
ie	believe	
	fiend	
	lien	

---

*Words marked thus are preferred spellings, that is, there are two acceptable spellings, but this one is preferred by the stylebook.

7.11   Words with the suffixes *-ege* and *-edge* are often misspelled:

knowledge	sacrilege
privilege	sacrilegious

7.12   These words from names are in common use:

nemesis
philistine
quixotic

7.13   These words frequently give trouble, some of them because their pronunciation does not indicate the presence of certain vowels or consonants:

aerial	
liaison	
parishioner	
provocateur	(provoke)
repetitious	(repeat)
skiing	(ski, skis, skied, skier)
stability	(stable)
subtlety, subtleties	(subtle)
temperament	
vacuum	
veterinarian	

7.14   These words are also susceptible to misspelling but do not fit any of the previous categories:

a lot	That's a lot of nonsense.
all right	It's all right to do it that way.

Other problem words:

accidentally	complexion
anecdote	consensus
asinine	defunct
aura	dietitian
caricature	disease
categorically	drought
cemetery	dumbbell
chauffeur	edifice
coconut	gauge

goodbye*
hypocrisy
immerse, immersion
inaugurate
incalculable, calculate
indict, indictment
innuendo
inoculate
intramural
kidnap, kidnapped,
    kidnapping, kidnapper*
minuscule
mold
oriented, orientation
paraphernalia
peninsula
picnic, but picnicked,
    picnicking, picnicker

plaque
predator
prejudice
preventive
rarefied
rehearsal
restaurateur
satellite
sergeant
soluble
strait jacket
strict, strictly
supersede
supposed, supposedly
temblor
tentacle
verbatim
vernacular

7.15   Some troublesome plurals:

alumna	alumnae
alumnus	alumni
attorney	attorneys
attorney general	attorneys general
court-martial	courts-martial
datum	data
Negro	Negroes
phenomenon	phenomena
tomato	tomatoes
tornado	tornadoes

7.16   Homophones, words that sound alike but that have different written forms, can cause spelling problems:

aural, oral	principle, principal
bear, bare	rite, right, write
bus, buss	shear, sheer
canvas, canvass	site, sight, cite
capital, capitol	straight, strait
compliment, complement	their, there, they're
cue, queue	to, two, too

*Words marked thus are preferred spellings, that is, there are two acceptable spellings, but this one is preferred by the stylebook.

7.17 Words that are similar in their written forms and often similar in pronunciation can cause difficulties because their meanings are quite different:

affect	effect
allude	elude
allusion	illusion
anecdote	antidote
apposite	opposite
appraise	apprise
censor	censure
consul	council, counsel
continual	continuous
eminent	imminent
empathy	apathy
expatiate	expiate
flout	flaunt
healthful	healthy
historical	historic
illusive	elusive
imply	infer
ingenious	ingenuous
nauseous	nauseated
odious	odorous
ordinance	ordnance
perspective	prospective
populous	populace
prostrate	prostitute
relic	relict
rend	render
straight	strait-laced
tenet	tenant
tortuous	torturous
uninterested	disinterested
venal	venial

Policy

8.1 Be prudent in the use of slang, expletives, profanity and obscenity in news stories. Many readers are offended by their use, and newspapers are generally conservative in this matter. Be especially cautious in using expletives and profanity that include references to the deity and in using so-called four-letter words. When such words or phrases are essential to a news story, include them. It is preferable, in this case, to spell the words out rather than using dashes or some other coy cover-up.

The question, as suggested by *The Washington Post Deskbook on Style,* is not "why not use it?" but rather, "why use it?"

In all matters covered by this section, consult your editor before you write.

8.2   Newspapers today generally avoid euphemisms in referring to diseases and acts once held to be unmentionable. It is preferable to say *rape* rather than to gloss it over by referring to a *statutory offense.* Use of standard and scientific terms is generally acceptable in news copy. Regular reading of daily newspapers will give you an idea of the range of permissibility, and the range seems to be growing all the time. Consult your editor when in doubt.

8.3   Do not use racial designations unless they are essential to the story. However, it is pointless to publish a description of a person being sought by police unless you do include race or color along with height, weight, sex, degree of baldness, shape of beard and so on.

8.4   Don't make fun of people or use pejorative names, nicknames or phrases that might embarrass or hold people up to ridicule. The following list is suggestive of the kinds of names to avoid, but it is not a complete list:

Dago	redneck
bog trotter	little people
hillbilly	sky pilot
gook	

Avoid using words or terms that tend to label or indict large groups of people with the offenses of a single individual or a few individuals:

teen-age drug addict	Sicilian gangster
student rioters	

8.5   Avoid sexual stereotyping in news stories. This is more a matter of point of view than use of a particular word. Do not assume maleness in all aspects of life. Do not treat women in a way you would not treat men.

In particular, avoid such things as referring to a female defense attorney as an attractive blonde if you would not refer to the male prosecuting attorney as a handsome blond. However, avoid unnecessarily complicated circumlocutions like *he or she.* Where male or female attributes are not relevant, you may use the masculine pronoun, as, *a reporter always protects his sources*, a grammatically correct and historically acceptable usage. Or you may prefer to rephrase it, as, *reporters always try to protect their sources*. In any case, don't write awkward or convoluted sentences in order to avoid the pronoun *his*.

Do not use *chairperson* or similar coinages indiscriminately. Generally, the proper term is *chairman*, a historically proper designation for a person running a meeting or heading a committee. In the case of governmental units, for example, legislative committees, *chairman* is the legally correct term. Some organizations do use *chairperson* — the American Civil Liberties Union, for example. ACLU meetings are run by a chairperson, their own designation, and you should use this form in your report of ACLU activities. In government, however, *chairperson* is inaccurate if ordinances or statutes designate committee heads as *chairmen*. Be as careful to use the right word in this matter as you would be to spell a person's name correctly.

8.6   In writing obituaries, avoid euphemisms like *passed away*. Just say that the person died.

8.7   Do not describe the method by which a person committed suicide. Someone may try to imitate it. It is usually enough to say that the person was found dead and that officials say he took his own life.

8.8   Use the word *innocent* in place of *not guilty*. There is always the possibility the word *not* will be lost:

> Smith pleaded innocent to the charge. (Safe)
> Smith pleaded not guilty to the charge. (Dangerous)

8.9   Don't use the word *allegedly* as a qualifier with criminal charges or accusations of wrongdoing. Mr. Smith the missing banker is not an alleged embezzler. He is being sought by police, who want to ask him about funds missing at the bank. He may, later, be charged with embezzlement. He may not be, either, and to label him an alleged embezzler may be injurious.

No matter how serious the charge, everyone is innocent until the accusation made has been proved in court.

> Smith, the alleged rapist, was jailed. (Questionable)
> Smith was jailed. Police said he would be charged
>   with rape. (Safe)

> Police are hunting the alleged killer. (Questionable)
> Police are hunting Smith for questioning about the
> death of his brother. (Safer)

8.10 Laws in many states prohibit the publication of names of juveniles in criminal cases.

Newspapers generally try to protect the anonymity of innocent victims in criminal cases, especially in cases of violent crime.

It often is best not to use the names of women who have been raped, even in stories about trials where the woman has testified in open court.

Courts today are giving wider recognition to the right to privacy. It is sometimes difficult to know whether a person is a public figure or whether a person innocently involved in a news event has a legitimate claim to privacy or should be identified in a news story.

Newspapers must be sensitive to the feelings of people who are involved in news stories. Consult your editor in doubtful situations. Right-to-privacy suits can be as expensive as libel suits.

Glossary

Add Any matter added to a news story at the end. See *Insert*.

Advance In press association parlance, a story transmitted some time prior to its intended use. For instance, a story transmitted to newspapers on Monday or Tuesday, but intended for use on the following Sunday. Also, frequently, any story written ahead for later use. Also a story written before an event.

Alive or **Live** Copy intended for use. Copy or assignments in the production channels. A live story is one on which a reporter is working and that will be used. See also *Kill*.

ANPA The American Newspaper Publishers Association.

AP Broadcast News Handbook A stylebook for broadcast journalists.

APME Editors of member newspapers have their own national professional association, the AP Managing Editors Association.

ASNE The American Society of Newspaper Editors.

Assignment Any duty given to a reporter, usually a story to cover or write.

Attribution The source of a news story or of a fact within a story. *To attribute* is to indicate the source of a story or fact and thus give the information authenticity.

Background Anything added to or inserted in a news story to explain earlier actions or events; facts intended to refresh the reader's memory about earlier actions or events.

Backgrounder A news story that explains the background or origins of an issue or situation. It may be mere explanation or it may be somewhat interpretive. Sometimes called a *situationer*.

491

Blind lead A lead in which a person is identified but not named until the second or third paragraph.

Body The main part of a news story after the lead. Sometimes called the *development*.

Boil Boiling is more drastic than *trimming*. It implies close paring of all sentences and the sacrifice of minor facts. Length of the story is substantially reduced.

Box To put a rule around a news story or picture. Any story that is enclosed in a rule.

Breaking news Unexpected, unplanned occurrences — for example, a plane crash. A story that must be covered quickly and without any advance preparation.

Bridge A transitional device for carrying the reader from the lead into the body of the story or from one part of a story to another. The bridge can be a word, a sentence or several sentences. See also *Swing paragraph* and *Transition*.

Brief A short news story, usually two or three paragraphs long. Newspapers often collect related short news stories under a single head, for instance, Business Briefs.

Bright A light, usually humorous or entertaining story used to lighten the newspaper and contrast with serious news.

Broadsheet The standard newspaper page size, approximately 14 by 22 inches but varying from newspaper to newspaper depending on the make and age of the press on which the newspaper is printed.

Byline The line that indicates who wrote a story, for example, "By John H. Smith." Bylines are usually used only on above-average stories, not on routine copy.

Cold type Opposite of *hot type*. Newspapers today are produced by the cold-type process, computer-controlled typesetting that produces images of news stories, advertising copy and headlines on paper. Copy is pasted up into pages and finally printing plates are made photographically.

Copy Anything written for publication.

Copy-editing marks Symbols used to indicate corrections or changes in news copy. Copy-editing marks are always made at the place a change is desired, as distinct from *proofreader's marks*, which are made in the margin of a proof. Proofreader's marks should never be used on copy.

Copy editor Also called *copyreader*. A newsman who reads all copy to check for errors, improve the story and add instructions for the composing room. Copy editors write headlines and insert subheads.

Copy paper The white or yellow newsprint on which news writers have traditionally written their copy.

Copy pencil A soft lead pencil used by reporters for taking notes or editing typewritten copy. Only a copy pencil is satisfactory for writing on the soft surface of copy paper.

Cut To eliminate all but the most important facts, those without which there would be no story or an incomplete one at best.

Dateline The words preceding news stories that indicate the place and, sometimes, the date of origin. Datelines are not used on local stories.

Dead Said of copy that has been killed. See *Alive* and *Kill*.

Deadline The time at which news copy is due or at which the last copy is due. Always meet deadlines. No one stops the presses. They just go without you if you miss a deadline.

Development Another name for the body of a news story.

Direct quote A speaker's exact words, a verbatim report enclosed in quotation marks. Sometimes slightly edited to improve syntax or correct grammar. See also *Indirect quote, Partial quote* and *Paraphrase*.

Down style Newspaper style that tends to avoid capitalization wherever possible. Non-distinguishing nouns in names, for example, are not capitalized in a down style, as in *Roosevelt hotel*. See also *Up style*.

Ed & Pub Abbreviation for *Editor & Publisher,* weekly news magazine of the newspaper industry. Required reading for those seriously interested in the newspaper world.

Edit Either to give a newspaper editorial direction or to actually carry out the steps of reporting, writing and preparing news for a newspaper's pages. To edit copy is to revise, correct and improve news stories. All good reporters carefully edit their own copy before turning it in.

Edition A specific version of one issue of a newspaper, for example, a *state edition* published for outlying areas or a *city edition* published for the newspaper's city and suburban readers. See also *Issue*.

Editor An editor is an executive or manager who supervises the reporting, writing and editing of the news; a skilled craftsman whose job requires education, experience and both intelligence and imagination. There are various categories of editors, titled according to the nature of the job: managing editor, city editor, sports editor and so on.

Editorial Having to do with the news side of a newspaper. Any news related matter, for example, an editorial decision or an editorial judgment.

Editorialize To inject one's own opinions into news copy. Traditionally, newspapers avoid editorializing in news stories and restrict the newspaper's opinions to the editorial page or to signed columns.

Editorial matter News, news copy.

Electronic carbons A system by which news stories offered by newspapers to the Associated Press go from a newspaper's computer directly to an AP computer.

Embargo See *Hold*.

End mark A symbol, usually ##, sometimes *30*, typed at the end of a story to indicate that the story is complete.

Feature (1) The main news angle or news peg of a story. A special point or twist to a story. (2) A type of news story, sometimes called a *news feature*. It is usually not breaking news but a story closely related to the news. Features are often interpretive, give background, play up human interest and convey the color of an event. (3) Non-news matter, for example, syndicated columns, comics, cartoons, horoscopes and so on, that appears regularly in the newspaper. (4) To give something prominence in a story; to emphasize something.

Featurize To play up an unusual angle or interesting point of a story rather than to rely on a bare recitation of the five Ws, the usual straight news approach, which might not make the best use of odd, unusual or interesting elements of a story.

First Amendment The First Amendment to the U.S. Constitution, which guarantees freedom of speech and of the press. The first article in the Bill of Rights and the cornerstone of the American citizen's civil liberties. Also guarantees freedom of religion, assembly and petition.

Five Ws The basic questions that news stories must answer: who, what, when, where, why and how.

Follow Sometimes *folo*. A story that follows another, giving new facts or bringing the story up to date. Also a *second-day story*.

Fourth Estate The press, a term attributed to Edmund Burke, who is reported to have called the reporter's gallery in Parliament "a Fourth Estate." The three estates of early English society were the clergy, the peerage and the commons.

Front-end system The electronic equipment — VDTs, computers, hard copy printers and peripheral equipment — on which the newsroom staff writes, edits and prepares the news for publication. Front-end systems have replaced the traditional composing room. Copy goes from the news writer's VDT to a computer, then back to an editor and from there to a phototypesetter.

Future book An editor's calendar of future meetings, programs and news events that must be covered. Editors keep a future book as one means of managing the coverage of the news.

FYI For your information. Frequently used to indicate that the material so marked is for background rather than for inclusion in a news story.

Guild The Newspaper Guild, the union for newsmen and other newspaper employees.

Handout A news story or other material prepared for distribution to newspapers, press associations, broadcast stations and other news outlets. The usual source is a public relations practitioner employed by a person, firm or group that wants a news story to appear in print. Handouts are useful and important sources of information but may be one-sided or incomplete and should always be carefully checked. Handouts often need to be rewritten. See also *Press release.*

Hard copy Any copy on paper, either original copy prepared by a news writer or a printout from the newsroom computer.

Hold To delay use of a story. Stories are often given to newspapers for later use and marked "hold for release" at a given time. Hold orders should not be ignored. AP indicates hold orders by marking stories "embargoed until (date — day — hour)."

Hole A gap in a news story. A hole in a story means that something essential to clarity or completeness is missing.

Hot type The process of producing a newspaper by mechanical means. The traditional system of newspaper production supplanted by computers, photocomposition and offset printing. In the hot-type process, type is cast, using molten lead, type metal. The heart of the hot-type production system was the linecasting machine: the Linotype, Intertype and Ludlow that set type a line at a time. Hot type also implies letterpress printing. See also *Cold type.*

Human interest An essential element of the news, a recognition of the fact that people are interested in what other people do. Especially strong human interest elements are love, children, success and misfortune, pets and animals.

Identification Facts used to identify a person, building, place or organization. The facts, for example, the age, street address, title or descriptive matter, that distinguish one person from another.

Indirect quote Not verbatim but rather a slightly edited or paraphrased version of a speaker's words. Indirect quotes are not enclosed in quotation marks. An indirect quote represents what a reporter tells us someone said. See also *Direct quote, Partial quote* and *Paraphrase.*

Insert To add matter within the body of a story already written. Copy written to be inserted is called an *insert.*

Inverted pyramid The basic news story form, with a summary lead at the beginning and minor facts at the end.

Issue A particular number of a newspaper or periodical, as "The story was published in the Globe in the issue of July 4, 1987."

Itemizing lead A lead that lists the several points a story will cover. Sometimes called a *1-2-3-4 lead.*

Journalism The trade, technique or profession of reporting news for the public by various means. Hence, newspaper journalism, broadcast journalism, magazine journalism and so on.

Journalism reviews Critical publications whose major interest is study and analysis of the press.

Journalist A formal name for a *newsman*. More used in England than the United States, where *reporter* and *newsman* seem to be preferred by those in the working press.

Journeyman A competent worker; a craftsman who has completed his apprenticeship.

Kill To destroy copy or type that is not to be used. "Kill" is a final order to prevent copy from being used. Kill orders must be strictly observed.

Lead The first paragraph or paragraphs of a news story. Pronounced "leed."

Legman A reporter who covers news but does not write it. To save time for the job of reporting, the legman hands over the writing chore to someone else. Legmen phone their stories in to the rewrite desk.

Localize To emphasize the local angle of a news story, usually by placing it in the lead or high in the story. Local news has high reader interest, and it always pays to emphasize local angles.

Lowercase Small letters, not capitals. Indicated by the initials *lc* or *LC*.

Media A term used to refer to the press — newspapers, magazines, television and radio. *Media* is plural. *Medium* is the singular form.

Memo A written memorandum. Never give oral messages or instructions. Always write — type — a memo.

More An instruction typed at the bottom of a page of copy to indicate that the story is not complete and that another page or pages follow.

Morgue Traditional term for the newspaper reference library where bound files of the newspaper, clippings files, photos and negatives were saved for reference or later use. The term *reference library* is replacing the old word, and data banks accessed by a computer terminal are replacing envelopes of clippings.

Must An instruction added to copy that means "this must be published."

New journalism A name given to a genre introduced by a number of writers in the 1960s, some journalists, some novelists, who began to report more accurately and more colorfully on the nuances of contemporary life. Their example encouraged new experiments in writing in many areas of the press and has led to much better writing overall in newspapers and magazines.

News hole The number of columns of space available for news in a newspaper. The space not devoted to advertising. The space available to a particular editor, for example, a sports editor, for use in that day's paper.

Newsman An employee of the news, or editorial, staff of a newspaper. A press association or news service employee. A man or woman who reports, writes or edits the news.

News peg The significant or interesting point on which a reporter hangs a story. The angle, feature or twist to a story that makes it interesting or important.

Newsprint A soft, rough paper made from wood pulp and used in printing newspapers. Waste at the end of newsprint rolls is cut into 8½-by-11 sheets to be used for copy paper.

No-news lead A lead empty of information, for example, the lead that begins "City Council met last night." The council met, but what did it accomplish?

Obituary An *obit*, a story about a death. An obit reports facts about a death, funeral arrangements, a list of surviving relatives and at least a brief biography.

Ombudsman A readers' representative who serves as a sort of middleman between the newspaper staff and the public.

Op ed Opposite editorial. The right-hand page facing the editorial page. Op ed pages carry additional opinion — columns, letters to the editor and editorial cartoons.

Optical character reader An electronic device that works much like a photocopier. A scanning light reads down the copy, but instead of producing a duplicate on paper, it creates an electronic version of the copy, which is transmitted to a computer. Also called an *OCR* or a *scanner*. The scanner bypasses the need to keyboard typewritten copy to enter it into a front-end system.

Overset Copy that was set into type ready for publication but was not published.

Pad To add superfluous matter to a story. A padded story has more words or details than necessary. A frequent order from the copy desk is "take the padding out of this" or "take the fat out of this."

Page brightener See *Bright*.

Paragraph An arbitrary division of written copy, usually from one to three or four sentences. Newspaper paragraphs tend to be shorter than those in other published work, primarily because newspaper columns are narrower than book columns and other columns.

Paraphrase Phrasing in the writer's words rather than in the words of a speaker or news source, usually done to report more concisely and briefly. See also *Direct quote*, *Indirect quote* and *Partial quote*.

Partial quote Verbatim, but less than a complete sentence. For best effect, partial quotes should be complete phrases rather than one or two words. Generally, it is best to avoid use of partial quotes in favor of complete sentences of direct quote or paraphrase. See also *Direct quote, Indirect quote* and *Paraphrase.*

Pica A printer's measurement. One pica is one-sixth of an inch.

Play up To emphasize a certain angle or fact in a news story. To give a story prominence by placing it on the front page.

Point A printer's measurement. Type size — the height of the face of a letter — is measured in points. There are 72 points to the inch. Hence, 8-point type runs nine lines to an inch set solid, that is, without space between the lines. An 8-point type set on a 9-point body runs eight lines to an inch. A 36-point typeface — display or headline type — is half an inch in height.

Precision journalism The technique of gathering data — facts or opinion — by quantitative methods. A good example is the measuring of public opinion by survey, that is, polling of a carefully selected sample of the public.

Press Originally, printed publications, chiefly newspapers and magazines, but now a broadened term that includes broadcast journalism. An older term and perhaps a better term than *media.*

Press release A news story prepared by a public relations practitioner for use by newspapers or wire services. See also *Handout.*

Print *To print* is to carry out the physical process of producing a newspaper, magazine or book by setting type, making up pages and printing on a press. The word *print* is not interchangeable with *publish,* which is the creative process of producing newspapers, periodicals and books. See also *Publish.*

Print media Newspapers, magazines and other periodicals. The terms *print media* and *newspaper* are not interchangeable.

Proofreader's marks Symbols used by proofreaders to make corrections on proofs. These differ in some instances from marks used by copy editors and are always placed in the margin of the proof. See also *Copy-editing marks.*

Public information A term commonly used to describe public relations activities and personnel in government and the military.

Public relations The business of presenting information, usually favorable, to the public about a person, firm or organization. Often referred to as *information services,* as in universities, or as *public information,* as in government.

Publish (1) To issue a newspaper or magazine, as "Gannett publishes 87 daily newspapers." (2) To include a story in an issue of a newspaper, as "The story was published in the Sunday paper." Publishing is a creative act by the editorial side of the newspaper. It is also managerial: Newspapers are published by their owners and managers.

Publisher The chief executive officer of a newspaper, responsible for the management of all aspects of the newspaper. The publisher manages a newspaper for the owners who publish it.

Q. and A. The device of reporting dialogue in the form of questions and answers. Frequently used to give verbatim reports of testimony at trials or public hearings.

Release date The date or time when a news story embargoed or marked "hold for release" may be published.

Reporter A newsman whose principal job is to gather the news and, usually, to write it.

Rewrite The rewrite desk. Also copy revised or rewritten is termed "a rewrite."

Rewriteman A newsman who not only rewrites stories to improve them, to bring them up to date or to change an angle, but also writes stories from information phoned in by reporters. See also *Legman*.

Round-up A story that pulls together various aspects of a newsworthy event. For example, a weekend round-up of auto accidents provided for Monday issues of newspapers by the wire services. A round-up assembles a number of stories of a similar nature under one lead. Another typical round-up is the weather round-up.

RTNDA The Radio and Television News Directors Association, an important organization for broadcast journalists.

Scanner An optical character reader. See also *Optical character reader*.

Second-day story A news story written or published on the day after the first story on a news event has been published. It does not tell a story for the first time but rather follows up on the earlier story. The second-day story provides new information or background that makes the original story more complete or understandable.

Set To arrange type into words and sentences preparatory to printing. To compose. Type can be set by hand, by linecasting machines or electronically by photocomposition machines controlled by computers.

Shirttail To add secondary matter to the end of a story. Also anything added in this way.

Sidebar A related story. A sidebar runs alongside another story and carries secondary details, background, color or human interest aspects of the story.

Slant The tone or direction deliberately given to a story. Sometimes, the emphasis of a story. A story directed to a certain segment of a newspaper's readership is said to be slanted for those readers, for example, a story may be slanted to teen-age readers. Another meaning is *bias*. In this sense, slanting is to be avoided.

Slug A one-word or two-word identification for a news story, typed at the top of each page of the story.

Speech tag Device for attributing a quote or a fact to its source, for example, "police said." Normal word order in a speech tag is name first, verb second.

Spot news Breaking news, unexpected news events.

State of the art Machinery or electronic equipment is said to be state of the art when it represents the most advanced state of development or technology. The latest model.

Stet A printer's term directing that a letter, word or other matter marked to be deleted or changed should be retained as it was in the first place. From Latin, "let it stand," from *stare*, "to stand." Used by proofreaders but also in copy editing.

Stick or **Stickful** A printer's term, used in the newsroom to indicate a few lines of type, the number of lines a printer's stick could hold. If you are asked to write a "stickful," write no more than five or six lines.

Story News written for publication, a report or account of an event. Newsmen prefer the word *story* to *article*.

Stringer Someone who reports or writes for a newspaper on a production basis, that is, is paid for what is published rather than as a full-time, salaried staff member.

Style Conventions or accepted usage regarding punctuation, capitalization, abbreviations, use of names and titles and other features of written language.

Stylebook A written guide to newspaper or wire service preferences in matters of style, for example, the *Associated Press Stylebook and Libel Manual*.

Summary A brief, inclusive statement of what a story is about. A summary lead tells concisely what happened. A summary paragraph briefly explains one or more aspects of a story.

Summary lead A lead that emphasizes the five Ws and summarizes concisely the main facts of a news story.

Suspended interest A type of news story in which the main point or outcome is withheld until the end of the story rather than being summarized at the beginning.

Swing paragraph Another term for a bridge or transitional paragraph, a device for moving the reader from the lead to the body of a story or from one part of a story to another. See also *Bridge* and *Transition*.

Tabloid A newspaper page half the size of a broadsheet.

Thirty The traditional newsroom symbol for the end of the copy. Used to indicate that the copy is complete, that there is no more to come. Origin of the term is obscure. Write as *thirty* or *30*.

Transition A word, phrase, sentence or paragraph that serves to carry a story from one part to another, often to indicate a shift from one speaker to another or from one topic to another. See also *Bridge* and *Swing paragraph.*

Trim To tighten up a story, chiefly by eliminating superfluous words and replacing loose phrases with single words that convey the same thought.

Tube The VDT — video display terminal — used in the newsroom for writing and editing news copy.

Update To bring a story up to date or to make it more timely. Sometimes news stories are updated from edition to edition as new information becomes available.

Uppercase Capital letters. Frequently abbreviated as *caps* or *UC.*

Up style Newspaper style that tends to capitalize when there is a choice. See also *Down style.* Newspaper style today is something of a compromise between up style and down style.

Video display terminal A VDT, an electronic typewriter with a cathode ray tube, like a small television screen, above the keyboard. You type on the keyboard, and your copy appears on a screen rather than on paper. The VDT is a word processor that enables the writer to write and rewrite copy and then store it in a computer data bank for further editing and later transmission to a phototypesetter. All newsrooms today are fully equipped with VDTs, the heart of a front-end system.

Wire Newspaper terminology for the press associations, the Associated Press and United Press International. Wire copy is the copy supplied by AP and UPI, though the copy no longer is transmitted by wire but is transmitted by radio by way of a satellite. Wire services refers to AP and UPI, and wire editors are the editors responsible for handling AP, UPI and supplemental news service copy.

Working press The newsmen who report, write and edit newspapers, magazines and other periodicals and who work in broadcast journalism. More particularly, the reporters who are in the front lines of journalism covering the news on a day-to-day basis. Also *newsmen* or *newswomen* or, less frequently, *journalists.*

A News Writer's Reference Shelf

These books and periodicals have proved of interest and use to journalism students and to the men and women who write for newspapers and news services.

Ad Age
> A weekly publication for the advertising industry. It carries a great deal of useful information about the newspaper industry. Address: 740 Rush St., Chicago, Ill. 60611.

Agee, Warren K., Phillip H. Ault and Edwin Emery. *Introduction to Mass Communications.* New York: Harper and Row, 1988.
> A primer for journalism students. Broad, informative discussion of the whole field of mass communications. Very useful bibliography.

American Newspaper Publishers Association. *Facts About Newspapers '87.* Washington, D.C.: American Newspaper Publishers Association, 1987.
> *Facts About Newspapers*, published annually, and other useful publications are available from the ANPA Public Affairs Department, The Newspaper Center, Box 17407, Dulles Airport, Washington, D.C. 20041.

AP Log
> A weekly newsletter reporting on the activities of AP bureaus and staffers and the performance of AP.

Associated Press. *The APME Red Book.* New York: Associated Press, annually.
> A report of the annual convention of the Associated Press Managing Editors Association and APME Continuing Study Committees.

503

Associated Press. *Stylebook and Libel Manual.* New York: Associated Press, 1986.

> This and other AP publications can be purchased from the AP, 50 Rockefeller Plaza, New York, N.Y. 10020.

Berner, R. Thomas. *Language Skills for Journalists,* 2nd ed. Boston: Houghton Mifflin Co., 1984.

> A grammar book written for journalists by an experienced journalist and teacher.

Bernstein, Theodore M. *The Careful Writer.* New York: Atheneum, 1965.

> A sound and practical guide to usage by an assistant managing editor of *The New York Times.* Should be in every news writer's library.

The Bulletin

> Published by the American Society of Newspaper Editors, *The Bulletin* helps keep editors informed about the issues that matter in the newspaper industry. Address: ASNE, 11600 Sunrise Valley Drive, Reston, Va. 22091.

Capon, Rene J. *The Word.* New York: Associated Press, 1982.

> A manual on good writing by the features editor of the Associated Press.

Columbia Journalism Review

> A bimonthly journal of comment, criticism and analysis, which reports on current issues and problems of the press. Published by the Columbia School of Journalism, 700 Journalism Building, Columbia University, New York, N.Y. 10027.

Copperud, Roy H. *A Dictionary of Usage and Style.* New York: Hawthorn Books, Inc., 1970.

> Basic and invaluable to the news writer for its sound and helpful guidance on problems of usage and news style.

Editor & Publisher

> A weekly trade publication, *Ed & Pub* reports on both the business and news sides of the newspaper industry. Address: 575 Lexington Ave., New York, N.Y. 10022.

Gannetteer

> Published for employees of the Gannett Co. Contains a great deal of interest to newspaper people generally. A regular feature is an insert on newsroom problems. Address: Gannett Co., Inc., 1100 Wilson Blvd., Arlington, Va. 22209.

Garst, Robert E., and Theodore M. Bernstein. *Headlines and Deadlines,* 4th ed. New York: Columbia University Press, 1982.

> A manual for copy editors but also instructive for the news writer.

The Guild Reporter

> Biweekly publication of the Newspaper Guild. Readable and informative. The Guild has been offering complimentary subscriptions to journalism teachers. The Newspaper Guild, 1125 Fifteenth St. N.W., Washington, D.C. 20005.

Harrigan, Jane T. *Read All About It!* Chester, Conn.: Globe Pequot Press, 1987.

An hour-by-hour account of how a daily newspaper — the Boston Globe — is produced: from editors to advertising sales reps, pasteup artists to pressmen.

JOB/NET

A placement service for minority journalists, a service of the nonprofit Institute for Journalism Education. Address: B28 Northgate Hall, University of California, Berkeley, Calif. 94720.

Journalism Scholarship Guide

A directory of college journalism programs and scholarships. Published annually by the Newspaper Fund, P.O. Box 300, Princeton, N.J. 08540.

Media Report to Women

A monthly newsletter for women in the media. Address: 3306 Ross Place N.W., Washington, D.C. 20008.

News

Publication of the Associated Managing Editors Association. Informative and current discussion of newsroom problems from the editor's point of view.

Newspaper Fund

A foundation established by Dow Jones & Co., Inc., to encourage talented young people to enter newspaper careers. The fund supports a number of programs for high school and college students, including programs for minorities, a summer intern program and programs for teachers. The fund publishes the useful *Journalism Scholarship Guide*. Address: P.O. Box 300, Princeton, N.J. 08540.

The New York Times

News writers should be newspaper readers. News writers and editors who want to be fully informed read this important newspaper regularly.

Presstime

A monthly magazine published by the American Newspaper Publishers Association. It is an important source of information about the economics and management of the newspaper industry.

Professional Communicator

Published by Women in Communications, Inc., for its members. A useful source of information about women in the mass media. Address: P.O. Box 9561, Austin, Texas 78766.

Publishers' Auxiliary

A biweekly trade journal published by the National Newspaper Association for the small town daily or weekly business. *Pub Aux* carries a wide range of stories on all aspects of community journalism. Address: 1627 K St. N.W., Suite 400, Washington, D.C. 20006.

Quill

Monthly magazine published by the Society of Professional Journalists, Sigma Delta Chi. Informed discussion by professionals about the problems of the press. Address: 53 W. Jackson Blvd., Suite 731, Chicago, Ill. 60604.

Still Here

A newsletter published by the Job/Scholarship Referral Service for minority students. Address: School of Communications, Howard University, Washington, D.C. 20059.

United Press International. *UPI Stylebook*. New York: United Press International, 1977.

UPI's version of the joint stylebook. Order from United Press International, 1400 I St., N.W., Washington, D.C. 20005.

Washington Journalism Review

Published 10 times a year. "The national media magazine from Washington." Somewhat more topical than *CJR*. Interesting and provocative. Address: 2233 Wisconsin Ave. N.W., Washington, D.C. 20007.

(Continuation of copyright page)

Text credits

Page 8: Selection from *The Editor & Publisher Year Book.* Reprinted by permission.

Page 9: Selection from *The Audit Bureau of Circulation.* Reprinted by permission.

Pages 26–27, 142–143, 211, 212, 213–214, 268–269, 309, 316, 336: Selections from *The Atlanta Journal & Constitution.* Copyright © 1982, 1983 *The Atlanta Constitution.* Reprinted by permission.

Pages 28–29, 340–341: Selections from *The Richmond Times-Dispatch.* Reprinted by permission.

Pages 58, 84–85, 129, 144–145, 195, 203, 284, 286, 290, 291, 291–293, 293–295, 296, 307, 308, 309, 311, 312, 349–350, ch. 18: Selections from *The Associated Press.* Reprinted by permission of *The Associated Press.*

Page 68: Selection from *The Bay City Times.* Reprinted by permission.

Pages 72, 82, 85–86, 101, 141, 173, 200, 230, 244–245, 301, 303, 306–307, 315, ch. 17, 406–407: Selections from *United Press International.* Reprinted by permission of *United Press International.*

Page 78: Selection from *The Los Angeles Herald Examiner.* Reprinted by permission.

Page 78: Selection from *The Berkshire Eagle.* Reprinted by permission.

Page 80: Selections from *The Miami Herald.* Reprinted with permission from *The Miami Herald.*

Pages 82, 91, 158, 179–180: Selections from *The St. Petersburg Times.* Reprinted by permission.

Pages 83, 164, 219: Selections from *The Milwaukee Sentinel.* Reprinted by permission.

Pages 89–90, 316: Selections from the 9/15/82 and 9/19/82 issues of *The Philadelphia Enquirer.* Reprinted by permission of *The Philadelphia Enquirer.*

Page 104: Selection from *The Post.* Reprinted with permission from *The Post,* West Palm Beach, Fla.

Pages 105, 174–175, 175: Selections from *The Asbury Park Press.* Reprinted by permission.

Pages 105, 202, 210, 210–211, 211: Selections by Stephen Maita, Jim Brewer, Erik Ingram, and Thomas G. Keane from the March 3, 1986, March 3, 1987, March 4, 1987 and March 7, 1987 issues of the *San Francisco Chronicle.* © SAN FRANCISCO CHRONICLE, 1986 and 1987. Reprinted by permission.

Pages 116–117, 136, 139: Selections from *The Jackson Sun.* Reprinted by permission.

Page 132: Selection from *The Sun-Tattler.* Reprinted by permission.

Page 135: Selection from *The Asheville Citizen.* Reprinted by permission.

Page 136: Selection from *The Lubbock Avalanche-Journal.* Reprinted by permission of *The Lubbock* (Tex.) *Avalanche-Journal.*

Page 148: Selection from *The Dallas News.* Reprinted by permission.

Page 150: Selection from *The Duluth News-Tribune.* Reprinted by permission.

Pages 160–161: Selection from *The Louisville Courier-Journal.* Copyright © 1982 *The Courier-Journal.* Reprinted with permission.

Pages 164–165, 215–216, 221, 304–305, 331, 350, 408: Selections from *The Milwaukee Journal.* Reprinted by permission.

Pages 176–177: Selection from *The Boston Globe.* Reprinted courtesy of *The Boston Globe.*

Pages 179, 314, 331–332: Selections from *The Detroit Free Press.* Reprinted by permission of *The Detroit Free Press.*

Pages 187–188, 226, 229, 275–276, 333: Selections from *The Rocky Mountain News.* Reprinted by permission.

Pages 190, 227, 229, 248, 347–348: Selections from 7/8/83 and 9/17/82, and selections by Larry Ingrassia, 1/16/78 and Paul Galloway, 2/22/76, from *The Chicago Sun-Times.* © With permission of *The Chicago Sun-Times, Inc.,* 1987.

Pages 192–193, 322–323: Selections from *The Seattle Times.* Reprinted by permission.

Page 196: From "Reporting on Polls: Some Helpful Hints," from *Canadian Daily Newspaper Publishers Association.* Reprinted by permission.

Page 201: Selection from *The Oregonian.* Reprinted by permission.

Pages 204–205, 264–266: Selections from *The Chicago Tribune.* Reprinted by permission.

Page 222: Selection from *The Island Packet.* Reprinted by permission.

Pages 233, 310: Selections from *The Times.* Reprinted by permission.

Pages 234, 311: Selections from *The Charlotte Observer.* Reprinted by permission from THE CHARLOTTE OBSERVER.

Pages 245–246: Selection from *The Arizona Republic.* Reprinted with permission from *The Arizona Republic.*

Pages 252, 254–255: Selections from *State News.* Reprinted by permission.

Page 253: Selection from *United Press International.* Reprinted with permission of *United Press International,* Copyright 1987.

Pages 271–272: Selection from *The Florida Times-Union.* Reprinted by permission of *The Florida Times-Union of Jacksonville.*

Pages 273–275: Selection from *The Enterprise.* Reprinted by permission of *The Falmouth* (Mass.) *Enterprise.*

Page 296: Taken from the NBC news copy of James Polk from 3/13/87. Reprinted by permission.

Pages 302–303: Selection from *The Oakland Press.* Reprinted by permission.

Pages 311, 342, 345, 346, 350, 350–351, 407: Selections from *The New York Times.* Copyright © 1965/1966/1969/1972/1985 by The New York Times Company. Reprinted by permission.

Pages 326–327: Selection from *The Charlotte News.* Reprinted by permission from THE CHARLOTTE NEWS.

Page 324, 325: Selections from *The Washington Post.* © *The Washington Post.* Reprinted by permission.

Page 419: Selection from *The Fort Worth Star-Telegram.* Reprinted by permission.

Index

511

To the Student

We need your help. By answering a few questions below, you can have a hand in shaping the next edition of *News Writing*. Please complete this questionnaire, tear it out and mail it to the following address:

Journalism Editor
College Division
Houghton Mifflin Co.
One Beacon St.
Boston, MA 02108

Thank you.

School name _____

Title of course(s) in which you used this book _____

_____

Is your school on a _____ quarter or _____ semester basis?

Instructor's name _____

Other books used in the course(s), if any _____

_____

1. What is your overall impression of the book? Did you find it

   _____ very useful _____ useful _____ not so useful. Comments, if any:

   _____

   _____

   _____

2. Did your teacher assign all sections and chapters of the book or only some? If any were omitted, please indicate which ones.

_____

_____

3. How did you find the reading level of the book?

_____ highly readable _____ generally interesting _____ fair

4. Did anything about the book surprise you? That is, did you find new material that you hadn't expected in a text of this kind?

_____ yes _____ no. If yes, be specific:

_____

_____

5. Is there any material you would like to see added to the book?

_____ yes _____ no. If yes, be specific:

_____

_____

6. Did your instructor test you on the book? _____ yes _____ no

Describe the tests: _____ objective _____ short essay _____ other

7. Did your teacher's lectures _____ usually cover the same ground as the book _____ introduce entirely different material _____ something in between (describe) _____

_____